The Beatles
Encyclopedia

The Beatles Encyclopedia

EVERYTHING FAB FOUR

Kenneth Womack

 GREENWOOD™

An Imprint of ABC-CLIO, LLC
Santa Barbara, California • Denver, Colorado

Library of Congress Cataloging-in-Publication Data

Names: Womack, Kenneth.
Title: The Beatles encyclopedia : everything Fab Four / Kenneth Womack.
Description: Santa Barbara, California : Greenwood, [2017] | Includes index.
Identifiers: LCCN 2016031213 (print) | LCCN 2016031872 (ebook) |
    ISBN 9781440844263 (paperback : alk. paper) | ISBN 9781440844270 (ebook)
Subjects: LCSH: Beatles—Encyclopedias.
Classification: LCC ML421.B4 W65 2017 (print) | LCC ML421.B4 (ebook) |
    DDC 782.42166092/2 [B] —dc23
LC record available at https://lccn.loc.gov/2016031213

ISBN: 978-1-4408-4426-3
EISBN: 978-1-4408-4427-0

21 20 19 18 17   1 2 3 4 5

This book is also available as an eBook.

Greenwood
An Imprint of ABC-CLIO, LLC

ABC-CLIO, LLC
130 Cremona Drive, P.O. Box 1911
Santa Barbara, California 93116-1911
www.abc-clio.com

This book is printed on acid-free paper ∞

Manufactured in the United States of America

Contents

Alphabetical List of Entries

Preface

This condensed version of *The Beatles Encyclopedia: Everything Fab Four* provides an overview of the lives and works of John Lennon, Paul McCartney, George Harrison, and Ringo Starr.

Nearly 50 years after their disbandment, the Beatles continue to exert a considerable influence upon global musical and popular culture. The most critically acclaimed and commercially successful artistic fusion of their generation and beyond, the Beatles altered the course of popular music in profound and lasting ways, widening the genre's demographics and elevating the concept of recording artistry at the same time. Since their professional inception in the early 1960s, the Beatles have sold more than 1 billion units, making them the most successful musical act of all time. Many of their seminal albums—namely, *Rubber Soul* (1965), *Revolver* (1966), *Sgt. Pepper's Lonely Hearts Club Band* (1967), *The Beatles* (*The White Album*) (1968), and *Abbey Road* (1969)—are widely considered to be central artistic touchstones in the history of 20th-century Western music.

This condensed version of *The Beatles Encyclopedia: Everything Fab Four* will appeal to readers at all levels, from the general public and students at the secondary and postsecondary ranks through advanced scholars and dyed-in-the-wool Beatlemaniacs. This reference work is designed so that it will be useful to high-school and college researchers alike, as well as to general readers and scholars. It provides a wealth of information devoted to the bandmates' lives and works in order to capture the nature and scope of the group's remarkable cultural achievements. To this end, it features a host of biographical information related to each band member, as well as to their immediate family and significant interpersonal relationships. In addition, it also includes biographical material associated with selected creative and business partners among the Beatles' circle. In order to provide an expansive portrait of the group's life and times, attention is devoted to the historical places associated with their career, as well as to important concert venues and key events in the Beatles' fascinating story.

The encyclopedia also affords readers with a wide-ranging compendium of the Beatles' musical corpus, with particular attention to their official catalog of singles and album releases. In contrast with the two-volume edition published in 2014, this condensed volume concentrates almost entirely upon the band's musical accomplishments during their heyday during the 1960s, while also providing a selection of entries devoted to their film and business interests. Each entry concludes with cross-references listing other pertinent entries.

STRUCTURE

This condensed encyclopedia is arranged alphabetically by entry, with some 360 topics ranging from *Abbey Road* to Zapple Records. Entries on songs and albums have a specific structure, designed to provide readers with as much detail as possible. Those entries associated with the Beatles' *songs* feature some or all of these elements:

- Authorship and Background: Whether written by one of the Beatles or by other songwriters, each song's entry provides the actual author or authors, especially useful for the large number of songs registered as by "Lennon–McCartney." Also gives details about the inspiration for or history of songs.
- Recording Sessions: Details on when and where the song was recorded, often with descriptions of issues about arrangements and performance.
- Personnel: A list of the people who performed on the recording. Whenever possible, details about the group's instrumentation include specific reference to the make and model of each bandmates' instruments.
- Legacy and Influence: If appropriate, details on whether the song has been ranked as one of the best (or worst) by various judging entities, such as *Rolling Stone* editors, polls, or information on whether the song has inspired other musicians.
- Album Appearances: The name of the album or albums on which the song appears.

Entries associated with the Beatles' *albums* provide similar information, with these elements:

- Background and Recording Sessions: Information on how the album was created, performed, and produced.
- Track Listing: A listing in order of all the songs on the album.
- Cover Artwork: Describes the designer, artist, and or photographer involved with the album.
- Chart Performance: How well the album has officially sold in both the United States and the United Kingdom.
- Legacy and Influence: Rankings from "Best Lists," by *Rolling Stone* magazine and other influential sources or polls; reports by other artists who have been influenced by the work.

SPECIAL FEATURES

The condensed version of *The Beatles Encyclopedia: Everything Fab Four* offers helpful additional features, including an alphabetic list of all the entries included in the work; a chronology of the Beatles, showing milestones in their lives, performances, and recordings; a thorough discography of the band's official U.K. and U.S. singles and album releases from the early 1960s through the present; and a bibliography of recommended resources with both print and online resources, preceding a comprehensive general index.

Acknowledgments

This special condensed version of *The Beatles Encyclopedia: Everything Fab Four* would not have been possible without the inspiration and support of a host of friends and colleagues, including Lynne Clay, Daphne Keller, Nancy Mezey, Judy Ramos, and Michael Thomas. For their scholarly influence and professional contributions, I am grateful to Andy Babiuk, Vincent Benitez, Jackie Edmondson, Walter Everett, Jude Southerland Kessler, Howard Kramer, Mark Lewisohn, Tim Riley, Bruce Spizer, and Jerry Zolten. I am also thankful for the encouragement of ABC-CLIO's George Butler, whose unflagging goodwill provided the catalyst for bringing this volume to fruition. Finally, I am grateful, as always, for the love and support of my family—Fred, Jennifer, Andy, Becca, Peter, Tori, Josh, Ryan, Chelsea, Emma, Landon, Justin, and Mellissa—and especially to my wife Jeanine, who makes all things possible.

Chronology

Note: All release dates refer to official entries in the Beatles' U.K. catalogue.

1940	**July 7**	Ringo Starr [Richard Starkey] is born in Liverpool, England.
	October 9	John Winston Lennon is born in Liverpool, England.
1942	**June 18**	James Paul McCartney is born in Liverpool, England.
1943	**February 25**	George Harrison is born in Liverpool, England.
1957	**July 6**	McCartney meets Lennon after a Quarry Men performance at the Woolton Parish Church Garden Fête in Liverpool.
1958	**February**	Harrison joins Lennon and McCartney as a member of the Quarry Men.
	June	The Quarry Men record "That'll Be the Day" and "In Spite of All the Danger" at P. F. Phillips Professional Tape and Disk Record Service in Liverpool.
1959	**August 29**	The Quarry Men begin an extensive engagement at Mona Best's Casbah Club in Liverpool.
	October	The Quarry Men change their name to Johnny and the Moondogs.
1960	**January**	Stuart Sutcliffe wins £65 for his prize-winning painting in the John Moores Exhibition. He purchases a Höfner bass at Lennon's behest and becomes the Quarry Men's bass guitarist.
	May	Allan Williams becomes the manager of Johnny and the Moondogs, who change their name—shortly thereafter—to Long John and the Silver Beetles.

	May 20–28	As the Silver Beetles, the band embarks upon a nine-day Scottish tour in support of Johnny Gentle.
	August 12	Drummer Pete Best joins the band, who changes their name to the Beatles in advance of their upcoming Hamburg engagement.
	August 17– November 29	The Beatles perform on the Reeperbahn in Hamburg, first at the Indra Club and later at the Kaiserkeller.
1961	**February 9**	The Beatles perform at Liverpool's Cavern Club, eventually becoming the establishment's regular lunchtime act.
	April 1–July 1	The Beatles perform on the Reeperbahn in Hamburg's Top Ten Club. During this period, McCartney replaces Sutcliffe as the band's regular bassist.
	June	The Beatles record several songs as the Beat Brothers, the backing band for musician Tony Sheridan.
	November 9	NEMS record-store owner Brian Epstein watches the Beatles perform at the Cavern Club.
	December 10	Epstein officially becomes the Beatles' manager.
1962	**January 1**	The Beatles audition, unsuccessfully, for Decca Records in London.
	January 5	"My Bonnie"/"The Saints" by Tony Sheridan and the Beatles is released by Polydor.
	April 10	Sutcliffe dies of a brain hemorrhage in Hamburg.
	April 13– May 31	The Beatles perform at Hamburg's Star-Club.
	June 6	The Beatles audition at EMI Studios for producer George Martin, who is impressed with their potential, with the exception of Best's drumming ability.
	August 16	Best is fired from the Beatles.
	August 18	Starr performs as the Beatles' drummer for the first time.
	August 23	Lennon marries Cynthia Powell.
	September 11	The Beatles record "Love Me Do," "Please Please Me," and "P.S. I Love You" at EMI Studios.

	October 5	"Love Me Do"/"P.S. I Love You" single is released by Parlophone. It reaches #17 on the British charts.
	October 17	The Beatles' first television appearance on Granada's *People and Places*.
	November 1–14	The Beatles return for a brief engagement at Hamburg's Star-Club.
	November 26	The Beatles record "Please Please Me" at EMI Studios.
	December 18–31	The Beatles' final engagement at Hamburg's Star-Club.
1963	**January 3–6**	Winter Scottish Tour.
	January 10– February 1	Winter U.K. Tour.
	January 11	"Please Please Me"/"Ask Me Why" single is released by Parlophone. It reaches the top position on the British charts.
	January 19	The Beatles appear before a nationally televised audience on *Thank Your Lucky Stars*.
	February 2–March 3	Helen Shapiro Tour.
	February 11	The Beatles record the *Please Please Me* album in a single day's session at EMI Studios.
	March 9–31	Tommy Roe/Chris Montez Tour.
	March 22	*Please Please Me* album is released by Parlophone.
	April 2–May 17	Spring U.K. Tour.
	April 11	"From Me to You"/"Thank You Girl" single is released by Parlophone.
	May 18–June 9	Roy Orbison/Beatles Tour.
	June 10– September 15	Summer U.K. Tour.
	August 23	"She Loves You"/"I'll Get You" single is released by Parlophone.
	October 5–7	The Beatles' Mini-Tour of Scotland.
	October 13	The Beatles perform before a national television audience of some 15 million viewers on the popular British variety show *Val Parnell's Sunday Night at the London Palladium*. Beatlemania is born.

	December 24– January 16	The Beatles' 1964 Christmas Show at the Odeon Cinema, London.
1965	February 11	Starr marries Maureen Cox.
	February–May	Principal photography for the *Help!* feature film.
	April 9	"Ticket to Ride"/"Yes It Is" single is released by Parlophone.
	June 20–July 3	The Beatles' European Tour.
	July 23	"Help!"/"I'm Down" single is released by Parlophone.
	July 29	*Help!* premieres at the London Pavilion.
	August 6	*Help!* album is released by Parlophone.
	August 15–31	The Beatles' American Tour.
	August 15	The Beatles perform at Shea Stadium in New York City before an audience of 55,600 fans.
	August 27	The Beatles meet Elvis Presley in Los Angeles.
	October– November	Recording sessions for *Rubber Soul.*
	October 26	The Beatles receive their MBEs [Member of the Order of the British Empire] from Queen Elizabeth II.
	December 3	"We Can Work It Out"/"Day Tripper" single is released by Parlophone.
	December 3	*Rubber Soul* album is released by Parlophone.
	December 3–12	The Beatles' British Tour.
1966	January 21	Harrison marries Pattie Boyd.
	April–June	Recording sessions for *Revolver.*
	June 10	"Paperback Writer"/"Rain" single is released by Parlophone.
	June 24–July 4	The Beatles' Tour of Germany and Japan.
	July 29	American magazine *Datebook* republishes Lennon's March 1966 interview in which he proclaims that the Beatles are "more popular than Jesus."
	August 12–29	The Beatles' Final American Tour.
	August 5	"Eleanor Rigby"/"Yellow Submarine" single is released by Parlophone.
	August 5	*Revolver* album is released by Parlophone.
	August 29	The Beatles play at San Francisco's Candlestick Park for their final concert before a paying audience.

	November 9	Lennon meets Yoko Ono at London's Indica Gallery.
	November–April	Recording sessions for *Sgt. Pepper's Lonely Hearts Club Band*.
1967	February 17	"Strawberry Fields Forever"/"Penny Lane" single is released by Parlophone.
	June 1	*Sgt. Pepper's Lonely Hearts Club Band* album is released by Parlophone.
	June 25	The Beatles perform "All You Need Is Love" on the *Our World* international telecast.
	July 7	"All You Need Is Love"/"Baby, You're a Rich Man" single is released by Parlophone.
	August 24	The Beatles meet the Maharishi Mahesh Yogi at the London Hilton.
	August 27	Epstein is found dead in London from an accidental drug overdose.
	September–October	Principal photography and recording sessions for the *Magical Mystery Tour* project.
	November 24	"Hello Goodbye"/"I Am the Walrus" single is released by Parlophone.
	December 8	*Magical Mystery Tour* EP is released by Parlophone.
	December 26	*Magical Mystery Tour* film is televised on the BBC.
1968	February–April	The Beatles visit the Maharishi's compound at Rishikesh, India.
	March 15	"Lady Madonna"/"The Inner Light" single is released by Parlophone.
	May 14	Lennon and McCartney announce the formation of Apple Corps at a New York City press conference.
	May–October	Recording sessions for *The Beatles* (*The White Album*).
	July 17	*Yellow Submarine* cartoon feature premieres at the London Pavilion.
	August 30	"Hey Jude"/"Revolution" single is released by Apple.
	November 22	*The Beatles* (*The White Album*) is released by Apple.
1969	January 2	Principal photography for the *Get Back* project commences at Twickenham Studios.

	January 17	*Yellow Submarine* album is released by Apple.
	January 30	The Beatles' Rooftop Concert at Apple Studios on Savile Row.
	March 12	McCartney marries Linda Eastman.
	March 20	Lennon marries Ono.
	March 21	Allen Klein is appointed as business manager for Apple Corps.
	April–August	Recording sessions for *Abbey Road*.
	April 11	"Get Back"/"Don't Let Me Down" single is released by Apple.
	May 30	"The Ballad of John and Yoko"/"Old Brown Shoe" single is released by Apple.
	August 22	The Beatles gather at Lennon and Ono's Tittenhurst Park estate for their final photo session.
	September 26	*Abbey Road* album is released by Apple.
	October 31	"Something"/"Come Together" single is released by Apple.
1970	**March 6**	"Let It Be"/"You Know My Name (Look Up the Number)" single is released by Apple.
	April 9	McCartney announces the Beatles' breakup.
	May 8	*Let It Be* album is released by Apple.
1973	**April 19**	*The Beatles, 1962–1966* and *The Beatles, 1967–1970* are released by Apple.
1976	**March 5**	"Yesterday"/"I Should Have Known Better" single is released by Parlophone.
	June 11	*Rock 'n' Roll Music* is released by Parlophone.
	June 25	"Back in the USSR"/"Twist and Shout" single is released by Parlophone.
1977	**May 6**	*The Beatles at the Hollywood Bowl* is released by Parlophone.
	November 19	*Love Songs* is released by Parlophone.
1978	**September 30**	"Sgt. Pepper's Lonely Hearts Club Band/With a Little Help from My Friends"/"A Day in the Life" single is released by Parlophone.
1979	**October 12**	*Rarities* is released by Parlophone.
1980	**December 8**	Lennon is assassinated in New York City.
1982	**March 22**	*Reel Music* is released by Parlophone.

	March 24	"The Beatles' Movie Medley"/"I'm Happy Just to Dance with You" is released by Parlophone.
	October 11	*20 Greatest Hits* is released by Parlophone.
1985	**July 13**	McCartney performs "Let It Be" at the Live Aid benefit concert at London's Wembley Stadium.
	October 9	Ono dedicates the Strawberry Fields memorial in New York City's Central Park.
1988		The Beatles are inducted into the Rock and Roll Hall of Fame.
1994		Lennon is inducted into the Rock and Roll Hall of Fame.
	November 30	*Live at the BBC* is released by Apple.
1995	**November**	The Beatles' televised *Anthology* documentary is broadcast in six parts on the U.K. ITV and the U.S. ABC TV networks.
	November 21	*Anthology 1* is released by Apple.
	December 4	"Free as a Bird"/"Christmas Time (Is Here Again)" is released by Apple.
1996		Martin is knighted by Queen Elizabeth II.
	March 4	"Real Love"/"Baby's in Black (Live)" is released by Apple.
	March 18	*Anthology 2* is released by Apple.
	October 28	*Anthology 3* is released by Apple.
1997		McCartney is knighted by Queen Elizabeth II.
1998	**April 17**	Linda McCartney dies of cancer in Tucson, Arizona.
1999		McCartney is inducted into the Rock and Roll Hall of Fame.
	September 13	*Yellow Submarine Songtrack* is released by Apple.
		Martin is inducted into the Rock and Roll Hall of Fame.
2000	**November 13**	*1* is released by Apple.
2001	**November 29**	Harrison dies of cancer in Los Angeles.
2003	**November 17**	*Let It Be . . . Naked* is released by Apple.
2004		Harrison is inducted posthumously into the Rock and Roll Hall of Fame.
2006	**June 30**	Cirque du Soleil's *Love* premieres at the Mirage in Las Vegas.

A

Abbey Road (LP)

September 26, 1969, Apple [Parlophone] PCS 7088 (stereo)
October 1, 1969, Apple [Capitol] SO 383 (stereo)

Abbey Road is the Beatles' 11th and final studio album. It was released on the Apple Records label on September 26, 1969, in the United Kingdom and October 1, 1969, in the United States. In pure chronological order, the band's 10th studio effort, originally intended to be released as the *Get Back* project, was formally released several months later, in May 1970, as the *Let It Be* soundtrack album, having been recorded, for the most part, in January 1969—and prior to the recording sessions that resulted in the *Abbey Road* album. As the Beatles' musical swan song, *Abbey Road* is considered to be one of the most widely influential albums of all time, while also bringing the band's monumental creative synthesis to a dramatic close.

Abbey Road was released as a stereo compact disc (CD), along with *Let It Be*, on October 19, 1987. *Abbey Road* was remastered and rereleased as a stereo CD on September 9, 2009.

BACKGROUND AND RECORDING SESSIONS

With Geoff Emerick back in the fold, having rejoined the Beatles' team as sound engineer for "The Ballad of John and Yoko" sessions, the group still needed to coax producer George Martin back into the studio. In spite of the band members' excitement about recording new material, Martin was clearly uncertain about their prospects for success after the emotional rancor associated with the *Get Back* sessions: "I really believed that was the end of the Beatles," he later recalled,

> And I assumed that I would never work with them again. I thought, "What a shame to end like this." So I was quite surprised when Paul rang me up and said, "We're going to make another record—would you like to produce it?" My immediate response was: "Only if you let me produce it the way we used to." (Beatles 2000, 337)

Although the lion's share of the recording sessions for *Abbey Road* occurred between July 2 and August 20, 1969, a February 22 session found the Beatles working on early takes of "I Want You (She's So Heavy)." In mid-April, with Martin at the helm, they continued crafting the new song before taking off the entire month of June in order to amass additional material for the eventual album. The months of July and August saw the Beatles hard at work on a "great medley" that was the album's centerpiece, with the band putting the finishing touches on "I Want You (She's So Heavy)" on August 20, having come full circle from their initial work back in February. In the interim, they crafted several new classic numbers, including "Something," "Come Together," and "Here Comes the Sun."

While the autumn of 1969 found John Lennon explicitly working toward the Beatles' disbandment, his enthusiasm at the outset of the *Abbey Road* sessions was palpable. As he noted during an interview with *Disc* magazine,

> If I could only get the time to myself, I think I could probably write about 30 songs a day. As it is, I probably average about 12 a night. Paul, too: he's mad on it. As soon as I leave here, I'm going 'round to Paul's place and we'll sit down and start work. The way we're writing at the moment, it's straightforward and there's nothing weird. The songs are like "Get Back," and a lot of that we did in one take. (Doggett 1998, 48)

The Beatles recorded the album with this very same fervor and drive—a stark contrast, in many ways, from the numerous sessions involved in the production of *Sgt. Pepper's Lonely Hearts Club Band* and *The White Album*. At one juncture during the project, the group worked simultaneously in three different studios at EMI, famously resorting to walkie-talkies in order to communicate between studios.

Abbey Road is noteworthy as the Beatles' first—and, indeed, last—sustained use of eight-track recording technology, given Abbey Road Studios' recent shift toward solid-state electronics in place of the vacuum tube–driven recording equipment that had marked the balance of their artistic career. The result is a perceptibly warmer tonality, a "mellower" quality, according to Emerick, that affords *Abbey Road* with a very different ambience than the Beatles' previous work (Emerick and Massey 2006, 277). In addition to the new studio technology, the album benefitted from Ringo Starr's newly acquired drum kit, a set of Ludwig Hollywoods that provided the drummer with greater clarity and punch. Working on *Abbey Road* "was tom-tom madness," Starr later recalled. "I had gotten this new kit made of wood, and calfskins, and the toms had so much depth. I went nuts on the toms. Talk about changes in my drum style—the kit made me change because I changed my kit" (Everett 1999, 245).

But for all of the favorable conditions under which *Abbey Road* seemed to be percolating—particularly Lennon's renewed enthusiasm—any genuine hopes of putting the *Get Back* project's corrosive atmosphere behind the group came to a sudden end during the first week of July. On July 1, fewer than 24 hours before the formal sessions for the album were set to begin, Lennon and Yoko Ono were involved in a devastating automobile accident when Lennon lost control of their Austin Maxi and drove off a steep embankment in northern Scotland. With six-year-old Julian and five-year-old Kyoko in the back seat, the newly married couple barely escaped with their lives, with Ono in particular suffering a concussion and several crushed vertebrae. After a five-day hospital stay, the couple finally made their way back to London, with John rejoining the group on July 9. As EMI engineer Phil McDonald later remembered:

> We were all waiting for them to arrive, Paul, George, and Ringo downstairs and us upstairs. They didn't know what state he would be in. There was a definite "vibe": they were almost afraid of Lennon before he arrived, because they didn't know what he would be like. I got the feeling that the three of them were a little bit scared of him. When he did come in it was a relief, and they got together fairly well. John was a powerful figure, especially with Yoko—a double strength. (Doggett 1998, 59, 60)

Given the state of her injuries and her high-risk pregnancy, Ono required constant bed rest—so much so, in fact, that Lennon had a double bed shipped to Abbey Road Studios from Harrods and a microphone positioned within easy reach so as to allow her to be in continuous communication with her husband.

But the cost of those nine days away from the band was hardly lost on Lennon. In spite of the severity of his injuries, his bandmates continued working throughout his absence on the album—a project for which he had evinced so much excitement only scant weeks before. While *Abbey Road* emerged as one of the band's master works, the interpersonal fissures of their final months together, as history well knows, truly took their toll on the group's ability to continue as a working creative unit.

TRACK LISTING

Side 1: "Come Together"; "Something"; "Maxwell's Silver Hammer"; "Oh! Darling"; "Octopus's Garden"; "I Want You (She's So Heavy)."

Side 2: "Here Comes the Sun"; "Because"; "You Never Give Me Your Money"; "Sun King"; "Mean Mr. Mustard"; "Polythene Pam"; "She Came in Through the Bathroom Window"; "Golden Slumbers"; "Carry That Weight"; "The End"; "Her Majesty" [unlisted].

COVER ARTWORK

The Beatles considered several titles before settling on *Abbey Road*, including *Four in the Bar*, *All Good Children Go to Heaven*, and the intentionally nonsensical *Billy's Left Foot*. At one point, they strongly considered naming the album *Everest* as homage to Emerick's favorite brand of cigarettes. As Paul McCartney later observed during an interview with Mark Lewisohn, "We were stuck for an album title, and the album didn't appear to have any obvious concept, except that it had all been done in the studio and it had been done by us. And Emerick used to have these packets of Everest cigarettes always sitting by him, and we thought, 'That's good. It's big and it's expansive' " (Lewisohn 1988, 13). But the idea eventually collapsed

Iconic cover of *Abbey Road,* 1969. Shown from left: George Harrison, Paul McCartney, Ringo Starr, and John Lennon. (Capitol/EMI/Photofest)

when the group realized that they couldn't be bothered to travel all of the way to Tibet for a photo shoot. In the end, it was Starr who afforded the Beatles' final studio album with its seminal name. "F—it," Starr dryly remarked. "Let's just step outside and name it *Abbey Road*" (Emerick and Massey 2006, 297).

As the central feature of creative director John Kosh's design, the album's iconic cover photograph was captured on Friday, August 8, 1969. With photographer Iain Macmillan standing atop a ladder while the London Metropolitan Police stayed Abbey Road's noontime traffic, the Beatles strolled across the zebra crossing only a few yards from the entrance to the studio where they had made their name.

CHART PERFORMANCE

U.K.: #1.

U.S.: #1 (certified by the RIAA as "12x Multi Platinum," with more than 12 million copies sold; certified by the RIAA as "Diamond," with more than 10 million copies sold).

LEGACY AND INFLUENCE

Abbey Road became the best-selling album of 1969 in both the United Kingdom and the United States, enjoying sales of more than 5 million copies worldwide. It became the first Beatles album to reach sales of 10 million, which the album achieved in 1980.

The zebra crossing near 3 Abbey Road that graces the album's cover has become a popular London tourist destination, with thousands of visitors making the annual pilgrimage to St. John's Wood to imitate the band's famous photo shoot. The Beatles' iconic pose has been widely imitated by other artists, namely the Red Hot Chili Peppers. The zebra crossing itself has been officially listed among the city's historical places. In 2010, Abbey Road Studios installed a webcam trained on the crosswalk. Over the years—and much to the chagrin of the studio's neighbors—fans have adorned the security wall in front of the studio with graffiti devoted to the Fab Four.

The album has often been the subject of homage. In April 1970, Booker T. and the M. G.'s released *McLemore Avenue*, a collection of soulful instrumental versions of *Abbey Road*'s contents. The cover art depicts the band walking across McLemore Avenue, the street in front of Memphis's Stax studio. In June 1970, American jazz guitarist George Benson released the well-received *The Other Side of Abbey Road*, a compilation that he began recording within weeks of the original album's release.

In 1970, *Abbey Road* was nominated for a Grammy Award for Album of the Year at the 12th Grammy Awards. It was also nominated for a Grammy for Contemporary Vocal Group Performance.

In 1995, *Abbey Road* was inducted into the National Academy of Recording Arts and Sciences Grammy Hall of Fame.

In 1998, the BBC ranked *Abbey Road* as #12 among its *Music of the Millennium* albums.

In 2000, *Q Magazine* ranked *Abbey Road* as #17 on the magazine's list of *The 100 Greatest British Albums Ever*.

In 2001, VH1 ranked *Abbey Road* as #8 among its *All Time Album Top 100*.

In 2003, *Rolling Stone* ranked *Abbey Road* as #14 on the magazine's list of *The 500 Greatest Albums of All Time*.

In 2005, *Mojo* magazine ranked *Abbey Road* as #24 on the magazine's list of *The 100 Greatest Albums Ever Made*.

In 2009, *Mojo* published a special issue that celebrated *Abbey Road*'s 40th anniversary, including a cover-mounted CD with contemporary cover versions of the album's entire contents entitled *Abbey Road Now!*

See also: Preston, Billy.

Abbey Road Studios (St. John's Wood, London)

Abbey Road Studios, the recording facility in which the Beatles produced the majority of their legendary catalog, is located at 3 Abbey Road amongst the stately Edwardian homes of London's St. John's Wood.

Built in 1830 as a luxurious residence that included five reception rooms, nine bedrooms, a wine cellar, a substantial garden, and servants' quarters, the home was purchased by the Gramophone Company in 1929. It officially opened its doors in November 1931—scant months after Columbia Graphophone had merged with the Gramophone Company and formed the EMI Group. In the early 1930s, English composer Edward Elgar conducted the historic recording sessions at EMI Studios for *Pomp and Circumstance*, the series of five marches that immortalized his name—the march entitled "The Land of Hope and Glory" emerged as a British sporting anthem, while "The Light of Life" became the signature melody for American graduation ceremonies. Ironically, while the Beatles are clearly responsible for the renown that Abbey Road Studios enjoys across the globe, the Greater London Council "blue plaque" affixed to its entryway commemorates the work of "Elgar, Sir Edward (1857–1934)." Aside from the ubiquitous graffiti on the complex's front wall, Abbey Road Studios offers no external commemoration for the work of its most famous clients.

The Abbey Road Studios complex comprises four studios, the largest of which is Studio One, where much of the facility's orchestral recording occurs (Harry 1992, 4). The Beatles carried out the vast majority of their work in Studio Two. As sound engineer Geoff Emerick describes it, "Studio Two was unusual at the EMI complex—in fact, unusual anywhere in the world—in that the control room was on the floor above the larger studio area where the musicians sat, overlooking it instead of being on the same level. Access between the two was navigated by a narrow flight of wooden stairs, and communications from the control room were transmitted over a pair of large speakers that hung on the far wall of the studio, directly over the emergency exit" (Emerick and Massey 2006, 41).

In 1970, given the worldwide success of the *Abbey Road* album, EMI rechristened the complex as Abbey Road Studios. In the ensuing years, Abbey Road Studios has become an increasingly popular tourist destination, with fans from across the globe alighting the Tube's Jubilee line in order to make the pilgrimage to St. John's Wood and have their photograph taken along the famous zebra crossing. In the Internet age, fans can visit Abbey Road virtually through the recording studios' 24-hour webcam, located at www.abbeyroad.com/crossing.

See also: Emerick, Geoff; Martin, George.

"Across the Universe" (Lennon–McCartney)

"Across the Universe" is a song on the Beatles' *Let It Be* album.

AUTHORSHIP AND BACKGROUND

Written by Lennon, "Across the Universe" is one of the songwriter's favorite compositions among his body of work.

As Lennon recalled,

> I was a bit more artsy-fartsy there. I was lying next to my first wife in bed, you know, and I was irritated. She must have been going on and on about something and she'd gone to sleep—and I kept hearing these words over and over, flowing like an endless stream. I went downstairs and it turned into a sort of cosmic song rather than an irritated song. . . . It's not a matter of craftsmanship—it wrote itself. It drove me out of bed. I didn't want to write it—and I couldn't get to sleep until I put it on paper. It's like being possessed—like a psychic or a medium. (Everett 1999, 156)

RECORDING SESSIONS

Produced by George Martin with postproduction by Phil Spector, "Across the Universe" was recorded on February 4, 1968, at Abbey Road Studios, with an additional overdubbing session on February 8 and an orchestral overdubbing session on April 1. During the latter session, Spector worked from Brian Rogers' orchestral arrangement and John Barham's choral arrangement for the song.

Recorded with Lennon on his Martin D-28 and Harrison on tamboura, the composition captures Lennon in one of his most earnest, lyrical, and hopeful performances. With "Across the Universe," Tim Riley remarks, "the free-floating imagery determines the musical flexibility—the words evoke the creative process as much as a creative state of mind" (Riley 1988, 296). As a work of metapoetry, "Across the Universe" captures both the aesthetic intensity of creative expression and the artist's struggle to rend language into meaning.

In the refrain for "Across the Universe," Lennon invokes the Sanskrit phrase "Jai guru deva om," which can be loosely translated as follows: Jai ("live forever") guru ("teacher") deva ("heavenly one") om ("the vibration of the universe"). The phrase can also be rendered as "victory to God divine" or, in the words of Maharishi Mahesh Yogi, "All Glory to Guru Dev."

"Across the Universe" underwent several different iterations, including the initial rendition, with a pair of acoustic guitars, a table harp, and Harrison's tamboura. During the second session, Lennon added his vocal, while Starr provided tom-tom accompaniment. Later that same evening, the Beatles invited a pair of Apple Scruffs—the Beatles' nickname for the horde of fans who trailed their every move—to sing harmony on "Across the Universe." Having been handpicked outside Abbey Road Studios by McCartney, an ecstatic Lizzie Bravo and Gayleen Pease provided backup vocals.

In October 1969, the Beatles shared a slightly sped-up version of "Across the Universe"—complete with Apple Scruffs and the sound of birds on the wing— with Spike Mulligan, who was organizing a charity LP for the World Wildlife Fund. The album was entitled *No One's Gonna Change Our World*, invoking Lennon's hopeful lyrics as the rallying call for the animal rights movement. In 1970, Spector slowed the song down and overdubbed an orchestral and choral arrangement.

The original February 4 version of "Across the Universe"—with the Apple Scruffs, bird sound effects, keyboards, and maracas mixed out—can be heard on the *Let It Be . . . Naked* (2003) version of the song.

PERSONNEL

Lennon: Vocal, Martin D-28
McCartney: Piano, Backing Vocal
Harrison: Tamboura
Starr: Maracas
Martin: Hammond Organ
Lizzie Bravo and Gayleen Pease (on World Wildlife Fund version): Backing Vocals
Studio Musicians: Orchestral and Choral Accompaniment (18 Violins, 4 Violas, 4 Cellos, 3 Trumpets, 3 Trombones, 2 Guitars, and 14 Female Singers) conducted by Spector (on *Let It Be* album version)

LEGACY AND INFLUENCE

In 2010, *Rolling Stone* ranked "Across the Universe" as #84 on the magazine's list of *The Beatles' 100 Greatest Songs*.

ALBUM APPEARANCES: *Let It Be*; *The Beatles, 1967–1970*; *Rarities* (U.K.); *Rarities* (U.S.); *Past Masters, Volume 2*; *Anthology 2*; *Let It Be . . . Naked*.

See also: *Let It Be* (LP); *Let It Be . . . Naked* (LP); Spector, Phil.

"Act Naturally" (Russell–Morrison)

"Act Naturally" is a song on the Beatles' *Help!* album.

AUTHORSHIP AND BACKGROUND

"Act Naturally" was written by Johnny Russell and Voni Morrison. In 1963, Buck Owens and the Buckaroos scored a No.1 U.S. country hit with the song. The song's first line comes from a remark by Russell, who broke a date with his girlfriend to go to a recording session in Los Angeles. As Russell recalled, "When she asked me why I was going to LA, I answered, 'They are going to put me in the movies and make a big star out of me.' We both laughed" (Collins 1996, 175).

RECORDING SESSIONS

Produced by George Martin, "Act Naturally" was recorded at Abbey Road Studios in 19 takes on June 17, 1965. It was the first song recorded after the Beatles completed principal photography for the *Help!* feature film.

During the recording sessions for *Help!*, Starr handled the lead vocals on both "Act Naturally" and a Lennon–McCartney composition entitled "If You've Got Trouble," which the Beatles left off the album in favor of the Russell–Morrison cover version. "Act Naturally" was the last cover version recorded by the Beatles until the *Get Back* sessions in January 1969. After "Act Naturally," the Beatles only recorded one more nonoriginal composition for any of their albums: the traditional 19th-century Liverpool ballad entitled "Maggie Mae," which was included on *Let It Be* and copyrighted to Lennon, McCartney, Harrison, and Starr as the composition's songwriters.

PERSONNEL

Lennon: Gibson J-160E
McCartney: Höfner 500/1, Backing Vocal
Harrison: Gretsch Tennessean
Starr: Vocal, Ludwig Oyster Black Pearl Drums

CHART PERFORMANCE

U.S.: "Yesterday"/"Act Naturally"; September 13, 1965, Capitol 5498: #1 (certified by the RIAA as "Gold," with more than 500,000 copies sold). As the B-side of "Yesterday," "Act Naturally" charted at #47.

ALBUM APPEARANCES: *Help!* (U.K.); *Yesterday . . . and Today*.

See also: *Help!* (U.K. LP).

"All I've Got to Do" (Lennon–McCartney)

"All I've Got to Do" is a song on the *With the Beatles* album.

AUTHORSHIP AND BACKGROUND

Written by Lennon, "All I've Got to Do" was composed with the sounds of Smokey Robinson and the Miracles on the songwriter's mind.

RECORDING SESSIONS

Produced by George Martin, "All I've Got to Do" was recorded in 14 takes at Abbey Road Studios on September 11, 1963.

PERSONNEL

Lennon: Vocal, Rickenbacker 325
McCartney: Höfner 500/1, Backing Vocal

Harrison: Gretsch Country Gentleman
Starr: Ludwig Oyster Black Pearl Drums

LEGACY AND INFLUENCE

In 2010, *Rolling Stone* ranked "All I've Got to Do" as #97 on the magazine's list of *The Beatles' 100 Greatest Songs.*

ALBUM APPEARANCES: *With the Beatles*; *Meet the Beatles!*

See also: *With the Beatles* (LP).

"All My Loving" (Lennon–McCartney)

"All My Loving" is a song on the *With the Beatles* album.

AUTHORSHIP AND BACKGROUND

Written by McCartney, "All My Loving" allegedly came to the songwriter while he was shaving one morning. "It was the first song I ever wrote," McCartney later recalled, "where I had the words before the music. I wrote the words on a bus on tour, then we got the tune when I arrived there." As Lennon later remarked, " 'All My Loving' is Paul, I regret to say. . . . Because it's a damn good piece of work. . . . But I play a pretty mean guitar in back" (Dowlding 1989, 49, 50).

RECORDING SESSIONS

Produced by George Martin, "All My Loving" was recorded at Abbey Road Studios in 11 takes in a single session on July 30, 1963. The song features neatly bookended verses with shrewdly positioned instances of stop-time between them that bring the track to a sudden halt, only to be reawakened by McCartney's buoyant singing, and, in one memorable instance, Harrison's Carl Perkins–inspired guitar break.

As Ian MacDonald points out, the song benefits from its "elegant simplicity," as well as from McCartney's double-tracked vocal, which is "irresistibly joyous" (MacDonald 1994, 72). The Beatles' deft usage of stop-time in the song finds its origins in African American popular music, with notable examples occurring in such compositions as Scott Joplin's "The Ragtime Dance" and Jelly Roll Morton's "King Porter Stomp." According to the Center for Black Music Research (2006), stop-time was originally contrived in order to provide audiences with moments in which to share their enthusiasm and applause.

On February 28, 1964, the Beatles recorded a second version of "All My Loving" for the BBC's *From Us to You* radio show that was later included on the *Live at the BBC* album. Overall, they recorded four versions of "All My Loving" for BBC Radio between December 1963 and February 1964.

PERSONNEL

Lennon: Rickenbacker 325, Backing Vocal
McCartney: Vocal, Höfner 500/1
Harrison: Gretsch Country Gentleman, Backing Vocal
Starr: Ludwig Oyster Black Pearl Drums

LEGACY AND INFLUENCE

In 1964, the Beatles received an Ivor Novello Award, awarded annually by the British Academy of Songwriters, Composers, and Authors, for "All My Loving."

In 2010, *Rolling Stone* ranked "All My Loving" as #44 on the magazine's list of *The Beatles' 100 Greatest Songs*.

ALBUM APPEARANCES: *With the Beatles*; *Meet the Beatles!*; *The Beatles, 1962–1966*; *The Beatles at the Hollywood Bowl*; *Live at the BBC*; *Anthology 1*.

See also: *The Ed Sullivan Show* (TV Series); *With the Beatles* (LP).

"All Together Now" (Lennon–McCartney)

"All Together Now" is a song on the Beatles' *Yellow Submarine* album.

AUTHORSHIP AND BACKGROUND

Written by McCartney with assistance from Lennon, "All Together Now" was composed expressly as an upbeat children's song for the *Yellow Submarine* animated feature film. Lennon composed the song's middle-eight.

As Lennon later recalled, "I enjoyed it when football crowds in the early days would sing 'All Together Now' " (Dowlding 1989, 212). As McCartney remarked, "When they were singing a song, to encourage the audience to join in they'd say 'all together now,' so I just took it and read another meaning into it, of—we are all together now. So I used the dual meaning. It's really a children's song. I had a few young relatives and I would sing songs for them" (Miles 1997, 481).

RECORDING SESSIONS

Produced by George Martin, the Beatles recorded "All Together Now" in nine takes at Abbey Road Studios on May 12, 1967. While Martin is credited as producer, he was absent that evening, leaving Geoff Emerick to supervise the session in his stead.

With Lennon strumming his Jumbo and playing harmonica on a Beatles track for the first time in two years, the instrumentation is rounded out by McCartney's Epiphone Texan, Starr on finger cymbals, and all four Beatles engaging in a light-hearted sing-along that gathers momentum before galloping into a sudden climax.

PERSONNEL

Lennon: Vocal, Ukulele, Harmonica, Plastic Sax
McCartney: Vocal, Epiphone Texan, Rickenbacker 4001S
Harrison: Backing Vocal
Starr: Ludwig Oyster Black Pearl Drums, Finger Cymbals, Backing Vocal

ALBUM APPEARANCES: *Yellow Submarine*; *Yellow Submarine Songtrack*.

See also: Emerick, Geoff; *Our World* (TV Special); *Yellow Submarine* (LP).

"All You Need Is Love" (Lennon–McCartney)

"All You Need Is Love" was a #1 single in the United Kingdom, where it was released on July 7, 1967. The song was later included on the Beatles' *Magical Mystery Tour* album.

AUTHORSHIP AND BACKGROUND

Written by Lennon, "All You Need Is Love" was written specifically as the Beatles' message to humankind for their globally televised *Our World* performance on June 25, 1967. The program was broadcast to a worldwide television audience of 400 million people in 26 countries.

As McCartney observed during the summer of 1967, "We had been told we'd be seen recording it by the whole world at the same time. So we had one message for the world—Love. We need more love in the world" (Cadogan 2008, 197). As Lennon later recalled,

> I think if you get down to basics, whatever the problem is, it's usually to do with love. So I think "All You Need is Love" is a true statement. I'm not saying, "All you have to do is . . ." because "All You Need" came out in the Flower Power Generation time. It doesn't mean that all you have to do is put on a phony smile or wear a flower dress and it's gonna be alright. Love is not just something that you stick on posters or stick on the back of your car, or on the back of your jacket or on a badge. I'm talking about real love, so I still believe that. Love is appreciation of other people and allowing them to be. Love is allowing somebody to be themselves and that's what we do need. (Cadogan 2008, 198)

The Beatles perform "All You Need Is Love" on *Our World*, the first live satellite uplink performance broadcast to the world, on June 25, 1967, in London, England. The show was watched by over 300 million people in 24 different countries. From left to right are Paul McCartney, John Lennon, Ringo Starr, and George Harrison. (Michael Ochs Archives/Getty Images)

With the worldwide groundswell of *Sgt. Pepper's Lonely Hearts Club Band* gradually receding in the band's rearview mirror, the Beatles made preparations to represent Great Britain on the international *Our World* telecast, slated for broadcast on June 25, 1967. Negotiated by Brian Epstein some months back and made public in mid-May, the Beatles' appearance on the satellite telecast required the proffering of a new song. With their internal rites of composition in full swing, Lennon and McCartney vied for the opportunity of displaying their wares on this most international of stages. While McCartney allegedly offered up "All Together Now" and "Your Mother Should Know" for consideration, Lennon suggested his latest composition entitled "All You Need Is Love," a rather obvious selection, given its universal theme. Bob Spitz claims that the McCartney entry was the recently penned "Hello, Goodbye," as opposed to "Your Mother Should Know" (Spitz 2005, 700). "It was an inspired song and they really wanted to give the world a message," Epstein remarked about "All You Need Is Love." "The nice thing about it is that it cannot be misinterpreted. It is a clear message saying that love is everything." For his part, Harrison later described "All You Need Is Love" as a "subtle bit of PR for God" (Beatles 2000, 257).

RECORDING SESSIONS

Produced by George Martin, "All You Need Is Love" went into production on June 14, 1967, at Olympic Sound Studio, where the Beatles recorded a 10-minute backing track for the upcoming global telecast. A few days later, they shortened the backing track to 6 minutes at an Abbey Road Studios session.

For the June 14 session, the group recorded 33 takes of "All You Need Is Love," with Lennon on harpsichord; McCartney playing a double bass, complete with bow; Starr on his Ludwigs; and Harrison plucking a violin, guitar-like, with mixed results. A few days later, Martin added a barrelhouse piano, while Lennon strummed a banjo, his lost mother Julia's instrument of choice. Given free rein to compose an orchestral score, the producer imagined an elaborate sound collage that begins with an intentionally stilted version of "La Marseillaise," in a barefaced attempt to conjure up stereotypical notions of the French as the world's greatest lovers, and concludes with a pastiche of musical quotations. In addition to the French national anthem, Martin concludes the song with an instrumental montage that features "Greensleeves"—a rather appropriate choice, given the 16th-century tune's despairing phrases about a heart that remains forever in captivity—as well as a fragment from Glenn Miller's "In the Mood," which subsequently resulted in an out-of-court settlement for copyright infringement. Martin also adorned the pastiche with a recurring phrase from Bach's *Two-Part Invention in F Major*, featuring the ever-faithful David Mason in a trumpet duet with Stanley Woods.

In itself, the *Our World* broadcast was the high-water mark for the Beatles' much-vaunted dreams for universal hope and tranquility. Leaving almost nothing to chance, Martin arranged for the group to accompany their prerecorded track, with a gum-chewing Lennon on lead vocals, McCartney on his Rickenbacker, Harrison playing his Casino on a four-bar solo, and Starr behind the drums. McCartney and Harrison's guitars were decked out in newly painted psychedelia for the occasion. Their clothes were even more flamboyant, with McCartney dressed in a white sport coat and a garish, hand-colored shirt; Lennon paradoxically wearing a conventional pin-striped suit; Harrison adorned in an orange paisley jacket; and Starr enveloped by a heavy, beaded getup consisting of suede, satin, and pseudo-fur (Spitz 2005, 702). Clearly, the days of coordinated suits and Beatle boots had been irrevocably lost among the staves of time. For his part, McCartney had painted his shirt himself: "I stayed up all night the night before. I didn't mean to but I was drawing on a shirt. I had these pen things that you used to draw with and the ink didn't wash out. I stayed up all night doing it, and the shirt was nicked the next day. Who has it, I don't know. One of these days Sotheby's will tell" (Flippo 1988, 241).

With a studio audience of friends and family belting out the chorus—including such rock 'n' roll glitterati as Mick Jagger, Keith Richards, Eric Clapton, Keith Moon, and Graham Nash, among others—EMI's Studio One enjoyed a festive atmosphere for the 7-minute broadcast, with a 13-piece orchestra, placard-toting extras, and a flourish of streamers, confetti, and balloons on global display. The placards included "All You Need Is Love" translated in four languages, as well as the mysterious "COME BACK MILLY! ALL IS FORGIVEN!" in reference to McCartney's aunt who had fled Liverpool for Australia. Fearing that Milly might never return, Paul's cousin Anne Danher hastily prepared the placard before the broadcast (Spitz 2005, 703). With an estimated audience of some 350 million people on five continents, it was flower power's finest moment. Martin's postproduction efforts for the upcoming single's release—which featured "Baby, You're a Rich Man" as its B-side—included the addition of Starr's introductory snare roll and some subtle tidying up of Lennon's vocals.

Rather fittingly, "All You Need Is Love" witnesses the Beatles bidding farewell, in a manner of speaking, to their early years, as well as to the naïve, idealistic visions of love that brought them world fame in the first place. As the song begins its protracted fade-out, Martin's arrangement of Bach's *Two-Part Invention* kicks into gear, with "Greensleeves" and "In the Mood" swirling joyfully in the background. Meanwhile, Lennon delivers a nonsequitur reference to "Yesterday," followed closely on the heels by his buoyant duet with McCartney, as they provide a brief refrain from "She Loves You." As Alan W. Pollack astutely remarks, "To my ears, their quote from 'She Loves You' goes beyond the merely clever literary association of the lyrics to become the more profound musical equivalent of the wax models [of the Beatlemania-era bandmates] on the cover of *Sgt. Pepper*" (Pollack 2000).

PERSONNEL

Lennon: Vocal, Harpsichord, Banjo
McCartney: Rickenbacker 4001S, Backing Vocal
Harrison: Sonic Blue Fender Stratocaster, Violin, Backing Vocal
Starr: Ludwig Oyster Black Pearl Drums
Martin: Piano
Jane Asher: Backing Vocal
Pattie Boyd: Backing Vocal
Marianne Faithfull: Backing Vocal
Mick Jagger: Backing Vocal
Gary Leeds: Backing Vocal
Michael McGear: Backing Vocal
Keith Moon: Brush Drums, Backing Vocal
Graham Nash: Backing Vocal
Keith Richards: Backing Vocal
Studio Musicians: Orchestral Accompaniment (2 Trumpets, 2 Trombones, 2 Saxophones, 4 Violins, 2 Cellos, and Accordion) conducted by Mike Vickers
David Mason: Piccolo Trumpet

CHART PERFORMANCE

U.K.: "All You Need Is Love"/"Baby, You're a Rich Man"; July 7, 1967, Parlophone R 5620: #1.

U.S.: "All You Need Is Love"/"Baby, You're a Rich Man"; July 17, 1967, Capitol 5964: #1 (certified by the RIAA as "Gold," with more than 500,000 copies sold).

LEGACY AND INFLUENCE

In 2004, *Rolling Stone* ranked "All You Need Is Love" as #370 on the magazine's list of *The 500 Greatest Songs of All Time*.

In 2010, *Rolling Stone* ranked "All You Need Is Love" as #21 on the magazine's list of *The Beatles' 100 Greatest Songs*.

In October 2012, BBC Local Radio listeners ranked "All You Need Is Love" as their fourth favorite Beatles song in a poll conducted in commemoration of the 50th anniversary of "Love Me Do," the band's first single.

ALBUM APPEARANCES: *Magical Mystery Tour*; *Yellow Submarine*; *The Beatles, 1967–1970*; *Reel Music*; *20 Greatest Hits*; *Yellow Submarine Songtrack*; *1*; *Love*.

See also: Epstein, Brian; *Magical Mystery Tour* (LP); *Our World* (TV Special).

"And I Love Her" (Lennon–McCartney)

"And I Love Her" is a song on the Beatles' *A Hard Day's Night* album.

AUTHORSHIP AND BACKGROUND

Largely written by McCartney with assistance from Lennon in terms of crafting the song's middle-eight, "And I Love Her" is one of the three principal compositions that McCartney prepared, along with "Can't Buy Me Love" and "Things We Said Today," for the film *A Hard Day's Night*.

"And I Love Her" "wasn't for anyone," McCartney later remembered. "Having the title start in midsentence, I thought that was clever. Well, Perry Como did 'And I Love You So' many years later. Tried to nick the idea. I like that. It was a nice tune, that one. I still like it" (Dowlding 1989, 71).

As Lennon recalled, " 'And I Love Her' is Paul again. I consider it his first 'Yesterday.' You know, the big ballad in *A Hard Day's Night*" (Lennon and Ono 2000, 173). "With one stroke," Tim Riley writes, McCartney "gains the status of standard balladeer composer" (Riley 1988, 104). "And I Love Her" has become one of the most widely covered compositions in popular music.

RECORDING SESSIONS

Produced by George Martin, "And I Love Her" was recorded at Abbey Road Studios on February 25, 1964, with additional remakes and overdubbing on February 26 and February 27.

PERSONNEL

Lennon: Gibson J-160E
McCartney: Vocal, Gibson J-160E
Harrison: José Ramírez Studio Guitar, Claves
Starr: Bongos

CHART PERFORMANCE

U.S.: "And I Love Her"/"If I Fell"; July 20, 1964, Capitol 5235: #12.

LEGACY AND INFLUENCE

In 2010, *Rolling Stone* ranked "And I Love Her" as #65 on the magazine's list of *The Beatles' 100 Greatest Songs*.

ALBUM APPEARANCES: *A Hard Day's Night* (U.S.); *A Hard Day's Night* (U.K.); *Something New*; *The Beatles, 1962–1966*; *Love Songs*; *Rarities* (U.S.); *Reel Music*; *Anthology 1*; *On Air: Live at the BBC, Volume 2*.

See also: *A Hard Day's Night* (Film); *A Hard Day's Night* (U.K. LP).

"And Your Bird Can Sing" (Lennon–McCartney)

"And Your Bird Can Sing" is a song on the Beatles' *Revolver* album.

AUTHORSHIP AND BACKGROUND

Written by Lennon, "And Your Bird Can Sing" found its origins in a gift that Cynthia Lennon presented to her husband. As Cynthia remembered, "I bought a clockwork bird in a gilded cage which I wrapped up carefully, just leaving the winding mechanism at the base exposed. Before handing it to John I wound it up. The imitation bird warbled loud and clear from its perch as John unwrapped the strange looking gift with an expression of sheer disbelief on his face" (Lennon 1978, 128).

For Lennon, the bird in the gilded cage offered increasing testimony about their ineffectual marriage, as well as regarding what he perceived to be her utter failure to understand him: As Lennon sings in the last line, "You don't get me."

In a 1995 interview, McCartney later described "And Your Bird Can Sing" as "one of my favorites," adding that "John and I got a fit of the giggles while we were doing the double-track. You couldn't have released it at the time. But now you can. Sounds great just hearing us lose it on a take." The early take of "And Your Bird Can Sing"—complete with John and Paul exploding into a series of giggles and guffaws—was included on the Beatles' *Anthology 2* release.

Speaking about "And Your Bird Can Sing" during one of his last interviews, Lennon was far less charitable about the song's quality, describing it as "another one of my throwaways—fancy paper around an empty box" (Lennon and Ono 2000, 180).

RECORDING SESSIONS

Produced by George Martin, "And Your Bird Can Sing" was recorded under the working title of "You Don't Get Me" at Abbey Road Studios on April 20, 1966, and remade on April 26. The song is characterized by the intricate guitar work by McCartney and Harrison on their dueling Epiphone Casinos: "We wrote [the guitar duet] at the session and learned it on the spot," McCartney recalled (Everett 1999, 46).

PERSONNEL

Lennon: Vocal, Epiphone Casino
McCartney: Rickenbacker 4001S, Epiphone Casino
Harrison: Epiphone Casino
Starr: Ludwig Oyster Black Pearl Drums, Tambourine

LEGACY AND INFLUENCE

In 2007, *Q Magazine* ranked "And Your Bird Can Sing" as #6 on the magazine's list of *The 20 Greatest Guitar Tracks*.

A 2008 issue of *Guitar World* magazine cites Harrison's solo on "And Your Bird Can Sing" as #69 on the magazine's list of the *100 Greatest Guitar Solos*.

In 2010, *Rolling Stone* ranked "And Your Bird Can Sing" as #78 on the magazine's list of *The Beatles' 100 Greatest Songs*.

ALBUM APPEARANCES: *Revolver* (U.K.); *Yesterday . . . and Today*; *Anthology 2*; *Tomorrow Never Knows*.

See also: Lennon, Cynthia Lillian; *Revolver* (U.K. LP).

"Anna (Go to Him)" (Alexander)

"Anna (Go to Him)" is a song on the Beatles' *Please Please Me* album.

AUTHORSHIP AND BACKGROUND

"Anna (Go to Him)" was written and originally performed by Arthur Alexander. Released in September 1962, Alexander's version became a Top 10 R&B hit.

RECORDING SESSIONS

Produced by George Martin, "Anna (Go to Him)" was recorded at Abbey Road Studios in three takes on February 11, 1963, with an overdubbing session on February 20.

PERSONNEL

Lennon: Vocal, Gibson J-160E
McCartney: Höfner 500/1, Backing Vocal
Harrison: Gretsch Duo-Jet, Backing Vocal
Starr: Premier Mahogany Duroplastic Drums

ALBUM APPEARANCES: *Please Please Me*; *The Early Beatles*; *On Air: Live at the BBC, Volume 2*.

See also: *Please Please Me* (LP).

"Another Girl" (Lennon–McCartney)

"Another Girl" is a song on the Beatles' *Help!* album.

AUTHORSHIP AND BACKGROUND

Written by McCartney, "Another Girl" was composed by the songwriter while vacationing at a Tunisian resort. For McCartney, "Another Girl" was written expressly to meet the quota of necessary songs for the *Help!* project. As McCartney later recalled, "It's a bit much to call them fillers because I think they were a bit more than that, and each one of them made it past the Beatles test. We all had to like it" (Miles 1997, 194).

RECORDING SESSIONS

Produced by George Martin, "Another Girl" was recorded at Abbey Road Studios on February 15, 1965, with additional overdubbing on February 16 in the form of McCartney's lead guitar solo. McCartney double-tracked his vocal.

PERSONNEL

Lennon: Gibson J-160E, Backing Vocal
McCartney: Vocal, Höfner 500/1, Epiphone Casino
Harrison: Sonic Blue Fender Stratocaster, Backing Vocal
Starr: Ludwig Oyster Black Pearl Drums

ALBUM APPEARANCES: *Help!* (U.K.); *Help!* (U.S.).

See also: *Help!* (Film); *Help!* (U.K. LP).

"Any Time at All" (Lennon–McCartney)

"Any Time at All" is a song on the Beatles' *A Hard Day's Night* album.

AUTHORSHIP AND BACKGROUND

Written by Lennon, who later recalled that "Any Time at All" was "an effort at writing 'It Won't Be Long'—same ilk. C to A minor, C to A minor with me shouting" (Lennon and Ono 2000, 195).

RECORDING SESSIONS

Produced by George Martin, "Any Time at All" was recorded at Abbey Road Studios on June 2, 1964.

"Any Time at All" features an artful solo in which McCartney's piano and Harrison's guitar create a clever opposition. Played with conspicuous classical overtones, the piano begins in a lower register and travels upward, while the guitar journeys, in converse fashion, from high to low. The result offers a powerful study in pop-music counterpoint.

PERSONNEL

Lennon: Vocal, Gibson J-160E
McCartney: Höfner 500/1, Piano, Backing Vocal
Harrison: Rickenbacker 360/12, Backing Vocal
Starr: Ludwig Oyster Black Pearl Drums

LEGACY AND INFLUENCE

In 2010, *Rolling Stone* ranked "Any Time at All" as #95 on the magazine's list of *The Beatles' 100 Greatest Songs*.

ALBUM APPEARANCES: *A Hard Day's Night* (U.K.); *Something New*; *Rock 'n' Roll Music*.

See also: *A Hard Day's Night* (U.K. LP).

Apple Corps, Ltd.

Apple finds its origins in the 1967 formation of Beatles and Co. As Stefan Granados observes in *Those Were the Days: An Unofficial History of the Beatles' Apple Organization, 1967–2001*,

> The first step towards creating this new business structure was to form a new partnership called Beatles and Co. in April 1967. To all intents and purposes, Beatles and Co. was an updated version on the Beatles' original partnership, Beatles Ltd. Under the new arrangement, however, each Beatle would own five percent of Beatles and Co. and a new corporation owned collectively by all four Beatles [which was soon known as Apple] would be given control of the remaining 80 percent of Beatles and Co. With the exception of individual song-writing royalties, which would still be paid directly to the writer or writers of a particular song, all of the money earned by the Beatles as a group would go directly to Beatles and Co. and would thus be taxed at a far lower corporate tax rate. (Granados 2002, 6)

While the company's name finds its roots in the common childhood saying, "A is for apple," McCartney was inspired to create the firm's logo during a 1967 visit from London art dealer Robert Fraser, who showed him René Magritte's painting *Le Jeu de Mourre* (1966). As McCartney later recalled,

> In my garden at Cavendish Avenue, which was a 100-year-old house I'd bought, Robert was a frequent visitor. One day he got hold of a Magritte he thought I'd love. Being Robert, he would just get it and bring it. I was out in the garden with some friends. I think I was filming Mary Hopkin with a film crew, just getting her to sing live in the garden, with bees and flies buzzing around, high summer. We were in the long grass, very beautiful, very country-like. We were out in the garden and Robert didn't want to interrupt, so when we went back in the big door from the garden to the living room, there on the table he'd just propped up this little Magritte. It was of a green apple. That became the basis of the Apple logo. Across the painting Magritte had written in that beautiful handwriting of his "Au revoir." And Robert had split. I thought that was the coolest thing anyone's ever done with me. (Vyner 1999, 317)

Apple Corps was famously launched by Lennon and McCartney during a May 1968 press conference at New York City's American Hotel. Speaking to the organization's goal of promoting hitherto obscure musicians and artists, McCartney remarked that:

> We really want to help people, but without doing it like a charity or seeming like ordinary patrons of the arts. We're in the happy position of not really needing any more money. So for the first time, the bosses aren't in it for profit. If you come and see me and say, "I've had such and such a dream," I'll say, "Here's so much money. Go away and do it." We've already bought all our dreams. So now we want to share that possibility with others. (Cross 2005, 180)

Lennon added that "the aim of this company isn't really a stack of gold teeth in the bank. We've *done* that bit. It's more of a trick to see if we can actually get artistic freedom within a business structure" (Cross 2005, 180).

In June 1968, the Beatles acquired 3 Savile Row in Mayfair, London—a five-story town house that had formally been "The Albany," a gentleman's club—as the head office for their fledgling organization. The basement area was later rebuilt to become Apple Studio and corporate offices were set up on the upper floors. Within weeks, the Apple Building, as it came to be known, was the chaotic home for hippies and other hangers-on, as well as the headquarters for the Beatles' ever-growing financial empire. As Alan Clayson and Spencer Leigh note:

> Out of his depth, a Beatle might commandeer a room at Savile Row, stick to conventional office hours and play company director until the novelty wore off. Initially, he'd look away from the disgusting realities of the half-eaten steak sandwich in a litter bin; the employee rolling a spliff of best Afghan hash; the typist who span out a single letter (in the house style, with no exclamation marks!) all morning before "popping out" and not returning until the next day. (Clayson and Leigh 2003, 256)

Its chaotic business practices notwithstanding, Apple Corps was overseen by managing director Ron Kass and divided into five overarching divisions, including Apple Electronics (managed by Yanni Alexis "Magic Alex" Mardas), Apple Films (managed by Denis O'Dell), Apple Publishing (managed by Terry Doran), Apple Records (managed by Peter Asher), and Apple Retail (managed by Pete Shotton). Apple Corps' contracts department was led by Brian Lewis, while long-time Beatles associates Alistair Taylor continued in his role as the band's chief fixer under the title of general manager, while his older brother Derek Taylor assumed the role of Apple press officer. In the organizational vacuum left in the wake of Brian Epstein's August 1967 death, Neil Aspinall became the Beatles' chief personal assistant and manager, a role that he continued under the auspices of Apple Corps during the company's early years before becoming its managing director from 1970 to 2007, when Jeff Jones assumed the post.

APPLE ELECTRONICS

Led by Mardas, the Apple Electronics division was spearheaded as a means for reimaging the consumer electronics market through Mardas' own innovations. As self-styled electronic wizard, Mardas originally established Apple Electronics as Fiftyshapes, Ltd. at 34 Boston Place in London's Westminster district. Under Mardas's leadership, Apple Corps lost some £300,000, given the technological unsound and commercially impractical nature of Magic Alex's ideas and designs. After Mardas's dismissal by Allen Klein during the 1969 reorganization of Apple Corps, the Apple Electronics division went on to oversee its greatest triumph—the redesign and implementation of the Apple Studio in the basement of the Apple Building.

APPLE FILMS

Led by Denis O'Dell, the Apple Films division was responsible for seven major film releases, the first of which was the Beatles' 1967 television movie *Magical Mystery Tour*. It also released the Beatles' *Yellow Submarine* (1968), directed by George Dunning, and *Let It Be* (1970), directed by Michael Lindsay-Hogg. Its other releases included the 1971 Ravi Shankar documentary *Raga*, directed by Howard Worth; *The Concert for Bangladesh* (1972), directed by Saul Swimmer; the Marc Bolan documentary *Born to Boogie* (1972), directed by Starr; *Son of Dracula* (1974), directed by Freddie Francis; and *Little Malcolm* (1974), directed by Stuart Cooper.

APPLE PUBLISHING

Led by Terry Doran, the Apple Publishing division served as the organization's music publishing arm. In its brief tenure, it was the home for numerous artists, the lion's share of which were associates of the Beatles and their entourage. In addition to Harrison and Starr—who later established Harrisongs and Startling Music, respectively, as their publishing arms—Apple Publishing served such clients as Badfinger, Yoko Ono, Billy Preston, and the Radha Krishna Temple, among others. As its imprint, Apple Books was also a short-lived success, responsible for very few releases, save for *The Beatles Get Back*, the paperback book featuring photographs by Ethan Russell that accompanied the initial release of the *Let It Be* soundtrack.

APPLE RECORDS

Led by Asher and, later, Aspinall, the Apple Records division was the organization's most successful unit, selling more than 16 million records from its inception in 1968 through 1970. Beginning with the "Hey Jude"/"Revolution" single, all new Beatles releases were distributed via the Apple Records label, although EMI held the copyrights and released Apple Records products with Parlophone/Capitol catalogue numbers.

In addition to the Beatles, Apple Records featured a slate of artists that included Badfinger, Mary Hopkin, Jackie Lomax, Preston, Radha Krishna Temple, Ravi Shankar, Ronnie Spector, James Taylor, and Doris Troy, among others. It also included the subsidiary label, Zapple Records, led by Barry Miles and spearheaded in order to release spoken word and avant-garde recordings. Between 1970 and the dissolution of the Beatles' partnership in the mid-1970s, the vast majority of Apple Records releases involved work by the former Beatles themselves.

APPLE RETAIL

Led by Lennon's boyhood friend Pete Shotton, the Apple Retail division was largely composed of the Apple Boutique, a retail clothing store located at London's 94 Baker Street. It was famous for its controversial multistory outdoor mural, designed by the Dutch collective the Fool, who also designed the boutique's hippie-chic merchandise. From its inception, it was plagued by shoplifting and its inability to turn a profit. After Shotton's resignation, John Lyndon assumed the store's managerial role until its closing on July 31, 1968, when the Beatles famously gave away the operation's remaining merchandise to the public.

In a press release about the closing of the Apple Boutique, McCartney noted that "our main business is entertainment, communication. Apple is mainly concerned with fun, not frocks. We want to devout all our energies to records, films, and our electronic adventures. We had to refocus." He added that "we decided to close down our Baker Street shop yesterday and instead of putting up a sign saying 'Business Will Be Resumed as Soon as Possible' and then auction off the goods, we decided to give them away. The shops were doing fine and making a nice profit on turnover. So far the biggest loss is in giving things away. But we did that deliberately. We came into the shops by the tradesman's entrance, but we're leaving by the front door."

In 1969, the mass disorganization and chaos associated with Apple Corps' early years came to a sudden end with the appointment of Allen Klein as the company's chairman. As Clayson and Leigh observed, "Overnight, glib lack of concern deferred to pointed questions. Which typist rings Canberra every afternoon? Why has so-and-so given himself a raise of 60 pounds a week? Why is he seen only on payday? Suddenly, lunch meant beans-on-toast in the office kitchen instead of Beluga caviar from Fortnum and Mason" (Clayson and Leigh 2003, 257). In a series of cost-saving efforts in order to ensure the survival of the Beatles' empire, Klein terminated most of the Apple Corps employees, including Aspinall, whom he rehired shortly thereafter after realizing his indispensable role, however complex, in the band's success. The dissolution of the Beatles' partnership in 1975 relegated Apple Corps as the band's holding company while bringing the usefulness of its various divisions to a close. After the conclusion of the Beatles' partnership, Apple Corps eventually relocated to 27 Ovington Square in London's Knightsbridge district. The company's ownership is controlled by McCartney, Starr, and the estates of Lennon and Harrison.

In later years, Apple has enjoyed a spectacular renaissance, revivifying the Apple Records label with *The Beatles Anthology* project in the 1990s, as well as the worldwide success of the Beatles' *1* album in the new century and the subsequent successes associated with the 2009 remasters and *The Beatles: Rock Band* video game. Apple Corps also settled its long-running trademark infringement lawsuit against Apple Computer, paving the way for the Beatles' long-awaited appearance on the latter's iTunes retailing site.

In 2007, Aspinall retired, succumbing to cancer within a matter of months, and Jeff Jones assumed the chief executive role that his predecessor had occupied for nearly four decades.

See also: Aspinall, Neil; *The Beatles: Rock Band* (Video Game); Epstein, Brian; iTunes; Klein, Allen; *Let It Be* (Film); Lindsay-Hogg, Michael; *Magical Mystery Tour* (TV Film); *1* (LP); Ono, Yoko; Preston, Billy; *Yellow Submarine* (Film); Zapple Records.

"Ask Me Why" (McCartney–Lennon)

"Ask Me Why" is a song on the Beatles' *Please Please Me* album.

AUTHORSHIP AND BACKGROUND

Written by Lennon, "Ask Me Why" evinces a clear influence from Smokey Robinson and the Miracles, one of the songwriter's favorite artists.

RECORDING SESSIONS

Produced by George Martin, "Ask Me Why" was recorded at Abbey Road Studios on June 6, 1962, as part of the Beatles' EMI audition. The band remade the song on November 26, 1962, while also recording the Lennon–McCartney composition "Tip of My Tongue" in an effort to select a B-side for the upcoming "Please Please Me" single. With "Tip of My Tongue" relatively unfinished at this juncture, the Beatles and Martin selected "Ask Me Why" as the B-side.

An earlier recording of "Ask Me Why" is one of the 17 demos on the "Hodgson Tape" that find their origins in the band's April and July 1960 recording sessions. All of the tracks were recorded on a Grundig reel-to-reel tape recorder that McCartney had borrowed from Charles Hodgson. In a November 1994 interview with Mark Lewisohn, McCartney recalled that "sometimes I'd borrow a tape recorder, a Grundig with a little green eye, and we'd sort of go 'round to my house and try and record things. . . . But those were very much home demos. Very bad quality" (Winn 2003a, 3). "Ask Me Why" is rumored to be one of the songs recorded during these sessions, although any recording of the song has not been publicly released.

PERSONNEL

Lennon: Vocal, Rickenbacker 325
McCartney: Höfner 500/1, Backing Vocal
Harrison: Gretsch Duo-Jet
Starr: Premier Mahogany Duroplastic Drums

CHART PERFORMANCE

U.K.: "Please Please Me"/"Ask Me Why"; January 11, 1963, Parlophone R 4983: #1. "Ask Me Why" did not chart.
U.S.: "Please Please Me"/"Ask Me Why"; February 25, 1963, Vee-Jay VJ 498: the first Vee-Jay release of "Please Please Me" did not chart.

ALBUM APPEARANCES: *Please Please Me*; *The Early Beatles*; *Live! at the Star-Club in Hamburg, Germany; 1962*; *On Air: Live at the BBC, Volume 2*.

See also: *Please Please Me* (LP).

Aspinall, Neil (1941–2008)

A lifelong friend of the Beatles, Neil Aspinall became the band's road manager and personal assistant, eventually spending the balance of his career managing Apple Corps, Ltd.

Aspinall was born on October 13, 1942, in Prestatyn, North Wales. As a 12-year-old, he studied English at the Liverpool Institute, where he met McCartney. In 1959, he left school to study accountancy and spent two years as a trainee accountant. In the early 1960s, he became the Beatles' road manager, having purchased a grey Comer van for £80. Soon, Aspinall was making more money shuttling the Beatles around the English countryside than he was as an accountant. When the Beatles returned from their July 1962 Hamburg engagement, he joined the group's entourage on a full-time basis and was employed by them for the rest of his life.

During this same period, Aspinall became close friends with drummer Pete Best, renting a room in the Best family home. He fell into a romantic relationship with Best's mother Mona, with whom Aspinall fathered a child, Vincent "Roag" Best, who was born in July 1962, only a few scant weeks before Pete Best was replaced by Starr as the Beatles' drummer.

In the ensuing years, Aspinall and Beatles roadie Mal Evans managed their concert tours. With Brian Epstein's untimely death in August 1967, Aspinall became more involved in the group's business affairs. He began managing Apple Corps after the organization's founding in April 1968. Apple Corps encompassed five divisions, including music, electronics, films, publishing, and retail. Much of Aspinall's early work at the firm involved establishing its business practices. As he later remarked during a 2004 interview with Stefan Granados, "We did not have one single piece of paper. No contracts. The lawyer, the accountants and Brian, whoever, had that. The Beatles had been given copies of various contracts, maybe—I don't know. I didn't know what the contract was with EMI, or with the film people or the publishers or anything at all. So it was a case of building up a filing system, find out what was going on while we were trying to continue doing something."

When Allen Klein took Apple Corps into receivership in 1969, Aspinall was dismissed along with much of the company's personnel. Klein quickly reinstated Aspinall, though, when he realized how integral Aspinall had become to the organization. During the early post-Beatles years, much of Aspinall's work involved managing the web of lawsuits, licensing, and copyright issues that regularly presented themselves at Apple Corps.

Aspinall deserves particular credit for the manner in which he consolidated the ex-Beatles' business affairs and continued to expand their financial empire. He was the driving force behind the enormously successful *Beatles Anthology* project, which he had earlier attempted with a 1970s film project entitled *The Long and Winding Road*. Aspinall also managed the Beatles' worldwide success with the *1* album in 2000, as well as the preparation of the remastering of their back catalogue.

In April 2007, Aspinall resigned from Apple Corps. At the time, the press reported that he felt the time was right to "move on." Aspinall was succeeded by Jeff Jones as Apple's chief executive.

Within a year, Aspinall succumbed to lung cancer, dying in New York City on March 24, 2008, at 66 years old. He was survived by Suzy Ornstein, his wife of nearly 40 years, as well as their four children Gayla, Dhara, Mandy, and Julian. He was interred at a private funeral in Twickenham. In attendance were Yoko Ono, Stella McCartney, Starr's wife Barbara Bach, George Martin, and Pete Best. Pete Townshend performed Bob Dylan's "Mr. Tambourine Man" in Aspinall's honor.

See also: Apple Corps, Ltd.; Bach, Barbara; Best, Pete; Epstein, Brian; Evans, Mal; Klein, Allen; *1* (LP); Ono, Yoko.

B

"Baby It's You" (Bacharach–Williams–David)

"Baby It's You" is a song on the Beatles' *Please Please Me* album.

AUTHORSHIP AND BACKGROUND

Written by Burt Bacharach, Barney Williams, and Hal David, "Baby It's You" became a Top 10 hit for the Shirelles in early 1962.

RECORDING SESSIONS

Produced by George Martin, "Baby It's You" was recorded at Abbey Road Studios on February 11, 1963, with an overdubbing session on February 20 in which Martin recorded a celesta solo.

The Beatles recorded a second cover version of "Baby It's You" on June 1, 1963, for the BBC radio program *Pop Go the Beatles*. This version was later included on the *Live at the BBC* album.

PERSONNEL

Lennon: Vocal, Gibson J-160E
McCartney: Höfner 500/1, Backing Vocal
Harrison: Gretsch Duo-Jet, Backing Vocal
Starr: Premier Mahogany Duroplastic Drums
Martin: Celesta

ALBUM APPEARANCES: *Please Please Me*; *The Early Beatles*; *Live at the BBC*.

See also: *Please Please Me* (LP).

"Baby, You're a Rich Man" (Lennon–McCartney)

"Baby, You're a Rich Man" is a song on the Beatles' *Magical Mystery Tour* album.

AUTHORSHIP AND BACKGROUND

Written by Lennon and McCartney, "Baby, You're a Rich Man" merges Lennon's verses with McCartney chorus, much like the collaborative format that spawned "A Day in the Life."

Lennon later remarked that "in 'Baby, You're a Rich Man' the point was, stop moaning. You're a rich man and we're all rich men, heh, heh, baby!" (Cott and Doudna 1982, 48). During one of his last interviews, Lennon observed that "Baby, You're a Rich Man" was "a combination of two separate pieces, Paul's and mine, put together and forced into one song. One-half was all mine. [sings] 'How does it feel to be one of the beautiful people / Now that you know who you are.' Then Paul comes in with [sings] 'Baby you're a rich man,' which was a lick he had around" (Riley 1988, 234, 235).

RECORDING SESSIONS

Produced by George Martin, "Baby, You're a Rich Man" was recorded at Olympic Sound Studios on May 11, 1967.

With Lennon playing the studio's handy Clavioline and sharing keyboard duties with McCartney on a Knight upright piano, "Baby, You're a Rich Man" offers up a psychedelic miasma, an aspect of the song that is heightened by Lennon's peripatetic Clavioline lines, McCartney's staccato bass riffs on his Rickenbacker, and a vibraphone part courtesy of tape operator Eddie Kramer. Rolling Stone Mick Jagger provides a backing vocal, while his bandmate Brian Jones turns in an oboe performance.

As the key sound in the introductory phrases of "Baby, You're a Rich Man," the Clavioline is an amplified keyboard that, when played, produces one note at a time.

PERSONNEL

Lennon: Vocal, Clavioline, Piano
McCartney: Rickenbacker 4001S, Piano, Backing Vocal
Harrison: Tambourine, Backing Vocal
Starr: Ludwig Oyster Black Pearl Drums
Jagger: Backing Vocal
Jones: Oboe
Kramer: Vibraphone

CHART PERFORMANCE

U.K.: "All You Need Is Love"/"Baby, You're a Rich Man"; July 7, 1967, Parlophone R 5620: #1. As the B-side of "All You Need Is Love," "Baby, You're a Rich Man" did not chart.

U.S.: "All You Need Is Love"/"Baby, You're a Rich Man"; July 17, 1967, Capitol 5964 #1 (certified by the RIAA as "Gold," with more than 500,000 copies sold). As the B-side of "All You Need Is Love," "Baby, You're a Rich Man" charted at #34.

LEGACY AND INFLUENCE

In 2010, *Rolling Stone* ranked "Baby, You're a Rich Man" as #68 on the magazine's list of *The Beatles' 100 Greatest Songs*.

ALBUM APPEARANCES: *Magical Mystery Tour*; *Yellow Submarine Songtrack*.

See also: Epstein, Brian; *Yellow Submarine* (Film).

"Baby's in Black" (Lennon–McCartney)

"Baby's in Black" is a song on *Beatles for Sale*.

AUTHORSHIP AND BACKGROUND

Written by Lennon and McCartney, "Baby's in Black" was the first song recorded for the album. The song's lyrics concern Astrid Kirchherr, the Beatles' friend from Hamburg who was engaged to be married to Stuart Sutcliffe at the time of his untimely April 1962 death.

As McCartney later recalled, "We wanted to write something a little bit darker, bluesy. It was very much co-written and we both sang it. Sometimes the harmony that I was writing in sympathy to John's melody would take over and become a stronger melody. When people wrote out the music score they would ask, 'Which one is the melody?' because it was co-written that you could actually take either. We rather liked this one" (Miles 1997, 175).

RECORDING SESSIONS

Produced by George Martin, "Baby's in Black" was recorded on August 11, 1964, at Abbey Road Studios. As with "If I Fell," Lennon and McCartney sing into the same microphone.

The Beatles perform "Baby's in Black" in a waltz-like Sauteuse structure with a 6/8 time signature. A Sauteuse refers to a leaping, Regency-era waltz.

PERSONNEL

Lennon: Vocal, Gibson J-160E
McCartney: Vocal, Höfner 500/1
Harrison: Gretsch Tennessean
Starr: Ludwig Oyster Black Pearl Drums, Tambourine

CHART PERFORMANCE

U.K.: "Real Love"/"Baby's in Black (Live)"; March 4, 1996, Apple RP 6425: #4. As the B-side of "Real Love," "Baby's in Black" did not chart.
U.S.: "Real Love"/"Baby's in Black (Live)"; March 4, 1996, Apple NR 8 58544 7: #11 (certified by the RIAA as "Gold," with more than 500,000 copies sold). As the B-side of "Real Love," "Baby's in Black" did not chart.

ALBUM APPEARANCES: *Beatles for Sale*; *Beatles '65*.

See also: *Beatles for Sale* (LP); Kirchherr, Astrid; Sutcliffe, Stuart.

Bach, Barbara (1947–)

Former actress and *Playboy* model Barbara Bach is Starr's second wife. Bach enjoyed starring film roles in the James Bond film *The Spy Who Loved Me* (1977), *Force 10 from Navarone* (1978), and *Caveman* (1981), where she met Starr, her costar, on the film set.

Born on August 27, 1947, in Queens, New York, Bach left school in order to pursue a modeling career. In 1968, she married Italian businessman Augusto Gregorini, with whom she had two children, Francesca Gregorini, a singer/songwriter, and Gianni Gregorini.

Over the years, Bach has performed roles in nearly 30 films, including McCartney's *Give My Regards to Broad Street* (1984). In *Caveman*, she played Lana, an alluring cavewoman who is the lustful object of forbidden desire for Atouk, Starr's scrawny caveman character. Bach and Starr met on the *Caveman* set in February 1980 and married on April 27, 1981, after the film's premiere.

In her post–film career, Bach earned a master's degree from UCLA in 1993 in psychology, later founding the Self Help Addiction Recovery Program with assistance from Harrison, Eric Clapton, and Pattie Boyd. Bach and Starr's own struggle with addiction included a six-week stay in a Tucson, Arizona, clinic in 1988. In 2008, Bach's sister Marjorie married Eagles guitarist Joe Walsh, one of Starr's closest friends and collaborators.

See also: Boyd, Pattie; Clapton, Eric; Starr, Ringo.

"Back in the USSR" (Lennon–McCartney)

"Back in the USSR" is the opening track on *The Beatles* (*The White Album*). It was released as a single backed with "Twist and Shout" in support of the *Rock 'n' Roll Music* compilation on June 25, 1976, in the United Kingdom.

AUTHORSHIP AND BACKGROUND

Written by McCartney during the Beatles' 1968 visit to India, "Back in the USSR" first came into being when Paul and Mike Love took to singing "I'm Backing the USSR" as a parody of the recent "I'm Backing Britain" campaign spearheaded by the government and endorsed by British Prime Minister Harold Wilson to lower the national debt (Everett 1999, 187). As the song took form, it became a tongue-in-check pastiche of Chuck Berry's "Back in the USA" and the Beach Boys' fun-in-the-sun, bikini-clad "California Girls." An early version of "Back in the USSR" was recorded in May 1968 at Harrison's Kinfauns studio as part of the Esher Tapes.

As McCartney remembered, "I wrote that as a kind of Beach Boys parody. And 'Back in the USA' was a Chuck Berry song, so it kinda took off from there. I just liked the idea of Georgia girls and talking about places like the Ukraine as if they were California, you know? It was also hands across the water, which I'm still conscious of. 'Cuz they like us out there, even though the bosses in the Kremlin may not. The kids do" (Dowlding 1989, 222).

RECORDING SESSIONS

Produced by George Martin, "Back in the USSR" was recorded at Abbey Road Studios on August 22, 1968, with an overdubbing session on August 23. The Beatles rehearsed the song during an August 22 session that went horribly awry when Starr—frustrated by his inability to play the requisite drum part and fed up with McCartney's increasingly proscriptive attitude—briefly quit the band. "I'm sure it pissed Ringo off when he couldn't quite get the drums to 'Back in the USSR,' and I sat in," McCartney remarked. "It's very weird to know that you can do a thing someone else is having trouble with" (Dowlding 1989, 222, 223).

"Back in the USSR" is a masterpiece of multitrack recording, with Lennon on his Gibson J-160E "Jumbo" acoustic guitar and six-string Fender bass; Harrison on his Fender Telecaster and Fender Jazz Bass; and McCartney on his Rickenbacker, his Casino, and playing Starr's vacant Ludwigs. With McCartney adopting his "Jerry Lee Lewis voice," Lennon and Harrison supply fantastic, soaring Beach Boys-like harmonies (Spizer 2003, 103).

In an effort to imbue the track with an appropriately international feel, Ken Scott created a tape loop of Viscount jet sounds from the EMI tape library's *Volume 17:*

Jet and Piston Engine Airplane. The result is a brilliant send-up of life behind the Iron Curtain, a world of ostensible mystery and danger—particularly from a Western ideological perspective nursed on *Sputnik* and James Bond—where "Moscow girls make me sing and shout," while the speaker entreats his listeners to "come and keep your comrade warm." In the song's most outrageous of its many puns, McCartney transposes the American South of Ray Charles's "Georgia on My Mind" with the comparatively icy clime of the Soviet Republic of Georgia.

PERSONNEL

Lennon: Gibson J-160E, Fender Bass VI
McCartney: Vocal, Rickenbacker 4001S, Piano, Epiphone Casino, Ludwig Oyster Black Pearl Drums
Harrison: Fender Jazz Bass, Fender Rosewood Telecaster

CHART PERFORMANCE

U.K.: "Back in the USSR"/"Twist and Shout"; June 25, 1976, Parlophone R 6016: #19.

LEGACY AND INFLUENCE

In 2010, *Rolling Stone* ranked "Back in the USSR" as #85 on the magazine's list of *The Beatles' 100 Greatest Songs.*

ALBUM APPEARANCES: *The Beatles* (*The White Album*); *The Beatles, 1967–1970*; *Rock 'n' Roll Music*; *Love*; *Tomorrow Never Knows.*

See also: The Beatles (*The White Album*) (LP).

"Bad Boy" (Williams)

"Bad Boy" was recorded in 1965 for release in the U.S. market, where it appeared on the *Beatles VI* album.

AUTHORSHIP AND BACKGROUND

Written by Larry Williams, "Bad Boy" was released as a single by Williams in 1959, although it failed to become a hit. The Beatles also covered Williams' "Dizzy Miss Lizzy" and "Slow Down."

RECORDING SESSIONS

Produced by George Martin, "Bad Boy" was recorded on May 10, 1965, between the recording sessions associated with the *Help!* album.

PERSONNEL

> Lennon: Vocal, Hammond Organ
> McCartney: Höfner 500/1
> Harrison: Gretsch Tennessean
> Starr: Ludwig Oyster Black Pearl Drums, Tambourine

ALBUM APPEARANCES: *Beatles VI*; *A Collection of Beatles Oldies*; *Rock 'n' Roll Music*; *Rarities* (U.K.); *Past Masters, Volume 1*.

See also: *Past Masters, Volume 1* (LP).

"The Ballad of John and Yoko" (Lennon–McCartney)

"The Ballad of John and Yoko" was the Beatles' sixth consecutive #1 single in the United Kingdom, where it was released on May 30, 1969. It was the band's final chart-topping single in their homeland.

AUTHORSHIP AND BACKGROUND

Written by Lennon, "The Ballad of John and Yoko" concerns the newly married couple's increasingly public escapades. Recorded under the working subtitle of "They're Gonna Crucify Me," the song witnesses its composer, as with "A Day in the Life," turning to the daily news for his inspiration—although in this case, John's *objet trouvé* finds Lennon sifting through his *own* newspaper clippings. In this sense, Lennon avails himself of a found object of a very different sort, an act of self-inscription in which he textualizes his madcap life with Ono for all time.

As Lennon later recalled,

> It's something I wrote, and it's like an old-time ballad. It's the story of us going along getting married, going to Paris, going to Amsterdam, all that. It's "Johnny B. Paperback Writer." The story came out that only Paul and I were on the record, but I wouldn't have bothered publicizing that. It doesn't mean anything. It just so happened that there were only two of us there—George was abroad and Ringo was on the film and he couldn't come that night. Because of that, it was a choice of either re-mixing or doing a new song—and you always go for doing a new one instead of fiddling about with an old one. So we did and it turned out well. (Beatles 2000, 333)

He later added that "I wrote that in Paris on our honeymoon. It's a piece of journalism. It's a folk song. That's why I called it 'The Ballad of . . . '" (Lennon and Ono 2000, 200).

As McCartney remembered,

> John came to me and said, "I've got this song about our wedding and it's called 'The Ballad of John and Yoko, Christ They're Gonna Crucify Me,'" and I said "Jesus Christ, you're kidding aren't you? Someone really is going to get upset about it." He said, "Yeah, but let's do it." I was a little worried for him because of the lyric, but he was going through a lot of terrible things. He came around to my house, wanting to do it really quick. He said, "Let's just you and me run over to the studio." I said, "Oh, alright, I'll play drums, I'll play bass." John played guitar. So we did it and stood back to see if the other guys would hate us for it—which I'm not sure about. They probably never forgave us. John was on heat, so to speak. He needed to record it so we just ran in and did it. (Lewisohn 1988, 14)

As Ono later recalled, "Paul knew that people were being nasty to John, and he just wanted to make it well for him. Paul has a very brotherly side to him" (Spignesi and Lewis 2009, 290).

RECORDING SESSIONS

Produced by George Martin, "The Ballad of John and Yoko" was recorded at Abbey Road Studios on April 14, 1969, less than a month after the Lennons' marriage on March 20 near Spain's Rock of Gibraltar. The recording session marked the return of Geoff Emerick to the Beatles' fold after his resignation during the sessions for *The White Album*. With an anxious Lennon determined to commit his latest creation to tape, the erstwhile Beatles sound engineer had been invited by Peter Brown to operate Abbey Road Studios' newly installed eight-track recording console.

With Harrison traveling abroad in the United States

John Lennon and Yoko Ono in a still image from the promotional film for "The Ballad of John and Yoko." (Fox Photos/Getty Images)

and Starr still toiling away on the set of *The Magic Christian*, the Beatles' personnel was limited to Lennon and McCartney, who recorded the song during the lengthy April 14, 1969, session. While Lennon handled the lead and rhythm guitar parts, McCartney provided a one-man rhythm section. In addition to his pounding bass lines and assorted piano flourishes, McCartney kept a steady beat on Starr's Ludwig Hollywoods. McCartney achieved a distinctive cracking drum sound courtesy of Emerick, who placed microphones both above and below the snare. Lennon and McCartney recorded the song in workmanlike fashion, clearly enjoying each other's company and the opportunity to revel in their musicianship. They couldn't resist good-naturedly acknowledging their conspicuously absent mates. "Go a bit faster, Ringo!" Lennon exclaimed to McCartney. "Okay, George!" he replied from behind Starr's kit. With McCartney's tinkling piano and the lyrics' whimsical progress from the Southampton docks to the Amsterdam Hilton, "The Ballad of John and Yoko" evinces seriocomic overtones, with Lennon effecting a martyr complex for the chorus: "They're gonna crucify me."

PERSONNEL

Lennon: Vocal, Epiphone Casino, Gibson J-160E
McCartney: Höfner 500/1, Piano, Ludwig Hollywood Maple Drums, Backing Vocal

CHART PERFORMANCE

U.K.: "The Ballad of John and Yoko"/"Old Brown Shoe"; May 30, 1969, Apple [Parlophone] R 5786: #1.
U.S.: "The Ballad of John and Yoko"/"Old Brown Shoe"; June 4, 1969, Apple [Capitol] 2531: #8 (certified by the RIAA as "Gold," with more than 500,000 copies sold).

LEGACY AND INFLUENCE

In 2010, *Rolling Stone* ranked "The Ballad of John and Yoko" as #48 on the magazine's list of *The Beatles' 100 Greatest Songs*.

CONTROVERSY

"The Ballad of John and Yoko" was banned by the BBC, as well as a majority of U.S. radio stations, for the song's "Christ, you know it ain't easy" refrain.

ALBUM APPEARANCES: *Hey Jude*; *The Beatles, 1967–1970*; *20 Greatest Hits*; *Past Masters, Volume 2*; *1*.

See also: Emerick, Geoff; Ono, Yoko.

The Beatals

In February 1960, the Quarry Men rechristened themselves under the short-lived name of the "Beatals." Legend has it that Stuart Sutcliffe suggested the notion of beetles as a reference to the biker gang in the 1953 Marlon Brando vehicle *The Wild One*, although Lennon and Sutcliffe later claimed to have chosen the name as an homage to Buddy Holly and the Crickets, changing the spelling from Beetles to Beatals in order to connote the idea of beat music. McCartney and Harrison took an immediate liking to the new name, and the days of the Quarry Men were over.

In April 1960, the Beatals gathered at McCartney's home at Forthlin Road, where they recorded demos for several songs on a Grundig reel-to-reel tape recorder that McCartney had borrowed from Charles Hodgson. These recordings eventually found their way onto the Hodgson Tape and the Kirchherr Tape, the surviving copy of the April 1960 recordings that was given by Sutcliffe to his fiancée Astrid Kirchherr. Together, these tapes represent some of the band's earliest rehearsals with Sutcliffe, their novice bass player.

In the spring of 1960, the Beatals dropped their latest name at the encouragement of Brian Casser of Cass and the Casanovas. The bandmates had come into Casser's orbit through Allan Williams, the owner of the Jacaranda Club who became their first manager.

See also: Kirchherr, Astrid; The Quarry Men; Sutcliffe, Stuart; Williams, Allan.

The Beatles (Name)

The Beatles' final name change occurred in August 1960, when manager Allan Williams arranged for the group to accept an extended engagement in the port city of Hamburg, West Germany. After recruiting Pete Best as their drummer, the band rechristened themselves as the Beatles, having scuttled the short-lived name, The Silver Beetles, and traveled to Hamburg's Reeperbahn. The band's name owes its genesis to original bassist Stuart Sutcliffe, who fashioned the word "Beatals" (later "Beatles") as a means for honoring Buddy Holly and the Crickets, as well as to reference the group's beat-music origins. Yet another legend has that Sutcliffe was referencing the name of the biker gang in the 1953 Marlon Brando vehicle *The Wild One*.

See also: The Beatals; Best, Pete; The Silver Beetles; Sutcliffe, Stuart; Williams, Allan.

The Beatles Anthology (TV Miniseries)

The Beatles Anthology miniseries premiered on ITV television in the United Kingdom and on ABC television in the United States in six parts in November 1995.

Originally released on VHS and laserdisc in 1996, the documentary was rereleased in 2003 as a multidisc DVD package with unreleased footage, special features, and music videos for "Free as a Bird" and "Real Love."

BACKGROUND

The Beatles Anthology television miniseries originated in *The Long and Winding Road*, Apple executive Neil Aspinall's 90-minute documentary on the history of the band. Completed in 1971, the project was inactive for many years, with the Beatles' involvement only beginning around 1980, when they began making plans for a reunion concert and recording new material. The background for *The Long and Winding Road* was made public in a 1980 legal deposition related to the Beatles' lawsuit against the *Beatlemania* musical. According to one source, Lennon remarked that he and the other three former Beatles had plans to stage a reunion concert that would serve as the would-be documentary's finale.

> Yoko Ono later reported that just days before his brutal death, John was making plans to go to England for a triumphant Beatles reunion. His greatest dream was to recreate the musical magic of the early years, with Paul, George, and Ringo. . . . [He] felt that they had travelled different paths for long enough. He felt that they had grown up and were mature enough to try writing and recording new songs. (Badman 2001, 273)

Lennon's December 8, 1980, murder put an end to any further work by Aspinall or others on *The Long and Winding Road*, but eventually the surviving Beatles involved themselves in the *Anthology* project in 1990, after the 1989 resolution of a long-standing lawsuit between McCartney and the other surviving Beatles regarding the unequal payment of royalties.

Directed by Geoff Wonfor and Bob Smeaton, the *Anthology* documentary took some five years to compile. Produced by Aspinall and Chips Chipperfield, the *Anthology* television miniseries consists of six hours of interviews and archival footage. Conducted by British musician and television personality Jools Holland, the early 1990s interviews with the surviving Beatles are interspersed with period audio and video interviews with Lennon. McCartney, Harrison, and Starr also recorded two new Beatles songs in support of the project, "Free as a Bird" and "Real Love." In the early 1990s, Harrison and Aspinall approached Ono about the idea of enhancing Lennon's Dakota-era demos for release. After McCartney delivered his induction speech on Lennon's behalf at the Rock and Roll Hall of Fame's January 1994 induction ceremony, Ono provided him with Lennon's demo tapes for "Free as a Bird," "Real Love," "Now and Then," and "Grow Old with Me." Before leaving the Dakota, McCartney later recalled,

> I checked it out with Sean, because I didn't want him to have a problem with it. He said, "Well, it'll be weird hearing a dead guy on lead vocal. But give it a try."

I said to them both, "If it doesn't work out, you can veto it." When I told George and Ringo I'd agreed to that they were going, "What? What if we love it?" It didn't come to that, luckily. I said to Yoko, "Don't impose too many conditions on us, it's really difficult to do this, spiritually. We don't know—we may hate each other after two hours in the studio and just walk out. So don't put any conditions, it's tough enough." (Huntley 2004, 249)

With Jeff Lynne handling production duties, Harrison, McCartney, and Starr completed new recordings for "Free as a Bird" and "Real Love."

In addition to the versions of "Free as a Bird" and "Real Love" by the Threetles, as they came to be known, the *Anthology* documentary also included some nearly six hours of audio material, which became the basis for three volumes' worth of multidisc *Anthology* albums.

In November 1995, the *Anthology* was broadcast on ITV and ABC television in the United Kingdom and the United States, respectively. As part of its promotion for the miniseries, ABC began identifying itself as "A-Beatles-C"—an allusion to legendary disk jockey Cousin Brucie's "77 W-A-Beatles-C" on the New York City AM airwaves in the early 1960s. ABC aired the series in three, two-hour installments on Sunday, November 19; Wednesday, November 22; and Thursday, November 23.

CONTENTS

Chapter 1 (July 1940–March 1963): "Liverpool: The Childhood Years"; "In My Life" montage; "Discovering Rock and Roll"; "John, Paul, and George: The Beginning of the Beatles"; "First Recordings, 1958–1960"; "Stuart Sutcliffe"; "Early Tours"; "Pete Best"; "Hamburg"; "Growing Pains"; "Stuart Sutcliffe Leaves"; excerpts from "I'm Down" and the Shadows' "FBI"; "The Cavern"; excerpts from "Long Tall Sally" and "Kansas City"; "Decca Sessions"; excerpts from "Three Cool Cats," "The Sheik of Araby," and "Bésame Mucho"; "George Martin"; "Ringo Arrives"; "Love Me Do"; " 'Please Please Me': 'We're No. 1' "; excerpts from the Beatles' "How Do You Do It" and Gerry and the Pacemakers' "How Do You Do It"; "Please Please Me"; "Leave My Kitten Alone."

Chapter 2 (March 1963–February 1964): "Racing Up the Ladder"; excerpts from "I'll Be on My Way," "Lonesome Tears in My Eyes," "That's All Right (Mama)," "If You're Irish, Come into the Parlour," and Helen Shapiro's "Look Who It Is" and "Thank You Girl"; *Please Please Me* album collage; "Touring Britain"; excerpts from Roy Orbison's "Oh, Pretty Woman," "From Me to You," "There's a Place," "It Won't Be Long," and "She Loves You"; "London: 1963"; excerpts from the Rolling Stones' "I Wanna Be Your Man" and the Beatles' "I Wanna Be Your Man"; "Early Television Appearances"; excerpts from the *Big Night Out* and *Morecambe and Wise*, along with "Moonlight Bay" and Eric Morecambe's "I Like It"; Abbey Road Studios audio montage, including excerpts from "One After 909," "I Saw

Her Standing There," "This Boy," "I Should Have Known Better," "Tell Me Why," "I Want to Hold Your Hand," "I'll Be Back," "Mr. Moonlight," "No Reply," and "What You're Doing"; "Reflections on Sudden Fame"; "This Boy"; "Beatlemania," including live performance on *Drop In*, along with video footage from "I Saw Her Standing There" and "Long Tall Sally"; "Royal Variety Performance," including excerpts from "From Me to You," "Till There Was You," and "Twist and Shout"; "Second Album: *With the Beatles*"; excerpts from "All My Loving," "Please Mister Postman," "Roll Over Beethoven," and "I Want to Hold Your Hand"; "Olympia Theatre, Paris: 1964"; " 'I Want to Hold Your Hand' Reaches #1 in the US"; "One After 909."

Chapter 3 (February 1964–July 1964): "Arrival in the US"; excerpt from Marvin Gaye's "Pride and Joy"; "First Appearance on *The Ed Sullivan Show*"; "All My Loving"; "The Coliseum Concert: Washington, DC"; footage of the Beatles performing "She Loves You," "I Saw Her Standing There," and "Please Please Me"; "Reception at the British Embassy"; "Miami Beach"; "I'll Follow the Sun" montage; "Second Appearance on *The Ed Sullivan Show*"; "Return to England"; "They're Going to Put Us in the Movies"; "Filming *A Hard Day's Night*," including "A Hard Day's Night," "I Should Have Known Better," "If I Fell," and "Can't Buy Me Love"; "*In His Own Write*," including footage from *Not Only . . . But Also*; "World Tour, 1964"; excerpts from "Long Tall Sally," "I'll Be Back," and "Any Time at All"; footage of the Beatles performing "All My Loving" and "You Can't Do That"; "World Premiere of *A Hard Day's Night*"; "Liverpool Homecoming"; "Things We Said Today"; "I'll Be Back."

Chapter 4 (August 1964–August 1965): "First Major US Tour, Summer 1964"; Hollywood Bowl footage of "All My Loving" and "She Loves You"; "Meeting Bob Dylan"; excerpts from Dylan's "The Times They Are a-Changin' " and "A Hard Rain's a-Gonna Fall"; "The Pressures of Touring"; excerpt from "Slow Down"; "Feedback: 'I Feel Fine' "; "Recording *Beatles for Sale*"; footage of "Kansas City"/"Hey-Hey-Hey-Hey!," "I'm a Loser," and "Everybody's Trying to Be My Baby"; "Filming *Help!*," including excerpts from "Another Girl," "The Night Before," "You're Going to Lose That Girl," "You've Got to Hide Your Love Away," and "Help!"; "Yesterday"; "I'm Down"; "*NME* Poll Winners' Concert," including footage of "I Feel Fine" and "She's a Woman"; "George Talks About His Songs"; "Act Naturally"; "Ticket to Ride"; "The Beatles Receive the MBE from the Queen"; "Eight Days a Week"; "If You've Got Trouble."

Chapter 5 (August 1965–July 1966): "Shea Stadium Concert," including footage of "I Feel Fine," "Baby's in Black," "I'm Down," and "Help!"; "Meeting Elvis Presley," including excerpts from Charlie Rich's "Mohair Sam" and Presley's "Hound Dog"; "More Tour Pressure," including excerpt from "Run for Your Life"; "New Musical Directions: *Rubber Soul* and *Revolver*"; *Rubber Soul* album montage, including "In My Life," "Drive My Car," and "Nowhere Man"; "Rāga Charu Kishi"; "Norwegian Wood (This Bird Has Flown)"; "Yellow Submarine"; "Taxman"; "Tomorrow Never Knows"; "Technical Limitations in the Studio," including footage of "Nowhere Man"; "LSD"; "Doctor Robert"; "Day Tripper"; "We Can

Work It Out"; "Taped Promotional Films," including excerpt from "I'm Looking Through You"; "Paperback Writer"; "Rain"; "World Tour, 1966"; footage of "Rock and Roll Music," "Paperback Writer," and "Yesterday"; "The Word"; "And Your Bird Can Sing."

Chapter 6 (July 1966–June 1967): "Trouble in the Philippines"; "Eleanor Rigby"; "I'm Only Sleeping"; "Touring Takes Its Toll"; "The Last Concert," including excerpt from "For No One"; "Individual Directions," including footage from *How I Won the War* and *The Family Way*, as well as the Tudor Minstrels performing "Music from *Family Way*" and "Love in the Open Air"; "The Making of 'Strawberry Fields Forever' "; "Penny Lane"; *Sgt. Pepper's Lonely Hearts Club Band* album montage, including excerpts from "Sgt. Pepper's Lonely Hearts Club Band," "With a Little Help from My Friends," and "Being for the Benefit of Mr. Kite!"; "A Day in the Life"; "Sgt. Pepper's Lonely Hearts Club Band (Reprise)"; "Reacting to *Sgt. Pepper's*"; footage of Jimi Hendrix's "Sgt. Pepper's Lonely Hearts Club Band"; "Drugs Reflect the Times"; "Baby, You're a Rich Man"; "Strawberry Fields Forever."

Chapter 7 (June 1967–July 1968): "Satellite Broadcast of 'All You Need Is Love' "; footage of "All You Need Is Love"; *Our World* performance; "Meeting the Maharishi"; "Brian Epstein's Death"; "You've Got to Hide Your Love Away" montage; *Magical Mystery Tour* movie montage, including "Magical Mystery Tour," "You Made Me Love You (I Didn't Want to Do It)," "The Fool on the Hill," "Your Mother Should Know," and "Flying"; "I Am the Walrus"; "Hello, Goodbye" promotional video; "The Apple Boutique"; "Rishikesh, India"; excerpts from "Across the Universe," "Dear Prudence," "I Will," Harrison's "Dera Dhun," and "Everybody's Got Something to Hide Except Me and My Monkey"; "Apple Records," including excerpts from Jackie Lomax's "Sour Milk Sea," James Taylor's "Something in the Way She Moves," the Iveys' "Maybe Tomorrow," Badfinger's "No Matter What," and Mary Hopkin's "Goodbye"; "Lady Madonna"; *Yellow Submarine* movie montage, including "Yellow Submarine" and "All Together Now"; "John Meets Yoko Ono," including excerpts from "Happiness Is a Warm Gun" and Lennon and Ono's "Unfinished Music No. 1: Two Virgins"; "While My Guitar Gently Weeps."

Chapter 8 (July 1968 to the End): *The White Album* montage, including excerpts from "Yer Blues," "Blackbird," "What's the New Mary Jane," "Ob-La-Di, Ob-La-Da," "Good Night," "Rocky Raccoon," "Sexy Sadie," "While My Guitar Gently Weeps," "Mother Nature's Son," "Piggies," "I Will," "Julia," "Why Don't We Do It in the Road?" "I'm So Tired," and "Don't Pass Me By"; "Revolution"; "The Apple Boutique Closes"; "Hey Jude"; footage of "Hey Jude" from *Frost on Sunday*; "Recording at Twickenham Studios," including excerpts from "I've Got a Feeling" and "For You Blue"; "Billy Preston Sits In"; "Get Back"; "The Long and Winding Road"; "The Rooftop Concert, January 30, 1969," including performances of "Don't Let Me Down" and "Get Back"; "Let It Be"; "Paul Marries Linda, John Marries Yoko"; "The Ballad of John and Yoko"; "Comments on the Breakup of the Band"; "Something"; *Abbey Road* album montage, including excerpts from

"Golden Slumbers," "Octopus's Garden," "Here Comes the Sun," "Come Together," "Because," and "The End"; footage from the last photo session on August 22, 1969; "Free as a Bird" video; musical montage, including "I Saw Her Standing There," "Got to Get You into My Life," "Misery," "Sie Liebt Dich," "And I Love Her," "Being for the Benefit of Mr. Kite!" "Rocky Raccoon," and "All You Need Is Love."

DVD Special Features Disc: "Recollections, June 1994," including excerpts from "Baby What You Want Me to Do," "Raunchy," "Thinking of Linking," "Blue Moon of Kentucky," and "Ain't She Sweet"; "Compiling the Anthology Albums," including an excerpt from "A Day in the Life"; "Back at Abbey Road, May 1995," including excerpts from "Golden Slumbers," "I'm Only Sleeping," and "Tomorrow Never Knows"; "Recording 'Free as a Bird' and 'Real Love'"; "Production Team"; "Making the 'Free as a Bird' Video"; "Real Love" video.

LEGACY AND INFLUENCE

In 1997, *The Beatles Anthology* earned a Grammy Award for Best Music Video, Long Form at the 39th Grammy Awards.

See also: Aspinall, Neil; Best, Pete; The Cavern Club; Decca Records Audition; Martin, George; Ono, Yoko; The Rooftop Concert.

The Beatles Anthology, Volume I (LP)

November 21, 1995, Apple [Parlophone] CDP 7243 8 34445 2
November 20, 1995, Apple [Capitol] CDP 7243 8 34445 2 6

The Beatles Anthology, Volume 1 was released in November 1995 in conjunction with the Beatles' *Anthology* television miniseries. As the first entry in the *Anthology* trilogy of albums, *The Beatles Anthology, Volume 1* contains "Free as a Bird," the first new Beatles recording since the January 1970 sessions in which the group completed work on "I Me Mine."

BACKGROUND

Also known as *Anthology 1*, *The Beatles Anthology, Volume 1* consists of studio outtakes, rare recordings, and live performances from the bandmates' early years, ranging from 1958 through 1964. Such rarities include recordings from the Quarry Men, the Beatles' Hamburg days with Tony Sheridan, and their Decca audition in 1962. In addition to rare performances with the Beatles by Stu Sutcliffe and Pete Best, the album includes material from the band's legend-making performance on *The Ed Sullivan Show* in February 1964 through the sessions for *Beatles for Sale*.

Produced by Jeff Lynne with Geoff Emerick as sound engineer, "Free as a Bird" is the much-publicized centerpiece of *The Beatles Anthology, Volume 1*. Released some 25 years after their disbandment, "Free as a Bird" was a 1995 hit single by the Beatles that the surviving band members recorded with a 1977 demo by Lennon as the song's basic track. It is one of the very few songs credited to all four Beatles as composers.

TRACK LISTING

Disc 1: "Free As a Bird"; "We Were Four Guys . . . That's All" (Speech); "That'll Be the Day"; "In Spite of All the Danger"; "Sometimes I'd Borrow" (Speech); "Hallelujah, I Love Her So"; "You'll Be Mine"; "Cayenne"; "First of All" (Speech); "My Bonnie"; "Ain't She Sweet"; "Cry for a Shadow"; "Brian Was a Beautiful Guy" (Speech); "I Secured Them" (Speech); "Searchin' "; "Three Cool Cats"; "The Sheik of Araby"; "Like Dreamers Do"; "Hello Little Girl"; "Well, the Recording Test" (Speech); "Bésame Mucho"; "Love Me Do"; "How Do You Do It"; "Please Please Me"; "One After 909" (Sequence); "One After 909" (Complete); "Lend Me Your Comb"; "I'll Get You"; "We Were Performers" (Speech); "I Saw Her Standing There"; "From Me to You"; "Money (That's What I Want)"; "You Really Got a Hold on Me"; "Roll Over Beethoven."

Disc 2: "She Loves You"; "Till There Was You"; "Twist and Shout"; "This Boy"; "I Want to Hold Your Hand"; "Boys, What Was I Thinking?" (Speech); "Moonlight Bay"; "Can't Buy Me Love" (Takes 1 and 2); "All My Loving" (*Ed Sullivan Show*); "You Can't Do That" (Take 6); "And I Love Her" (Take 2); "A Hard Day's Night" (Take 1); "I Wanna Be Your Man"; "Long Tall Sally"; "Boys"; "Shout"; "I'll Be Back" (Take 2); "I'll Be Back" (Take 3); "You Know What to Do" (Demo); "No Reply" (Demo); "Mr. Moonlight" (Takes 1 and 4); "Leave My Kitten Alone" (Take 5); "No Reply" (Take 2); "Eight Days a Week" (Sequence); "Eight Days a Week" (Complete); Medley: "Kansas City"/"Hey-Hey-Hey-Hey!" (Take 2).

CHART PERFORMANCE

U.K.: #2 (certified by the BPI as "2x Platinum," with more than 600,000 copies sold).

U.S.: #1 (certified by the RIAA as "8x Multi Platinum," with more than 8 million copies sold).

COVER ARTWORK

The cover for *The Beatles Anthology, Volume 1* features the first third of Klaus Voormann's *Anthology* collage—an assortment of layers, torn and peeled back upon each other, of period photographs and album covers. In a symbolic gesture, the record sleeve for *The Savage Young Beatles* album depicted at the center of the *Anthology 1* cover reveals former drummer Pete Best's face removed in favor of

Starr's, his successor in the band. Best later used the missing part from Voormann's collage as the cover art for the Pete Best Band's 2008 album *Haymans Green*.

LEGACY AND INFLUENCE

In 1997, *The Beatles Anthology, Volume 1* was honored at the American Music Awards for Favorite Pop/Rock Album.

See also: *The Beatles Anthology, Volume 1* (LP); Aspinall, Neil; Best, Pete; The Cavern Club.

The Beatles Anthology, Volume 2 (LP)

March 18, 1996, Apple [Parlophone] CDP 7243 8 34448 2
March 18, 1996, Apple [Capitol] CDP 7243 8 34448 4 7

The Beatles Anthology, Volume 2 was released in March 1996 in conjunction with the Beatles' *Anthology* television miniseries. As the second entry in the *Anthology* trilogy of albums, *The Beatles Anthology, Volume 2* contains "Real Love," the second new Beatles recording, after "Free as a Bird," since the January 1970 sessions in which the group completed work on "I Me Mine."

BACKGROUND

Also known as *Anthology 2*, *The Beatles Anthology, Volume 2* consists of studio outtakes, rare recordings, and live performances from the bandmates' mid-period, ranging from 1965 through 1968. Such rarities include unreleased outtakes from the Beatles' *Help!* sessions, as well as the unreleased "12-Bar Original" instrumental from their *Rubber Soul* period. The contents of *Anthology 2* bring the Beatles' middle years to a close with their recordings in February 1968 before the group traveled to Rishikesh on their voyage of spiritual enlightenment with Maharishi Mahesh Yogi.

Produced by Jeff Lynne with Geoff Emerick as sound engineer, "Real Love" sets *The Beatles Anthology, Volume 2* into motion. Released some 25 years after their disbandment, "Real Love" was a 1996 hit single by the Beatles that the surviving band members recorded with a 1979 demo by Lennon as the song's basic track. Notably absent from *Anthology 2* is "Carnival of Light," the Beatles' January 1967 avant-garde recording that had been invited for presentation at *The Million Volt Light and Sound Rave* art festival. Harrison vetoed the track's inclusion on the album.

TRACK LISTING

Disc 1: "Real Love"; "Yes It Is" (Takes 2 and 14); "I'm Down" (Take 1); "You've Got to Hide Your Love Away" (Takes 1, 2, and 5); "If You've Got Trouble"

(Take 1); "That Means a Lot" (Take 1); "Yesterday" (Take 1); "It's Only Love" (Takes 2 and 3); "I Feel Fine"; "Ticket to Ride"; "Yesterday"; "Help!"; "Everybody's Trying to Be My Baby"; "Norwegian Wood (This Bird Has Flown)" (Take 1); "I'm Looking Through You" (Take 1); "12-Bar Original" (Edited Take 2); "Tomorrow Never Knows" (Take 1); "Got to Get You into My Life" (Take 5); "And Your Bird Can Sing" (Take 2); "Taxman" (Take 11); "Eleanor Rigby" (Take 14); "I'm Only Sleeping" (Rehearsal); "I'm Only Sleeping" (Take 1); "Rock and Roll Music"; "She's a Woman."

Disc 2: "Strawberry Fields Forever" (Demo Sequence); "Strawberry Fields Forever" (Take 1); "Strawberry Fields Forever" (Take 7 and Edit Piece); "Penny Lane" (Take 9); "A Day in the Life" (Takes 1, 2, 6, and Orchestra); "Good Morning, Good Morning" (Take 8); "Only a Northern Song" (Takes 3 and 12); "Being for the Benefit of Mr. Kite!" (Takes 1 and 2); "Being for the Benefit of Mr. Kite!" (Take 7 and Effects Tape); "Lucy in the Sky with Diamonds" (Takes 6, 7, and 8); "Within You, Without You" (Instrumental); "Sgt. Pepper's Lonely Hearts Club Band (Reprise)" (Take 5); "You Know My Name (Look Up the Number)" (Composite); "I Am the Walrus" (Take 16); "The Fool on the Hill" (Demo); "Your Mother Should Know" (Take 27); "The Fool on the Hill" (Take 4); "Hello, Goodbye" (Take 16 and Overdubs); "Lady Madonna" (Takes 3 and 4); "Across the Universe" (Take 2).

CHART PERFORMANCE

U.K.: #1 (certified by the BPI as "Platinum," with more than 300,000 copies sold).
U.S.: #1 (certified by the RIAA as "4x Multi Platinum," with more than 4 million copies sold).

COVER ARTWORK

The cover for *The Beatles Anthology, Volume 2* features the second third of Klaus Voormann's *Anthology* collage—an assortment of layers, torn and peeled back upon each other, of period photographs and album covers.

See also: *The Beatles Anthology, Volume 2* (LP); Lynne, Jeff; Voormann, Klaus.

The Beatles Anthology, Volume 3 (LP)

October 25, 1996, Apple [Parlophone] CDP 7243 8 34451 2 7
October 29, 1996, Apple [Capitol] CDP 7243 8 34451 2 7

The Beatles Anthology, Volume 3 was released in October 1996. *The Beatles Anthology, Volume 3* is the final entry in the *Anthology* trilogy of albums.

BACKGROUND

Also known as *Anthology 3*, *The Beatles Anthology, Volume 3* consists of studio outtakes, rare recordings, and live performances from the bandmates' late period, ranging from 1968 through their last photo session in August 1969. Such rarities include unreleased outtakes from the Beatles' *White Album* sessions, as well as the unreleased "Not Guilty" and "What's the New Mary Jane." The contents of *Anthology 3* bring the Beatles' career to a close with their recordings for the *Get Back* project—including rare footage from the much-heralded rooftop concert—through the *Abbey Road* sessions.

In contrast with *Anthology 1* and *Anthology 2*, *Anthology 3* does not feature any new tracks by the Threetles, as Harrison, McCartney, and Starr abandoned work on the Lennon demo "Now and Then" because of issues with the source track's sound quality—namely, a persistent hum that producer Jeff Lynne was unable to mitigate.

TRACK LISTING

Disc 1: "A Beginning"; "Happiness Is a Warm Gun" (Esher Demo); "Helter Skelter" (Edited Take 2); "Mean Mr. Mustard" (Esher Demo); "Polythene Pam" (Esher Demo); "Glass Onion" (Esher Demo); "Junk" (Esher Demo); "Piggies" (Esher Demo); "Honey Pie" (Esher Demo); "Don't Pass Me By" (Takes 3 and 5); "Ob-La-Di, Ob-La-Da" (Take 5); "Good Night" (Rehearsal and Take 34); "Cry Baby Cry" (Take 1); "Blackbird" (Take 4); "Sexy Sadie" (Take 6); "While My Guitar Gently Weeps" (Demo); "Hey Jude" (Take 2); "Not Guilty" (Take 102); "Mother Nature's Son" (Take 2); "Glass Onion" (Take 33); "Rocky Raccoon" (Take 8); "What's the New Mary Jane" (Take 4); "Step Inside Love"/"Los Paranoias"; "I'm So Tired" (Takes 3, 6, and 9); "I Will" (Take 1); "Why Don't We Do It in the Road?" (Take 4); "Julia" (Take 2).

Disc 2: "I've Got a Feeling"; "She Came in Through the Bathroom Window" (Rehearsal); "Dig a Pony"; "Two of Us"; "For You Blue"; "Teddy Boy"; Medley: "Rip It Up"/"Shake, Rattle, and Roll"/"Blue Suede Shoes"; "The Long and Winding Road"; "Oh! Darling" (Edited); "All Things Must Pass" (Demo); "Mailman, Bring Me No More Blues"; "Get Back" (Rooftop Concert); "Old Brown Shoe" (Demo); "Octopus's Garden" (Takes 2 and 8); "Maxwell's Silver Hammer" (Take 5); "Something" (Demo); "Come Together" (Take 1); "Come and Get It" (Demo); "Ain't She Sweet" (Jam); "Because" (A Cappella Version); "Let It Be"; "I Me Mine" (Take 16); "The End" (Remix).

CHART PERFORMANCE

U.K.: #4 (certified by the BPI as "Gold," with more than 100,000 copies sold).
U.S.: #1 (certified by the RIAA as "3x Multi Platinum," with more than 3 million copies sold).

COVER ARTWORK

The cover for *The Beatles Anthology, Volume 3* features the final third of Klaus Voormann's *Anthology* collage—an assortment of layers, torn and peeled back upon each other, of period photographs and album covers. As with his 1966 cover for the *Revolver* album, Voormann offers a contemporary self-portrait in the artwork for *Anthology 2*.

See also: *The Beatles Anthology, Volume 3* (LP); Lynne, Jeff; Voormann, Klaus.

"The Beatles Are Bigger than Jesus Christ"

In March 1966, the *London Evening Standard* published Maureen Cleave's latest interview with Lennon. Having recently read Hugh J. Schonfield's best seller, *The Passover Plot* (1965), the Beatle was anxious to share his views regarding the plight of contemporary religion. During their discussion, Lennon remarked that "Christianity will go. It will vanish and shrink. . . . We're more popular than Jesus now; I don't know which will go first—rock and roll or Christianity. Jesus was all right, but his disciples were thick and ordinary. It's them twisting it that ruins it for me" (Lange 2001, 143).

Lennon's comments passed without notice in the British press, but on July 31, 1966, the American magazine *Datebook* republished the interview. Within days, radio stations across the nation's Bible Belt were sponsoring "Beatle-burnings" in which they invited the public to torch their Beatles records. As the group prepared to travel to the United States, Lennon took to calling their upcoming spate of American concerts the "Jesus Christ Tour." He had no idea how accurate his words would prove to be. By the time that the Beatles alighted on American shores, Lennon's remarks to Cleave had set off a public-relations controversy that Epstein and the Beatles could scarcely have imagined. At a press conference in Chicago, Lennon attempted to quell the storm: "I wasn't saying whatever they're saying I was saying," he told the media. "I'm sorry I said it really. I never meant it to be a lousy anti-religious thing. I apologize if that will make you happy. I still don't know quite what I've done. I've tried to tell you what I did do, but if you want me to apologize, if that will make you happy, then okay, I'm sorry." Years later, Lennon quipped that "I should have said television is more popular than Jesus; then I might have got away with it" (Beatles 2000, 226).

But the controversy didn't ebb so easily, and neither did the group's distaste for the relentless circus of Beatlemania. On August 19, 1966, the band played a concert at the Mid-South Coliseum in Memphis, Tennessee, where the Ku Klux Klan staged a protest, and a firecracker exploded on the stage. For a split second, they thought that they were under attack, that one of them had been assassinated. As Lennon remembered, "There had been threats to shoot us, the Klan were burning Beatle records outside, and a lot of the crew-cut kids were joining in with them.

Somebody let off a firecracker and every one of us—I think it's on film—look at each other, because each thought it was the other that had been shot. It was that bad" (Beatles 2000, 227).

For the Beatles, the controversy surrounded Lennon's remark exposed the brutal underbelly of Beatlemania when pop culture collides with personal ideology. For Lennon, the 1966 American Tour came to be known as the "Jesus Christ Tour," and on August 29, 1966, in San Francisco it spelled the end of the Beatles' touring lives forever.

See also: Tours, 1960–1966.

The Beatles at the Hollywood Bowl (LP)

May 6, 1977, Parlophone EMTV 4
May 4, 1977, Capitol SMAS 11638

The Beatles at the Hollywood Bowl is a live album, now deleted from the Beatles' catalogue, that was released in the United Kingdom and the United States in May 1977.

BACKGROUND

The Beatles at the Hollywood Bowl was compiled from the group's live performances at the famed Los Angeles–area venue in August 1964 and August 1965. Capitol Records had originally planned to record the Beatles' February 12, 1964, concerts at Carnegie Hall in New York City, but proved unable to procure the required permits from the Musicians Union. In August 1964, Capitol recorded the Beatles' Hollywood Bowl performance for the express purpose of releasing a live album, although the sound quality of the recording was considered too poor for release. A year later, Capitol commissioned the recording of the band's August 1965 recording with similarly unsatisfactory results. Until the 1977 release of *The Beatles at the Hollywood Bowl*, the only available recording from the Beatles' Hollywood Bowl appearances was an August 1964 excerpt of "Twist and Shout" that was included on *The Beatles Story*.

In the years after the group's disbandment, Phil Spector initially began preparing the live recordings for release, although the album never materialized. The catalyst for *The Beatles at the Hollywood Bowl* finally came in the form of the impending release of *Live! at the Star-Club in Hamburg, Germany; 1962*. Determined to counter the legal, albeit unauthorized release of the Beatles' poorly recorded early efforts in Hamburg, EMI asked George Martin to revisit the Hollywood Bowl recordings. As Martin recalled in the album's liner notes:

It was with some misgivings . . . that I agreed to listen to those early tapes at the request of Bhaskar Menon, Capitol's president. The fact that they were the only live recordings of the Beatles in existence (if you discount inferior bootlegs) did not impress me. What did impress me, however, was the electric atmosphere and raw energy that came over. And so, together with my recording engineer, Geoff Emerick, I set to work to bring the performance back to life. It was a labor of love, for we did not know if we could make them good enough for the world to hear—let alone John, Paul, George and Ringo.

In order to enhance the quality of the recorded performances, Martin and Emerick "transferred the vintage three track tapes to modern multi-track, remixed, filtered, equalized, and generally polished the tapes. Then, by careful editing from the two performances, we produced the performance that you hear now, obviously there has been no overdubbing. All the voices and instruments are the original performance (some of the vocal balances, with three singers on one track are evidence enough). But it is a piece of history that will not occur again."

Given that *The Beatles at the Hollywood Bowl* is compiled from two separate concert tours, a number of songs were omitted from the album. The August 1964 compositions not included consist of "Twist and Shout," "You Can't Do That," "Can't Buy Me Love," "If I Fell," "I Want to Hold Your Hand," and "A Hard Day's Night"; while the August 1965 compositions not included consist of "I Feel Fine," "Everybody's Trying to Be My Baby," "Baby's in Black," "I Wanna Be Your Man," and "I'm Down." The August 1965 recording of "Baby's in Black" was later released as the B-side of the "Real Love" single in 1995. Additionally, a segment from the August 1964 recording of "I Want to Hold Your Hand" was remixed into the original studio version of the song as part of the *Love* soundtrack album in 2006.

TRACK LISTING

Side 1: "Twist and Shout"; "She's a Woman"; "Dizzy Miss Lizzy"; "Ticket to Ride"; "Can't Buy Me Love"; "Things We Said Today"; "Roll Over Beethoven."
Side 2: "Boys"; "A Hard Day's Night"; "Help!"; "All My Loving"; "She Loves You"; "Long Tall Sally."

COVER ARTWORK

The simple cover art for *The Beatles at the Hollywood Bowl* depicted a pair of concert tickets with an illustration of the Hollywood Bowl in the background. Martin provided extensive liner notes, writing that "those of us who were lucky enough to be present at a live Beatle concert—be it in Liverpool, London, New York,

Washington, Los Angeles, Tokyo, Sydney, or wherever—will know how amazing, how unique those performances were. . . . It may be a poor substitute for the reality of those times, but it is now all there is."

CHART PERFORMANCE

U.K.: #1 (certified by the BPI as "Gold," with more than 100,000 copies sold).
U.S.: #2 (certified by the RIAA as "Platinum," with more than 1 million copies sold).

See also: *The Beatles Story* (LP); Emerick, Geoff; *Live! at the Star-Club in Hamburg, Germany; 1962* (LP); *Love* (LP); Martin, George; Spector, Phil.

The Beatles Bootleg Recordings 1963 (LP)

December 17, 2013, Apple/Universal Music

Released exclusively through iTunes, *The Beatles Bootleg Recordings 1963* compilation features 59 unreleased recordings from the band's recording sessions in 1962.

BACKGROUND

Originally slated only to be available for a few hours in order to protect the recordings from entering the public domain, *The Beatles Bootleg Recordings 1963* has enjoyed worldwide distribution. The compilation is composed of 15 studio outtake recordings, along with 44 previously unreleased tracks from the band's BBC sessions. *The Beatles Bootleg Recordings 1963* also features Lennon and McCartney's acoustic guitar demo version of "Bad to Me" and Lennon's piano demo for "I'm in Love."

CONTENTS

"There's a Place" (Takes 5 and 6); "There's a Place" (Take 8); "There's a Place" (Take 9); "Do You Want to Know a Secret" (Take 7); "A Taste of Honey" (Take 6); "I Saw Her Standing There" (Take 2); "Misery" (Take 1); "Misery" (Take 7); "From Me to You" (Takes 1 and 2); "From Me to You" (Take 5); "Thank You Girl" (Take 1); "Thank You Girl" (Take 5); "One After 909" (Takes 1 and 2); "Hold Me Tight" (Take 21); "Money (That's What I Want)" (Studio outtake); "Some Other Guy"; "Love Me Do"; "Too Much Monkey Business"; "I Saw Her Standing There"; "Do You Want to Know a Secret"; "From Me to You"; "I Got to Find My Baby"; "Roll Over Beethoven"; "A Taste of Honey"; "Love Me Do"; "Please Please Me"; "She Loves You"; "I Want to Hold Your Hand"; "Till There Was You"; "Roll Over

Beethoven"; "You Really Got a Hold on Me"; "The Hippy Hippy Shake"; "Till There Was You"; "A Shot of Rhythm and Blues"; "A Taste of Honey"; "Money (That's What I Want)"; "Anna (Go to Him)"; "Love Me Do"; "She Loves You"; "I'll Get You"; "A Taste of Honey"; "Boys"; "Chains"; "You Really Got a Hold on Me"; "I Saw Her Standing There"; "She Loves You"; "Twist and Shout"; "Do You Want to Know a Secret"; "Please Please Me"; "Long Tall Sally"; "Chains"; "Boys"; "A Taste of Honey"; "Roll Over Beethoven"; "All My Loving"; "She Loves You"; "Till There Was You"; "Bad to Me" (Demo); "I'm in Love" (Demo).

CHART PERFORMANCE

U.K.: Did not chart.
U.S.: #172.

See also: *Live at the BBC* (LP); *On Air: Live at the BBC, Volume 2.*

The Beatles Cartoons (TV Series)

The brainchild of King Features Syndicate producer Al Brodax, the Beatles Cartoons aired as a half-hour production from September 15, 1965, through September 7, 1969. Financed by toy magnate A.C. Gilmer, the ABC series became an instant hit in the Nielsen Weekly Ratings for its Saturday morning time slot.

Each show consisted of two musical numbers, which formed the basis for every episode's plot. The first of the series' 39 installments featured "I Want to Hold Your Hand" and "A Hard Day's Night." In each episode, the lyrics appeared on the screen in order to encourage viewers to sing along with the band. The voices of the Beatles' cartoon personae were supplied by Paul Frees (Lennon and Martin) and Lance Percival (McCartney and Starr).

The animation for the Beatles cartoons was produced by TVC Animation of London and Astransa, an Australian firm. TVC later performed the bulk of the animation duties for the Beatles' feature-length cartoon *Yellow Submarine*. According to Chris Cuddington, one of the animators for the series, "It took about four weeks to animate each film, and I enjoyed it immensely. The characters were easy to draw, and the stories were simple and uncomplicated."

The show's final two seasons consisted entirely of reruns. In 1968, ABC moved the series to Sundays, where it remained until its cancellation in the fall of 1969. Buoyed by the initial success of the Beatles cartoons, King Features Syndicate briefly considered similar ventures on behalf of such 1960s musical standouts as Herman's Hermits and Freddie and the Dreamers.

In a 1972 interview with Roy Carr, Lennon warmly recalled that "I still get a blast out of watching the Beatles cartoons on TV." During a 1999 interview with Timothy White, Harrison remembered that "I always kind of liked [the cartoons].

They were so bad or silly that they were good, if you know what I mean. And I think the passage of time might make them more fun now" (Axelrod 1999, Back Cover).

The theme music shifted over the duration of the series, with the theme music for Season 1 including the introductory riff from "A Hard Day's Night" transitioning into "Can't Buy Me Love." For Season 2, the show's theme was "Help!"; for Season 3, the theme was "And Your Bird Can Sing."

SEASON I (1965–1966)

1. "A Hard Day's Night"/"I Want to Hold Your Hand" (Sing-along: "Not a Second Time"/"Devil in Her Heart")
2. "Do You Want to Know a Secret"/"If I Fell" (Sing-along: "A Hard Day's Night"/"I Want to Hold Your Hand")
3. "Please Mister Postman"/"Devil in Her Heart" (Sing-along: "If I Fell"/"Do You Want to Know a Secret")
4. "Not a Second Time"/"Slow Down" (Sing-along: "Baby's in Black"/"Misery")
5. "Baby's in Black"/"Misery" (Sing-along: "I'll Get You"/"Chains")
6. "You Really Got a Hold on Me"/"Chains" (Sing-along: "Slow Down"/"Honey Don't")
7. "I'll Get You"/"Honey Don't" (Sing-along: "You Really Got a Hold on Me"/"Any Time at All")
8. "Any Time at All"/"Twist and Shout" (Sing-along: "I'll Be Back"/"Little Child")
9. "Little Child"/"I'll Be Back" (Sing-along: "Long Tall Sally"/"Twist and Shout")
10. "Long Tall Sally"/"I'll Cry Instead" (Sing-along: "I'll Follow the Sun"/"When I Get Home")
11. "I'll Follow the Sun"/"When I Get Home" (Sing-along: "I'll Cry Instead"/"Everybody's Trying to Be My Baby")
12. "Everybody's Trying to Be My Baby"/"I Should Have Known Better" (Sing-along: "I'm a Loser"/"I Wanna Be Your Man")
13. "I'm a Loser"/"I Wanna Be Your Man" (Sing-along: "No Reply"/"I'm Happy Just to Dance with You")
14. "Don't Bother Me"/"No Reply" (Sing-along: "It Won't Be Long"/"I Should Have Known Better")
15. "I'm Happy Just to Dance with You"/"Mr. Moonlight" (Sing-along: "Don't Bother Me"/"Can't Buy Me Love")
16. "Can't Buy Me Love"/"It Won't Be Long" (Sing-along: "Anna (Go to Him)"/"Mr. Moonlight")
17. "Anna (Go to Him)"/"I Don't Want to Spoil the Party" (Sing-along: "Matchbox"/"Thank You Girl")

18. "Matchbox"/"Thank You Girl" (Sing-along: "I Don't Want to Spoil the Party"/"Help!")
19. "From Me to You"/"Boys" (Sing-along: "Please Mister Postman"/"I Saw Her Standing There")
20. "Dizzy Miss Lizzy"/"I Saw Her Standing There" (Sing-along: "Ticket to Ride"/"From Me to You")
21. "What You're Doing"/"Money (That's What I Want)" (Sing-along: "Dizzy Miss Lizzy"/"All My Loving"
22. "Komm, Gib Mir Deine Hand"/"She Loves You" (Sing-along: "Bad Boy"/ "Tell Me Why")
23. "Bad Boy"/"Tell Me Why" (Sing-along: "Please Please Me"/"Hold Me Tight")
24. "I Feel Fine"/"Hold Me Tight" (Sing-along: "What You're Doing"/"There's a Place")
25. "Please Please Me"/"There's a Place" (Sing-along: "Roll Over Beethoven"/ "Rock and Roll Music")
26. "Roll Over Beethoven"/"Rock and Roll Music" (Sing-along: "I Feel Fine"/ "She Loves You")

SEASON 2 (1966)

27. "Eight Days a Week"/"I'm Looking Through You" (Sing-along: "Run for Your Life"/"Girl")
28. "Help!"/"We Can Work It Out" (Sing-along: "The Night Before"/"Day Tripper")
29. "I'm Down"/"Run for Your Life" (Sing-along: "Eight Days a Week"/ "Paperback Writer")
30. "Drive My Car"/"Tell Me What You See" (Sing-along: "Yesterday"/"We Can Work It Out")
31. "I Call Your Name"/"The Word" (Sing-along: "I Feel Fine"/"Wait")
32. "All My Loving"/"Day Tripper" (Sing-along: "I'm Looking Through You"/ "Nowhere Man")
33. "Nowhere Man"/"Paperback Writer" (Sing-along: "And I Love Her"/ "Michelle")

SEASON 3 (1967)

34. "Penny Lane"/"Strawberry Fields Forever" (Sing-along: "Good Day Sunshine"/"Rain")
35. "And Your Bird Can Sing"/"Got to Get You into My Life" (Sing-along: "Penny Lane"/"Eleanor Rigby")

36. "Good Day Sunshine"/"Ticket to Ride" (Sing-along: "Strawberry Fields Forever"/"And Your Bird Can Sing")

37. "Taxman"/"Eleanor Rigby" (Sing-along: "Got to Get You into My Life"/ "Here, There, and Everywhere")

38. "Tomorrow Never Knows"/"I've Just Seen a Face" (Sing-along: "She Said She Said"/"Long Tall Sally")

39. "Wait"/"I'm Only Sleeping" (Sing-along: "Penny Lane"/"Eleanor Rigby")

See also: *Yellow Submarine* (Film).

The Beatles' Christmas Records (1963–1969)

Conceived as a means of providing holiday greetings to their legions of loyal fans, the Beatles' annual Christmas messages were distributed via their fan clubs in the United Kingdom and the United States, respectively, as flexi-disc and cardboard record releases. While compilation albums were released to their fan clubs in 1970, the Beatles have never officially released their Christmas recordings, save for the inclusion of "Christmas Time (Is Here Again)," which was released as part of *The Beatles Anthology* project.

BACKGROUND

Entitled as *The Beatles' Christmas Record*, the group's 1963 release was written and produced by Tony Barrow and recorded on October 17, 1963, at the Dick James House, the studio owned and operated by their music publisher on London's Oxford Street. For the recording, the Beatles sing the Christmas carol "Good King Wenceslas" and the comic "Rudolph the Red-Nosed Ringo." The U.K. fan club version was distributed on December 6, 1963 (Lyntone [EMI] LYN 492), with an edited version released via the U.S. fan club in December 1964.

Entitled as *Another Beatles Christmas Record*, the band's 1964 release was written and produced by Barrow and recorded on October 26, 1964, at the Dick James House. For the recording, the Beatles sing the Christmas carol "Jingle Bells" and the traditional "Did You Wash Your Father's Shirt?" while gently mocking Barrow's prepared holiday greeting. The U.K. fan club version was distributed on December 18, 1964 (Lyntone [EMI] LYN 757). While American fans received the 1963 version of the recording in December 1964, *Another Beatles Christmas Record* was not made available for U.S. fans until its inclusion on 1970's *The Beatles' Christmas Album* compilation.

Entitled as *The Beatles' Third Christmas Record*, the band's 1965 release was produced by Barrow, cowritten by Barrow and the Beatles, and recorded on

November 8, 1965, at the Dick James House. For the recording, the Beatles sing the traditional "Auld Lang Syne," as well as excerpts from "Yesterday" and the Four Tops' "It's the Same Old Song." Lennon also sings an original composition "Happy Christmas to Ya List'nas," while the recording concludes with an original Beatles poem entitled "Christmas Comes But Once a Year." The recording was distributed to U.K. fans on December 18, 1965 (Lyntone [EMI] LYN 948). American fans merely received a postcard, inscribed with the words "Seasons Greetings— Paul, Ringo, George, John," without the recording itself, which was finally released in the United States on 1970's *The Beatles' Christmas Album* compilation. The U.S. fan club's *Beatle Bulletin* later reported that *The Beatles' Third Christmas Record* arrived too late to be released for the 1965 holiday season; hence, the postcard was distributed in its stead.

Entitled as *The Beatles' Fourth Christmas Record*, the band's 1966 release was produced by George Martin, written by the Beatles, and recorded on November 8, 1966, at the Dick James House. For the recording, which was made during a break from the "Strawberry Fields Forever" sessions, the Beatles perform a series of skits, including "Podgy the Bear and Jasper" and "Felpin Mansions." With McCartney on piano accompaniment, the group sings McCartney's hastily improvised compositions "Everywhere It's Christmas," "Orowainya," and "Please Don't Bring Your Banjo Back." The recording was distributed to U.K. fans on December 16, 1966 (Lyntone [EMI] LYN 1145). As with 1965, American fans merely received a postcard without benefit of the recording itself, which was finally released in the United States on 1970's *The Beatles' Christmas Album* compilation.

Entitled as *Christmas Time (Is Here Again)*, the band's 1967 release was produced by Martin, written by the Beatles, and recorded on November 28, 1967, at Abbey Road Studios. For the recording, the Beatles concocted a six-minute narrative in which various groups audition for a BBC radio show, with "Christmas Time (Is Here Again)" serving as the track's periodic refrain. The song's comic spirit was likely inspired by the BBC Radio 1's Bonzo Dog Doo Dah Band, while also sharing the same free-form hilarity inherent in the Beatles' "You Know My Name (Look Up the Number)," which the Beatles had recorded in large part during the previous summer. The four Beatles voice various characters ranging from game-show contestants and musicians (the Ravellers) to actors in a fictive radio program entitled *Theatre Hour*. In addition to each Beatle offering a spoken-word seasonal greeting to the band's fans, the recording concludes with Lennon reading his Joycean, nonsensical poem entitled "When Christmas Time Is Over" with "Auld Lang Syne" as his musical accompaniment. The recording was distributed to U.K. fans on December 15, 1967 (Lyntone [EMI] LYN 1360).

Entitled as *The Beatles' 1968 Christmas Record*, the band's 1968 release was produced by British DJ Kenny Everett and recorded in separate locations by the bandmates in November and December 1968. The recording includes individual Beatles messages, along with McCartney's song "Happy Christmas, Happy New

Year" and Lennon's poems "Jock and Yono" and "Once Upon a Pool Table." Recent Beatles recordings of "Birthday," "Helter Skelter," and "Ob-La-Di, Ob-La-Da" appear in the mix, as does a cover version of "Nowhere Man" by Tiny Tim with ukulele accompaniment. *The Beatles' 1968 Christmas Record* was distributed to U.K. fans on December 20, 1968 (Lyntone [EMI] LYN 1743). In contrast with the previous three holiday seasons in which they received postcards, American fans were finally provided with actual copies of the recording itself (Lyntone [EMI] LYN 1744).

Entitled as *The Beatles' Seventh Christmas Record* (1969), the Fab Four's final holiday recording was produced by British DJ Maurice Cole and recorded in separate locations by the group members, now effectively disbanded, in November and December 1969. The recording features brief greetings from Harrison and Starr, with McCartney singing "This Is to Wish You a Merry, Merry Christmas." Much of the recording originates from a session with Lennon and Yoko Ono at their Tittenhurst Park estate. *The Beatles' Seventh Christmas Record* concludes with the bandmates' guitar solos from *Abbey Road*'s "The End," along with Ono interviewing Lennon. The recording was distributed to U.K. fans on December 19, 1969 (Lyntone [EMI] LYN 1970). As with 1968's Christmas record, American Beatles fans also received the record as their 1969 holiday greeting (Lyntone [EMI] LYN 1971).

In 1970, the Beatles' Christmas records were subsequently compiled and released to the band's fan clubs in the United Kingdom and the United States, respectively, as *From Then to You* and *The Beatles' Christmas Album*.

While the Beatles' Christmas recordings have not been officially released in their entirety, "Christmas Time (Is Here Again)" was released as the B-side of 1994's "Free as a Bird" single. Excerpts of dialogue from *The Beatles' Third Christmas Record* and *The Beatles' Fourth Christmas Record* were also featured on the 2006 *Love* project. Finally, for the 2010 holiday season, *The Beatles' Christmas Record* was made available as a free download from iTunes.

See also: *Abbey Road* (LP); Abbey Road Studios; iTunes; Martin, George; Ono, Yoko.

Beatles for Sale (LP)

December 4, 1964, Parlophone PMC 1240 (mono)/PCS 3062 (stereo)

Beatles for Sale is the Beatles' fourth studio album. It was released on the Parlophone label on December 4, 1964, in the United Kingdom. In the United States, several of the songs on *Beatles for Sale* were released on *Beatles '65*, released on December 15, 1964, and *Beatles VI*, released on June 14, 1965.

Beatles for Sale became standardized among U.S. album releases with the February 26, 1987, distribution of the band's first four albums as mono CD releases. It was remastered and rereleased as a stereo CD on September 9, 2009. A remastered mono release was also made available at this time as part of a limited edition box set entitled *The Beatles in Mono*.

BACKGROUND AND RECORDING SESSIONS

Produced by George Martin with Norman "Normal" Smith as his sound engineer, *Beatles for Sale* was recorded sporadically on four-track equipment over several sessions during the latter months of 1964. For the Beatles, it arrived at the tail-end of an unprecedented and incredibly hectic year. "They were rather war-weary during *Beatles for Sale*," Martin recalled. "One must remember that they'd been battered like mad throughout 1964, and much of 1963. Success is a wonderful thing, but it is very, very tiring. They were always on the go" (Dowlding 1989, 82). As it turned out, the Beatles had very little to offer in the way of new material by that period. Although many of the band's critics—and even their producer—malign *Beatles for Sale* as one of their weakest efforts, there is little doubt that it contains moments of profound change and insight. While the album includes eight original compositions, it is rounded out by a whopping six cover versions—the most amongst any of their studio albums.

Despite their paucity in number, *Beatles for Sale*'s original compositions find the songwriters, especially Lennon, in their most revealing and self-analytical guises to date. In contrast with *A Hard Day's Night*, the Beatles had very little time in the studio to complete *Beatles for Sale*. After recording "Baby's in Black" on August 11, 1964, the Beatles devoted six additional sessions at Abbey Road Studios during the production of the album, with seven days allotted in the control room for the mixing and mastering processes associated with *Beatles for Sale*. Sessions for the album were completed on October 26. Not since *Please Please Me* had the Beatles been so rushed to churn out a new product—and, starting with their next album, they never hurried in quite the same fashion again.

Beatles for Sale notably begins with a trio of songs that Beatles scholars have dubbed as the "Lennon trilogy" in an effort to reflect the progressive nature of the group's work—and Lennon's work as songwriter, in particular—on "No Reply," "I'm a Loser," and "Baby's in Black." Devin McKinney shrewdly describes *Beatles for Sale* as "half a great album; but that half is so great it shoots energy through the rest and elevates the field" (McKinney 2003, 398). From its heady beginnings in Paris and New York City through the band's sessions at Abbey Road Studios at the end of the year, 1964 was a signal moment in the group's career. They had succeeded in reinvigorating their musical and lyrical aesthetic by taking more creative risks, on the one hand, and strengthening their vice grip on their massive international audience, on the other, by generating a seemingly endless series of hit songs—and with apparent ease, no less. It was a bountiful period that reaped artistic dividends in the ensuing years, an era in which the band was forced to contend with a growing unease with life on the road and a fervent desire to improve their art with every passing composition. As Thomas MacFarlane observes, "The Beatles' early period (1962–1964) is characterized by a consolidation of composition forms inherited from previous musical eras (rock, blues, country), which the group then proceeded to integrate into a highly distinctive personal style" (MacFarlane 2004, 26).

TRACK LISTING

Side 1: "No Reply"; "I'm a Loser"; "Baby's in Black"; "Rock and Roll Music"; "I'll Follow the Sun"; "Mr. Moonlight"; Medley: "Kansas City" /"Hey-Hey-Hey-Hey!"

Side 2: "Eight Days a Week"; "Words of Love"; "Honey Don't"; "Every Little Thing"; "I Don't Want to Spoil the Party"; "What You're Doing"; "Everybody's Trying to Be My Baby."

COVER ARTWORK

The *Beatles for Sale* album cover photograph was shot by Robert Freeman at dusk near London's Hyde Park. Freeman's photograph depicts the Beatles amidst the autumnal colors of late fall. It was the first Beatles album to feature a gatefold design. The cover's interior offered a montage of photographs of the bandmates. Beatles press officer Derek Taylor authored the album's liner notes, writing that "there's priceless history between these covers. When, in a generation or so, a radioactive, cigar-smoking child, picnicking on Saturn, asks you what the Beatle affair was all about, don't try to explain all about the long hair and the screams! Just play them a few tracks from this album and he'll probably understand. The kids of AD2000 will draw from the music much the same sense of well being and warmth as we do today."

CHART PERFORMANCE

U.K.: #1. (In the United States, *Beatles for Sale* has been certified by the RIAA as "Platinum," with more than 1 million copies sold.)

LEGACY AND INFLUENCE

Beatles for Sale assumed the #1 spot in the U.K. album charts on December 9, 1964, replacing *A Hard Day's Night*. It held the #1 position for nine weeks.

See also: *Beatles '65* (LP); *Beatles VI* (LP); *A Hard Day's Night* (U.K. LP); *Please Please Me* (LP).

"The Beatles' Movie Medley" (Lennon–McCartney)

Released in 1982 in support of the *Reel Music* compilation, "The Beatles' Movie Medley" was inspired by the success of the smash-hit Beatles sound-alike "Stars on 45" medley.

AUTHORSHIP AND BACKGROUND

"The Beatles' Movie Medley" includes songs culled from the group's five movies: *A Hard Day's Night*, *Help!*, *Magical Mystery Tour*, *Yellow Submarine*, and *Let It Be*. The songs excerpted in the medley include "Magical Mystery Tour," "All You Need Is Love," "You've Got to Hide Your Love Away," "I Should Have Known Better," "A Hard Day's Night," "Ticket to Ride," and "Get Back."

"The Beatles' Movie Medley" holds the distinction of being the only Beatles' single that has not been released on CD or any other digital format. It has never been included, moreover, on a Beatles album release.

CHART PERFORMANCE

U.K.: "The Beatles' Movie Medley"/"I'm Happy Just to Dance with You"; March 24, 1982, Parlophone R6055: #10.

U.S.: "The Beatles' Movie Medley"/"I'm Happy Just to Dance with You"; March 24, 1982, Capitol B5107: #12.

See also: *A Hard Day's Night* (Film); *Help!* (Film); *Let It Be* (Film); *Magical Mystery Tour* (TV Film); *Reel Music* (LP); *Yellow Submarine* (Film).

The Beatles, 1962–1966 (LP)

April 19, 1973, Apple [Parlophone] PCSP 717
April 2, 1973, Apple [Capitol] SKBO 3403

Along with *The Beatles, 1967–1970*, *The Beatles, 1962–1966* is the Beatles' first authorized compilation. It was released on the Apple Records label on April 2, 1973, in both the United Kingdom and the United States.

The Beatles, 1962–1966 was released as a stereo CD, along with *The Beatles, 1967–1970*, on September 20, 1993. It was remastered and rereleased as a stereo

CD on October 18, 2010, in the United Kingdom, and on October 19, 2010, in the United States.

BACKGROUND

Known among fans as the "Red Album" because of its cover design's familiar red border, *The Beatles, 1962–1966* was the brainchild of Beatles manager Allen Klein, who conceived the album as a direct response to a bootleg Beatles greatest hits collection entitled *Alpha Omega*. Hawked in U.S. television and radio advertisements in late 1972 and early 1973, *Alpha Omega* was a pirated Beatles compilation sold via mail order.

The original vinyl release of *The Beatles, 1962–1966* contains variant recordings. The American release includes the "James Bond Theme," George Martin and His Orchestra's 21-second introductory piece for "Help!" Meanwhile, the British release includes a variant version of "I Feel Fine" with incidental whispering at the beginning of the mix. The original release of *The Beatles, 1962–1966* also marks the American album debut of "From Me to You" and "A Hard Day's Night." The "James Bond Theme" and the whispering intro to "I Feel Fine" were deleted from the compilation's 1993 CD release.

TRACK LISTING

Side 1: "Love Me Do"; "Please Please Me"; "From Me to You"; "She Loves You"; "I Want to Hold Your Hand"; "All My Loving"; "Can't Buy Me Love."
Side 2: "A Hard Day's Night"; "And I Love Her"; "Eight Days a Week"; "I Feel Fine"; "Ticket to Ride"; "Yesterday."
Side 3: "Help!"; "You've Got to Hide Your Love Away"; "We Can Work It Out"; "Day Tripper"; "Drive My Car"; "Norwegian Wood (This Bird Has Flown)."
Side 4: "Nowhere Man"; "Michelle"; "In My Life"; "Girl"; "Paperback Writer"; "Eleanor Rigby"; "Yellow Submarine."

COVER ARTWORK

Designed by Tom Wilkes, the cover artwork for *The Beatles, 1962–1966* features Angus McBean's March 5, 1963, photograph of the Beatles on the EMI House staircase that originally graced the *Please Please Me* album. The back cover for *The Beatles, 1962–1966* reproduces McBean's May 13, 1969, EMI House photograph that had originally been shot for the *Get Back* project. As with *The Beatles, 1967–1970*, the "Red Album" features a gatefold design with a photograph from the Beatles' "Mad Day Out" photo session on July 28, 1968. Taken by veteran war photographer Don McCullin, the gatefold photo depicts the group mingling with a crowd near St. Pancras Old Church and Gardens near London's Regent's Park.

CHART PERFORMANCE

U.K.: #3 (certified by the BPI as "Platinum," with more than 300,000 copies sold).
U.S.: #3 (certified by the RIAA as "15x Multi Platinum," with more than 15 million copies sold; certified by the RIAA as "Diamond," with more than 10 million copies sold).

See also: *The Beatles, 1967–1970* (LP); *Get Back* Project.

The Beatles, 1967–1970 (LP)

April 19, 1973, Apple [Parlophone] PCSP 718
April 2, 1973, Apple [Capitol] SKBO 3404

Along with *The Beatles, 1962–1966*, *The Beatles, 1967–1970* is the Beatles' first authorized compilation. It was released on the Apple Records label on April 2, 1973, in both the United Kingdom and the United States.

The Beatles, 1967–1970 was released as a stereo CD, along with *The Beatles, 1962–1966*, on September 20, 1993. It was remastered and rereleased as a stereo CD on October 18, 2010, in the United Kingdom, and on October 19, 2010, in the United States.

BACKGROUND

Known among fans as the "Blue Album" because of its cover design's familiar blue border, *The Beatles, 1967–1970* was the brainchild of Beatles manager Allen Klein, who conceived the album as a direct response to a bootleg Beatles greatest hits collection entitled *Alpha Omega*. Hawked in U.S. television and radio advertisements in late 1972 and early 1973, *Alpha Omega* was a pirated Beatles compilation sold via mail order. Klein originally considered the inclusion of Beatles solo material for *The Beatles, 1967–1970*, although the idea was later dropped because of space considerations.

TRACK LISTING

Side 1: "Strawberry Fields Forever"; "Penny Lane"; "Sgt. Pepper's Lonely Hearts Club Band"; "With a Little Help from My Friends"; "Lucy in the Sky with Diamonds"; "A Day in the Life"; "All You Need Is Love."
Side 2: "I Am the Walrus"; "Hello, Goodbye"; "The Fool on the Hill"; "Magical Mystery Tour"; "Lady Madonna"; "Hey Jude"; "Revolution."
Side 3: "Back in the USSR"; "While My Guitar Gently Weeps"; "Ob-La-Di, Ob-La-Da"; "Get Back"; "Don't Let Me Down"; "The Ballad of John and Yoko"; "Old Brown Shoe."

Side 4: "Here Comes the Sun"; "Come Together"; "Something"; "Octopus's Garden"; "Let It Be"; "Across the Universe"; "The Long and Winding Road."

COVER ARTWORK

Designed by Wilkes, the cover artwork for *The Beatles, 1967–1970* features McBean's May 13, 1969, EMI House photograph that had originally been shot for the *Get Back* project. The back cover for *The Beatles, 1967–1970* reproduces McBean's March 5, 1963, photograph of the Beatles on the EMI House staircase that originally graced the *Please Please Me* album. As with *The Beatles, 1962–1966*, the "Red Album" features a gatefold design with a photograph from the Beatles' "Mad Day Out" photo session on July 28, 1968. Taken by veteran war photographer Don McCullin, the gatefold photo depicts the group mingling with a crowd near St. Pancras Old Church and Gardens near London's Regent's Park.

CHART PERFORMANCE

U.K.: #2 (certified by the BPI as "Platinum," with more than 300,000 copies sold).

U.S.: #1 (certified by the RIAA as "17x Multi Platinum," with more than 17 million copies sold; certified by the RIAA as "Diamond," with more than 10 million copies sold).

See also: *The Beatles, 1962–1966* (LP); *Get Back* Project.

The Beatles: Rock Band (Video Game)

Released on September 9, 2009, along with the Beatles' remastered stereo and mono recordings, *The Beatles: Rock Band* video game resulted from a collaboration between Apple Corps and Harmonix Music Systems. The game was published by MTV Games and distributed by Electronic Arts.

BACKGROUND

The Beatles: Rock Band has sold more than 3 million units worldwide. The game featured critical input from McCartney and Starr, as well as Dhani Harrison and Giles Martin, who prepared the Beatles' music for the game's soundtrack.

The Beatles: Rock Band consists of 52 standard songs, ranging from the group's early years, the heights of Beatlemania, the studio years, to the rooftop concert. It featured custom instrumental peripherals, including replica game controllers for Lennon's Rickenbacker 325 guitar, McCartney's Höfner 500/1 bass, Harrison's Gretsch Duo-Jet guitar, and Starr's Ludwig Oyster Black Pearl drum set.

The game's standard 52 songs includes 45 tracks from the Beatles' official U.K. album releases, as well as six nonalbum singles and the "Within You, Without You"/"Tomorrow Never Knows" mash-up from the *Love* album. In addition to "All You Need Is Love," players have the option of downloading the full album contents for *Abbey Road, Rubber Soul,* and *Sgt. Pepper's Lonely Hearts Club Band.*

The Beatles: Rock Band earned a number of industry awards, including GameSpot's Best Music/Rhythm Game award. Its opening cinematic video received considerable acclaim, including the 2009 British Animation Award for Best Commissioned Animation. The opening cinematic video also won a Silver Clio Award for Television/Cinema/Digital Technique. In addition to the impressive global sales for *The Beatles: Rock Band,* it sold a remarkable quarter of its inventory during its first week of release alone.

See also: *Abbey Road* (LP); Apple Corps, Ltd.; *Love* (LP); Martin, Giles; The Rooftop Concert; *Rubber Soul* (U.K. LP); *Sgt. Pepper's Lonely Hearts Club Band* (LP).

The Beatles' Second Album (LP)

April 10, 1964, Capitol T 2080 (mono)/ST 2080 (stereo)

The Beatles' Second Album was the third Beatles album released in the United States. It was released on the Capitol label on April 10, 1964. Several of the songs on *The Beatles' Second Album* were culled from *With the Beatles,* which was released in the United Kingdom on November 22, 1963; as well as tracks from the *Long Tall Sally* EP, released in the United Kingdom on June 19, 1964; and the *A Hard Day's Night* album, released in the United Kingdom on July 10, 1964. *The Beatles' Second Album* also included both sides of the "She Loves You"/"I'll Get You" single, which was released in the United Kingdom on August 23, 1963, and "Thank You Girl," the B-side of the "From Me to You" single, released in the United Kingdom on April 11, 1963.

The Beatles' Second Album was deleted from the Beatles' catalogue in 1987, when the group's U.K. albums were distributed as CD releases. A remastered mono and stereo release of *The Beatles' Second Album* was released on November 15, 2004, as part of the box set entitled *The Capitol Albums, Volume 1.*

BACKGROUND

Given the runaway success of *Meet the Beatles!*, Capitol Records met the consumer desire for new product from the band through the release of *The Beatles' Second Album*, which bridged the gap until new material associated with the *A Hard Day's Night* feature film emerged in the summer of 1964. *The Beatles' Second Album* is noteworthy for additional echo and reverb effects intentionally added to the mix by Capitol's Dave Dexter, Jr., who wanted to afford the album with a "live" feel.

TRACK LISTING

Side 1: "Roll Over Beethoven"; "Thank You Girl"; "You Really Got a Hold on Me"; "Devil in Her Heart"; "Money (That's What I Want)"; "You Can't Do That."

Side 2: "Long Tall Sally"; "I Call Your Name"; "Please Mister Postman"; "I'll Get You"; "She Loves You."

COVER ARTWORK

The cover art for *The Beatles' Second Album* featured a collage of period photographs of the group, along with a banner announcing "Electrifying Big-Beat Performances by England's Paul McCartney, John Lennon, George Harrison and Ringo Starr." The back cover's liner notes stated that "never before has show business seen and heard anything like them. And here they are! The world's most popular foursome singing and playing their new collection of hits."

CHART PERFORMANCE

U.S.: #1 (certified by the RIAA as "2x Multi Platinum," with more than 2 million copies sold).

LEGACY AND INFLUENCE

When *The Beatles' Second Album* captured the #1 spot on the American album charts during the week of May 2, 1964, it replaced *Meet the Beatles!*, which had held the top position for 11 weeks. It marked the first instance in which a recording artist displaced itself from the top spot on the U.S. album charts.

See also: *The Capitol Albums, Volume 1* (Box Set); *A Hard Day's Night* (U.K. LP); *Meet the Beatles!* (LP); *With the Beatles* (LP).

Beatles '65 (LP)

December 15, 1964, Capitol T 2228 (mono)/ST 2228 (stereo)

Beatles '65 was the seventh Beatles album released in the United States—the fifth on Capitol Records, along with Vee-Jay Records' *Introducing . . . the Beatles* and United Artists' soundtrack for the *A Hard Day's Night* feature film. It was released on the Capitol label on December 15, 1964. Eight of the songs on *Beatles '65* were culled from the *Beatles for Sale* album, released in the United Kingdom on December 4, 1964. It also included "I'll Be Back" from *A Hard Day's Night*, released in the United Kingdom on July 10, 1964, and the "I Feel Fine"/"She's a Woman" single, released in the United Kingdom on November 27, 1964, and in the United States on November 23, 1964.

Beatles '65 was deleted from the Beatles' catalogue in 1987, when the group's U.K. albums were distributed as CD releases. A remastered mono and stereo release of *Beatles '65* was released on November 15, 2004, as part of the box set entitled *The Capitol Albums, Volume 1*.

BACKGROUND

The December 1964 release of *Beatles '65* capped the group's amazingly successful first year in the American marketplace. As with other Beatles American releases, Capitol's Dave Dexter, Jr., added reverb and echo effects to the tracks. The version of "Mr. Moonlight" on *Beatles '65* is noteworthy for the track's elongated fade-out in comparison with the song's original release on *Beatles for Sale*.

TRACK LISTING

Side 1: "No Reply"; "I'm a Loser"; "Baby's in Black"; "Rock and Roll Music"; "I'll Follow the Sun"; "Mr. Moonlight."

Side 2: "Honey Don't"; "I'll Be Back"; "She's a Woman"; "I Feel Fine"; "Everybody's Trying to Be My Baby."

COVER ARTWORK

Beatles '65's front cover artwork consists of a photographic collage of the Beatles—the largest of which, representing winter, finds the bandmates in playful repose with a quartet of umbrellas. The other three photographs represent spring, summer, and autumn (from left to right, respectively). The album's cover art was photographed by Robert Whitaker at London's Farringdon Studio in late 1964.

As with the marketing hype associated with the era, the album's liner notes speak to the Beatles' remarkable and sustained success:

> Some said it couldn't really be happening; that it was just publicity. And the fabulous Beatles proved them wrong. Others said they couldn't last more than a month or two; that nobody could hang onto that kind of fame. The Beatles, of course, proved them wrong too. . . . But you, the Beatles' fans, knew all along. You knew that the Beatles really do have a style and a sound like there's never been before. And it's simply because you like them (and they like you) that this fantastic success story has happened, and continues to happen more and more all the time. . . . These are the new favorites by the four boys who have proven themselves to be the biggest favorites of all. Here's *Beatles '65!*

CHART PERFORMANCE

U.S.: #1 (certified by the RIAA as "3x Multi Platinum," with more than 3 million copies sold).

LEGACY AND INFLUENCE

As testimony to the band's phenomenal appeal, *Beatles '65* debuted at #98 before rocketing to the #1 position on the U.S. album charts during the following week.

See also: *Beatles for Sale* (LP); *The Capitol Albums, Volume 1* (Box Set); *A Hard Day's Night* (U.K. LP).

The Beatles Stereo Box Set

September 9, 2009, Apple [Parlophone] 5099969944901
September 9, 2009, Apple [Capitol] 5099969944901

The Beatles Stereo Box Set offers remastered versions of the Beatles' standard musical catalogue. The 16-disc collection was released in concert with *The Beatles: Rock Band* video game and *The Beatles in Mono* box set.

BACKGROUND

As with the mono box set, *The Beatles Stereo Box Set* was supervised by EMI's senior engineers Allan Rouse and Guy Massey. The remastering process for the Beatles' catalogue was conducted over a four-year period at London's Abbey Road Studios and involved painstaking efforts to employ both state-of-the-art recording technology along with vintage studio equipment. In this manner, the engineers hoped to preserve the authenticity of the band's original analogue recordings.

The Beatles Stereo Box Set includes all 12 Beatles albums in stereo, with the first four Beatles albums—*Please Please Me*, *With the Beatles*, *A Hard Day's Night*, and *Beatles for Sale*—making their stereo debut. Originally released with the Beatles' 1987 CD collection, *Past Masters, Volume 1* and *Past Masters, Volume 2* have been combined into a single title, *Past Masters*. While the engineers attempted to provide remastered versions of the Beatles' entire corpus, their efforts were challenged by the band's early singles, "Love Me Do"/"P. S. I Love You" and "She Loves You"/"I'll Get You." The master tapes of these tapes were erased or reused, which was EMI's practice during that era. Two other tracks in the band's catalogue were only mixed in mono, including "Only a Northern Song" and "You Know My Name (Look Up the Number)."

Each remastered album features the visual components inherent in the original U.K. cover artwork, as well as the accompanying illustrations and liner notes.

Each album's booklet offers detailed historical and recording notes. Each of the original U.K. releases includes a mini-documentary, directed by Bob Smeaton, that contains archival footage, rare photographs, and studio chatter from the bandmates.

In a press release, Beatles historian Bruce Spizer observed that "these new CDs sound significantly better than what was first mastered 22 years ago," adding that "the engineers at Abbey Road captured the spirit of the original recordings. They resisted the temptation to drastically boost the bass to make it sound more contemporary. There is none of the harshness and muddiness that was often found on CDs mastered in the eighties. The vocals and instruments have stunning clarity. You'll hear details in the music that you've never heard before. The remasters provide a fabulous listening experience."

In subsequent years, EMI rereleased *The Beatles, 1962–1966, The Beatles, 1967–1970,* and *Yellow Submarine Songtrack* with the inclusion of the tracks created during the remastering process associated with *The Beatles Stereo Box Set.* EMI's engineering team also began remastering the solo catalogues of Lennon and McCartney.

In 2011, *The Beatles Stereo Box Set* won the Grammy Award for Best Historical Album at the 53rd Grammy Awards.

CONTENTS

Disc 1: *Please Please Me*
Disc 2: *With the Beatles*
Disc 3: *A Hard Day's Night*
Disc 4: *Beatles for Sale*
Disc 5: *Help!*
Disc 6: *Rubber Soul*
Disc 7: *Revolver*
Disc 8: *Sgt. Pepper's Lonely Hearts Club Band*
Disc 9: *Magical Mystery Tour*
Disc 10: *The Beatles (The White Album)*
Disc 11: *Yellow Submarine*
Disc 12: *Abbey Road*
Disc 13: *Let It Be*
Disc 14: *Past Masters*

CHART PERFORMANCE

U.K.: #24.
U.S.: #15 (certified by the RIAA as "3x Multi Platinum," with more than 3 million copies sold).

See also: Abbey Road Studios; *Abbey Road* (LP); *Beatles for Sale* (LP); *The Beatles, 1962–1966* (LP); *The Beatles, 1967–1970* (LP); *The Beatles Stereo Box Set*; *The Beatles (The White Album)* (LP); *A Hard Day's Night* (U.K. LP); *Help!* (U.K. LP); *Let It Be* (LP); *Magical Mystery Tour* (LP); *Past Masters* (LP); *Please Please Me* (LP); *Revolver* (U.K. LP); *Rubber Soul* (U.K. LP); *Sgt. Pepper's Lonely Hearts Club Band* (LP); *With the Beatles* (LP); *Yellow Submarine* (LP); *Yellow Submarine Songtrack* (LP).

The Beatles Story (LP)

November 23, 1964, Capitol TBO 2222 (mono)/STBO 2222 (stereo)

The Beatles Story was a documentary double album, now deleted, that was released specifically for the U.S. market.

BACKGROUND

Produced by Gary Usher and Roger Christian, *The Beatles Story* featured interviews, press conferences, and song extracts. It was released by Capitol Records in an express effort to counter the recent release of *Hear the Beatles Tell All*, a Vee-Jay Records compilation of Beatles interviews with Los Angeles radio disc jockeys Dave Hull and Jim Steck.

The Beatles Story also included audio outtakes from the Beatles' 1964 appearance at the Hollywood Bowl. The material was later included in its entirety in the 1977 release of *The Beatles at the Hollywood Bowl*.

TRACK LISTING

Side 1: "On Stage with the Beatles"; "How Beatlemania Began"; "Beatlemania in Action"; "Man Behind the Beatles—Brian Epstein"; "John Lennon"; "Who's a Millionaire." (Side 1 includes extracts from "I Want to Hold Your Hand"; "Slow Down"; and "This Boy.")

Side 2: "Beatles Will Be Beatles"; "Man Behind the Music—George Martin"; "George Harrison." (Side 2 includes extracts from "You Can't Do That"; "If I Fell"; and "And I Love Her.")

Side 3: "*A Hard Day's Night*—Their First Movie"; "Paul McCartney"; "Sneaky Haircuts and More about Paul." (Side 3 includes extracts from "A Hard Day's Night" and "And I Love Her.")

Side 4: "The Beatles Look at Life"; " 'Victims' of Beatlemania"; "Beatle Medley"; "Ringo Starr"; "Liverpool and All the World!" (Side 4 includes extracts from "Twist and Shout" (live); "Things We Said Today"; "I'm Happy Just to Dance with You"; "Long Tall Sally"; "She Loves You"; and "Boys.")

COVER ARTWORK

The Beatles Story features the Beatles' individual photographs by Joe Cavello arrayed atop the Union Jack. Written by John Babcock, the album's liner notes describe *The Beatles Story* as "a narrative and musical biography of Beatlemania." As Babcock writes, "It's Like Spending a Very Special Evening in the Company of the Beatles Themselves!" In his liner notes, Babcock observes that "millions of words have been written about them. Thousands on thousands of pictures have been printed. All in an effort to capture for fans the world over the fascinating truth and substance about four wonderful guys named John, George, Paul and Ringo. Here, at last, *is* the whole story and the real story about the Beatles, authoritatively researched, produced, and recorded on two lively long-play records by Capitol Records."

CHART PERFORMANCE

U.S.: #7 (certified by the RIAA as "Gold," with more than 500,000 copies sold).

See also: *The Beatles at the Hollywood Bowl* (LP).

The Beatles (The White Album) (LP)

November 22, 1968, Apple [Parlophone] PMC 7067–7068 (mono)/PCS 7067–7068 (stereo)
November 22, 1968, Apple [Capitol] SWBO 101 (stereo)

The Beatles (*The White Album*) is the Beatles' ninth studio album. It is also the only double album among their studio efforts. It was released on the Apple Records label on November 22, 1968, in the United Kingdom and the United States.

The White Album was released as a stereo CD, along with *Yellow Submarine*, on August 24, 1987. *The White Album* was remastered and rereleased as a stereo CD on September 9, 2009. A remastered mono release was also made available at this time as part of a limited edition box set entitled *The Beatles in Mono*.

BACKGROUND AND RECORDING SESSIONS

Produced by George Martin, *The White Album* was recorded on four- and eight-track equipment between May 30 and October 14, 1968. Early versions of several songs were recorded in May 1968 at Harrison's Kinfauns studio as part of the Esher Tapes. Several songs were produced by Chris Thomas during Martin's extended holiday. By July, tensions in the studio drove longtime sound engineer Geoff Emerick to resign from the project. The double album took longer than any other Beatles studio album to record.

On October 16, Lennon and McCartney conducted a 24-hour session at Abbey Road Studios in which they organized the songs in an effort to establish thematic unity. As Lennon later recalled, "Paul and I sat up putting *The White Album* in order until we were going crazy" (Lennon and Ono 2000, 55). Their strategy distributed the heavier rock 'n' roll tracks on Side 3, with the animal-oriented songs relegated to Side 2. In order to create a sense of balance, they apportioned Harrison's songs across all four sides. With Martin, Ken Scott, and John Smith in tow, they cross-faded and edited the tracks, ensuring that the album, like *Sgt. Pepper's Lonely Hearts Club Band*, was mastered without rills. The daylong session made for one of the most self-conscious moments in the history of the Beatles' artistry. Some eight months earlier, *The White Album* had found its origins in the Maharishi's ashram, only to be rehearsed and recorded at Kinfauns, reborn at EMI and Trident Studios, and transformed for the ages by Lennon and McCartney in the control room.

Although he didn't participate in the October 16 session at Abbey Road Studios, Harrison ended up making a belated and very significant contribution to the album's production. While visiting the Capitol Tower in Los Angeles, he listened to test pressings for *The White Album*. Aghast at their subpar quality, Harrison insisted that he be allowed to work with Capitol's engineers during the mastering process. Capitol's production team had employed a limiter to compress the volume range, and the results were disastrous (Spizer 2003, 118). "If George had not heard it in time and taken the tape away to work on it himself and returned it the way it should be," Mal Evans later remarked, "the American LP might have been a bit of a mess! It was a lot of work for George but worthwhile" (Ryan and Kehew 2006, 494).

Several tracks were recorded during the sessions for *The White Album* but omitted from the album's final contents, including Harrison's "Circles," "Not Guilty," and "Sour Milk Sea"; Lennon's "Child of Nature" (later remade as "Jealous Guy") and "What's the New Mary Jane"; and McCartney's "Jubilee" (later remade as "Junk") and "Teddy Boy." In addition to an unreleased 27-minute version of "Helter Skelter," the recording sessions for *The White Album* also saw the Beatles working on a mysterious unreleased McCartney composition entitled "Et Cetera." The Beatles also tinkered with early versions of such songs as "The Long and Winding Road," "Mean Mr. Mustard," "Polythene Pam," and "Something."

In the ensuing years, there has been unremitting conjecture about the Beatles' motives in producing a double album in the first place. Some argue that they were trying to hasten the completion of their latest EMI contract. Perhaps they were attempting to satisfy their seemingly relentless creative impulses with the expansive artistic spaces of four long-playing sides? Yet others have suggested that the Beatles, competitive to the end, were trying to match, if not exceed, the critical success of Bob Dylan's two-record masterwork *Blonde on Blonde*. In spite of all the speculation, Martin has never minced words regarding his feelings about *The White Album*'s sprawl: "I thought we should probably have made a very, very good single album, rather than a double." In retrospect, Starr has argued that it should have been released as two separate LPs—"the *White* and the *Whiter* albums" (Beatles 2000, 305)—while Harrison felt that 30 songs was "a bit heavy" (Spitz 2005, 794). For McCartney, the question was moot. Self-reflexively withdrawing from himself and the band's art, he made no bones about the indisputable quality of their achievement. As he remarked in the Beatles' *Anthology* documentary, "It's great. It sold. It's the bloody Beatles' *White Album*. Shut up!"

As Harrison later recalled, *The White Album* "felt more like a band recording together. There were a lot of tracks where we just played live." Meanwhile, Starr saw the record as a sign of the Beatles' artistic renaissance: "As a band member, I've always felt *The White Album* was better than *Sgt. Pepper* because by the end it was more like a real group again. There weren't so many overdubs like on *Pepper*. With all those orchestras and whatnot, we were virtually a session group on our own album" (Ryan and Kehew 2006, 476). Although he later described *The White Album* as the "tension album," McCartney appreciated the opportunity to simplify and reconsolidate the group's sound, to retreat from the highly orchestrated production of their 1966- and 1967-era recordings. Perhaps even more so than McCartney, Lennon was absolutely delighted to dispense with their previously elaborate production efforts in favor of a spare and more conventional rock 'n' roll sound. And while he later portrayed *The White Album* as a series of solo recordings by each of the individual Beatles with the others acting as each other's session men, he was quick to point out that, in reality, their demeanor in the studio hadn't changed all that much since the early days: "We were no more openly critical of each other's music in 1968, or later, than we had always been" (Dowlding 1989, 219).

TRACK LISTING

Side 1: "Back in the USSR"; "Dear Prudence"; "Glass Onion"; "Ob-La-Di, Ob-La-Da"; "Wild Honey Pie"; "The Continuing Story of Bungalow Bill"; "While My Guitar Gently Weeps"; "Happiness Is a Warm Gun."

Side 2: "Martha My Dear"; "I'm So Tired"; "Blackbird"; "Piggies"; "Rocky Raccoon"; "Don't Pass Me By"; "Why Don't We Do It in the Road?"; "I Will"; "Julia."

Side 3: "Birthday"; "Yer Blues"; "Mother Nature's Son"; "Everybody's Got Something to Hide Except Me and My Monkey"; "Sexy Sadie"; "Helter Skelter"; "Long, Long, Long."

Side 4: "Revolution 1"; "Honey Pie"; "Savoy Truffle"; "Cry Baby Cry"; "Can You Take Me Back?" [unlisted]; "Revolution 9"; "Good Night."

COVER ARTWORK

For several months, the group considering entitling the album *A Doll's House* at the suggestion of Lennon, who wanted to pay homage to Norwegian playwright Henrik Ibsen. They even went so far as to commission a cover illustration by

Scottish artist "Patrick" (John Byrne). But with the July 1968 release of Family's *Music in a Doll's House*, the Beatles were forced to go back to the drawing board. At the suggestion of Robert Fraser, McCartney met with pop art designer Richard Hamilton, who proposed that the cover effect a dramatic contrast with the colorful albums of their recent psychedelic past. Hamilton recommended a plain white cover imprinted with individual numbers in order to assume the exclusive quality of a limited edition—although in this case, it was a limited edition composed, quite ironically, of some 5 million copies. At Hamilton's urging, the bandmates decided to name the album *The Beatles*, a deliberately simple title in relation to *Sgt. Pepper's Lonely Hearts Club Band*. But as the album's title, *The Beatles* never really stood a chance. With its stark white cover art, the two-record set became known as *The White Album* within scant days of its release.

The White Album's packaging included four individual color photographs of the Beatles, taken by John Kelly (1944–2008), along with a poster-sized lyric sheet adorned with a collage of additional photographs. *The White Album* is the only Beatles studio album not to feature the bandmates' image on the cover.

CHART PERFORMANCE

U.K.: #1.

U.S.: #1 (certified by the RIAA as "19x Multi Platinum," with more than 19 million copies sold; certified by the RIAA as "Diamond," with more than 10 million copies sold).

LEGACY AND INFLUENCE

In 1998, the BBC ranked *The Beatles (The White Album)* as #10 among its *Music of the Millennium* albums.

In 2000, *The Beatles (The White Album)* was inducted into the National Academy of Recording Arts and Sciences Grammy Hall of Fame.

In 2000, *Q Magazine* ranked *The Beatles (The White Album)* as #7 on the magazine's list of *The 100 Greatest British Albums Ever*.

In 2001, VH1 ranked *The Beatles (The White Album)* as #11 among its *All Time Album Top 100*.

In 2003, *Rolling Stone* ranked *The Beatles (The White Album)* as #10 on the magazine's list of *The 500 Greatest Albums of All Time*.

In 2005, *Mojo* magazine ranked *The Beatles (The White Album)* as #19 on the magazine's list of *The 100 Greatest Albums Ever Made*.

Charles Manson employed the lyrics of several songs from *The White Album* as his justification for attacking White establishment culture and creating a race war during the infamous Tate–LaBianca murders in August 1969. On January 19, 1971, *The White Album* was played during the subsequent trial in order to address its possible role in subliminally inciting the Manson family to carry out the Tate–LaBianca killings.

Hamilton's poster collage, originally included in the package associated with *The White Album*, is on display at the British Museum.

In 1979, American author Joan Didion adopted *The White Album* as the title of her best-selling collection of autobiographical literary essays. *The White Album* traces the social unrest associated with 1960s-era life in Los Angeles, California.

The White Album has frequently been the subject of artistic homage. On Halloween night in 1994, jam band Phish performed *The White Album* in its entirety. The concert was later released as *Live Phish, Volume 13* (2002). For *The Grey Album* (2004), DJ Danger Mouse sampled several songs from *The White Album* for his mash-ups with the tracks on Jay-Z's *The Black Album* (2003). In protest of EMI's efforts to thwart *The Grey Album*'s distribution, activist groups organized "Grey Tuesday," a coordinated Internet effort on February 24, 2004, designed to create widespread distribution of Danger Mouse's recordings. More than 100,000 copies of the album were ultimately downloaded on Grey Tuesday.

In 2008, *Mojo* magazine published a special issue that celebrated *The White Album*'s 40th anniversary, including a cover-mounted CD with contemporary cover versions of the album's entire contents entitled *The White Album Recovered*.

See also: Clapton, Eric; Martin, George; Thomas, Chris.

Beatles VI (LP)

June 14, 1965, Capitol T 2358 (mono)/ST 2358 (stereo)

Beatles VI was the ninth Beatles album to be released in the United States—the seventh on Capitol Records, along with Vee-Jay Records' *Introducing . . . the Beatles* and United Artists' soundtrack for the *A Hard Day's Night* feature film. It was released on the Capitol label on June 14, 1965. Six of the songs on *Beatles VI* were culled from the *Beatles for Sale* album, released in the United Kingdom on December 4, 1964. Two of the tracks were culled from the forthcoming *Help!* album, which was released in the United Kingdom on August 6, 1965. *Beatles VI* also included "Yes It Is," the B-side of the "Ticket to Ride" single, released in the United Kingdom on April 9, 1965, and in the United States on April 19, 1965.

Beatles VI was deleted from the Beatles' catalogue in 1987, when the group's U.K. albums were distributed as CD releases. A remastered mono and stereo release of *Beatles VI* was released on April 11, 2006, as part of the box set entitled *The Capitol Albums, Volume 2*.

BACKGROUND

The June 1965 release of *Beatles VI* was the ninth Beatles album to be released on American shores within the past 18 months. As with other Beatles American releases, Dexter, Jr., added reverb and echo effects to the tracks, particularly "Yes

It Is." It also includes "Bad Boy" among its contents—a track that was not released in the United Kingdom until December 1966 with the compilation entitled *A Collection of Beatles Oldies*. Along with "Dizzy Miss Lizzy," "Bad Boy" was recorded specifically for the U.S. release of *Beatles VI*—the only instance in which the Beatles intentionally recorded tracks for distribution on an American album.

TRACK LISTING

Side 1: Medley: "Kansas City"/"Hey-Hey-Hey-Hey!"; "Eight Days a Week"; "You Like Me Too Much"; "Bad Boy"; "I Don't Want to Spoil the Party"; "Words of Love."

Side 2: "What You're Doing"; "Yes It Is"; "Dizzy Miss Lizzy"; "Tell Me What You See"; "Every Little Thing."

COVER ARTWORK

The front cover artwork for *Beatles VI* features a photograph by Robert Whitaker from the same session in which the Beatles posed for the photographs that grace the cover of *Beatles '65*. The album's cover art was photographed by Whitaker at London's Farringdon Studio in late 1964. The back cover art for *Beatles VI* includes a collage of photographs taken in Abbey Road Studio Two during the sessions for *Beatles for Sale*.

CHART PERFORMANCE

U.S.: #1 (certified by the RIAA as "Platinum," with more than 1 million copies sold).

See also: *Beatles for Sale* (LP); *Beatles '65* (LP); *A Collection of Beatles Oldies* (LP).

"Because" (Lennon–McCartney)

"Because" is a song on the Beatles' *Abbey Road* album.

AUTHORSHIP AND BACKGROUND

Lennon was inspired to write "Because" after hearing Yoko Ono play the first movement of Beethoven's *Moonlight Sonata* on the piano. Intrigued by its delicate structure and counterpoint, he asked her to play the sonata backward, and "Because" was born.

As Lennon remembered, "I was lying on the sofa in our house, listening to Yoko play Beethoven's 'Moonlight Sonata' on the piano. Suddenly, I said, 'Can you play those chords backward?' She did, and I wrote 'Because' around them. The song sounds like 'Moonlight Sonata,' too. The lyrics are clear, no bullshit, no imagery, no obscure references" (Lennon and Ono 2000, 191).

RECORDING SESSIONS

Produced by George Martin, "Because" was recorded at Abbey Road Studios on August 1, 1969, with additional overdubbing sessions on August 4 and 5. The song's most salient feature—Lennon, McCartney, and Martin's exquisite three part-harmony—was overdubbed three times in order to achieve a blissful layered effect.

PERSONNEL

Lennon: Vocal (middle register), Epiphone Casino
McCartney: Vocal (high register), Rickenbacker 4001S
Harrison: Vocal (low register), Moog Synthesizer
Martin: Electric Baldwin Harpsichord

LEGACY AND INFLUENCE

In 2010, *Rolling Stone* ranked "Because" as #77 on the magazine's list of *The Beatles' 100 Greatest Songs*.

ALBUM APPEARANCES: *Abbey Road*; *Anthology 3*; *Love*.

See also: *Abbey Road* (LP); *The Beatles Anthology, Volume 3* (LP); *Love* (LP); Martin, George; Ono, Yoko.

"Being for the Benefit of Mr. Kite!" (Lennon–McCartney)

"Being for the Benefit of Mr. Kite!" is a song on the Beatles' *Sgt. Pepper's Lonely Hearts Club Band* album.

AUTHORSHIP AND BACKGROUND

Written by Lennon, "Being for the Benefit of Mr. Kite!" finds its origins in a 19th-century circus poster that the songwriter discovered and purchased during a break in the filming of the "Strawberry Fields Forever" promotional video in Sevenoaks, Kent.

Lennon transcribed the lyrics nearly verbatim from the poster, which advertised a circus near Rochdale, Lancashire, in February 1843. Lennon later described his musical interpretation of this found object—the found "poetry" of the circus poster—as "pure, like a painting, a pure watercolor" (Dowlding 1989, 173). By taking the existing language of the circus poster and setting it to music in an entirely different venue, Lennon creates a mixed-media production in "Being for the Benefit of Mr. Kite!"

As Lennon remembered,

> "Mr. Kite" was a straight lift. I had all the words staring me in the face one day when I was looking for a song. It was from this old poster I'd bought at an antique shop. We'd been down to Surrey or somewhere filming a piece. There was a break, and I went into this shop and bought an old poster advertising a variety show which starred Mr. Kite. It said the Hendersons would also be there, late of Pablo Fanques Fair. There would be hoops and horses and someone going through a hogs head of real fire. Then there was Henry the Horse. The band would start at ten to six. All at Bishopsgate. Look, there's the bill—with Mr. Kite topping it. I hardly made up a word, just connecting the lists together. Word for word, really. (Cadogan 2008, 195)

RECORDING SESSIONS

Produced by George Martin, "Being for the Benefit of Mr. Kite!" was recorded at Abbey Road Studios on February 17, 1967, with additional overdubbing sessions on February 20, as well as March 28, 29, and 31.

With Lennon playing the Hammond organ and Martin working the counter-melody on a carnivalesque Wurlitzer, the track's instrumentation finds McCartney concocting a lively, imaginative bass part on his Rickenbacker and Harrison and Starr—along with Beatles associates Mal Evans and Neil Aspinall—on a quartet of harmonicas. On February 20, 1967, Martin and Emerick diced up small sections of old calliope tapes of Sousa marches, tossed them in the air, and then randomly reassembled them during the song's pair of middle-eight musical interludes.

PERSONNEL

Lennon: Vocal, Hammond Organ
McCartney: Rickenbacker 4001S, Epiphone Texan
Harrison: Harmonica
Starr: Ludwig Oyster Black Pearl Drums, Harmonica, Tambourine
Martin: Harmonium, Lowrey Organ, Wurlitzer Organ
Evans: Harmonica
Aspinall: Harmonica

CONTROVERSY

As with "Fixing a Hole," some listeners claim that "Being for the Benefit of Mr. Kite!" makes explicit references to heroin abuse. To the contrary, Lennon vehemently claims that "the story that Henry the Horse meant 'heroin' was rubbish" (Cadogan 2008, 195). The song was subsequently banned from radio airplay by the BBC.

ALBUM APPEARANCES: *Sgt. Pepper's Lonely Hearts Club Band*; *Anthology 2*; *Love*.

See also: Aspinall, Neil; *The Beatles Anthology, Volume 2* (LP); Evans, Mal; *Love* (LP); Martin, George; *Sgt. Pepper's Lonely Hearts Club Band* (LP).

"Bésame Mucho" (Velázquez–Skylar)

The Beatles recorded "Bésame Mucho" as part of their EMI audition on June 6, 1962. The Beatles' version of the song was styled after the 1960 recording by the Coasters.

AUTHORSHIP AND BACKGROUND

Written by Mexican songwriter Consuelo Velázquez, "Bésame Mucho" was inspired by the piano arrangement for "Quejas, o la Maja y el Ruiseñor" from Spanish composer Enrique Granados's *Goyescas* (1911). Sunny Skylar later composed an English-language version of the lyrics for "Bésame Mucho," which translates literally as "kiss me a lot."

Pedro Infante sang an English-language cover version of "Bésame Mucho" in his 1951 film *A Toda Maquina*, while Lucho Gatica enjoyed an international hit with the song in 1953.

RECORDING SESSIONS

Produced by George Martin, the Beatles recorded "Bésame Mucho" as part of their Parlophone Records debut session at Abbey Road Studios on June 6, 1962. As McCartney recalled, "We'd got a fairly silly repertoire at the time, George doing 'Sheik of Araby' and I was still doing 'Bésame Mucho'" (Miles 1997, 89).

In 1984, Geoff Emerick remixed "Bésame Mucho" in preparation for the unreleased Beatles *Sessions* project. In 1994, Martin remixed "Bésame Mucho" for release as part of the Beatles' *Anthology* project.

PERSONNEL

Lennon: Guitar, Backing Vocal
McCartney: Vocal, Bass
Harrison: Guitar, Backing Vocal
Best: Drums

ALBUM APPEARANCES: *Live! at the Star-Club in Hamburg, Germany; 1962*; *Anthology 1*.

See also: Best, Pete; Emerick, Geoff.

Best, Pete (1941–)

Born Randolph Peter Best on November 24, 1941, Best was the inaugural drummer for the Beatles. The son of Mona Best, who owned Liverpool's Casbah Coffee Club during the Beatles' formative years, Best was born in Madras, India, where his father John served as an army athletic training instructor. The family returned to England in 1944, eventually settling into a spacious home in Liverpool's West Derby district. As a budding drummer in the late 1950s, the strapping Best played regular gigs with Ken Brown's band, the Black Jacks, at the Casbah, where the Silver Beetles had been hanging out of late. The Silver Beetles at the time comprised John Lennon, Paul McCartney, George Harrison, and Stuart Sutcliffe, with various drummers. With a two-month booking at Bruno Koschmider's Indra Club in the offing for the band beginning in August 1960, McCartney wasted little time in inviting Best to join the group. After a hasty audition on August 12 that he couldn't possibly have failed, Best was offered membership in the band, which shortly thereafter changed its name to the Beatles.

For the next two years, Best served as the group's drummer, as well as their chief booking agent until manager Brian Epstein joined the fold in November 1961. Best's days as the group's timekeeper were numbered after the Beatles' June 1962 Parlophone Records session with producer George Martin. While the producer liked the band's raw potential and their acerbic sense of humor, he wasn't fond of the work of Best, whom he felt that the band should replace—at least in the recording studio. And, for Epstein and the Beatles, Best had now become expendable. For quite some time, he had been estranged from his bandmates—preferring not to fraternize with them, for the most part, nor to adopt their hairstyles or irreverent mannerisms. There is little question, moreover, that they were jealous of Best's popularity among the band's growing legion of female fans. But the final straw was clearly his musicianship. He could maintain a steady, pounding beat in a dancehall, to be sure, but his skills had proven to be remarkably limited in the recording studio, where subtlety and finesse, rather than his ham-fisted drumming style, were more suitable. The June 6 recording of "Love Me Do" is resoundingly clear in this regard—particularly during the bridge, as Best's cadence very perceptibly lags before lumbering back into the chorus.

Between the EMI audition on June 6, 1962, and the end of July, Epstein booked the Beatles for a staggering 61 gigs over a period of eight weeks. By the time that August arrived, Best's fate was sealed. His final performance with the band occurred at the Cavern on the evening of August 15. The group felt that it was Epstein's duty, as manager, to do the dirty work. The next morning, Epstein summoned Best to his office and dismissed him from the Beatles. "The boys want you out," Epstein told him, "and it's already been arranged that Ringo will join the band on Saturday" (Spitz 2005, 330). In a state of utter shock, Best nursed his wounds in a sea of ale at the Grapes, a pub across Matthew Street from the Cavern, in the company of Neil Aspinall. Best was flummoxed, under-standably, by his bandmates' betrayal. After all, he had been in the group for just over two years, and before Epstein's arrival, he took it upon himself to handle most of their book-ing and managerial responsi-bilities. His mother Mona had worked indefatigably on behalf

The Beatles' original drummer Pete Best in 1965. (AP Photo)

of their ambitions to boot. When Aspinall offered to quit the band's employ in protest, his friend graciously talked him out of it in spite of his own despair. Amaz-ingly, Epstein asked Best if he wouldn't mind playing the remaining three gigs before Starr's inaugural performance—and even more amazingly, Best agreed. By the time of the next show, though, he had clearly rethought his decision, and Johnny Hutchinson, the drummer for the Big Three, sat in for him. The Big Three were enormously popular in Liverpool at the time, and Epstein had reportedly invited Hutchinson to join the band before formally inviting Starr to join the group as the Beatles' drummer.

For Best, of course, the Beatles' incredible success overshadowed the rest of his life. As an act of consolation, Epstein found work for Best as the drummer for the Liverpool group Lee Curtis and the All-Stars. Renamed Pete Best and the All-Stars after Curtis's exit in 1964, the band released an unsuccessful single, "I'm Gonna Knock on Your Door," for Decca. In 1965, he reportedly attempted suicide by gassing himself. Over the next several years, he led the Pete Best Four and later the Pete Best Combo, which released an album entitled *Best of the Beatles* (1966). By the end of the decade, he was working as a Liverpool baker before embarking upon a career as a civil servant. In 1978, he was hired as a technical advisor for the ABC television production of *Birth of the Beatles*, and, in later years, he has emerged as a regular staple at Beatles conventions. In 1988, Best formed the Pete Best Band with his half-brother Roag, the son of his mother and Beatles' associate and Apple executive director Neil Aspinall. In 2008, they released an album entitled *Haymans Green*, and in 2011, Liverpool honored the drummer by designating a city street as Pete Best Drive.

See also: Aspinall, Neil; Epstein, Brian; Martin, George.

"Birthday" (Lennon–McCartney)

"Birthday" is a song on *The Beatles* (*The White Album*).

AUTHORSHIP AND BACKGROUND

Written largely by McCartney, "Birthday" was improvised by the Beatles in the studio. As Lennon later observed, "I think Paul wanted to write a song like 'Happy Birthday, Baby,' the old '50s hit" (Dowlding 1989, 238). Ted Goranson has suggested that McCartney was thinking about the Tuneweavers' 1957 hit "Happy, Happy Birthday" when he devised the song's central guitar riff.

RECORDING SESSIONS

Produced by Chris Thomas during George Martin's absence, "Birthday" was recorded at Abbey Road Studios on September 18, 1968. Beatle wives Pattie Boyd and Yoko Ono provided backing vocals during the session. McCartney's piano was heavily treated with STEED (single-tape echo and echo delay) in order to achieve a live-sounding echo effect.

The Beatles took a brief respite from the recording session to watch the 1956 rock musical *The Girl Can't Help It* on television at McCartney's home on nearby Cavendish Avenue.

PERSONNEL

Lennon: Vocal, Epiphone Casino
McCartney: Vocal, Epiphone Casino, Piano
Harrison: Fender Bass VI, Backing Vocal
Starr: Ludwig Oyster Black Pearl Drums, Tambourine
Boyd: Backing Vocal
Ono: Backing Vocal

ALBUM APPEARANCES: *The Beatles* (*The White Album*); *Rock 'n' Roll Music*.

See also: *The Beatles* (*The White Album*) (LP); Boyd, Pattie; Ono, Yoko; *Rock 'n' Roll Music* (LP).

"Blackbird" (Lennon–McCartney)

"Blackbird" is a song on *The Beatles* (*The White Album*).

AUTHORSHIP AND BACKGROUND

Written by McCartney in Scotland during the spring of 1968, the folksy "Blackbird" imagines a contemplative metaphor for the United States' civil rights struggles during the 1960s. As McCartney later observed, "I had in my mind a black woman rather than a bird. Those were the days of the civil rights movement, which all of us cared passionately about. So this way really a song from me to a black woman experiencing these problems in the States: 'Let me encourage you to keep trying, to keep your faith, there is hope' " (Ryan and Kehew 2006, 484). Based on Bach's *Bourée for Lute in E Minor*, which McCartney and Harrison had learnt in their youth, McCartney's distinctive acoustic guitar melody for "Blackbird" alternates among 3/4, 4/4, and 2/4 time signatures.

An early version of "Blackbird" was recorded in May 1968 at Harrison's Kinfauns studio as part of the Esher Tapes.

RECORDING SESSIONS

Produced by George Martin, "Blackbird" was recorded at Abbey Road Studios on June 11, 1968. Sound engineer employed three microphones to capture the recording. The tapping sound heard throughout the song is not a metronome, as one might reasonably conclude, but rather the sound of McCartney's feet gently rapping on the floor of Studio Two.

Martin had originally suggested adding a brass accompaniment to "Blackbird," although McCartney ultimately rejected the idea.

The sweet sound of a chirping blackbird—a European *Turdus merula*, to be exact—was culled from the EMI tape library's *Volume 7: Birds of Feather*. McCartney recorded two additional compositions on June 11, 1968, including "Gone Tomorrow, Here Today" and "You Came My Way."

PERSONNEL

McCartney: Vocal, Martin D-28

LEGACY AND INFLUENCE

In 2010, *Rolling Stone* ranked "Blackbird" as #38 on the magazine's list of *The Beatles' 100 Greatest Songs*.

ALBUM APPEARANCES: *The Beatles* (*The White Album*); *Anthology 3*; *Love*.

See also: *The Beatles Anthology, Volume 3* (LP); *The Beatles* (*The White Album*) (LP); *Love* (LP).

"Blue Jay Way" (Harrison)

"Blue Jay Way" is a song on the Beatles' *Magical Mystery Tour* album.

AUTHORSHIP AND BACKGROUND

Written by Harrison, "Blue Jay Way" was composed on August 1, 1967, during a visit by Harrison and wife Pattie Boyd to Los Angeles, where they stayed in a rented house on Blue Jay Way in the Hollywood Hills overlooking Sunset Boulevard. He wrote the song while awaiting the arrival of Beatles associate Derek Taylor.

RECORDING SESSIONS

Produced by George Martin, "Blue Jay Way" was recorded at Abbey Road Studios on September 6, 1967, with additional overdubbing on September 7 and October 6. Harrison double-tracked his lead vocal.

The recording for "Blue Jay Way" finds Harrison and Lennon playing hypnotic passages in a psychedelic duet of dueling Hammond organs. The track sports a pointedly hazy texture created through the use of phasing, which had been deployed to great effect on the Small Faces' recent hit "Itchycoo Park." A recording technique in which slight changes in the interaction of related audio signals result in a flanging effect, phasing was the most salient feature of "Blue Jay Way," imbuing the speaker's words of concern with an eerie sense of paranoia.

PERSONNEL

Lennon: Hammond Organ, Tambourine, Backing Vocal
McCartney: Rickenbacker 4001S, Backing Vocal
Harrison: Vocal, Hammond Organ
Starr: Ludwig Oyster Black Pearl Drums, Cymbal
Studio Musician: String Accompaniment conducted by Martin
Uncredited musician: Cello

ALBUM APPEARANCES: *Magical Mystery Tour*; *Love*.

See also: Boyd, Pattie; *Love* (LP); *Magical Mystery Tour* (LP); *Magical Mystery Tour* (TV Film).

Boyd, Pattie (1944–)

Born as Patricia Anne Boyd in Taunton, Somerset, on March 17, 1944, Pattie Boyd is an English model, photographer, and the first wife of Harrison, later marrying Harrison's longtime friend and collaborator Eric Clapton. In 1962, she began her modeling career, later appearing on the covers of *Vogue* and other leading magazines. In 1964, she met Harrison while working as an extra on the set of *A Hard Day's Night*. At the time, she was in a serious relationship with photographer Eric Swayne, although she soon broke up with him to date the Beatle. After moving in together at Harrison's Kinfauns home, Boyd and Harrison became engaged on December 25, 1965, later marrying on January 21, 1966, in Esher's Upper High Street Registry Office, with McCartney serving as best man. She was a regular fixture in the Beatles' lives, attending the June 1967 *Our World* live simulcast and joining them in Rishikesh, India, for the group's February 1968 visit to Maharishi Mahesh Yogi's ashram. In 1970, Boyd and Harrison relocated to Friar Park, the former Beatle's enormous Victorian mansion in Henley-on-Thames.

By 1973, the Harrisons' relationship was disintegrating, with Boyd having an extramarital affair with the Rolling Stones' Ron Wood, while Harrison had an affair of his own with Starr's wife Maureen. In 1974, the couple separated; their divorce was finalized in 1977. Over the years, Harrison had written numerous songs for Boyd, including the top-charting Beatles hit "Something." On May 19, 1979, Boyd married Clapton, who had nurtured his love for Harrison's wife since the late 1960s, culminating in the legendary Derek and the Dominos' album *Layla and Other Assorted Love Songs* (1970). The album's title track, based on *The Story of Layla* by 12th-century Persian poet Nizami Ganjavi, describes

Musician George Harrison and actress Pattie Boyd are seen in the backseat of a car after their wedding at the Epsom registry office outside London on January 21, 1966. The two met in March 1964 during the filming of the Beatles' *A Hard Day's Night.* (AP Photo)

Clapton's unrequited love for Boyd. Clapton later composed the Top 20 U.S. hit "Wonderful Tonight" with Boyd as his inspiration. Harrison, McCartney, and Starr attended Boyd and Clapton's wedding, famously performing an impromptu concert that included a rendition of "Sgt. Pepper's Lonely Hearts Club Band."

In 1984, Boyd and Clapton separated after what Boyd later claimed to be Clapton's alcoholism and numerous infidelities. The couple were formally divorced in 1989. In 2007, she published her best-selling autobiography entitled *Wonderful Tonight: George Harrison, Eric Clapton, and Me*.

See also: Clapton, Eric; *A Hard Day's Night* (Film); Harrison, George; Maharishi Mahesh Yogi; Tigrett, Maureen Cox (Starkey).

"Boys" (Dixon–Farrell)

"Boys" is a song on the Beatles' *Please Please Me* album.

AUTHORSHIP AND BACKGROUND

Written by Luther Dixon and Wes Farrell, "Boys" was originally performed by the Shirelles. In November 1960, the group released "Boys" as the B-side of their single "Will You Love Me Tomorrow."

The Beatles had been performing "Boys" since their days at the Cavern. Prior to Starr joining the band, Pete Best handled the song's lead vocal. For his part, Starr had performed "Boys" with Rory Storm and the Hurricanes before joining the Beatles in August 1962.

RECORDING SESSIONS

Produced by George Martin, "Boys" was recorded at Abbey Road Studios in a single take on February 11, 1963, with an overdubbing session on February 20. The song, with its "bop shoo-op" chorus, became a fan favorite during the Beatles' live performances throughout 1963.

PERSONNEL

Lennon: Rickenbacker 325, Backing Vocal
McCartney: Höfner 500/1, Backing Vocal
Harrison: Gretsch Duo-Jet, Backing Vocal
Starr: Vocal, Premier Mahogany Duroplastic Drums

CHART PERFORMANCE

U.S.: "Kansas City"/"Boys"; October 11, 1965, Capitol 6066: Did not chart. As the B-side of the "Kansas City" single, "Boys" charted at #102.

ALBUM APPEARANCES: *Please Please Me*; *The Early Beatles*; *Rock 'n' Roll Music*; *The Beatles at the Hollywood Bowl*; *Anthology 1*; *On Air: Live at the BBC, Volume 2*.

See also: *The Beatles Anthology, Volume 1* (LP); *Please Please Me* (LP).

C

"Can You Take Me Back?" (Lennon–McCartney)

"Can You Take Me Back?" is a song on *The Beatles* (*The White Album*).

AUTHORSHIP AND BACKGROUND

Written by Paul McCartney, "Can You Take Me Back?" was improvised in the studio with Ringo Starr during the sessions associated with "I Will."

RECORDING SESSIONS

Produced by George Martin, "Can You Take Me Back?" was recorded at Abbey Road Studios on September 16, 1968.

PERSONNEL

McCartney: Vocal, Martin D-28
Starr: Ludwig Oyster Black Pearl Drums

ALBUM APPEARANCES: *The Beatles* (*The White Album*); *Love*.

See also: *The Beatles* (*The White Album*) (LP); *Love* (LP).

"Can't Buy Me Love" (Lennon–McCartney)

"Can't Buy Me Love" is a song on the Beatles' *A Hard Day's Night* album. It was the band's fifth consecutive #1 single in the United Kingdom, where it was released on March 20, 1964.

AUTHORSHIP AND BACKGROUND

Written by McCartney, "Can't Buy Me Love" is one of the three principal compositions that McCartney prepared, along with "And I Love Her" and "Things We Said Today," for the film *A Hard Day's Night*.

McCartney composed "Can't Buy Me Love" on an upright piano at the George V Hotel in Paris, where the Beatles were booked for an extended run at the

Olympia Theatre. As McCartney recalled, " 'Can't Buy Me Love' is my attempt to write a bluesy mode. The idea behind it was that all these material possessions are all very well but they won't buy me what I really want" (Badman 2001, 97).

RECORDING SESSIONS

Produced by George Martin, "Can't Buy Me Love" was recorded at Pathé Marconi Studios in Paris on January 29, 1964, with additional sessions at Abbey Road Studios on February 25 and March 10. In the studio, Martin cleverly suggested that the band reorient the song's structure. "We've got to have an introduction," he remarked, "something that catches the ear immediately, a hook. So let's start out with the chorus" (Cross 2005, 327).

Played on his Gretsch Country Gentleman, George Harrison's guitar solo is a masterwork of energy and style that benefits, in eerie fashion, from the guitarist's earlier attempts at the solo, which can be heard leaking into the mix in the extreme background.

In March 1964, the Beatles recorded a version of "Can't Buy Me Love" for the BBC's *From Us to You* radio show.

PERSONNEL

Lennon: Gibson J-160E
McCartney: Vocal, Höfner 500/1
Harrison: Gretsch Country Gentleman
Starr: Ludwig Oyster Black Pearl Drums
Norman Smith: Hi-Hat

CHART PERFORMANCE

U.K.: "Can't Buy Me Love"/"You Can't Do That"; March 20, 1964, Parlophone R 5114: #1.
U.S.: "Can't Buy Me Love"/"You Can't Do That"; March 16, 1964, Capitol 5150: #1 (certified by the RIAA as "Gold," with more than 500,000 copies sold).

LEGACY AND INFLUENCE

"Can't Buy Me Love" was a hit even before it was released, enjoying some 2.1 million advance orders. When "Can't Buy Me Love" assumed the #1 position on the U.S. charts on April 4, 1964, the entire Top 5 spots on the Hot 100 were occupied by the Beatles, including "Twist and Shout," "She Loves You," "I Want to Hold Your Hand," and "Please Please Me," respectively; at the same time, the Beatles held the Top 2 spots on the album charts, with *Meet the Beatles!* and *Introducing . . . the Beatles*. During the song's second week at #1, the Beatles charted 14 different songs in the Hot 100.

In 1965, the Beatles received an Ivor Novello Award, awarded annually by the British Academy of Songwriters, Composers, and Authors, for "Can't Buy Me Love."

In 2004, *Rolling Stone* ranked "Can't Buy Me Love" as #295 on the magazine's list of *The 500 Greatest Songs of All Time*.

In 2010, *Rolling Stone* ranked "Can't Buy Me Love" as #29 on the magazine's list of *The Beatles' 100 Greatest Songs*.

ALBUM APPEARANCES: *A Hard Day's Night* (U.S.); *A Hard Day's Night* (U.K.); *A Collection of Beatles Oldies*; *Hey Jude*; *The Beatles, 1962–1966*; *The Beatles at the Hollywood Bowl*; *Reel Music*; *20 Greatest Hits*; *Live at the BBC*; *Anthology 1*; *1*.

See also: *A Hard Day's Night* (U.K. LP).

The Capitol Albums, Volume I (Box Set)

November 15, 2004, Apple [Capitol] 07243 875348 2 7
November 16, 2004, Apple [Capitol] CDP 7243 8 66878 2 1

The Capitol Albums, Volume 1 box set collects the Beatles' 1964 U.S. Capitol Records releases.

BACKGROUND

Remastered for compact-disc (CD) release, *The Capitol Albums, Volume 1* box set consists of the Beatles' first four Capitol Records' album releases in North America. The remastered albums, which feature mono and simulated stereo versions of the original tracks, were created from the submaster tapes original prepared by Capitol Records' A&R executive Dave Dexter, Jr. The American versions of the original recordings are known for the additional reverb that Dexter added during the mastering process.

In 2004, a promotional CD was released in advance of *The Capitol Albums, Volume 1* box set. The sampler disc included stereo and mono versions of "All My Loving," "I Wanna Be Your Man," "I Call Your Name," "Roll Over Beethoven," "Things We Said Today," "If I Fell," "She's a Woman," and "I'm a Loser."

CONTENTS

Disc 1: *Meet the Beatles!*
Disc 2: *The Beatles' Second Album*
Disc 3: *Something New*
Disc 4: *Beatles '65*

CHART PERFORMANCE

U.K.: Did not chart.
U.S.: #35 (certified by the RIAA as "Platinum," with more than 1 million copies sold).

See also: *Beatles' Second Album* (LP); *Beatles '65* (LP); *Meet the Beatles!* (LP); *Something New* (LP).

The Capitol Albums, Volume 2 (Box Set)

April 11, 2006, Apple [Capitol] 0946 3 603352 5
April 11, 2006, Apple [Capitol] CDP 0946 3 57716 2 6

The Capitol Albums, Volume 2 box set collects the Beatles' 1965 U.S. Capitol Records releases.

BACKGROUND

Remastered for CD release, *The Capitol Albums, Volume 2* box set consists of the Beatles' 1965 Capitol Records' album releases in North America. The remastered albums, which feature mono and simulated stereo versions of the original tracks, were created from the submaster tapes original prepared by Capitol Records' A&R executive Dave Dexter, Jr. The American versions of the original recordings are known for the additional reverb that Dexter added during the mastering process.

A minor controversy erupted when early versions of *The Capitol Albums, Volume 2* were released with the incorrect mono mixes associated with the original American *Beatles VI* and *Rubber Soul* albums. New pressings were later completed with the correct vintage mono mixes provided for the *Beatles VI* and *Rubber Soul* albums.

In 2006, a promotional CD was released in advance of *The Capitol Albums, Volume 2* box set. The sampler disc included stereo and mono versions of "Baby It's You," "Boys," "What You're Doing," "I Don't Want to Spoil the Party," "The Night Before," "You've Got to Hide Your Love Away," "Think for Yourself," and "I've Just Seen a Face."

CONTENTS

Disc 1: *The Early Beatles*
Disc 2: *Beatles VI*
Disc 3: *Help!*
Disc 4: *Rubber Soul*

CHART PERFORMANCE

U.K.: Did not chart.

U.S.: #46 (certified by the RIAA as "Gold," with more than 500,000 copies sold).

See also: *Beatles VI* (LP); Capitol Records; *The Early Beatles* (LP); *Help!* (U.S. LP); *Rubber Soul* (U.S. LP).

"Carnival of Light" (Lennon–McCartney)

Along with the unreleased "Et Cetera" and the 27-minute version of "Helter Skelter," "Carnival of Light" is one of the most elusive and mysterious recordings in the Beatles' corpus.

AUTHORSHIP AND BACKGROUND

Attempted at McCartney's behest, "Carnival of Light" is an avant-garde recording that had been invited for presentation by the organizers of *The Million Volt Light and Sound Rave*, an art festival of electronic music and light shows that debuted on January 28, 1967, at London's Roundhouse Theatre. By turns hypnotic, surreal, and frightening, "Carnival of Light" consists of nearly 14 minutes' worth of electronic noise, prefiguring the experimental soundscapes of *The White Album*'s "Revolution 9" in the process.

In an April 2002 interview with Mark Ellen on the Rocking Vicar website (therockingvicar.com), McCartney recalled that "we recorded ['Carnival of Light'] in about fifteen minutes. It's very *avant-garde* . . . I instigated it. No there's no lyrics, it's *avant-garde* music. You would class it as—well you wouldn't class it actually, but it would come in the Stockhausen/John Cage bracket. John Cage would be the nearest."

RECORDING SESSIONS

Produced by George Martin, "Carnival of Light" was recorded at Abbey Road Studios on January 5, 1968, during a vocal overdubbing session for "Penny Lane" during the onset of what became the sessions for the *Sgt. Pepper's Lonely Hearts Club Band* album.

With assistance from Starr—along with bemused looks from Martin and Harrison, who were decidedly unimpressed with the recording—Lennon and McCartney superimposed a host of distorted drum and organ sounds onto the track, as well as tape echo and random interjections by the duo, including "Are you alright?" and "Barcelona!" "Carnival of Light" also featured McCartney vamping a version of "Fixing a Hole" on the piano.

Having listened to the recording, Barry Miles observed that

The tape has no rhythm. . . . The Beatles make literally random sounds, although they sometimes respond to each other; for instance, a burst of organ notes answered by a rattle of percussion. The basic track was recorded slow so that some of the drums and organ were very deep and sonorous, like the bass notes of a cathedral organ. Much of it is echoed and it is often hard to tell if you are listening to a slowed-down cymbal or a tubular bell. John and Paul yell with massive amounts of reverb on their voices, there are Indian war cries, whistling, close-miked gasping, genuine coughing and fragments of studio conversation, ending with Paul asking, with echo, "Can we hear it back now?" (Miles 1997, 309)

According to Mark Lewisohn, "Track one of the tape was full of distorted, hypnotic drum and organ sounds; track two had a distorted lead guitar; track three had the sounds of a church organ, various effects (the gargling of water was one) and voices; track four featured various indescribable sound effects with heaps of tape echo and manic tambourine" (Lewisohn 1988, 92). As sound engineer Geoff Emerick later recalled, "When they had finished George Martin said to me, 'This is ridiculous, we've got to get our teeth into something more constructive'" (Lewisohn 1988, 92).

With the session complete, a mono version of "Carnival of Light" was prepared for the organizers of *The Million Volt Light and Sound Rave* for playback later that month.

PERSONNEL

Lennon, McCartney, Harrison, and Starr: Vocals, Tape Effects, Piano, Organ, Guitar, Tambourine

See also: Emerick, Geoff; *Sgt. Pepper's Lonely Hearts Club Band* (LP).

"Carry That Weight" (Lennon–McCartney)

"Carry That Weight" is a song on the Beatles' *Abbey Road* album. It is the seventh song in the *Abbey Road* medley.

AUTHORSHIP AND BACKGROUND

McCartney's "Carry That Weight" was debuted, along with "Golden Slumbers," as a single unit on January 7, 1969, during the *Get Back* sessions (Sulpy and Schweighardt 1997, 80). Harrison's arpeggiated guitar part reprises the musical themes inherent in "You Never Give Me Your Money," affording the medley with a striking sense of internal musical cohesion.

"Carry That Weight" explicitly references the band's growing interpersonal difficulties, particularly in terms of McCartney's recognition of his own culpability. In the documentary *Imagine: John Lennon* (1988), Lennon confirmed this aspect of the song, adding that McCartney was "singing about all of us."

As McCartney later recalled, "I'm generally quite upbeat, but at certain times things get to me so much that I just can't be upbeat anymore and that was one of those times. 'Carry that weight a long time'—like forever! That's what I meant . . . in this heaviness there was no place to be. It was serious, paranoid heaviness, and it was just very uncomfortable" (Miles 1997, 557).

RECORDING SESSIONS

Produced by George Martin, "Carry That Weight" was recorded at Abbey Road Studios on July 2, 1969. Additional overdubbing sessions occurred throughout July, concluding on August 15. Lennon was absent from the primary recording sessions for "Golden Slumbers" due to his car wreck in Scotland.

PERSONNEL

Lennon: Vocal
McCartney: Vocal, Epiphone Casino, Piano
Harrison: Vocal, Fender Jazz Bass, Fender Rosewood Telecaster
Starr: Vocal, Ludwig Hollywood Maple Drums
Studio Musicians: Orchestral Accompaniment (12 Violins, 4 Violas, 4 Cellos, Double Bass, 4 Horns, 3 Trumpets, Trombone, Bass Trombone) conducted by Martin

ALBUM APPEARANCE: *Abbey Road.*

See also: *Abbey Road* (LP).

The Cavern Club (Liverpool)

Owned by Alan Sytner and named after Le Caveau Français Jazz Club in Paris, the Cavern opened its doors on Liverpool's Mathew Street in January 1957. Lennon's band, the Quarry Men, played their fourth gig at the club, which was located in a basement just below street level. As a skiffle group, the Quarry Men found it to be tough going in a club that catered to a jazz-loving audience. After Lennon turned in raucous renditions of Elvis Presley's "Hound Dog" and "Blue Suede Shoes," Sytner sent a note to the stage in which he ordered the band to "cut out the bloody rock!" (Lewisohn 1986, 20).

The Beatles performed 292 shows at the Cavern Club, often playing lunchtime concerts, from February 1961 to August 1963. The Cavern Club also marked the location of the Beatles' fateful performance in November 1961 in which Epstein first

The Beatles perform onstage at the Cavern Club in February 1961 in Liverpool, England. From left to right are George Harrison, Paul McCartney, Pete Best, and John Lennon. (Michael Ochs Archives/Getty Images)

came into the band's orbit. The Cavern closed in 1973 following a performance by Dutch act, the Focus, and the building's basement was filled in during construction associated with the city's underground rail system. In 1984, the club was rebuilt using much of the original space—not to mention the Cavern's brickwork—and it reopened intermittently until 1991, when Liverpudlians Bill Heckle and Dave Jones began operating the club on a permanent basis. In the ensuing years, it has become a popular tourist attraction. In 1999, it famously served as a venue for McCartney, who performed a set in support of his *Run Devil Run* album.

See also: The Quarry Men.

"Cayenne" (McCartney)

The Beatles recorded the instrumental "Cayenne" under their short-lived name "the Beatals" during their April 1960 home recording sessions.

AUTHORSHIP AND BACKGROUND

Credited to McCartney, "Cayenne" is a 12-bar blues composition written in the style of the Shadows. The origins of the song's name are uncertain—perhaps being an homage to the capital of French Guiana or, more likely, to the fiery hot pepper used in cooking spicy dishes.

RECORDING SESSIONS

In April 1960, the Beatals gathered at the McCartneys' Liverpool home at 20 Forthlin Road, where they recorded demos for eight songs on a Grundig reel-to-reel tape recorder that McCartney had borrowed from Charles Hodgson. Known as the Kirchherr Tape, the surviving copy of the April 1960 recordings was given by Stuart Sutcliffe to his fiancée Astrid Kirchherr. In 1994, she presented it to Harrison (Winn 2003a, 3).

Recorded in the McCartneys' bathroom, "Cayenne," with its Latin samba rhythm, reveals some intriguing guitar work, especially in the delicate counterpoint delivered by the Beatals' trio of guitarists against the tentative bass line established by Sutcliffe in the recording's extreme background.

PERSONNEL

Lennon: Guitar
McCartney: Guitar
Harrison: Guitar
Sutcliffe: Bass

ALBUM APPEARANCE: *Anthology 1.*

See also: *The Beatles Anthology, Volume 1* (LP); Kirchherr, Astrid; Sutcliffe, Stuart.

"Chains" (Goffin–King)

"Chains" is a song on the Beatles' *Please Please Me* album.

AUTHORSHIP AND BACKGROUND

Written by celebrated Brill Building songwriters Gerry Goffin and Carole King, "Chains" became a Top 20 hit for the Cookies, Little Eva's backing singers, in December 1962.

RECORDING SESSIONS

Produced by George Martin, "Chains" was recorded at Abbey Road Studios on February 11, 1963, with an overdubbing session on February 20.

PERSONNEL

Lennon: Rickenbacker 325, Backing Vocal
McCartney: Höfner 500/1, Backing Vocal
Harrison: Vocal, Gretsch Duo-Jet
Starr: Premier Mahogany Duroplastic Drums

ALBUM APPEARANCES: *Please Please Me*; *The Early Beatles*.

See also: *Please Please Me* (LP).

"Christmas Time (Is Here Again)" (Harrison–Lennon–McCartney–Starr)

December 15, 1967, Lyntone [EMI] LYN 1360

Originally recorded for the Beatles' 1967 Christmas record, "Christmas Time (Is Here Again)" is one of the very few songs credited to all four Beatles as composers.

AUTHORSHIP AND BACKGROUND

"Christmas Time (Is Here Again)" was composed as the 1967 entry for the Beatles' annual fan club Christmas records. The song's comic spirit was likely inspired by the BBC Radio 1's Bonzo Dog Doo Dah Band, while also sharing the same free-form hilarity inherent in the Beatles' "You Know My Name (Look Up the Number)," which the Beatles had recorded in large part during the previous summer.

RECORDING SESSIONS

Produced by George Martin, the Beatles recorded "Christmas Time (Is Here Again)" at Abbey Road Studios on November 28, 1967. The six-minute Christmas record centered around a narrative in which various groups audition for a BBC radio show, with "Christmas Time (Is Here Again)" serving as the track's periodic refrain. The four Beatles voice various characters ranging from game-show contestants and musicians (the Ravellers) to actors in a fictive radio program entitled *Theatre Hour.*

The track itself begins with Lennon ad-libbing the words "Interplanetary remix! Page four hundred and forty four!" At the conclusion of "Christmas Time (Is Here Again)," each Beatle offers a spoken-word seasonal greeting to the band's fans:

"This is Paul McCartney here. I'd just like to wish you everything you wished yourself for Christmas."

"This is John Lennon saying on behalf of the Beatles, have a very Happy Christmas and a good New Year."

"George Harrison speaking. I'd like to take this opportunity to wish you a very Merry Christmas, listeners everywhere."

"This is Ringo Starr, and I'd just like to say Merry Christmas and a really Happy New Year to all listeners."

With "Auld Lang Syne" as his accompaniment, Lennon brings "Christmas Time (Is Here Again)" to a close with a reading of his Joycean, nonsensical poem entitled "When Christmas Time Is Over": One line says, "Happy breastling to you people all out best from me to you."

As with the other fan club records, "Christmas Time (Is Here Again)" was distributed to British fans in December 1967 via a seven-inch flexi-disc in a decorated picture sleeve, while American fans received a postcard with seasons greeting. In December 1968, American fan club members began receiving flexi-discs as well.

In 1984, Geoff Emerick remixed "Christmas Time (Is Here Again)" in preparation for the unreleased Beatles *Sessions* project. In 1994, Martin remixed "Christmas Time (Is Here Again)" for release as the B-side for "Free as a Bird" in conjunction with the Beatles' *Anthology* project.

PERSONNEL

Lennon: Vocal, Bass Drum
McCartney: Vocal, Piano
Harrison: Vocal, Gibson J-160E
Starr: Vocal, Ludwig Oyster Black Pearl Drums
Martin: Vocal
Victor Spinetti: Vocal

CHART PERFORMANCE

U.K.: "Free as a Bird"/"Christmas Time (Is Here Again)"; December 4, 1995, Apple R6422: #2. As the B-side of "Free as a Bird," "Christmas Time (Is Here Again)" did not chart.

U.S.: "Free as a Bird"/"Christmas Time (Is Here Again)"; December 12, 1995, Apple NR 7243 8 58497 7 0: #6 (certified by the RIAA as "Gold," with more than 500,000 copies sold). As the B-side of "Free as a Bird," "Christmas Time (Is Here Again)" did not chart.

See also: The Beatles' Christmas Records.

Clapton, Eric (1945–)

Born on March 30, 1945, in Ripley, Surrey, Eric Clapton is one of the most gifted and celebrated guitarists of his generation. Clapton began playing the guitar in earnest at age 15, later attending the Kingston College of Art before leaving the institution to pursue a professional career in music. Over the next several years, he came to prominence as a leading figure in the British Blues Boom. After cutting his teeth as a member of the Yardbirds, he left the band to become a member of John Mayall and the Bluesbreakers. During this period—in which Clapton earned his fabled nickname "Slowhand"—the guitarist went on to form Cream, a power trio with drummer Ginger Baker and Jack Bruce. The band sold more than 15 million records, scoring hits with "I Feel Free," "Sunshine of Your Love," "White Room," and "Badge," which Clapton co-authored with Harrison, with whom he became lifelong friends in the mid-1960s.

In 1968, Clapton famously provided the lead guitar solo on Harrison's "While My Guitar Gently Weeps" on the Beatles' *White Album*. On September 5, Harrison had invited Clapton to join the group at Abbey Road Studios. For Harrison, Clapton's appearance altered the band's dynamics dramatically, changing their behavior for the better. "Just bringing in a stranger among us made everybody cool out," Harrison later remarked (Beatles 2000, 306). Clapton played his magnificent, driving solo on a Gibson Les Paul Standard. At Clapton's request, the solo was heavily treated with ADT (automatic double-tracking) in order to achieve a more "Beatley" sound. "I was given the grand job of waggling the oscillator on the 'Gently Weeps' mixes," Chris Thomas recalled. "We did this flanging thing, really wobbling

Eric Clapton (right) joins good friend George Harrison on stage at the former Beatle's charity benefit, the Concert for Bangladesh, at Madison Square Garden on August 1, 1971. The pair dueled on "While My Guitar Gently Weeps," the Beatles' *White Album* song for which Clapton had supplied a memorable guitar solo. (Bettmann/Getty Images)

the oscillator in the mix. I did that for hours" (Babiuk 2001, 229). In 1969, Harrison composed his final Beatles song, "Here Comes the Sun," while strolling around Clapton's Hurtwood mansion garden on a break from the group's relentless Apple Corps business meetings: "The relief of not having to go and see all those dopey accountants was wonderful," Harrison later recalled, "and I was walking around the garden with one of Eric's acoustic guitars and wrote 'Here Comes the Sun'" (Dowlding 1989, 285). Clapton also participated in Harrison's charity benefit *The Concert for Bangladesh*, for which Clapton performed "While My Guitar Gently Weeps" with Harrison in a suite of dueling guitar solos.

During the 1970s, Clapton spearheaded the legendary Derek and the Dominos' album *Layla and Other Assorted Love Songs* (1970), which explored the guitarist's long-nurtured love for Harrison's wife Pattie Boyd. The album's title track, based on *The Story of Layla* by 12th-century Persian poet Nizami Ganjavi, describes Clapton's unrequited love for Boyd. On May 19, 1979, Clapton married Boyd, with Clapton later composing the Top 20 U.S. hit "Wonderful Tonight" with Boyd as his inspiration. Harrison, McCartney, and Starr attended Clapton and Boyd's wedding, famously performing an impromptu concert that included a rendition of "Sgt. Pepper's Lonely Hearts Club Band." In 1984, Boyd and Clapton separated after what Boyd later claimed to be issues with Clapton's alcoholism and numerous infidelities. The couple were formally divorced in 1989. In 2007, Boyd published her best-selling autobiography entitled *Wonderful Today: George Harrison, Eric Clapton, and Me*.

In 1991, Clapton enjoyed a resurgence in his career following the release of his *Unplugged* album, which included a popular acoustic interpretation of "Layla," as well as the chart-topping "Tears in Heaven," which describes Clapton's grief over the death of his four-year-old son Conor. Later that year, Clapton persuaded Harrison to mount a Japanese tour with him, resulting in Harrison's *Live in Japan* (1992), which marked Harrison's first live album since 1971's *The Concert for Bangladesh*. The concerts featured a range of solo hits by Harrison and Clapton, as well as several Beatles songs. In 2002, after Harrison's death from cancer in 2001, Clapton performed several songs, including "While My Guitar Gently Weeps," "Wah-Wah," "If I Needed Someone," and "Something," as part of the *Concert for George* celebration of Harrison's life at London's Royal Albert Hall.

Clapton is the Rock and Roll Hall of Fame's only three-time inductee—including his work as a solo artist and as a member of the Yardbirds and Cream. In addition to winning 17 Grammy Awards, Clapton was ranked by *Rolling Stone* magazine in 2003 as one of the *100 Greatest Guitarists of All Time*—second only to Jimi Hendrix.

See also: The Beatles (*The White Album*) (LP); Boyd, Pattie; Harrison, George; Thomas, Chris.

A Collection of Beatles Oldies (LP)

December 9, 1966, Parlophone PMC 7016 (mono)/PCS 7016 (stereo)

A Collection of Beatles Oldies was released by Parlophone in the United Kingdom on December 9, 1966. The album marked the band's first official greatest hits compilation.

A Collection of Beatles Oldies was deleted from the Beatles' catalogue in 1987, when the group's U.K. studio albums were distributed as CD releases.

BACKGROUND

Fearing that too much time had elapsed since the last Beatles release, Parlophone released the band's first greatest hits compilation, *A Collection of Beatles Oldies*, in Great Britain in early December 1966. Sporting the subtitle of *But Goldies!*, *A Collection of Beatles Oldies* marks the U.K. debut of "Bad Boy," a Larry Williams cover version that had been released in the American marketplace on *Beatles VI* (1965). *A Collection of Beatles Oldies* also marked the U.K. album debut of six tracks that had previously been released as singles: "From Me to You," "We Can Work It Out," "I Feel Fine," "Day Tripper," "Paperback Writer," and "I Want to Hold Your Hand."

TRACK LISTING

Side 1: "She Loves You"; "From Me to You"; "We Can Work It Out"; "Help!"; "Michelle"; "Yesterday"; "I Feel Fine"; "Yellow Submarine."

Side 2: "Can't Buy Me Love"; "Bad Boy"; "Day Tripper"; "A Hard Day's Night"; "Ticket to Ride"; "Paperback Writer"; "Eleanor Rigby"; "I Want to Hold Your Hand."

COVER ARTWORK

A Collection of Beatles Oldies features a cover design by David Christian, including a colorful collage of mid-1960s images, most notably a stylish gentleman done up in his Carnaby Street finery. The back cover features a candid 1966-era photograph of the Fab Four by Robert Whitaker.

CHART PERFORMANCE

U.K.: #7.

See also: *Beatles VI.*

"Come Together" (Lennon–McCartney)

"Come Together" is the opening track on the Beatles' *Abbey Road* album. It was also a hit double A-side single, backed with "Something," which was released in the United Kingdom on October 31, 1969, and in the United States on October 6, 1969.

AUTHORSHIP AND BACKGROUND

Written shortly after his Scottish car accident on July 1, 1969, "Come Together" was one of the last compositions that Lennon wrote expressly for the Beatles. The idea for the song had first occurred to him on May 30, when Timothy Leary met with Lennon during the famous Bed-In for peace, which Lennon and Yoko Ono held at Montreal's Hôtel Reine-Elizabeth. The counterculture guru asked Lennon to compose a song based on the slogan for Leary's 1970 California gubernatorial campaign, "Come Together—Join the Party!"

In spite of its titular call for coalition, "Come Together" shares little in common with Leary's unifying political slogan, which went for naught after the candidate was jailed for a 1968 drug arrest. In composing "Come Together," Lennon was influenced by Chuck Berry's 1956 hit, "You Can't Catch Me," in which the pioneering rock 'n' roller sings, "Here come up flattop he was movin' up with me." The Beatles had improvised a version of "You Can't Catch Me" on January 14, 1969, during the *Get Back* sessions.

RECORDING SESSIONS

Produced by George Martin, "Come Together" was recorded at Abbey Road Studios on July 21, 1969, along with several overdubbing sessions throughout the rest of the month. Lennon later described it as "gobbledygook" that the band had improvised in the studio (Lennon and Ono 2000, 201). In addition to Lennon's soulful lead vocal, the song is particularly memorable because of the slick tom-tom roll that Starr fashioned as the song's motto.

McCartney achieved a distinctive looping bass sound on his Rickenbacker, while also playing a bluesy riff on the Fender Rhodes electric piano: "Whenever [John] did praise any of us, it was great praise, indeed, because he didn't dish it out much," McCartney later recalled. "If ever you got a speck of it, a crumb of it, you were quite grateful. With 'Come Together,' for instance, he wanted a piano lick to be very swampy and smoky, and I played it that way and he liked it a lot. I was quite pleased with that" (Dowlding 1989, 277).

As with the sessions that concluded the *Get Back* project, the group's work on "Come Together" was loose and effortless, with Lennon good-naturedly ad-libbing "got to get some bobo" and "Eartha Kitt, man!" (Winn 2003b, 332). Lyrically, the song's nonsensicality most closely resembles the idiosyncratic verbal textures of "I Am the Walrus," as opposed to the superficial automobile homage afforded by Berry's "You Can't Catch Me." Lennon and Ono's recent experiments with heroin are referenced rather explicitly, moreover, when Lennon sings "shoot me" during the song's introductory phrases.

PERSONNEL

Lennon: Vocal, Epiphone Casino
McCartney: Rickenbacker 4001S, Electric Piano
Harrison: Gibson Les Paul Standard
Starr: Ludwig Hollywood Maple Drums, Maracas

CHART PERFORMANCE

U.K.: "Something"/"Come Together"; October 31, 1969, Apple [Parlophone] R 5814: #4. As a double A-side with "Something," "Come Together" charted at #4.

U.S.: "Something"/"Come Together"; October 6, 1969, Apple [Capitol] 26543: #3 (certified by the RIAA as "2x Multi Platinum," with more than 2 million copies sold). As a double A-side with "Something," "Come Together" charted at #1.

LEGACY AND INFLUENCE

"It's a funky record," Lennon remembered. "It's one of my favorite Beatles tracks" (Dowlding 1989, 277).

Walter Everett interprets "Come Together" as Lennon's attempt to provide listeners with a composite rendering of the individual Beatles' personae: "The gobbledygook may be heard as a disguise for Lennon's portrayal of the band members, one per verse: George as the long-haired holy roller, Paul as the good-looking player of Muddy Waters licks, and Lennon himself through images of the Walrus, Ono, and Bag Productions and a 'spinal cracker' reference to his car accident, but Ringo is harder to make out so clearly" (Everett 1999, 246).

In 2004, *Rolling Stone* ranked "Come Together" as #202 on the magazine's list of *The 500 Greatest Songs of All Time.*

In 2010, *Rolling Stone* ranked "Come Together" as #9 on the magazine's list of *The Beatles' 100 Greatest Songs.*

CONTROVERSY

In the United Kingdom, the BBC banned "Come Together" because of Lennon's reference to Coca-Cola, which the network determined to be inappropriate advertising.

Lennon's slight revisioning of the song's lyric into "Here come 'ol flattop he was movin' up slowly" found him on the losing end, at least initially, of a protracted lawsuit with Chuck Berry's publisher Morris Levy. In his out-of-court settlement with Berry's publisher, Lennon promised to record other songs in Levy's stable, several of which appeared on the former Beatle's 1975 solo album *Rock 'n' Roll*. The saga involving "Come Together" involved various other permutations, including Phil Spector's absconding of the album's master tapes, which led to Capitol Records paying some $90,000 in ransom to the eccentric producer for their return. Impatient with Lennon over the disposition of the out-of-court settlement, Levy marketed a television mail-order version of the album's rough mix entitled *Roots*. Capitol Records' subsequent lawsuit against Levy plunged the music publisher's label Adam VIII, Ltd., into bankruptcy. In a bizarre twist to the original complaint, the lawsuit directed Levy to pay Lennon some $85,000 in damages for harming his professional reputation.

ALBUM APPEARANCES: *Abbey Road*; *The Beatles, 1967–1970*; *20 Greatest Hits*; *Anthology 3*; *1*; *Love*.

See also: *Abbey Road* (LP); Spector, Phil.

Compact Disc Releases (1987–1988)

The Beatles joined the digital revolution in 1987 with the coordinated CD release of the Beatles' U.K. albums, along with the compilations *Past Masters, Volume 1* and *Past Masters, Volume 2* to account for the band's nonalbum tracks. In 1988, all 15 titles comprising the Beatles' CD releases were collected as *The Beatles Box Set*. In 2009, the Beatles' original CD releases were superseded by the remastered release of the Beatles' entire catalogue.

The Beatles' CD releases occurred in a series of seven, highly coordinated batches in order to create buzz among the band's audience. Although the CD releases were criticized for their dearth of original artwork, EMI's reissue campaign was ultimately successful, as a number of the albums reentered the American charts. *Please Please Me*, *With the Beatles*, and *A Hard Day's Night* charted at Nos. 32, 40, and 30, respectively, while *Abbey Road* reentered the U.S. charts at #30. The most successful of the reissues was *Sgt. Pepper's Lonely Hearts Club Band*, which charted at #3, while *The Beatles* (*The White Album*) charted at #18. The batches were released as follows:

Batch 1: *Please Please Me*, *With the Beatles*, *A Hard Day's Night*, and *Beatles for Sale* released as mono CDs on February 26, 1987.

Batch 2: *Help!*, *Rubber Soul*, and *Revolver* released as stereo CDs on April 30, 1987.

Batch 3: *Sgt. Pepper's Lonely Hearts Club Band* released as a stereo CD on June 1, 1987.

Batch 4: *The Beatles* (*The White Album*) and *Yellow Submarine* released as stereo CDs on August 24, 1987.

Batch 5: *Magical Mystery Tour* released as a stereo CD on September 21, 1987.

Batch 6: *Abbey Road* and *Let It Be* released as stereo CDs on October 19, 1987.
Batch 7: *Past Masters, Volume 1* and *Past Masters, Volume 2* released as stereo CDs on March 7, 1988.

See also: *Abbey Road* (LP); *Beatles for Sale* (LP); *The Beatles* (*The White Album*) (LP); *A Hard Day's Night* (U.K. LP); *Help!* (U.K. LP); *Let It Be* (LP); *Magical Mystery Tour* (LP); *Past Masters, Volume 1* (LP); *Past Masters, Volume 2* (LP); *Please Please Me* (LP); *Revolver* (U.K. LP); *Rubber Soul* (U.K. LP); *Sgt. Pepper's Lonely Hearts Club Band* (LP); *With the Beatles* (LP); *Yellow Submarine* (LP).

"The Continuing Story of Bungalow Bill" (Lennon–McCartney)

"The Continuing Story of Bungalow Bill" is a song on *The Beatles* (*The White Album*).

AUTHORSHIP AND BACKGROUND

Written by Lennon, "The Continuing Story of Bungalow Bill" finds its origins during the Beatles' 1968 visit to India. Lennon based the melody for the song on Mack Gordon and Henry Revel's "Stay as Sweet as You Are." In the Rishikesh compound, Lennon had become acquainted with Nancy Cooke de Herrera, one of the Maharishi's devoted followers. During the Beatles' stay in India, de Herrera's eldest son Rik Cooke had shot and killed a tiger during a hunt with his mother in the Sitabani Forest, providing perfect fodder for Lennon's simple tale about an "all American bullet-headed Saxon mother's son."

As Lennon later recalled, " 'Bungalow Bill' was written about a guy in Maharishi's meditation camp who took a short break to go shoot a few poor tigers, and then came back to commune with God. There used to be a character called Jungle Jim, and I combined him with Buffalo Bill. It's sort of a teenage social-comment song and a bit of a joke" (Lennon and Ono 2000, 200).

An early version of "The Continuing Story of Bungalow Bill" was recorded in May 1968 at Harrison's Kinfauns studio as part of the Esher Tapes.

RECORDING SESSIONS

Produced by George Martin, the Beatles recorded "The Continuing Story of Bungalow Bill" between midnight and dawn on October 9, 1968—Lennon's 28th birthday.

The distinctive flamenco guitar introduction in "The Continuing Story of Bungalow Bill" was played by an uncredited Chris Thomas on the Mellotron Mark II. Thomas employed the instrument's mandolin stop during the song's verses and the bassoon stop during the coda that precedes "While My Guitar Gently Weeps."

PERSONNEL

Lennon: Vocal, Gibson J-160E
McCartney: Rickenbacker 4001S, Backing Vocal
Harrison: Gibson J-200, Backing Vocal
Starr: Ludwig Oyster Black Pearl Drums, Tambourine, Backing Vocal
Ono: Vocal Solo, Backing Vocal
Maureen Starkey: Backing Vocal
Thomas: Mellotron Mark II

ALBUM APPEARANCE: *The Beatles* (*The White Album*).

See also: *The Beatles* (*The White Album*) (LP); Thomas, Chris.

"Cry Baby Cry" (Lennon–McCartney)

"Cry Baby Cry" is a song on *The Beatles* (*The White Album*).

AUTHORSHIP AND BACKGROUND

Written by Lennon, "Cry Baby Cry" finds its origins during the Beatles' 1968 visit to India. Lennon later claimed that he was influenced by an advertisement proclaiming "Cry baby cry / Make your mother buy." "Cry Baby Cry" is overtly based upon the children's nursery rhyme "Sing a Song of Sixpence." As with such classic Lennon songs as "I Am the Walrus," "Cry Baby Cry" is composed of nonsensical lyrics.

In a 1968 interview, Lennon recalled composing the music to "Cry Baby Cry": "I've been playing it over and over on the piano. I've let it go now, but it will come back if I really want it. Sometimes I get up from the piano as if I've been in a trance, and I know I have let a few things slip away, which I could have caught had I wanted something."

An early version of "Cry Baby Cry" was recorded in May 1968 at Harrison's Kinfauns studio as part of the Esher Tapes.

RECORDING SESSIONS

Produced by George Martin, "Cry Baby Cry" was recorded at Abbey Road Studios on July 15, 1968, with overdubbing sessions on July 16 and 18. Sound engineer Geoff Emerick resigned on July 16, still smarting from the interpersonal fallout associated with the "Ob-La-Di, Ob-La-Da" sessions.

PERSONNEL

Lennon: Vocal, Gibson J-160E, Piano, Hammond Organ
McCartney: Rickenbacker 4001S

Harrison: Gibson Les Paul Standard
Starr: Ludwig Oyster Black Pearl Drums, Tambourine
Martin: Harmonium

ALBUM APPEARANCES: *The Beatles (The White Album)*; *Anthology 3*; *Love*.

See also: *The Beatles (The White Album)*.

"Cry for a Shadow" (Harrison–Lennon)

"Cry for a Shadow" was recorded by Tony Sheridan and the Beat Brothers [The Beatles] in Hamburg in June 1961. It was released as the A-side of a single in the United Kingdom on February 28, 1964, to capitalize on the marketing power of Beatlemania.

AUTHORSHIP AND BACKGROUND

Written by Harrison and Lennon, the instrumental "Cry for a Shadow" was an explicit parody of the Shadows, British singer Cliff Richard's backing band. Composed under the working title of "Beatle Bop," "Cry for a Shadow" finds the Beatles imitating the Shadows' musical mannerisms, including guitarist Hank Marvin's telltale licks and Jet Harris's melodic bass runs. Inspired most directly by the Shadows' "Apache" instrumental, "Cry for a Shadow" even finds McCartney imitating Harris's enthusiastic yells during the song's middle-eight.

As Harrison remembered,

> In Hamburg we had to play so long, we actually used to play "Apache." . . . But John and I were just bullshitting one day, and he had this new little Rickenbacker with a funny kind of wobble bar on it. And he started playing that off, and I just came in, and we made it up right on the spot. (Everett 2001, 98)

RECORDING SESSIONS

Produced by German bandleader Bert Kämpfert with assistance from sound engineer Karl Hinze, "Cry for a Shadow" was recorded at Hamburg's Friedrich-Ebert-Halle on June 22, 1961. Kämpfert had caught the Beatles' act with Tony Sheridan at the Top Ten Club. Kämpfert subsequently offered Sheridan a contract with Polydor Records and signed up the Beatles as his backup band. For Sheridan's recordings, the Beatles temporarily refashioned themselves as the Beat Brothers. In German slang, *Pidels*, which sounds a lot like *Beatles*, is the plural form of penis. It was a connotation that Kämpfert was entirely unwilling to risk. The Beatles were paid 300 marks for the session.

"Cry for a Shadow" was one of eight songs that the Beatles recorded during their session with Sheridan at Friedrich-Ebert-Halle in June 1961.

As Harrison later recalled, "It was a bit disappointing because we'd been hoping to get a record deal for ourselves. Although we did 'Ain't She Sweet' and the instrumental 'Cry for a Shadow' without Sheridan, they didn't even put our name on the record" (Beatles 2000, 59).

As Beatlemania came into full force in 1964, Polydor and MGM released a single version of "Cry for a Shadow" in the United Kingdom and the United States, respectively. In the United Kingdom, Polydor released "Cry for a Shadow" as an A-side, while MGM released the instrumental in the United States as the B-side of Sheridan's "Why (Can't You Love Me Again)" to capitalized on the Beatles' popularity.

PERSONNEL

Lennon: Guitar
McCartney: Bass, Yelling
Harrison: Guitar
Pete Best: Drums

CHART PERFORMANCE

U.K.: "Cry for a Shadow"/"Why (Can't You Love Me Again)"; February 28, 1964, Polydor NH 52–275 (as the Beatles with Sheridan): Did not chart.

U.S.: "Why (Can't You Love Me Again)"/"Cry for a Shadow"; March 27, 1964, MGM K-13227 (as the Beatles with Sheridan): #88. As the B-side of "Why (Can't You Love Me Again)," "Cry for a Shadow" did not chart.

ALBUM APPEARANCES: *Anthology 1.*

See also: Sheridan, Tony.

D

"A Day in the Life" (Lennon–McCartney)

"A Day in the Life" is a song on the Beatles' *Sgt. Pepper's Lonely Hearts Club Band* album. Critics and fans alike consider it to be one of the band's central aesthetic achievements.

AUTHORSHIP AND BACKGROUND

"A Day in the Life" was written as two principal sections by Lennon and McCartney. As with "She's Leaving Home," Lennon originally discovered his muse for "A Day in the Life" in the found objects of newspaper headlines. A December 19, 1966, issue of the *Daily Sketch* published a photo of Tara Browne's grisly car crash. There were some reports that the 21-year-old heir to the Guinness brewery fortune had "blown his mind out in a car" from drugs, leading to speeding through the streets of South Kensington in his sleek Lotus Elan with his girlfriend, runway model Suki Potier, in tow. Blazing through a traffic light at more than 100 mph, he smashed the sports car into a truck that was parked across the intersection. Browne was killed instantly. Amazingly, Potier survived the collision and was relatively unscathed. Lennon brought his composition to fruition with imagery from a January 17, 1967, article in the *Daily Mail* on "The Holes in Our Roads." As Lennon later recalled, it "was a story about 4,000 potholes in Blackburn, Lancashire, that needed to be filled." After hearing Lennon's original verses for "A Day in the Life," McCartney shared the song that eventually comprised the middle-eight for Lennon's original text. McCartney had borrowed the passage's opening phrase from the first line of Dorothy Fields's 1930 hit "On the Sunny Side of the Street." McCartney was also responsible for crafting "I'd love to turn you on" into the song's one-line chorus, which Lennon described as a "damn good piece of work" (Lennon and Ono 2000, 184).

As Lennon remembered,

> I was writing the song with the *Daily Mail* propped up in front of me on the piano. I had it open to the "News In Brief" or whatever they call it. There was a paragraph about four thousand holes being discovered in Blackburn Lancashire. And when we came to record the song there was still one word missing from that verse. I knew the line had to go, "Now they know how many holes it takes to—something—the Albert Hall." For some reason I couldn't think of the verb.

What did the holes do to the Albert Hall? It was Terry Doran who said "fill" the Albert Hall. And that was it. Then we thought we wanted a growing noise to lead back into the first bit. We wanted to think of a good end and we had to decide what sort of backing and instruments would sound good. Like all our songs, they never become an entity until the very end. They are developed all the time as we go along. (Cadogan 2008, 197)

As Lennon later added,

"A Day in the Life" was a good piece of work between Paul and me. I had the "I read the news today" bit, and it turned Paul on. Now and then we really turn each other on with a bit of song, and he just said "yeah"—bang bang, like that. It just sort of happened beautifully, and we arranged it and rehearsed it, which we don't often do, the afternoon before. So we all knew what we were playing, we all got into it. It was a real groove, the whole scene on that one. Paul sang half of it and I sang half. I needed a middle-eight for it, but Paul already had one there. (Cott and Doudna 1982, 49)

As McCartney later recalled,

I remember being very conscious of the words "I'd love to turn you on" and thinking, "Well, that's about as risqué as we dare get at this point." Well, the BBC banned it. It said, "Now they know how many holes it takes to fill the Albert Hall" or something. But I mean that there was nothing vaguely rude or naughty in any of that. "I'd love to turn you on" was the rudest line in the whole thing. But that was one of John's very good ones. I wrote—that was co-written. The orchestra crescendo and that was based on some of the ideas I'd been getting from Stockhausen and people like that, which is more abstract. So we told the orchestra members to just start on their lowest note and end on their highest note and go in their own time, which orchestras are frightened to do. That's not the tradition. But we got 'em to do it. (Dowlding 1989, 184)

RECORDING SESSIONS

Produced by George Martin, "A Day in the Life" was recorded under the working title of "In the Life of . . ." at Abbey Road Studios on January 19 and 20, 1967, with an orchestral overdubbing session on February 10 and the recording of the song's final chord on February 22. The Beatles began recording "A Day in the Life" on January 19, with Lennon counting off the first take by muttering "sugar plum fairy, sugar plum fairy" in rhythm with the ensuing acoustic guitar part that he strummed on his Jumbo. In addition to Lennon's echo-laden lead vocal, the instrumentation included McCartney on piano, Harrison on maracas, and Starr on the bongos. Take four featured Mal Evans counting out 24 bars in order to afford space for future musical adornment before setting off an alarm clock (at the 2:18 mark in the song) to note McCartney's entrance during the middle-eight. Lennon had originally brought the windup alarm clock into Studio Two as a joke, according to Geoff Emerick, "saying that it would come in handy for waking up Ringo when he was needed to do an overdub" during the lengthy sessions for *Sgt. Pepper* (Emerick and Massey 2006, 147). In later years, Starr grew fond of saying that *Sgt. Pepper* was the album during which he learned to play chess. As for the sound of the alarm clock itself, Emerick spent a significant amount of time attempting to delete it from the recording, eventually giving up when he realized it was impossible to separate it from the mix.

The next evening, McCartney overdubbed a bass track on his Rickenbacker and recorded a rough version of his lead vocal. During the February 3 session, McCartney rerecorded his vocal, with the alarm clock appropriately sounding a split second before he sings, "Woke up, fell out of bed." That same day, Starr came up with one of his most inventive drum parts on record. Despite the drummer's words of protests—"Come on, Paul, you know how much I hate flashy drumming"—McCartney talked Starr into trying out the fantastic, innovative tom-tom fills that punctuate the lyrics of "A Day in the Life" (Emerick and Massey 2006, 149). The band's producer remembered things differently: "That was entirely [Starr's] own idea," Martin recollected. "Ringo has a tremendous feel for a song, and he always helped us hit the right tempo the first time. He was rock solid, and this made the recording of all the Beatles' songs so much easier" (Lewisohn 1988, 95). Emerick punched up the sound of Starr's drums by removing the bottom heads from his tom-toms and placing microphones directly beneath them.

On February 10, 1967, the Beatles made history during one of their most chaotic sessions to date. With seven movie cameras running, McCartney directed a 40-piece orchestra, its membership having been culled from the London Philharmonic and the Royal Philharmonic. Their mission? To fill in Evans's 24 empty bars with the sound of pure apocalypse. Instead of asking Martin to provide the musicians with a score, McCartney distributed written instructions to the players, as opposed to musical notation: "We just wrote it down like a cooking recipe," McCartney recalled. "Twenty-four bars, on the ninth bar the orchestra will take off and it will go from its lowest note to its highest note." In an effort to establish the appropriately zany atmosphere in cavernous Studio One, the Beatles asked the guest musicians, whose number included Alan Civil and David Mason, to dress the part. As Ian Peel points out, McCartney was evoking the "outlandish performance art of Stockhausen" by requesting that the orchestra members attend the session in formal evening dress, while wearing funny masks, false teeth, and bulbous noses (Peel 2002, 39). For his own part, McCartney donned a kitchen apron for the occasion. A variety of rock 'n' roll personalities were present, including Mick Jagger, Marianne Faithfull, Keith Richards, Donovan, and Michael Nesmith. Meanwhile, Lennon—with a bald wig perched awkwardly on his head—wore an outrageous blue-velvet coat (Winn 2003b, 97).

In spite of the convivial mood, the classically trained musicians were not very keen on performing in such an unscripted fashion. The orchestral passages for "A

Day in the Life" required them to create a massive crescendo in the space of two dozen measures. As McCartney later recalled,

> I went around to all the trumpet players and said, "Look all you've got to do is start at the beginning of the 24 bars and go through all the notes on your instrument from the lowest to the highest—and the highest has to happen on that 24th bar, that's all. So you can blow 'em all in that first thing and then rest, then play the top one there if you want, or you can steady them out." And it was interesting because I saw the orchestra's characters. The strings were like sheep—they all looked at each other: "Are you going up? I am!" and they'd all go up together, the leader would take them all up. The trumpeters were much wilder. (Lewisohn 1988, 14)

According to Martin, both composers had suggested the orchestral passages, with McCartney hoping for a "freak-out" and Lennon desiring a "tremendous build-up, from nothing up to something absolutely like the end of the world" (Everett 1999, 118). Emerick recorded the musicians on two separate tape machines in order to delay the signal at varying intervals. This tactic was supplemented by the pioneering use of ambiophonics on the track. The process of creating "ambiophony" involved the placement of 100 loudspeakers along all four walls of Studio One. A forerunner of contemporary surround-sound, ambiophonics assisted Emerick in capturing the orchestra's powerful crescendos. With the work of the studio musicians complete, the Beatles turned to the conclusion of "A Day in the Life," a composition that demanded the appropriate punctuation mark for the most evocative rallying call to consciousness in the Lennon–McCartney songbook. The initial ending for the track was going to be a "choir of voices" singing a long "hummmmmm," an effect that they attempted during the February 10 session (Lewisohn 1995, 244). But within a few weeks, they had scrapped the hummmmmm idea altogether in favor of the famous 53-second piano chord—an E major—played by Lennon, McCartney, Starr, and Evans on a trio of pianos. Martin supplemented the awe-inspiring sound on the studio's harmonium. Not surprisingly, it took nine takes before they all succeeded in pounding the chord simultaneously. In order to enhance the sound of the chord, Emerick allowed for a 45-second sustain. "I reached full volume," he recalled, "and the gain was so high that you could literally hear the quiet swoosh of the studio's air conditioners" (Emerick and Massey 2006, 161). It may not have been the end of the world, but it certainly sounded like it.

The chord's metaphorical open-endedness suggests—in dramatic contrast with the self-contained love songs of the Beatles' musical youth—the proffering of a larger philosophical question for which there is no immediate answer. "A song not of disillusionment with life itself but of disenchantment with the limits of mundane perception," Ian MacDonald observes, " 'A Day in the Life' depicts the 'real' world as an unenlightened construct that reduces, depresses, and ultimately destroys" (MacDonald 1994, 181). In "A Day in the Life," the songwriters revisit the vexing relationship that invariably exists between the self and the outside world. They consider the distressing double-bind inherent in our interhuman bond, an interrelationship that possesses the power for engendering genuine love and connection, on the one hand, while creating untold loneliness and neglect on the other. By trumpeting "I'd love to turn you on" to the anxious ears of a waiting world—and ensuring that the song was ultimately banned by the BBC in the process—the Beatles dared their audience to embrace self-awareness and mind-consciousness in spite of the harrowing headlines that seem to foretell humanity's doom on a daily basis. Modernists to a fault, the Beatles never stopped experimenting with their art, they never ceased exploiting ironies of distance and situation, and they refused to silence their narrative without first reminding us that there is an ethical center out there somewhere—we simply have to keep questing for it, no matter what the cost. As Walter Everett astutely writes, " 'A Day in the Life' represents the Beatles' wake-up call for whomever might be listening. The song is not merely a warning of an ashy apocalypse, as it has often been taken, but suggests that there is yet hope for the phoenix" (Everett 1999, 116).

PERSONNEL

Lennon: Vocal, Gibson J-160E, Piano

McCartney: Vocal, Rickenbacker 4001S, Piano

Harrison: Maracas

Starr: Ludwig Oyster Black Pearl Drums, Congas, Piano

Evans: Alarm Clock, Piano

Studio Musicians: Orchestral Accompaniment conducted by Martin and McCartney

John Marston: Harp

Erich Gruenberg, Granville Jones, Bill Monro, Jürgen Hess, Hans Geiger, D. Bradley, Lionel Bentley, David McCallum, Donald Weekes, Henry Datyner, Sidney Sax, Ernest Scott: Violin

John Underwood, Gwynne Edwards, Bernard Davis, John Meek: Viola

Francisco Gabarro, Dennis Vigay, Alan Delziel, Alex Nifosi: Cello

Cyril Mac Arther, Gordon Pearce: Double Bass

Roger Lord: Oboe

Basil Tschaikov, Jack Brymer: Clarinet

N. Fawcett, Alfred Waters: Bassoon

Clifford Seville, David Sandeman: Flute

Alan Civil, Neil Sanders: Horn

David Mason, Monty Montgomery, Harold Jackson: Trumpet

Raymond Brown, Raymond Premru, T. Moore: Trombone

Michael Barnes: Tuba

Tristan Fry: Tympani

CHART PERFORMANCE

U.K.: "Sgt. Pepper's Lonely Hearts Club Band/With a Little Help from My Friends"/"A Day in the Life"; September 30, 1978, Parlophone R6022: #63.

As the B-side of "Sgt. Pepper's Lonely Hearts Club Band/With a Little Help from My Friends," "A Day in the Life" did not chart.

U.S.: "Sgt. Pepper's Lonely Hearts Club Band/With a Little Help from My Friends"/"A Day in the Life"; September 30, 1978, Capitol 4612: #71. As the B-side of "Sgt. Pepper's Lonely Hearts Club Band/With a Little Help from My Friends," "A Day in the Life" did not chart.

LEGACY AND INFLUENCE

"A Day in the Life" is included among the Rock and Roll Hall of Fame's *500 Songs That Shaped Rock and Roll*.

In 1968, "A Day in the Life" was nominated for a Grammy Award for Best Instrumental Arrangement Accompanying Vocalist(s) at the 10th Grammy Awards.

In 2004, *Rolling Stone* ranked "A Day in the Life" as #28 on the magazine's list of *The 500 Greatest Songs of All Time*.

In 2006, *Pitchfork* ranked "A Day in the Life" as #5 on the Web magazine's list of *The 200 Greatest Songs of the 1960s*.

In 2006, *Q Magazine* ranked "A Day in the Life" as #4 on the magazine's list of *The 100 Greatest Songs of All Time*.

In 2010, *Rolling Stone* ranked "A Day in the Life" as #1 on the magazine's list of *The Beatles' 100 Greatest Songs*.

CONTROVERSY

"A Day in the Life" was subsequently banned by the BBC because of McCartney's reference, during the song's middle-eight, to having "a smoke," which the network interpreted as an allusion to marijuana usage. The BBC also took issue with the lyric involving "4,000 holes in Blackburn, Lancashire," which was interpreted as a reference to the track marks on a heroin junkie's arm. Ironically, the line perceived by McCartney to be the song's most "risqué" line—"I'd love to turn you on"—was not cited in the BBC's decision to ban "A Day in the Life" from receiving radio airplay.

ALBUM APPEARANCES: *Sgt. Pepper's Lonely Hearts Club Band*; *The Beatles, 1967–1970*; *Anthology 2*; *Love.*

See also: *The Beatles Anthology, Volume 2* (LP); "Paul Is Dead" Hoax; *Sgt. Pepper's Lonely Hearts Club Band* (LP).

"Day Tripper" (Lennon–McCartney)

"Day Tripper" was a hit double A-side single, backed with "We Can Work It Out," which was released in the United Kingdom on December 3, 1965, and in the United

States on December 6, 1965. Together, "Day Tripper" and "We Can Work It Out" marked the band's 10th consecutive #1 single in the United Kingdom. Along with "We Can Work It Out," it was released contemporaneously with *Rubber Soul*.

AUTHORSHIP AND BACKGROUND

Written by Lennon with contributions from McCartney, "Day Tripper"—as with "I Feel Fine"—was inspired by Bobby Parker's "Watch Your Step."

As Lennon recalled, "That's mine. Including the guitar lick, the guitar break, and the whole bit. It's just a rock 'n' roll song. Day trippers are people who go on a day trip, right? Usually on a ferry boat or something. But it was kind of—you know, you're just a weekend hippie. Get it?" (Badman 2001, 194).

RECORDING SESSIONS

Produced by Martin, "Day Tripper" was recorded at Abbey Road Studios on October 16, 1965.

PERSONNEL

Lennon: Vocal, Rickenbacker 325
McCartney: Höfner 500/1
Harrison: Gibson ES-345
Starr: Ludwig Oyster Black Pearl Drums, Tambourine

CHART PERFORMANCE

U.K.: "We Can Work It Out"/"Day Tripper"; December 3, 1965, Parlophone R 5389: #1. As a double A-side with "We Can Work It Out," "Day Tripper" charted at #1.

U.S.: "We Can Work It Out"/"Day Tripper"; December 6, 1965, Capitol 5555: #1 (certified by the RIAA as "Gold," with more than 500,000 copies sold). As a double A-side with "We Can Work It Out," "Day Tripper" charted at #5.

LEGACY AND INFLUENCE

In 2010, *Rolling Stone* ranked "Day Tripper" as #39 on the magazine's list of *The Beatles' 100 Greatest Songs*.

ALBUM APPEARANCES: *A Collection of Beatles Oldies*; *The Beatles, 1962–1966*; *20 Greatest Hits*; *Past Masters, Volume 2*; *1*.

See also: *Rubber Soul* (U.K. LP).

"Dear Prudence" (Lennon–McCartney)

"Dear Prudence" is a song on *The Beatles* (*The White Album*).

AUTHORSHIP AND BACKGROUND

Written by Lennon, "Dear Prudence" finds its origins during the Beatles' 1968 visit to India. The group was joined in the Maharishi's compound by actress Mia Farrow and her reclusive younger sister Prudence, who refused to leave her room, prompting various members of the compound to alight outside her door, speaking and singing to her in an effort to draw her forth. An early version of "Dear Prudence" was recorded in May 1968 at Harrison's Kinfauns studio as part of the Esher Tapes.

As Lennon remembered,

> "Dear Prudence" is me. Written in India. A song about Mia Farrow's sister, who seemed to go slightly balmy, meditating too long, and couldn't come out of the little hut we were livin' in. They selected me and George to try and bring her out because she would trust us. If she'd been in the West, they would have put her away. . . . We got her out of the house. She'd been locked in for three weeks and was trying to reach God quicker than anybody else. That was the competition in Maharishi's camp—who was going to get cosmic first. What I didn't know was I was "already" cosmic. (Clayson 2003a, 232)

RECORDING SESSIONS

Produced by Martin, "Dear Prudence" was recorded at Trident Studios on August 28, 1968, with overdubbing sessions on August 29 and 30, during Starr's brief hiatus from the band. Lennon and Harrison overdubbed their guitar parts several times in order to create a luminous, layered effect. The bandmates were joined in the studio by Evans, Apple artist Jackie Lomax, and McCartney's cousin John.

PERSONNEL

Lennon: Vocal, Epiphone Casino
McCartney: Rickenbacker 4001S, Piano, Flügelhorn, Ludwig Oyster Black Pearl Drums, Backing Vocal
Harrison: Fender Rosewood Telecaster, Gibson Les Paul Standard, Backing Vocal
Evans: Backing Vocal, Tambourine
Lomax: Backing Vocal
John McCartney: Backing Vocal

LEGACY AND INFLUENCE

In 2010, *Rolling Stone* ranked "Dear Prudence" as #63 on the magazine's list of *The Beatles' 100 Greatest Songs*.

ALBUM APPEARANCES: *The Beatles* (*The White Album*); *Love*.

See also: *The Beatles* (*The White Album*) (LP).

Decca Records Audition

Having secured the Beatles' management contract, Brian Epstein vowed to win them a record deal with a major label. Without missing a beat, Epstein began expanding his contacts throughout the music world. To this end, Epstein had played "My Bonnie" for Ron White, the marketing manager for the monolithic EMI, as well as to Tony Barrow, the *Liverpool Echo*'s music reporter who also served as a publicity representative for Decca Records. Epstein was known for the brash confidence that he brought to such meetings, often touting the Beatles' destiny as being "bigger than Elvis." For his part, Barrow contacted Dick Rowe, Decca's chief A&R (Artists and Repertoire) man, and Rowe dispatched one of his producers, Mike Smith, to Liverpool. On December 13, 1961, Smith visited the Cavern and was duly impressed with the energy and charisma inherent in the Beatles' performance. Later that evening, Smith told Epstein that "we've got to have them down for a bash in the studio at once. Let's see what they can do" (Spitz 2005, 285).

On New Year's Eve, the Beatles made the nine-hour trek to London, with Neil Aspinall behind the wheel of their van, in a driving snowstorm. Just before 11 A.M. on Monday, January 1, 1962, the band members, understandably nervous and grumpy, arrived at Decca's Russell Square recording studios. They performed 15 songs for the label's consideration, including several staples from their stage act—"Till There Was You," "The Sheik of Araby," "Three Cool Cats," and "Bésame Mucho"—as well as three original numbers, including "Like Dreamers Do," "Hello Little Girl," and "Love of the Loved." As Lennon later reported, "I remember when we made our first recording. We didn't sound natural. Paul sang 'Till There Was You' and he sounded like a woman. I sang 'Money,' and I sounded like a madman. By the time we made our demos of 'Hello Little Girl' and 'Love of the Loved,' we were okay, I think" (Winn 2003a, 7). Yet, for all of their concern and unease, Smith seemed pleased with their performance. "I can't see any problems," he told them as they left the studio. "You should record" (Spitz 2005, 287).

Yet, to everyone's surprise, EMI's Ron White sent his formal rejection of the band in mid-January, asserting that the label already had plenty of vocal groups under contract at the time. Finally, on February 1, 1962, Rowe offered Decca's response, curtly reporting that "groups with guitars are on the way out." Besides which, Rowe added, the Beatles "sound too much like the Shadows" (Spitz 2005, 293). In a symbolic gesture that demonstrated their increasing estrangement from their drummer, the other Beatles didn't bother to inform Pete Best about the Decca rejection for several days. But the Decca saga was hardly over. Fearing that Decca would lose their precious retail record contracts with NEMS (North End Music Stores), Rowe turned up at the Cavern on February 3 in order to hear the band for himself. Rowe arrived in Liverpool during a deluge, and when he finally reached the club's entrance, he couldn't make his way through the throng of kids packing themselves into the Cavern's sweaty archways to see the Beatles.

Rowe returned to London, where, several days later, he met with Epstein yet again in order to assuage the manager, who felt as though he had been slighted by the music conglomerate. "You have a good record business in Liverpool," Rowe told him. "Stick to that" (Spitz 2005, 294). Mark Lewisohn notes that Decca's decision may have had its roots in geographical preference. As it happens, Smith auditioned two groups on January 1, 1962, the Beatles and Brian Poole and the Tremeloes, yet Rowe only allowed Smith to sign one of the bands: Smith "chose the latter group," Lewisohn observes, "not because they were more promising but purely and simply because they were based in Barking, just eight miles from his office. They would be far easier, and cheaper, to work with than a group based 200 miles away. So Decca Records let the Beatles go, and, more than coincidentally, began their slide into oblivion" (Lewisohn 1986, 91, 92).

Anthology 1 includes the Beatles' Decca performances of "Like Dreamers Do," "The Sheik of Araby," "Hello Little Girl," "Three Cool Cats," and "Searchin'."

DECCA AUDITION SET LIST

"Like Dreamers Do"
"Money (That's What I Want)"
"Till There Was You"
"The Sheik of Araby"
"To Know Her Is to Love Her"
"Take Good Care of My Baby"
"Memphis, Tennessee"
"Sure to Fall (In Love with You)"
"Hello Little Girl"
"Three Cool Cats"
"Crying, Waiting, Hoping"
"Love of the Loved"
"September in the Rain"
"Bésame Mucho"
"Searchin'"

PERSONNEL

Lennon: Vocals, Guitar
McCartney: Vocals, Bass

Harrison: Vocals, Guitar
Best: Drums

See also: *The Beatles Anthology, Volume 1* (LP); Epstein, Brian.

"Devil in Her Heart" (Drapkin)

"Devil in Her Heart" is a song on the *With the Beatles* album.

AUTHORSHIP AND BACKGROUND

"Devil in His Heart" was written by Richard P. Drapkin, a songwriter and musician who recorded under the name Ricky Dee. The Donays, an early 1960s girl group, released the song as a single in 1962, although it failed to crack the Top 40.

RECORDING SESSIONS

Produced by Martin, "Devil in Her Heart" was recorded in three takes at Abbey Road Studios on July 18, 1963. Harrison double-tracked his lead vocal.

PERSONNEL

Lennon: Rickenbacker 325, Backing Vocal
McCartney: Höfner 500/1, Backing Vocal
Harrison: Vocal, Gretsch Country Gentleman
Starr: Ludwig Oyster Black Pearl Drums, Maracas

ALBUM APPEARANCES: *With the Beatles*; *The Beatles' Second Album*; *On Air: Live at the BBC, Volume 2*.

See also: *With the Beatles* (LP).

"Dig a Pony" (Lennon–McCartney)

"Dig a Pony" is a song on the Beatles' *Let It Be* album.

AUTHORSHIP AND BACKGROUND

Written by Lennon, "Dig a Pony" was originally written as two separate songs entitled "All I Want Is You" and "Dig a Pony." As Lennon later recalled, "I was just having fun with words. It was literally a nonsense song. You just take words and you stick them together, and you see if they have any meaning. Some of them do and some of them don't" (Cadogan 2008, 225). The songwriter proved to be less charitable during one of his last interviews, remarking that "Dig a Pony" was "another piece of garbage" (Lennon and Ono 2000, 205).

RECORDING SESSIONS

Produced by Martin with postproduction by Phil Spector, "Dig a Pony" was recorded during the Beatles' rooftop concert on January 30, 1969. The band had earlier conducted rehearsals for the song at Apple Studio on January 22 and 28.

"Dig a Pony" features an arresting guitar preface in 3/4 time—an "aggressive ostinato riff," in Alan W. Pollack's words—that introduces the speaker's unabashed, free-form ruminations about falling in love (Pollack 2000). Lennon's oblique reference to picking a "moondog" offers an allusion to the band's fleeting existence way back in November 1959 as Johnny and the Moondogs.

At the beginning of "Dig a Pony" on the *Let It Be* album, Starr can be heard yelling "Hold it!" to his bandmates because he was not ready to perform, holding a cigarette in one hand and a single drumstick in the other. In addition, the song originally included McCartney singing "All I want is you" as his backing vocal, although it was deleted from both the *Let It Be* and *Let It Be . . . Naked* releases. McCartney's backing vocal is preserved on the *Anthology 3* version of "Dig a Pony."

The *Let It Be . . . Naked* (2003) version of "Dig a Pony" is a remixed version of the original rooftop concert recording without the false start that is included on the *Let It Be* soundtrack album.

PERSONNEL

Lennon: Vocal, Epiphone Casino
McCartney: Höfner 500/1, Backing Vocal
Harrison: Fender Rosewood Telecaster, Backing Vocal
Starr: Ludwig Hollywood Maple Drums
Preston: Fender Rhodes Electric Piano

LEGACY AND INFLUENCE

In 2010, *Rolling Stone* ranked "Dig a Pony" as #92 on the magazine's list of *The Beatles' 100 Greatest Songs*.

ALBUM APPEARANCES: *Let It Be*; *Anthology 3*; *Let It Be . . . Naked*.

See also: *Let It Be* (LP); *Let It Be . . . Naked* (LP); Preston, Billy; Spector, Phil.

"Dig It" (Harrison–Lennon–McCartney–Starr)

"Dig It" is a song on the Beatles' *Let It Be* album. It is one of the very few songs credited to all four Beatles as composers.

AUTHORSHIP AND BACKGROUND

Improvised by all four Beatles, "Dig It" is a free-form, improvisational rant of some 12 minutes that at one point featured Lennon in an unlikely duet with six-year-old Heather Eastman, the daughter of McCartney's fiancée Linda Eastman. Peter Doggett describes "Dig It" as a "slice of late '60s hippie slang" (Doggett 1998, 82).

RECORDING SESSIONS

Produced by Martin with postproduction by Spector, "Dig It" was recorded at Apple Studio on January 24, 1969, with an additional overdubbing session on January 26.

PERSONNEL

Lennon: Vocal, Fender Bass VI
McCartney: Piano
Harrison: Fender Rosewood Telecaster
Starr: Ludwig Hollywood Maple Drums
Preston: Hammond Organ
Martin: Shaker

ALBUM APPEARANCE: *Let It Be.*

See also: *Let It Be* (LP); *Let It Be . . . Naked* (LP); McCartney, Linda Eastman; Preston, Billy; Spector, Phil.

"Dizzy Miss Lizzy" (Williams)

"Dizzy Miss Lizzy" is a song on the Beatles' *Help!* album.

AUTHORSHIP AND BACKGROUND

Written by Larry Williams, "Dizzy Miss Lizzy" was released as a single by Williams in 1958, although it failed to become a hit. The original single was backed with "Slow Down," another Williams composition covered by the Beatles.

RECORDING SESSIONS

Produced by Martin, "Dizzy Miss Lizzy" was recorded at Abbey Road Studios on May 10, 1965. In June 1965, the Beatles recorded another version of "Dizzy Miss Lizzy" for the BBC's *Ticket to Ride* radio show.

PERSONNEL

Lennon: Vocal, Hammond Organ
McCartney: Höfner 500/1
Harrison: Gretsch Tennessean
Starr: Ludwig Oyster Black Pearl Drums, Cowbell

ALBUM APPEARANCES: *Help!* (U.K.); *Beatles VI*; *The Beatles at the Hollywood Bowl*; *Live at the BBC*.

See also: *Help!* (U.K. LP); Plastic Ono Band.

"Do You Want to Know a Secret" (McCartney–Lennon)

"Do You Want to Know a Secret" is a song on the Beatles' *Please Please Me* album.

AUTHORSHIP AND BACKGROUND

Written by Lennon, "Do You Want to Know a Secret" finds its inspiration in Walt Disney's *Snow White and the Seven Dwarfs* (1937), which Lennon's mother Julia used to sing for him during his childhood. In the film, Snow White offers a spoken introduction to the movie's first song, "I'm Wishing": "Wanna know a secret?" she asks a clutch of adoring doves. "Promise not to tell?" Lennon had recently composed the song in the Liverpool flat that he and Cynthia were borrowing from Epstein.

RECORDING SESSIONS

Produced by Martin, "Do You Want to Know a Secret" was recorded at Abbey Road Studios on February 11, 1963, with an overdubbing session on February 20.

PERSONNEL

Lennon: Rickenbacker 325, Backing Vocal
McCartney: Höfner 500/1, Backing Vocal
Harrison: Vocal, Gretsch Duo-Jet
Starr: Premier Mahogany Duroplastic Drums

CHART PERFORMANCE

U.S.: "Do You Want to Know a Secret"/"Thank You Girl"; March 23, 1964, Vee-Jay VJ 587: #2.

ALBUM APPEARANCES: *Please Please Me*; *The Early Beatles*; *On Air: Live at the BBC, Volume 2*.

See also: *Please Please Me* (LP).

"Doctor Robert" (Lennon–McCartney)

"Doctor Robert" is a song on the Beatles' *Revolver* album.

AUTHORSHIP AND BACKGROUND

Written by Lennon, "Doctor Robert" finds the Beatles presenting their first overt reference to the drug usage that had been altering their lives and their songwriting aesthetic appreciably since their fateful meeting with Bob Dylan some 20 months earlier. It makes specific mention of New York physician Robert Freymann, who was well-known for prescribing a range of hallucinogenic drugs—specifically vitamin shots mixed with amphetamines—to his celebrity clientele.

In addition to Freymann, "Doctor Robert" may have been a veiled reference to John Riley, the dentist who, without their knowledge, had sent Lennon and Harrison on their first acid trip in early April 1965. At first, Riley attempted to keep his guests from leaving, given their onrushing hallucinogenic condition. Fearing that their host was attempting to detain the Beatles and their wives for an orgy, the two couples drove off in Harrison's Mini Cooper to the Ad Lib Club. They eventually made their way to Kinfauns, the Harrisons' Esher bungalow, where Lennon imagined himself to be captaining a giant submarine. For Harrison, the experience was a revelation: "It was like I had never tasted, smelled, or heard anything before. For me, it was like a flash. It just opened up something inside of me, and I realized a lot of very heavy things. From that moment on, I wanted to have that depth and clarity of perception" (Badman 2001, 147).

To Lennon's mind, the acid trip served as validation for the surrealistic imagery that he had been experiencing his entire life, particularly in terms of having surrealistic or psychedelic visions. As Lennon remembered, "Doctor Robert" was "another of mine. Mainly about drugs and pills. It was about myself. I was the one that carried all the pills on tour—later on the roadies did it. We just kept them in our pockets, loose, in case of trouble" (Lennon and Ono 2000, 180).

RECORDING SESSIONS

Produced by Martin, "Doctor Robert" was recorded at Abbey Road Studios on April 17, 1966, with an additional overdubbing session on April 19 in which Lennon double-tracked his lead vocal.

Lennon later observed that *"Rubber Soul* was the pot album, and *Revolver* was the acid," yet "Doctor Robert" evinces an archly satirical tone—especially in terms of Lennon's characterization of the errant physician (Beatles 2000, 194). Although the Beatles' creative accomplishments during this period are often attributed to the influence of illicit drugs—and there is little doubt that they consumed considerable amounts of hallucinogens, especially Lennon—the bandmates were intensely focused and painstaking in the studio. "We were really hard workers," Starr recalled, and "we worked like dogs to get it right" (Spitz 2005, 606). While their hallucinogenic activities surely contributed to the band's evolving consciousness and creativity, the group required, as with most artists, to maintain their wits in their working environment. "The Beatles said they preferred not to work high," Lewisohn notes, but "they took their high experiences into the studio" (2004, 182).

PERSONNEL

> Lennon: Vocal, Epiphone Casino, Harmonium
> McCartney: Rickenbacker 4001S, Backing Vocal
> Harrison: Epiphone Casino, Maracas
> Starr: Ludwig Oyster Black Pearl Drums

ALBUM APPEARANCES: *Revolver* (U.K.); *Yesterday . . . and Today.*

See also: *Revolver* (U.K. LP).

"Don't Bother Me" (Harrison)

"Don't Bother Me" is a song on the *With the Beatles* album.

AUTHORSHIP AND BACKGROUND

According to Harrison, "Don't Bother Me" was "the first song I wrote—as an exercise to see if I *could* write a song. I wrote it in a hotel in Bournemouth, where we were playing a summer season in 1963. I was sick in bed—maybe that's why it turned out to be 'Don't Bother Me'" (Dowlding 1989, 50).

RECORDING SESSIONS

Produced by Martin, "Don't Bother Me" was recorded at Abbey Road Studios on September 11 and 12, 1963. Harrison double-tracked his lead vocal.

PERSONNEL

> Lennon: Rickenbacker 325, Tambourine
> McCartney: Höfner 500/1, Claves

Harrison: Vocal, Gretsch Country Gentleman
Starr: Ludwig Oyster Black Pearl Drums, Bongos, Loose-Skinned Arabian
Bongo

ALBUM APPEARANCES: *With the Beatles*; *Meet the Beatles!*

See also: With the Beatles (LP).

"Don't Let Me Down" (Lennon–McCartney)

"Don't Let Me Down" is the B-side of the Beatles' "Get Back" single, which was released in the United Kingdom on April 11, 1969, and in the United States on May 5, 1969.

AUTHORSHIP AND BACKGROUND

Written by Lennon, "Don't Let Me Down" was inspired by the songwriter's intense admiration and desire for Ono, to whom he dedicated the song. In *The Beatles: An Illustrated Record* (1975), Roy Carr and Tony Tyler described "Don't Let Me Down" as a "superb sobber from misery-expert J.W.O. Lennon, MBE. And still one of the most highly underrated Beatle underbellies" (Carr and Tyler 1975, 78).

"That's me, singing about Yoko," Lennon observed during one of his final interviews (Lennon and Ono 2000, 204). As McCartney remembered, "It was a very tense period. John was with Yoko, and had escalated to heroin and all the accompanying paranoias and he was putting himself out on a limb. I think that, as much as it excited and amused him, at the same time it secretly terrified him. So 'Don't Let Me Down' was a genuine plea" (Doggett 2009, 62).

RECORDING SESSIONS

Credited to the Beatles with Preston, "Don't Let Me Down" was produced by Martin and recorded at Apple Studio on January 28, 1969. During a January 22 rehearsal of the song, Lennon pointedly urged Starr to effect a heavy cymbal crash: "Give me a big 'kzzzsshhhh!' Give me the courage to come screaming in."

While the January 28 Apple Studio recording was used for the B-side of "Get Back," the two January 30 rooftop recordings of the song were edited together for the version of "Don't Let Me Down" included on the *Let It Be . . . Naked* version of the song that was released in November 2003.

PERSONNEL

Lennon: Vocal, Epiphone Casino
McCartney: Höfner 500/1

Harrison: Fender Rosewood Telecaster
Starr: Ludwig Hollywood Maple Drums
Preston: Fender Rhodes Electric Piano

CHART PERFORMANCE

U.K.: "Get Back"/"Don't Let Me Down"; April 11, 1969, Apple [Parlophone] R 5777 (as the Beatles with Preston): #1. As the B-side of "Get Back," "Don't Let Me Down" did not chart.

U.S.: "Get Back"/"Don't Let Me Down"; May 5, 1969, Apple [Capitol] 2490 (as the Beatles with Preston): #1 (certified by the RIAA as "2x Multi Platinum," with more than 2 million copies sold). As the B-side of "Get Back," "Don't Let Me Down" charted at #35.

LEGACY AND INFLUENCE

In 2010, *Rolling Stone* ranked "Don't Let Me Down" as #46 on the magazine's list of *The Beatles' 100 Greatest Songs*.

ALBUM APPEARANCES: *Hey Jude*; *The Beatles, 1967–1970*; *Past Masters, Volume 2*; *Let It Be . . . Naked*.

See also: *Let It Be* (LP); *Let It Be . . . Naked* (LP); Lindsay-Hogg, Michael; Ono, Yoko; The Rooftop Concert.

"Don't Pass Me By" (Starr)

"Don't Pass Me By" is a song on *The Beatles* (*The White Album*).

AUTHORSHIP AND BACKGROUND

Written by Starr during the Beatles' 1968 visit to India, "Don't Pass Me By" marks the drummer's first complete composition, with Starr having received partial credit for "What Goes On" and "Flying."

Originally entitled "Ringo's Tune (Untitled)" and later "Some Kind of Friendly," "Don't Pass Me By" was a watershed moment for Starr. As he later recalled, "I'd write tunes that were already written and just change the lyrics and the other three would have hysterics just tellin' me what I'd rewritten" (Dowlding 1989, 235).

RECORDING SESSIONS

Produced by Martin, "Don't Pass Me By" was recorded at Abbey Road Studios on June 5, 1968, with overdubbing sessions on June 6, July 12, and July 22. The introductory piano piece was added by McCartney during the final overdubbing session.

Martin composed an orchestral introduction for "Don't Pass Me By" entitled "A Beginning." While the Beatles left it off of *The White Album*, "A Beginning" was later included on *Anthology 3*.

PERSONNEL

McCartney: Rickenbacker 4001S, Piano
Starr: Vocal, Piano, Ludwig Oyster Black Pearl Drums, Sleigh Bell
Jack Fallon: Violin

ALBUM APPEARANCES: *The Beatles* (*The White Album*); *Rarities* (U.S.); *Anthology 3*.

See also: *The Beatles* (*The White Album*) (LP); *Let It Be . . . Naked* (LP); "Paul Is Dead" Hoax; Ringo Starr and His All-Starr Band.

"Drive My Car" (Lennon–McCartney)

"Drive My Car" is a song on the Beatles' *Rubber Soul* album.

AUTHORSHIP AND BACKGROUND

Written by McCartney with a significant Lennon contribution, "Drive My Car" was later described by McCartney—along with "Norwegian Wood (This Bird Has Flown)"—as one of *Rubber Soul*'s two "comedy numbers." According to McCartney, the notion of "driving my car" was an old blues connotation for sex (Miles 1997, 270).

As McCartney later recalled,

This is one of the songs where John and I came nearest to having a dry session. The lyrics I brought in were something to do with golden rings, which are always fatal (to songwriting). "Rings" is fatal anyway—"rings" always rhymes with "things" and I knew it was a bad idea. I came in and I said, "These aren't good lyrics but it's a good tune." Well, we tried, and John couldn't think of anything, and we tried, and eventually it was, "Oh let's leave it, let's get off this one." "No, no. We can do it, we can do it." So we had a break, then we came back to it, and somehow it became "drive-my-car" instead of "golden rings," and then it was wonderful—because this nice tongue-in-cheek idea came. (Miles 1997, 269)

RECORDING SESSIONS

Produced by Martin, "Drive My Car" was recorded at Abbey Road Studios on October 13, 1965.

As Harrison later recalled, his guitar solo for "Drive My Car" was derived from "a lick off 'Respect,' you know, the Otis Redding version. And I played the line on the guitar and Paul laid that with me on the bass. We laid that track down like that. We played the lead part later on top of it" (Dowlding 1989, 114).

PERSONNEL

Lennon: Epiphone Casino
McCartney: Vocal, Höfner 500/1
Harrison: Sonic Blue Fender Stratocaster
Starr: Ludwig Oyster Black Pearl Drums, Cowbell

LEGACY AND INFLUENCE

In 2010, *Rolling Stone* ranked "Drive My Car" as #43 on the magazine's list of *The Beatles' 100 Greatest Songs*.

ALBUM APPEARANCES: *Rubber Soul* (U.K.); *Yesterday . . . and Today*; *The Beatles, 1962–1966*; *Rock 'n' Roll Music*; *Love*.

See also: *Rubber Soul* (U.K. LP).

E

The Early Beatles (LP)

March 22, 1965, Capitol T 2309 (mono)/ST 2309 (stereo)

The Early Beatles was the eighth Beatles album to be released in the United States—the sixth on Capitol Records, along with Vee-Jay Records' *Introducing . . . the Beatles* and United Artists' soundtrack for the *A Hard Day's Night* feature film. It was released on the Capitol label on March 22, 1965. Eleven of the songs on *The Early Beatles* were culled from the *Please Please Me* album—with the exception of "I Saw Her Standing There" (released on *Meet the Beatles!*), "Misery," and "There's a Place"—released in the United Kingdom on March 11, 1963. *The Early Beatles* includes the same contents as the second issue of *Introducing . . . the Beatles*, released by Vee-Jay Records on February 10, 1964. With Vee-Jay's license to distribute Beatles tracks having expired in October 1964, Capitol Records was legally permitted to release the tracks for themselves.

The Early Beatles was deleted from the Beatles' catalogue in 1987, when the group's U.K. albums were distributed as compact-disc releases. A remastered mono and stereo release of *The Early Beatles* was released on April 11, 2006, as part of the box set entitled *The Capitol Albums, Volume 2.*

BACKGROUND

The March 1965 release of *The Early Beatles* marks the only Capitol Records album for which the Beatles failed to chart in the Top 10 during their years as a working rock band. As with other Beatles American releases, Capitol's Dave Dexter, Jr., added reverb and echo effects to the tracks, particularly "Twist and Shout."

TRACK LISTING

Side 1: "Love Me Do"; "Twist and Shout"; "Anna (Go to Him)"; "Chains"; "Boys"; "Ask Me Why."

Side 2: "Please Please Me"; "P.S. I Love You"; "Baby It's You"; "A Taste of Honey"; "Do You Want to Know a Secret."

COVER ARTWORK

The Early Beatles' front cover artwork features the photograph originally printed on the back cover of the *Beatles for Sale* album in the United Kingdom. The photograph was shot by Robert Freeman at dusk near London's Hyde Park. The album's liner notes wax nostalgically about the Beatles' first blush of success, scarcely a year before, on American shores: "Early birds all over the United States—millions of them—got the bug for the Beatles in the first weeks of 1964. The eleven great songs in this album were among those that launched the Beatles. They appeared then on another record label. They appear now for the first time on Capitol—added, with pride and pleasure, to the fine Capitol treasury of Beatles recordings which, together, constitute an unprecedented phenomenon of entertainment history."

CHART PERFORMANCE

U.S.: #43 (certified by the RIAA as "Platinum," with more than 1 million copies sold).

See also: *Beatles for Sale* (LP); *A Hard Day's Night* (Film); *Please Please Me* (LP).

The Ed Sullivan Show (TV Series)

The Beatles' legendary first appearance on Ed Sullivan's popular variety show on February 9, 1964, enjoyed a massive television audience of some 73 million viewers. In many ways, the international phenomenon known as Beatlemania was born that evening when nearly 40 percent of the U.S. population tuned in to witness the band's American debut.

The Beatles had originally come into the orbit of Sullivan (1901–1974) on the morning of October 31, 1963, having just landed at London's Heathrow Airport. Sullivan had flown in from the United States to scout out talent for his popular CBS variety show, when he and his wife Sylvia encountered the thousands of ecstatic fans who had gathered at the airport to welcome their idols home. On November 11, Beatles manager Brian Epstein flew to New York City in order to consummate a deal with the American television impresario, who offered $10,000, plus expenses for the band to perform on three consecutive installments of Sullivan's program.

After "I Want to Hold Your Hand" became the Beatles' first #1 single in the United States on February 1, 1964, Capitol Records invested the unheard-of sum of $40,000 in promoting the band's inaugural American visit. Arriving at New York City's newly christened John F. Kennedy Airport on February 7, the Beatles were greeted with a mob of some 3,000 ecstatic fans. The United States was still reeling from President Kennedy's assassination in November 1963, and the Beatles seemed to offer the kind of good-natured diversion that the nation desperately needed.

As the Beatles prepared for their first performance on *The Ed Sullivan Show*, the CBS Television office was deluged with requests for more than 50,000 passes for a studio that held a mere 703 patrons. Legend has it that criminal activity came to a virtual standstill during the Beatles' first appearance on the show. The Beatles performed five songs in the following order: "All My Loving," "Till There Was You," "She Loves You," "I Saw Her Standing There," and "I Want to Hold Your Hand." Earlier that day, the Beatles taped performances of "Twist and Shout," "Please Please Me," and "I Want to Hold Your Hand" for their second appearance on *The Ed Sullivan Show* on February 16, 1964.

The Beatles appeared on *The Ed Sullivan Show* on six more occasions over the ensuing years. On May 24, 1964, the show broadcast an interview with the band and a taped performance of "You Can't Do That." As the Beatles prepared for their famous Shea Stadium concert in August 1965, they taped six songs for the show's

In one of the most defining moments in music and television history, the Beatles perform on *The Ed Sullivan Show* in New York City on February 9, 1964. From left, in front, are Paul McCartney, George Harrison, and John Lennon. Ringo Starr plays the drums. (AP Photo)

September 12 episode, including "I Feel Fine," "I'm Down," "Act Naturally," "Ticket to Ride," "Yesterday," and "Help!" *The Ed Sullivan Show* broadcast videos for "Rain" and "Paperback Writer" on the June 5, 1966, installment of the program. On February 12, 1967, the band debuted their videos for "Penny Lane" and "Strawberry Fields Forever" on *The Ed Sullivan Show*, which also broadcast their video for "Hello, Goodbye" on the November 26, 1967, episode. The Beatles' final appearance on the show occurred on February 15, 1970, when they debuted their videos for "Two of Us" and "Let It Be."

While the band clearly enjoyed a long and storied relationship with *The Ed Sullivan Show*, their February 1964 appearance left an indelible imprint on the American cultural memory. Comedian Frank Gorshin watched the Beatles' first American performance from the wings of the Ed Sullivan Theater, where he observed the birth of Beatlemania:

> Pandemonium broke out. It was nothing but screams. Kids jumping up and down. I had never witnessed that kind of adulation. The Beatles did their numbers, but I didn't really hear them. I heard nothing but the screams. I was consumed with the idea that they could do this to people—that they could get this kind of reaction. (Gorshin 1999)

The Beatles' legendary appearances on the program were commemorated by the 2006 video release of *The Four Historic Ed Sullivan Shows Featuring the Beatles*, which includes unabridged versions of each episode of the variety show.

See also: Shea Stadium.

"Eight Days a Week" (Lennon–McCartney)

"Eight Days a Week" is a song on the *Beatles for Sale* album. It was the band's second consecutive #1 hit single in the United States, where it was released on February 15, 1965.

AUTHORSHIP AND BACKGROUND

Written by John Lennon and McCartney, "Eight Days a Week" was composed as the Beatles' next U.K. singles release until Lennon's "I Feel Fine" emerged as the favorite, relegating "Eight Days a Week" to inclusion on the *Beatles for Sale* album instead.

As Lennon later recalled, "Both of us wrote it. I think we wrote this when we were trying to write the title song for *Help!* because there was at one time the thought of calling the film, *Eight Arms To Hold You*" (Dowlding 1989, 87).

Often erroneously attributed to Starr, the genesis of the song's title finds its origins in one of McCartney's road trips from London to suburban Weybridge to visit Lennon. "I remember asking the chauffeur once if he was having a good week," McCartney recalled, and the chauffer said, " 'I'm very busy at the moment. I've been working eight days a week.' And I thought, 'Eight days a week! Now there's a title' " (Everett 2001, 262).

"Eight Days a Week" offers yet another example of a purported "Ringoism." Credited as the originator of various malapropisms like some kind of rock 'n' roll Yogi Berra, Starr has also been inaccurately cited as the source for the aforementioned "A Hard Day's Night." Perhaps his well-known—and correctly attributed—title for *Revolver*'s "Tomorrow Never Knows" has prompted his biographers to toast him as pop music's King Malaprop with broad, uncritical strokes?

RECORDING SESSIONS

Produced by Martin, "Eight Days a Week" was recorded at Abbey Road Studios on October 6, 1964, with an additional session on October 18 to append the song's conclusion. "Eight Days a Week" pointedly begins with a fade-in.

PERSONNEL

Lennon: Vocal, Gibson J-160E
McCartney: Höfner 500/1, Backing Vocal
Harrison: Gretsch Country Gentleman
Starr: Ludwig Oyster Black Pearl Drums

CHART PERFORMANCE

U.S.: "Eight Days a Week"/"I Don't Want to Spoil the Party"; February 15, 1965, Capitol 5371: #1 (certified by the RIAA as "Gold," with more than 500,000 copies sold).

LEGACY AND INFLUENCE

In 2010, *Rolling Stone* ranked "Eight Days a Week" as #34 on the magazine's list of *The Beatles' 100 Greatest Songs*.

ALBUM APPEARANCES: *Beatles for Sale*; *Beatles VI*; *The Beatles, 1962–1966*; *20 Greatest Hits*; *Anthology 1*; *1*.

See also: *Beatles for Sale* (LP); *Help!* (Film); *Revolver* (U.K. LP).

"Eleanor Rigby" (Lennon–McCartney)

"Eleanor Rigby" is a song on the Beatles' *Revolver* album. It was the band's 12th consecutive #1 single in the United Kingdom, where it was released on August 5, 1966, as a double A-side with "Yellow Submarine," which also topped the charts.

AUTHORSHIP AND BACKGROUND

Written by McCartney with assistance from Lennon, "Eleanor Rigby" is one of the most contested compositions, along with "In My Life," in the Lennon–McCartney catalogue.

McCartney had seen the name "Rigby" on a storefront in Bristol, where Jane Asher was starring in a production of John Dighton's *The Happiest Days of Your Life*. His protagonist's first name found its inspiration in Eleanor Bron, the British actress who played one of the Eastern cult leaders in *Help!* As for the song's musical origins, McCartney recalls that "I wrote it at the piano, just vamping an E-minor chord; letting that stay as a vamp and putting a melody over it, just danced over the top of it. It has almost Asian Indian rhythms" (Miles 1997, 281). With the threads of the melody in hand, he began tinkering with a variety of different lyrics: "I was just mumbling around and eventually came up with these words: 'Picks up the rice in a church where the wedding has been.' Those words just fell out like stream-of-consciousness stuff, but they started to set the tone of it all, because you then have to ask yourself, what did I mean?" (Miles 1997, 282). After establishing the character of Eleanor Rigby as one of the song's central characters, McCartney opted to turn the song over to Lennon because the lyrics were incomplete (Miles 1997, 283). McCartney recalled a convivial writing session with his songwriting partner: "We sat around, laughing, got stoned and finished it off" (Dowlding 1989, 134).

In sharp contrast with McCartney's recollections, Lennon remembered composing some "70 percent" of the lyrics for "Eleanor Rigby." McCartney's response? "Yeah. About half a line" (Dowlding 1989, 134, 135). Lennon admits that McCartney and Harrison invented the song's familiar chorus—"Ah, look at all the lonely people"—during the first session: "He and George were settling on that as I left the studio to go to the toilet, and I heard the lyric and turned around and said, 'That's *it!*'" Otherwise, Lennon attributes the first verse to McCartney, while claiming that "the rest [of the lyrics] are basically mine" (Lennon and Ono 2000, 139, 140). Yet Pete Shotton agreed entirely with McCartney's memories about the composition of "Eleanor Rigby." Shotton visited the studio during the session in which the song was first recorded: "Though John was to take credit, in one of his last interviews, for most of the lyrics," Shotton averred, "my own recollection is that 'Eleanor Rigby' was one 'Lennon–McCartney' classic in which John's contribution was virtually nil" (Dowlding 1989, 134, 135). It is worth noting that Lennon's own memories of the session were considerably tainted by what he perceived to be McCartney's intentionally hurtful behavior:

> Well, he knew he had a song. But by that time he didn't want to ask for my help, and we were sitting around with Mal Evans and Neil Aspinall, so he said to us, "Hey, you guys, finish up the lyrics." Now I was there with Mal, a telephone installer who was our road manager, and Neil, who was a student accountant [and the Beatles' personal assistant], and I was insulted and hurt that Paul had

just thrown it out in the air. He actually meant he wanted *me* to do it, and of course there isn't a line of theirs in the song. But . . . that's the kind of person he is. "Here, finish these lyrics up," like to *anybody* around." (Lennon and Ono 2000, 139)

As Lennon remarked about McCartney during a September 1980 interview, "How *dare* he throw it out in the air like that?" (Everett 1999, 11).

While Lennon and McCartney disputed the nature of the authorship for "Eleanor Rigby" and "In My Life," McCartney later pointed out that "I find it very gratifying that out of everything we wrote, we only appear to disagree over two songs" (Miles 1997, 278).

RECORDING SESSIONS

Produced by Martin, the instrumental track for "Eleanor Rigby" was recorded at Abbey Road Studios on April 28, 1966, with overdubbing sessions for the vocals on April 29 and June 6.

Martin created the song's haunting string arrangement—ostensibly after receiving detailed instructions from McCartney—during the lengthy first session on April 28, 1966, in which Lennon and McCartney conversed with the producer via the studio's intercom system (Lewisohn 1988, 219). According to Lennon, McCartney's idea for a string accompaniment for "Eleanor Rigby" came via Asher, who had recently introduced him to the work of Vivaldi. As McCartney later recalled, "I thought of the backing, but it was George Martin who finished it off. I just go bash, bash on the piano. He knows what I mean" (Dowlding 1989, 135).

For his arrangement for "Eleanor Rigby," Martin claimed to have drawn his inspiration from Bernard Herrmann's recent orchestral score for François Truffaut's *Fahrenheit 451* (1966). Yet as Kevin Ryan and Brian Kehew observe, it is difficult to believe that *Fahrenheit 451* served as Martin's primary influence, given that it "was not released until November of 1966, seven months after the recording of 'Eleanor Rigby'; indeed, Herrmann reportedly only wrote the score in June of that year. The more obvious source of inspiration was Herrmann's 1960 score for Alfred Hitchcock's *Psycho*, which prominently featured the same scraping staccato string effect Martin employed here in 1966" (Ryan and Kehew 2006, 422). As the composer behind the terrifying soundtrack for Alfred Hitchcock's *Psycho* (1960), Herrmann might seem, at first blush, an unlikely model for the musical arrangement of a pop song. Yet in retrospect, Martin's choice was a stroke of genius. With its razor-sharp tempo, Martin's arrangement imbues McCartney's narrative about the perils of loneliness with an appropriately chilling veneer. Instructed by McCartney to establish a "really biting" sound, Geoff Emerick attempted to capture the songwriter's vision by placing the microphones unusually close to the string octet, which consisted of four violins, two violas, and two cellos. The studio musicians were visibly irritated by the idea of playing in front of microphones that were as little as an inch away from their strings. As Emerick recalled, "The musicians were horrified! One of them gave me a look of disdain, rolled his eyes to the ceiling, and said under his breath, 'You can't do that, you know.'" When Emerick returned to the control room, he could clearly hear the studio musicians sliding their chairs away from the microphones that he had just set up. The musicians finally complied with Emerick's mike placement, but only after Martin ordered them to remain in position (Emerick and Massey 2006, 127). As for McCartney's vocal, the singer double-tracked his voice, which occurs in the right channel of the mono recording, only to return to both channels when Lennon and Harrison join him for the chorus. It makes for a genuinely eerie effect that is bolstered by Martin's striking arrangement.

PERSONNEL

Lennon: Harmony Vocal
McCartney: Vocal
Harrison: Harmony Vocal
Studio Musicians: String Octet Accompaniment conducted by Martin
Tony Gilbert, Sidney Sax, John Sharpe, Jürgen Hess: Violin
Stephen Shingles, John Underwood: Viola
Derek Simpson, Norman Jones: Cello

CHART PERFORMANCE

U.K.: "Eleanor Rigby"/"Yellow Submarine"; August 5, 1966, Parlophone R 5493: #1.

U.S.: "Eleanor Rigby"/"Yellow Submarine"; August 8, 1966, Capitol 5715: #11 (certified by the RIAA as "Gold," with more than 500,000 copies sold).

LEGACY AND INFLUENCE

In 1967, "Eleanor Rigby" earned a Grammy Award for Best Contemporary Solo Vocal Performance at the 9th Grammy Awards.

In 1967, "Eleanor Rigby" was honored as the *New Musical Express*'s "Single of the Year."

In 2000, *Mojo* magazine ranked "Eleanor Rigby" as #19 on the magazine's list of *The 100 Greatest Songs of All Time.*

In 2002, "Eleanor Rigby" was inducted into the National Academy of Recording Arts and Sciences Grammy Hall of Fame.

In 2004, *Rolling Stone* ranked "Eleanor Rigby" as #138 on the magazine's list of *The 500 Greatest Songs of All Time.*

In 2006, *Pitchfork* ranked "Eleanor Rigby" as #47 on the Web magazine's list of *The 200 Greatest Songs of the 1960s.*

In 2010, *Rolling Stone* ranked "Eleanor Rigby" as #22 on the magazine's list of *The Beatles' 100 Greatest Songs.*

In October 2012, BBC Local Radio listeners ranked "Eleanor Rigby" as their 5th favorite Beatles song in a poll conducted in commemoration of the 50th anniversary of "Love Me Do," the band's first single.

ALBUM APPEARANCES: *Revolver* (U.K.); *Revolver* (U.S.); *A Collection of Beatles Oldies*; *The Beatles, 1962–1966*; *20 Greatest Hits*; *Anthology 2*; *Yellow Submarine Songtrack*; *1.*

See also: *Revolver* (U.K. LP).

Emerick, Geoff (1946–)

Born in London in 1946, Emerick had joined the staff of EMI's (Electrical and Mechanical Industries) Abbey Road Studios as an assistant engineer at the tender age of 16. His second day on the job was September 6, 1962, the very date of the evening session when the Beatles recorded "How Do You Do It" and "Love Me Do." He also worked the July 1963 session in which the group first unveiled "She Loves You" for Martin's consideration, and he later took part in the equally historic recording sessions for "I Want to Hold Your Hand" and "A Hard Day's Night." For quite some time after that—as the young EMI staffer was promoted from assistant engineer to lacquer cutter to mastering engineer to balance engineer—the Beatles worked outside of Emerick's earshot. During this period, he worked on recordings by Judy Garland and the Hollies, while also serving as sound engineer for Manfred Mann's #1 U.K. hit "Pretty Flamingo."

At Martin's invitation, Emerick became the Beatles' sound engineer in 1966 after Norman "Normal" Smith left their mixing board in order to produce Pink Floyd's debut album. His first recording as the Beatles' sound engineer was "Tomorrow Never Knows" for the *Revolver* album in 1966. For the track, he famously recorded Lennon's vocal through a rotating Leslie speaker in order to capture the sound that he wanted. The following year, he was instrumental in the recording of the band's landmark *Sgt. Pepper's Lonely Hearts Club* album. In July 1968, he left the Beatles' fold after becoming exhausted with the bandmates' increasing tensions, as well as with fledgling producer Chris Thomas. In 1969, Lennon and McCartney coaxed Emerick's return by inviting him to work on "The Ballad of John and Yoko" single, setting the stage for Emerick's efforts on the Beatles' swan song *Abbey Road.* In the post-Beatles years, he worked on behalf of Apple Corps, overseeing the construction and the installation of Apple Studio in the basement of Apple's Savile Row headquarters.

Since 1970, Emerick has worked on several recordings for McCartney, including Wings' *Band on the Run* (1973) and *London Town* (1973), as well as his *Flaming Pie* (1997) solo album. He has worked with numerous other acts, including

Elvis Costello, Badfinger, Cheap Trick, Jeff Beck, Supertramp, Split Enz, America, and Kate Bush, among others. In 2004, he enjoyed critical acclaim for his efforts on Nellie McKay's debut album *Get Away from Me*. In 2007, he produced a 40th-anniversary tribute to *Sgt. Pepper's Lonely Hearts Club Band* for broadcast on BBC Radio, with contributions from such artists as Oasis and the Killers.

Since 1984, Emerick has lived in Los Angeles. In 2006, he published his memoirs, entitled *Here, There, and Everywhere: My Life Recording the Music of the Beatles*, with music journalist Howard Massey. He has received four Grammy Awards, including three for his work on the *Sgt. Pepper's Lonely Hearts Club Band*, *Revolver*, and *Band on the Run* albums.

See also: *Abbey Road* (LP); Martin, George; *Revolver* (U.K. LP); *Revolver* (U.S. LP); *Sgt. Pepper's Lonely Hearts Club Band* (LP); Thomas, Chris.

"The End" (Lennon–McCartney)

"The End" is a song on the Beatles' *Abbey Road* album. It is the eighth and final song in the *Abbey Road* Medley.

AUTHORSHIP AND BACKGROUND

McCartney's "The End"—with key contributions from his bandmates in the form of a series of memorable solos—affords the medley with a concluding piece in the form of an old-time rock 'n' roll revue in which each musician shows off his chops. McCartney appropriately concludes the song and the medley with a quasi-Shakespearean couplet.

As Lennon later observed,

> That's Paul again, the unfinished song, right? Just a piece at the end. He had a line in it, "And in the end the love you take / Is equal to the love you make," which is a very cosmic, philosophical line—which again proves that if he wants to, he can think. (Dowlding 1989, 292)

RECORDING SESSIONS

Produced by Martin, "The End" was recorded at Abbey Road Studios on July 23, 1969, with several overdubbing sessions held in August. It was recorded under the working title of "Ending." Emerick captured the sound of Starr's rumbling drum solo by placing a dozen microphones around Starr's kit.

Lennon, McCartney, and Harrison followed Starr's solo with a series of two-bar guitar solos. As Emerick later recalled, "John, Paul, and George looked like they had gone back in time, like they were kids again, playing together for the sheer enjoyment of it. More than anything, they reminded me of gunslingers, with their guitars strapped on, looks of steely-eyed resolve, determined to outdo one another. Yet there was no animosity, no tension at all—you could tell that they were simply having fun" (Emerick and Massey 2006, 295).

PERSONNEL

Lennon: Epiphone Casino
McCartney: Vocal, Rickenbacker 4001S, Fender Esquire, Piano
Harrison: Gibson Les Paul Standard
Starr: Ludwig Hollywood Maple Drums
Studio Musicians: Orchestral Accompaniment (12 Violins, 4 Violas, 4 Cellos, Double Bass, 4 Horns, 3 Trumpets, Trombone, Bass Trombone) conducted by Martin

LEGACY AND INFLUENCE

In 2007, *Q Magazine* ranked "The End" as #7 on the magazine's list of *The 20 Greatest Guitar Tracks*.

ALBUM APPEARANCES: *Abbey Road*; *Anthology 3*; *Love*; *Tomorrow Never Knows*.

See also: *Abbey Road* (LP); *The Beatles Anthology, Volume 3* (LP).

Epstein, Brian (1934–1967)

Born in Liverpool to Harry and Malka "Queenie" Epstein on September 19, 1934, Brian Samuel Epstein had been educated at a succession of schools before settling upon Wrekin College in Shropshire. In 1950, he entered the business world as a furniture salesman in his father Harry's prosperous department store on Walton Road. After a stint in the National Service, he returned to Liverpool, and Harry subsequently assigned his son to manage the record department. He only completed half of his two-year term in the National Service. At one point, he was charged with impersonating an officer after being saluted, incorrectly, by a sentry. As a result, he was confined to barracks and later discharged on "medical grounds." With his wide-ranging knowledge of classical music, he transformed it into a profitable business in short order. Yet to his parents' great chagrin, he decided to leave Liverpool in order to pursue an actor's life at London's Royal Academy of Dramatic Art (RADA). After dropping out of the RADA in his third term, he returned to his hometown once again. His indefatigable father then opened Clarendon Furnishings, an upscale furniture store on the Wirral peninsula, and installed him as manager. In 1958, Harry decided to capitalize on the booming record business by opening up a NEMS (North End Music Stores) location at Great Charlotte Street under his management. Although his early years had been distinguished by a general inability to fit in—he was homosexual, which was criminalized in Great Britain at the time—Epstein had proved highly adept at consolidating NEMS's success, and within a few years, he was in charge of the family's entire record operation. His homosexuality forced him to lead a double-life. Given his elite social status in Liverpool, he was often the target of blackmailers and consequently enjoyed few genuinely happy love affairs. As Philip Norman points out, he was "attracted to what homosexuals call the rough trade—to the dockers and laborers of whom their kind go in greatest mortal terror. Those who sought the rough trade in Liverpool in 1957 paid a high price, even in that currency of damnation. Rebuffed or accepted, they still went in fear. If there were not a beating up, then there would probably, later on, be extortion and blackmail" (Norman 1981, 132).

With the August 3, 1961, issue of *Mersey Beat*, Epstein had even begun authoring a regular column entitled "Record Releases by Brian Epstein of NEMS."

By the early 1960s, Epstein operated two NEMS outlets in Liverpool, including stores on Great Charlotte Street and Whitechapel, the latter of which was less than 200 yards away from the Cavern Club. On October 28, 1961, a patron named Raymond Jones reportedly entered NEMS—the largest record outlet in Liverpool and throughout the North Country—and requested a copy of the Beatles' "My Bonnie" from the store's owner, 27-year-old Epstein. In his autobiography *A Cellarful of Noise* (1964), he claims to have been unfamiliar with the Beatles before Jones's visit on that fateful day: "The name 'Beatle' meant nothing to me though I vaguely recalled seeing it on a poster advertising a university dance at New Brighton Tower, and I remembered thinking it was an odd and purposeless spelling" (Epstein 1998, 94, 95). Given his association with *Mersey Beat*—and its regular cover stories about the band—it is doubtful that the Beatles had so thoroughly eluded his notice. In addition to the *Mersey Beat*'s lavish attention upon the band, the Beatles were featured on numerous posters throughout Epstein's record stores. As Bill Harry pointed out, "He would have had to have been blind—or ignorant—not to have noticed their name" (Spitz 2005, 266). A number of music historians have gone so far as to suggest that Epstein manufactured Jones out of thin air (Lewisohn 1988, 34). Yet in Epstein's defense, Spencer Leigh recently located the elusive Raymond Jones, now retired and living in Spain. As Jones remarked, "No one will ever take away from me that it was me who spoke to Brian Epstein and then he went to the Cavern to see [the Beatles] for himself" (Leigh 2004, 21).

In an event, on November 9, 1961, Epstein attended a lunchtime performance by the group at the Cavern in the company of his assistant manager at NEMS, Alistair Taylor. They descended into the cellar, where the club's DJ, Bob Wooler, announced that Epstein of NEMS (North End Music Stores) was in attendance. Mesmerized by their performance, Epstein met with the Beatles backstage, where he was greeted by Harrison: "Hello there. What brings Mr. Epstein here?" As with so many others who encountered the group, Epstein enjoyed their charm and good humor. But more important, he was impressed with the reaction that they garnered from the kids in the audience. "They gave a captivating and honest show and they had very considerable magnetism," he wrote in his autobiography. "I loved their ad-libs and I was fascinated by this, to me, new music with its pounding bass beat and its vast engulfing sound" (Epstein 1998, 98, 99).

Even as he walked away from the Cavern that day, Epstein was already thinking about managing the band. After an initial meeting on December 3, 1961, with the group—sans McCartney, who was allegedly at home taking a bath—Epstein began to make inquiries about the Beatles. Not surprisingly, Allan Williams warned him about what he believed to be the band's lack of ethics. "I wouldn't touch 'em with a f—ing barge pole," he told Epstein (Spitz 2005, 274). But Epstein was once and truly hooked, and at a meeting on December 10, the Beatles accepted Epstein as their manager. They signed a formal, five-year contract with him on January 24, 1962, at Pete Best's house. Epstein pointedly declined to sign the contract in order to allow his clients to withdraw from the agreement at any time. Over the next few months, he entreated the band to improve their demeanor on stage—no more swearing, no more eating between songs. For his part, he ensured that their regular fee at the Cavern Club was doubled, and he vowed, more important, to win them a record deal with a major label. While the Beatles were famously rejected

by Decca Records after their January 1962 audition in London, Epstein doggedly pursued a record deal for the band, eventually winning a Parlophone Records contract for them after a June 1962 audition with Martin.

Over the next four years, Epstein emerged as a genuine rock 'n' roll impresario, working as the veritable architect of Beatlemania—both in England and abroad—by consolidating the band's fame through thousands of concert appearances, press conferences, and photo opportunities. He also shrewdly negotiated the Beatles' intermittent film appearances in the mid-1960s, allowing them to circulate their music and image among a variety of different demographics.

Brian Epstein, manager of the Beatles. (Michael Ochs Archives/Getty Images)

While he suffered key missteps along the way—most notably, the disastrous Seltaeb negotiation that forfeited many of the band's key marketing rights, as well as the traumatic Far Eastern leg of their German and Japanese tour during the summer of 1966—the Beatles' manager succeeded in exporting the Mersey Beat sound associated with a host of the group's Liverpool contemporaries. In so doing, he was a central cog in the establishment of the British Invasion that swept across North American shores in the months and years after the Beatles' legendary February 9, 1964, appearance on *The Ed Sullivan Show*. In addition to negotiating such landmark Beatles moments as their appearances at Carnegie Hall, the Hollywood Bowl, and Shea Stadium, Epstein assisted the bandmates in traversing the minefield associated with "The Beatles Are Bigger than Jesus Christ" controversy during the summer of 1966 that culminated in their final paying concert appearance at San Francisco's Candlestick Park on August 9 of that same year.

Yet for Epstein, the posttouring world made for a bitter, unfulfilling life. As the architect of Beatlemania, he had been on a high-octane entertainment carousel for nearly five years, and toiling in its shadow was too much for him to bear. In late September 1966, he had dinner at his posh Chapel Street home with Peter Brown, who had recently moved into the manager's house in order to look after him in his erratic state. Later that evening, Brown discovered that his roommate had fallen unconscious in his bedroom. Unable to rouse Epstein, Brown took him to a private hospital in Richmond, where the medical staff pumped his stomach and saved his life. While Epstein described the event as a "foolish accident," Brown knew better. The next morning, he found an empty bottle of Nembutal and the manager's would-be suicide note: "I can't deal with this anymore," Epstein had written. "It's beyond me, and I just can't go on" (Spitz 2005, 647). For some members of Epstein's inner circle, his words proved to be prophetic. On August 27, 1967, as the Beatles enjoyed their spiritual excursion to Wales in the company of Maharishi Mahesh Yogi, the world learned the news of Epstein's untimely death, at the relatively tender age of 32.

As it happens, during one of his last interviews, Epstein expressed his all-consuming fear of loneliness: "I hope I'll never be lonely, although, actually, one inflicts loneliness on oneself to a certain extent" (Badman 2001, 299). When the London nightlife failed to rouse his aching soul during that fateful final weekend, he drove home in his beloved Bentley, dying alone in his bedroom. "At that time," Taylor remembered, "Brian was taking all sorts of medication. He lived on pills—pills to wake him up, pills to send him to sleep, pills to keep him lively, pills to quieten him down, pills to cure his indigestion" (Taylor 2003, 187). While the shadow of suicide lingered over Epstein's sudden death, his passing was officially ruled as an accidental overdose of barbiturates mixed with alcohol. As Harrison later recalled, "In those days everybody was topping themselves accidentally" (Spitz 2005, 718). But nothing could have prepared the Beatles for life without

Epstein. They loved him, to be sure, and they were thunderstruck with grief. But they also intuitively understood his role as the architect of Beatlemania and their attendant superstardom. The tragedy of his untimely death notwithstanding, he also existed—for better or worse—at the center of their financial vortex. He had been the keeper of their business affairs, and his sudden absence from their world had left a power vacuum in his place. And it was a void that they were in absolutely no way prepared to fill. "I knew that we were in trouble then," Lennon later remarked. "I didn't really have any misconceptions about our ability to do anything other than play music. And I was scared. I thought, 'We've f—ing had it'" (Lennon 1970, 25).

Epstein's death indeed had far-reaching ramifications, as the Beatles' business affairs began to spiral out of control during the development of Apple Corps, the fallout associated with Lennon and McCartney's unsuccessful 1969 effort to acquire Northern Songs, and the eventual receivership of their collective affairs under the aegis of American businessman Allen Klein. Although it is perhaps disingenuous to suggest that the band's autumn 1969 disbandment might have been delayed or even avoided with Epstein at the band's helm, it is worth noting that Epstein successfully guided the group's business affairs by employing the finest minds in the London financial establishment to guide their business empire. With his death, the Beatles no longer followed such a course, paving the way for other parties—such as Robert Stigwood and later Klein—to enter the fray, while also leaving the bandmates themselves to attempt to create their own business solutions through Apple Corps and similarly half-baked efforts.

In a 1997 BBC interview, McCartney remarked that "if anyone was the fifth Beatle, it was Brian." In one of the most poignant memorials to Epstein, Lennon composed "You've Got to Hide Your Love Away" for the Beatles' *Help!* album in 1965. The composition is generally understood to be Lennon's coy allusion to Epstein's homosexuality—and the associated pain that comes from secreting the very truth and nature about oneself from the world. In "You've Got to Hide Your Love Away," Lennon does his best Bob Dylan impersonation and sings about loneliness and the bitter effects that it stamps upon its victims. Epstein was also memorialized in the group's "Free as a Bird" video as part of *The Beatles Anthology* project in the mid-1990s. As the video nears its conclusion, Epstein can be seen donning a scarf. In 2012, it was announced that British actor Benedict Cumberbatch would play Epstein in the as-of-yet-untitled biographical film about the Beatles' manager to be directed by Paul McGuigan. Over the years, Epstein has appeared as a character in several movies about the Beatles. Brian Jameson played the role of Epstein in *Birth of the Beatles* (1979), while Jamie Glover plays him in the 2000 television movie *In His Life: The John Lennon Story*. In the most notorious film about the Beatles' manager, Christopher Münch's *The Hours and Times* (1991) offers a fictive imagining of an intimate encounter between Lennon and the Beatles' manager during a 1963 Spanish vacation.

See also: Apple Corps, Ltd.; "The Beatles Are Bigger than Jesus Christ"; Best, Pete; The Cavern Club; *The Ed Sullivan Show* (TV Series); *Help!* (U.K. LP); Klein, Allen; Tours, 1960–1966; Williams, Allan.

Evans, Mal (1935–1976)

Born in Liverpool on May 27, 1935, Mal Evans was a close friend and associate of the Beatles, working as their road manager and confidant for many years. In his early years, he worked as a telephone engineer and as a bouncer at the Cavern Club. In 1961, he married his wife Lily, and their son Gary was born later that same year. Known as the "Gentle Giant" and "Big Mal," the imposing Evans was a natural choice to serve as bouncer at the Cavern, where he came into the orbit of the Beatles and their manager Brian Epstein, who hired Evans as the band's road manager in August 1962. Along with Neil Aspinall, Evans ferried the Beatles around in the band's van and set up their equipment while on tour. In addition to being the Beatles all-around gofer during this period, he also forged numerous autographs for them, given their deluge of fan requests.

Evans was with the Beatles during many of the most memorable moments in their career, including meeting Bob Dylan in 1964, playing their famous Hollywood Bowl shows in 1964 and 1965, their near-disastrous visit to the Philippines in July 1966, and their farewell concert at San Francisco's Candlestick Park in August 1966. After an impromptu visit to Kenya with McCartney in 1966, he and the Beatles' bassist created the concept that eventually flowered into the *Sgt. Pepper's Lonely Hearts Club Band* (1967) album. In addition to assisting with the filming of the *Magical Mystery Tour* television movie, he accompanied the band to visit the Maharishi Mahesh Yogi in Rishikesh, India, in February 1968. He was also present when McCartney married Linda Eastman in March 1969 at the Marylebone Registry Office. Later that year, he worked as roadie for the Plastic Ono Band's concert debut at the one-day Sweet Toronto Peace Festival in September 1969. He held an executive-level position with Apple Corps until Klein's reorganization of the company. Klein fired Evans in 1970, only to reinstate him after complaints from the now-former Beatles.

Over the years, Evans participated in numerous Beatles recordings, including his work as a member of the chorus on "Yellow Submarine." He later played harmonica on "Being for the Benefit of Mr. Kite!" For "A Day in the Life," he famously set the alarm clock before McCartney's middle-eight. In addition to playing the trumpet on "Helter Skelter," he provided sound effects for "You Know My Name (Look Up the Number)." He also appeared in the Beatles' movies, including *A Hard Day's Night*, *Help!*, *Magical Mystery Tour*, and *Let It Be*, where he can be seen quite prominently during the Rooftop Concert.

In the post-Beatles years, Evans continued to work for Apple Corps, producing Badfinger's Top 10 hit "No Matter What." He also assisted Harrison with *All Things*

Must Pass and Lennon with the *John Lennon/Plastic Ono Band* album. He coauthored "You and Me (Babe)" with Harrison for Starr's best-selling *Ringo* album. In 1973, he separated from his wife and relocated to Los Angeles, where Lennon was in the throes of his "Lost Weekend." At the time, he was working on his memoirs, to be entitled *Living the Beatles' Legend.* Suffering from depression during this period, he was living in Los Angeles with his girlfriend Fran Hughes. On January 5, 1976, a groggy and confused Evans, who had recently taken Valium, was killed after he fled to his bedroom with an air rifle. Police officers arrived shortly afterwards, firing six shots at Evans and killing him instantly. In later years, Evans' diaries, personal papers, photographs, Beatles lyrics, and

Mal Evans, former Beatles' road manager, assists Ringo Starr in a London recording studio in June 1971. (Estate Of Keith Morris/Redferns/ Getty Images)

other effects have slowly paraded through auction houses and have been traded among private collectors. In August 2012, a one-man play about Evans' life entitled *Beatle Mal's Legendary Band* was staged at the Edinburgh Festival Fringe.

See also: Aspinall, Neil; The Cavern Club; Epstein, Brian; *A Hard Day's Night* (Film); *Help!* (Film); *Let It Be* (Film); *Magical Mystery Tour* (TV Film); Plastic Ono Band; *Sgt. Pepper's Lonely Hearts Club Band* (LP).

"Every Little Thing" (Lennon–McCartney)

"Every Little Thing" is a song on the *Beatles for Sale* album.

AUTHORSHIP AND BACKGROUND

Written by McCartney, "Every Little Thing" was composed in the music room of Asher's home on 57 Wimpole Street in London.

As McCartney later observed, " 'Every Little Thing,' like most of the stuff I did, was my attempt at the next single, but it became an album filler rather than the great almighty single. It didn't have quite what was required" (Miles 1997, 174).

RECORDING SESSIONS

Produced by Martin, "Every Little Thing" was recorded in nine takes at Abbey Road Studios on September 29 and 30, 1964.

During the recording, Starr pounded on a tympani to punctuate the chorus: "Every little thing she does [boom! boom!] she does for me, / And you know the things she does [boom! boom!] she does for me."

PERSONNEL

Lennon: Vocal, Gibson J-160E
McCartney: Vocal, Höfner 500/1, Piano
Harrison: Rickenbacker 360/12
Starr: Ludwig Oyster Black Pearl Drums, Tympani

LEGACY AND INFLUENCE

In 2010, *Rolling Stone* ranked "Every Little Thing" as #91 on the magazine's list of *The Beatles' 100 Greatest Songs*.

ALBUM APPEARANCES: *Beatles for Sale*; *Beatles VI*.

See also: *Beatles for Sale* (LP); *Let It Be . . . Naked* (LP).

"Everybody's Got Something to Hide Except Me and My Monkey" (Lennon–McCartney)

"Everybody's Got Something to Hide Except Me and My Monkey" is a song on *The Beatles* (*The White Album*).

AUTHORSHIP AND BACKGROUND

Written by Lennon, "Everybody's Got Something to Hide Except Me and My Monkey" finds its origins during the Beatles' 1968 visit to India. "Come on is such a joy" was a favorite saying of the Maharishi's (Spizer 2003, 112).

"It was about me and Yoko," Lennon later remarked. "Everybody seemed to be paranoid except for us two, who were in the glow of love" (Dowlding 1989, 241). Lennon later admitted that the song's monkey references offered a subtle allusion to the couple's growing heroin habit at the time.

An early version of "Everybody's Got Something to Hide Except Me and My Monkey" was recorded in May 1968 at Harrison's Kinfauns studio as part of the Esher Tapes.

RECORDING SESSIONS

Produced by Martin, "Everybody's Got Something to Hide Except Me and My Monkey" was recorded under the working title of "Come On, Come On" at Abbey Road Studios on June 27, 1968, with overdubbing sessions on July 1 and 23.

The thundering entrance of the guitar and bass riffs at the conclusion of "Everybody's Got Something to Hide Except Me and My Monkey" were achieved through double-tracking the instruments.

PERSONNEL

Lennon: Vocal, Epiphone Casino
McCartney: Rickenbacker 4001S
Harrison: Gibson SG Standard, Fire Bell
Starr: Ludwig Oyster Black Pearl Drums

LEGACY AND INFLUENCE

In 2010, *Rolling Stone* ranked "Everybody's Got Something to Hide Except Me and My Monkey" as #73 on the magazine's list of *The Beatles' 100 Greatest Songs*.

ALBUM APPEARANCE: *The Beatles (The White Album)*.

See also: *The Beatles (The White Album)* (LP).

"Everybody's Trying to Be My Baby" (Perkins)

"Everybody's Trying to Be My Baby" is a song on the *Beatles for Sale* album.

AUTHORSHIP AND BACKGROUND

Written by Carl Perkins, "Everybody's Trying to Be My Baby" borrows its title from a 1930s-era song by country songwriter Rex Griffin. Originally included on the *Dance Album of . . . Carl Perkins* (1957), "Everybody's Trying to Be My Baby" was later anthologized on Perkins's *Teen Beat: The Best of Carl Perkins* (1958). The latter album also included "Honey Don't" and "Matchbox," two additional songs for which the Beatles recorded cover versions.

RECORDING SESSIONS

Produced by Martin, "Everybody's Trying to Be My Baby" was recorded at Abbey Road Studios on October 18, 1964. Harrison's vocal is heavily treated with STEED (single-tape echo and echo delay) in order to achieve a live-sounding echo effect. In November 1964, the Beatles recorded a version of "Everybody's Trying to Be My Baby" for the BBC's *Saturday Club* radio show that was later included on the *Live at the BBC* album. In June 1963, they recorded yet another version for the BBC's *Pop Go the Beatles* program.

PERSONNEL

    Lennon: Gibson J-160E, Tambourine
    McCartney: Höfner 500/1
    Harrison: Vocal, Gretsch Country Gentleman
    Starr: Ludwig Oyster Black Pearl Drums

ALBUM APPEARANCES: *Beatles for Sale*; *Beatles '65*; *Rock 'n' Roll Music*; *Live! at the Star-Club in Hamburg, Germany; 1962*; *Live at the BBC*; *Anthology 2*.

See also: *Beatles for Sale* (LP).

F

"Fixing a Hole" (Lennon–McCartney)

"Fixing a Hole" is a song on the Beatles' *Sgt. Pepper's Lonely Hearts Club Band* album.

AUTHORSHIP AND BACKGROUND

Written by McCartney, "Fixing a Hole" may have found its roots in the songwriter's contemporaneous repairs to the roof of his farm near Campbeltown, Scotland.

Interestingly, McCartney later remarked that

> "Fixing a Hole" is really about the fans who hang around outside your door day and night. . . . If they only knew the best way to get in is not to do that, because obviously anyone who is going to be straight and be like a real friend is going to get in—but they simply stand there and give off the impression, "Don't let us in." I actually do enjoy having them in. I used to do it more, but I don't as much now because I invited one in once and the next day she was in *The Daily Mirror* with her mother saying we were going to get married. (Cadogan 2008, 194)

"That's Paul," Lennon remembered during one of his last interviews, "again writing a good lyric" (Cadogan 2008, 194).

RECORDING SESSIONS

Produced by Martin, "Fixing a Hole" was recorded at London's Regent Sound Studio on February 9, 1967, with an additional overdubbing session on February 21 at Abbey Road Studios. The Regent Sound session marked a rare Beatles session that had occurred beyond the confines of Abbey Road Studios, which was unavailable that evening. It was the first time the Beatles had worked outside of Abbey Road since their recordings at Paris's Pathé Marconi Studios in January 1964.

With McCartney effecting a sprightly harpsichord and George Harrison playing a quirky distorted solo on his Sonic Blue Strat, "Fixing a Hole" finds McCartney refashioning a line—"Well, there's a hole in the roof where the rain pours in"—from Elvis Presley's "We're Gonna Move" (Everett 1999, 107).

The evening of the first "Getting Better" recording session was noteworthy for other reasons. "Strange story," McCartney later recalled, "the night we went to record that, a guy turned up at my house who announced himself as Jesus. So I took him to the session. You know—couldn't harm, I thought. Introduced Jesus to the guys. Quite reasonable about it. But that was it. Last we ever saw of Jesus" (Dowlding 1989, 170).

PERSONNEL

> Lennon: Fender Jazz Bass
> McCartney: Vocal, Harpsichord
> Harrison: Sonic Blue Fender Stratocaster
> Starr: Ludwig Oyster Black Pearl Drums, Maracas

CONTROVERSY

For some listeners, "Fixing a Hole" takes on associations with heroin abuse. Yet as McCartney observed, "This song is just about the hole in the road where the rain gets in; a good old analogy—the hole in your make-up which lets the rain and stops your mind from going where it will. It's you interfering with things. If you're a junkie sitting in a room fixing a hole then that's what it will mean to you, but when I wrote it I meant if there's a crack or the room is uncolorful, then I'll paint it" (Cadogan 2008, 194).

ALBUM APPEARANCE: *Sgt. Pepper's Lonely Hearts Club Band.*

See also: *Sgt. Pepper's Lonely Hearts Club Band* (LP).

"Flying" (Harrison–Lennon–McCartney–Starr)

"Flying" is a song on the Beatles' *Magical Mystery Tour* album. It is one of the very few songs credited to all four Beatles as composers.

AUTHORSHIP AND BACKGROUND

"Flying" was written explicitly as soundtrack music for the *Magical Mystery Tour* made-for-television film.

As McCartney later recalled, " 'Flying' was an instrumental that we needed for [the film] *Magical Mystery Tour* so in the studio one night I suggested to the guys that we made something up. I said, 'We can keep it very, very simple, we can make it a 12-bar blues. We need a little bit of a theme and a little bit of a backing.' I wrote the melody, otherwise it's just a 12-bar backing thing. It's played on the Mellotron, on a trombone setting. It's credited to all four [Beatles], which is how you would credit a non-song" (Miles 1997, 358).

RECORDING SESSIONS

Produced by Martin, "Flying" was recorded at Abbey Road Studios on September 8, 1967, with an additional overdubbing session on September 28.

"Flying" had gone under the working title of "Aerial Tour Instrumental" in reference to its role in the movie's psychedelic interlude. With the Mellotron's trumpet setting toggled, the group sang along, doubling the faux brass sounds in wordless "la la" style, before concluding with a prerecorded Mellotron tape of a Dixieland band in full swing (Winn 2003b, 134). Lennon later added flute sounds on the Mellotron, while also concocting tape loops composed of electronic effusions, organ melodies, and chimes. When played in reverse, the tape loops were substituted for the Dixieland ending (now deleted from the Beatles' catalogue), imbuing "Flying" with its mysterious, otherworldly terminus.

PERSONNEL

Lennon: Vocal, Mellotron Mark II, Hammond Organ
McCartney: Vocal, Rickenbacker 4001S
Harrison: Vocal, Gibson J-160E
Starr: Vocal, Ludwig Oyster Black Pearl Drums, Maracas

ALBUM APPEARANCE: *Magical Mystery Tour.*

See also: *Magical Mystery Tour* (LP); *Magical Mystery Tour* (TV Film).

"The Fool on the Hill" (Lennon–McCartney)

"The Fool on the Hill" is a song on the Beatles' *Magical Mystery Tour* album.

AUTHORSHIP AND BACKGROUND

Written by McCartney, the songwriter debuted the composition for Lennon during the March 1967 session in which they wrote "With a Little Help from My Friends." At Lennon's urging, McCartney wrote down the lyrics for "The Fool on the Hill" in order to capture them for a later date.

As McCartney later recalled, " 'Fool on the Hill' was mine and I think I was writing about someone like the Maharishi. His detractors called him a fool. Because of his giggle he wasn't taken too seriously. I was sitting at the piano at my father's house in Liverpool hitting a D6 chord, and I made up 'Fool on the Hill' " (Miles 1997, 365). As Lennon later observed, "Now that's Paul. Another good lyric. Shows he's capable of writing complete songs" (Lennon and Ono 2000, 186).

Beatles associate Alistair Taylor remembers the origins of "The Fool on the Hill" differently, recalling a bizarre incident that occurred when he was strolling with

McCartney on Primrose Hill in London's Regent Park. To their surprise, a mysterious man appeared and inexplicably disappeared; later that day, McCartney and Taylor contemplated the existence of God.

RECORDING SESSIONS

Produced by Martin, "The Fool on the Hill" was recorded at Abbey Road Studios on September 25, 1967, with additional overdubbing sessions on September 26 and October 20.

"The Fool on the Hill" was assembled, as with "I Am the Walrus," in several increasingly elaborate layers. The early takes feature McCartney on "Mrs. Mills"— the nickname for Studio Two's upright piano—a concord of flutes and recorders, and Starr on the finger cymbals. In addition to double-tracking his vocal, McCartney added a plaintive recorder solo, while Lennon and Harrison played harmonicas in downbeat accompaniment. In addition to scoring an arrangement for a trio of flutes, Martin inserted an unusual tape effect at 2:40—an intensely fluid, meandering sound that hearkens back to the birdlike noises that adorn "Tomorrow Never Knows" (Everett 1999, 138).

PERSONNEL

Lennon: Harmonica
McCartney: Vocal, Rickenbacker 4001S, Recorder, Piano, Epiphone Texan
Harrison: Gibson J-160E, Harmonica
Starr: Ludwig Oyster Black Pearl Drums, Maracas, Finger Cymbals
Studio Musicians: Woodwind Accompaniment conducted by Martin
Jack Ellory, Christopher Taylor, Richard Taylor: Flute

ALBUM APPEARANCES: *Magical Mystery Tour*; *The Beatles, 1967–1970*; *Anthology 2*; *Love*.

See also: *Magical Mystery Tour* (LP); *Magical Mystery Tour* (TV Film).

"For No One" (Lennon–McCartney)

"For No One" is a song on the Beatles' *Revolver* album.

AUTHORSHIP AND BACKGROUND

Possibly inspired by the Rolling Stones' "Lady Jane," "For No One" was originally entitled "Why Did It Die?"

As McCartney recalled, "I wrote that on a skiing holiday in Switzerland. In a hired chalet amongst the snow" (Dowlding 1989, 142). McCartney later remarked that "I suspect it was about another argument. I don't have easy relationships with women, I never have. I talk too much truth" (Sounes 2010, 144). As Lennon remembered, "One of my favorites of his. A nice piece of work" (Lennon and Ono 2000, 180).

RECORDING SESSIONS

Produced by Martin, "For No One" was recorded at Abbey Road Studios on May 9, 1966, with a vocal overdubbing session on May 16, followed by the recording of a French horn solo by Alan Civil, the principal horn player for the London Philharmonic Orchestra, on May 19.

For the recording of "For No One," McCartney plays a rented Clavichord, a European keyboard that creates sound when a series of tiny metal blades known as tangents strike the instrument's brass or iron strings. During the recording session on May 19 in Studio Three, Civil blanched at Martin's arrangement for the solo, which required him to play beyond his instrument's normal range. As McCartney remembered, "On the session, Alan Civil said, 'George?' and looked at us both. He said, 'George, you've written a D,' and George and I just looked at him and held our nerve and said, 'Yes?' And he gave us a crafty look and went, 'Okay'" (Miles 1997, 289).

PERSONNEL

McCartney: Vocal, Rickenbacker 4001S, Clavichord
Starr: Ludwig Oyster Black Pearl Drums, Tambourine
Civil: Horn

LEGACY AND INFLUENCE

In 2010, *Rolling Stone* ranked "For No One" as #40 on the magazine's list of *The Beatles' 100 Greatest Songs*.

ALBUM APPEARANCES: *Revolver* (U.K.); *Revolver* (U.S.); *Love Songs*.

See also: *Revolver* (U.K. LP).

"For You Blue" (Harrison)

"For You Blue" is a song on the Beatles' *Let It Be* album.

AUTHORSHIP AND BACKGROUND

Written by Harrison for his wife Pattie, "For You Blue" shares much in common with Elmore James's "Madison Blues," an aspect that Harrison does absolute nothing to conceal, at one point ad-libbing "Elmore James got nothing on this baby" during the eventual recording. It went under the title of "George's Blues (Because You're Sweet and Lovely)." As Harrison later recalled, " 'For You Blue' is a simple 12-bar song following all the normal 12-bar principles, except that it's happy-go-lucky!" (Badman 2001, 13).

RECORDING SESSIONS

Produced by Martin with postproduction by Phil Spector, "For You Blue" was recorded at Apple Studio on January 25, 1969. With McCartney playing a nifty honky-tonk piano, this 12-bar blues effusion is noteworthy for Lennon's slide-guitar solo—played with a Höfner 5140 Hawaiian Standard resting on his knees. Harrison can be heard saying, "Go, Johnny, go!" as Lennon works the slide guitar to his obvious delight.

For the song's *Let It Be . . . Naked* release (2003), "For You Blue" was remixed from the January 1969 Apple Studio session.

PERSONNEL

Lennon: Höfner 5140 Hawaiian Standard
McCartney: Piano
Harrison: Vocal, Gibson J-200
Starr: Ludwig Hollywood Maple Drums

CHART PERFORMANCE

U.S.: "The Long and Winding Road"/"For You Blue"; 11 May 1970, Apple [Capitol] 2832: #1 (certified by the RIAA as "Gold," with more than 500,000 copies sold). As the B-side of "The Long and Winding Road," "For You Blue" did not chart.

ALBUM APPEARANCES: *Let It Be*; *Anthology 3*; *Let It Be . . . Naked*.

See also: *Let It Be* (LP); *Let It Be . . . Naked* (LP).

"Free as a Bird" (Harrison–Lennon–McCartney–Starr)

Released some 25 years after their disbandment, "Free as a Bird" was a 1995 hit single by the Beatles that the surviving band members recorded with a 1977 demo by Lennon as the song's basic track. It is one of the very few songs credited to all four Beatles as composers.

AUTHORSHIP AND BACKGROUND

Written by Lennon, "Free as a Bird" was composed at his home with Yoko Ono in New York City's Dakota apartment building. In 1977, Lennon recorded a demo version of the song, with vocal and piano accompaniment recorded on a single microphone, on a cassette player. On the original recording, Lennon can be heard introducing the song as "Free as a Boid [Bird]" in an exaggerated New Yorker's accent.

As the surviving Beatles—often referred to as "The Threetles"—compiled their *Anthology* documentary in the early 1990s, Harrison and Apple Corps executive Neil Aspinall approached Ono about the idea of enhancing Lennon's demos for release. After McCartney delivered his induction speech on Lennon's behalf at the Rock and Roll Hall of Fame's January 1994 induction ceremony, Ono provided him with Lennon's demo tapes for "Free as a Bird," "Real Love," "Now and Then," and "Grow Old with Me."

RECORDING SESSIONS

While Martin was originally considered for the production duties associated with "Free as a Bird," the aging producer bowed out of the project because of problems with his hearing. As McCartney later remarked in a 1995 interview with *Bass Player* magazine,

> George doesn't want to produce much any more 'cause his hearing's not as good as it used to be. He's a very sensible guy, and he says, "Look, Paul, I like to do a proper job," and if he doesn't feel he's up to it he won't do it. It's very noble of him, actually—most people would take the money and run. (Badman 2001, 439)

Jeff Lynne, who had produced Harrison's *Cloud Nine* album (1987), was subsequently tapped as the song's coproducer, along with Lennon, McCartney, Harrison, and Starr.

Given Lennon's glaring absence from the proceedings, Starr suggested a scenario in which his bandmates pretended that the fallen Beatle had gone out to lunch or for a cup of tea. Meanwhile, McCartney, Harrison, and Starr retired to McCartney's Hog Hill Mill studio in Sussex for a series of February and March 1994 recording sessions in which they recorded additional vocals and instrumentation around Lennon's basic track.

In true Beatles style, "Free as a Bird" ends with a free-form coda, complete with Harrison strumming a madcap ukulele part and Lennon's voice, recorded backward in the final mix, quoting Liverpudlian entertainer George Formby's signature catchphrase, "Turned out nice again." In the finished version of "Free as a Bird," Lennon's backward phrase sounds eerily as if the late Beatle is saying his own name.

PERSONNEL

Lennon: Vocal, Piano
McCartney: Vocal, Höfner 500/1, Double Bass, Acoustic Guitar, Piano
Harrison: Vocal, Model "T" Hamburguitar, Acoustic Guitar, Ukulele
Starr: Drums, Percussion

CHART PERFORMANCE

U.K.: "Free as a Bird"/"Christmas Time (Is Here Again)"; December 4, 1995, Apple R6422: #2.
U.S.: "Free as a Bird"/"Christmas Time (Is Here Again)"; December 12, 1995, Apple NR 7243 8 58497 7 0: #6 (certified by the RIAA as "Gold," with more than 500,000 copies sold).

LEGACY AND INFLUENCE

In 1997, "Free as a Bird" earned Grammy Awards for Best Music Video, Short Form and for Best Pop Performance by a Duo or Group with Vocal at the 39th Grammy Awards.

ALBUM APPEARANCE: *Anthology 1.*

See also: *The Beatles Anthology, Volume 1* (LP); Lynne, Jeff; Ono, Yoko.

"From Me to You" (McCartney–Lennon)

"From Me to You" was the Beatles' second consecutive #1 single in the United Kingdom, where it was released on April 11, 1963.

AUTHORSHIP AND BACKGROUND

Lennon and McCartney had written the band's next single, "From Me to You," on the tour bus on February 28, 1963. The idea had come to them while discussing the regular *New Musical Express* column "From You to Us," which McCartney decided to personalize by refashioning the phrase in the first person as "From Me to You." In McCartney's thinking, this allowed them to speak directly to their audience, as they had previously done with "I Saw Her Standing There" (Miles 1997, 149).

RECORDING SESSIONS

Produced by Martin, "From Me to You" was recorded in 13 takes at Abbey Road Studios on March 5, 1963. During the band's early years, they rehearsed their new compositions in Studio Two in front of Martin, who sat above them on a tall stool. While they readily ascribed this position of authority to their producer, the group intuitively recognized the importance of their collaboration with the elder Martin, who—despite his many producing spoken-word and novelty records—possessed a genuine knack for recognizing and crafting hit songs.

"The Beatles had marvelous ears when it came to writing and arranging their material," assistant producer Ron Richards observed, "but George had real taste—and an innate sense of what worked" (Spitz 2005, 386). When he first heard "From Me to You" with its original guitar introduction, Martin suggested that Lennon and McCartney sing the opening motto—"da-da-da da-da-dun-dun-da"—along with an overdubbed harmonica part by Lennon. Having forgotten his harmonica that day, Lennon borrowed one from Malcolm Davies, a disc-cutter at Abbey Road Studios.

PERSONNEL

Lennon: Vocal, Harmonica, Rickenbacker 325
McCartney: Vocal, Höfner 500/1
Harrison: Gretsch Duo-Jet
Starr: Premier Mahogany Duroplastic Drums

The Beatles pose for a photo during a recording session in London on March 5, 1963, that included "From Me To You," "Thank You Girl," and "One After 909." From left to right are George Harrison, Paul McCartney, Ringo Starr, and John Lennon. (Michael Ochs Archives/Getty Images)

CHART PERFORMANCE

U.K.: "From Me to You"/"Thank You Girl"; April 11, 1963, Parlophone R 5015: #1.

U.S.: "From Me to You"/"Thank You Girl"; May 27, 1963, Vee-Jay VJ 522: #116.

U.S.: "Please Please Me"/"From Me to You"; January 30, 1964, Vee-Jay VJ 581: #3. As the B-side of the "Please Please Me" single, "From Me to You" charted at #41.

LEGACY AND INFLUENCE

In 2010, *Rolling Stone* ranked "From Me to You" as #72 on the magazine's list of *The Beatles' 100 Greatest Songs*.

ALBUM APPEARANCES: *A Collection of Beatles Oldies*; *The Beatles, 1962–1966*; *20 Greatest Hits*; *Past Masters, Volume 1*; *Anthology 1*; *1*; *On Air: Live at the BBC, Volume 2*.

See also: Royal Command Variety Performance.

G

"Get Back" (Lennon–McCartney)

"Get Back" was the band's fifth consecutive #1 single in the United Kingdom, where it was released on April 11, 1969. It is also a song on the Beatles' *Let It Be* album.

AUTHORSHIP AND BACKGROUND

Written by McCartney, "Get Back" was improvised at Twickenham Film Studios and later at Apple Studio during the January 1969 *Get Back* sessions.

As McCartney remarked shortly after the song's release, "We were sitting in the studio and we made it up out of thin air. We started to write words there and then. When we finished it, we recorded it at Apple Studio and made it into a song to rollercoast by" (Dowlding 1989, 269). Lennon added that "we'd been talking about it since we recorded it, and we kept saying, 'That's a single.' Eventually we got so fed up talking about it we suddenly said 'Okay, that's it. Get it out tomorrow'" (Cadogan 2008, 215). In a March 1969 interview with Nick Logan, Starr described "Get Back" as "a lovely little toetapper. If you can sit down when this one is on, then you're a stronger man than I am."

During one of his final interviews in 1980, Lennon characterized "Get Back" as "a better version of 'Lady Madonna.' You know—a potboiler rewrite" (Lennon and Ono 2000, 201).

RECORDING SESSIONS

Credited to the Beatles with Billy Preston, "Get Back" was produced by Martin with postproduction by Phil Spector. It was recorded at Apple Studio on January 27 and 28, 1969, after numerous rehearsals.

Over the course of 17 days in January 1969, the Beatles rehearsed some 59 iterations of "Get Back." In so doing, they slogged through a seemingly endless parade of false starts and bouts of sloppy instrumentation on the way to perfecting the distinctive galloping groove of "Get Back." It had been born way back on January 7, when McCartney toyed with the bass riff that drives Lulu's "I'm a Tiger" before happening upon the melody of his latest composition. He had borrowed a portion of the song's lyrics from Harrison's "Sour Milk Sea," one of May

1968's Esher demos in which Harrison sings "Get back to the place you should be." An earlier version of "Get Back" witnessed McCartney indulging in a comparatively rare moment of political satire. On January 9, Lennon and McCartney had improvised a number entitled "Commonwealth" in which they derided the Conservative Party's repatriation movement to limit the sudden influx of thousands of Indian and Pakistani immigrants who had been denied the right to work in Kenya. Things had come to a head in April 1968, when British politician Enoch Powell delivered his controversial "Rivers of Blood" speech in response to the Labour Government's introduction of antidiscrimination legislation. According to Powell, the pending race relations bill "would make colored people a privileged class" (Sulpy and Schweighardt 1997, 157, 158). As "Get Back" began to emerge from the Beatles' chaotic mid-January sessions, McCartney satirized Powell's anti-immigration position, singing "Don't dig no Pakistanis taking all the people's jobs."

But within a few days, "Get Back" took a decidedly different, more playful turn. Originally known as Joe and Teresa, McCartney's quirky "Get Back" characters eventually morphed into pot-smoking Jo-Jo and Sweet Loretta Martin, an enigmatic drag queen. But the real story of "Get Back" involves the song's music, rather than its eccentric, albeit one-dimensional story line. With an infectious forward momentum provided by Starr's relentless snare, "Get Back" finds McCartney contributing an unforgettable, near-falsetto vocal, while Lennon concocts a wonderfully funky guitar solo on his Epiphone Casino. The 45-RPM single version of the song, which became an international hit come April, features a classic false ending, Beatles-style, with McCartney gleefully ad-libbing the coda.

For the song's Let It Be . . . Naked release (2003), "Get Back" consists of the January 27, 1969, single version of the song, albeit without the January 28 coda or the incidental framing dialogue.

PERSONNEL

Lennon: Epiphone Casino, Backing Vocal
McCartney: Vocal, Höfner 500/1
Harrison: Fender Rosewood Telecaster, Backing Vocal
Starr: Ludwig Hollywood Maple Drums
Preston: Fender Rhodes Electric Piano

CHART PERFORMANCE

U.K.: "Get Back"/"Don't Let Me Down"; April 11, 1969, Apple [Parlophone] R 5777 (as the Beatles with Preston): #1.

U.S.: "Get Back"/"Don't Let Me Down"; May 5, 1969, Apple [Capitol] 2490 (as the Beatles with Preston): #1 (certified by the RIAA as "2x Multi Platinum," with more than 2 million copies sold).

LEGACY AND INFLUENCE

In 1970, the Beatles received an Ivor Novello Award, awarded annually by the British Academy of Songwriters, Composers, and Authors, for "Get Back."

In 2010, *Rolling Stone* ranked "Get Back" as #41 on the magazine's list of *The Beatles' 100 Greatest Songs*.

ALBUM APPEARANCES: *Let It Be*; *The Beatles, 1967–1970*; *Rock 'n' Roll Music*; *Reel Music*; *20 Greatest Hits*; *Past Masters, Volume 2*; *Anthology 3*; *1*; *Let It Be . . . Naked*; *Love*.

See also: *Get Back* Project; *Let It Be* (LP); *Let It Be . . . Naked* (LP); Preston, Billy; Tigrett, Maureen Cox (Starkey).

Get Back Project

The idea for the so-called *Get Back* project finds its origins in the wee hours of September 5, 1968. Having recorded the promotional films for "Hey Jude" and "Revolution" the previous evening, the Beatles had stayed up much of the night with Denis O'Dell and director Michael Lindsay-Hogg. As they downed one convivial scotch-and-Coke after another, the group reminisced about performing in front of the studio audience that Mal Evans had assembled. As the newly appointed director of Apple Films recalled, "Collectively, they said, 'Denis, this was a great evening. Now we must talk about doing a big show together.'" The group had been exhilarated by their performance—not only because of their interaction with the audience, but more importantly in terms of the simple joy that they experienced in playing together as a band. "They were jamming and having a good time and having a better time than they thought they were going to have," Lindsay-Hogg remembered. "So they sort of thought maybe there is some way they can do something again in some sort of performance way" (Matteo 2004, 18).

And with that, the *Get Back* project was born. Over the years, the sessions have come to be associated with the group's notion—particularly evinced by Lennon—of "getting back" to their musical roots, of recapturing the live sound and sense of spontaneity that characterized their earlier work. While this was certainly true, given the sparse approach that the Beatles took regarding the project's instrumentation and its overall lack of elaborate studio production, the group had something entirely different, even unexpected, in mind. Buoyed by the audience response to "Hey Jude" and "Revolution," they intended to rehearse a new live act and unveil it in the new year. It would be their triumphant return to the stage.

In order to document their preparation for the concert, the Beatles tasked Lindsay-Hogg with the job of filming their rehearsals at Twickenham Film Studios, the very same soundstage where they had shot *A Hard Day's Night* five years earlier. As the group honed their plans for the project, which at one point included the possibility of a television special, Lindsay-Hogg devised a scheme of his own. In December, he had directed the Rolling Stones' *Rock and Roll Circus*, a production originally slated to debut as a television program in which performances by the Stones, the Who, Jethro Tull, and Clapton, among others, were introduced by playful banter among the assembled glitterati, which included Lennon and Ono in an inspired cameo. But for the Beatles, Lindsay-Hogg had something very different in mind. He dispensed with the plasticine veneer of big-top spectacle and strive instead for the brute, gritty truth of authenticity. Using a pair of Nagra tape recorders and two cameramen, he intended to shoot the documentary in *audio vérité* style. As with *cinema vérité*—which roughly translates as the "cinema of truth"—the idea behind *audio vérité* is to seize upon the essential human truth inherent in the text. As an unscripted documentary production, *audio vérité* necessitates an unmediated presentation of the subject. With reels of tape at the ready, Lindsay-Hogg hoped to capture the Beatles' music and conversations in excruciating detail. He acted as a shameless participant in the proceedings, provoking the group into a series of exchanges about their plans for live performance, the evolving nature of the songs being rehearsed, and their shifting internal politics. In so doing, his *audio vérité* approach managed to record the Beatles at a critical crossroads in the twilight of their career.

The *Get Back* project began at Twickenham during the late morning of Thursday, January 2, 1969. As with nearly all of the rehearsals during the Beatles' fortnight at the soundstage, the first day's proceedings were determined by the sporadic arrival of the bandmates, especially Lennon, who, along with Ono, often was the last member to arrive on the scene. In addition to the film crew, the Beatles were joined by Martin and Glyn Johns, who had been hired to supervise the sound recording for the television broadcast. As the project progressed, he began to assume to the role of sound engineer, overseeing the recording and playback of their rehearsals. After the complexities of *The White Album*, Martin was excited about what he perceived to be the "brilliant" concept behind the band's latest project: "The original idea was that we should record an album of new material and rehearse it, then perform it before a live audience for the first time—on record and film. In other words, make a live album of new material, which no one had ever done before." For his part, Lennon wanted the resulting LP to be an "honest album"; in Lennon's mind that meant no editing or overdubbing: "We just record a song and that's it," he told the producer (Ryan and Kehew 2006, 504). In spite of his initial enthusiasm, Martin only made himself available sporadically throughout the *Get Back* sessions, growing increasingly bewildered as the band went through one fragmented rehearsal after another trying to knock their new material into shape. With the hazy lens of historical hindsight, Lennon derided Twickenham's sterile atmosphere and the experience of working under the watchful eyes and ears of Lindsay-Hogg's production unit:

We couldn't get into it. It was just a dreadful, dreadful feeling in Twickenham Studio, being filmed all the time. I just wanted them [the film crew] to go away.

You couldn't make music at eight in the morning or ten or whatever it was, in a strange place with people filming you and colored lights. (Doggett 1998, 10)

The group had become used to working evening sessions at EMI Studios, and the sudden shift to daylight must have been understandably jarring. In striking contrast with Lennon's memories, Johns recalled the *Get Back* sessions with fondness:

The whole mood was wonderful. . . . There was all this nonsense going on at the time about the problems surrounding the group. . . . In fact, they were having a wonderful time and being incredibly funny. I didn't stop laughing for six weeks. (Doggett 1998, 78)

During the first rehearsal, the Beatles worked through rudimentary versions of Lennon's bluesy new composition "Don't Let Me Down," Harrison's meditative "All Things Must Pass," and a pair of up-tempo rock 'n' roll tunes by McCartney, "I've Got a Feeling" and "Two of Us." As the sessions continued, conversation was dominated by discussion about the location for the upcoming live performance, which they planned to undertake, impractical as it may seem, by mid-January. They initially considered a lavish concert at the Royal Albert Hall, with Apple recording artists Mary Hopkin and James Taylor on the bill, before settling, for a short while, on the comparatively intimate Roundhouse, the unofficial headquarters for the London underground music scene. Other ideas included performing in a Roman amphitheater in North Africa, or perhaps onboard a ship at sea, or even by torchlight in the middle of the Sahara desert. At one point, Lennon suggested, half-jokingly, that a concert in an insane asylum might be more appropriate, given the band's recent spate of interpersonal problems. Starr made it known on several occasions that he refused to go abroad, prompting McCartney to tease the drummer that they would be forced to replace him with Jimmie Nicol. While O'Dell suggested that they film the concert with the band performing in the middle of one of London's renowned art museums, Ono had become particularly intrigued by the avant-garde concept of the Beatles playing a concert before 20,000 empty seats in order to signify "the invisible nameless everybody in the world" (Doggett 1998, 20). In one instance, she even suggested that they reorient the documentary so as to film the Beatles' personal activities, reality-television style, from dusk to dawn in their private homes. The group's outlandish concert ideas began to wane rather precipitously, however, when Ono pointed out that "after 100,000 people in Shea Stadium, everything else sucks" (Matteo 2004, 48).

In addition to rehearsing new material, the *Get Back* sessions found the Beatles manically improvising one song after another, including a wide range of classic rock 'n' roll numbers like "Shake, Rattle, and Roll," "Johnny B. Goode," "Lawdy Miss Clawdy," "Lucille," "You Really Got a Hold on Me," "Mailman, Bring Me No More Blues," "Little Queenie," "Rock and Roll Music," "Blue Suede Shoes," and "Be-Bop-a-Lula," among a host of others. Surprisingly, they improvised very few original songs, with the exception of a risqué tune entitled "Suzy's Parlor."

As the *Get Back* sessions proceeded, Lennon and McCartney slowly began to surmount this tendency, delving deeper and deeper into their writerly heritage. At one juncture, the songwriters revisited "Just Fun," one of their first compositions together back in the late 1950s, later attempting versions of such juvenilia as "Thinking of Linking" and "I Lost My Little Girl," the latter of which found Lennon taking lead vocals on McCartney's early composition about his mother Mary's untimely demise. Yet as January rolled along, the Beatles seemed increasingly unable to concentrate on the project at hand, with Lennon and McCartney persistently "playing riffs and half-snatches of melodies on their guitars." This "aimless noodling," in the words of Doug Sulpy and Ray Schweighardt, finally began to irritate McCartney in spite of his own culpability in distracting his mates (Sulpy and Schweighardt 1997, 85). Fed up with being the band's solitary cheerleader, the normally well-mannered Beatle became unhinged during the January 7, 1969, session: "We've been very negative since Mr. Epstein passed away," he remarked. "I don't see why any of you, if you're not interested, get yourselves into this. What's it for? It can't be for the money. Why are you here?"(Doggett 1998, 24, 25). Worse yet, he attributed the band's inability to move forward creatively as the ruinous work of their own suffocating nostalgia: "When we do get together, we just talk about the f—ing past. We're like OAPs [old-age pensioners], saying, 'Do you remember the days when we used to rock?' Well, we're here now, we can still do it" (Doggett 1998, 27). If nothing else, McCartney's angry words of wisdom served to revive his flagging partner, who seemed to be unable to rouse the necessary creative energy to generate new material. When McCartney finally confronted him about his inability to produce new compositions beyond "Don't Let Me Down," Lennon responded with his classic defensive posture, a combination of sarcasm and petulance:

MCCARTNEY: "Haven't you written anything?"
LENNON: "No."
MCCARTNEY: "We're going to be facing a crisis."
LENNON: "When I'm up against the wall, Paul, you'll find that I'm at my best."
MCCARTNEY: "I wish you'd come up with the goods."
LENNON: "I think I've got Sunday off."
MCCARTNEY: "I hope you can deliver."
LENNON: "I'm hoping for a little rock-and-roller." (Doggett 1998, 29)

Lennon's lethargy was understandable, given the band's considerable output and activity during the previous year, not to mention his escapades with Ono and the personal tragedy of her miscarriage. Lennon and Ono's protracted heroin abuse may have been taking its toll—at one juncture during the Twickenham sessions, Ono joked about shooting heroin as the couple's form of exercise (Doggett 1998, 34).

By this point, Lennon may have been equally annoyed by Harrison's obvious profundity of new material, but there is little question that their growing personal feud involved Harrison's exasperation with Ono's constant presence in the studio, particularly when she spoke up for Lennon, while her silent boyfriend nervously plucked at his guitar. For his part, Lennon had been distressed over his bandmates' refusal to embrace the love of his life, to understand his fervent need to be in Ono's company during his every waking moment. But Harrison made little effort to hide his vexation with Ono's unremitting presence, and on Friday, January 10, 1969—after enduring a morning session in which McCartney goaded him about how to perform his guitar part—Harrison abruptly quit the group. After a heated argument with Lennon during lunch, Harrison made a hasty exit, uttering "See you 'round the clubs" as he left the soundstage. Either out of spite or ennui—or both—Lennon began improvising the Who's "A Quick One While He's Away" within minutes of Harrison's departure. At one point, he sarcastically called for an absent Harrison to play the guitar solo (Sulpy and Schweighardt 1997, 170).

Back at Kinfauns, Harrison burned off his anger with a bout of songwriting that produced "Wah-Wah," a song that was later included on Harrison's *All Things Must Pass* solo recording. As a pun on the name of the popular guitar effects pedal, "Wah-Wah" became Harrison's euphemism for a pounding headache: "You've given me a wah-wah." The song's autobiographical elements are undeniable, and they speak, in particular, to the complex nature of his uneasy relationship with Lennon, the older, more experienced boy whom he had looked up to during his early teen years. The composition makes specific reference to his indebtedness to Lennon: "You made me such a big star / Being there at the right time." Not long after Harrison's departure, Lennon began calling for the group to replace him with Clapton, a caustic suggestion, given Harrison's close friendship with the renowned guitarist: "The point is: if George leaves, do we want to carry on the Beatles? I do," Lennon told McCartney and Starr. "We should just get other members and carry on" (Doggett 1998, 33). The day's session ended with a spate of improvised jamming, including a rendition of "Martha My Dear" in which Ono provided a screeching solo, screaming Lennon's name over and over. Meanwhile, McCartney played on, seemingly unfazed by the chaos around him (Sulpy and Schweighardt 1997, 176).

On Sunday, the Beatles gathered at Brookfields, Starr's Surrey estate, and the rift between Lennon and Harrison grew even wider when the guitarist refused to return to Twickenham. The next day, Lennon, McCartney, and Starr ran through sloppy versions of McCartney's "Get Back," and by Wednesday, the sessions had ground to a halt. That afternoon, the group met yet again, this time settling their differences to everyone's apparent satisfaction. The truce involved at least two considerations: first, that they would abandon Twickenham's dour atmosphere immediately in favor of Apple's newfangled basement studio; and second, that they would dispense with the concept of a live performance, staging instead a concert for Lindsay-Hogg's cameras without benefit of an audience. The shift from Twickenham to Apple effectively spelled the end for the television production, with the Beatles now setting their sights on recording a new album and a concomitant documentary. Although their fantasy of making a spectacular return to the stage had perished, the idea for a new studio album had been born—and if the Beatles knew nothing else, they understood implicitly how to make an LP.

The sessions would have begun on the following Monday, were it not for Magic Alex, who had promised to build a 72-track recording studio for the group in the basement of the Apple building at 3 Savile Row in Soho. Magic Alex also dreamt of devising an invisible force field to serve as the sound screen for Starr's drums. When Martin arrived at the studio, he was shocked to discover 16 speakers arrayed along the basement walls, with Magic Alex's multitrack system nowhere in evidence. As Harrison later recalled,

> Alex's recording studio was the biggest disaster of all time. He was walking around with a white coat on like some sort of chemist, but he didn't have a clue what he was doing. It was a 16-track system, and he had 16 tiny little speakers all around the walls. You only need two speakers for stereo sound. It was awful. The whole thing was a disaster, and it had to be ripped out. (Doggett 1998, 36)

To make matters worse, Magic Alex's ostensibly state-of-the-art mixing desk "looked like it had been built with a hammer and chisel," second engineer Alan Parsons remarked. "None of the switches fitted properly, and you could almost see the metal filings. It was rough, all right, and it was all very embarrassing, because it just didn't do anything" (Babiuk 2001, 236). Consequently, Martin and Johns spent the next two days turning Apple's basement into a respectable recording studio by bringing in two mobile four-track mixing consoles from EMI, overhauling the basement's amateurish soundproofing, and attempting to quiet the building's noisy heating system.

On Wednesday, January 22, 1969, Harrison officially returned to the fold, performing a duet of "You Are My Sunshine" with Lennon in order to signify their renewed camaraderie. Later that day, Harrison decided to alter the band's chemistry, as he had done so successfully back in September 1968 with Clapton, by inviting ace keyboard player Billy Preston to lend his talents to the Beatles. As luck would have it, Harrison and Clapton had seen Preston performing in Ray Charles's band on January 19. The Beatles had first met Preston back in Hamburg in 1962 when he was a member of Little Richard's backup band. "I pulled in Billy Preston," Harrison later recalled in the Beatles' *Anthology* documentary. "It helped because the others would have to control themselves a bit more. John and Paul mainly, because they had to, you know, act more handsomely," he continued. "It's interesting to see how people behave nicely when you bring a guest in because they don't want everyone to know that they're so bitchy" (Ryan and Kehew 2006, 506). Harrison's gambit worked its magic, with Lennon lobbying hard for Preston to become a permanent member of the group, although McCartney demurred at the thought of five Beatles: "It's bad enough with four!" he exclaimed (Sulpy and Schweighardt 1997, 232; Doggett 1998, 38). For the next several days, the five bandmates rehearsed with a vengeance. Time was clearly of the essence, as Starr was due to star in *The Magic Christian* with Peter Sellers in early February. Meanwhile, Johns was scheduled to record an album with the Steve Miller Band in the United States, and Preston was about to embark upon a concert tour back in his native Texas. If the Beatles were going to salvage the *Get Back* project, something had to happen—and soon.

And to the Beatles' own amazement, something *did* happen. Over the next five days, they committed no less than four classic songs to tape—"Don't Let Me Down," "Get Back," "Let It Be," and "The Long and Winding Road"—as well as at least two near-classics to boot, including "I've Got a Feeling" and "Two of Us." And they performed their legendary January 30, 1969, rooftop concert in the bargain. Riding on an incredible burst of energy, no doubt assisted by the good vibes and superb musicianship of Preston, they transformed their own hostility into the stuff of rock music history. All told, Lindsay-Hogg's documentary work had resulted in the accrual of 223 rolls of audio and film, tallying up some 60 hours' worth of sound and footage from the group's 10 days at Twickenham Film Studios. A staggering 530 more rolls had been amassed after the project's relocation to Apple (Sulpy and Schweighardt 1997, 317).

In early March 1969, Lennon and McCartney turned the virtual mountain of audiotapes associated with the *Get Back* project over to Johns. In so doing, they set a series of events into motion that spiraled out of their control, resulting in the tortuous saga of the album's release more than a year later. As Johns later recalled, "They pointed to a big pile of tapes in the corner and said, 'Remember that idea you had about putting together an album? Well, there are the tapes. Go and do it'" (Doggett 1998, 45). Johns prepared at least two full-length versions of the *Get Back* album over the next nine months. Lennon and McCartney were confident enough in Johns' ability to whip the material into shape that they commissioned Angus McBean to shoot a cover photograph for an LP to be entitled *Get Back, Don't Let Me Down, and Twelve Other Songs*.

And it might have worked, too, were it not for the slipshod efforts of Johns, who, in historical hindsight, had probably taken Lennon and McCartney's notion of getting back to the basics far too literally. In May 1969, Johns debuted his preliminary mix of *Get Back* for the Beatles' inspection, and it was an ungodly mess. Brimming with studio banter and false starts, his version of the album was clearly designed to seem rough and spontaneous in contrast with their previous LPs. If nothing else, Johns succeeded in adhering to Lennon's dictum against the slick "jiggery-pokery" of professional studio production. But Johns didn't fail in his attempt to make the album appear impulsive and unstructured. Rather, Johns' presumptive mistake involved his textual choices for the LP's contents. In sober backcast, it's difficult to imagine what led him to select ineffectual versions of the songs for inclusion when he had so many different renditions, thanks to Lindsay-Hogg's no-holds barred recording effort, from which to choose. As it turns out, he made highly suspect decisions throughout the postproduction process, selecting subpar recordings of key songs when much stronger versions were available—particularly in terms of the tracks that the Beatles had recorded during that last burst of creative energy in Apple's basement studio (as well as on its rooftop) at the end of January. His biggest sin, by far, involved his selection of a comparatively unfinished version of "Don't Let Me Down" from the January 22 session when an extant rendition from the January 28 session was tighter and more polished in almost every possible respect. Even the rooftop version was superior, in spite of Lennon's inability to remember the lyrics for the second verse, for which he resorted to conjuring up some gibberish on the spot as an impromptu guide vocal. Amazingly, Johns resorted to the same procedure for "Dig a Pony" and "I've Got a Feeling." The Beatles had performed far better versions of both songs on the roof, yet Johns had selected earlier and comparatively sloppier takes for inclusion on the album. In the case of "I've Got a Feeling," Johns opted for a rendition from the January 24 session that features a shoddy introduction, and, worse yet, that falls into utter collapse during its conclusion. Johns also selected a sluggish version of "Two of Us" recorded on the very same day as "I've Got a Feeling," once again choosing an inferior take when a significantly stronger version was available. Whether it had been done in haste or the producer had been overly concerned with preserving the immediacy of the sessions, Johns had missed a crucial opportunity to bring the project to fruition, allowing the tapes to remain in limbo—and just long enough to permit other hands to intervene.

As the months rolled by, it became increasingly apparent that the Beatles would scuttle Johns' version of the *Get Back, Don't Let Me Down, and Twelve Other Songs* album altogether. Although Johns later substituted a comparatively more professional January 1970 mix for his May 1969 version of the album, by then it was much too late. While McCartney apparently approved of Johns' work—praising, in particular, the producer's attempt to preserve the album's spare sonic textures—Lennon despised *Get Back*, later claiming that it would succeed, for better or for worse, in breaking the Beatles' myth: "That's us, with no trousers on and no glossy paint over the cover and no sort of hope," he remarked. "This is what we are like with our trousers off, so would you please end the game now?" (Beatles 2000, 322). By the early spring of 1970, the tapes had fallen into the hands of renowned American producer Phil Spector—the esteemed progenitor of the "wall of sound." Lennon had recently worked with Spector on his hit solo single "Instant Karma," and he had been impressed enough with the producer's lightning-quick results to turn the *Get Back* tapes over to him with little concern—and, perhaps more significantly, without McCartney's knowledge. In December, the Beatles' revolving management had sold the rights to Lindsay-Hogg's documentary to United Artists, who reincarnated the project as a feature film. The Beatles subsequently altered the title of their album from *Get Back* to *Let It Be* in order to synchronize the marketing of its release with the movie of the same name.

JOHNS' PROPOSED TRACK LISTING FOR *GET BACK, DON'T LET ME DOWN, AND TWELVE OTHER SONGS*

Side 1: "One After 909"; "Rocker"; "Save the Last Dance for Me"; "Don't Let Me Down"; "Dig a Pony"; "I've Got a Feeling"; and "Get Back."

Side 2: "For You Blue"; "Teddy Boy"; "Two of Us"; "Maggie Mae"; "Dig It"; "Let It Be"; "The Long and Winding Road"; and "Get Back (Reprise)."

Over the course of their January 1969 sessions at Twickenham Film Studios and Apple Studio, the Beatles produced a massive corpus of debut compositions, improvisations, and unreleased cover versions (listed below). In addition to the songs that eventually comprised the *Let It Be* album, the Beatles' January 1969 recordings of "Blue Suede Shoes," "Mailman, Bring Me No More Blues," "Rip It Up," and "Shake, Rattle, and Roll" were later included on *Anthology 3*.

See also: Clapton, Eric; Evans, Mal; Johns, Glyn; *Let It Be* (Film); *Let It Be* (LP); Ono, Yoko.

"Getting Better" (Lennon–McCartney)

"Getting Better" is a song on the Beatles' *Sgt. Pepper's Lonely Hearts Club Band* album.

AUTHORSHIP AND BACKGROUND

Written by McCartney with Lennon, "Getting Back" came into being on a spring day in 1967 when McCartney recalled the optimistic words of Nicol, who employed "getting better" as his stock phrase during his brief stint as Starr's replacement in the early summer of 1964.

As McCartney later remembered,

[I] wrote that at my house in St. John's Wood. All I remember is that I said, "It's getting better all the time," and John contributed the legendary line, "It couldn't get much worse." Which I thought was very good. Against the spirit of that song, which was all super-optimistic—then there's that lovely little sardonic line. Typical John. (Dowlding 1989, 168)

As Lennon recalled,

"Getting Better" is a diary form of writing. All that "I used to be cruel to my woman / I beat her and kept her apart from the things that she loved" was me. I used to be cruel to my woman, and physically—any woman. I was a hitter. I couldn't express myself and I hit. I fought men and I hit women. That is why I am always on about peace, you see. It is the most violent people who go for love and peace. Everything's the opposite. But I sincerely believe in love and peace. I am a violent man who has learned not to be violent and regrets his violence. I will have to be a lot older before I can face in public how I treated women as a youngster. (Jackson 2012, 38)

RECORDING SESSIONS

Produced by Martin, "Getting Better" was recorded at Abbey Road Studios on March 9, 1967, with additional overdubbing sessions on March 10, 21, and 23.

For the recording, Lennon took his Rickenbacker 325 out of mothballs to join McCartney's pulsing Fender Esquire and Harrison's droning tamboura, an unfretted, lute-like, four-stringed Indian instrument.

The March 9, 1967, session was famously interrupted by an untimely Lennon acid trip. Concerned about his colleague's anxious demeanor and unaware of his recent ingestion of LSD, Martin took Lennon on the roof of Abbey Road Studios to get some fresh air. Realizing that Lennon could easily fall off the roof in his altered state, the other Beatles rushed upstairs in the nick of time (Badman 2001, 271). It was one of the few occasions, interestingly enough, when the band's legendary drug usage interrupted their work in the studio.

PERSONNEL

Lennon: Rickenbacker 325
McCartney: Vocal, Rickenbacker 4001S, Fender Esquire
Harrison: Tamboura
Starr: Ludwig Oyster Black Pearl Drums, Bongos
Martin: Hammond Organ

ALBUM APPEARANCE: *Sgt. Pepper's Lonely Hearts Club Band.*

See also: *Sgt. Pepper's Lonely Hearts Club Band* (LP).

"Girl" (Lennon–McCartney)

"Girl" is a song on the Beatles' *Rubber Soul* album.

AUTHORSHIP AND BACKGROUND

Written by Lennon and McCartney, "Girl" was the last song completed for the *Rubber Soul* album.

As Lennon later remarked, "That's me, writing about this dream girl—the one that hadn't come yet. It was Yoko" (Lennon and Ono 2000, 197). As Paul observed, "It was John's original idea, but it was very much co-written. I remember writing 'the pain and pleasure,' and 'a man must break his back'" (Miles 1997, 275).

RECORDING SESSIONS

Produced by Martin, "Girl" was recorded at Abbey Road Studios on November 11, 1965, the last session for *Rubber Soul.*

As Paul later remarked,

It was amusing to see if we could get a naughty word on the record. The Beach Boys had a song out where they'd done "la la la la" and we loved the innocence of that and wanted to copy it, but not use the same phrase. So we were looking around for another phrase—"dit dit dit dit," which we decided to change it in our waggishness to "tit tit tit tit." And it gave us a laugh. It was good to get some light relief in the middle of this real big career that we were forging. If we could put in something that was a little bit subversive then we would. George Martin would say, "Was that dit-dit or tit-tit you were singing?" "Oh! dit-dit, George, but it does sound a bit like that, doesn't it?" Then we'd get in the car and break down laughing. (Miles 1997, 276)

For "Girl," Harrison simulates a bouzouki-like sound on his Hootenanny, playing an intricate Greek melody that affords the track with an Old World resonance. "Girl" is also recognizable for Lennon's intensely breathy vocals. As McCartney later remarked, "Listen to John's breath on 'Girl.' We asked the engineer to put it on treble, so you get this huge intake of breath and it sounds just like a percussion instrument" (Dowlding 1989, 121).

PERSONNEL

Lennon: Vocal, Gibson J-160E
McCartney: Höfner 500/1, Epiphone Texan, Backing Vocal
Harrison: Framus 12-string Hootenanny, Backing Vocal
Starr: Ludwig Oyster Black Pearl Drums

LEGACY AND INFLUENCE

In 2010, *Rolling Stone* ranked "Girl" as #62 on the magazine's list of *The Beatles' 100 Greatest Songs*.

ALBUM APPEARANCES: *Rubber Soul* (U.K.); *Rubber Soul* (U.S.); *The Beatles, 1962–1966*; *Love Songs*; *Love*.

See also: *Love Songs* (LP); Ono, Yoko; *Rubber Soul* (U.K. LP).

"Glass Onion" (Lennon–McCartney)

"Glass Onion" is a song on *The Beatles* (*The White Album*).

AUTHORSHIP AND BACKGROUND

Written by Lennon, "Glass Onion" finds its origins during the Beatles' 1968 visit to India. Lennon's composition refers to a wide range of Beatles characters and songs—from "Lady Madonna" and "The Fool on the Hill" to "Fixing a Hole" and "Strawberry Fields Forever," ultimately conveying a carpentry metaphor, presumably about the toil and difficulty of songwriting, with the lyric "Trying to make a dove-tail joint." An early version of "Glass Onion" was recorded as a home demo by Lennon at his Kenwood estate.

RECORDING SESSIONS

Produced by Chris Thomas during Martin's extended holiday, "Glass Onion" was recorded at Abbey Road Studios on September 11, 1968, with overdubbing sessions on September 12, 13, 16, and October 10. Starr plays the drums on "Glass Onion," having returned to the fold a week earlier, his drum kit smothered in flowers, courtesy of Evans. As balance engineer Ken Scott later observed,

> The classic for me is in the song "Glass Onion." There's a drum thing that goes *blat blat*. It happens three times in the song. Well, with that drum part, even though it was on the basic track, we double- and triple-tracked the snare drum onto one separate track, imbuing Ringo's drum work with its impudent, highly layered thud. (Scott 2005, 40)

Tea towels were used to dampen Starr's drums, particularly his snare, which was fortified with a pack of Everest cigarettes—Geoff Emerick's favorite brand—sitting on the drum head in order to enhance the effect.

Searching for an innovative means for bringing the composition to a close, Lennon supervised a bizarre late-September session in which he overdubbed the sound of broken glass, a ringing telephone, and BBC soccer commentator Kenneth Wolstenholme exclaiming "It's a goal!" over a roaring football crowd (Spizer 2003, 104). When Martin returned shortly thereafter from his vacation, he was suitably unimpressed with Lennon's inexplicably arcane epilogue. By superimposing an arrangement for four violins, two violas, and two cellos onto the track, Martin afforded "Glass Onion" with an eerie string coda. The "It's a goal!" version of "Glass Onion" is included on *Anthology 3*.

PERSONNEL

Lennon: Vocal, Gibson J-160E
McCartney: Fender Jazz Bass, Piano, Soprano Recorder
Harrison: Epiphone Casino
Starr: Ludwig Oyster Black Pearl Drums, Tambourine
Studio Musicians: String Accompaniment conducted by Martin
Eric Bowie, Henry Datyner, Norman Lederman, Ronald Thomas: Violin
Keith Cummings, John Underwood: Viola
Eldon Fox, Reginald Kilby: Cello

ALBUM APPEARANCES: *The Beatles* (*The White Album*); *Anthology 3*; *Love*.

See also: *The Beatles Anthology, Volume 3* (LP); *The Beatles* (*The White Album*) (LP); "Paul Is Dead" Hoax; Thomas, Chris.

"Golden Slumbers" (Lennon–McCartney)

"Golden Slumbers" is a song on the Beatles' *Abbey Road* album. It is the sixth song in the *Abbey Road* Medley.

AUTHORSHIP AND BACKGROUND

McCartney's "Golden Slumbers" was debuted, along with "Carry That Weight," as a single unit on January 7, 1969, during the *Get Back* sessions (Sulpy and Schweighardt 1997, 80). A traditional English lullaby originally penned by Elizabethan playwright Thomas Dekker, "Golden Slumbers" came into McCartney's orbit during a visit to his father's Cheshire home in 1968. The elder McCartney had married 34-year-old Angela Williams back in November 1964, and her 9-year-old daughter Ruth was trying her hand at the piano when her 26-year-old Beatle stepbrother encountered "Golden Slumbers" in one of her piano books. Inspired by the 400-year-old poem, McCartney began writing his own musical accompaniment to Dekker's original lyrics.

RECORDING SESSIONS

Produced by Martin, "Golden Slumbers" was recorded at Abbey Road Studios on July 2, 1969. Additional overdubbing sessions occurred throughout July, concluding on August 15. Lennon was absent from the primary recording sessions for "Golden Slumbers" due to his car wreck in Scotland.

As Lennon remembered,

> Paul laid the strings on after we finished most of the basic track. I personally can't be bothered with strings and things, you know. I like to do it with the group or with electronics. And especially going through that hassle with musicians and all that bit, you know, it's such a drag trying to get them together. But Paul digs that, so that's his scene. It was up to him where he went with violins and what he did with them. And I think he just wanted a straight kind of backing, you know. Nothing freaky. (Cadogan 2008, 22)

PERSONNEL

McCartney: Vocal, Epiphone Casino, Piano
Harrison: Fender Jazz Bass, Fender Rosewood Telecaster
Starr: Ludwig Hollywood Maple Drums

Studio Musicians: Orchestral Accompaniment (12 Violins, 4 Violas, 4 Cellos, Double Bass, 4 Horns, 3 Trumpets, Trombone, Bass Trombone) conducted by Martin

ALBUM APPEARANCE: *Abbey Road.*

See also: *Abbey Road* (LP).

"Good Day Sunshine" (Lennon–McCartney)

"Good Day Sunshine" is a song on the Beatles' *Revolver* album.

AUTHORSHIP AND BACKGROUND

Written by McCartney with assistance from Lennon, "Good Day Sunshine" was the songwriter's explicit attempt to one-up the Lovin' Spoonful's smash-hit "Daydream."

As McCartney recalled, "'Good Day Sunshine' was me trying to write something similar to 'Daydream.' John and I wrote it together at Kenwood, but it was basically mine and he helped me with it" (Miles 1997, 288). As Lennon remembered, "'Good Day Sunshine' is Paul's. Maybe I threw in a line or something" (Beatles 2000, 209).

RECORDING SESSIONS

Produced by Martin, "Good Day Sunshine" was recorded at Abbey Road Studios on June 8, 1966, with an additional overdubbing session on June 9.

"Good Day Sunshine" involves an intricate time-signature in which the song's musical components shift among common, 5/4, and 3/4 time. Martin performs a honky-tonk piano solo using his wound-up piano effect.

PERSONNEL

Lennon: Backing Vocal
McCartney: Vocal, Rickenbacker 4001S, Piano
Harrison: Backing Vocal
Starr: Ludwig Oyster Black Pearl Drums
Martin: Piano

LEGACY AND INFLUENCE

In 2010, *Rolling Stone* ranked "Good Day Sunshine" as #89 on the magazine's list of *The Beatles' 100 Greatest Songs*.

ALBUM APPEARANCES: *Revolver* (U.K.); *Revolver* (U.S.).

See also: *Revolver* (U.K. LP).

"Good Morning, Good Morning" (Lennon–McCartney)

"Good Morning, Good Morning" is a song on the Beatles' *Sgt. Pepper's Lonely Hearts Club Band* album.

AUTHORSHIP AND BACKGROUND

Written by Lennon, "Good Morning, Good Morning" was inspired, rather appropriately, by a television commercial for Kellogg's cornflakes: "Good morning, good morning, / The best to you each morning, / Sunshine breakfast, Kellogg's Corn Flakes, / Crisp and full of fun."

As Lennon later recalled, "I often sit at the piano, working at songs with the television on low in the background. If I'm a bit low and not getting much done, the words from the telly come through. That's when I heard the words, 'Good Morning, Good Morning'" (Dowlding 1989, 178). McCartney later added that "Good Morning, Good Morning" was "our first major use of sound effects, I think. We had horses and chickens and dogs and all sorts running through it" (Dowlding 1989, 179).

RECORDING SESSIONS

Produced by Martin, "Good Morning, Good Morning" was recorded at Abbey Road Studios on February 8, 1967, with additional overdubbing sessions on February 16, as well as March 13, 28, and 29.

Shifting wildly amongst 5/4, 3/4, and 4/4 time signatures, "Good Morning, Good Morning" offers a masterpiece of electrical energy, with Lennon's kinetic vocal—heavily treated with ADT and with the singer's inner boredom at the very thought of enduring yet another day of unchecked tedium—as well as with McCartney's inventive, blistering guitar solo on his Fender Esquire.

Overdubbed on March 29, 1967, the sound effects in "Good Morning, Good Morning" were courtesy of the EMI tape library's *Volume 35: Animals and Bees* and *Volume 57: Fox-Hunt*. As Emerick recalled, "John said to me during one of the breaks that he wanted to have the sound of animals escaping and that each successive animal should be capable of frightening or devouring its predecessor. So those are not just random effects. There was actually a lot of thought put into all that" (Dowlding 1989, 178). The animal sounds were inspired by the coda for "Caroline, No," a track on the Beach Boys' *Pet Sounds* album (1966).

"During the mix," Emerick added, "I also enjoyed whacking the faders all the way up for Ringo's huge tom hit during the stop-time—so much so that the limiters nearly overloaded, but it definitely gets the listener's attention! Add in the flanged brass, miked in an unorthodox way, and it's all icing on the cake; take those effects off and the recording doesn't have the same magic. That song serves as a good example of how simple manipulation can improve a track sonically" (Emerick and Massey 2006, 179).

On April 19, 1967, Martin came up with the notion of using the final cluck of the hen as the innovative transitional device from "Good Morning, Good Morning" into "Sgt. Pepper's Lonely Hearts Club Band (Reprise)." As Martin later remarked,

> The order we had worked out for the album meant that that track was to be followed by a reprise of the "Sgt. Pepper" song, and of course I was trying to make the whole thing flow. So imagine my delight when I discovered that the sound of a chicken clucking at the end of "Good Morning" was remarkably like the guitar sound at the beginning of "Sgt. Pepper." I was able to cut and mix the two tracks in such a way that the one actually turned into the other. That was one of the luckiest edits one could ever get. . . . Sgt. Pepper himself was breathing life into the project by this time. (Lewisohn 1988, 109)

PERSONNEL

Lennon: Vocal, Piano
McCartney: Rickenbacker 4001S, Fender Esquire
Harrison: Epiphone Casino
Starr: Ludwig Oyster Black Pearl Drums, Tambourine
Studio Musicians: Brass and Saxophone Arrangement featuring Sounds Incorporated (3 saxophones, 2 trombones, and a horn) conducted by Martin

ALBUM APPEARANCES: *Sgt. Pepper's Lonely Hearts Club Band*; *Anthology 2*.

See also: *Sgt. Pepper's Lonely Hearts Club Band* (LP).

"Good Night" (Lennon–McCartney)

"Good Night" is a song on *The Beatles* (*The White Album*).

AUTHORSHIP AND BACKGROUND

Written by Lennon, "Good Night" was composed as a lullaby for the songwriter's five-year-old son Julian.

As McCartney remembered,

> I think John felt it might not be good for his image for him to sing it, but it was fabulous to hear him do it, he sang it great. We heard him sing it in order to teach it to Ringo, and he sang it very tenderly. John rarely showed his tender side, but

my key memories of John are when he was tender, that's what has remained with me—those moments where he showed himself to be a very generous, loving person. (Miles 1997, 487)

RECORDING SESSIONS

Produced by Martin, "Good Night" was recorded on June 28, 1968, followed by an overdubbing session on July 2. The song underwent a remake on July 22.

Having been tasked by Lennon to arrange the song in an intentionally "corny" style, Martin ornamented "Good Night" with a harp, a 30-piece orchestra, and a choir of four boys and four girls. An early version of "Good Night" includes Starr's spoken introduction: "Come along, children, it's time to toddle off to bed" (Dowlding 1989, 250). Backing vocals were provided by the Mike Sammes Singers.

"Good Night" was a lullaby written by John Lennon for his son, Julian. The two are shown here at home on February 11, 1968, a few months before the song, a track from The Beatles' White Album, was recorded. (SSPL/Getty Images)

PERSONNEL

Starr: Vocal
Martin: Celesta
The Mike Sammes Singers: Backing Vocals
Studio Musicians: Orchestral and Choral Accompaniment (12 Violins, 3 Violas, 3 Cellos, 3 Flutes, Clarinet, Horn, Vibraphone, Double Bass, Harp) conducted by Martin

ALBUM APPEARANCES: *The Beatles* (*The White Album*); *Anthology 3*.

See also: *The Beatles* (*The White Album*) (LP).

"Got to Get You into My Life" (Lennon–McCartney)

"Got to Get You into My Life" is a song on the Beatles' *Revolver* album.

AUTHORSHIP AND BACKGROUND

Written by McCartney, "Got to Get You into My Life" celebrates the songwriter's feelings about marijuana's mind-opening effects.

As McCartney later observed,

> I'd been a rather straight working class lad, but when we started to get into pot it seemed to me to be quite uplifting. It didn't seem to have too many side effects like alcohol or some of the other stuff, like pills, which I pretty much kept off. I kind of liked marijuana and to me it seemed it was mind-expanding, literally mind-expanding. So "Got to Get You into My Life" is really a song about that. It's not to a person, it's actually about pot. It's saying, "I'm going to do this. This is not a bad idea." So it's actually an ode to pot, like someone else might write an ode to chocolate or a good claret. (Harry 2002, 384)

As Lennon remembered, "I think that was one of his best songs, too, because the lyrics are good and I didn't write them. You see? When I say that he could write lyrics if he took the effort—here's an example" (Beatles 2000, 209).

RECORDING SESSIONS

Produced by Martin, "Got to Get You into My Life" was recorded at Abbey Road Studios on April 7 and 8, 1966, with additional overdubbing sessions on April 11, May 18, and June 17.

In addition to the song's mind-expanding impetus, "Got to Get You into My Life" also finds McCartney offering yet another valentine to the Beatles' American influences. In this instance, the track captures the sound of Motown, especially the flavor of such Supremes hits as "Where Did Our Love Go" and "Baby Love." Under Martin's arrangement, "Got to Get You into My Life" features a crisp musical attack courtesy of a quintet of studio musicians—three trumpets and two tenor saxophones. In order to achieve a more robust and all-encompassing sound, Emerick later double-tracked the brass. As the song closes in on the two-minute mark, Harrison overdubbed a guitar solo on his Sonic Blue Fender Stratocaster.

PERSONNEL

Lennon: Vocal, Epiphone Casino, Harmonium
McCartney: Rickenbacker 4001S, Backing Vocal
Harrison: Sonic Blue Fender Stratocaster, Maracas
Starr: Ludwig Oyster Black Pearl Drums
Martin: Hammond Organ
Studio Musicians: Brass and Saxophone Accompaniment conducted by Martin
Les Condon, Ian Hamer, Eddie Thornton: Trumpet
Alan Branscombe, Peter Coe: Tenor Saxophone

CHART PERFORMANCE

U.S.: "Got to Get You into My Life"/"Helter Skelter"; May 31, 1976, Capitol 4274: #7 (certified by the RIAA as "Gold," with more than 500,000 copies sold).

LEGACY AND INFLUENCE

In 2010, *Rolling Stone* ranked "Got to Get You into My Life" as #50 on the magazine's list of *The Beatles' 100 Greatest Songs*.

ALBUM APPEARANCES: *Revolver* (U.K.); *Revolver* (U.S.); *Rock 'n' Roll Music*; *Anthology 2*.

See also: *Revolver* (U.K. LP).

Graves, Elsie Gleave (Starkey) (1914–1987)

Born in Liverpool on October 19, 1914, Elsie was the mother of Richard Henry Parkin Starkey, Jr. (Ringo Starr), with her first husband Richard Henry Parkin Starkey, Sr., known as "Big Ritchie." On October 24, 1936, Elsie married Starkey, whom she had met in the Liverpool dance halls. After Starr's birth on July 7, 1940, Big Ritchie was entirely unprepared for the responsibilities of fatherhood, preferring instead to continue making the rounds of the dance halls where he and Elsie had begun their courtship only a few years before. Within a year of their son's birth, the Starkeys had separated. By 1943, they had divorced, leaving Elsie to raise young Ritchie by herself until she married Harry Graves in 1953. Starr claimed that he saw his birth father no more than three more times throughout his life, observing that he had "no real memories" of Big Ritchie.

As a mother, Elsie was devoted to Starr, whose childhood was overshadowed by rampant illness, including dangerous bouts of appendicitis and peritonitis before his seventh birthday. Throughout his early years, Starr made little progress in school, spending inordinate periods under hospitalization with his mother by his side. In 1952, Starr was stricken with tuberculosis, which had reached epidemic proportions in Liverpool—particularly in the Dingle neighborhood where he lived with Elsie. Eventually, the boy ended up at Royal Liverpool Children's Hospital, where he convalesced in the sanitarium. During his lengthy stay at the hospital, Starr was encouraged to keep his mind alert by participating in the makeshift hospital band, which consisted of young patients playing rudimentary percussion along with prerecorded music (Spitz 2005, 338). For Starr, the experience was a revelation, sparking his interest in playing the drums, which Elsie's second husband Harry Graves supported by purchasing the boy's first drum kit. Starr remained close with Elsie and Graves for the remainder of their lives—through the Beatles years and beyond. Elsie died in 1987 at age 73.

See also: Graves, Harry; Starr, Ringo; Starkey, Richard Henry Parkin, Sr.

Graves, Harry (1907–1994)

Born in 1907, Graves became Starr's stepfather on April 17, 1953, when he married Elsie Gleave. A Liverpool Corporation housepainter, Graves had previously lived in London only to retreat to Liverpool after a failed marriage. Starr developed a lasting affection for Graves, whom he lovingly called his "step-ladder." Graves had a deep love for popular music—ranging from vocal stylists like Dinah Shore and Sarah Vaughan to pop stars in the vein of Frankie Lane and Johnnie Ray—and he shared this passion with his stepson, whose own interest in music deepened with the advent of the skiffle craze. Using an old washboard for percussion, Starr joined the Eddie Clayton Skiffle Group. In December 1957, Graves presented his stepson with a used drum kit, which he had bought in London for £10. With his drum set in tow, Starr became a professional drummer, thanks to Graves, as the Eddie Clayton Skiffle Group began booking a series of small-time local engagements. Graves remained a constant presence throughout Starr's life—across the tremors of Beatlemania, the post-Beatles years, and Elsie's death in 1987. Graves died on August 24, 1994, at age 87.

See also: Graves, Elsie Gleave (Starkey); Starr, Ringo.

H

"Happiness Is a Warm Gun" (Lennon–McCartney)

"Happiness Is a Warm Gun" is a song on *The Beatles* (*The White Album*).

AUTHORSHIP AND BACKGROUND

Lennon had been inspired to write the song after George Martin showed him a magazine cover with the phrase "Happiness Is a Warm Gun." As Lennon later remarked, "I just thought it was a fantastic, insane thing to say. A warm gun means you just shot something" (Lennon 1970, 115). The article in the gun magazine was no doubt alluding to Charles Schultz's well-known early 1960s *Peanuts* cartoon. With the caption "Happiness is a warm puppy," the cartoon depicts beloved beagle Snoopy locked in the brawny embrace of Lucy Van Pelt (Spizer 2003, 108).

As Lennon later recalled, "A gun magazine was sitting around and the cover was the picture of a smoking gun. The title of the article, which I never read, was 'Happiness Is a Warm Gun.' I took it right from there. I took it as the idea of happiness after having shot somebody. Or some animal" (Harry 2011, 309).

In addition to portraying "Happiness Is a Warm Gun" as a miniature "history of rock and roll," Lennon described the composition's three principal sections as "the Dirty Old Man," "the Junkie," and "the Gunman" (Beatles 2000, 307). The song's final section likely shares its origins with the May 1968 Esher recording of "I'm So Tired," in which Lennon improvises the song's lyrics, concluding with "I wonder should I get up and go to the funny farm."

RECORDING SESSIONS

Produced by Martin, "Happiness Is a Warm Gun" was recorded at Abbey Road Studios in 45 takes on September 23, 1968, with another 25 takes attempted on the following day. Additional overdubs were added on September 25, when the song's principal sections were edited together. An early version of "Happiness Is a Warm Gun" was recorded as a home demo by Lennon at his Kenwood estate.

While the first section is undergirded by Lennon and Harrison's arpeggiated guitars, the second and third sections offer a feast of shifting time signatures. In the song's final section, an homage to 1950s-era rock 'n' roll, McCartney and Harrison provide Lennon with deft backing vocals, singing "bang-bang, shoot-shoot" in perfect doo-wop harmony.

PERSONNEL

Lennon: Vocal, Epiphone Casino, Tambourine
McCartney: Rickenbacker 4001S, Backing Vocal
Harrison: Gibson Les Paul Standard, Backing Vocal
Starr: Ludwig Oyster Black Pearl Drums

LEGACY AND INFLUENCE

In 2010, *Rolling Stone* ranked "Happiness Is a Warm Gun" as #24 on the magazine's list of *The Beatles' 100 Greatest Songs*.

CONTROVERSY

"Happiness Is a Warm Gun" was banned by the BBC for its prurient sexual language.

ALBUM APPEARANCES: *The Beatles* (*The White Album*); *Anthology 3*.

See also: *The Beatles* (*The White Album*) (LP); Martin, George.

A Hard Day's Night (Film)

Based on a screenplay by Alun Owen and produced on a budget of some $350,000, the movie *A Hard Day's Night* was filmed at London's Paddington Station, Twickenham Film Studios, and various other locations in March and April 1964, premiering on July 6 at the London Pavilion in Piccadilly Circus. In 1965, McCartney was nominated for Most Promising Newcomer to Leading Film Roles at BAFTA, the 18th British Film Awards.

Directed by Richard Lester, the movie grossed $11 million worldwide and $1.3 million in the first week of its American release—both of which were astounding figures for that era. It was a defining moment for the Beatles in terms of its commercial success, as well as for its myth-making power. When Epstein negotiated their contract with United Artists for *A Hard Day's Night* in October 1963, they wanted to make the movie "for the express purpose of having a soundtrack album," according to the film's producer Walter Shenson. In one instance, Lennon even told Epstein that "we don't fancy being Bill Haley and the Bellhops, Brian" (Barrow 1993, 5).

As a work of film, *A Hard Day's Night* capitalizes on each band member's image as it had been established by their adeptly choreographed press conferences and their appearances on such popular fare as *Thank Your Lucky Stars* and *The Ed Sullivan Show*. Perhaps even more significantly, the audience for the Beatles' films were already well-schooled in the generic, myth-making conventions of the pop musical by such movies as *The Girl Can't Help It* (1956) and *Rock Around the Clock*

The Beatles have their hair combed by stylists on the set of their first movie production, *A Hard Day's Night*, at Twickenham Film Studios in England, on March 12, 1964. From left are George Harrison, Ringo Starr, Paul McCartney and John Lennon. Behind Harrison is his future wife, Pattie Boyd. (AP Photo)

(1956), not to mention Elvis Presley's various cinematic forays. The audience's desire to see their heroes fulfill their preconceived roles as the Fab Four allows them to anticipate—and thus share in the construction of—the existing characters and plot mechanisms inherent in *A Hard Day's Night*. As with the Beatles cartoons that premiered on ABC in September 1965, *A Hard Day's Night* assisted the band in promoting the mythology about their different personalities that lingers to the present day.

As a pop musical that splices together micronarratives about each band members' experiences during a "hard day's night," the film features various montages and performance pieces devoted to the six new Beatles songs recorded explicitly for the movie. Bob Neaverson contends that films such as *A Hard Day's Night* attempt to draw their audiences into a voyeuristic relationship with their subjects, to afford their spectators with a glimpse into the band's constructed "lives." "The audience is allowed to see a pop group in intimate, 'behind-the-scenes' scenarios which are essentially 'real,' or at least, realistic," Neaverson writes. "Ultimately, [the film] enabled them to leave the cinema feeling that they had come to 'know' (and love) the group as 'real' people, rather than that they had merely been 'entertained' by a pop group acting out a totally fictitious plot" (Neaverson 1997, 21).

As for the *A Hard Day's Night* music, the songs in order of their appearance in the movie included

"A Hard Day's Night"
"I Should Have Known Better"
"I Wanna Be Your Man" (excerpt)
"Don't Bother Me" (excerpt)
"All My Loving" (excerpt)
"If I Fell"
"Can't Buy Me Love"
"And I Love Her"
"I'm Happy Just to Dance with You"
"This Boy"
"Tell Me Why"
"She Loves You"

See also: *A Hard Day's Night* (U.K. LP); Lester, Richard.

"A Hard Day's Night" (Lennon–McCartney)

"A Hard Day's Night" is a song on the Beatles' *A Hard Day's Night* album. It was the band's seventh consecutive #1 single in the United Kingdom, where it was released on July 10, 1964.

AUTHORSHIP AND BACKGROUND

Written by Lennon, "A Hard Day's Night" was composed in breakneck fashion. As Lennon remembered,

> It was an off-the-cuff remark by Ringo. You know, one of those malapropisms. A Ringo-ism, where he said it not to be funny—just said it. So Dick Lester said, "We are going to use that title." And the next morning I brought in the song 'cuz there was a little competition between Paul and I as to who got the A-side— who got the hits. If you notice, in the early days the majority of singles, in the movies and everything, were mine. In the early period I'm dominating the group. (Harry 2011, 312)

RECORDING SESSIONS

Produced by Martin, "A Hard Day's Night" was recorded at Abbey Road Studios on April 16, 1964. When all was said and done, "A Hard Day's Night" had been written, rehearsed, and recorded in fewer than 24 hours. The Beatles also recorded a version of the song for BBC Radio's *Top Gear* program.

"A Hard Day's Night" opens in unforgettable style with Harrison's distinctive, chiming chord—a G7-suspended played on his Rickenbacker 12-string: "We knew it would open both the film and the soundtrack LP," Martin recalled, "so we wanted a particularly strong and effective beginning. The strident guitar chord was the perfect launch" (Lewisohn 1988, 43).

In "A Hard Day's Night," Harrison's remarkable guitar solo was achieved via Martin's wound-up piano technique. With the producer "doubling" Harrison's guitar solo on "Mrs. Mills"—Studio Two's upright piano—sound engineer Geoff Emerick rolled the tape at half-speed in the control room above. With only one free track available on the mixing desk, Emerick watched the "two Georges—Harrison and Martin—working side by side in the studio, foreheads furrowed in concentration as they played the rhythmically complex solo in tight unison on their respective instruments" (Emerick and Massey 2006, 84).

In itself, Harrison's guitar solo for "A Hard Day's Night" represents a signal moment in the Beatles' career, given that it was all but impossible for him to reproduce the solo on stage. Indeed, if the band could hear above the din of their screaming fans—a near-impossibility in and of itself—the group could reasonably hope to produce a note-perfect rendition of "Can't Buy Me Love" in concert. Yet the sheer velocity of the solo in "A Hard Day's Night," achieved via Martin's wound-up piano effect, resulted in a guitar figure that could only find flight in the recording studio.

This by-product of the group's evolving studio complexity is demonstrated on the recording of the Beatles performing "A Hard Day's Night" on *Live at the BBC* (1994). According to producer Bernie Andrews, the band initially hoped to reproduce the intricate solo on stage with Martin's musical assistance. When Martin couldn't make it for the BBC session, Andrews opted to splice in the prerecorded wound-up piano effect that Martin had created in the studio with the Beatles (Russell 2006, 291). For the group's 1964–1965 live performances of "A Hard Day's Night," Harrison improvised a contrastingly simplistic guitar solo that mimicked the song's melody.

PERSONNEL

Lennon: Vocal, Rickenbacker 325
McCartney: Vocal, Höfner 500/1
Harrison: Rickenbacker 360/12
Starr: Ludwig Oyster Black Pearl Drums
Martin: Piano

CHART PERFORMANCE

U.K.: "A Hard Day's Night"/"Things We Said Today"; July 10, 1964, Parlophone R 5160: #1.

U.S.: "A Hard Day's Night"/"I Should Have Known Better"; July 13, 1964, Capitol 5122: #1 (certified by the RIAA as "Gold," with more than 500,000 copies sold).

LEGACY AND INFLUENCE

In 1964, "A Hard Day's Night" earned a Grammy Award for Best Performance by a Vocal Group at the 6th Grammy Awards. It was also nominated for a Grammy Award for Best Contemporary Song.

In 2004, *Rolling Stone* ranked "A Hard Day's Night" as #154 on the magazine's list of *The 500 Greatest Songs of All Time.*

In 2008, *Rolling Stone* ranked "A Hard Day's Night" as #22 on the magazine's list of *The 100 Greatest Guitar Songs of All Time.*

In 2010, *Rolling Stone* ranked "A Hard Day's Night" as #11 on the magazine's list of *The Beatles' 100 Greatest Songs.*

ALBUM APPEARANCES: *A Hard Day's Night* (U.S.); *A Hard Day's Night* (U.K.); *A Collection of Beatles Oldies*; *The Beatles, 1962–1966*; *The Beatles at the Hollywood Bowl*; *Reel Music*; *20 Greatest Hits*; *Live at the BBC*; *Anthology 1*; *1*.

See also: *A Hard Day's Night* (Film).

A Hard Day's Night (U.K. LP)

July 10, 1964, Parlophone PMC 1230 (mono)/PCS 3058 (stereo)

A Hard Day's Night is the Beatles' third studio album. It was released on the Parlophone label on July 10, 1964, in the United Kingdom. It was the first Beatles album to be comprised entirely of original compositions and the only Beatles album to consist entirely of songs by Lennon and McCartney. In the United States, several of the songs on *A Hard Day's Night* were released on United Artists' *A Hard Day's Night* soundtrack on June 26, 1964, with any remaining tracks being held over in the United States for *Something New*, released on July 20, 1964; *Beatles '65*, released on December 15, 1964; and *Hey Jude*, released on February 26, 1970.

A Hard Day's Night became standardized among U.S. album releases with the February 26, 1987, distribution of the band's first four albums as mono compact-disc (CD) releases. *A Hard Day's Night* was remastered and rereleased as a stereo CD on September 9, 2009. A remastered mono release was also made available at this time as part of a limited edition box set entitled *The Beatles in Mono*.

BACKGROUND AND RECORDING SESSIONS

For all of the chaos in their Beatlemania-era lives, the Beatles enjoyed a reasonable working pace in the studio during the production of *A Hard Day's Night*.

Produced by Martin with Norman "Normal" Smith as his sound engineer, the album was recorded sporadically on four-track equipment over several sessions between February 25, 1964—earlier if you count their stint at Pathé Marconi in January—and June 2. The February 25 sessions witnessed the emergence of two additional compositions, "And I Love Her" and "I Should Have Known Better"—each of which were written in haste for the still-untitled feature film, which was scheduled to begin principal photography on March 2.

The album's title was delivered from the lips of Starr, who, after a particularly long and difficult day in Beatledom, was said to have uttered, "It's been a hard day's night." Lennon employed Starr's malapropism in "Sad Michael," a short story collected in his 1964 book *In His Own Write*. "He'd had a hard day's night that day," Lennon wrote, "for Michael was a Cocky Watchtower" (Beatles 2000, 134). Alan Clayson perceptively notes that, with all due deference to Starr, the phrase had more likely come into the Beatles' universe by way of Eartha Kitt, whose song "I Had a Hard Day Last Night" was the B-side of her 1963 single "Lola Lola" (Clayson 2003b, 380).

On June 3, 1964, the day after sessions for the album concluded, Starr collapsed from exhaustion during a photo session, later being diagnosed with acute tonsillitis. Starr's illness forced him to miss the Beatles' concerts in Denmark, the Netherlands, Hong Kong, and Australia. During his absence, Jimmie Nicol filled in as the band's drummer.

TRACK LISTING

Side 1: "A Hard Day's Night"; "I Should Have Known Better"; "If I Fell"; "I'm Happy Just to Dance with You"; "And I Love Her"; "Tell Me Why"; "Can't Buy Me Love."

Side 2: "Any Time at All"; "I'll Cry Instead"; "Things We Said Today"; "When I Get Home"; "You Can't Do That"; "I'll Be Back."

COVER ARTWORK

Photographed and designed by Robert Freeman, the distinctive album cover for *A Hard Day's Night* was employed in a coordinated marketing campaign for both the album and the feature film. As with the Beatles' previous albums, Beatles press officer Tony Barrow authored the album's liner notes, writing that

Alun Owen began work on the original screenplay late last autumn. Producer Walter Shenson and director Richard Lester watched their newest screen stars at work over Christmas and the New Year on the stage of the Finsbury Park "Astoria" in London. John and Paul began to compile a collection of new compositions for the soundtrack while The Beatles were appearing at the Paris "Olympia" last January. One morning early in March a specially chartered train moved out of Paddington station and the first day's shooting of the Beatles' first film got underway. Reel upon reel of precious film had filled the camera crew's metal cans before a title had been selected for the United Artists picture. Then Ringo casually came up with the name at the end of a particularly strenuous session on the film set. "It's been a hard day's night that was!" he declared, squatting for a moment in the arm of his canvas chair behind the line of cameras and technicians. The film, which also stars Wilfred Brambell in the role of Paul's (mythical) Irish grandfather, was promptly named *A Hard Day's Night*.

CHART PERFORMANCE

U.K.: #1 (In the United States, *A Hard Day's Night* has been certified by the RIAA as "4x Multi Platinum," with more than 4 million copies sold).

LEGACY AND INFLUENCE

In 2000, *Q Magazine* ranked *A Hard Day's Night* as #5 on the magazine's list of *The 100 Greatest British Albums Ever*.

In 2003, *Rolling Stone* ranked *A Hard Day's Night* as #307 on the magazine's list of *The 500 Greatest Albums of All Time*.

In 2005, *Mojo* magazine ranked *A Hard Day's Night* as #81 on the magazine's list of *The 100 Greatest Albums Ever Made*.

See also: *A Hard Day's Night* (Film); Martin, George.

A Hard Day's Night (U.S. LP)

June 26, 1964, United Artists UA 6366 (mono)/UAS 6366 (stereo)

A Hard Day's Night was the fourth Beatles album to be released in the United States. It was released on the United Artists label on June 26, 1964. The American version of *A Hard Day's Night* includes the seven songs included in the feature film, along with "I'll Cry Instead," which had originally been written, though later passed over, for the movie. The soundtrack is rounded out by Martin's instrumental arrangements of four Lennon–McCartney compositions—"I Should Have Known Better," "And I Love Her," "This Boy (Ringo's Theme)," and "A Hard Day's Night"—as performed by George Martin and His Orchestra. In 1979, the EMI Group acquired United Artists, and the soundtrack for *A Hard Day's Night* was released on the Capitol label on August 17, 1980.

The American version of *A Hard Day's Night* was deleted from the Beatles' catalogue in 1987, when the group's U.K. albums were distributed as CD releases.

BACKGROUND

A Hard Day's Night topped the American album charts for 14 weeks—the most of any album during the 1964 calendar year. With United Artists having released the

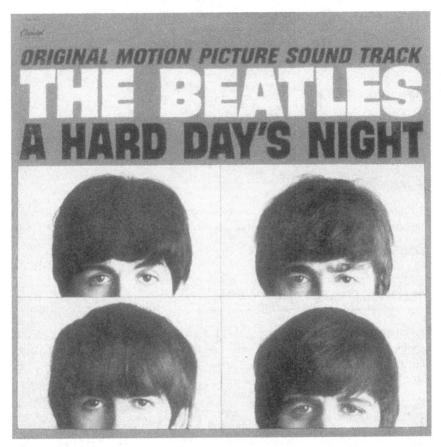

Album cover of the Beatles' *A Hard Day's Night,* which was released in the United States on July 10, 1964. Clockwise from bottom left are George Harrison, Paul McCartney, John Lennon, and Ringo Starr. (Michael Ochs Archives/Getty Images)

soundtrack for *A Hard Day's Night*, Capitol Records countered a few weeks later with *Something New*, a collection of eight songs from the original British release of *A Hard Day's Night*.

TRACK LISTING

Side 1: "I'll Cry Instead"; "Things We Said Today"; "Any Time at All"; "When I Get Home"; "Slow Down"; "Matchbox."

Side 2: "Tell Me Why"; "And I Love Her"; "I'm Happy Just to Dance with You"; "If I Fell"; "Komm, Gib Mir Deine Hand" ["I Want to Hold Your Hand"].

CHART PERFORMANCE

U.S.: #1 (certified by the RIAA as "4x Multi Platinum," with more than 4 million copies sold).

COVER ARTWORK

For the U.S. soundtrack for *A Hard Day's Night*, Freeman's composite cover photographs for the album cover were drawn from his distinctive design for the U.K. version of *A Hard Day's Night*.

LEGACY AND INFLUENCE

In 2000, *A Hard Day's Night* was inducted into the National Academy of Recording Arts and Sciences Grammy Hall of Fame.

See also: *A Hard Day's Night* (U.K. LP).

Harrison, George (1943–2001)

Having joined the Quarry Men in 1958, Harrison was the Beatles' lead guitarist, as well as a highly successful solo artist with three #1 hits in "My Sweet Lord," "Give Me Love (Give Me Peace on Earth)," and "Got My Mind Set on You," the last #1 song by any of the former Beatles.

EARLY YEARS

Harrison was born in Liverpool on February 25, 1943, to father Harold, a Liverpool bus driver, and mother Louise, who worked in a grocery shop. He was the youngest of four children, with older siblings Louise, Harry, and Pete. For much of his life, he believed that he was born on February 25, although he claimed in later years that family records proved that he had entered the world on the previous day at 11:50 P.M. Harold and Louise's meager occupations ensured that the Harrisons, much like the McCartneys, scarcely rose above the succession of council houses that life afforded them. Good fortune shined on them, though, when the family was chosen amongst a deep well of housing applicants to relocate from modest Arnold Grove into a new council house on Upton Green in Speke—and less than a mile away from the McCartney abode on Forthlin Road.

Nicknamed Geo (pronounced as "Joe") by his family, he had been a sterling student at Dovedale Primary, yet he had transformed, in his incipient adolescence, into a lackluster, uninterested pupil at the Liverpool Institute:

I felt then that there was some hypocrisy going on, even though I was only about 11-years-old. . . . It seemed to be the same on every housing estate in

English cities: on one corner they'd have a church and on the other corner a pub. Everybody's out there getting pissed and then just goes in the church, says three "Hail Marys" and one "Our Father" and sticks a fiver in the plate. It felt so alien to me. Not the stain-glass window or the pictures of Christ; I like that a lot, and the smell of the incense and the candles. I just didn't like the bullshit. After Communion, I was supposed to have Confirmation, but I thought "I'm not going to bother with that, I'll just confirm it later myself." (Beatles 2000, 26)

Harrison was fortunate, nevertheless, to grow up in a generally convivial environment—no doubt fostered by his mother Louise, who filled their home with music courtesy of the BBC, and Harold, who, despite his paltry paycheck, was genuinely proud of his work as a bus driver.

As with Lennon and McCartney, Harrison's musical passions had been roused by skiffle. In the autumn of 1956, he had attended a Lonnie Donegan concert with his older brother Harold and was mesmerized by the performance. After buying his own copy of "Rock Island Line," he talked his mother into purchasing a three-quarter sized, Dutch-made Egmond guitar. His initial attempts at playing the instrument were met with failure. Months later, though, he was buoyed by the imported American sounds of Elvis Presley, and he turned his attentions back on the guitar with a vengeance. With his friend Arthur Kelly in tow, he took weekly lessons from a local guitarist who displayed his talents at a nearby pub known as the Cat. "He taught us a few basic root chords straightaway," Kelly remembered. "The first number we learned was 'Your Cheatin' Heart,' by Hank Williams. We hated the song but were thrilled, at least, to be changing from C to F to G7" (Spitz 2005, 122). Soon thereafter, Harrison and Kelly formed a skiffle band of their own that they christened the Rebels. With his brother Pete on tea-chest bass, they plowed

George Harrison in 1968. (Photofest)

George Harrison poses for a childhood snapshot while playing an acoustic guitar, ca. 1954, in Liverpool, England. (Michael Ochs Archives/ Getty Images)

through a handful of songs in his bedroom. They even played a gig at the local British Legion, where they served as the opening act for a magician.

By this time, Harrison had begun to lose interest in skiffle, having discovered such legendary American guitarists as Chet Atkins and Carl Perkins. He honed his skills by devoting hour upon hour of meticulous practice in order to master the sounds that he heard on Radio Luxembourg and the American records that he and his friends found— and mostly shoplifted—at Lewis's department store on the banks of the Mersey. Meanwhile, his friendship with McCartney began to blossom during their schooldays together at the Liverpool Institute. Before long, McCartney was hanging out at the Harrisons' amiable home on weekends. A month after attending the Quarry Men's performance at Wilson Hall, Harrison met up with the group at a skiffle club in West Oakhill Park. As the band (which included McCartney and Lennon as well as other friends) looked on, he broke into a slick, note-perfect rendition of "Guitar Boogie," a relatively complicated composition that impressed the group almost immediately. He subsequently wowed them with a painstaking version of "Raunchy." Intuitively realizing that he was in the presence of a budding virtuoso, Lennon overlooked his age and invited him into the group.

"The Quarry Men had other members," Harrison recalled, "who didn't seem to be doing anything, so I said, 'Let's get rid of them, then I'll join'" (Beatles 2000, 30). His emergence in the band quickly spelled the end for Griffiths, who was dismissed when Lennon and McCartney intentionally neglected to invite him to a rehearsal, leaving Hanton to inform the guitarist about the change in personnel. Not long afterward, Garry contracted tubercular meningitis, and his protracted confinement led to his estrangement from the band. Only Hanton remained from Lennon's original formation of the Quarry Men, but the difference in overall quality was palpable. With Lennon, McCartney, and Harrison as the band's trio of burgeoning guitarists, their sound had noticeably brightened, and their creative energy had blossomed like never before. Their garage-band origins were shifting, slowly but surely, into serious musical aspirations. For this reason alone, Harrison's membership in the Quarry Men had been a genuine boon for the band. He continued as the band's guitarist through its various permutations as the Beatals, the Silver Beetles, and, finally, the Beatles in August 1960, when the group traveled to Hamburg, with then-members Best and Sutcliffe, for the extended musical apprenticeship that served as a prelude to the onset of their global fame in the early 1960s.

MARRIAGE AND FAMILY

In 1964, Harrison met model Pattie Boyd, who was working as an extra on the set of *A Hard Day's Night*. After moving in together at his Kinfauns home, Boyd and Harrison became engaged on December 25, 1965, later marrying on January 21, 1966, in Esher's Upper High Street Registry Office, with McCartney serving as best man. In 1974, the couple separated; their divorce was finalized in 1977. On May 19, 1979, Boyd married Harrison's close friend, guitar icon Eric Clapton, who had nurtured his love for Harrison's wife since the late 1960s. Harrison met his second wife, Olivia Trinidad Arias, at A&M Records, in Los Angeles, where she was working as a secretary. They were married on September 2, 1978, at the Henley-on-Thames Registry Office. A month earlier, their son Dhani had been born on August 1, 1978. Dhani later became a professional musician in his own right, most notably as vocalist and guitarist for thenewno2.

SOLO YEARS

Harrison enjoyed a very successful solo career, and, at least initially, was the first of the former Beatles to find critical and commercial acclaim as an artist in his own right. After releasing the largely experimental *Wonderwall Music* (1968) and *Electronic Sound* (1969), his breakthrough LP was *All Things Must Pass* (1970), a triple album coproduced with Spector and the progenitor of a trio of hit songs in "My Sweet Lord," "What Is Life," and "Isn't It a Pity." The album's success was later overshadowed by a protracted lawsuit regarding the similarities between "My Sweet Lord" and the Chiffons' "He's So Fine." Composed by Ronald Mack, "He's So Fine" was recorded by the Chiffons and released as a single in December 1962 and become a #1 hit in the United States in 1963. In September 1976, Harrison was ordered to pay damages in the amount of $1.6 million.

On the heels of *All Things Must Pass*, Harrison staged *The Concert for Bangladesh*, which included two benefit concerts held on the afternoon and evening of Sunday, August 1, 1971, at New York City's Madison Square Garden. Harrison and Ravi Shankar organized the concerts in order to raise awareness and relief funds following the 1970 Bhola cyclone and Bangladeshi civil war atrocities. With such guest artists as Starr, Bob Dylan, Clapton, Billy Preston, Leon Russell, and Badfinger, *The Concert for Bangladesh* resulted in a best-selling live album and concert film. By the mid-1980s, more than $12 million had been raised through Harrison and Shankar's efforts. In 1973, *The Concert for Bangladesh* earned a Grammy Award for Album of the Year at the 15th Grammy Awards.

In the ensuing years, Harrison enjoyed best-selling albums with *Living in the Material World* (1973), which featured the hit single "Give Me Love (Give Me Peace on Earth)," and *Dark Horse* (1974), for which he embarked on his only post-Beatles U.S. tour. While he found commercial success with such 1970s-era albums as *Extra Texture (Read All About It)* (1975), *Thirty Three & 1/3* (1976), and *George Harrison* (1979), this period was marked by various shifts in sound as he attempted to replicate the success of his work at the beginning of the decade. The latter album is noteworthy for "Blow Away," a Top 20 U.S. hit. In the 1980s, his *Somewhere in England* (1981) was highlighted by "All Those Years Ago," which the former Beatle had fashioned in honor of Lennon, who had been murdered on December 8, 1980, and recorded with McCartney and Starr, among others. His subsequent album *Gone Troppo* (1982) was a critical and cultural failure for him; yet in 1987, he returned to the pop scene with a vengeance with the platinum-selling *Cloud Nine*. Coproduced by Jeff Lynne, the album featured the #1 hit single "Got My Mind Set on You," as well as the nostalgic Beatles-oriented "When We Was Fab."

During subsequent years, Harrison enjoyed success as a member of the Traveling Wilburys, a rock supergroup formed in the late 1980s by Harrison, Dylan, Lynne, Roy Orbison, and Tom Petty, along with Jim Keltner. The band's first album, *Traveling Wilburys, Volume 1* (1988), was a considerable critical and commercial success and featured the hit single "Handle with Care." It subsequently won the Grammy Award for Best Rock Performance by a Duo or Group in 1989. A second album, *Traveling Wilburys, Volume 3*, was released in 1990. As a solo artist, his career was rounded out by a solo tour, accompanied by Clapton, of Japan in 1991. The concerts were commemorated with the release of his *Live in Japan* in 1992. His final solo album, *Brainwashed*, was coproduced with Lynne and his son Dhani and released posthumously in 2002. In 2004, the album's "Marwa Blues" earned a Grammy Award for Best Pop Instrumental Performance at the 46th Grammy Awards. *Brainwashed* was nominated for a Grammy Award for Best Pop Vocal Album, while the song "Any Road" was nominated for a Grammy Award for Best Male Pop Vocal Performance.

LATER YEARS AND DEATH

On December 30, 1999, Harrison and wife Olivia were attacked at their Friar Park estate in Henley-on-Thames by a mentally ill intruder, Michael Abram, whom

Olivia subdued by hitting over the head with a table lamp. Harrison had been stabbed multiple times and was rushed to the hospital. In 2001, he was diagnosed with lung cancer. In spite of numerous surgical efforts, the cancer spread and he died at age 58 in Los Angeles on November 29, 2001, with Olivia and Dhani by his side. The following year, Olivia staged the memorial *Concert for George* at London's Royal Albert Hall. In addition to McCartney and Starr, the guest musicians included Clapton, Lynne, Preston, Shankar, and Petty, among others. Proceeds from the event went to Harrison's Material World Charitable Foundation.

LEGACY

As with the other Beatles, Harrison was appointed as a member of the Order of the British Empire during the Queen's Birthday Honours on June 12, 1965, receiving his insignia from Queen Elizabeth II at Buckingham Palace on October 26. On August 31, 1984, his legacy was commemorated with the naming of a minor planet, 4149 Harrison, by Brian A. Skiff at the Lowell Observatory's Anderson Mesa Station. In 1988, the Beatles were inducted into the Rock and Roll Hall of Fame. In December 1992, Harrison was the inaugural recipient of the Billboard Century Award. In 2003, he was ranked #11 on *Rolling Stone* magazine's list of the 100 Greatest Guitarists of All Time. In 2004, he was inducted posthumously into the Rock and Roll Hall of Fame as a solo artist. On April 14, 2009, he was honored with a star on Hollywood's Walk of Fame by the Hollywood Chamber of Commerce. As with the other Beatles, his star is located on North Vine Street in front of the Capitol Records Building. In 2011, Harrison's life and work were explored in the award-winning documentary film *George Harrison: Living in the Material World*, directed by Martin Scorsese.

See also: Boyd, Pattie; Clapton, Eric; Harrison, Harold Hargreaves; Harrison, Louise French; Harrison, Olivia Trinidad Arias; Lennon, John; Lynne, Jeff; McCartney, Paul; The Traveling Wilburys.

Harrison, Harold Hargreaves (1909–1978)

Born in Liverpool on May 2, 1909, Harold Harrison is George Harrison's father. A former steward on a ship on the British White Star Line, he was later employed as a Liverpool bus driver. In 1929, he met Louise French, who worked in a grocery shop, and married her the next year. Two children, Louise and Harry, followed in quick succession, and by 1936, Harold brought his seafaring days to an end in order to seek out a more lucrative profession. The long reach of the Great Depression left him unemployed for another two years until he landed a position as a bus driver on the Liverpool Corporation's Speke–Liverpool route. In 1941, the Harrisons' third child Peter was born, and on February 25, 1943, they rounded out the family with George.

After his wife Louise died in 1970, Harold spent the remainder of his days battling emphysema. In his final years, he lived with George at his Friar Park estate, passing away in May 1978 just shy of his 79th birthday and only a few months before his grandson Dhani was born.

See also: The Cavern Club; Harrison, George; Harrison, Louise French; The Quarry Men.

Harrison, Louise French (1911–1970)

Born in Liverpool on March 10, 1911, Louise French is George Harrison's mother. In 1929, she met Harold Harrison, a steward on the British White Star Line. Together, they shared a love of music and dancing, joining Liverpool's Depot Social Club together. Harold and Louise married in 1930, and two children, Louise and Harry, followed. In 1941, the Harrisons' third child Peter was born, and on February 25, 1943, George was born. Louise was particularly influential in igniting George's early musical interests via BBC radio, later purchasing him a three-quarter sized, Dutch-made Egmond guitar. Soon thereafter, a friend of Harold's taught George how to play such songs as "Whispering," "Sweet Sue," and "Dinah." George's parents were strong supporters of his musical interests, later allowing the Quarry Men to rehearse in their home and attending Beatles shows at the Cavern Club.

Louise died on July 7, 1970, at age 59.

See also: The Cavern Club; Harrison, George; Harrison, Harold Hargreaves; The Quarry Men.

Harrison, Olivia Trinidad Arias (1948–)

Born in Mexico City on May 18, 1948, Olivia is George Harrison's widow. The daughter of a dry cleaner and a seamstress, she grew up in Southern California, graduating from high school in 1965. She met Harrison in the mid-1970s at A&M Records, where she worked as a secretary. They were married on September 2, 1978, at the Henley-on-Thames Registry Office. A month earlier, their son Dhani had been born on August 1, 1978. On December 30, 1999, she and Harrison were attacked at their Friar Park estate by Michael Abram, whom she subdued by hitting over the head with a table lamp. Harrison was severely wounded by Abram, who had a knife and who was judged mentally ill. In 2001, Harrison was diagnosed with lung cancer. In spite of numerous surgical efforts, the cancer spread and Harrison died in Los Angeles on November 29, 2001, with Olivia and Dhani by his side. The following year, she staged the memorial *Concert for George* at London's Royal Albert Hall. In addition to McCartney and Starr, the guest musicians included Eric Clapton, Jeff Lynne, Billy Preston, Ravi Shankar, and Tom Petty, among others. Proceeds from the event went to Harrison's Material World Charitable Foundation. In the ensuing years, Olivia has maintained an active presence at Beatles-related events, including the June 1, 2009, press conference with Starr, McCartney, and Ono to mark the release of *The Beatles: Rock Band* video game. She also coproduced the documentary *George Harrison: Living in the Material World* (2011), directed by Scorsese.

See also: *The Beatles: Rock Band* (Video Game); Clapton, Eric; Harrison, George; Ono, Yoko; Preston, Billy.

"Hello, Goodbye" (Lennon–McCartney)

"Hello, Goodbye" was the band's second consecutive #1 single in the United Kingdom, where it was released on November 24, 1967. It was later included on the Beatles' *Magical Mystery Tour* album.

AUTHORSHIP AND BACKGROUND

Written by McCartney, "Hello, Goodbye" was composed as a kind of pop-musical update of George and Ira Gershwin's "Let's Call the Whole Thing Off." It had been written by McCartney in the company of Alistair Taylor, who sat at the harmonium with the Beatle and improvised a series of antonyms: "You say yes, I say no / You say stop, and I say go go go." Taylor later remarked that "I wonder whether Paul really made up that song as he went along or whether it was running through his head already" (Turner 1994, 139, 140).

As McCartney later recalled,

> "Hello, Goodbye" was one of my songs. There are Geminian influences here I think—the twins. It's such a deep theme of the universe, duality—man woman, black white, high low, right wrong, up down, hello goodbye—that it was a very easy song to write. It's just a song of duality, with me advocating the more positive. You say goodbye, I say hello. You say stop, I say go. I was advocating the more positive side of the duality, and I still do to this day. (Cadogan 2008, 198)

As Lennon remembered, "That's another McCartney. An attempt to write a single. It wasn't a great piece. The best bit was at the end, which we all ad-libbed in the studio, where I played the piano. Like 'Ticket to Ride,' where we just threw something in at the end" (Lennon and Ono 2000, 198).

RECORDING SESSIONS

Produced by Martin with Ken Scott assisting Emerick as sound engineer, "Hello, Goodbye" was recorded at Abbey Road Studios on October 2, 1967, with additional overdubbing sessions on October 19, 20, and 25, with a final session on November 2.

Initially rehearsed under the working title of "Hello Hello," "Hello, Goodbye" benefited from one of the group's most inspired moments of creative caprice when they concocted the song's impromptu "hela-heba-hello-a" finale in the studio. In its finished state, the recording of "Hello, Goodbye" is something of a misnomer in the Beatles' corpus, evincing acute instrumental separation with piano and drums on the extreme left channel, while the backing vocals, strings, and electric guitars occupy the far right.

PERSONNEL

Lennon: Hammond Organ, Backing Vocal
McCartney: Vocal, Rickenbacker 4001S, Piano, Bongos, Congas
Harrison: Epiphone Casino, Backing Vocal
Starr: Ludwig Oyster Black Pearl Drums, Maracas, Tambourine, Backing Vocal
Studio Musicians: String Accompaniment conducted by Martin
Leo Birnbaum, Kenneth Essex: Viola

CHART PERFORMANCE

U.K.: "Hello, Goodbye"/"I Am the Walrus"; November 24, 1967, Parlophone R 5655: #1.

U.S.: "Hello, Goodbye"/"I Am the Walrus"; November 27, 1967, Capitol 2056: #1 (certified by the RIAA as "Gold," with more than 500,000 copies sold).

LEGACY AND INFLUENCE

In 2010, *Rolling Stone* ranked "Hello, Goodbye" as #100 on the magazine's list of *The Beatles' 100 Greatest Songs*.

CONTROVERSY

In 1967, the BBC banned the promotional video for "Hello, Goodbye" from television broadcast because McCartney intentionally demonstrated that he was lip-syncing his lead vocal, which violated the standing rules of the British Musicians' Union. To skirt the ban on lip-syncing vocals, British musicians often recorded their vocals live, as McCartney did for the Beatles' 1968 promotional video for "Hey Jude."

ALBUM APPEARANCES: *Magical Mystery Tour*; *The Beatles, 1967–1970*; *20 Greatest Hits*; *Anthology 2*; *1*.

See also: *Magical Mystery Tour* (LP).

"Hello Little Girl" (Lennon–McCartney)

"Hello Little Girl" is purportedly the first song ever composed by Lennon. The Beatles recorded it during a homemade recording session in July 1960 and later as part of their Decca Records audition in January 1962.

AUTHORSHIP AND BACKGROUND

Written by Lennon in 1957, "Hello Little Girl" was inspired by an old "Thirties or Forties song"—likely "It's De-Lovely," by Cole Porter from his 1936 musical *Red Hot and Blue*—that his mother Julia once sang to him. As Lennon later recalled, "That was me. That was actually my first song. 'When I see you every day I say mmm hmm, hello little girl.' I remember some Thirties or Forties song which was [singing] 'You're delightful, you're delicious, and da dada / Isn't it a pity that you are such a scatterbrain.' That always fascinated me for some reason or another. It's also connected to my mother. It's all very Freudian. She used to sing that one. So I made 'Hello Little Girl' out of it" (Lennon and Ono 2000, 172).

RECORDING SESSIONS

The July 1960 recording of "Hello Little Girl" was produced in the McCartney family's bathroom using a Grundig tape recorder. Known as the Braun Tape, the recordings survived in the possession of Hans-Walther "Icke" Braun, one of the band's Hamburg friends, who was entrusted with the tape in the spring of 1961 (Winn 2003a, 4). Seventeen demos survive from the July 1960 recordings, including early versions of the Lennon–McCartney compositions "One After 909," "I'll Follow the Sun," and "Hello Little Girl." In addition to Lennon, McCartney, and Harrison, the July 1960 version of "Hello Little Girl" features Sutcliffe on bass.

The January 1962 recording of "Hello Little Girl," produced by Mike Smith, is considerably more evolved, with Lennon on lead vocals, McCartney playing bass, and Best behind the drum kit.

PERSONNEL

July 1960 Home Demo:
Lennon: Vocal, Guitar
McCartney: Guitar, Backing Vocal
Harrison: Guitar
Sutcliffe: Bass
Decca Records Audition:
Lennon: Vocal, Guitar
McCartney: Bass, Backing Vocal

Harrison: Guitar, Backing Vocal
Best: Drums

ALBUM APPEARANCE: *Anthology 1*.

See also: *The Beatles Anthology, Volume 1* (LP); Decca Records Audition.

Help! (Film)

Originally entitled *Eight Arms to Hold You*, the film's screenplay had been written as a vehicle for Sellers, who turned it down in order to star in *What's New Pussycat?*, a movie in which he portrayed a sex therapist for an inveterate ladies' man played by Peter O'Toole. Rechristened as *Help!*, the screenplay had been tailored to fit the Beatles' on-screen personae, and it received an ample budget of some $600,000.

With *Help!*, the Beatles cemented the collective, carefree image that they began fashioning in *A Hard Day's Night*, while also creating additional opportunities for deepening the highly orchestrated nature of their public "personalities." Directed by Lester and filmed between February 23 and May 11, 1965, in such diverse locations as the Bahamas and London's Twickenham Film Studios, *Help!*'s narrative relies upon the same zany humor as *A Hard Day's Night*. In contrast with the band's earlier film, *Help!* employs a James Bond–inspired spy text as its central crisis: Starr, it seems, has come into the possession of an exotic diamond ring that is coveted by various desperate people, including a cult of Eastern mystics, hit men, and mad scientists, among a host of others. Numerous car chases and skiing shenanigans ensue as the drummer's mates attempt to rescue him from his predicament. In *Help!*, one can glimpse the future of such derivative screwball oddities as the Monkees and the *Banana Splits* (children's 1970 television show) in the film's campy ridiculousness.

As with *A Hard Day's Night*, *Help!* labors to maintain the mythology of the group's collective identity. In one unforgettable scene, the Beatles return home to four adjacent row houses. After unlocking each of their separate doors in unison, each member enters what turns out to be a single, gigantic flat that they all share. For the bandmates themselves, the irony of that scene must have been simply staggering at the time. As Ann Pacey, a critic for the London *Sun*, observes, the Beatles seem "as trapped as four flies" in *Help!* (Neaverson 1997, 42).

As for the *Help!* music, the songs in order of their appearance in the movie included:

"Help!"
"You're Going to Lose That Girl"
"You've Got to Hide Your Love Away"
"Ticket to Ride"
"I Need You"
"The Night Before"

"Another Girl"
"She's a Woman" (excerpt)
"A Hard Day's Night" (instrumental)
"I'm Happy Just to Dance with You" (instrumental)
"You Can't Do That" (instrumental)
"Help!"

See also: *A Hard Day's Night* (Film); Lester, Richard.

"Help!" (Lennon–McCartney)

"Help!" is a song on the Beatles' *Help!* album. It was the band's ninth consecutive #1 single in the United Kingdom, where it was released on July 23, 1965. It was also the band's fourth consecutive #1 hit single in the United States, where it was released on July 19, 1965.

AUTHORSHIP AND BACKGROUND

Written largely by Lennon, "Help!" was originally a slow-tempo composition that evoked the anxiety of Lennon's lyrics. The song's tempo was intentionally sped up in the studio to make it more commercially viable—a move that Lennon deeply regretted.

As Lennon later recalled,

> The whole Beatle thing was just beyond comprehension. When "Help!" came out, I was actually crying out for help. Most people think it's just a fast rock 'n' roll song. I didn't realize it at the time; I just wrote the song because I was commissioned to write it for the movie. But later, I knew I really was crying out for help. So it was my fat Elvis period. You see the movie: He—I—is very fat, very insecure, and he's completely lost himself. And I am singing about when I was so much younger and all the rest, looking back at how easy it was. Now I may be very positive—yes, yes—but I also go through deep depressions where I would like to jump out the window, you know. It becomes easier to deal with as I get older; I don't know whether you learn control or, when you grow up, you calm down a little. Anyway, I was fat and depressed and I was crying out for help. (Everett 2001, 296)

RECORDING SESSIONS

Produced by Martin, "Help!" was recorded at Abbey Road Studios in 12 takes on April 13, 1965.

Having rehearsed the tempo change in the studio, the Beatles adorned the track with a shower of descending 16th notes from Harrison's lead guitar, a distinguishing feature that was added on the track's 12th and final take. McCartney echoes this motif with a descending bass figure of his own during the verses. In addition to the composition's innovative call-and-response backing vocals, the song's confessional quality is highlighted in the latter third of the song, as Lennon returns to the first verse—"When I was younger so much younger than today," he sings. "I never needed anybody's help in any way."

The song's musical phrasings contribute to the band's unnerving depiction of the songwriter's psychological malaise. As Tim Riley observes, "Since Paul and George anticipate nearly every line Lennon sings in the verse, the effect is of voices inside the same head, prodding, goading [the listener] to chilling consequences. By the time Lennon sings 'open up the doors,' the voices are completely caught up in the nightmare" (Riley 1988, 139).

PERSONNEL

> Lennon: Vocal, Framus 12-string Hootenanny
> McCartney: Höfner 500/1
> Harrison: Gretsch Tennessean
> Starr: Ludwig Oyster Black Pearl Drums, Tambourine

CHART PERFORMANCE

> U.K.: "Help!"/"I'm Down"; July 23, 1965, Parlophone R 5305: #1.
> U.S.: "Help!"/"I'm Down"; July 19, 1965, Capitol 5476: #1 (certified by the RIAA as "Gold," with more than 500,000 copies sold).

LEGACY AND INFLUENCE

"Help!" is included among the Rock and Roll Hall of Fame's *500 Songs That Shaped Rock and Roll.*

In 1966, "Help!" was nominated for a Grammy Award for Contemporary Rock and Roll Group Vocal Performance at the 8th Grammy Awards. It was also nominated for a Grammy Award for Vocal Group Performance.

In 2004, *Rolling Stone* ranked "Help!" as #29 on the magazine's list of *The 500 Greatest Songs of All Time.*

In 2010, *Rolling Stone* ranked "Help!" as #15 on the magazine's list of *The Beatles' 100 Greatest Songs.*

In 2008, "Help!" was inducted into the National Academy of Recording Arts and Sciences Grammy Hall of Fame.

ALBUM APPEARANCES: *Help!* (U.K.); *Help!* (U.S.); *A Collection of Beatles Oldies; The Beatles, 1962–1966; Rarities* (U.S.); *The Beatles at the Hollywood Bowl; Reel Music; 20 Greatest Hits; Anthology 2; 1; Love.*

See also: *Help!* (Film); *Help!* (U.K. LP).

Help! (U.K. LP)

August 6, 1965, Parlophone PMC 1255 (mono)/PCS 3071 (stereo)

Help! is the Beatles' fifth studio album. It was released on the Parlophone label on August 6, 1965, in the United Kingdom. In the United States, several of the songs on *Help!* were released on *Beatles '65*, released on December 15, 1964; *Beatles VI*, released on June 14, 1965; the *Help!* soundtrack, released on August 13, 1965; and *Yesterday . . . and Today*, released on June 20, 1966.

    Help! became standardized among U.S. album releases with the April 30, 1987, distribution of *Help!*, *Rubber Soul*, and *Revolver* as stereo CD releases. It was remastered and rereleased as a stereo CD on September 9, 2009. A remastered mono release was also made available at this time as part of a limited edition box set entitled *The Beatles in Mono*.

BACKGROUND AND RECORDING SESSIONS

Produced by Martin with Norman "Normal" Smith as his sound engineer, *Help!* was recorded on four-track equipment over several lengthy sessions in mid-February and mid-June 1965, with an additional pair of sessions conducted on April 13 and May 10. Yet for all of the album's strides in terms of musical sophistication and autobiographical nuance, *Help!* was a hodgepodge in terms of its overall content. There were moments of unparalleled beauty ("You've Got to Hide Your Love Away" and "Yesterday") in the midst of some of the band's least substantial efforts ("Act Naturally" and "You Like Me Too Much"). The period in which the group recorded *Help!* finds the Beatles making a number of musical advancements, with McCartney playing lead guitar for the first time ("Another Girl" and "Ticket to Ride") and Harrison discovering the 21-stringed sitar and Indian music during the filming of the *Help!* feature film. The album also saw the emergence of McCartney's "Yesterday," the most widely covered song in the history of popular music.

    The songs that make up the first half of the album account for the soundtrack associated with the film ("Help!" through "Ticket to Ride"), while the second half accounts for the group's non–soundtrack material. Directed by Lester and filmed between February 23 and May 11, 1965, in such diverse locations as Austria, the Bahamas, and London's Twickenham Film Studios, *Help!*'s filmic narrative relies upon the same zany humor as *A Hard Day's Night*. Originally entitled *Eight Arms to Hold You*, the screenplay had been written as a vehicle for Sellers. Rechristened as *Help!*, the screenplay had been tailored to fit the Beatles' on-screen personae. United Artists also provided a budget of some $600,000, a considerable increase over their previous film. As with the soundtrack albums in the United Kingdom and the United States, the feature film was a tremendous international success, although the Beatles found their second effort less satisfying than the first. As Lennon later recalled, Lester "forgot about who and what we were. And that's why the film didn't work. It was like having clams in a movie about frogs" (Dowlding 1989, 96).

TRACK LISTING

Side 1: "Help!"; "The Night Before"; "You've Got to Hide Your Love Away"; "I Need You"; "Another Girl"; "You're Going to Lose That Girl"; "Ticket to Ride."

Side 2: "Act Naturally"; "It's Only Love"; "You Like Me Too Much"; "Tell Me What You See"; "I've Just Seen a Face"; "Yesterday"; "Dizzy Miss Lizzy."

COVER ARTWORK

As with the band's three previous album covers, the *Help!* album cover photograph was shot by Freeman. The cover art depicts the group flashing a distress signal—"LP U.S." in semaphore. To accomplish this end, the original photograph on the album cover was reverse-printed. Hence, holding the photograph up to a mirror reveals the letters "LP U.S." In contrast with the band's first four albums, *Help!* does not include explanatory liner notes.

CHART PERFORMANCE

U.K.: #1 (In the United States, *Help!* has been certified by the RIAA as "3x Multi Platinum," with more than 3 million copies sold).

LEGACY AND INFLUENCE

In 2003, *Rolling Stone* ranked *Help!* as #332 on the magazine's list of *The 500 Greatest Albums of All Time*.

See also: *Help!* (Film); Martin, George.

Help! (U.S. LP)

August 13, 1965, Capitol MAS 2386 (mono)/SMAS 2386 (stereo)

Help! was the 10th Beatles album to be released in the United States—the 8th on Capitol Records, along with Vee-Jay Records' *Introducing . . . the Beatles* and United Artists' soundtrack for the *A Hard Day's Night* feature film. It was released on the Capitol label on August 13, 1965. The album includes the songs from the *Help!* feature film, along with Ken Thorne's incidental soundtrack music performed by George Martin and His Orchestra.

The American version of *Help!* was deleted from the Beatles' catalogue in 1987, when the group's U.K. albums were distributed as CD releases. A remastered mono and stereo release of *Help!* was released on April 11, 2006, as part of the box set entitled *The Capitol Albums, Volume 2*.

BACKGROUND

The American version of *Help!* was a substantial success, holding down the top spot on the U.S. album charts for nine weeks. George Martin and His Orchestra's "Another Hard Day's Night" is noteworthy for the appearance of the sitar—arguably, the first appearance of the Indian instrument on a major Western album release.

TRACK LISTING

Side 1: "James Bond Theme" [unlisted]; "Help!"; "The Night Before"; "From Me to You Fantasy" (Instrumental); "You've Got to Hide Your Love Away"; "I Need You"; "In the Tyrol" (Instrumental).

Side 2: "Another Girl"; "Another Hard Day's Night" (Instrumental); "Ticket to Ride"; "The Bitter End"/"You Can't Do That" (Instrumental); "You're Going to Lose That Girl"; "The Chase" (Instrumental).

COVER ARTWORK

As with the U.K. release, the front-cover artwork for *Help!* features a photograph from the lens of Freeman. The cover art depicts the group flashing a distress signal—"LP U.S." in semaphore. To accomplish this end, the original photograph on the album cover was reverse-printed. Hence, holding the photograph up to a mirror reveals the letters "LP U.S." In addition to Freeman's photograph, the U.S. cover includes the logo from the *Help!* feature film.

CHART PERFORMANCE

U.S.: #1 (certified by the RIAA as "3x Multi Platinum," with more than 3 million copies sold).

LEGACY AND INFLUENCE

In 1966, *Help!* was nominated for a Grammy Award for Album of the Year at the 8th Grammy Awards. It was also nominated for a Grammy Award for Best Original Score Written for a Motion Picture or Television Show.

See also: *Help!* (Film); *Help!* (U.K. LP); Martin, George.

"Helter Skelter" (Lennon–McCartney)

"Helter Skelter" is a song on *The Beatles* (*The White Album*).

AUTHORSHIP AND BACKGROUND

McCartney had been inspired to write "Helter Skelter" after learning that the Who's latest single, "I Can See for Miles," was being described by Pete Townshend in *Melody Maker* as "the raunchiest, loudest, most ridiculous rock and roll record you've ever heard" (Beatles 2000, 311). McCartney composed the song with the explicit goal of one-upping the Who. The phrase "helter-skelter" refers to the spiral slides on the English playgrounds of the Beatles' youth.

As McCartney later observed, "The Who had made some track that was the loudest, the most raucous rock 'n' roll, the dirtiest thing they'd ever done. It made me think, 'Right. Got to do it.' I like that kind of geeking up. And we decided to do the loudest, nastiest, sweatiest rock number we could" (Dowlding 1989, 242).

RECORDING SESSIONS

Produced by Martin, "Helter Skelter" was recorded at Abbey Road Studios on July 18, 1968. During that drug-addled session, the Beatles created a 27-minute version of the song that is much slower in comparison with the final version. An edited track of this version appears on *Anthology 3*. As Starr later recalled, " 'Helter Skelter' was a track we did in total madness and hysterics in the studio. Sometimes you just had to shake out the jams" (Beatles 2000, 311).

On September 18, 1968, the band attempted a remake, with McCartney playing his Casino and turning in a larynx-searing lead vocal, Lennon on his Fender Jazz Bass, and Harrison on his Gibson Les Paul Standard—nicknamed "Lucy," it was his guitar of choice during the making of *The White Album*. Meanwhile, Mal Evans played a dyspeptic trumpet, while Starr pounded away on the drums through some 18 versions of the song during rehearsal (Spizer 2003, 113). After the final take, Starr reportedly threw his drumsticks across Studio Two and screamed, "I've got blisters on my fingers!"

PERSONNEL

Lennon: Fender Jazz Bass, Epiphone Casino
McCartney: Vocal, Epiphone Casino
Harrison: Gibson Les Paul Standard
Starr: Ludwig Oyster Black Pearl Drums
Evans: Trumpet

CHART PERFORMANCE

U.S.: "Got to Get You into My Life"/"Helter Skelter"; May 31, 1976, Capitol 4274: #7 (certified by the RIAA as "Gold," with more than 500,000 copies sold). As the B-side of "Got to Get You into My Life," "Helter Skelter" did not chart.

LEGACY AND INFLUENCE

In 2005, *Q Magazine* ranked "Helter Skelter" as #5 on the magazine's list of *100 Greatest Guitar Tracks*.

In 2010, *Rolling Stone* ranked "Helter Skelter" as #52 on the magazine's list of *The Beatles' 100 Greatest Songs*.

In 2011, McCartney's performance of "Helter Skelter" on his 2009 live album *Good Evening New York City* earned a Grammy Award for Best Solo Rock Vocal Performance at the 53rd Grammy Awards.

ALBUM APPEARANCES: *The Beatles* (*The White Album*); *Rock 'n' Roll Music*; *Rarities* (U.S.); *Anthology 3*; *Love*; *Tomorrow Never Knows*.

See also: *The Beatles Anthology, Volume 3* (LP); *The Beatles* (*The White Album*) (LP).

"Her Majesty" (Lennon–McCartney)

"Her Majesty" is a song on the Beatles' *Abbey Road* album. Before the advent of the group's CD releases of the album, the song appeared as a "hidden track" at the end of the LP.

AUTHORSHIP AND BACKGROUND

Composed by McCartney, "Her Majesty" is a gentle acoustic paean to Queen Elizabeth II (1926–), the British monarch whose reign began in 1952.

As McCartney recalled, "I was in Scotland, and I was just writing this little tune. I can never tell, like, how tunes come out. I just wrote it as a joke" (Cadogan 2008, 223).

RECORDING SESSIONS

Produced by Martin, "Her Majesty" was recorded at Abbey Road Studios in three takes on July 2, 1969. It was recorded on the same day as the Beatles' first session for "Golden Slumbers" and "Carry That Weight." In the final mix of the *Abbey Road* Medley, "Her Majesty" begins 14 seconds after the conclusion of "The End."

As it happens, the location of "Her Majesty" at the conclusion of the LP was more a matter of accident than design. In an earlier dry run at mixing the medley on July 30, 1969, "Her Majesty" followed "Mean Mr. Mustard"—indeed, in the song's final mix, listeners can still hear the final chord of "Mean Mr. Mustard" at the beginning of "Her Majesty."

After listening to the dry run of the medley, McCartney informed sound engineer John Kurlander that "I don't like 'Her Majesty,' throw it away." Kurlander promptly edited the song out of the medley, but expressly ignored McCartney's order about throwing the track out. "I'd been told never to throw anything away," Kurlander later recalled, "so after he left I picked it up off the floor, put about 20 seconds of red leader tape before it, and stuck it onto the end of the edit tape" (Dowlding 1989, 294). Later, when McCartney heard "Her Majesty" in its new position as an impromptu coda after "The End," he liked it and opted to include it in the album's final mix. "Typical Beatles," McCartney later remarked, "an accident."

PERSONNEL

McCartney: Vocal, Martin D-28

ALBUM APPEARANCE: *Abbey Road.*

See also: *Abbey Road* (LP).

"Here Comes the Sun" (Harrison)

"Here Comes the Sun" is a song on the Beatles' *Abbey Road* album.

AUTHORSHIP AND BACKGROUND

"Here Comes the Sun" was Harrison's final composition as a member of the Beatles. Harrison had written the song's lush melody while strolling around Clapton's Hurtwood mansion garden on a break from the group's relentless Apple business meetings: "The relief of not having to go and see all those dopey accountants was wonderful," Harrison later recalled, "and I was walking around the garden with one of Eric's acoustic guitars and wrote 'Here Comes the Sun' " (Dowlding 1989, 285).

RECORDING SESSIONS

Produced by Martin, the band recorded multiple takes of "Here Comes the Sun" on July 7 and 8, 1969, with overdubbing sessions on July 16 and several additional dates in August. Lennon was absent from the primary recording sessions for "Here Comes the Sun" due to his car wreck in Scotland. Harrison performed the song's distinctive melody on his Gibson J-200 acoustic with a capo affixed to the seventh fret. The song's introductory motto is distinguished by Harrison's luminous Moog synthesizer part, which Emerick gently pans from left to right in the recording mix.

PERSONNEL

McCartney: Rickenbacker 4001S
Harrison: Vocal, Gibson J-200, Moog Synthesizer
Starr: Ludwig Hollywood Maple Drums
Studio Musicians: Orchestral Accompaniment (4 Violas, 4 Cellos, Double Bass, 2 Piccolos, 2 Flutes, 2 Alto Flutes, 2 Clarinets) conducted by Martin

LEGACY AND INFLUENCE

In 2010, *Rolling Stone* ranked "Here Comes the Sun" as #28 on the magazine's list of *The Beatles' 100 Greatest Songs*.

In October 2012, BBC Local Radio listeners ranked "Here Comes the Sun" as their #6th favorite Beatles song in a poll conducted in commemoration of the 50th anniversary of "Love Me Do," the band's first single.

ALBUM APPEARANCES: *Abbey Road*; *The Beatles, 1967–1970*; *Love*.

See also: *Abbey Road* (LP); Clapton, Eric.

"Here, There, and Everywhere" (Lennon–McCartney)

"Here, There, and Everywhere" is a song on the Beatles' *Revolver* album.

AUTHORSHIP AND BACKGROUND

Written by McCartney, "Here, There, and Everywhere" was inspired by "God Only Knows" from the Beach Boys' *Pet Sounds* album (1966).

As McCartney recalled,

> I sat out by [John's] pool on one of the sun chairs with my guitar and started strumming in E. . . . And soon [I] had a few chords, and I think by the time he'd woken up, I had pretty much written the song, so we took it indoors and finished it up. (Miles 1997, 285)

As Lennon remembered, "That's Paul's song completely, I believe. And one of my favorite songs of the Beatles" (Lennon and Ono 2000, 179).

RECORDING SESSIONS

Produced by Martin, "Here, There, and Everywhere" was recorded at Abbey Road Studios on June 14, 1966, with overdubbing sessions on June 16 and 17.

"Here, There, and Everywhere" was *Revolver*'s penultimate recording. Later admitting that he opted to sing the song in the style of Marianne Faithfull, McCartney's vocal introduction shifts from 9/8 to 7/8 to common time in the space of a dozen words: "To lead a better life, / I need my love to be here." The song also offers an example of the Beatles' penchant for varispeed recording during this period and beyond. As with ADT [automatic double- tracking], varispeed allowed them to manipulate their sound in an innovative fashion. As with several other instances on *Revolver*, "Here, There, and Everywhere" finds Martin and Emerick recording the track at a slower speed. During playback, varispeed recording results in a higher pitch—in this case, with the rendering of McCartney's lead vocal at a higher frequency.

PERSONNEL

McCartney: Vocal, Epiphone Texan, Rickenbacker 4001S
Harrison: Rickenbacker 360/12
Starr: Ludwig Oyster Black Pearl Drums

LEGACY AND INFLUENCE

In 2000, *Mojo* magazine ranked "Here, There, and Everywhere" as #4 on the magazine's list of *The 100 Greatest Songs of All Time*.

In 2010, *Rolling Stone* ranked "Here, There, and Everywhere" as #25 on the magazine's list of *The Beatles' 100 Greatest Songs*.

ALBUM APPEARANCES: *Revolver* (U.K.); *Revolver* (U.S.); *Love Songs*; *Anthology 2*.

See also: *Revolver* (U.K. LP).

"Hey Bulldog" (Lennon–McCartney)

"Hey Bulldog" is a song on the Beatles' *Yellow Submarine* album.

AUTHORSHIP AND BACKGROUND

Written by Lennon with assistance from McCartney, "Hey Bulldog" was the last song that the Beatles recorded before traveling to India in February 1968. It was composed and rehearsed under the working title of "Hey Bullfrog." As Lennon remembered, "It's a good sounding record that means nothing" (Dowlding 1989, 214).

RECORDING SESSIONS

Produced by Martin, "Hey Bulldog" was recorded at Abbey Road Studios on February 11, 1968. With Lennon on piano, McCartney on his Rickenbacker, Harrison on his Gibson SG Standard, and Starr flailing away on the drums, the song features a deftly constructed terraced effect in which the instrumentation slowly builds in advance of a lead vocal that witnesses Lennon at his fiery, throat-searing best: "If you're lonely, you can talk to me!" he screams. Lennon matches the intensity of his singing with a razor-edged guitar solo that he plays with a Vox Wah-Wah pedal engaged, likely having borrowed Harrison's Gibson SG. The entire session finds the Beatles in top form, losing their artistic inhibitions to create one of their most energetic and appealing performances on record. The proceedings come to a fantastic close as Lennon and McCartney howl, bulldog-like, into the fade-out.

PERSONNEL

Lennon: Vocal, Epiphone Casino, Piano
McCartney: Rickenbacker 4001S
Harrison: Gibson SG Standard
Starr: Ludwig Oyster Black Pearl Drums, Tambourine

LEGACY AND INFLUENCE

In 2010, *Rolling Stone* ranked "Hey Bulldog" as #81 on the magazine's list of *The Beatles' 100 Greatest Songs*.

ALBUM APPEARANCES: *Yellow Submarine*; *Rock 'n' Roll Music*; *Yellow Submarine Songtrack*; *Tomorrow Never Knows*.

See also: *Yellow Submarine* (Film); *Yellow Submarine* (LP).

"Hey Jude" (Lennon–McCartney)

"Hey Jude" was a hit double A-side single, backed with "Revolution," which was released by the Beatles in the United Kingdom on August 30, 1968, and in the United States on August 26, 1968. "Hey Jude" was also the band's fourth consecutive #1 single in the United Kingdom.

AUTHORSHIP AND BACKGROUND

Written by McCartney, "Hey Jude" finds its origins in McCartney's mid-1968 visit to Weybridge in an effort to console Lennon's estranged wife Cynthia and five-year-old Julian after Lennon's defection for Ono. In the Beatles' *Anthology* documentary, McCartney remembered driving out to the suburbs in his Aston Martin, when he started "coming up with these words in my own mind. I was talking to Julian: 'Hey Jules, don't take it bad. Take a sad song and make it better.' " Realizing that "Hey Jules" was a "bit of a mouthful," McCartney changed the name to "Jude." McCartney drew his musical inspiration for "Hey Jude" from the Drifters' "Save the Last Dance for Me."

Thrilled with his new composition, McCartney played it for Lennon and Ono. "These words won't be on the finished version," he told them in reference to the cryptic lyric, "the movement you need is on your shoulder." As McCartney later recalled, "John was saying, 'It's great!' I'm saying, 'It's crazy. It doesn't make any sense at all.' He's saying, 'Sure it does, it's great' " (Dowlding 1989, 203). Sagely heeding his partner's advice, McCartney allowed the lyric to survive.

During one of his last interviews, Lennon described "Hey Jude" as "one of [McCartney's] masterpieces" (Lennon and Ono 2000, 186).

RECORDING SESSIONS

Produced by Martin, the recording session for "Hey Jude" began on July 29, 1968, when the Beatles gathered at Abbey Road Studios to rehearse the song. At one point, Harrison wanted to play a guitar riff that echoed the melody, an idea that McCartney sternly rebuffed. "It was a bit of a number for me to dare to tell George Harrison—one of the greatest, I think—to not play," he later remarked. "It was like an insult, almost" (Babiuk 2001, 224). In spite of McCartney's squabble with Harrison, the initial session was jovial, with Lennon ad-libbing "goo goo g'Jude" and McCartney adopting his "Elvis voice" and singing "Here come the Jude!" (Winn 2003b, 213).

The recording sessions were relocated on July 31, 1968, to Trident Studios, with its state-of-the-art eight-track recording facilities and its exquisite Bechstein concert grand piano.

Paul McCartney holds four-year-old Julian, son of his colleague John Lennon, during a holiday near Athens in Greece in July 1967. The following year McCartney, trying to console the boy during his parents' marital difficulties, composed the song that would become one of the Beatles' most beloved, "Hey Jude" (originally titled "Hey Jules"). (Central Press/Getty Images)

According to McCartney, Starr was in the bathroom at the beginning of the final take: "He heard me starting," McCartney remembered. "He does up his fly, leaps back into the studio, and I suddenly see him tiptoeing past my back, rather quickly, trying to get to his drums. And, just as he got to his drums, boom boom boom—his timing was absolutely impeccable." On the evening of August 1, Martin recorded a 40-piece orchestra to accompany the song's lengthy coda, "a wordless four-minute mantra," according to Everett, that includes an extended sing-along and fade-out (Everett 1999, 192). Legend has it that a member of the orchestra left the session in a huff, stating that "I'm not going to clap my hands and sing Paul McCartney's bloody song!" (Cross 2005, 368). The Beatles completed "Hey Jude" on August 2, with the band receiving their customary acetate copies in advance of the single's release.

During the rehearsals for the song, McCartney and Harrison vehemently disagreed over the guitar arrangement for "Hey Jude." Harrison originally wanted to echo McCartney's vocals with his guitar part, a creative idea that McCartney soundly rejected. As McCartney later reflected, "I did want to insist that there shouldn't be an answering guitar phrase in 'Hey Jude'—and that was important to me—but of course if you tell a guitarist that, and he's not as keen on the idea as you are, it looks as if you're knocking him out of the picture. I think George felt that: it was like, 'Since when are you going to tell me what to play? I'm in the Beatles too.' So I can see his point of view" (Beatles 2000, 316). During the production of the Beatles' *Anthology* documentary in the mid-1990s, McCartney and Harrison laughed about the incident, with McCartney saying, "I realize I was a bossy git," to which Harrison replied, "Oh no, Paul, you never did anything like that!" As Ron Richards later recalled, McCartney could be "oblivious to anyone else's feelings in the studio" because he was driven to make the best possible recording at any cost (Spitz 2005, 783).

PERSONNEL

> Lennon: Gibson J-200, Backing Vocal
> McCartney: Vocal, Fender Jazz Bass, Piano
> Harrison: Sonic Blue Fender Stratocaster, Backing Vocal
> Starr: Ludwig Oyster Black Pearl Drums, Tambourine
> Studio Musicians: Orchestral and Vocal Accompaniment (10 Violins, 3 Violas, 3 Cellos, 2 Flutes, 2 Clarinets, Bass Clarinet, Bassoon, Contrabassoon, 4 Trumpets, 2 Horns, 4 Trombones, Percussion) conducted by Martin

CHART PERFORMANCE

> U.K.: "Hey Jude"/"Revolution"; August 30, 1968, Apple [Parlophone] R 5722: #1.

U.S.: "Hey Jude"/"Revolution"; August 26, 1968, Apple [Capitol] 2276: #1 (certified by the RIAA as "4x Multi Platinum," with more than 4 million copies sold).

LEGACY AND INFLUENCE

"Hey Jude" is included among the Rock and Roll Hall of Fame's *500 Songs That Shaped Rock and Roll.*

In 1969, "Hey Jude" was honored as the *New Musical Express*'s "Single of the Year."

In 1969, "Hey Jude" was nominated for a Grammy Award for Record of the Year at the 11th Grammy Awards. It was also nominated for a Grammy Award for Best Pop Performance by a Duo or Group with Vocals.

In 1969, the Beatles received an Ivor Novello Award, awarded annually by the British Academy of Songwriters, Composers, and Authors, for "Hey Jude."

In 2000, *Mojo* magazine ranked "Hey Jude" as #29 on the magazine's list of *The 100 Greatest Songs of All Time.*

In 2001, "Hey Jude" was inducted into the National Academy of Recording Arts and Sciences Grammy Hall of Fame.

In 2004, *Rolling Stone* ranked "Hey Jude" as #8 on the magazine's list of *The 500 Greatest Songs of All Time.*

In 2006, *Q Magazine* ranked "Hey Jude" as #23 on the magazine's list of *The 100 Greatest Songs of All Time.*

In 2008, "Hey Jude" was ranked as #8 on *Billboard* magazine's *All Time Hot 100 Songs.*

In 2010, *Rolling Stone* ranked "Hey Jude" as #7 on the magazine's list of *The Beatles' 100 Greatest Songs.*

In October 2012, BBC Local Radio listeners ranked "Hey Jude" as their favorite Beatles song in a poll conducted in commemoration of the 50th anniversary of "Love Me Do," the band's first single.

ALBUM APPEARANCES: *Hey Jude*; *The Beatles, 1967–1970*; *20 Greatest Hits*; *Past Masters, Volume 2*; *Anthology 3*; *1*; *Love.*

See also: Lennon, Cynthia Lillian; Lindsay-Hogg, Michael.

Hey Jude (LP)

February 26, 1970, Apple [Capitol] SW 385 (stereo)

Hey Jude is a compilation album, now deleted from the Beatles' catalogue, that was released on February 26, 1970, in the United States. Originally entitled *The Beatles Again*, the album's contents are now available during the digital era on *A Hard Day's Night* (U.K. LP) and *Past Masters*.

BACKGROUND

After taking Apple Corps into receivership and renegotiating the band's contract in 1969, Allen Klein conceived the idea for *The Beatles Again* in order to fill the gulf between the release of *Abbey Road* and the forthcoming soundtrack album for *Let It Be*. Its songs were chosen by Allan Steckler, an ABKCO executive, who compiled a range of unreleased singles material for U.S. distribution. Klein and Steckler renamed the LP in order to capitalize on the worldwide success of "Hey Jude." Much of the early material included on *Hey Jude* had not been included on a U.S. album release because of the band's contract with United Artists, which released the soundtrack for *A Hard Day's Night* (U.S. LP), or because the material had only been released as singles.

TRACK LISTING

Side 1: "Can't Buy Me Love"; "I Should Have Known Better"; "Paperback Writer"; "Rain"; "Lady Madonna"; "Revolution."

Side 2: "Hey Jude"; "Old Brown Shoe"; "Don't Let Me Down"; "The Ballad of John and Yoko."

COVER ARTWORK

The album's cover art, consisting of photos by American photographer Ethan Russell (1945–), was taken during the group's final photo shoot—indeed, their final day together—on August 22, 1969, on the lush grounds of the Lennons' newly purchased Tittenhurst estate. Several other photographers were in attendance, including the *Daily Mail*'s Monte Fresco, Linda McCartney, and Beatles assistant Mal Evans, who shot amateur film footage of the occasion. Russell's cover shot for *Hey Jude* depicts the band posed in front of the estate's old Victorian assembly hall, complete with its enigmatic stone busts. For all of the dark portents of the band's last summer together, the finality of the occasion was clearly lost on the Beatles, who may still have wondered if they could best their own demons and survive to record another day. "It was just a photo session," Starr later remembered. "I wasn't there thinking, 'Okay, this is the last photo session'" (Beatles 2000, 345).

CHART PERFORMANCE

U.S.: #2 (certified by the RIAA as "3x Multi Platinum," with more than 3 million copies sold).

See also: Klein, Allen; McCartney, Linda Eastman; Ono, Yoko.

"Hold Me Tight" (Lennon–McCartney)

"Hold Me Tight" is a song on the *With the Beatles* album.

AUTHORSHIP AND BACKGROUND

Written by McCartney, "Hold Me Tight" was influenced by the American girl groups of the early 1960s. As McCartney later remarked, "I can't remember much about that one. Certain songs were just 'work' songs—you haven't got much of a memory of them. That's one of them. You just knew you had a song that would work, a good melody. 'Hold Me Tight' never really had that much of an effect on me. It was a bit Shirelles" (Dowlding 1989, 54).

RECORDING SESSIONS

Produced by Martin, "Hold Me Tight" was recorded at Abbey Road Studios on September 12, 1963.

PERSONNEL

> Lennon: Rickenbacker 325, Backing Vocal
> McCartney: Vocal, Höfner 500/1
> Harrison: Gretsch Country Gentleman, Backing Vocal
> Starr: Ludwig Oyster Black Pearl Drums

ALBUM APPEARANCES: *With the Beatles*; *Meet the Beatles!*

See also: *Please Please Me* (LP); *With the Beatles* (LP).

"Honey Don't" (Perkins)

"Honey Don't" is a song on the *Beatles for Sale* album.

AUTHORSHIP AND BACKGROUND

Written by Carl Perkins, "Honey Don't" is emblematic of the classic rockabilly sound popularized by Perkins, Elvis Presley, and a myriad of other American artists. "Honey Don't" was released in January 1956 as the B-side of Perkins's "Blue Suede Shoes."

RECORDING SESSIONS

Produced by Martin, "Honey Don't" was recorded at Abbey Road Studios on October 26, 1964, which marked the final day of recording sessions for the *Beatles for*

Sale album. On August 1, 1963, the Beatles recorded a version of "Honey Don't" for the BBC's *Pop Go the Beatles* radio show. In contrast with the studio recording for *Beatles for Sale*, Lennon appears on lead vocals instead of Starr. This version of "Honey Don't" was later included on the *Live at the BBC* album. A second live recording of "Honey Don't" from the band's BBC sessions was later included on the Beatles' *On Air: Live at the BBC, Volume 2*.

PERSONNEL

Lennon: Rickenbacker 325/12
McCartney: Höfner 500/1
Harrison: Gretsch Tennessean
Starr: Vocal, Ludwig Oyster Black Pearl Drums

ALBUM APPEARANCES: *Beatles for Sale*; *Beatles '65*; *Live at the BBC*; *On Air: Live at the BBC, Volume 2*.

See also: *Beatles for Sale* (LP).

"Honey Pie" (Lennon–McCartney)

"Honey Pie" is a song on *The Beatles* (*The White Album*).

AUTHORSHIP AND BACKGROUND

Written by McCartney, "Honey Pie" celebrates the dance-hall sound of yesteryear. As with "When I'm Sixty-Four," "Honey Pie" exists in a long line of nods by the songwriter to the music of his father's generation, including such McCartney tunes as "You Gave Me the Answer," "Baby's Request," and "My Valentine."

As McCartney remembered,

> I very much liked that old crooner style—the strange fruity voice that they used, so "Honey Pie" was me writing one of them to an imaginary woman, across the ocean, on the silver screen, who was called Honey Pie. It's another of my fantasy songs. We put a sound on my voice to make it sound like a scratchy old record. So it's not a parody. It's a nod to the vaudeville tradition that I was raised on. (Miles 1997, 497)

An early version of "Honey Pie" was recorded in May 1968 at Harrison's Kinfauns studio as part of the Esher Tapes.

RECORDING SESSIONS

Produced by Martin, "Honey Pie" was recorded on October 1, 1968, at Trident Studios, with overdubbing sessions on October 2 and 4. To provide the song with the necessary ambience, the track begins with the white noise of a phonograph needle alighting a 78-rpm record. For "Honey Pie," Lennon turns in a terrific retro guitar solo on his Casino. "John played a brilliant solo on 'Honey Pie,'" Harrison later recalled. It "sounded like Django Reinhardt or something" (Dowlding 1989, 245).

PERSONNEL

Lennon: Epiphone Casino
McCartney: Vocal, Epiphone Casino, Piano
Harrison: Fender Bass VI
Starr: Ludwig Oyster Black Pearl Drums
Harry Klein: Clarinet

ALBUM APPEARANCES: *The Beatles* (*The White Album*); *Anthology 3*.

See also: *The Beatles* (*The White Album*).

I

"I Am the Walrus" (Lennon–McCartney)

"I Am the Walrus" is a song on the Beatles' *Magical Mystery Tour* album. It was the B-side of "Hello, Goodbye," which was the band's second consecutive #1 single in the United Kingdom, where it was released on November 24, 1967.

AUTHORSHIP AND BACKGROUND

Written by John Lennon, the idea behind "I Am the Walrus" likely originated from Lennon's hallucinogenic experiences, as well as Lewis Carroll's nonsensical poem "The Walrus and the Carpenter" from *Through the Looking-Glass*, and the verbal and textual convolutions of Bob Dylan's "Desolation Row," the lyrical tour de force that acts as the climax for *Highway 61 Revisited* (1965). Lennon ultimately trumps his antecedents' penchant for verbal esoterica with a series of disjunctive, acid-soaked images—word pictures that, by virtue of their tightly packed visual imagery, defy easy interpretation.

As Lennon explained,

> We write lyrics, and I write lyrics that you don't realize what they mean till after. Especially some of the better songs or some of the more flowing ones, like "Walrus." The whole first verse was written without any knowledge. With "I Am the Walrus," I had "I am he as you are he as we are all together." I had just these two lines on the typewriter, and then about two weeks later I ran through and wrote another two lines and then, when I saw something, after about four lines, I just knocked the rest of it off. Then I had the whole verse or verse and a half and then sang it. I had this idea of doing a song that was a police siren, but it didn't work in the end [sings like a siren] "I-am-he-as-you-are-he-as . . ." You couldn't really sing the police siren. (Cott and Doudna 1982, 51)

As Lennon added during one of his last interviews,

> The first line was written on one acid trip one weekend. The second line was written on the next acid trip the next weekend, and it was filled in after I met Yoko. Part of it was putting down Hare Krishna. All these people were going on about Hare Krishna, Allen Ginsberg in particular. The reference to "Elementary penguin" is the elementary, naïve attitude of going around chanting, "Hare Krishna," or putting all your faith in any one idol. I was writing obscurely, à la

217

Dylan, in those days. It's from "The Walrus and the Carpenter" [from] *Alice in Wonderland*. To me, it was a beautiful poem. It never dawned on me that Lewis Carroll was commenting on the capitalist and social system. I never went into that bit about what he really meant, like people are doing with the Beatles' work. Later, I went back and looked at it and realized that the walrus was the bad guy in the story and the carpenter was the good guy. I thought, "Oh, shit, I picked the wrong guy." I should have said, "I am the carpenter." But that wouldn't have been the same, would it? (Harry 2011, 139)

In *Beatlesongs* (1989), William J. Dowlding offers yet another possibility for the origins of "I Am the Walrus," writing that "the song's genesis came" when Lennon's boyhood friend Pete Shotton and Lennon "read a fan letter from a student at Quarry Bank, their old school. The fan wrote, much to their amusement, that the school's literature class was analyzing the Beatles' songs. This prompted them to remember a song they used to sing while attending the school: 'Yellow matter custard, green slop pie / All mixed together with a dead dog's eye' " (Dowlding 1989, 198).

In a 1967 interview, George Harrison remarked that "people don't understand. In John's song, 'I Am the Walrus' he says: 'I am he as you are he as you are me.' People look for all sorts of hidden meanings. It's serious, but it's also not serious. It's true, but it's also a joke."

RECORDING SESSIONS

Produced by George Martin, "I Am the Walrus" was recorded at Abbey Road Studios on September 5, 1967, with overdubbing sessions on September 6 and 27.

On September 5, 1967, the Beatles recorded 16 takes of the song's basic rhythm track in which the shaping of "I Am the Walrus" can be plainly heard. With Lennon on electric piano, Paul McCartney on his Rickenbacker, Harrison on his Fender Strat, and Ringo Starr behind the drums, the session begins with the Beatles lumbering rather tentatively around the song's chord patterns and rhythmic foundations before slowly gaining confidence and shifting more deftly among the number's complex of structural elements. In spite of their musical finesse, the lingering sadness over Brian Epstein's death some nine days earlier remained palpable. "I distinctly remember the look of emptiness on all their faces while they were playing 'I Am the Walrus,' " Geoff Emerick later recalled. "It's one of the saddest memories I have of my time with the Beatles" (Emerick and Massey 2006, 214).

With a basic track in place, the group began adorning "I Am the Walrus" with one layer after another of words and music, timbre, and sound. With the addition of each new textual stratum, the song's levels of meaning become even more oblique. With his vocal treated with ADT [automatic double-tracking], Lennon's chorus of "goo goo g'joob" provides a kind of doo-wop-infused jabberwocky, while the recurrent "I am the eggman" seems positively creepy, if not downright frightening in Lennon's hyperkinetic performance. Although he disliked the chaotic nature of "I Am the

Walrus" from the start, Martin created a stirring string arrangement, with 16 musicians participating in the orchestral overdub in Studio One.

Meanwhile, the Mike Sammes Singers plied their craft on that very same evening in Studio Three, where the eight male and eight female singers gathered to record some of the most outrageous backing vocals in Beatledom. At Lennon's behest, the choral group recorded the positively devilish "ho-ho-ho, hee-hee-hee, ha-ha-ha!" After shouting "oompah, oompah, stick it up your jumper!" the singers chanted "got one, got one, everybody's got one" before devolving into a spate of high-pitched whooping sounds (Lewisohn 1995, 268). A few days later, Lennon was fumbling with the radio in Studio Two's control room, where he aimlessly dialed up a BBC production of Shakespeare's *The Tragedy of King Lear*. Featuring a selection from Act IV, Scene VI—which Emerick fed directly onto the master tape—the passages from *King Lear* include audible lines from Oswald ("O, untimely death!") and Edgar ("Sit you down, father; rest you"). With the found object of *King Lear* in place, the multifaceted sound collage of "I Am the Walrus" had reached its fruition.

As the last burst of the Beatles' self-conscious psychedelia, "I Am the Walrus" functions—on both a lyrical and musical level—as a brilliant tirade against the ills of enforced institutionalism and runaway consumerism. Teeming with stunning wordplay and linguistic imagery—"obscurity for obscurity's sake" (Roos 1984, 26)—"I Am the Walrus" pits Lennon's bitter vocals against a surrealistic musical tableau composed of McCartney's hypnotic bass, Harrison and Starr's playful percussion, and Martin's exhilarating string arrangements. "I Am the Walrus" opens with Lennon's Mellotron-intoned phrasings designed to replicate the monotonous cry of a police siren. As the song's spectacular lyrics unfold—"I am he as you are he and you are me and we are altogether"—Starr's wayward snare interrupts the proceedings and sets Lennon's intentionally absurd, Whitmanesque catalogue of images into motion. While an assortment of cryptic voices and diabolical laughter weave in and out of the mix, Lennon's pungent lyrics encounter an array of ridiculous characters, including that madman of literary effrontery himself, Edgar Allan Poe.

When "I Am the Walrus" finally recedes amongst its ubiquitous mantra of "goo goo g'joob," the song dissolves into the scene from *King Lear*, and the whole production suddenly dies by its own hand in a symbolic meta-suicide denoting the spiritual death of the individual in a Western world beset by corporate monoliths and identity politics. As with "A Day in the Life," "I Am the Walrus" prods its listeners into consciousness through brute force. In the former song, the Beatles harness the thunder of a symphony orchestra run amok. For "I Am the Walrus," they muster the noise of discordant sound and language in order to rock our worlds. Described by Ian MacDonald as "the most idiosyncratic protest song ever written" (MacDonald 1994, 216), "I Am the Walrus" features Lennon's most inspired verbal and aural textures, as well as the Beatles' supreme moment of narrative paradox: in one sense, "I Am the Walrus" seems utterly devoid of meaning, yet at the same time its songwriter's rants about prevailing social strictures absolutely beg for interpretation, its layers of meaning fecundating and expanding with every listening.

PERSONNEL

Lennon: Vocal, Electric Piano
McCartney: Rickenbacker 4001S
Harrison: Sonic Blue Fender Stratocaster
Starr: Ludwig Oyster Black Pearl Drums
Studio Musicians: String, Brass, Woodwind, and Vocal Accompaniment (8 Violins, 4 Cellos, 3 Horns) conducted by Martin
The Mike Sammes Singers: Backing Vocals

CHART PERFORMANCE

U.K.: "Hello, Goodbye"/"I Am the Walrus"; November 24, 1967, Parlophone R 5655: #1. As the B-side of "Hello, Goodbye," "I Am the Walrus" did not chart.
U.S.: "Hello, Goodbye"/"I Am the Walrus"; November 27, 1967, Capitol 2056: #1 (certified by the RIAA as "Gold," with more than 500,000 copies sold). As the B-side of "Hello, Goodbye," "I Am the Walrus" charted at #56.

LEGACY AND INFLUENCE

In 2006, *Pitchfork* ranked "I Am the Walrus" as #26 on the Web magazine's list of *The 200 Greatest Songs of the 1960s*.

In 2010, *Rolling Stone* ranked "I Am the Walrus" as #33 on the magazine's list of *The Beatles' 100 Greatest Songs*.

CONTROVERSY

The BBC banned "I Am the Walrus" from radio airplay because of its lewd references to "pornographic priestess" and "knickers." As Lennon later observed, "We chose the word [knickers] because it is a lovely expressive word. It rolls off the tongue. It could *mean* anything" (Beatles 2000, 274). In a 1967 interview, McCartney added that "everyone keeps preaching that the best way is to be 'open' when writing for teenagers. Then when we do we get criticized. Surely the word 'knickers' can't offend anyone. Shakespeare wrote words a lot more naughtier than knickers!"

ALBUM APPEARANCES: *Magical Mystery Tour*; *The Beatles, 1967–1970*; *Rarities* (U.S.); *Reel Music*; *Anthology 2*; *Love*.

See also: *Magical Mystery Tour* (LP); *Magical Mystery Tour* (TV Film); "Paul Is Dead" Hoax.

"I Call Your Name" (Lennon–McCartney)

"I Call Your Name" is a song on the Beatles' *Long Tall Sally* EP, released in the United Kingdom on June 19, 1964.

AUTHORSHIP AND BACKGROUND

Written by Lennon, "I Call Your Name" is a pre-Beatles composition. As Lennon later recalled, "That was my song. When there was no Beatles and no group, I just had it around. It was my effort as a kind of blues originally, and then I wrote the middle-eight just to stick it in the album when it came out years later. The first part had been written before Hamburg even. It was one of my *first* attempts at a song" (Everett 2001, 372).

RECORDING SESSIONS

Produced by Martin, "I Call Your Name" was recorded at Abbey Road Studios on March 1, 1964. Lennon double-tracked his lead vocal.

Lennon performs a guitar solo during the song's middle-eight that he later revealed to be a rudimentary attempt at ska, a form of Jamaican music that merges elements of calypso with American jazz and rhythm and blues.

PERSONNEL

Lennon: Vocal, Rickenbacker 325
McCartney: Höfner 500/1
Harrison: Rickenbacker 360/12
Starr: Ludwig Oyster Black Pearl Drums, Cowbell

ALBUM APPEARANCES: *The Beatles' Second Album*; *Rock 'n' Roll Music*; *Rarities* (U.K.); *Past Masters, Volume 1*.

See also: Lester, Richard; Lynne, Jeff.

"I Don't Want to Spoil the Party" (Lennon–McCartney)

"I Don't Want to Spoil the Party" is a song on the *Beatles for Sale* album.

AUTHORSHIP AND BACKGROUND

Written by Lennon, "I Don't Want to Spoil the Party" was influenced by Lesley Gore's 1963 smash hit, "It's My Party." As Lennon later remembered, "'I Don't Want to Spoil the Party' was a very personal one of mine" (Dowlding 1989, 90).

RECORDING SESSIONS

Produced by Martin, "I Don't Want to Spoil the Party" was recorded in 19 takes at Abbey Road Studios on September 29, 1964.

PERSONNEL

Lennon: Vocal, Gibson J-160E
McCartney: Vocal, Höfner 500/1
Harrison: Gretsch Tennessean
Starr: Ludwig Oyster Black Pearl Drums, Tambourine

CHART PERFORMANCE

U.S.: "Eight Days a Week"/"I Don't Want to Spoil the Party"; February 15, 1965, Capitol 5371: #1 (certified by the RIAA as "Gold," with more than 500,000 copies sold). As the B-side of "Eight Days a Week," "I Don't Want to Spoil the Party" charted at #39.

ALBUM APPEARANCES: *Beatles for Sale*; *Beatles VI*.

See also: *Beatles for Sale* (LP).

"I Feel Fine" (Lennon–McCartney)

"I Feel Fine" was the band's sixth consecutive #1 single in the United Kingdom, where it was released on November 27, 1964. "I Feel Fine" was also the first of six consecutive #1 singles in the United States, where it was released on November 23, 1964.

AUTHORSHIP AND BACKGROUND

Written by Lennon, "I Feel Fine" marks the first time that feedback was intentionally used on a recording.

As Lennon remembered,

That's me completely. Including the guitar lick with the first feedback anywhere. I defy anybody to find a record—unless it is some old blues record from 1922—that uses feedback that way. So I claim it for the Beatles. Before Hendrix, before the Who, before anybody. The first feedback on record. (Cross 2005, 315)

The central guitar riff in "I Feel Fine" finds its origins in Bobby Parker's 1961 composition "Watch Your Step," which the Beatles included in their live repertoire in 1961–1962.

As Harrison recalled,

A lot of Lennon–McCartney songs had other people involved, whether it's lyrics, or structures, or circumstance. A good example is "I Feel Fine." I'll tell you exactly how that came about: We were crossing Scotland in the back of an Austin Princess, singing "Matchbox" in three-part harmony. And it turned into "I Feel Fine." The guitar part was from Bobby Parker's "Watch Your Step," just a bastardized version. I was there for the whole of its creation—but it's still a Lennon–McCartney. (Everett 2001, 265)

John Lennon poses with his Gibson acoustic guitar in 1964. The memorable feedback sound in that year's "I Feel Fine" was the result of Lennon leaning his Gibson, which had an electric pick-up, against an amplifier, accidentally creating a sound that the group loved and used in the recording. (Michael Ochs Archives/Getty Images)

Everett points out, however, that Harrison's historical memory about the occasion of the composition of "I Feel Fine" may, in fact, be in error: "The Beatles did not take this trip across Scotland until *after* the recording of 'I Feel Fine.' (Perhaps they were instead returning to London from the far-northern Hull, a trip that directly preceded the session in question?)" (Everett 2001, 265).

McCartney has pointed out that the drum part in "I Feel Fine" was influenced by Ray Charles's "What'd I Say."

RECORDING SESSIONS

Produced by Martin, "I Feel Fine" was recorded at Abbey Road Studios on October 18, 1964. The feedback that begins the song occurred entirely by accident in the studio. As McCartney later recalled,

> John had a semi-acoustic Gibson guitar. It had a pick-up on it so it could be amplified. We were just about to walk away to listen to a take when John leaned his guitar against the amp. I can still see him doing it, and it went, "Nnnnnnwahhhhh!" And we went, "What's that? Voodoo!" "No, it's feedback."

"Wow, it's a great sound!" George Martin was there so we said, "Can we have that on the record?" "Well, I suppose we could, we could edit it on the front." It was a found object—an accident caused by leaning the guitar against the amp. The song itself was more John's than mine. We sat down and co-wrote it with John's original idea. John sang it. I'm on harmonies. (Miles 1997, 172)

On November 17, 1964, the Beatles recorded a second version of "I Feel Fine" at London's Playhouse Theatre for the BBC's *Top Gear* radio show on November 26. The recording was later rebroadcast on the *Saturday Club* radio program on December 26. A live studio outtake of the song from the band's BBC sessions was later included on the Beatles' *On Air: Live at the BBC, Volume 2.*

PERSONNEL

Lennon: Vocal, Rickenbacker 325
McCartney: Höfner 500/1, Backing Vocal
Harrison: Gretsch Tennessean, Backing Vocal
Starr: Ludwig Oyster Black Pearl Drums

CHART PERFORMANCE

U.K.: "I Feel Fine"/"She's a Woman"; November 27, 1964, Parlophone R 5200: #1.

U.S.: "I Feel Fine"/"She's a Woman"; November 23, 1964, Capitol 5327: #1 (certified by the RIAA as "Gold," with more than 500,000 copies sold).

LEGACY AND INFLUENCE

In 2010, *Rolling Stone* ranked "I Feel Fine" as #42 on the magazine's list of *The Beatles' 100 Greatest Songs.*

ALBUM APPEARANCES: *Beatles '65*; *A Collection of Beatles Oldies*; *The Beatles, 1962–1966*; *20 Greatest Hits*; *Past Masters, Volume 1*; *Live at the BBC*; *Anthology 2*; *1*; *On Air: Live at the BBC, Volume 2.*

See also: *The Ed Sullivan Show* (TV Series); *Live at the BBC* (LP).

"I Me Mine" (Harrison)

"I Me Mine" is a song on the Beatles' *Let It Be* album.

AUTHORSHIP AND BACKGROUND

Written by Harrison, "I Me Mine" was later described by the songwriter as the explicit result of his experiences with LSD, which forced him to reconceive his personal ego as the function of a larger, collective force: "The big I; i.e., Om, the complete whole," Harrison wrote, a "universal consciousness that is void of duality and ego" (Harrison 1980, 158). In addition to its obvious critique of his bandmates' selfish behavior, the song also owes its genesis to the *Bhagavad Gita*, which states that "They are forever free who renounce all selfish desires and break away from the ego-cage of 'I,' 'me,' and 'mine' to be united with the Lord. This is the supreme state. Attain to this, and pass from death to immortality" (2: 71, 72).

As Harrison later remarked,

"I Me Mine" is the ego problem. I looked around and everything I could see was relative to my ego. You know, like "that's my piece of paper," and "that's my flannel," or "give it to me," or "I am." It drove me crackers—I hated everything about my ego—it was a flash of everything false and impermanent which I disliked. But later I learned from it—to realize that there is somebody else in here apart from old blabbermouth. "Who am I" became the order of the day. Anyway, that's what came out of it: "I Me Mine"—it's about the ego, the eternal problem. (Harrison 1980, 158)

Harrison's musical inspiration for "I Me Mine" originated from an Austrian marching band's incidental soundtrack music during a BBC television program, *Europa: The Titled and the Untitled*, which he saw on January 7, 1969. He debuted the song for the other Beatles on January 8 at Twickenham Film Studios.

RECORDING SESSIONS

Produced by Martin with postproduction by Phil Spector, "I Me Mine" was recorded at Abbey Road Studios on January 3, 1970, with an orchestral overdubbing session on April 1. During the latter session, Spector worked from Richard Hewson's orchestral arrangement and John Barham's choral arrangement for the song.

During the January 8, 1969, rehearsal of "I Me Mine" during the *Get Back* sessions, Lennon "jokes that a collection of freaks can dance along with George's waltz," before telling the guitarist "to get lost—that the Beatles only play rock and roll and there's no place in the group's playlist for a Spanish waltz" (Sulpy and Schweighardt 1997, 124). As if on cue, McCartney took to singing "I Me Mine" while feigning a Spanish accent.

With the estranged Lennon on a lengthy vacation with Yoko Ono in Denmark—he had announced that he wanted a "divorce" from the Beatles the previous September—Harrison, McCartney, and Starr remade the song at Abbey Road Studios on January 3, 1970. As they prepared to record "I Me Mine," Harrison acknowledged Lennon's absence with a wry reference to the popular British band Dave Dee, Dozy, Beaky, Mick, & Tich: "You all will have read that Dave Dee [Lennon] is no longer with us, but Mickey and Tich and I [McCartney, Starr, and Harrison] have decided to carry on the good work that's always gone down in [Abbey Road Studios'] Number Two" (Harry 1992, 548). With a potent dose of musical drama supplied by the songwriter's vocal and McCartney's ominous Hammond organ work, Harrison's waltzing composition offers a knowing critique of humanity's penchant for elevating the desires of the self over the welfare of the community. Their rendition of the song clocked in at less than two minutes, a constraint that Spector remedied by repeating various portions of the track in order to make it seem more robust.

Twenty-four years later, McCartney, Harrison, and Starr reunited to record two of Lennon's 1970s-era demos, "Free as a Bird" and "Real Love," for the Beatles' *Anthology* project.

The *Let It Be . . . Naked* album (2003) features a remixed track of Spector's edited version of the January 1970 recording—albeit without the addition of Spector's orchestral and choral overdubbing session.

PERSONNEL

> McCartney: Rickenbacker 4001S, Electric Piano, Hammond Organ, Backing Vocal
> Harrison: Vocal, Gibson J-200, Fender Rosewood Telecaster
> Starr: Ludwig Hollywood Maple Drums
> Studio Musicians: Orchestral Accompaniment (18 Violins, 4 Violas, 4 Cellos, Harp, 3 Trumpets, 3 Trombones) conducted by Spector

ALBUM APPEARANCES: *Let It Be*; *Anthology 3*; *Let It Be . . . Naked*.

See also: *Let It Be* (LP); *Let It Be . . . Naked* (LP).

"I Need You" (Harrison)

"I Need You" is a song on the Beatles' *Help!* album.

AUTHORSHIP AND BACKGROUND

Written by Harrison, "I Need You" refers to Pattie Boyd, whom Harrison was missing while the Beatles were filming *Help!* in the Bahamas. In March 1964, Harrison met Boyd, a British fashion model, on the set of *A Hard Day's Night*. "George was in love," Cynthia Lennon recalled. "Pattie, on the other hand, was well and truly involved with a very steady boyfriend. George proceeded to work to a plan of campaign to woo Pattie away from her steady and make her his own" (Badman 2001, 96). Harrison's scheme apparently succeeded, and he married Pattie in January 1966, leaving McCartney as the only remaining bachelor among the Beatles.

RECORDING SESSIONS

Produced by Martin, "I Need You" was recorded at Abbey Road Studios on February 15, 1965, with additional overdubbing on February 16. Harrison double-tracked his vocal. Harrison achieves the song's signature effect on his guitar using a volume pedal, the first instance of the Beatles using pedal-effects technology in the studio.

PERSONNEL

> Lennon: Gibson J-160E, Backing Vocal
> McCartney: Höfner 500/1, Backing Vocal
> Harrison: Vocal, Gretsch Tennessean
> Starr: Ludwig Oyster Black Pearl Drums, Cowbell

ALBUM APPEARANCES: *Help!* (U.K.); *Help!* (U.S.); *Love Songs*.

See also: Boyd, Pattie; *Help!* (U.K. LP).

"I Saw Her Standing There" (McCartney–Lennon)

"I Saw Her Standing There" is a song on the Beatles' *Please Please Me* album.

AUTHORSHIP AND BACKGROUND

Written by McCartney, "I Saw Her Standing There" had gone under the working title of "17" over the past few years. Beginning with McCartney's brisk count-off—"one, two, three, four!"—"I Saw Her Standing There" inaugurates the Beatles' first album-length recording in arresting fashion. Written years before in the McCartney family's front parlor on 20 Forthlin Road, "I Saw Her Standing There" offers a clear example of the manner in which Lennon and McCartney shared in the crafting of each other's lyrics. McCartney had originally written the song's initial phrases as "Well, she was just seventeen / Never been a beauty queen."

In Lennon's revision, the lyrics take on an entirely different aspect altogether—"Well, she was just seventeen," McCartney sings, "you know what I mean"—thus informing the composition with an ironic, knowing sense of suggestiveness in contrast with the speaker's fairly innocent experience. McCartney's opening lyric echoes Chuck Berry's "Little Queenie"—"too cute to be a minute over seventeen"—and he borrows his walking-bass line directly from Berry's "I'm Talking about You." "We were the biggest nickers in town," McCartney later admitted. "Plagiarists extraordinaires" (MacDonald 1994, 144).

As Lennon later recalled, "That's Paul doing his usual job of producing what George Martin used to call a 'potboiler.' I helped with a couple of the lyrics" (Lennon and Ono 2000, 194).

RECORDING SESSIONS

Produced by Martin, "I Saw Her Standing There" was recorded at Abbey Road Studios on February 11, 1963, with an overdubbing session on February 20. In October 1963, the Beatles recorded a version of "I Saw Her Standing There" for the BBC's *Easy Beat* radio show, which was broadcast on October 20 and later included on the *Live at the BBC* album. Overall, the group recorded "I Saw Her Standing There" on 11 occasions for BBC Radio between March 1963 and May 1964. Yet another live recording of "I Saw Her Standing There" from the band's BBC sessions was later included on the Beatles' *On Air: Live at the BBC, Volume 2.*

PERSONNEL

Lennon: Rickenbacker 325
McCartney: Vocal, Höfner 500/1
Harrison: Gretsch Duo-Jet
Starr: Premier Mahogany Duroplastic Drums

CHART PERFORMANCE

U.S.: "I Want to Hold Your Hand"/"I Saw Her Standing There," December 26, 1963, Capitol 5112: #1 (certified by the RIAA as "Gold," with more than 500,000 copies sold). As the B-side of "I Want to Hold Your Hand," "I Saw Her Standing There" charted at #14.

LEGACY AND INFLUENCE

In 2004, *Rolling Stone* ranked "I Saw Her Standing There" as #140 on the magazine's list of *The 500 Greatest Songs of All Time.*

In 2008, *Rolling Stone* ranked "I Saw Her Standing There" as #45 on the magazine's list of *The 100 Greatest Guitar Songs of All Time.*

In 2010, *Rolling Stone* ranked "I Saw Her Standing There" as #16 on the magazine's list of *The Beatles' 100 Greatest Songs.*

ALBUM APPEARANCES: *Please Please Me*; *Rock 'n' Roll Music*; *Live! at the Star-Club in Hamburg, Germany; 1962*; *Live at the BBC*; *Anthology 1*; *On Air: Live at the BBC, Volume 2.*

See also: *Live at the BBC* (LP); *Please Please Me* (LP).

"I Should Have Known Better" (Lennon–McCartney)

"I Should Have Known Better" is a song on the Beatles' *A Hard Day's Night* album.

AUTHORSHIP AND BACKGROUND

Written by Lennon specifically for the feature film *A Hard Day's Night*, "I Should Have Known Better" was mimed by the Beatles during the movie's train compartment scene. The scene was actually filmed inside a van, with crew members rocking the vehicle back and forth to simulate train travel.

RECORDING SESSIONS

Produced by Martin, "I Should Have Known Better" was recorded at Abbey Road Studios on February 25, 1964. The Beatles remade the song the following day, and Lennon double-tracked his vocal.

PERSONNEL

Lennon: Vocal, Gibson J-160E, Harmonica
McCartney: Höfner 500/1
Harrison: Rickenbacker 360/12
Starr: Ludwig Oyster Black Pearl Drums

CHART PERFORMANCE

U.S.: "A Hard Day's Night"/"I Should Have Known Better"; July 13, 1964, Capitol 5122: #1 (certified by the RIAA as "Gold," with more than 500,000 copies sold). As the B-side of "A Hard Day's Night," "I Should Have Known Better" charted at #53.
U.K.: "Yesterday"/"I Should Have Known Better"; March 5, 1976, Parlophone R 6013: #8. As the B-side of "Yesterday," "I Should Have Known Better" did not chart.

LEGACY AND INFLUENCE

In 2010, *Rolling Stone* ranked "I Should Have Known Better" as #36 on the magazine's list of *The Beatles' 100 Greatest Songs*.

ALBUM APPEARANCES: *A Hard Day's Night* (U.K.); *A Hard Day's Night* (U.S.); *Hey Jude*; *Reel Music*.

See also: *A Hard Day's Night* (U.K. LP).

"I Wanna Be Your Man" (Lennon–McCartney)

"I Wanna Be Your Man" is a song on the *With the Beatles* album.

AUTHORSHIP AND BACKGROUND

"I Wanna Be Your Man" figured prominently in the Beatles' growing friendship with an up-and-coming rhythm and blues quintet who called themselves the Rolling Stones. The Beatles first met the Rolling Stones in April 1963 at London's Crawdaddy Club, and a chance encounter in September between Lennon and McCartney and the Stones' manager and publicist Andrew Loog Oldham brought "I Wanna Be Your Man" into the fledgling band's orbit. Lennon and McCartney actually completed the composition, which was inspired by Benny Spellman's "Fortune Teller," in the presence of Oldham and the Rolling Stones, whose version of the song features Brian Jones on slide guitar and a lead vocal performance by Mick Jagger.

RECORDING SESSIONS

Produced by Martin, "I Wanna Be Your Man" was recorded at Abbey Road Studios on September 11 and 12, 1963, with additional sessions on October 3 and 23. Starr double-tracked his lead vocal. On February 28, 1964, the Beatles recorded a second version of "I Wanna Be Your Man" for the BBC's *From Us to You* radio show that was later included on the *Live at the BBC* album.

PERSONNEL

    Lennon: Rickenbacker 325, Harmony Vocal
    McCartney: Höfner 500/1, Harmony Vocal
    Harrison: Gretsch Country Gentleman
    Starr: Vocal, Ludwig Oyster Black Pearl Drums, Maracas
    Martin: Hammond Organ

ALBUM APPEARANCES: *With the Beatles*; *Meet the Beatles!*; *Rock 'n' Roll Music*; *Live at the BBC*; *Anthology 1*.

See also: *Live at the BBC* (LP); *With the Beatles* (LP).

"I Want to Hold Your Hand" (Lennon–McCartney)

"I Want to Hold Your Hand" was the Beatles' first #1 single in the United States, where it was released on December 26, 1963. It was the band's fourth consecutive

#1 single in the United Kingdom, where it was released on November 29, 1963. By the end of January 1964, "I Want to Hold Your Hand" had sold more than 1.5 million copies in the United Kingdom.

AUTHORSHIP AND BACKGROUND

Composed by Lennon and McCartney, "I Want to Hold Your Hand" was written after Epstein urged the band to aspire for a distinctly American sound. The result was a pleasing blend of African American rhythm and blues, West Coast surf music, and high-octane rock 'n' roll. Working at the piano in the basement of Jane Asher's home on 57 Wimpole Street in London, Lennon and McCartney composed the classic tune that later altered the band's fortunes across the globe.

Paul McCartney and John Lennon perform "I Want To Hold Your Hand" on *Late Scene Extra,* on November 25, 1963, in Manchester, England, days before the song's release as a U.K. single. Within weeks, it had displaced the band's "She Loves You" at the top of the British charts, and helped kick off the Beatles' U.S. invasion. (David Redfern/Getty Images)

As Lennon later recalled,

We wrote a lot of stuff together, one on one, eyeball to eyeball. Like in "I Want To Hold Your Hand," I remember when we got the chord that made the song. We were in Jane Asher's house, downstairs in the cellar playing on the piano at the same time. And we had, "Oh you-u-u/got that something. . . ." And Paul hits this chord, and I turn to him and say, "That's *it!*" I said, "Do that again!" In those days, we really used to absolutely write like that—both playing into each other's noses. (Sounes 2010, 92)

RECORDING SESSIONS

Produced by Martin, "I Want to Hold Your Hand" was recorded in 17 takes at Abbey Road Studios on October 17, 1963. It was the first Beatles recording to benefit from four-track technology.

The Beatles recorded a German-language version, "Komm, Gib Mir Deine Hand," on January 29, 1964, at Pathé Marconi Studios in Paris. It was later included on the U.S. album release *Something New* (1964).

Prior to "I Want to Hold Your Hand," Capitol Records, as EMI's U.S. subsidiary, had refused to release the Beatles to an American audience. But having just racked up nearly 300,000 advance orders for *With the Beatles* alone, EMI could simply no longer wait for its American subsidiary to come around. Capitol Records had subsequently been ordered by EMI's managing director L. G. Wood to release the Beatles' next single without delay. With the band slated to perform on the *Ed Sullivan Show* on February 9, 1964, American promoter Sid Bernstein signed them for a pair of shows at Carnegie Hall that same week. Having originally planned to press a mere 5,000 copies of "I Want to Hold Your Hand," Capitol earmarked the impressive sum of $40,000 to promote the single in the United States (Spitz 2005, 443, 444), and American Beatlemania was born.

PERSONNEL

Lennon: Vocal, Rickenbacker 325
McCartney: Vocal, Höfner 500/1
Harrison: Gretsch Country Gentleman
Starr: Ludwig Oyster Black Pearl Drums

CHART PERFORMANCE

U.K.: "I Want to Hold Your Hand"/"This Boy"; November 29, 1963, Parlophone R 5084: #1.

U.S.: "I Want to Hold Your Hand"/"I Saw Her Standing There," December 26, 1963, Capitol 5112: #1 (certified by the RIAA as "Gold," with more than 500,000 copies sold).

LEGACY AND INFLUENCE

"I Want to Hold Your Hand" is included among the Rock and Roll Hall of Fame's *500 Songs That Shaped Rock and Roll.*

In 1964, the Beatles received an Ivor Novello Award, awarded annually by the British Academy of Songwriters, Composers, and Authors, for "I Want to Hold Your Hand."

In 1964, "I Want to Hold Your Hand" was nominated for a Grammy Award for Record of the Year at the 6th Grammy Awards.

In 1998, "I Want to Hold Your Hand" was inducted into the National Academy of Recording Arts and Sciences Grammy Hall of Fame.

In 2004, *Rolling Stone* ranked "I Want to Hold Your Hand" as #16 on the magazine's list of *The 500 Greatest Songs of All Time.*

In 2006, *Pitchfork* ranked "I Want to Hold Your Hand" as #58 on the Web magazine's list of *The 200 Greatest Songs of the 1960s.*

In 2007, *Mojo* magazine ranked "I Want to Hold Your Hand" as #2 on the magazine's list of *Big Bangs: 100 Records That Changed the World.*

In 2008, "I Want to Hold Your Hand" was ranked as #39 on *Billboard* magazine's *All Time Hot 100 Songs.*

In 2010, *Rolling Stone* ranked "I Want to Hold Your Hand" as #2 on the magazine's list of *The Beatles' 100 Greatest Songs.*

In October 2012, BBC Local Radio listeners ranked "I Want to Hold Your Hand" as their ninth favorite Beatles song in a poll conducted in commemoration of the 50th anniversary of "Love Me Do," the band's first single.

ALBUM APPEARANCES: *Meet the Beatles!*; *A Collection of Beatles Oldies*; *The Beatles, 1962–1966*; *Rock 'n' Roll Music*; *20 Greatest Hits*; *Past Masters, Volume 1*; *Anthology 1*; *1*; *Love*; *On Air: Live at the BBC, Volume 2.*

See also: *Meet the Beatles!* (LP).

"I Want to Tell You" (Harrison)

"I Want to Tell You" is a song on the Beatles' *Revolver* album.

AUTHORSHIP AND BACKGROUND

Written by Harrison, "I Want to Tell You" went under the working titles of "I Don't Know," as well as "Granny Smith" and "Laxton's Superb"—both of which commemorate apple varietals. Harrison's "I Want to Tell You" inaugurates the sort of existential philosophy that will characterize his finest Beatles recordings from "Within You, Without You" and "The Inner Light" to "While My Guitar Gently Weeps" and "I Me Mine."

Clearly written with Eastern notions of karma in mind, "I Want to Tell You" addresses the individual as the result of a set of totalizing, lived experiences. Harrison makes a point in the song of underscoring the significance of personal responsibility and the self-negating ills of ego-consciousness. He later described "I Want to Tell You" as being "about the avalanche of thoughts that are so hard to write down or say or transmit" (Beatles 2000, 209).

RECORDING SESSIONS

Produced by Martin, "I Want to Tell You" was recorded at Abbey Road Studios on June 2, 1966, with an additional overdubbing session on June 3 in which McCartney overdubbed his bass. Harrison also double-tracked his vocal.

PERSONNEL

Lennon: Tambourine, Maracas, Backing Vocal
McCartney: Rickenbacker 4001S, Piano, Backing Vocal
Harrison: Vocal, Epiphone Casino
Starr: Ludwig Oyster Black Pearl Drums

ALBUM APPEARANCES: *Revolver* (U.K.); *Revolver* (U.S.).

See also: *Revolver* (U.K. LP).

"I Want You (She's So Heavy)" (Lennon–McCartney)

"I Want You (She's So Heavy)" is a song on the *Abbey Road* album.

AUTHORSHIP AND BACKGROUND

Written by Lennon to celebrate his love for Ono, "I Want You (She's So Heavy)" offers a hearty blend of electric blues with equal doses of heavy metal guitar rock. It was ironically both the first and last song recorded by the Beatles for the *Abbey Road* album.

RECORDING SESSIONS

Produced by Martin, the sessions for "I Want You (She's So Heavy)" began on February 22, 1969, at Trident Studios. The original recording session featured Lennon on his Casino, McCartney on his Rickenbacker, and Starr behind the drums. In mid-April, Lennon and Harrison began constructing the composition's massive guitar sound by doubling the existing arpeggiated Casino track and adding two more layers via Harrison's heavily distorted Les Paul. A few days later, Billy

Preston contributed a groovy Hammond organ part, while Starr punctuated the lengthy musical bridge—as McCartney's funky Rickenbacker solo took center stage—with a supple conga.

On April 20, 1969, the distinctive white noise toward the conclusion of "I Want You (She's So Heavy)" was generated by Starr on a wind machine from Abbey Road's Studio Two percussion cupboard, with Lennon augmenting the din by playing Harrison's Moog. As with "Strawberry Fields Forever," "I Want You (She's So Heavy)" was made possible by editing various discrete sections together. During an August 20 session, the song was assembled with the introductory passages transitioning into Lennon and Harrison's guitar strata prior to the extended musical bridge. Lennon's vocal proper reemerges in the vicinity of the composition's midway point, before achieving its scorching climax with the needle literally driving into the red at 4:28.

For the remaining three minutes, "I Want You (She's So Heavy)" increases perceptibly in intensity. "Louder! Louder!" Lennon implored Emerick during the mixing process. "I want the track to build and build and build, and then I want the white noise to completely take over and blot out the music altogether." With only 21 seconds remaining of the original recording, "all of a sudden he barked out an order" to the Beatles' engineer, "Cut the tape here!" (Emerick and Massey 2006, 301). Martin and the Beatles mixed the song during a session on August 20, the last day they ever worked together in the same recording studio.

Interestingly, "I Want You (She's So Heavy)" was originally supposed to conclude the album, with the *Abbey Road* Medley running its thematic course on side one instead. While the decision to bring the album and the Beatles' recording career to a close with a symphonic suite makes perfect sense, the sudden, unexpected resolution of "I Want You (She's So Heavy)" made for an alarming end to *Abbey Road*, as well as to the Fab Four's musical career, in and of itself.

PERSONNEL

Lennon: Lead Vocal, Epiphone Casino, Moog Synthesizer
McCartney: Rickenbacker 4001S, Backing Vocal
Harrison: Gibson Les Paul Standard, Backing Vocal
Starr: Ludwig Hollywood Maple Drums, Wind Machine
Preston: Hammond Organ

LEGACY AND INFLUENCE

In 2010, *Rolling Stone* ranked "I Want You (She's So Heavy)" as #59 on the magazine's list of *The Beatles' 100 Greatest Songs*.

ALBUM APPEARANCES: *Abbey Road*; *Love*.

See also: *Abbey Road* (LP); Ono, Yoko.

"I Will" (Lennon–McCartney)

"I Will" is a song on *The Beatles* (*The White Album*).

AUTHORSHIP AND BACKGROUND

Written by McCartney, "I Will" finds its origins during the Beatles' 1968 visit to India.

As McCartney remembered,

> I was doing a song, "I Will," that I had as a melody for quite a long time but I didn't have lyrics to it. I remember sitting around (in India) with Donovan, and maybe a couple of other people. We were just sitting around one evening after our day of meditation and I played him this one and he liked it, and we were trying to write some words. We kicked around a few lyrics, something about the moon, but they weren't very satisfactory and I thought the melody was better than the words. It's still one of my favorite melodies that I've written. You just occasionally get lucky with a melody and it becomes rather complete and I think this is one of them—quite a complete tune. (Miles 1997, 420)

RECORDING SESSIONS

Produced by Martin, "I Will" was recorded in 67 takes at Abbey Road Studios on September 16, 1968, with an additional overdubbing session on September 17.

PERSONNEL

Lennon: Cymbals, Maracas
McCartney: Vocal, Martin D-28, Scat Bass
Starr: Bongos

ALBUM APPEARANCES: *The Beatles* (*The White Album*); *Love Songs*; *Anthology 3*.

See also: *The Beatles* (*The White Album*) (LP).

"If I Fell" (Lennon–McCartney)

"If I Fell" is a song on the Beatles' *A Hard Day's Night* album.

AUTHORSHIP AND BACKGROUND

Written by Lennon, "If I Fell" was later described by the songwriter as a turning point in his life as an artist. As Lennon recalled,

That was my first attempt at a ballad proper. That was the precursor to "In My Life." It has the same chord sequences as "In My Life"—D and B minor and E minor, those kinds of things. And it's semi-autobiographical, but not consciously. It shows that I wrote sentimental love ballads—silly love songs—way back when. (Lennon and Ono 2000, 194)

RECORDING SESSIONS

Produced by Martin, "If I Fell" was recorded at Abbey Road Studios on February 27, 1964. Singing into the same microphone during the session, Lennon and McCartney share vocals on the track during what McCartney later described as their "close-harmony period."

PERSONNEL

Lennon: Vocal, Gibson J-160E
McCartney: Vocal, Höfner 500/1
Harrison: Rickenbacker 360/12
Starr: Ludwig Oyster Black Pearl Drums

CHART PERFORMANCE

U.K.: "If I Fell"/"Tell Me Why"; December 4, 1964, Parlophone DP 562 (originally intended for export, this U.K. single was sold sporadically by British retailers; it did not chart).
U.S.: "And I Love Her"/"If I Fell"; July 20, 1964, Capitol 5235: #12. As the B-side of "And I Love Her," "If I Fell" charted at #53.

LEGACY AND INFLUENCE

In 2010, *Rolling Stone* ranked "If I Fell" as #26 on the magazine's list of *The Beatles' 100 Greatest Songs*.

ALBUM APPEARANCES: *A Hard Day's Night* (U.K.); *A Hard Day's Night* (U.S.); *Something New*; *Love* Songs.

See also: *A Hard Day's Night* (U.K.).

"If I Needed Someone" (Harrison)

"If I Needed Someone" is a song on the Beatles' *Rubber Soul* album.

AUTHORSHIP AND BACKGROUND

Written by Harrison, the songwriter later mocked "If I Needed Someone" for its lack of musical variation: " 'If I Needed Someone' was like a million other songs written around one chord," he remarked. "A 'D' chord actually" (Badman 2001, 193).

RECORDING SESSIONS

Produced by Martin, "If I Needed Someone" was recorded at Abbey Road Studios on October 16, 1965, with an additional overdubbing session on October 18.

With Martin on harmonium, "If I Needed Someone" features Harrison's distinctive shimmering guitar introduction—played on his capoed Rickenbacker 360—which was inspired by the Byrds' "The Bells of Rhymney." Harrison double-tracked his vocal.

PERSONNEL

Lennon: Tambourine, Backing Vocal
McCartney: Höfner 500/1, Backing Vocal
Harrison: Vocal, Rickenbacker 360/12
Starr: Ludwig Oyster Black Pearl Drums
Martin: Harmonium

LEGACY AND INFLUENCE

In 2010, *Rolling Stone* ranked "If I Needed Someone" as #51 on the magazine's list of *The Beatles' 100 Greatest Songs*.

ALBUM APPEARANCES: *Rubber Soul* (U.K.); *Yesterday . . . and Today*.

See also: Clapton, Eric; *Rubber Soul* (U.K. LP).

"If You've Got Trouble" (Lennon–McCartney)

"If You've Got Trouble" was recorded during the sessions for *Help!* and remained unreleased until the Beatles' *Anthology* project during the 1990s.

AUTHORSHIP AND BACKGROUND

Written by Lennon, "If You've Got Trouble" was composed expressly to be Starr's vocal contribution to the *Help!* album, although the Beatles selected "Act Naturally" for inclusion on the project instead.

RECORDING SESSIONS

Produced by Martin, "If You've Got Trouble" was recorded at Abbey Road Studios on February 18, 1965, the same day in which the Beatles worked on "Tell Me

What You See" and "You've Got to Hide Your Love Away." Starr double-tracked his vocal for "If You've Got Trouble."

In 1984, Emerick remixed "If You've Got Trouble" in preparation for the unreleased Beatles *Sessions* project. In 1994, Martin remixed "If You've Got Trouble" for release as part of the Beatles' *Anthology* project.

PERSONNEL

Lennon: Rickenbacker 325, Backing Vocal
McCartney: Höfner 500/1, Backing Vocal
Harrison: Gretsch Tennessean
Starr: Vocal, Ludwig Oyster Black Pearl Drums

ALBUM APPEARANCE: *Anthology 2.*

See also: *The Beatles Anthology, Volume 2* (LP); *Help!* (U.K. LP).

"I'll Be Back" (Lennon–McCartney)

"I'll Be Back" is a song on the Beatles' *A Hard Day's Night* album.

AUTHORSHIP AND BACKGROUND

Written by Lennon, "I'll Be Back" was inspired by Del Shannon's "Runaway." As Lennon later observed, " 'I'll Be Back' is me completely. My variation of the chords in a Del Shannon song" (Lennon and Ono 2000, 173). As Bill Harry observes, "Lennon just reworked the chords of the Shannon number and came up with a completely different song" (Harry 1992, 542, 543).

MacDonald describes the song as "a surprisingly downbeat farewell and a token of coming maturity" (MacDonald 1994, 94).

RECORDING SESSIONS

Produced by Martin, "I'll Be Back" was recorded in 16 takes at Abbey Road Studios on June 1, 1964.

PERSONNEL

Lennon: Vocal, Gibson J-160E
McCartney: Gibson J-160E, Höfner 500/1, Backing Vocal
Harrison: Gibson J-160E, Backing Vocal
Starr: Ludwig Oyster Black Pearl Drums

ALBUM APPEARANCES: *A Hard Day's Night* (U.K.); *Beatles '65*; *Love Songs*; *Anthology 1*.

See also: *A Hard Day's Night* (U.K. LP).

"I'll Cry Instead" (Lennon–McCartney)

"I'll Cry Instead" is a song on the Beatles' *A Hard Day's Night* album.

AUTHORSHIP AND BACKGROUND

Written by Lennon, "I'll Cry Instead" pointedly refers to "a chip on my shoulder that's bigger than my feet," a sentiment that, according to the songwriter, reflects his frustrated mental state during the song's creation.

As Lennon later remembered, "I wrote that for *A Hard Day's Night*, but Dick Lester didn't even want it. He resurrected 'Can't Buy Me Love' for that sequence instead. I like the middle-eight to that song" (Dowlding 1989, 75).

RECORDING SESSIONS

Produced by Martin, "I'll Cry Instead" was recorded at Abbey Road Studios on June 1, 1964. The track was completed by editing two sections together. An extended version of the song appears on the United Artists release of the soundtrack for *A Hard Day's Night*.

PERSONNEL

Lennon: Vocal, Gibson J-160E
McCartney: Höfner 500/1
Harrison: Gretsch Country Gentlemen
Starr: Ludwig Oyster Black Pearl Drums, Tambourine

CHART PERFORMANCE

U.S.: "I'll Cry Instead"/"I'm Happy Just to Dance with You"; July 20, 1964, Capitol 5234: #25.

ALBUM APPEARANCES: *A Hard Day's Night* (U.K.); *A Hard Day's Night* (U.S.); *Something New*.

See also: *A Hard Day's Night* (U.K. LP).

"I'll Follow the Sun" (Lennon–McCartney)

"I'll Follow the Sun" is a song on *Beatles for Sale*.

AUTHORSHIP AND BACKGROUND

Written by McCartney, "I'll Follow the Sun" was originally recorded at the McCartney's family home in July 1960.

As McCartney later recalled,

> I wrote that in my front parlour in Forthlin Road. I was about 16. There was a few from then—"Thinking of Linking," ever heard of that one? So "I'll Follow the Sun" was one of those very early ones. I seem to remember writing it just after I'd had the flu. I remember standing in the parlour looking out through lace curtains of the window and writing that one. We had this hard R&B image in Liverpool, so I think songs like "I'll Follow the Sun," ballads like that, got pushed back to later. (Everett 2001, 268)

RECORDING SESSIONS

Produced by Martin, "I'll Follow the Sun" was recorded at Abbey Road Studios on October 8, 1964. Starr kept time during the acoustic "I'll Follow the Sun" by slapping his knees with his palms.

The July 1960 recording of "I'll Follow the Sun" was produced in the McCartney family's bathroom using a Grundig tape recorder. Known as the Braun Tape, the recordings survived in the possession of Hans-Walther "Icke" Braun, one of the band's Hamburg friends, who was entrusted with the tape in the spring of 1961 (Winn 2003a, 4). Seventeen demos survive from the July 1960 recordings, including early versions of the Lennon–McCartney compositions "One After 909," "I'll Follow the Sun," and "Hello Little Girl." In addition to Lennon, McCartney, and Harrison, the July 1960 version of "I'll Follow the Sun" features Sutcliffe on bass.

PERSONNEL

July 1960 Version:
Lennon: Guitar, Backing Vocal
McCartney: Vocal, Guitar
Harrison: Guitar
Sutcliffe: Bass
October 1964 Version:
Lennon: Gibson J-160E
McCartney: Vocal, Epiphone Texan
Harrison: Gretsch Country Gentleman
Starr: Percussion

LEGACY AND INFLUENCE

In 2010, *Rolling Stone* ranked "I'll Follow the Sun" as #79 on the magazine's list of *The Beatles' 100 Greatest Songs*.

ALBUM APPEARANCES: *Beatles for Sale*; *Beatles '65*; *Love Songs*; *On Air: Live at the BBC, Volume 2*.

See also: *Beatles for Sale* (LP); Sutcliffe, Stuart.

"I'll Get You" (Lennon–McCartney)

"I'll Get You" was the B-side of the Beatles' "She Loves You" single.

AUTHORSHIP AND BACKGROUND

Written by Lennon and McCartney at Lennon's Aunt Mimi's Menlove Avenue home, "I'll Get You" was influenced by Joan Baez's folk rendition of "All My Trials." MacDonald notes the song's subterranean cheekiness—with its "mock-naïve love framed by sardonic 'oh yeahs'" and an "air of dry self-sendup" (MacDonald 1994, 65).

In a 1963 interview, McCartney observed that if "we write one song, then we can get going after that and get more ideas. We wrote 'I'll Get You,' which is the B-side, first. And then 'She Loves You' came after that. You know—we got ideas from that. Then we recorded it."

RECORDING SESSIONS

Produced by Martin, "I'll Get You" was recorded at Abbey Road Studios on July 1, 1963. The song went under the working title of "Get You in the End."

PERSONNEL

Lennon: Vocal, Gibson J-160E
McCartney: Vocal, Höfner 500/1
Harrison: Gretsch Country Gentleman, Backing Vocal
Starr: Ludwig Oyster Black Pearl Drums

CHART PERFORMANCE

U.K.: "She Loves You"/"I'll Get You"; August 23, 1963, Parlophone R 5055: #1. As the B-side of "She Loves You," "I'll Get You" did not chart.
U.S.: "She Loves You"/"I'll Get You"; September 16, 1963; rereleased January 25, 1964, Swan 4152: #1. As the B-side of "She Loves You," "I'll Get You" did not chart.

U.S.: "Sie Liebt Dich" ["She Loves You"]/"I'll Get You"; May 21, 1964, Swan 4182: #97. As the B-side of "She Loves You," "I'll Get You" did not chart.

ALBUM APPEARANCES: *The Beatles' Second Album*; *Rarities* (U.K.); *Past Masters, Volume 1*; *Anthology 1*; *On Air: Live at the BBC, Volume 2*.

See also: Smith, Mimi Stanley.

"I'm a Loser" (Lennon–McCartney)

"I'm a Loser" is a song on *Beatles for Sale*.

AUTHORSHIP AND BACKGROUND

Written by Lennon, "I'm a Loser" finds the songwriter becoming more confessional and autobiographical in his work. As Lennon recalled, "That's me in my Dylan period. Part of me suspects I'm a loser, and part of me thinks I'm God almighty" (Harry 2011, 383).

RECORDING SESSIONS

Produced by Martin, "I'm a Loser" was recorded on August 14, 1964, in eight takes at Abbey Road Studios. On November 26, 1964, the Beatles recorded another version of "I'm a Loser" for the BBC's *Top Gear* radio show, which was broadcast on November 26 and later included on the *Live at the BBC* album. The group recorded yet another version for BBC Radio on May 26, 1965, with Lennon irreverently ad-libbing "Beneath this wig, I am wearing a tie."

PERSONNEL

Lennon: Vocal, Gibson J-160E, Harmonica
McCartney: Höfner 500/1
Harrison: Gretsch Tennessean
Starr: Ludwig Oyster Black Pearl Drums, Tambourine

LEGACY AND INFLUENCE

In 2010, *Rolling Stone* ranked "I'm a Loser" as #71 on the magazine's list of *The Beatles' 100 Greatest Songs*.

ALBUM APPEARANCES: *Beatles for Sale*; *Beatles '65*; *Live at the BBC*.

See also: *Beatles for Sale* (LP); *Live at the BBC* (LP).

"I'm Down" (Lennon–McCartney)

"I'm Down" is the B-side of the Beatles' "Help!" single, which was released in the United Kingdom on July 23, 1965, and in the United States on July 19, 1965.

AUTHORSHIP AND BACKGROUND

Written by McCartney, "I'm Down" was composed by the songwriter as an homage to Little Richard.

As McCartney later recalled,

> I could do Little Richard's voice which is a wild, hoarse, screaming thing—it's like an out-of-body experience. You have to leave your current sensibilities and go about a foot above your head to sing it. A lot of people were fans of Little Richard so I used to sing his stuff, but there came a point when I wanted to do one of my own, so I wrote "I'm Down." (Harry 2002, 442)

RECORDING SESSIONS

Produced by Martin, "I'm Down" was recorded at Abbey Road Studios on June 14, 1965, the same day in which the Beatles recorded "I've Just Seen a Face" and "Yesterday." During the session, McCartney can be heard saying "Plastic soul, man"—the phrase that later transformed into the Beatles' album *Rubber Soul*.

PERSONNEL

Lennon: Hammond Organ, Backing Vocal
McCartney: Vocal, Höfner 500/1
Harrison: Gretsch Tennessean
Starr: Ludwig Oyster Black Pearl Drums, Bongos

CHART PERFORMANCE

U.K.: "Help!"/"I'm Down"; July 23, 1965, Parlophone R 5305: #1.
U.S.: "Help!"/"I'm Down"; July 19, 1965, Capitol 5476: #1 (certified by the RIAA as "Gold," with more than 500,000 copies sold). As the B-side of "Help!" "I'm Down" charted at #101.

LEGACY AND INFLUENCE

In 2010, *Rolling Stone* ranked "I'm Down" as #56 on the magazine's list of *The Beatles' 100 Greatest Songs*.

ALBUM APPEARANCES: *Rock 'n' Roll Music*; *Rarities* (U.K.); *Past Masters, Volume 1*; *Anthology 2*; *Tomorrow Never Knows*.

See also: *Rubber Soul* (U.K. LP).

"I'm Happy Just to Dance with You" (Lennon–McCartney)

"I'm Happy Just to Dance with You" is a song on the Beatles' *A Hard Day's Night* album.

AUTHORSHIP AND BACKGROUND

"I'm Happy Just to Dance with You" was written by Lennon expressly for Harrison to undertake as a lead vocalist—"I couldn'ta sung it," Lennon confessed (Dowlding 1989, 70). As McCartney later observed, "We wrote 'I'm Happy Just to

From left, Paul McCartney, George Harrison, John Lennon, and Ringo Starr perform "I'm Happy Just to Dance with You" on the set of *A Hard Day's Night* at the Scala Theatre on March 1, 1964. Lennon, who wrote it as a lead vocal part for Harrison, comments at the end, "Oh, very good that, George!" (Redferns/Getty Images)

Dance with You' for George in the film. It was a bit of a formula song. We knew that in (the key of) E if you went to an A-flat-minor, you could always make a song with those chords. That change pretty much always excited you" (Everett 2001, 390).

RECORDING SESSIONS

Produced by Martin, "I'm Happy Just to Dance with You" was recorded at Abbey Road Studios on March 1, 1964.

PERSONNEL

Lennon: Rickenbacker 325, Backing Vocal
McCartney: Höfner 500/1, Backing Vocal
Harrison: Vocal, Rickenbacker 360/12
Starr: Ludwig Oyster Black Pearl Drums, Loose-Skinned Arabian Bongo

CHART PERFORMANCE

U.S.: "I'll Cry Instead"/"I'm Happy Just to Dance with You"; July 20, 1964, Capitol 5234: #25. As the B-side of "I'll Cry Instead," "I'm Happy Just to Dance with You" charted at #95.

U.K.: "The Beatles' Movie Medley"/"I'm Happy Just to Dance with You"; March 24, 1982, Parlophone R6055: #10. As the B-side of "The Beatles' Movie Medley," "I'm Happy Just to Dance with You" did not chart.

U.S.: "The Beatles' Movie Medley"/"I'm Happy Just to Dance with You"; March 24, 1982, Capitol B5107: #12. As the B-side of "The Beatles' Movie Medley," "I'm Happy Just to Dance with You" did not chart.

ALBUM APPEARANCES: *A Hard Day's Night* (U.K.); *A Hard Day's Night* (U.S.); *Something New.*

See also: *A Hard Day's Night* (U.K. LP).

"I'm Looking Through You" (Lennon–McCartney)

"I'm Looking Through You" is a song on the Beatles' *Rubber Soul* album.

AUTHORSHIP AND BACKGROUND

Written by McCartney, "I'm Looking Through You" was composed after an argument with Asher. At the time, McCartney was separated from Asher, who was in Bristol on a theater tour.

As McCartney later recalled, "As is one's wont in relationships, you will from time to time argue or not see eye to eye on things, and a couple of the songs around this period were that kind of thing. I would write it out in a song and then I've got rid of the emotion. I don't hold grudges so that gets rid of that little bit of emotional baggage" (Miles 1997, 276).

RECORDING SESSIONS

Produced by Martin, "I'm Looking Through You" was recorded at Abbey Road Studios on October 24, 1965. It was remade on November 6 and again on November 10, with additional overdubbing on November 11, when McCartney double-tracked his lead vocal.

In 1984, Emerick remixed an alternate take of "I'm Looking Through You" in preparation for the unreleased Beatles *Sessions* project. In 1994, Martin remixed "I'm Looking Through You" for release as part of the Beatles' *Anthology* project.

PERSONNEL

Lennon: Gibson J-160E, Tambourine, Backing Vocal
McCartney: Vocal, Höfner 500/1
Harrison: Epiphone Casino, Backing Vocal
Starr: Ludwig Oyster Black Pearl Drums, Hammond Organ

ALBUM APPEARANCES: *Rubber Soul* (U.K.); *Rubber Soul* (U.S.); *Anthology 2.*

See also: *Rubber Soul* (U.K. LP).

"I'm Only Sleeping" (Lennon–McCartney)

"I'm Only Sleeping" is a track on the Beatles' *Revolver* album.

AUTHORSHIP AND BACKGROUND

Written by Lennon with assistance from McCartney, "I'm Only Sleeping" benefits from the eerie, hypnotic effect of Harrison's backward guitar solo. As Lennon later recalled, "It's got backwards guitars—that's me dreaming my life away" (Lennon and Ono 2000, 198). As McCartney remembered, "It was a nice idea—'There's nothing wrong with it. I'm not being lazy, I'm only sleeping, I'm yawning, I'm meditating, I'm having a lay-in.' The luxury of all that was what it was all about. The song was co-written but from John's original idea" (Cadogan 2008, 187).

RECORDING SESSIONS

Produced by Martin, "I'm Only Sleeping" was recorded in 16 takes on April 27, 1966, with an overdubbing session for the lead vocal on April 29 and the backing vocals on May 6. The backward guitar solo was overdubbed on May 5.

As Emerick remembered, the process for recording Harrison's backward guitar solo took some nine hours: "I can still picture George hunched over his guitar for hours on end," Emerick recalled, "headphones clamped on, brows furrowed in concentration" (Emerick and Massey 2006, 124).

PERSONNEL

Lennon: Vocal, Gibson J-160E
McCartney: Rickenbacker 4001S
Harrison: Sonic Blue Fender Stratocaster
Starr: Ludwig Oyster Black Pearl Drums

LEGACY AND INFLUENCE

In 2010, *Rolling Stone* ranked "I'm Only Sleeping" as #57 on the magazine's list of *The Beatles' 100 Greatest Songs*.

ALBUM APPEARANCES: *Revolver* (U.K.); *Yesterday . . . and Today*; *Rarities* (U.S.); *Anthology 2*.

See also: Emerick, Geoff; *Revolver* (U.K. LP).

"I'm So Tired" (Lennon–McCartney)

"I'm So Tired" is a song on *The Beatles* (*The White Album*).

AUTHORSHIP AND BACKGROUND

Written by Lennon, "I'm So Tired" finds its origins during the Beatles' 1968 visit to India, when the songwriter was plagued by insomnia during his extended study of Transcendental Meditation. The notion of insomnia is a frequent theme in Lennon's work, including the Beatles song "I'm Only Sleeping" and his posthumous solo hit single "Watching the Wheels."

An early version of "I'm So Tired" was recorded in May 1968 at Harrison's Kinfauns studio as part of the Esher Tapes.

RECORDING SESSIONS

Produced by Martin, "I'm So Tired" was recorded on October 8, 1968, at Abbey Road Studios.

Lennon later described "I'm So Tired" as "one of my favorite tracks. I just like the sound of it, and I sing it well" (Dowlding 1989, 232).

PERSONNEL

Lennon: Vocal, Epiphone Casino, Hammond Organ
McCartney: Rickenbacker 4001S, Backing Vocal
Harrison: Fender Stratocaster
Starr: Ludwig Oyster Black Pearl Drums

LEGACY AND INFLUENCE

In 2010, *Rolling Stone* ranked "I'm So Tired" as #83 on the magazine's list of *The Beatles' 100 Greatest Songs*.

ALBUM APPEARANCES: *The Beatles* (*The White Album*); *Anthology 3*.

See also: *The Beatles* (*The White Album*) (LP); "Paul Is Dead" Hoax.

"In My Life" (Lennon–McCartney)

"In My Life" is a song on the Beatles' *Rubber Soul* album.

AUTHORSHIP AND BACKGROUND

Written by Lennon with assistance from McCartney, "In My Life" is one of the most contested compositions, along with "Eleanor Rigby," in the Lennon–McCartney catalogue.

"In My Life" finds its origins in the words of English journalist Kenneth Allsop, who suggested to Lennon that he write a song about his childhood. To this end, Lennon's "In My Life" also benefits from the songwriter's youthful reading of Charles Lamb's 18th-century poem "The Old Familiar Faces": "For some they have died, and some they have left me, / *And some are taken from me*; all are departed; / All, all are gone, the old familiar faces."

As the song began to take shape, "In My Life" came to represent one of Lennon and McCartney's most complicated instances of writerly dispute. As Lennon remembers, "It was, I think, my first real major piece of work. Up till then it had all been sort of glib and throwaway. And that was the first time I consciously put my literary part of myself into the lyric" (Lennon and Ono 2000, 178, 179). Lennon recalled "writing a first draft of the song in which he struggled for days and hours trying to write clever lyrics" (Lennon and Ono 2000, 193):

> "In My Life" started out as a bus journey from my house on 250 Menlove Avenue to town, mentioning every place that I could remember. And it was ridiculous. This is before even "Penny Lane" was written and I had Penny Lane, Strawberry

Field, Tram Sheds—Tram Sheds are the depots just outside of Penny Lane—and it was the most boring sort of "What I Did on My Holiday's Bus Trip" song and it wasn't working at all. (Lennon and Ono 2000, 152)

In Lennon's estimation, the song's lyrics improved after he began waxing nostalgically about the friends, lovers, and places of his Liverpudlian past. Lennon pointedly recalls that "the whole lyrics were already written before Paul even heard it. In 'In My Life,'" he adds, "[Paul's] contribution melodically was the harmony and the middle-eight itself" (Lennon and Ono 2000, 153).

McCartney's recollections about the composition of "In My Life" vary to a considerable degree from Lennon's version of events. McCartney remembered a writing session in which Lennon had already completed the song's opening stanzas: "But as I recall, he didn't have a tune to it." McCartney allegedly devoted half an hour to composing the song's musical structure in its entirety:

And I went down to the half-landing, where John had a Mellotron, and I sat there and put together a tune based on Smokey Robinson and the Miracles. Songs like "You Really Got a Hold on Me" and "Tears of a Clown" had really been an influence. You refer back to something you've loved and try and take the spirit of that and write something new. So I recall writing the whole melody. And it actually does sound very like me, if you analyze it. I was obviously working to lyrics. The melody's structure is very me. (Miles 1997, 277)

While they often dispute Robinson's influence on the composition of the song's musical structure, a number of musicologists agree that "In My Life" evinces a McCartneyesque flavor. The song's "angular verticality, spanning an octave in typically wide—and difficult—leaps, certainly shows more of his touch than Lennon's, despite fitting the latter's voice snugly," MacDonald writes. "As for the middle-eight, there isn't one, [with] the song alternating between its verse and an extended chorus" (MacDonald 1994, 136, 137). Everett, for one, disagrees with MacDonald's somewhat definitive conclusion about McCartney's musical contributions to "In My Life." Everett argues that "John and Paul had such a long history of writing 'into each others' noses' that the origins of even such Beatles-marking details can't be securely placed with one or the other" (Everett 2001, 320). While Lennon and McCartney disputed the authorship of "In My Life" and "Eleanor Rigby," McCartney later pointed out that "I find it very gratifying that out of everything we wrote, we only appear to disagree over two songs" (Miles 1997, 278).

RECORDING SESSIONS

Produced by Martin, "In My Life" was recorded in three takes at Abbey Road Studios on October 18, 1965.

Fittingly, "In My Life" features Martin's wistful piano solo, which he later described as his "Bach inversion." Four days after the Beatles completed their work on the song, Martin went to Abbey Road Studios before the band members arrived in order to record the keyboard solo, which was made possible via his wound-up piano effect and which replaced the Vox Continental organ solo that he had recorded earlier as a space-saver (Lewisohn 1988, 202, 203). As part of his wound-up piano technique, Martin recorded his solo at half-tempo, doubling the tape speed for the final recording. The result was an exquisite, harpsichord-like sound. As Martin later recalled,

> "In My Life" is one of my favorite songs because it is so much John. A super track and such a simple song. There's a bit where John couldn't decide what to do in the middle and, while they were having their tea break, I put down a baroque piano solo which John didn't hear until he came back. What I wanted was too intricate for me to do live, so I did it with a half-speed piano, then sped it up, and he liked it. (Beatles 2000, 197)

PERSONNEL

Lennon: Vocal, Gibson J-160E
McCartney: Höfner 500/1, Backing Vocal
Harrison: Sonic Blue Fender Stratocaster, Backing Vocal
Starr: Ludwig Oyster Black Pearl Drums, Tambourine, Bells
Martin: Piano

LEGACY AND INFLUENCE

In 2000, *Mojo* magazine ranked "In My Life" as #1 on the magazine's list of *The 100 Greatest Songs of All Time*.

In 2004, *Rolling Stone* ranked "In My Life" as #23 on the magazine's list of *The 500 Greatest Songs of All Time*.

In 2010, *Rolling Stone* ranked "In My Life" as #5 on the magazine's list of *The Beatles' 100 Greatest Songs*.

In 2006, *Q Magazine* ranked "In My Life" as #57 on the magazine's list of *The 100 Greatest Songs of All Time*.

ALBUM APPEARANCES: *Rubber Soul* (U.S.); *Rubber Soul* (U.K.); *The Beatles, 1962–1966*; *Love Songs*.

See also: Martin, George; *Rubber Soul* (U.K. LP); Sutcliffe, Stuart.

"In Spite of All the Danger" (McCartney–Harrison)

In July 1958, "In Spite of All the Danger" was the second song recorded by the Quarry Men. It was first released as part of the *Anthology* project in 1995.

AUTHORSHIP AND BACKGROUND

Written by McCartney with assistance from Harrison, "In Spite of All the Danger" was inspired by Presley's "Trying to Get to You" from the rock pioneer's Sun Records era. As McCartney remembered, "It was my song. It's very similar to an Elvis song. It's me doing an Elvis, but I'm a bit loathe to say which! I know which one! It was one that I'd heard at scout camp when I was younger and I'd loved it. And when I came to write the first couple of songs at the age of about 14 that was one of them" (McCartney 1988, 7).

McCartney added that

It says on the label that it was me and George but I think it was actually written by me, and George played the guitar solo! We were mates and nobody was into copyrights and publishing, nobody understood—we actually used to think when we came down to London that songs belonged to everyone. I've said this a few times but it's true, we really thought they just were in the air, and that you couldn't actually own one. So you can imagine the publishers saw us coming! "Welcome boys, sit down. That's what you think, is it?" So that's what we used to do in those days—and because George did the solo we figured that he "wrote" the solo. (Lewisohn 1988, 6)

RECORDING SESSIONS

The Quarry Men—Lennon, McCartney, Harrison, Colin Hanton, and John "Duff" Lowe—recorded "In Spite of All the Danger" on Saturday, July 12, 1958, three days before Julia Lennon's untimely death on Menlove Avenue. The Quarry Men had pooled their money in order to record a demo at P. F. Phillips Professional Tape and Disk Record Service, a fancy name for a back room in the 38 Kensington Street home of Percy Phillips, who had built a primitive recording studio with a Vortexion reel-to-reel tape recorder, an MSS portable disc-cutting machine, and a trio of microphones. With Phillips's assistance, the group cut a 78-rpm single. The Quarry Men had intended to record several takes in Phillips' studio, but their host was having none of it. For the bargain-basement price of 17 shillings, they were going "straight to vinyl," which meant that they would be recording directly onto a shellac disc. It also meant that the band had to turn in flawless takes in order to get their money's worth.

As McCartney later recalled,

I remember we all went down on the bus with our instruments—amps and guitars—and the drummer went separately. We waited in the little waiting room outside while somebody else made their demo and then it was our turn. We just went in the room, hardly saw the fella because he was next door in a little control booth. "OK, what are you going to do?" We ran through it very quickly, quarter of an hour, and it was all over. (Lewisohn 1988, 7)

For their second performance that day—following Buddy Holly's "That'll Be the Day"—the Quarry Men tackled an original composition at McCartney's urging. "In Spite of All the Danger" featured "doo-wop" backing vocals arrayed against Lowe's tinkling piano. As Lowe later recalled, "I can well remember even at the rehearsal at his house in Forthlin Road, Paul was quite specific about how he wanted it played and what he wanted the piano to do. There was no question of improvising. We were told what we had to play. There was a lot of arranging going on even back then" (Turner 1994, 193).

The Quarry Men agreed to share the record amongst themselves, with each member taking temporary ownership of the prize for a week at a time. Lennon, McCartney, Harrison, and Hanton duly passed the disc amongst themselves, and when the record was in Hanton's custody, the drummer talked his friend Charles Roberts into playing it over the P.A. system in the lounge at Littlewood's gaming hall, where it received a surly response from the staff. The disc next alighted in the hands of Lowe, who stowed it away in a linen drawer where it languished for years. McCartney purchased the disc from Lowe in 1981 for an undisclosed amount.

PERSONNEL

> Lennon: Vocal, Guitar
> McCartney: Guitar, Backing Vocal
> Harrison: Guitar, Backing Vocal
> Lowe: Piano
> Hanton: Drums

ALBUM APPEARANCE: *Anthology 1*.

See also: *The Beatles Anthology, Volume 1* (LP); The Quarry Men.

"The Inner Light" (Harrison)

"The Inner Light" was the B-side of the Beatles' "Lady Madonna" single, which was released in the United Kingdom on March 15, 1968, and in the United States on March 18, 1968.

AUTHORSHIP AND BACKGROUND

Written by Harrison, "The Inner Light" was composed at the suggestion of Cambridge Sanskrit scholar Juan Mascaró. Harrison authored "The Inner Light" based on the professor's translation of a poem by Lao Tzŭ—from *Tao Te Ching*, the seminal sixth-century work of Chinese scripture (Everett 1999, 152).

Harrison observed that

In the original poem, the verse says "Without going out of my door, I can know the ways of heaven." And so to prevent any misinterpretations—and also to make the song a bit longer—I did repeat that as a second verse but made it: "Without going out of your door / You can know all things on earth / Without looking out of your window / You can know the ways of heaven"—so that it included everybody. (Harrison 1980, 118)

As McCartney later remarked, "Forget the Indian music and listen to the melody. Don't you think it's a beautiful melody? It's really lovely" (Everett 1999, 153).

RECORDING SESSIONS

Produced by Martin, the Indian instrumental music for "The Inner Light" was recorded under Harrison's direction at EMI Studios in Bombay, India, on January 12, 1968. Harrison was in Bombay to work on his soundtrack album entitled *Wonderwall Music*.

Harrison overdubbed his lead vocal for "The Inner Light" back at Abbey Road Studios on February 6, 1968, with Lennon and McCartney overdubbing their backing vocals on February 8. As Abbey Road Studios tape operator Jerry Boys later recalled, "George had this big thing about not wanting to sing it because he didn't feel confident that he could do the song justice. I remember Paul saying, 'You must have a go, don't worry about it, it's good'" (Lewisohn 1988, 133).

PERSONNEL

Lennon: Backing Vocal
McCartney: Backing Vocal
Harrison: Vocal
Studio Musicians: Indian Instrumental Accompaniment
Hariprasad Chaurasia: Bansuri
Rijram Desad: Harmonium
Hanuman Jadev: Shehnai
Aashish Khan: Sarod
Mahapurush Misra: Pakhavaj

CHART PERFORMANCE

U.K.: "Lady Madonna"/"The Inner Light"; March 15, 1968, Parlophone R 5675: #1. As the B-side of "Lady Madonna," "The Inner Light" did not chart.
U.S.: "Lady Madonna"/"The Inner Light"; March 18, 1968, Capitol 2138: #4 (certified by the RIAA as "Platinum," with more than 1 million copies sold). As the B-side of "Lady Madonna," "The Inner Light" charted at #96.

ALBUM APPEARANCES: *Rarities* (U.K.); *Rarities* (U.S.); *Past Masters, Volume 2*; *Love*.

See also: Lynne, Jeff.

"It's All Too Much" (Harrison)

"It's All Too Much" is a song on the Beatles' *Yellow Submarine* album.

AUTHORSHIP AND BACKGROUND

Written by Harrison, "It's All Too Much" finds the songwriter offering his first and last meditation on his experiences with LSD.

In a 1999 *Billboard* interview with Timothy White, Harrison remarked that " 'It's All Too Much' was written in a childlike manner from realizations that appeared during and after some LSD experiences and which were later confirmed in meditation" (Everett 1999, 127).

Harrison swore off acid within a scant few months of authoring "It's All Too Much." In August 1967, Harrison and his wife Pattie Boyd visited San Francisco's Haight-Ashbury district, ground zero for American hippiedom and the Summer of Love. Harrison described the San Francisco drug scene as being like the "Bowery," a netherworld of "bums" and "dropouts." For Harrison, it was a moment of epiphany from which he simply couldn't turn back, and the Beatle ceased taking LSD on the spot. As he later recalled, "That was the turning point for me—that's when I went right off the whole drug cult and stopped taking the dreaded lysergic acid. I had some in a little bottle (it was liquid). I put it under a microscope and it looked like bits of old rope. I thought that I couldn't put that into my brain anymore" (Beatles 2000, 259).

RECORDING SESSIONS

Produced by Martin, "It's All Too Much" was recorded under the working title of "Too Much" at London's De Lane Lea Recording Studios on May 25, 1967, with additional overdubbing sessions on May 26 and June 2.

Martin was conspicuously absent during the first session for "It's All Too Much," having skipped a number of sessions of late because he had become exasperated with the Beatles' aimless demeanor. "Sometimes," the producer recalled, "they would jam for hours in the studio, and we would be expected to tape it all, recognizing the moment of great genius when it came through. The only trouble was, it never did come through" (Martin 1979, 138). During the chaotic first session, the Beatles created a basic rhythm track for "Too Much," which included the recording of a 25-minute jam session based on the rather convoluted composition. With the assistance of the De Lane Lea personnel, the song was eventually mixed down to a more reasonable eight minutes, which featured Lennon and Harrison on heavily distorted Casinos and McCartney turning in an uninspired bass part on his Rickenbacker. The "Too Much" chant that concludes the song morphed, at various instances, into "tuba" and "Cuba," as Lennon and McCartney's backing vocals devolved into further chaos (Lewisohn 1988, 112; 1995, 256).

The June 1, 1967, session for "Too Much"—occurring on the very day of the much-heralded release of *Sgt. Pepper*—found the group at De Lane Lea yet again, where their work on "Too Much" produced hour after hour of mindless instrumental jam sessions, with little real progress being made on the song. Martin rejoined the proceedings the next evening, and in spite of the chaos of additional instrumental jamming, managed to assemble a parcel of studio musicians, including David Mason, in order to bring the rambling song to an end. Although "It's All Too Much" ultimately exists as a rather minor track in the Beatles' canon, it features a variety of intriguing elements, including trumpet quotations from Jeremiah Clarke's "Prince of Denmark's March" (often incorrectly identified as the "Trumpet Voluntary"), as well as Harrison's borrowing of a lyric from the Merseys' 1966 hit single "Sorrow": "With your long blonde hair and your eyes of blue." Even more interesting is the arresting prefatory guitar work. Described by Tim Riley as "the resplendent surge of a Hendrix electric fireball," Harrison's introduction, played on the hollow-bodied Casino, finds the guitarist engaging the instrument's Bigsby bar in searing, full vibrato force (Riley 1988, 243). Yet for the most part, "It's All Too Much" witnesses the band squeezing the life out of a two-chord guitar figure before settling in for a seemingly interminable coda. As Mark Lewisohn observes, "The single-minded channeling of their great talent so evident on *Sgt. Pepper* did seem, for the moment at least, to have disappeared" (Lewisohn 1995, 256).

PERSONNEL

Lennon: Epiphone Casino, Backing Vocal
McCartney: Rickenbacker 4001S, Backing Vocal, Cowbell
Harrison: Vocal, Epiphone Casino, Hammond Organ
Starr: Ludwig Oyster Black Pearl Drums
Studio Musicians: Brass and Woodwind Accompaniment conducted by Martin
David Mason and three uncredited musicians: Trumpet
Paul Harvey: Bass Clarinet

ALBUM APPEARANCES: *Yellow Submarine*; *Yellow Submarine Songtrack*; *Tomorrow Never Knows*.

See also: *Yellow Submarine* (Film); *Yellow Submarine* (LP).

"It's Only Love" (Lennon–McCartney)

"It's Only Love" is a song on the Beatles' *Help!* album.

AUTHORSHIP AND BACKGROUND

Written by Lennon with assistance from McCartney under the working title "That's a Nice Hat (Cap)," "It's Only Love" was first released in the United States on the *Rubber Soul* album.

As Lennon later observed, " 'It's Only Love' is mine. I always thought it was a lousy song. The lyrics are abysmal. I always hated that song" (Lennon and Ono 2000, 177). As McCartney later recalled, "Sometimes we didn't fight it if the lyric came out rather bland on some of those filler songs like 'It's Only Love.' If a lyric was really bad we'd edit it. But we weren't that fussy about it, because it's only a rock 'n' roll song. I mean, this is not literature" (Miles 1997, 200).

RECORDING SESSIONS

Produced by Martin, "It's Only Love" was recorded at Abbey Road Studios on June 15, 1965.

PERSONNEL

Lennon: Vocal, Framus 12-string Hootenanny
McCartney: Höfner 500/1
Harrison: Gretsch Tennessean
Starr: Ludwig Oyster Black Pearl Drums, Tambourine

ALBUM APPEARANCES: *Help!* (U.K.); *Rubber Soul* (U.S.); *Anthology 2.*

See also: *Help!* (U.K. LP).

iTunes

In November 2010, Apple Corps released the Beatles' newly remastered catalogue on computer and entertainment behemoth Apple's iTunes Store. In so doing, the release of the Beatles' music brought to an end the long-standing dispute between Apple Corps and Apple, Inc., which had originally been named by Steve Jobs and Steve Wozniak during the 1970s as an homage to the Beatles.

The dispute between Apple Corps and Apple, Inc. (formerly Apple Computer) originally involved a trademark conflict between the Beatles' EMI subsidiary and the computer giant. In 1991, the warring companies reaching an agreement about the manner in which each corporation would deploy its trademark. Apple, Inc., paid Apple Corps $27 million as part of an agreement that Apple, Inc., would not involve itself in the music distribution business using the Apple name and logo. In 2003, Apple Corps sued Apple, Inc., arguing that the computer corporation violated the 1991 agreement by opening the iTunes Store. Apple, Inc., finally prevailed after a U.K. judge ruled that the 1991 agreement had not been broken because the iTunes Store sold prerecorded music as opposed to original music under the Apple logo. In 2007, the latest dispute was resolved when Apple, Inc., agreed not to distribute music through physical media such as CDs.

With the latest round of disputes having been quieted, the way was paved for Apple Corps to reach an agreement for the sale of Beatles music on Apple's iTunes Store. For the first time, the Beatles were available in a legitimate downloadable format, making them one of the last blockbuster music acts to join the digital revolution. The iTunes Store heralded the historic release with a teaser on its website, announcing that "tomorrow is just another day. That you'll never forget." In a press release, Apple's Jobs was ecstatic about the Beatles' unveiling on the iTunes virtual sales floor: "We love the Beatles and are honored and thrilled to welcome them to iTunes. It has been a long and winding road to get here. Thanks to the Beatles and EMI, we are now realizing a dream we've had since we launched iTunes ten years ago."

As the iTunes press release demonstrates, the surviving Beatles and the estates of Harrison and Lennon were equally pleased, with McCartney remarking, "We're really excited to bring the Beatles' music to iTunes. It's fantastic to see the songs we originally released on vinyl receive as much love in the digital world as they did the first time around." Starr added, "I am particularly glad to no longer be asked when the Beatles are coming to iTunes. At last, if you want it—you can get it now—the Beatles from Liverpool to now!" Olivia Harrison simply stated, "The Beatles on iTunes—Bravo!" while Ono stated that "in the joyful spirit of 'Give Peace a Chance,' I think it is so appropriate that we are doing this on John's 70th birthday year."

See also: Apple Corps, Ltd.; *The Beatles Stereo Box Set*; Harrison, Olivia Trinidad Arias; Ono, Yoko; *Sgt. Pepper's Lonely Hearts Club Band* (LP).

"It Won't Be Long" (Lennon–McCartney)

"It Won't Be Long" is a song on the *With the Beatles* album.

AUTHORSHIP AND BACKGROUND

Written by Lennon, "It Won't Be Long" involves a play on words between "be long" and "belong." Vocally, the song features a call-and-response chorus of "yeah, *yeah*, yeah, *yeah*, yeah, *yeah*."

RECORDING SESSIONS

Produced by Martin, "It Won't Be Long" was recorded in 17 takes at Abbey Road Studios on July 30, 1963. "It Won't Be Long" is the opening track on the album, as well as the first song recorded specifically for the project.

PERSONNEL

Lennon: Vocal, Rickenbacker 325
McCartney: Höfner 500/1, Backing Vocal
Harrison: Gretsch Country Gentleman, Backing Vocal
Starr: Ludwig Oyster Black Pearl Drums

LEGACY AND INFLUENCE

In 2010, *Rolling Stone* ranked "It Won't Be Long" as #53 on the magazine's list of *The Beatles' 100 Greatest Songs*.

ALBUM APPEARANCES: *With the Beatles*; *Meet the Beatles!*

See also: *With the Beatles* (LP).

"I've Got a Feeling" (Lennon–McCartney)

"I've Got a Feeling" is a song on the Beatles' *Let It Be* album.

AUTHORSHIP AND BACKGROUND

Written by Lennon and McCartney, "I've Got a Feeling" is the merge of three unrecorded compositions: McCartney's "I've Got a Feeling," Lennon's "Everybody Had a Hard Year," and "Watching Rainbows," which McCartney, Lennon, and Starr had improvised during a January 14, 1969, rehearsal of "Mr. Mean Mustard" at Twickenham Film Studios. At the time, Harrison was briefly estranged from the band, having walked out during a January 10 session at Twickenham.

Interestingly, McCartney's "I've Got a Feeling" combines his optimism about his newfound love for Linda Eastman with Lennon's contrasting pessimism in "Everybody Had a Hard Year" about Ono's recent miscarriage, his divorce from Cynthia Lennon, his recent arrest for drug possession, and his precarious emotional place with the Beatles.

RECORDING SESSIONS

Produced by Martin with postproduction by Spector, "I've Got a Feeling" was recorded during the Beatles' rooftop concert on January 30, 1969, after extensive rehearsals at Apple Studio on January 22, 24, 27, and 28.

"I've Got a Feeling" features Billy Preston on his Fender Rhodes Electric Piano and the band whipping up a groovy gruel of guitar rock. The song's bridge offers one of the Beatles' most explosive middle-eights courtesy of McCartney's ferocious lead vocal. In a searing, gut-wrenching performance, McCartney packs as much emotion and meaning into those nine measly seconds as he does in nearly any other song in his massive corpus. It's a bravura moment in which he lays himself bare.

The raw power of the middle-eight in "I've Got a Feeling" is underscored by Harrison's elongated, subtly descending guitar figure. During the rehearsals for the song, McCartney can be heard outlining his vision for the guitar lick, briefly chastising Harrison for rushing the phrase—"It's coming down too fast—the note"—before describing how the guitar lick should come to fruition: "There shouldn't be any recognizable jumps. Falling . . . Falling . . ."

"I've Got a Feeling" finally segues into Lennon's "Everybody Had a Hard Year." After the first iteration of Lennon's verses, McCartney returns to the introductory stanza, joining his partner in a quodlibet structure in which their superimposed voices merge in a cathartic counterpoint.

For the song's *Let It Be . . . Naked* release (2003), "I've Got a Feeling" exists as a composite from both performances during the Beatles' rooftop concert.

PERSONNEL

Lennon: Vocal, Epiphone Casino
McCartney: Vocal, Höfner 500/1
Harrison: Fender Rosewood Telecaster
Starr: Ludwig Hollywood Maple Drums
Preston: Fender Rhodes Electric Piano

LEGACY AND INFLUENCE

In 2010, *Rolling Stone* ranked "I've Got a Feeling" as #64 on the magazine's list of *The Beatles' 100 Greatest Songs.*

ALBUM APPEARANCES: *Let It Be; Anthology 3; Let It Be . . . Naked; Tomorrow Never Knows.*

See also: *Let It Be* (LP); *Let It Be . . . Naked* (LP); The Rooftop Concert; Spector, Phil.

"I've Just Seen a Face" (Lennon–McCartney)

"I've Just Seen a Face" is a song on the Beatles' *Help!* album.

AUTHORSHIP AND BACKGROUND

Written by McCartney, "I've Just Seen a Face" went under the working title of "Auntie Gin's Theme."

As McCartney remembered, "I think of this as totally by me. It was slightly country and western from my point of view. It was faster, though. It was a strange up-tempo thing. I was quite pleased with it. The lyric works. It keeps dragging you forward—it keeps pulling you to the next line. There's an insistent quality about it" (Harry 2002, 444).

RECORDING SESSIONS

Produced by Martin, "I've Just Seen a Face" was recorded at Abbey Road Studios on June 14, 1965.

PERSONNEL

Lennon: Gibson J-160E
McCartney: Vocal, Höfner 500/1, Epiphone Texan
Harrison: Framus 12-string Hootenanny
Starr: Ludwig Oyster Black Pearl Drums, Maracas

LEGACY AND INFLUENCE

In 2010, *Rolling Stone* ranked "I've Just Seen a Face" as #58 on the magazine's list of *The Beatles' 100 Greatest Songs*.

ALBUM APPEARANCES: *Help!* (U.K.); *Rubber Soul* (U.S.).

See also: *Help!* (U.K. LP).

J

Johnny and the Moondogs

In November 1959, the Quarry Men briefly refashioned themselves as Johnny and the Moondogs and auditioned for British hit-maker Carroll Levis, the emcee of the "Search for a Star" talent competition. It had been more than two years since their previous appearance as the Quarry Men before "Mr. Star-Maker," and this time they made it through two trial heats in Liverpool before trundling off to Manchester in November 1959 in order to try their luck yet again in one of Levis' star-searching contests. With McCartney and Harrison on guitar—Lennon had recently lost or sold his Höfner Club 40—the group performed Buddy Holly's "Think It Over," with Lennon on lead vocals and McCartney and Harrison handling the harmonies, in an attempt to vie for the top prize.

Forced to leave the venue in order to make the 9:47 train back to Liverpool—the group simply didn't have the money to spend the night in Manchester—Johnny and the Moondogs were long gone by the time that Levis bestowed the honors on the lucky winners. Yet the evening wasn't a total loss, as Lennon landed another electric guitar by stealing an old, tattered cutaway job on their way out of the Manchester Hippodrome. With the dawning of the 1960s, the group quickly shed the name of Johnny and the Moondogs in favor of several different monikers before settling on the Beatles.

See also: The Quarry Men.

Johns, Glyn (1942–)

Born in Epsom, Surrey, on February 15, 1942, Johns is a celebrated record producer and sound engineer, having worked with such artists as the Beatles, Bob Dylan, the Band, the Rolling Stones, the Who, Led Zeppelin, the Eagles, Eric Clapton, and the Clash, among others. After working at London's IBC Studios as a sound engineer, he came into the Beatles' orbit in January 1969 after being hired to supervise the sound recording for the *Get Back* project.

A few months later, Lennon and McCartney turned the virtual mountain of audio tapes associated with the *Get Back* project over to Johns, who recalled that "they pointed to a big pile of tapes in the corner and said, 'Remember that idea you had about putting together an album? Well, there are the tapes. Go and do it'" (Doggett 1998, 45). Johns prepared at least two full-length versions of an album to be entitled *Get Back, Don't Let Me Down, and Twelve Other Songs* over the next nine months; yet in each case, the band rejected his mix. By the end of the year, the project had fallen into the hands of Spector, and Johns' vision of an album in which the Beatles "get back" to basics was scuttled until 2003's *Let It Be . . . Naked* release. In the years after his postproduction work with the Beatles, Johns recorded a number of albums by the Who, including *Who's Next*, *The Who By Numbers*, and *Who Are You*, while also working on Led Zeppelin's debut album and the first three album releases by the Eagles. On April 14, 2012, Johns was inducted into the Rock and Roll Hall of Fame.

See also: *Get Back* Project; *Let It Be* (LP); *Let It Be . . . Naked* (LP); The Rooftop Concert; Spector, Phil.

"Julia" (Lennon–McCartney)

"Julia" is a song on *The Beatles* (*The White Album*). It was released as the B-side of a single backed with "Ob-La-Di, Ob-La-Da" on November 8, 1976, in the United States.

AUTHORSHIP AND BACKGROUND

Written by Lennon, "Julia" finds its origins during the Beatles' 1968 visit to India. With his capoed Gibson J-160E "Jumbo" guitar, Lennon tries his hand at the highly arpeggiated finger-picking style—the distinctive "claw hammer"—that he had picked up from Donovan back in Rishikesh.

For "Julia," Lennon had borrowed two of the song's key phrases from Lebanese poet Kahlil Gibran's *Sand and Foam: A Book of Aphorisms* (1926), including "Half of what I say is meaningless, but I say it so that the other half may reach you" and "When Life does not find a singer to sing her heart she produces a philosopher to speak her mind" (Gibran 1995, 14).

Lennon's "Julia" memorializes the songwriter's late mother while simultaneously addressing his spiritual deliverance at the hands of his newfound soul mate, the "ocean child" Yoko Ono. In Jaepanese, Ono's name translates literally as "child of the sea."

As Lennon remembered, "Julia was my mother. But it was sort of a combination of Yoko and my mother blended into one. That was written in India. We wrote tons of songs in India" (Lennon and Ono 2000, 190).

An early version of "Julia" was recorded in May 1968 at Harrison's Kinfauns studio as part of the Esher Tapes.

RECORDING SESSIONS

Produced by Martin, "Julia" was recorded at Abbey Road Studios on October 13, 1968. During the session, Lennon double-tracked both his vocal and guitar parts.

John Lennon as a child in 1949, with his mother Julia Lennon. (Mark and Colleen Hayward/Getty Images)

PERSONNEL

Lennon: Vocal, Gibson J-160E

CHART PERFORMANCE

U.S.: "Ob-La-Di, Ob-La-Da"/"Julia"; November 8, 1976, Capitol 4347: #49. As the B-side of "Ob-La-Di, Ob-La-Da," "Julia" did not chart.

LEGACY AND INFLUENCE

In 2010, *Rolling Stone* ranked "Julia" as #69 on the magazine's list of *The Beatles' 100 Greatest Songs*.

ALBUM APPEARANCES: *The Beatles* (*The White Album*); *Anthology 3*; *Love*.

See also: *The Beatles* (*The White Album*) (LP); Lennon, Julia Stanley.

K

"Kansas City"/"Hey-Hey-Hey-Hey!" (Leiber–Stoller/Penniman)

The medley "Kansas City"/"Hey-Hey-Hey-Hey!" is a song on the *Beatles for Sale* album.

AUTHORSHIP AND BACKGROUND

Written by Jerry Leiber and Mike Stoller, "Kansas City"—originally known as "K.C. Loving"—was released as a single in 1952 by Little Willie Littlefield. In 1959, it became a #1 hit for Wilbert Harrison. It is one of the most widely covered compositions in rock music history.

Written by Richard Penniman [Little Richard], "Hey-Hey-Hey-Hey" was released in 1958 by Little Richard as the B-side of "Good Golly Miss Molly."

RECORDING SESSIONS

Produced by George Martin, "Kansas City"/"Hey-Hey-Hey-Hey!" was recorded at Abbey Road Studios on October 18, 1964. The Beatles fashioned their version after the medley popularized by Little Richard, who first recorded the songs as a medley in 1959. Having toured with Little Richard during the early 1960s, the Beatles had the opportunity to see him perform the medley in person on multiple occasions.

In July 1963, the Beatles recorded yet another cover version of "Kansas City"/"Hey-Hey-Hey-Hey!" for the BBC's *Pop Go the Beatles* radio show that was later included on the *Live at the BBC* album. Yet another live recording of the medley from the band's BBC sessions was later included on the Beatles' *On Air: Live at the BBC, Volume 2*.

PERSONNEL

Lennon: Rickenbacker 325, Backing Vocal
McCartney: Vocal, Höfner 500/1
Harrison: Gretsch Country Gentleman
Starr: Ludwig Oyster Black Pearl Drums
Martin: Piano

CHART PERFORMANCE

U.S.: "Kansas City"/"Boys"; October 11, 1965, Capitol 6066: did not chart. As the B-side of the "Kansas City" single, "Boys" charted at #102.

LEGACY AND INFLUENCE

Wilbert Harrison's recording of "Kansas City" is included among the Rock and Roll Hall of Fame's *500 Songs That Shaped Rock and Roll*.

ALBUM APPEARANCES: *Beatles for Sale*; *Beatles VI*; *Rock 'n' Roll Music*; *Live! at the Star-Club in Hamburg, Germany; 1962*; *Anthology 1*; *On Air: Live at the BBC, Volume 2*.

See also: *Beatles for Sale* (LP).

Kaufman, "Murray the K." (1922–1982)

Born in New York City on February 14, 1922, "Murray the K." Kaufman was an influential disc jockey from the 1950s through the 1970s. He is perhaps most famous for his self-described status as the "Fifth Beatle" after the emergence of American Beatlemania in February 1964. A World War II veteran, he made his name as a radio DJ in 1958, when he joined WINS AM radio for the all-night "Swingin' Soiree" show. Not long afterward, WINS DJ Alan Freed, who coined the term "rock 'n' roll," was indicted for tax evasion and forced out of the business. After taking over Freed's time slot, Kaufman rose to national prominence. When the Beatles arrived on American shores on February 7, 1964, he befriended the bandmates, proving to be one of their most fervent supporters, a role that was augmented by his status as New York City's most popular DJ. He broadcast his show from the group's Plaza Hotel suite, hung out backstage at *The Ed Sullivan Show*, and followed the band to Washington, D.C., and Miami. He later claimed that his status as the "Fifth Beatle" was derived by George Harrison on the train ride from New York City to Washington, D.C. He continued his relationship with the band over the years, visiting them on the set of *A Hard Day's Night* and later singing backup vocals, along with Timothy Leary, Allen Ginsberg, and Derek Taylor, on John Lennon and Yoko Ono's peace anthem "Give Peace a Chance," which was recorded on June 1, 1969, in Room 1742 of Montreal's Hôtel Reine-Elizabeth. In 1978, Kaufman played himself in Robert Zemeckis' *I Wanna Hold Your Hand*. He died on February 21, 1982, at age 60 after a lengthy battle with cancer.

See also: *The Ed Sullivan Show* (TV Series).

Kirchherr, Astrid (1938–)

Born in Hamburg on May 20, 1938, Astrid Kirchherr is a gifted photographer, per-haps most well known for her early photographs of the Beatles, as well as her ill-fated romance with artist and bass player Stuart Sutcliffe. Along with her then-boyfriend Klaus Voormann and friend Jürgen Vollmer, Kirchherr first met the Beatles during their summer 1960 residency in Hamburg. As McCartney later recalled, "One of those days we were doing our stuff and some slightly strange-looking people arrived who didn't look like anyone else. Immediately we felt, 'Wey-hey . . . kindred spirits . . . something's going on here.' They came in and sat down and they were Astrid, Jürgen, and Klaus" (Beatles 2000, 50).

The Beatles' relationship with Kirchherr and Voormann led to the band's famous Beatle haircut. As Harrison recalled, "Astrid and Klaus were very influential. I remember we went to the swimming baths once and my hair was down from the water and they said, 'No, leave it, it's good.' I didn't have my Vaseline anyway, and I was thinking, 'Well, these people are cool—if they think it's good, I'll leave it like this.' They gave me that confidence and when it dried off it dried naturally down, which later became 'the look'" (Beatles 2000, 58).

Kirchherr first met Sutcliffe after the Beatles' performance at Hamburg's Kai-serkeller club, and within two months, Sutcliffe and Kirchherr were engaged. The couple's affection for each other was palpable, but Sutcliffe's newfound love was interrupted, as time went on, by intense seizures, as well as by paralyzing head-aches that left him in a state of utter agony until the pain finally ceased. In 1961, Sutcliffe made plans to attend Hamburg's prestigious State College of Art. For the time being, he remained as the Beatles' bassist, even boldly venturing into the spot-light to sing Elvis Presley's "Love Me Tender." Eventually, he left the band, given growing tensions with McCartney, as well as to pursue his art. Yet tragedy struck on April 10, 1962, when Sutcliffe died at age 21 from a brain hemorrhage after complaining for months on end about a relentless series of headaches. His autopsy declared the official cause of death as "cerebral paralysis due to bleeding into the right ventricle of the brain" (Harry 1992, 638).

In later years, Kirchherr pursued a career as a freelance photographer, eventu-ally holding exhibitions across the globe in such diverse locales as London, Liv-erpool, New York City, Tokyo, and the Rock and Roll Hall of Fame and Museum in Cleveland, Ohio. She married twice, including a seven-year union with Gibson Kemp, the drummer who replaced Starr in Rory Storm and the Hurricanes. In 1994, she worked as a consultant on Ian Softley's *Backbeat*, which documents the Bea-tles' early, prefame years in Hamburg. She was played in the film by actress Sheryl Lee. She currently owns and operates a vintage photography shop in Hamburg.

See also: Sutcliffe, Stuart; Voormann, Klaus.

Klein, Allen (1931–2009)

Born on December 18, 1931, in Newark, New Jersey, Klein was an American businessman and record company executive, known especially for his work with the Beatles and the Rolling Stones. After working in the music industry as a bookkeeper, he consolidated his efforts when he established the company that eventually became ABKCO Industries. Originally founded in 1961 as Allen Klein and Company, ABKCO Industries served as his umbrella corporation, beginning in 1968, to carry out his management and music publishing operations. He managed such artists as Bobby Darin and Sam Cooke, later serving as the business manager for the Beatles and the Rolling Stones. As an acronym for Allen and Betty Klein and Company, ABKCO oversaw the licensing policies for a host of artists, including Chubby Checker and Bobby Rydell.

In addition to his work as the Rolling Stones' business manager, Klein became embroiled in the Beatles' affairs in 1969 at Lennon's invitation. In short order, Lennon, Harrison, and Starr supported Klein as the band's new manager, while McCartney favored his father-in-law Lee Eastman for the role of Brian Epstein's successor instead. Begrudgingly, McCartney was forced to accept his minority position, and Klein became the Beatles' representative. Not too long afterward, Klein renegotiated the Beatles' contract with EMI, making them the highest paid artists at that time. He also enacted sweeping changes at Apple Corps, making many staff members redundant, while working to improve the company's ailing balance sheets. At this juncture, Klein's success on his clients' behalf was clear, with McCartney admitting that "if you are screwing us, I don't see how."

As the 1970s wore on, the former Beatles' relationship with Klein began to sour, with the manager's slipshod business dealings complicating the proceeds associated with *The Concert for Bangladesh*. In 1979, he was convicted of tax evasion for embezzling a portion of the aforementioned proceeds and was sentenced to two months in prison. In 1977, the Beatles and ABKCO settled an ongoing lawsuit in ABKCO's favor for some $4.2 million after the group failed to fulfill their ABKCO-negotiated contract with EMI that lapsed in 1976. During his recording sessions for "Beware of Darkness" on his *All Things Must Pass* album, Harrison ad-libbed the lyrics as "Beware of ABKCO." Lennon also refers to Klein derisively in "Steel and Glass," a song from *Walls and Bridges*.

In the late 1990s, ABKCO was famously involved in the lawsuit involving the Verve's sampling of Andrew Loog Oldham Orchestra's cover version of the Rolling Stones' "The Last Time" in their international hit song "Bitter Sweet Symphony." While the Verve had negotiated a license to sample the Andrew Loog Oldham Orchestra's recording of "The Last Time" in their recording of "Bitter Sweet Symphony," ABKCO successfully demonstrated that the group had sampled too much from the original recording under the strictures of the license. As part of the lawsuit's resolution, copyright for "Bitter Sweet Symphony" was awarded to ABKCO with songwriting credit reverting to Mick Jagger and Keith Richards in spite of the fact that the cover version of "The Last Time" that the Verve had sampled had been arranged by Oldham.

In 2008, ABKCO enjoyed yet another legal victory on the Rolling Stones' behalf, demonstrating that Lil Wayne had engaged in copyright infringement with his song "Playing with Fire" from his album *Tha Carter III*. Having proven that Wayne's song finds its origins in the Rolling Stones' "Play with Fire," Wayne was ordered to delete "Playing with Fire" from the online distribution of *Tha Carter III*.

Klein died on July 4, 2009, from complications associated with Alzheimer's disease. Since Klein's death, his son Jody has served as president of ABKCO, working actively toward the remastering of seminal 1960s works by the Rolling Stones, the Animals, and Herman's Hermits, among others.

See also: Apple Corps, Ltd.; Epstein, Brian.

"Komm, Gib Mir Deine Hand" (Lennon–McCartney)

As the Beatles' German-language version of "I Want to Hold Your Hand," "Komm, Gib Mir Deine Hand" was recorded specifically to stimulate the band's sales in the West German marketplace.

AUTHORSHIP AND BACKGROUND

As with "Sie Liebt Dich," "Komm, Gib Mir Deine Hand" was translated into German by Luxembourg songwriter and musician Camillo Felgen, who used the pseudonym Jean Nicolas. Felgen acted at the request of EMI's Germany producer Otto Demler. Along with Martin and Norman Smith, Felgen traveled in January 1964 to Paris, where the Beatles were booked for an extended run at the Olympia Theatre, to join the group for a recording session to prepare German-language versions of "I Want to Hold Your Hand" and "She Loves You" for distribution by West Germany's Odeon label. EMI's West German division, Electrola Gesellschaft, had appealed to Epstein and Martin that the Beatles would make a greater impact upon the West German marketplace if their hits were translated into German-language versions. With a key EMI subsidiary pressuring their parent company for a Beatles release in their mother tongue, Epstein and Martin still had to persuade the Beatles, who were reluctant to comply because they believed foreign-language versions of their songs were unnecessary to break into non-English-speaking markets.

"Komm, gib mir deine hand" translates as "come on, give me your hand." In its most literal and correct German translation, "I want to hold your hand" translates as "Ich möchte deine hand halten."

RECORDING SESSIONS

Produced by Martin, the Beatles recorded the vocals for "Komm, Gib Mir Deine Hand" in 11 takes on January 29, 1964, at Pathé Marconi Studios in Paris. Martin was able to dub the Beatles' German-language vocals onto the original instrumental track for "I Want to Hold Your Hand" recorded in October 1963. The mono mix of the song was dispatched to West Germany and the United States. On March 13—while the Beatles were filming *A Hard Day's Night*—Martin mixed a stereo version of "Komm, Gib Mir Deine Hand" for release.

During the January 29, 1964, session, Felgen assisted the Beatles in learning how to pronounce the songs' German-lyrics phonetically. For Martin, the experience of persuading the Beatles to join him at Pathé Marconi made for one of his less heartening memories of his life with the group. Relaxing in their suite at the George V Hotel, the band had decided, without informing their producer, not to attend the session. Martin was livid, to say the least:

I barged into their suite, to be met by this incredible sight, right out of the Mad Hatter's tea party. Jane Asher—Paul's girlfriend—with her long red hair, was pouring tea from a china pot, and the others were sitting around her like March Hares. They took one look at me and *exploded*, like in a school room when the headmaster enters. Some dived into the sofa and hid behind cushions, others dashed behind curtains. "You are bastards!" I screamed, to which they responded with impish little grins and roguish apologies. (Lewisohn 1988, 38)

Within minutes, to Martin's great relief, the Beatles were on their way to the studio.

PERSONNEL

Lennon: Vocal, Rickenbacker 325
McCartney: Vocal, Höfner 500/1
Harrison: Gretsch Country Gentleman
Starr: Ludwig Oyster Black Pearl Drums

ALBUM APPEARANCES: *Something New*; *Rarities* (U.K.); *Past Masters, Volume 1*.

See also: *Past Masters, Volume 1*.

L

"Lady Madonna" (Lennon–McCartney)

"Lady Madonna" was the band's third consecutive #1 single in the United Kingdom, where it was released on March 15, 1968.

AUTHORSHIP AND BACKGROUND

Written by Paul McCartney, "Lady Madonna" found its inspiration in a magazine photograph of an African woman holding a baby. McCartney was especially intrigued by the caption, which described the woman as a "Mountain Madonna" (Everett 1999, 153).

As McCartney remarked, " 'Lady Madonna' is all women. How do they do it?—bless 'em. Baby at your breast, how do they get the time to feed them? Where do they get the money? How do you do this thing that women do?" (Dowlding 1989, 201). He later added that "the original concept was the Virgin Mary, but it quickly became symbolic of every woman—the Madonna image but as applied to ordinary working-class women. 'Lady Madonna' was me sitting down at the piano trying to write a bluesy boogie-woogie thing. It reminded me of Fats Domino for some reason, so I started singing a Fats Domino impression. It took my voice to a very odd place" (Inglis 2009, 115).

Ringo Starr later observed that " 'Lady Madonna' sounds like Elvis, doesn't it? No, it doesn't sound like Elvis—it *is* Elvis. Even those bits where he goes very high" (Dowlding 1989, 201). As John Lennon remembered, the song was composed by Paul. "Good piano lick, but the song never really went anywhere. Maybe I helped him on some of the lyrics" (Lennon and Ono 2000, 201).

RECORDING SESSIONS

Produced by George Martin, "Lady Madonna" was recorded at Abbey Road Studios on February 3, 1968, with an additional overdubbing session on February 8.

In addition to concocting a driving bass part on his Rickenbacker, McCartney liberally borrowed his piano arrangement for "Lady Madonna" from "Bad Penny Blues," a 1956 hit produced by Martin for jazz musician Humphrey Lyttelton. With his "Elvis voice" in full flower—and well-supported by a zesty tenor sax solo by the legendary Ronnie Scott—McCartney tells the heartrending story of a woman desperately attempting to provide sustenance for her growing brood. As Geoff Emerick later recalled, "We spent a lot of time getting the right piano sound for 'Lady Madonna.' We ended up using a cheaper type of microphone and heavy compression and limiting" (Dowlding 1989, 200). McCartney plays the piano part for "Lady Madonna" on "Mrs. Mills"—the nickname for Studio Two's upright piano.

PERSONNEL

> Lennon: Epiphone Casino
> McCartney: Vocal, Rickenbacker 4001S, Piano
> Harrison: Sonic Blue Fender Stratocaster
> Starr: Ludwig Oyster Black Pearl Drums
> Studio Musicians: Saxophone Accompaniment conducted by Martin
> Bill Povey, Ronnie Scott: Tenor Saxophone
> Bill Jackman, Harry Klein: Baritone Saxophone

CHART PERFORMANCE

> U.K.: "Lady Madonna"/"The Inner Light"; March 15, 1968, Parlophone R 5675: #1.
> U.S.: "Lady Madonna"/"The Inner Light"; March 18, 1968, Capitol 2138: #4 (certified by the RIAA as "Platinum," with more than 1 million copies sold).

LEGACY AND INFLUENCE

In 2010, *Rolling Stone* ranked "Lady Madonna" as #86 on the magazine's list of *The Beatles' 100 Greatest Songs*.

ALBUM APPEARANCES: *Hey Jude*; *The Beatles, 1967–1970*; *20 Greatest Hits*; *Past Masters, Volume 2*; *Anthology 2*; *1*; *Love*.

See also: *Past Masters, Volume 2*.

"Leave My Kitten Alone" (John–McDougal–Turner)

"Leave My Kitten Alone" is a song on the Beatles' *Anthology 1*.

AUTHORSHIP AND BACKGROUND

Written by Little Willie John, James McDougal, and Titus Turner, "Leave My Kitten Alone" was released as single in 1959 by Little Willie John, who enjoyed a Top 20 hit with the tune. In 1961, Johnny Preston released a cover version of "Leave My Kitten Alone" that charted at #73 on the Hot 100.

RECORDING SESSIONS

Produced by Martin, "Leave My Kitten Alone" was recorded at Abbey Road Studios in five takes on August 14, 1964, during the sessions associated with the *Beatles for Sale* album. At the time, "Leave My Kitten Alone" was not remixed for release.

Some 18 years later, EMI's John Barrett remixed "Leave My Kitten Alone" for an Abbey Road Studios public tour presentation entitled "The Beatles at Abbey Road." In 1984, Emerick remixed "Leave My Kitten Alone" in preparation for the unreleased Beatles *Sessions* project. In 1994, Martin remixed "Leave My Kitten Alone" for release as part of the Beatles' *Anthology* project.

PERSONNEL

Lennon: Vocal, Rickenbacker 325
McCartney: Höfner 500/1, Piano
Harrison: Gretsch Tennessean
Starr: Ludwig Oyster Black Pearl Drums, Tambourine

ALBUM APPEARANCE: *Anthology 1.*

See also: *The Beatles Anthology, Volume 1* (LP); *Beatles for Sale* (LP).

Lennon, Alfred (1912–1976)

Alfred "Freddie" Lennon was born in Liverpool on December 12, 1912. In the late 1930s, Freddie met Julia Stanley, a talented singer, banjo player, and dancer. On December 3, 1938, Freddie and Julia married. After having gone through a succession of odd jobs, he became a merchant seaman in order to support his young bride, with whom he lived in the Stanleys' home at 9 Newcastle Road. As with so many men of his generation, he made his living by putting out to sea on voyages to the Mediterranean, North Africa, and the West Indies—to wherever the shipping lanes would take him. He was away at sea on the evening of October 9, 1940, when his son John Winston Lennon was born at the Oxford Street Maternity Hospital. By 1942, Julia had tired of staying home in wait for a sea-bound husband, and she began venturing out amongst Liverpool's nightclubs and saloons. Eventually, she took up with Taffy Williams, a Welsh soldier. Pregnant with Williams' baby, Julia gave birth to a daughter, whom she named Victoria, in June 1945 at the Elmswood Nursing Home. The baby was given up for adoption soon thereafter, and Freddie, distraught with his wife's unfaithfulness and his own failings, put out to sea yet again. That same year, Freddie saw Julia for the last time after he took his young son to Blackpool with the intention of taking him abroad to New Zealand. When Lennon's aunt, Mimi Smith, heard about Freddie's plans, she thwarted them by alerting Julia. Freddie reentered Lennon's life after the rise of Beatlemania, attempting to contact his son during the film production of *A Hard Day's Night*. While Lennon refused to see his father, in 1965 Freddie succeeded in meeting Lennon's wife Cynthia and his young son Julian at the Lennon's Weybridge estate. In 1968, Freddie married Pauline Jones, with whom he fathered two sons, David and Robin. Lennon spoke with his father on a few occasions during the 1970s before Freddie succumbed to cancer on April 1, 1976. In a gesture of goodwill, Lennon offered to pay for his father's funeral expenses, although his widow demurred.

See also: Lennon, Cynthia Lillian; Lennon, John; Lennon, Julia Stanley; Smith, Mimi Stanley.

Lennon, Cynthia Lillian (1939–2015)

Born on September 10, 1939, in Blackpool, Cynthia Lillian Powell grew up in Liverpool's Hoylake section on the Wirral Peninsula. Cynthia met Lennon in calligraphy class at the Liverpool of College of Art. After she became pregnant, she married Lennon on August 23, 1962, at Liverpool's Mount Pleasant Registry Office with McCartney and Harrison in attendance. That evening, Lennon performed with the Beatles at Chester's Riverpark Ballroom. The couple belatedly celebrated their honeymoon on September 16 in Paris. The Lennons' son Julian was born on April 8, 1963; when Lennon met his son for the first time three days later, he remarked that "he's bloody marvelous" and that he's "gonna be a famous rocker like his dad" (Wiener 1991, 51). During the early years of Beatlemania, the Beatles' handlers maintained strict secrecy about the existence of Lennon's wife and child, fearing that they would dispel the media-created myth of his bachelorhood. By the end of 1963, though, Cynthia and Julian had become known to the media after the infant's christening. The young family moved to a three-bedroom flat in London, later purchasing their Kenwood estate in Weybridge. Cynthia accompanied her husband on the Beatles' first U.S. visit, the only time that she joined the band on tour.

In 1965, Cynthia met her husband's father Alfred, who arrived unexpectedly with his 19-year-old fiancée Pauline Jones at the Lennons' Kenwood estate, where he also met his grandson Julian. In 1968, she accompanied Lennon and the other Beatles on their February 1968 visit to Maharishi Mahesh Yogi's ashram in Rishikesh, India. During their return flight to England, Lennon became drunk and confessed to thousands of infidelities. A few weeks later, he encouraged his wife to take a vacation to Greece in the company of Apple Corps' "Magic Alex" Mardas and musician Donovan, among others. Upon her return on May 22, 1968, she discovered that Ono had joined her husband in their Kenwood estate. Fleeing the scene of Lennon's betrayal, Cynthia spent the night in the apartment of Jenny Boyd, the sister of Harrison's wife Pattie. That evening, Cynthia was forced to fend off the advances of Magic Alex, who later claimed to have had an illicit affair with her. Later, after Ono became pregnant, an enraged Cynthia filed for divorce in August 1968. After reaching a £100,000 settlement, the Lennons were formally divorced on November 8, 1968.

On July 31, 1970, Cynthia married Italian hotelier Robert Bassanini. After the couple divorced in 1973, she owned and operated a Welsh restaurant, Oliver's Bistro, along with a bed and breakfast. During this period, she saw Lennon for the last time during his "Lost Weekend" separation from Ono. On May 1, 1976, she married John Twist, a British engineer. In 1978, she published her best-selling memoirs entitled *A Twist of Lennon*. She was informed about Lennon's December 1980 murder by Starr. In 1981, she separated from Twist, and the couple divorced in 1983, after which she sold Oliver's Bistro. After her separation from Twist, she entered a long-term romantic relationship with Jim Christie, a Liverpool chauffeur. They lived in Penrith, Cumbria, the Isle of Man, and later in Normandy before separating in 1998. In 2002, she married nightclub owner Noel Charles, living with him in Majorca, Spain, until his death in March 2013.

In later years, Cynthia published a second collection of her memoirs entitled *John* (2005). The following year, she attended the Las Vegas premiere of the Beatles' *Love*, making a rare appearance with Ono. On October 9, 2010, Cynthia and Julian unveiled the John Lennon Peace Monument at Liverpool's Chavasse Park. While her story was glossed over in *Nowhere Boy* (2009), Cynthia was played by Jennifer Ehle in Ian Softley's *Backbeat* (1994), a film that details the Beatles' formative years. On April 1, 2015, she died, aged 75, in Majorca, Spain, after a long struggle with cancer.

See also: Lennon, John; *Love* (LP); Maharishi Mahesh Yogi; Ono, Yoko.

Lennon, John (1940–1980)

Having founded the Quarry Men in 1957, John Ono Winston Lennon was the Beatles' lead vocalist and rhythm guitarist, as well as a member of the highly successful Lennon–McCartney songwriting team. During the post-Beatles years, he notched four #1 hits in "Imagine," "Whatever Gets You Thru the Night," "(Just Like) Starting Over," and "Woman."

EARLY YEARS

John Winston Lennon was born in Liverpool on October 9, 1940, as the son of merchant seaman Alfred "Freddie" Lennon and Julia Stanley Lennon, who honored her son by drawing his middle name from Great Britain's esteemed prime minister, Sir Winston Churchill. Freddie was away at sea on the evening that he was born at the Oxford Street Maternity Hospital. As his devoted aunt, Mimi Stanley Smith, remembered, "There was shrapnel falling and gunfire, and when there was a little lull I ran into the hospital ward and there was this beautiful little boy" (Spitz 2005, 24). Within a few years, Julia tired of Freddie's seafaring ways, and took up with Taffy Williams, a Welsh soldier. Pregnant with Williams' baby, Julia gave birth to a daughter, whom she named Victoria, in June 1945 at the Elmswood Nursing Home. Lennon's half-sister was given up for adoption soon thereafter, and Freddie, distraught with his wife's unfaithfulness and his own failings, put out to sea yet again.

Not long afterward, Julia set up housekeeping with John Dykins, a Liverpool wine steward. Disgusted with her sister's behavior and determined to provide her nephew with a proper upbringing, Mimi and her husband George Smith, a dairy farmer, took custody of Lennon. "Julia had met someone else, with whom she had a chance of happiness," Mimi remembered, "and no man wants another man's child. That's when I said I wanted to bring John to Menlove Avenue to live with George and me. I wouldn't even let him risk being hurt or feeling he was in the way. I made up my mind that I'd be the one to give him what every child has the right to—a safe and happy home life" (Norman 1981, 18). Ultimately, Mimi saw to it that her nephew was forcibly removed from her sister's home, eventually enlisting the aid of social services after learning that Lennon shared the same cramped bedroom with Julia and her lover. Mimi and George raised Lennon in the middle-class neighborhood of Woolton. Their home, which they nicknamed "Mendips," was a semidetached, wood and stucco house near Penny Lane and across from the Allerton Golf Course. "Mimi told me my parents had fallen out of love," Lennon recalled. "She never said anything directly against my father and mother. I soon forgot my father. It was like he was dead. But I did see my mother now and again, and my feeling never died off for her. I often thought about her, though I never realized for a long time that she was living no more than five or ten miles away" (Beatles 2000, 7).

During his earliest years at Dovedale Primary School, Lennon was a model student who had developed into an avid reader—he devoured Lewis Carroll and Edgar Allan Poe—as well as a gifted cartoonist. Around this time, he also obtained his first musical instrument: a harmonica. "I can remember why I took it up in the first place," he recalled. "I must have picked one up very cheap. [Mimi] used to take in students, and one of them had a mouth organ and said he'd buy me one if I could learn a tune by the next morning. So I learned about two. I was somewhere between eight and twelve at the time—in short pants, anyway" (Babiuk 2001, 7). At 12-years-old, he moved to Quarry Bank Grammar School, accompanied by Pete Shotton. "We went through it like Siamese twins," Shotton later remembered. "We started in our first year at the top and gradually sank together into the subbasement" (Norman 1981, 23). Indeed, Lennon's life had taken a turn for the worse during his first year at Quarry Bank, especially after his Uncle George died, quite suddenly, from a hemorrhage. During his last years at Dovedale, he ran with a group of friends known for cutting class and pulling off the occasional shoplifting. By the time that he reached Quarry Bank, he had graduated to full-blown rambunctiousness. Within a few years, Lennon and Shotton had begun skipping school in order to take the bus to Spring Wood, where Julia now lived. For Lennon, Julia seemed more like an older sister than his mother. "She'd do these tricks just to make us laugh," Shotton recalled. "She used to wear these old woolen knickers on her head while she did the housework. She'd open the door to us with the knicker legs hanging down her back. She didn't care. She was just like John" (Norman 1981, 25).

In addition to rediscovering his mother, Lennon had also discovered skiffle, which Lonnie Donegan had exploded into a national phenomenon with the hit song "Rock Island Line," an up-tempo rendition of Leadbelly's three-chord ditty about a railroad line that brings trainloads of livestock to market in New Orleans. Great Britain's aspiring teenaged musicians loved skiffle for its simple nature, as well as for its relative inexpensiveness. Skiffle's sounds could be easily reproduced with unconventional instruments like kazoos, washboards, or jugs—and, for its more affluent practitioners, sometimes in combination with conventional instruments such as guitars and drums. With skiffle on his mind—and rock 'n' roll in his heart after first encountering the raw power of Elvis Presley's "Heartbreak Hotel" in May 1956—Lennon finally persuaded Aunt Mimi to purchase a £5 guitar for him in March 1957. It was a steel-stringed instrument that he had spotted in an advertisement in *Reveille* magazine. A Gallotone Champion, the smallish guitar was constructed out of lacquered wide-grain maple. Having talked his friends Eric Griffiths, Ivan Vaughan, and Nigel Walley to start up a band with Shotton and himself, Lennon formed the Black Jacks, which soon morphed into the Quarry Men. Not long afterward, Griffiths introduced them to drummer Colin Hanton. Griffiths remembered the boys' first experiences playing the guitar—and how Julia taught them to play chords: "John's mother had played the banjo, so she re-tuned our guitars to banjo tuning and taught us banjo chords, maybe three or four at the most. And that was it: instant guitar playing" (Babiuk 2001, 10). A few months and a couple of personnel changes later, the Quarry Men took their show, which consisted of skiffle tunes along with a dash of imported American rock 'n' roll, on the road. Their first gig, a local qualifying audition for radio and television personality "Mr. Star-Maker" Carroll Levis, was on June 9, 1957, at the Empire Theatre on Liverpool's Lime Street. After losing the audition to the Sunnyside Skiffle Group, the Quarry Men played at an outdoor party on June 22 hosted by Marjorie Roberts, a resident of Roseberry Street who organized the festivities in order to commemorate the 550th anniversary of King John issuing a royal charter inviting Liverpool's citizenry to become landowners. The event ended rather badly for the Quarry Men after a local gang threatened to beat them up—especially "that Lennon" (Lewisohn 1986, 19). The Quarry Men's next gig, the garden fête at St. Peter's Church Hall, brought them into the orbit of McCartney, who wowed the bandmates with his renditions of "Twenty Flight Rock" and "Be-Bop-a-Lula." Within a few weeks, the 15-year-old McCartney was a member of the band, with Harrison following several months later, and by the following year the Lennon–McCartney partnership was born.

Meanwhile, Lennon's young life was struck by tragedy on the evening of July 15, 1958, when he was spending the night at Julia's house with her husband John

Dykins, whom he had irreverently nicknamed "Twitchy." Returning from visiting her sister at Mendips, Julia was hit by a car driven by Eric Clague, an off-duty police officer, as he made a sharp turn around a hedge on Menlove Avenue. By the time Mimi reached her sister, it was clear that she had perished instantly. Legend has it that Clague was drunk at the time of the incident, a story that Lennon echoes in numerous interviews (Beatles 2000, 13). Clague stood trial for Julia's death, but was acquitted. As Clague recalled, "Mrs. Lennon just ran straight out in front of me. I just couldn't avoid her. I was not speeding. I swear it. It was just one of those terrible things that happen" (Badman 2001, 18). Julia was just 44 years old.

Devastated in his grief, Lennon turned inwardly and buried his pain in silent misery. "It was the worst thing that ever happened to me," he recalled years later. "I lost her twice. Once when I was moved in with my auntie. And once again at 17 when she actually, physically died. That was very traumatic for me. That was really a hard time for me. It made me very, very bitter. The underlying chip on my shoulder that I had got really big then. Being a teenager and a rock-and-roller and an art student and my mother being killed just when I was re-establishing a relationship with her" (Beatles 2000, 13). Even music failed to provide a tonic for him, and he was frequently seen drowning his sorrows at Ye Cracke, a local saloon where he salved his wounds with whiskey and beer. Only McCartney, it seemed, could draw Lennon out of his stupor, arranging for sporadic gigs and rehearsals in order to rejuvenate his bewildered friend. "That became a very big bond between John and me, because he lost his mum early on, too. We both had this emotional turmoil which we had to deal with, and, being teenagers, we had to deal with it very quickly. We both understood that something had happened that you couldn't talk about—but we could laugh about it, because each of us had gone through it. . . . Occasionally, once or twice in later years, it would hit in. We'd be sitting around, and we'd have a cry together, not often, but it was good" (Beatles 2000, 19). Lennon was haunted by his mother's memory for the remainder of his life, as evidenced by such songs as *The White Album*'s "Julia," as well as "Mother" and "My Mummy's Dead," which were included on his 1970 *John Lennon/Plastic Ono Band* album.

With the dawning of the 1960s, Lennon enrolled at the Liverpool College of Art, where he met artist Stuart Sutcliffe and eventually convinced him to become the group's bass guitarist. As with McCartney and Harrison, Lennon continued as a member of the Quarry Men through its various permutations as the Beatals, the Silver Beetles, and, finally, the Beatles in August 1960, when the group traveled to Hamburg for the extended musical apprenticeship that served as a prelude to the onset of their global fame in the early 1960s.

MARRIAGE AND FAMILY

Lennon met Cynthia Lillian Powell in calligraphy class at the Liverpool of College of Art. After she became pregnant, Lennon married Cynthia on August 23,

1962, at Liverpool's Mount Pleasant Registry Office with McCartney and Harrison in attendance. The Lennons' son Julian was born on April 8, 1963; Julian later pursued a musical career in the 1980s, when he recorded the hit single "Valotte." In November 1966, Lennon met avant-garde artist Yoko Ono at London's Indica Gallery. Lennon and Ono consummated their relationship in May 1968, when Cynthia was away on a vacation in Greece. Upon her return on May 22, 1968, Cynthia discovered that Ono had joined her husband in their Kenwood estate. After reaching a financial settlement, the Lennons were formally divorced on November 8, 1968. Ono and Lennon were married the following year, on March 29, 1969, near the

John Lennon in 1968. (Photofest)

Rock of Gibraltar. In April 1969, Lennon officially added the middle name "Ono" in honor of his new wife. The couple, however, took an 18-month hiatus beginning in 1973 that Lennon later referred to as his "Lost Weekend." By 1975, Ono and Lennon had ended their separation. Their son Sean Taro Ono Lennon was born on Lennon's birthday on October 9, 1975. Sean went on to pursue a musical career of his own, most recently as a member of the duo (with girlfriend Charlotte Kemp Muhl) known as the Ghost of Saber Tooth Tiger.

SOLO YEARS

Lennon's solo career unfolded with a trio of experimental albums in conjunction with Ono, including *Unfinished Music No. 1: Two Virgins* (1968), with its controversial cover art; *Unfinished Music No. 2: Life with the Lions* (1969); and *Wedding Album* (1969). The duo's peace activism created international headlines during the late 1960s and early 1970s. Their efforts culminated in such hit singles as the peace anthems "Give Peace a Chance" and "Happy Xmas (War Is Over)." During this period, Lennon and Ono also conceptualized the Plastic Ono Band as a means for translating their art and activism to the music scene. The band's first album was the concert recording *Live Peace in Toronto 1969*, which was compiled from the one-day Sweet Toronto Peace Festival held on September 13, 1969, at the University of Toronto's Varsity Stadium. In 1970, Lennon and Ono completed the twin LP releases, *John Lennon/Plastic Ono Band* and *Yoko Ono/ Plastic Ono Band*. Produced by Lennon, Ono, and Phil Spector, *John Lennon/ Plastic Ono Band* is widely considered to be Lennon's post-Beatles masterwork. The album is the result of Lennon's experiences with primal-scream therapy, while also finding the former Beatle exorcising his Fab Four past with "God," the album's existential centerpiece.

Lennon followed the critically acclaimed *John Lennon/Plastic Ono Band* with *Imagine* (1971), the LP that produced his signature anthem in "Imagine," as well as his excoriation of McCartney in "How Do You Sleep?" A significant critical and commercial success, *Imagine* was succeeded by Lennon and Ono's *Sometime in New York City* (1972), the duo's blunt return to political activism, with Elephant's Memory serving as their backup band, and the nadir of Lennon's solo career. The production of Lennon's next trio of studio albums coincided with his separation from Ono during his "Lost Weekend" period in which he was involved romantically with May Pang at his estranged wife's urging. With the exception of the album's title track, *Mind Games* (1973) finds Lennon in one of his most uninspired artistic eras—largely due to his marital dilemmas and his protracted immigration battle to stay in the United States. While *Walls and Bridges* (1974) spawned two hit singles in "Whatever Gets You Thru the Night" and "#9 Dream," it was Lennon's *Rock 'n' Roll* (1975) album that marked the former Beatle's return to form as he recorded cover versions of a host of rock standards, including "Stand by Me." *Rock 'n' Roll* also marked Lennon's final studio album before his five-year, self-imposed retirement in 1975.

Lennon's final burst of creative activity resulted in *Double Fantasy* (1980) and the posthumously released *Milk and Honey* (1984). The former album—a self-styled "Heart Play" between Lennon and Ono—finds its origins in Lennon's visit to Bermuda, accompanied by son Sean, during the summer of 1980. After a harrowing experience at sea, Lennon's creative forces were reignited. Produced by Jack Douglas, the sessions for *Double Fantasy* commenced shortly after Lennon's return to the United States. Released on November 17, some three weeks before his senseless murder, *Double Fantasy* included a trio of hit singles, including "(Just Like) Starting Over," "Woman," and "Watching the Wheels." It later earned a Grammy Award for Album of the Year at the 24th Grammy Awards. Its lead single "(Just Like) Starting Over" was nominated for a Grammy Award for Record of the Year. During their 1980 sessions together, Douglas and the Lennons produced an abundance of material—so much so, in fact, that they made plans to prepare a second album of new material to be entitled *Milk and Honey*. Eventually released in 1984, *Milk and Honey* included Lennon's last solo hit single in "Nobody Told Me," as well as "Grow Old with Me," one of his final demo recordings.

DEATH

On December 8, 1980, Lennon was assassinated by Mark David Chapman, a deranged fan, as he returned to the Dakota apartment building with Ono from a New York City recording studio. He was 40 years old. Within minutes, sports commentator Howard Cosell announced Lennon's death to a national U.S. television audience during ABC's *Monday Night Football*. Over the next several days, thousands of fans gathered in front of the Dakota to mourn together, singing Beatles and Lennon solo songs. Forgoing a funeral in concert with her husband's wishes, Ono had Lennon's remains cremated at Westchester's Ferncliff Cemetery. On December 14, she asked for 10 minutes of silence to honor Lennon's memory. Some 225,000 fans gathered in Central Park, while New York City's radio stations went off the air in compliance with Ono's request.

Over the years, Lennon has been the subject of numerous tributes, including Harrison's "All Those Years Ago" (1981) and McCartney's "Here Today" (1982). Other musical commemorations include Elton John's "Empty Garden (Hey, Hey Johnny)" (1982), Queen's "Life Is Real (Song for Lennon)" (1982), Paul Simon's "The Late Great Johnny Ace" (1983), and Bob Dylan's "Roll On John" (2012), among a host of others. Lennon's untimely passing also resulted in a number of noteworthy memorials. In 1985, the Strawberry Fields Memorial was dedicated in

More than 100,000 people cram the streets outside John Lennon's New York apartment building, the Dakota, to mourn his death, December 1980. (AP Photo/ David Bookstaver)

New York City's Central Park. In 2002, Liverpool's international airport was rededicated as Liverpool John Lennon Airport, including a bronze statue in the main terminal. On what would have been Lennon's 67th birthday, Ono dedicated the Imagine Peace Tower on October 9, 2007, on Iceland's Viðey Island.

LEGACY

As with the other Beatles, Lennon was appointed as a member of the Order of the British Empire (MBE) during the Queen's Birthday Honours on June 12, 1965, receiving his insignia from Queen Elizabeth II at Buckingham Palace on October 26. In 1969, he ceremoniously returned his MBE in protest over Great Britain's support of the United States' involvement in the Vietnam War. On January 12, 1983, his legacy was commemorated with the naming of a minor planet, 4147 Lennon, by Brian A. Skiff at the Lowell Observatory's Anderson Mesa Station. In 1988, the Beatles were inducted into the Rock and Roll Hall of Fame. On September 30, 1988, Lennon was honored with a star on Hollywood's Walk of Fame by the Hollywood Chamber of Commerce. As with the other Beatles, his star is located on North Vine Street in front of the Capitol Records Building. In 1994, he was inducted posthumously into the Rock and Roll Hall of Fame as a solo artist. In a 2002 BBC poll, he was ranked #8 on a list of the 100 Greatest Britons. Over the years, *Rolling Stone* magazine has ranked Lennon as #5 on its list of the 100 Greatest Singers of All Time and as #38 on its list of the 100 Greatest Artists of All Time.

See also: Harrison, George; Lennon, Alfred; Lennon, Cynthia Lillian; Lennon, Julia Stanley; McCartney, Paul; Ono, Yoko; Smith, Mimi Stanley; Spector, Phil; Sutcliffe, Stuart.

Lennon, Julia Stanley (1914–1958)

Born on March 12, 1914, in Liverpool, Julia Stanley was the fourth of five sisters, including her eldest sister Mimi. A talented singer, banjo player, and dancer, Julia was known as Judy amongst her family and for her great beauty throughout the city. "Judy was feminine, she was beautiful," a niece recalled. "You never saw her with her hair undone. She went to bed with makeup on so that she'd look beautiful in the morning" (Spitz 2005, 22). On December 3, 1938, 24-year-old Julia stunned her tightly knit family with the news that she had married a charming 29-year-old bachelor named Freddie Lennon. After having gone through a succession of odd jobs, Freddie became a merchant seaman in order to support his young bride, with whom he lived in the Stanleys' home at 9 Newcastle Road. As with so many men of his generation, Freddie made his living by putting out to sea on voyages to the Mediterranean, North Africa, and the West Indies—to wherever the shipping lanes would take him. Lennon had no illusions about his origins:

Ninety percent of the people on this planet, especially in the West, were born out of a bottle of whiskey on a Saturday night, and there was no intent to have children. Ninety percent of us were accidents—I don't know anybody who has planned a child. All of us were Saturday night specials. (Beatles 2000, 7)

Not surprisingly, Freddie was at sea on the evening that his son John was born at the Oxford Street Maternity Hospital. Although his father was away in parts unknown, Lennon was quickly joined by his devoted aunt, Mimi Stanley Smith, who ensured that she was with her sister that night. By 1942, Julia had grown tired of awaiting Freddie's return. After taking up with Taffy Williams, a Welsh soldier, she gave birth to his daughter Victoria, born in June 1945. In later years, Victoria went by her adopted name, Ingrid Marie Pedersen.

Before too long, the still-married Julia set up housekeeping with Dykins, a Liverpool wine steward. Disgusted with her sister's behavior and determined to provide her nephew with a proper upbringing, Mimi and her husband George Smith, a dairy farmer, took custody of Lennon and raised him at "Mendips," their Menlove Avenue home in Liverpool. Meanwhile, Julia and Dykins had two children together, including Julia Baird (born March 5, 1947) and Jacqueline (born October 26, 1949). Unbeknownst to young Lennon, his mother Julia lived only a few miles away during his childhood years. By the time that Lennon began attending Quarry Bank during his high school years, he developed a relationship with her that was more akin to an older sister than to an authority figure.

In addition to rediscovering his mother, Lennon had also discovered skiffle. In March 1957, he finally persuaded his Aunt Mimi to purchase a £5 guitar for him. It was a steel-stringed instrument that he had spotted in an advertisement in *Reveille* magazine. A Gallotone Champion, the smallish guitar was constructed out of lacquered wide-grain maple. Having talked his friends into joining his band, he formed the Black Jacks, which soon morphed into the Quarry Men. Griffiths remembered the boys' first experiences playing the guitar—and how Julia taught them to play chords: "John's mother had played the banjo, so she re-tuned our guitars to banjo tuning and taught us banjo chords, maybe three or four at the most. And that was it: instant guitar playing" (Babiuk 2001, 10).

June 1958 was also notable for the Quarry Men's performance at a dinner dance at St. Barnabas Hall in Penny Lane. In attendance that evening was Lennon's mother Julia, who, in recent months, had rekindled her relationship with her son with a fervor. They enjoyed a closeness that, for Lennon, was rendered all the more special by her new role in his life as a treasured confidante and friend. "Between numbers she was the only person who clapped every time—and loud," Hanton remembered. "If that didn't get things going, she put her fingers in her teeth and whistled. She probably liked us just fine, but she would have done anything to encourage John" (Spitz 2005, 144).

Yet Lennon and Julia's renewed relationship proved to be short-lived. On the evening of July 15, 1958, Lennon was spending the night at Julia's house with her husband John Dykins, nicknamed by John as "Twitchy." Returning from visiting her sister at Mendips, Julia was hit by a car driven by Eric Clague, as he made a sharp turn around a hedge on Menlove Avenue. By the time that Mimi reached her sister, it was clear that she had perished instantly. Legend has it that Clague was drunk at the time of the incident, a story that John echoes in numerous interviews (Beatles 2000, 13). Clague stood trial for Julia's death, but was acquitted. As Clague recalled, "Mrs. Lennon just ran straight out in front of me. I just couldn't avoid her. I was not speeding. I swear it. It was just one of those terrible things that happen" (Badman 2001, 18). Julia was just 44 years old.

Lennon was haunted by his mother's memory for the remainder of his life, as evidenced by such songs as *The White Album*'s "Julia," as well as "Mother" and "My Mummy's Dead," which were included on his 1970 *John Lennon/Plastic Ono Band* album. In April 1963, Lennon and his first wife Cynthia's son Julian was named in his mother's memory. Julia was also memorialized in such feature films as *In His Life: The John Lennon Story* (2000), in which she was played by Christine Cavanaugh, and *Nowhere Boy* (2009), in which she was played by Anne-Marie Duff.

See also: *The Beatles* (*The White Album*) (LP); Lennon, Alfred; Lennon, John; McCartney, Paul; The Quarry Men; Smith, Mimi Stanley.

Lester, Richard (1932–)

Born on January 19, 1932, in Philadelphia, Richard Lester is a celebrated American filmmaker, credited with adding to the Beatles' fame and critical approval by directing their two movies, *A Hard Day's Night* (1964) and *Help!* (1965), which were both generally considered charming and witty. After beginning his formal education at the University of Pennsylvania at age 15, he relocated to London, where he began his career as a filmmaker. After making his debut director episodes for the *Mark Saber* detective series, he collaborated with Peter Sellers on a series of TV comedy shows before directing such feature films as *The Running Jumping and Standing Still Film* (1960) and *The Knack . . . and How to Get It* (1965). In the mid-1960s, Lester directed the Beatles' movie musicals *A Hard Day's Night* (1964) and *Help!* (1965). He also directed Lennon's solo acting debut in the antiwar movie *How I Won the War* (1967). In the 1970s, he director several well-known feature films, including *The Three Musketeers* (1973), *The Four Musketeers* (1974), and *Robin and Marian* (1976). He later directed Christopher Reeve in *Superman II* (1980) and *Superman III* (1983).

See also: *A Hard Day's Night* (Film); *Help!* (Film); Lennon, John.

Let It Be (Film)

Directed by Michael Lindsay-Hogg, *Let It Be* is a 1970 documentary that captures the Beatles rehearsing new songs during the making of the ill-fated *Get*

Back project. The production was originally planned as an effort to record the Beatles as they prepared to "get back" to their roots and rehearse for an upcoming concert.

Filming commenced on January 2, 1969, with the Beatles having assembled at Twickenham Film Studios. After Harrison briefly quit the band, filming resumed on January 21 at Apple Studio in the basement of Apple Corps' Savile Row headquarters. At this juncture, the Beatles were joined by American keyboard player Billy Preston. Eventually, the bandmates scuttled the idea of a concert, preferring to document the production of their next album instead. With this concept in mind, Lindsay-Hogg filmed the group as they prepared a raft of new compositions, including "Two of Us," "Let It Be," and "The Long and Winding Road," which were filmed on January 31 in Apple Studio. He also filmed the band's impromptu final concert, which they held on the building's rooftop on January 30.

Lindsay-Hogg previewed a rough cut of the movie—entitled *Get Back* at that juncture—for the Beatles on July 20, 1969. The original version was an hour longer than the final cut, prompting the bandmates to suggest various edits in order to reduce the amount of acrimony that the movie depicted. In the early months of 1970, the name of the movie was altered to *Let It Be* in order to synchronize it with the Beatles' upcoming album release of the same name. The movie premiered in New York City on May 13, 1970, with a London premiere held the following week at the London Pavilion. In 1971, *Let It Be* won an Oscar for Best Music (Original Song Score) at the 43rd Academy Awards. Producer Quincy Jones accepted the award on the bandmates' behalf. In the 1980s, *Let It Be* was released on VHS video and laserdisc, although it has never been released on DVD. Apple Corps remastered the movie's original 16-mm negative in 1992 in preparation for the Beatles' *Anthology* documentary series.

As for the *Let It Be* music, the songs in order of their appearance in the movie included

"Paul's Piano Intro"
"Don't Let Me Down"
"Maxwell's Silver Hammer"
"Two of Us"
"I've Got a Feeling"
"Oh! Darling"
"One After 909"
"Jazz Piano Song"
"Across the Universe"
"Dig a Pony"
"Suzy Parker"
"I Me Mine"
"For You Blue"
"Bésame Mucho"
"Octopus's Garden"

"You Really Got a Hold on Me"
"The Long and Winding Road"
Medley: "Rip It Up"/"Shake, Rattle, and Roll"
Medley: "Kansas City"/"Miss Ann"/"Lawdy Miss Clawdy"
"Dig It"
"Let It Be"
"Get Back"

See also: Apple Corps, Ltd.; *Get Back* Project; *Let It Be* (LP); Lindsay-Hogg, Michael; Ono, Yoko; Preston, Billy; The Rooftop Concert.

"Let It Be" (Lennon–McCartney)

"Let It Be" was a hit single, backed with "You Know My Name (Look Up the Number)," which was released in the United Kingdom on March 6, 1970, and in the United States on March 11, 1970. "Let It Be" is also the title track for the Beatles' *Let It Be* album.

AUTHORSHIP AND BACKGROUND

Written by McCartney, "Let It Be" was inspired by a dream in which the songwriter's late mother Mary came to visit him to remind her son to release his worldly troubles—to let it all be. "It was such a sweet dream," McCartney later recalled. "I woke up thinking, Oh, it was really great to visit with her again. I felt very blessed to have that dream. So that got me writing the song 'Let It Be.' I literally started off 'Mother Mary,' which was her name, 'When I find myself in times of trouble,' which I certainly found myself in. The song was based on that dream" (Lange 2001, 7). Earlier versions of the song found McCartney singing "There will be no sorrow" and leading into the title of the song "Let It Be," a lyric that he sagely revised as "There will be an answer," affording the composition with a more optimistic mien.

Later reflecting on the dream that inspired "Let It Be," McCartney remarked that

> I had a lot of bad times in the '60s. We used to lie in bed and wonder what was going on and feel quite paranoid. Probably all the drugs. I had a dream one night about my mother. She died when I was fourteen so I hadn't really heard from her in quite a while, and it was very good. It gave me some strength. (Cadogan 2008, 223)

During one of his last interviews, Lennon observed that

> That's Paul. What can you say? Nothing to do with the Beatles. It could've been Wings. I don't know what he's thinking when he writes "Let It Be." I think it was inspired by "Bridge Over Troubled Water." That's my feeling, although I

have nothing to go on. I know he wanted to write a "Bridge Over Troubled Water."
(Lennon and Ono 2000, 202)

RECORDING SESSIONS

Produced by Martin with postproduction by Spector, "Let It Be" was first recorded
on January 25, 1969, and remade during a January 31 session from which the eventual single and album versions of the song were culled. Additional overdubbing
sessions were held on April 30, 1969, and January 4, 1970—the last Beatles session until the surviving Beatles reunited in February and March 1994 to record
"Free as a Bird." During the latter session, Martin conducted and overdubbed his
orchestral arrangement for the song.

During the April 1969 session, Harrison remade his guitar solo, playing a deliberately subdued rendition in comparison with the January 1969 performance in
the *Let It Be* documentary. The remade version of the solo was used for the single
version of "Let It Be," while the album version of the song featured yet another
remade solo, played on the guitarist's Leslied Rosewood Telecaster, that Harrison
recorded during the January 1970 session.

Released in March 1970, the single version of "Let It Be" reveals a more overt
sense of religiosity—with Preston's Hammond organ and the choir-like backing
vocals elevated in the mix, effecting the ambience of a hymn. The single version
also featured Harrison along with Paul and Linda McCartney providing backing
vocals during the January 1970 session. On March 26, 1970, Spector enhanced
Martin's existing orchestral arrangement during the production of the *Let It Be*
album version of the song.

For the song's *Let It Be . . . Naked* release (2003), "Let It Be" consists of a remix
of the original version recorded on January 31, 1969, without Spector's enhanced
orchestral overdubs.

PERSONNEL

Single Version:
Lennon: Fender Bass VI
McCartney: Vocal, Piano
Harrison: Fender Rosewood Telecaster, Backing Vocal
Starr: Ludwig Hollywood Maple Drums
Preston: Hammond Organ
Linda McCartney: Backing Vocal

Album Version:
Lennon: Fender Bass VI
McCartney: Vocal, Piano
Harrison: Fender Rosewood Telecaster (Leslied), Backing Vocal
Starr: Ludwig Hollywood Maple Drums

Studio Musicians: Orchestral Accompaniment (2 Trumpets, 2 Trombones, Tenor Saxophone, Cello) conducted by Martin

CHART PERFORMANCE

U.K.: "Let It Be"/"You Know My Name (Look Up the Number)"; March 6, 1970, Apple [Parlophone] R 5833: #2.

U.S.: "Let It Be"/"You Know My Name (Look Up the Number)"; March 11, 1970, Apple [Capitol] 2764: #1 (certified by the RIAA as "2x Multi Platinum," with more than 2 million copies sold).

LEGACY AND INFLUENCE

In 1971, "Let It Be" was nominated for a Grammy Award for Record of the Year at the 13th Grammy Awards.

In 2000, *Mojo* magazine ranked "Let It Be" as #60 on the magazine's list of *The 100 Greatest Songs of All Time*.

In 2004, "Let It Be" was inducted into the National Academy of Recording Arts and Sciences Grammy Hall of Fame.

In 2004, *Rolling Stone* ranked "Let It Be" as #20 on the magazine's list of *The 500 Greatest Songs of All Time.*

In 2010, *Rolling Stone* ranked "Let It Be" as #8 on the magazine's list of *The Beatles' 100 Greatest Songs.*

In October 2012, BBC Local Radio listeners ranked "Let It Be" as their 3rd favorite Beatles song in a poll conducted in commemoration of the 50th anniversary of "Love Me Do," the band's first single.

ALBUM APPEARANCES: *Let It Be*; *The Beatles, 1967–1970*; *Reel Music*; *20 Greatest Hits*; *Past Masters, Volume 2*; *Anthology 3*; *1*; *Let It Be . . . Naked.*

See also: *Get Back* Project; *Let It Be* (LP); *Let It Be . . . Naked* (LP); McCartney, Linda Eastman; Spector, Phil.

Let It Be (LP)

May 8, 1970, Apple [Parlophone] PCS 7096 (stereo)
May 18, 1970, Apple [Capitol] AR 34001 (stereo)

Let It Be is the Beatles' tenth studio album. It was released on the Apple Records label on May 8, 1970, in the United Kingdom and May 18, 1970, in the United States. In pure chronological order, the band's eleventh and final studio effort, *Abbey Road*, had been formally released the previous year on September 26, 1969, in the United Kingdom and October 1, 1969, in the United States. Originally intended to be released as the *Get Back* project, the *Let It Be* soundtrack album had been recorded, for the most part, in January 1969, and prior to the recording sessions that resulted in the *Abbey Road* album.

Let It Be was released as a stereo CD, along with *Abbey Road*, on October 19, 1987. On November 17, 2003, the Beatles released *Let It Be . . . Naked*, which included comparatively sparse remastered versions of the original recordings without Spector's 1970 orchestral and choral overdubs. *Let It Be* was remastered and rereleased as a stereo CD on September 9, 2009.

BACKGROUND AND RECORDING SESSIONS

Produced by Martin with postproduction efforts by Glyn Johns and Spector, *Let It Be* is easily the Beatles' most complex and circuitous album. Originally devised as the *Get Back* project in which the group would reconnect with their musical roots, *Let It Be* was recorded sporadically over 26 months, ranging from key recording sessions in February 1968 and January 1969 with additional sessions in January 1970 culminating in a mammoth orchestral and choral overdubbing session in early April of that year. The Beatles' work took place in a variety of venues, including Abbey Road Studios, Twickenham Film Studios, their newly fashioned basement Apple Studio, and even the rooftop of the Apple Corps building itself at 3 Savile Row in London.

For the balance of 1969, Johns toiled of the resulting master tapes, attempting on several occasions to assemble an LP's worth of material that met the Beatles'—namely, Lennon and McCartney's—liking. His mission, in keeping with the spirit of the *Get Back* sessions in January 1969, was to showcase the Beatles as a working rock band attempting to reconnect with their musical roots. Yet time and time again, Johns presented the bandmates with a slipshod compilation, which was hardly surprising, given the convoluted nature of the recording sessions associated with the *Get Back* project. But as the months rolled by, it became increasingly apparent that the Beatles would scuttle Johns' version of a potential *Get Back, Don't Let Me Down, and Twelve Other Songs* album altogether. Although Johns later substituted a comparatively more professional January 1970 mix for his May 1969 version of the album, by then it was much too late. While McCartney apparently approved of Johns' work—praising, in particular, the producer's attempt to preserve the album's spare sonic textures—Lennon despised *Get Back*, later claiming that it would succeed, for better or for worse, in breaking the Beatles' myth.

By the early spring of 1970, the tapes had fallen into the hands of renowned American producer Phil Spector—the esteemed progenitor of the "wall of sound." Lennon had recently worked with Spector on his hit solo single "Instant Karma," and he had been impressed enough with the producer's lightning-quick results to turn the *Get Back* tapes over to him with little concern—and, perhaps more significantly, without McCartney's knowledge. In December, the Beatles' revolving management had sold the rights to Lindsay-Hogg's documentary to United

Artists, who reincarnated the project as a feature film. The Beatles subsequently altered the title of their album from *Get Back* to *Let It Be* in order to synchronize the marketing of its release with the movie of the same name.

In late March, Spector began his postproduction activities, culminating in a massive overdubbing session in Abbey Road Studio One on April 1, in which he edited and remixed the *Get Back* recordings in order to prepare the soundtrack album for release. With orchestral arrangements provided by Richard Hewson, Spector applied his wall of sound to "Across the Universe," "The Long and Winding Road," and "I Me Mine," which the Beatles remade in January 1970 for the soundtrack, given the song's relatively conspicuous place in the movie.

In contrast with more coherent and unified albums such as *Sgt. Pepper* and *The White Album*, *Let It Be* (and, for that matter, the *Magical Mystery Tour* project) ultimately suffers for its lack, in Allan F. Moore's perceptive words, of "authorial control" (Moore 1997, 71). With three different producers at the helm and a filmmaker to boot, the project's overriding sense of creative incongruity should have been a foregone conclusion. In Spector's hands, the LP retained much of the studio banter that had given Johns' version a sense of charm in comparison to its rough exterior. Yet the wall of sound overdubbing sessions succeeded in altogether mitigating the project's philosophy of getting back to the basics.

TRACK LISTING

Side 1: "Two of Us"; "Dig a Pony"; "Across the Universe"; "I Me Mine"; "Dig It"; "Let It Be"; "Maggie Mae."

Side 2: "I've Got a Feeling"; "One After 909"; "The Long and Winding Road"; "For You Blue"; "Get Back."

COVER ARTWORK

As the *Get Back* project gathered momentum, the Beatles prepared *Get Back, Don't Let Me Down, and Twelve Other Songs* for their next album release. On May 13, 1969, Angus McBean and the Beatles convened at EMI House, where McBean positioned the bandmates in the same fashion as they had appeared six years earlier for the cover of *Please Please Me*. In retrospect, it was a clever idea—a means of bookending their career, as well as underscoring their intent to return to the unadulterated rock 'n' roll sound that brought them fame and fortune in the first place. Long after the *Get Back* project was finally scrapped in favor of the *Let It Be* documentary, McBean's twin photographs of the early- and latter-day Beatles was recycled as the covers for the 1973 compilations of *The Beatles, 1962–1966* and *The Beatles, 1967–1970*, respectively.

Meanwhile, Apple Records prepared *Let It Be* for its May 1970 release with John Kosh, the creative artist behind the *Abbey Road* cover design, serving as the project's director. Kosh's sleeve design initially used McBean's EMI House photograph of the band in a March 1970 mock-up for *Let It Be*'s cover art, although it was later replaced by January 1969 still photographs by Ethan Russell of the group in various states of rock 'n' roll performance. In the United Kingdom, the album's original release included a book of color photographs entitled *The Beatles Get Back*.

The album's back-cover liner notes quietly and, in retrospect, rather diplomatically offer "thanks to George Martin/Glyn Johns/Billy Preston/Mal Davies/Peter Brown/Richard Hewson/Brian Rogers." More prominently, the liner notes describe *Let It Be* as "a new phase Beatles album. Essential to the content of the film *Let It Be* was that they performed live for many of the tracks; in comes the warmth and the freshness of a live performance; as reproduced for disc by Phil Spector." For McCartney, *Let It Be*'s simulated "warmth and freshness" were nothing but an empty ruse. "When the *Let It Be* album came out," he later remarked, "there was a little bit of hype on the back of the sleeve for the first time ever on a Beatles album. At the time, the Beatles were very strained with each other. It said it was a 'new phase' Beatles album and nothing was further from the truth. That was the last Beatles album and everybody knew it. There was no 'new phase' about it at all. Klein had it reproduced because he said it didn't sound commercial enough" (Badman 2001, 13).

CHART PERFORMANCE

U.K.: #1.

U.S.: #1 (certified by the RIAA as "4x Multi Platinum," with more than 4 million copies sold).

LEGACY AND INFLUENCE

In 1971, *Let It Be* earned a Grammy Award for Best Original Score Written for a Motion Picture or Television Show at the 13th Grammy Awards. It was also nominated for a Grammy Award for Contemporary Vocal Group Performance.

In 1971, *Let It Be* was honored as the *New Musical Express*'s "Album of the Year."

In 1988, Slovenian band Laibach recorded a full-length cover version of the *Let It Be* album, with the notable exception of the title track itself, as a series of military style interpretations and choral pieces.

In 2003, *Rolling Stone* ranked *Let It Be* as #86 on the magazine's list of *The 500 Greatest Albums of All Time*.

In 2010, *Mojo* magazine published a special issue that celebrated *Let It Be*'s 40th anniversary, including a cover-mounted CD with contemporary cover versions of the album's entire contents entitled *Let It Be Revisited*.

In 2013, American author Chad Gayle adopted *Let It Be* as the title of his debut novel, a nostalgic story of loss and redemption set in 1970s-era Amarillo, Texas.

See also: *Get Back* Project; Johns, Glyn; *Let It Be* (LP); *Let It Be . . . Naked* (LP); Martin, George; Spector, Phil.

Let It Be . . . Naked (LP)

November 17, 2003, Apple CDP 7243 5 95713 2 4

Let It Be . . . Naked is the authorized remixing of the Beatles' Let It Be album, which was originally released in May 1970. Released on November 17, 2003, Let It Be . . . Naked included comparatively sparse remastered versions of the original recordings without Spector's orchestral arrangements.

BACKGROUND AND RECORDING SESSIONS

Let It Be . . . Naked finds its origins in a chance meeting between McCartney and Lindsay-Hogg, the director behind the Let It Be documentary. McCartney and Lindsay-Hogg pondered the idea of remixing the original soundtrack in advance of a possible future DVD release of the film. Energized by the notion of revisiting the Let It Be album—and with the late Harrison's assent—McCartney enlisted the help of Abbey Road Studios sound engineers Paul Hicks, Guy Massey, and Allan Rouse to comb through some 30 reels of audiotape in order to produce a stripped-down version of the original recordings. In so doing, McCartney clearly hoped to recapture the driving spirit behind the original Get Back project.

As with the original album, Let It Be . . . Naked involves the Beatles recordings produced on February 4, 1968; January 2–31, 1969; and January 3–4, 1970. As the remixed album's producers, Hicks, Massey, and Rouse jettisoned "Dig It" and "Maggie Mae" in favor of "Don't Let Me Down." They also deleted the original soundtrack's incidental studio chatter. More important, Let It Be . . . Naked affords listeners with a remixed version of the original recordings without benefit of the postproduction sheen of Spector's "wall of sound."

Hicks, Massey, and Rouse's editorial work establishes a vastly different version of the album. For the Let It Be . . . Naked version of the song, "Get Back" consists of the January 27, 1969, single version of the song, albeit without the January 28 coda or the incidental framing dialogue. "Dig a Pony" is a remixed version of the original rooftop concert recording without the false start that is included on the Let It Be soundtrack album. "For You Blue" was remixed from the January 1969 Apple Studio session. As one of the most controversial recordings from the original soundtrack, "The Long and Winding Road" was remixed from the composition's final take, recorded on January 31, 1969, albeit without Spector's orchestral and choral overdubbing efforts. The Let It Be . . . Naked version of "Two of Us" consists of a remix of the January 31 Apple Studio recording. The remixed version of "I've Got a Feeling" exists as a composite from both performances during the Beatles' rooftop concert. Likewise, "One After 909" was remixed from the rooftop concert version, albeit without Lennon's ad-lib. For "Don't Let Me Down," the two January 30 rooftop recordings of the song were edited together for the version of "Don't Let Me Down." Harrison's "I Me Mine" features a remixed track of Spector's edited version of the January 1970 recording—albeit without the addition of Spector's orchestral and choral overdubbing session. The original February 4, 1968, version of "Across the Universe"—with the Apple Scruffs, bird sound effects, keyboards, and maracas mixed out—can be heard on the *Let It Be . . . Naked* version of the song. Finally, "Let It Be" consists of a remix of the original version recorded on January 31, 1969, without Spector's enhanced orchestral overdubs.

For the *Let It Be . . . Naked* album, Hicks, Massey, and Rouse also made a number of key editorial alterations to the original recordings. Although "Get Back" did not require significant editorial intervention, for "Dig a Pony," the engineers corrected Lennon's vocal error in the second verse. "For You Blue" finds the producers including a previously unheard acoustic guitar track, while "The Long and Winding Road" has been remixed to delete McCartney's vocal ad-lib during Preston's keyboard solo. In "Two of Us," the producers correct an errant guitar note played by Lennon on his acoustic guitar just prior to his whistling solo. For "I've Got a Feeling," the two rooftop performances are edited together, as they are for the remix of "Don't Let Me Down," where the mergence of the two rooftop performances allow the producers to correct the song's lyrics, which Lennon had fumbled during both performances of the tune. "I Me Mine" is a rarity among the *Let It Be . . . Naked* contents, as it retains Spector's original editing scheme, albeit with different mixes associated with the guitar and organ parts. For "Across the Universe," the producers return to the song's original master, while "Let It Be" finds Hicks, Massey, and Rouse editing two performances—takes 27A and 27B—together and correcting an errant piano chord by McCartney.

The *Let It Be . . . Naked* package is supplemented by a special "Fly on the Wall" disc that contains nearly 22 minutes of song excerpts and dialogue from the numerous hours of audiotape produced during the January 1969 *Get Back* sessions. Compiled and edited by Kevin Howlett, the "Fly on the Wall" material includes excerpts from "Dig It" and "Maggie Mae," which had been omitted from *Let It Be . . . Naked*, along with references to such Beatles works as "Back in the USSR," "Every Little Thing," and "She Came in Through the Bathroom Window," among a host of others.

TRACK LISTING

Disc 1: "Get Back"; "Dig a Pony"; "For You Blue"; "The Long and Winding Road"; "Two of Us"; "I've Got a Feeling"; "One After 909"; "Don't Let Me Down"; "I Me Mine"; "Across the Universe"; "Let It Be."

Fly on the Wall Bonus Disc 2: "Sun King"; "Don't Let Me Down"; "One After 909"; "Because I Know You Love Me So"; "Don't Pass Me By"; "Taking a Trip to Carolina"; "John's Piano Piece"; "Child of Nature" ["Jealous Guy"]; "Back in the USSR"; "Every Little Thing"; "Don't Let Me Down"; "All Things Must Pass"; "John's Jam"; "She Came in Through the Bathroom Window";

"Paul's Bass Jam"; "Paul's Piano Piece"; "Get Back"; "Two of Us"; "Maggie Mae"; "Fancy My Chances with You"; "Can You Dig It?"; "Get Back."

COVER ARTWORK

The *Let It Be . . . Naked* cover art features a monochromatic negative of the original *Let It Be* cover, which consisted of a composite of Russell's January 1969 still photographs of the band. Harrison's original image from *Let It Be* has been replaced by a photograph of him playing his guitar, in keeping with the photographs of the other Beatles in various acts of performance.

CHART PERFORMANCE

U.K.: #7 (certified by the BPI as "Gold," with more than 100,000 copies sold). U.S.: #5 (certified by the RIAA as "Platinum," with more than 1 million copies sold).

See also: *Get Back* Project; Johns, Glyn; *Let It Be* (LP); Martin, George; Spector, Phil.

Lindsay-Hogg, Michael (1940–)

Born on May 5, 1940, in New York City, Lindsay-Hogg in an American film and stage director who was born as Sir Michael Edward Lindsay-Hogg, Fifth Baronet. He was the son of actress Geraldine Fitzgerald and Sir Edward Lindsay-Hogg, Fourth Baronet. In later years, he learned that his biological father was in actuality the celebrated actor and film director Orson Welles. As a director, Lindsay-Hogg made his debut for the 1960s British television series *Ready Steady Go!* In 1968, he directed *The Rolling Stones Rock and Roll Circus*, which was not formally released until 1996. His work with the Beatles includes promotional videos for "Paperback Writer," "Rain," "Hey Jude," and "Revolution." In January 1969, he began filming the Beatles' ill-fated *Get Back* project at London's Twickenham Film Studios, which later resulted in Lindsay-Hogg's full-length documentary *Let It Be*. In the ensuing years, he directed numerous music videos for the Rolling Stones, as well as for McCartney and Wings. In 2000, he directed VH1's television movie, *Two of Us*, which offers a fictionalized account of Lennon and McCartney's day together on April 24, 1976. His film credits include a film adaptation of *Waiting for Godot*, Simon and Garfunkel's *The Concert in Central Park*, and *The Object of Beauty*, among others. In 2011, he published his autobiography entitled *Luck and Circumstance: A Coming of Age in Hollywood, New York, and Points Beyond*.

See also: *Get Back* Project; *Let It Be* (Film).

"Little Child" (Lennon–McCartney)

"Little Child" is a song on the *With the Beatles* album.

AUTHORSHIP AND BACKGROUND

Written by Lennon and McCartney, "Little Child" finds the songwriters borrowing the line "I'm so sad and lonely" from Elton Hayes's "Whistle My Love," which was featured in Walt Disney's *The Story of Robin Hood and His Merrie Men* (1952).

As McCartney later recalled, "Certain songs were inspirational and you just followed that. 'Little Child' was a work job" (Miles 1997, 153).

RECORDING SESSIONS

Produced by Martin, "Little Child" was recorded at Abbey Road Studios on September 11 and 12, 1963, with additional work on October 3.

PERSONNEL

Lennon: Vocal, Rickenbacker 325, Harmonica
McCartney: Vocal, Höfner 500/1, Piano
Harrison: Gretsch Country Gentleman
Starr: Ludwig Oyster Black Pearl Drums

ALBUM APPEARANCES: *With the Beatles*; *Meet the Beatles!*

See also: *With the Beatles* (LP).

Live at the BBC (LP)

November 30, 1994, Apple [Parlophone] PCSP 726
December 6, 1994, Apple [Capitol] CDP 7243–8–31796–2-6

Released in 1994, *Live at the BBC* marks the first compilation to include live performances by the band since *The Beatles at the Hollywood Bowl* in 1977 and the first including unreleased material since 1970's *Let It Be*. In November 2013, a remastered version of *Live at the BBC* was released concomitantly with *On Air: Live at the BBC, Volume 2*.

BACKGROUND

Live at the BBC features 56 songs, along with 13 dialogue tracks, recorded as BBC Light Programme radio shows from January 1963 through May 1965—a period that captures the emergence of British Beatlemania during the autumn of 1963 through the band's ascendance toward unquestionable global fame. The material on *Live at the BBC* was culled from some 275 performance of 88 different songs, the majority of which were cover versions. The band's first appearance on BBC Radio occurred in March 1962 with a recording for *Teenager's Turn: Here We Go*. Their run on BBC Radio ended with their appearance on the May 1965 special *The Beatles Invite You to Take a Ticket to Ride*. While several of the songs included on *Live at the BBC* were performed live, the lion's share was recorded in advance for future broadcasts.

Live at the BBC had been in development since 1989. The project had likely been inspired, at least initially, by the BBC's 1982 two-hour radio special entitled *The Beatles at the Beeb*, which celebrated the 20th anniversary of the group's original appearance on the Light Programme. Another, more comprehensive series was broadcast in 1988 on BBC Radio 1 as 14 half-hour episodes. The tracks on *Live at the BBC* were selected by George Martin, who was assisted by Abbey Road sound engineer Peter Mew.

Notably, *Live at the BBC* includes "I'll Be on My Way," the only Lennon–McCartney composition that the group recorded for the BBC without a subsequent studio version by the band. "I'll Be on My Way" was subsequently released by Billy J. Kramer with the Dakotas as the B-side for their "Do You Want to Know a Secret" single, which become a 1963 #2 hit for the group, who were also managed by Brian Epstein.

TRACK LISTING

Disc 1: "Beatle Greetings" (Speech); "From Us to You"; "Riding on a Bus" (Speech); "I Got a Woman"; "Too Much Monkey Business"; "Keep Your Hands Off My Baby"; "I'll Be on My Way"; "Young Blood"; "A Shot of Rhythm and Blues"; "Sure to Fall (In Love with You)"; "Some Other Guy"; "Thank You Girl"; "Sha La La La La!" (Speech); "Baby It's You"; "That's All Right (Mama)"; "Carol"; "Soldier of Love"; "A Little Rhyme" (Speech); "Clarabella"; "I'm Gonna Sit Right Down and Cry (Over You)"; "Crying, Waiting, Hoping"; "Dear Wack!" (Speech); "You Really Got a Hold on Me"; "To Know Her Is to Love Her"; "A Taste of Honey"; "Long Tall Sally"; "I Saw Her Standing There"; "The Honeymoon Song"; "Johnny B. Goode"; "Lucille"; "Can't Buy Me Love"; "From Fluff to You" (Speech); "Till There Was You."

Disc 2: "Crinsk Dee Night" (Speech); "A Hard Day's Night"; "Have a Banana!" (Speech); "I Wanna Be Your Man"; "Just a Rumour" (Speech); "Roll Over Beethoven"; "All My Loving"; "Things We Said Today"; "She's a Woman"; "Sweet Little Sixteen"; "1822!" (Speech); "Lonesome Tears in My Eyes"; "Nothin' Shakin' (But the Leaves on the Trees)"; "Hippy Hippy Shake"; "Glad All Over"; "I Just Don't Understand"; "So How Come (No One Loves Me)"; "I Feel Fine"; "I'm a Loser"; "Everybody's Trying to Be My Baby"; "Rock and Roll Music"; "Ticket to Ride"; "Dizzy Miss Lizzy"; Medley: "Kansas

City"/"Hey-Hey-Hey-Hey!"; "Set Fire to That Lot!" (Speech); "Matchbox"; "I Forgot to Remember to Forget"; "Love These Goon Shows!" (Speech); "I Got to Find My Baby"; "Ooh! My Soul"; "Ooh! My Arms" (Speech); "Don't Ever Change"; "Slow Down"; "Honey Don't"; "Love Me Do."

COVER ARTWORK

The album's front and back cover art depicts the Beatles in front of the BBC's Paris Studio in London's Waterloo Place. Shot in December 1963, the photograph was taken by Dezo Hoffmann (1918–1986). In his September 1994 liner notes for *Live at the BBC*, Derek Taylor writes that "this collection is of a distant era; when London was six/eight hours from Liverpool, when London was 'The Big Time' and almost still 'The Big Smoke.' Trains were still steam. There was no take-away save fish and chips. No *Sun*. The rudest thing in newsprint was *Reveille*. Television was black and white; there were two channels."

Taylor takes particular note of the Beatles' usage of radio in order to consolidate their fame and increase their popularity. As Taylor adds, "That the Beatles were woven into the fabric of British life was due in large part to the regularity of their attention to good habits—the Christmas messages to fans, the package tours, the visits home to Liverpool families, an honest paying of all the expected dues and in no small measure to the BBC, who provided that unparalleled broadcasting expertise to keep the nation in touch with 'the boys' through fifty-two broadcasts. Radio allowed them to 'be themselves' and that was always enough for the Beatles and for their followers."

CHART PERFORMANCE

- U.K.: #1 (certified by the BPI as "2x Platinum," with more than 600,000 copies sold).
- U.S.: #3 (certified by the RIAA as "4x Multi Platinum," with more than 4 million copies sold).

LEGACY AND INFLUENCE

In 1996, *Live at the BBC* was nominated for a Grammy Award for Best Historical Album at the 38th Grammy Awards.

See also: Martin, George; *On Air: Live at the BBC, Volume 2* (LP).

Live! at the Star-Club in Hamburg, Germany; 1962 (LP)

April 8, 1977, Lingasong LNL1
June 13, 1977, Atlantic LS 2 7001

Recorded during the Beatles' fifth and final Hamburg residency, *Live! at the Star-Club in Hamburg, Germany; 1962* offers an important early record of the band's formative years in West Germany.

BACKGROUND

The Beatles spent the last few days of 1962 in Hamburg, where their concerts on December 28 and 31 were recorded by Star-Club soundman Adrian Barber, who also played guitar for the Big Three. Several of the tapes ended up in the hands of Ted "Kingsize" Taylor, who later claimed that Lennon gave him the rights to the live recordings in exchange for a round of drinks (Winn 2003a, 21). Several of the songs recorded during the December 28 and 31 performances were released in 1977 as *Live! at the Star-Club in Hamburg, Germany; 1962* on CBS's Lingasong label. Although the low-fidelity sound quality is questionable throughout, the album is of considerable historical value, given that it comprises their fifth and final extended engagement on the Reeperbahn. The Beatles' standard lineup appears on all of the tracks, save for "Be-Bop-a-Lula," which features Star-Club waiter Fred Fascher on lead vocals, and "Hallelujah, I Love Her So," which features Star-Club manager Horst Fascher singing lead vocals.

Harrison later took issue with Taylor's claim, arguing that his suggestion that Lennon gave Taylor permission for making the recording was "a load of rubbish." As Harrison remarked,

> Even if John had given Taylor his permission to tape the Beatles' performance, that does not make it legal for the tape to be turned into an album. One drunken person recording another bunch of drunks does not constitute a business deal. It just did not happen. It certainly didn't take place in my company or my lifetime. Neither Paul nor Ringo heard it either. The only person who allegedly heard anything about it is the one who is dead—who can't actually come here and say it's a load of rubbish. If we had been sitting around the table and Ted Taylor was saying, "Hey Lads, I am going to record you and I'll make this live record that will come back to haunt you for the rest of your lives," and John was saying, "Great, you can do it," then I would have said, "You are not recording me." We had a record contract, and we were on a roll. The last thing we needed was one little bedroom recording to come out. The Star-Club recording was the crummiest recording ever made in our name! (Unterberger 2006, 41)

In 1998, the Beatles were awarded the rights to the 1962 Hamburg recordings on the strength of Harrison's testimony, bringing their long-standing legal conflict with Taylor to an end. Ironically, the Beatles had strongly considering skipping their final residency in Hamburg, but ultimately honored their contract at manager Brian Epstein's insistence.

TRACK LISTING (U.K.)

Side 1: "I Saw Her Standing There"; "Roll Over Beethoven"; "Hippy Hippy Shake"; "Sweet Little Sixteen"; "Lend Me Your Comb"; "Your Feet's Too Big."

Side 2: "Twist and Shout"; "Mr. Moonlight"; "A Taste of Honey"; "Bésame Mucho"; "Reminiscing"; Medley: "Kansas City"/"Hey-Hey-Hey-Hey!"

Side 3: "Nothin' Shakin' (But the Leaves on the Trees)"; "To Know Her Is to Love Her"; "Little Queenie"; "Falling in Love Again (Can't Help It)"; "Ask Me Why"; "Be-Bop-a-Lula"; "Hallelujah, I Love Her So."

Side 4: "Red Sails in the Sunset"; "Everybody's Trying to Be My Baby"; "Matchbox"; "I'm Talking About You"; "Shimmy Like Kate"; "Long Tall Sally"; "I Remember You."

TRACK LISTING (U.S.)

Side 1: "I'm Gonna Sit Right Down and Cry (Over You)"; "Roll Over Beethoven"; "Hippy Hippy Shake"; "Sweet Little Sixteen"; "Lend Me Your Comb"; "Your Feet's Too Big."

Side 2: "Where Have You Been All My Life"; "Mr. Moonlight"; "A Taste of Honey"; "Bésame Mucho"; "Till There Was You"; Medley: "Kansas City"/"Hey-Hey-Hey-Hey!"

Side 3: "Nothin' Shakin' (But the Leaves on the Trees)"; "To Know Her Is to Love Her"; "Little Queenie"; "Falling in Love Again (Can't Help It)"; "Sheila"; "Be-Bop-a-Lula"; "Hallelujah, I Love Her So."

Side 4: "Red Sails in the Sunset"; "Everybody's Trying to Be My Baby"; "Matchbox"; "I'm Talking About You"; "Shimmy Like Kate"; "Long Tall Sally"; "I Remember You."

CHART PERFORMANCE

U.K.: Did not chart.
U.S.: #111.

See also: Epstein, Brian.

"The Long and Winding Road" (Lennon–McCartney)

"The Long and Winding Road" was a hit single, backed with "For You Blue," which was released in the United States on May 11, 1970. It is also a song on the Beatles' *Let It Be* album. It was the Beatles' last #1 single in the United States.

AUTHORSHIP AND BACKGROUND

Written by McCartney, "The Long and Winding Road" finds the songwriter working to produce a soul-rending number in the style of Ray Charles. As for the circuitous road of the title, McCartney was undoubtedly referring to the B842 in Scotland, which winds its way through the Mull of Kintyre peninsula near the songwriter's rustic Campbeltown farm.

As McCartney recalled,

> It's rather a sad song. I like writing sad songs, it's a good bag to get into because you can actually acknowledge some deeper feelings of your own and put them in it. It's a good vehicle, it saves having to go to a psychiatrist. Songwriting often performs that feat—you say it, but you don't embarrass yourself because it's only a song, or is it? You are putting the things that are bothering you on the table and you are reviewing them, but because it's a song, you don't have to argue with anyone. It's a sad song because it's all about the unattainable; the door you never quite reach. This is the road that you never get to the end of. (Miles 1997, 539)

During one of his last interviews, Lennon remarked that that's "Paul again. He had a little spurt just before we split" (Lennon and Ono 2000, 205).

RECORDING SESSIONS

Produced by Martin with postproduction by Spector, "The Long and Winding Road" was recorded at Apple Studio on January 31, 1969, after an earlier rehearsal of the song on January 26. An orchestral and choral overdubbing session was conducted by Spector on April 1, 1970. During the latter session, Spector worked from Richard Hewson's orchestral arrangement and John Barham's choral arrangement for the song.

With McCartney on Apple Studio's Blüthner grand piano, the January 1969 recording effects a somber quietude, a gentle musing on the vexing emotional difference between a sentimentalized past and an agonizing present. The song's inherent beauty is unnecessarily blemished by Lennon's slipshod work on the Fender Bass VI, a guitar part that McCartney had numerous opportunities to refine as the ensuing album went through its various iterations over the course of the spring, summer, and fall months of 1969. In *Revolution in the Head: The Beatles' Records and the Sixties*, Ian MacDonald catalogues key instances involving Lennon's erratic bass playing on "The Long and Winding Road": "Recurring wrong notes at 0:28, 2:10, and 3:07; mis-strikes at 2:39 and 2:52; drop-outs at 2:59 and 3:14; a fumble at 0:19; a vague glissando at 1:03; a missed final push at 3:26. (One can hear McCartney grin at his partner's incompetence at 1:59)" (MacDonald 1994, 271).

But as history proved, the challenges of bringing McCartney's artistic vision for "The Long and Winding Road" to fruition were only just beginning. As McCartney remarked in April 1970,

The album was finished a year ago, but a few months ago American record producer Phil Spector was called in by John Lennon to tidy up some of the tracks.
But a few weeks ago, I was sent a remixed version of my song "The Long and
Winding Road" with harps, horns, an orchestra, and a women's choir added. No
one had asked me what I thought. I couldn't believe it. The record came with a
note from Allen Klein saying he thought the changes were necessary. I don't
blame Phil Spector for doing it, but it just goes to show that it's no good me sitting here thinking I'm in control because obviously I'm not. Anyway, I've sent
Klein a letter asking for some things to be altered, but I haven't received an
answer yet. (Badman 2001, 6)

McCartney's disgust with Spector's alteration of "The Long and Winding Road"
resounded for years to come. In truth, the songwriter's angst had nothing to do with
Lennon's bass playing and everything to do with the track's post-*Get Back* history.
Although it is impossible to deny McCartney's anger at not being consulted about
the album's disposition, he directed much of his vitriol toward Spector's decision to
imbue "The Long and Winding Road" with a 33-piece orchestra, a 14-member choir,
two studio musicians on guitar, and one drummer—ironically, Starr, the last Beatle to join the band and the last member to play on a Beatles session. At one point,
McCartney even attempted, albeit unsuccessfully, to block the album's release.
Although McCartney vehemently objected to the manner in which Spector
recorded orchestral and choral tracks onto his songs from the *Get Back* sessions,
Lennon later defended Spector's efforts on the disintegrating band's behalf: "He
worked like a pig on it," Lennon recalled. "He'd always wanted to work with the
Beatles, and he was given the *shittiest* load of badly recorded shit—and with a
lousy feeling to it . . . and he made *something* out of it" (Lennon 1970, 101, 102).

Quite obviously, McCartney couldn't have agreed less. His vision for one of
his most personal of compositions had been shattered—and entirely without his
permission. Tim Riley proves to be equally unforgiving in his analysis of the song:
"All of the sudden," he writes, "it's as if we're in the showroom of a large casino,
and Paul is cruising into a schmaltzy ballad" (Riley 1988, 301). Riley was only
the latest in a long line of critical voices besieging Spector's work on "The Long
and Winding Road." Martin felt that the track's orchestral arrangement wreaked
of the saccharine sounds of Mantovani and Muzak, while John Mendelsohn called
the song "oppressive mush" and "virtually unlistenable with hideously cloying
strings and a ridiculous choir." Nicholas Schaffner blamed Spector's orchestration
for destroying the "sense of intimacy, informality, and honesty" that the song possessed in its original form (Schaffner 1977, 138). There is little question, moreover, that Spector's orchestration works at variance with Martin's consistent efforts
over the years to afford the Beatles' tracks with tasteful, fashion- and time-defying
arrangements that contributed to the band's musical aspirations without overpow-
ering them. Yet on the other hand, there is something to be said for Spector's full-
blown rendering of the song in spite of its apparent divergence from the songwriter's

intentions. MacDonald, for instance, praises Spector's version as an elemental study of illusion and nostalgia. " 'The Long and Winding Road' was so touching in its fatalistic regret, and so perfect as a downbeat finale to the Beatles' career," he writes, "that it couldn't fail, however badly dressed" (MacDonald 1994, 273).

Interestingly, by the early years of the 21st century, no less than six additional versions of "The Long and Winding Road" had been made available on various McCartney projects, including four telling concert performances of the track. The first of these later versions of the Beatles' final American hit single surfaced during McCartney's celebrated return to the international stage, an event that was commemorated by the release of *Wings over America* (1976). The album features a somber rendering of the Beatles classic, complete with a plaintive trumpet accompaniment. Yet another version of "The Long and Winding Road" appeared on McCartney's 1990 concert album, *Tripping the Live Fantastic*. While this latest rendition of the song imitated the simple melody of the preorchestral version of "The Long and Winding Road," McCartney's backup band clearly attempts to replicate the violin solo created during Spector's postproduction work in 1970. Similar concert performances were included on *Back in the US* (2002) and the *Live 8* DVD (2005). McCartney's various interpretations of the song reached their ridiculous nadir in yet another rendering of "The Long and Winding Road" on his 1984 album, *Give My Regards to Broad Street*. In an outrageous jazz reading of the song, McCartney offers an overproduced, saxophone-accompanied performance. The original, pre-Spector version of the song finally became available on *Anthology 3*. Reproduced without Spector's string and choral arrangement, "The Long and Winding Road" seems to have come full circle, ostensibly satisfying McCartney's artistic designs for the song for the first time.

For the song's *Let It Be . . . Naked* release (2003), "The Long and Winding Road" was remixed from the composition's final take, recorded on January 31, 1969, albeit without Spector's orchestral and choral overdubbing efforts.

PERSONNEL

Lennon: Fender Bass VI
McCartney: Vocal, Piano
Harrison: Fender Rosewood Telecaster
Starr: Ludwig Hollywood Maple Drums
Preston: Hammond Organ
Studio Musicians: Orchestral and Choral Accompaniment (18 Violins, 4 Violas, 4 Cellos, 3 Trumpets, 3 Trombones, 2 Guitars, 14 Female Singers) conducted by Spector

CHART PERFORMANCE

U.S.: "The Long and Winding Road"/"For You Blue"; 11 May 1970, Apple [Capitol] 2832: #1 (certified by the RIAA as "Gold," with more than 500,000 copies sold).

LEGACY AND INFLUENCE

In 2000, *Mojo* magazine ranked "The Long and Winding Road" as #43 on the magazine's list of *The 100 Greatest Songs of All Time*.

In 2010, *Rolling Stone* ranked "The Long and Winding Road" as #90 on the magazine's list of *The Beatles' 100 Greatest Songs*.

In October 2012, BBC Local Radio listeners ranked "The Long and Winding Road" as their seventh favorite Beatles song in a poll conducted in commemoration of the 50th anniversary of "Love Me Do," the band's first single.

ALBUM APPEARANCES: *Let It Be*; *The Beatles, 1967–1970*; *Love Songs*; *Reel Music*; *20 Greatest Hits*; *Anthology 3*; *1*; *Let It Be . . . Naked*.

See also: *Get Back* Project; *Let It Be* (LP); *Let It Be . . . Naked* (LP); Spector, Phil.

"Long, Long, Long" (Harrison)

"Long, Long, Long" is a song on *The Beatles* (*The White Album*).

AUTHORSHIP AND BACKGROUND

Written by Harrison, "Long, Long, Long" finds its origins during the Beatles' 1968 visit to India.

"Long, Long, Long" went under the working title of "It's Been a Long, Long, Long Time." Harrison borrowed the song's chord structure, while alternating the time signature between 6/8 and 3/8, from Bob Dylan's "Sad-Eyed Lady of the Lowlands," the haunting, epic track that brings the *Blonde on Blonde* album (1966) to a close.

As Harrison later observed, "The 'you' in 'Long, Long, Long' is God. I can't recall much about it except the chords, which I think were coming from [Dylan's] 'Sad Eyed Lady of the Lowlands'—D to E minor, A, and D—those three chords and the way they moved" (Dowlding 1989, 244).

RECORDING SESSIONS

Produced by Martin, "Long, Long, Long" was recorded at Abbey Road Studios on October 7, 1968, with additional overdubbing sessions on October 8 and 9. Producer Chris Thomas contributed an uncredited piano part.

PERSONNEL

Lennon: Martin D-28
McCartney: Rickenbacker 4001S, Hammond Organ
Harrison: Vocal, Gibson J-200

Starr: Ludwig Oyster Black Pearl Drums
Thomas: Piano

LEGACY AND INFLUENCE

In 2010, *Rolling Stone* ranked "Long, Long, Long" as #98 on the magazine's list of *The Beatles' 100 Greatest Songs*.

ALBUM APPEARANCE: *The Beatles* (*The White Album*).

See also: *The Beatles* (*The White Album*) (LP).

"Long Tall Sally" (Blackwell–Johnson–Penniman)

"Long Tall Sally" is a song on the Beatles' *Long Tall Sally* EP, released in the United Kingdom on June 19, 1964.

AUTHORSHIP AND BACKGROUND

Written by Robert "Bumps" Blackwell, Enotris Johnson, and Richard Penniman [Little Richard], "Long Tall Sally" is a 12-bar blues song.

Written under the working titles of "The Thing" and later as "Bald Headed Sally," "Long Tall Sally" was released by Little Richard as a single in March 1956, becoming a Top 10 hit in the United States and the United Kingdom alike. The song has emerged as one of popular music's most widely covered compositions.

RECORDING SESSIONS

Produced by Martin, "Long Tall Sally" was recorded in a single take at Abbey Road Studios on March 1, 1964. The Beatles also recorded seven versions of "Long Tall Sally" for broadcast on BBC Radio between July 1963 and July 1964. Their July 16, 1963, recording was included on the band's *Live at the BBC* album. Yet another live recording of the song from the Beatles' BBC sessions was later included on *On Air: Live at the BBC, Volume 2*.

PERSONNEL

Lennon: Rickenbacker 325
McCartney: Vocal, Höfner 500/1
Harrison: Gretsch Tennessean
Starr: Ludwig Oyster Black Pearl Drums
Martin: Piano

LEGACY AND INFLUENCE

Little Richard's recording of "Long Tall Sally" is included among the Rock and Roll Hall of Fame's *500 Songs That Shaped Rock and Roll.*

In 2004, *Rolling Stone* ranked "Long Tall Sally" as #56 on the magazine's list of *The 500 Greatest Songs of All Time.*

ALBUM APPEARANCES: *The Beatles' Second Album*; *Rock 'n' Roll Music*; *The Beatles at the Hollywood Bowl*; *Live! at the Star-Club in Hamburg, Germany; 1962*; *Rarities* (U.K.); *Live at the BBC*; *Past Masters, Volume 1*; *Anthology 1*; *On Air: Live at the BBC, Volume 2.*

See also: *Live at the BBC* (LP).

Love (LP)

November 20, 2006, Apple [Parlophone] 0946 3 79808 2 8
November 21, 2006, Apple [Capitol] CDP 0946 3 79810 2 3

Produced by George Martin and his son Giles, *Love* consists of remixes and mash-ups of Beatles recordings for the soundtrack for Cirque du Soleil's acclaimed 2006 theatrical production.

BACKGROUND

Originally conceived as the soundtrack for Cirque du Soleil's long-running Las Vegas production at the Mirage, *Love* combines musical components from some 130 different Beatles recordings. For the project, Martin and his son Giles painstakingly mixed and edited segments from the Beatles' massive corpus. *Love* also challenged the duo to carry out difficult production decisions in order to maintain the integrity of the source material, yet provide audience members with the opportunity to hear the band's familiar music in new and different ways. In the album's liner notes, Martin recalled:

> We agonized over the inclusion of "Yesterday" in the show. It is such a famous song, the icon of an era, but had it been heard too much? The story of the addition of the original string quartet is well known, however few people know how limited the recording was technically, and so the case for not including it was strong, but how could anyone ignore such a marvelous work? We introduce it with some of Paul's guitar work from "Blackbird" and hearing it now, I know that I was right to include it. Its simplicity is so direct; it tugs at the heartstrings.

In the liner notes, Martin also recognized the responsibility that editing the Beatles' music entails, noting that "during the process I was asked to write a string score for an early take of George's poignant 'While My Guitar Gently Weeps.' I was aware of such a responsibility but thankfully everyone approved of the result. 'Yesterday' was the first score I had written for a Beatle song way back in 1965 and this score, forty-one years later, is the last. It wraps up an incredible period of my life with those four amazing men who changed the world."

Echoing his father's sentiments, Giles remarked in the liner notes that

> At the beginning of the project, I knew that no one would ever hear my mistakes as we'd been secretively shut away, so I thought I'd start by trying to combine a few tracks to see what the result would be. Feeling like I was painting a moustache on *The Mona Lisa* I started work mixing the bass and drums of "Tomorrow Never Knows" with George's track "Within You Without You." The end result is what you hear on the album today, and it is the Beatles open-mindedness and support combined with my dad's great musical insight that has made *Love* possible.

For the Beatles themselves, the Martins' work proved to be astounding. As McCartney later observed in the press release celebrating *Love*'s premiere, "This album puts the Beatles back together again because suddenly there's John and George with me and Ringo." Starr added, "George and Giles did such a great job combining these tracks. It's really powerful for me, and I even heard things I'd forgotten we'd recorded." Released in October 2008, the documentary *All Together Now* commemorates the production of the Beatles' collaborative project with Cirque du Soleil, as well as the making of *Love*.

TRACK LISTING

"Because"; "Get Back"; "Glass Onion"; "Eleanor Rigby"/"Julia"; "I Am the Walrus"; "I Want to Hold Your Hand"; "Drive My Car"/"The Word"/"What You're Doing"; "Gnik Nus"; "Something"/"Blue Jay Way"; "Being for the Benefit of Mr. Kite!"/"I Want You (She's So Heavy)"/"Helter Skelter"; "Help!"; "Blackbird"/"Yesterday"; "Strawberry Fields Forever"; "Within You, Without You"/"Tomorrow Never Knows"; "Lucy in the Sky with Diamonds"; "Octopus's Garden"/"Sun King"; "Lady Madonna"; "Here Comes the Sun"/"The Inner Light"; "Come Together"/"Dear Prudence"/"Cry Baby Cry"; "Revolution"/"Back in the USSR"; "While My Guitar Gently Weeps"; "A Day in the Life"; "Hey Jude"; "Sgt. Pepper's Lonely Hearts Club Band (Reprise)"; "All You Need Is Love."

Bonus Tracks: "The Fool on the Hill"; "Girl."

COVER ARTWORK

The cover art for *Love*, designed by Drew Lorimer, Janina Bunjamin, and Philippe Meunier, features Cirque du Soleil's Beatles logo for the theatrical production on a field of yellow.

CHART PERFORMANCE

U.K.: #3 (certified by the BPI as "2x Platinum," with more than 600,000 copies sold).

U.S.: #4 (certified by the RIAA as "2x Multi Platinum," with more than 2 million copies sold).

LEGACY AND INFLUENCE

In 2008, *Love* earned a Grammy Award for Best Compilation Soundtrack Album at the 50th Grammy Awards. *Love* also earned a Grammy Award for Best Surround-Sound Album.

See also: Martin, George; Martin, Giles.

"Love Me Do" (Lennon–McCartney)

"Love Me Do" is a song on the Beatles' *Please Please Me* album. It was the Beatles' first single in the United Kingdom, where it was released on October 5, 1962.

AUTHORSHIP AND BACKGROUND

Written by McCartney and Lennon during their teen years, "Love Me Do" finds McCartney and Lennon, like the Everly Brothers, sharing lead vocals. By the time that the Beatles arrived at Abbey Road Studios for their Parlophone audition, the group had been performing the song for years. Dissatisfied with Pete Best's timing on "Love Me Do" during the band's June 6, 1962, audition, George Martin informed Brian Epstein that he would be employing a professional studio musician during future sessions. The Best audition recording of the song from June 6 can be heard on *Anthology 1*.

RECORDING SESSIONS

When the Beatles returned to Abbey Road Studios on September 6, 1962, Best had been dismissed from the group and replaced by Starr, who—at least to Martin's ears—struggled through some 15 takes of "Love Me Do." True to his word, Martin hired professional drummer Andy White for the Beatles' next session on September 11, relegating Starr to tambourine duty.

Starr was understandably incensed at the turn of events:

They started "P.S. I Love You" with this other bloke playing the drums and I was given the f—in' maracas. I thought, that's the end. They're doing a Pete Best on me. And then they decided to record the other side again ["Love Me Do"], the one on which I'd originally played the drums. I was given the tambourine this time. (Cross 2005, 399)

Satisfied with the September 11, 1962, recording of "Love Me Do," Martin selected the song as the band's debut single. Interestingly, Starr's drumwork can be heard on the single release of "Love Me Do," as opposed to the album track, where Starr can be heard playing the tambourine while White keeps time on the drums.

The Beatles also recorded eight different versions of "Love Me Do" for BBC Radio, including a July 10, 1963, version for the BBC's *Pop Go the Beatles* radio show that was later included on the *Live at the BBC* album.

PERSONNEL

Single Version:
Lennon: Vocal, Harmonica, Gibson J-160E
McCartney: Vocal, Höfner 500/1
Harrison: Gibson J-160E
Starr: Premier Mahogany Duroplastic Drums
Album Version:
Lennon: Vocal, Harmonica, Gibson J-160E
McCartney: Vocal, Höfner 500/1
Harrison: Gibson J-160E
Starr: Tambourine
White: Drums

CHART PERFORMANCE

U.K.: "Love Me Do"/"P.S. I Love You"; October 5, 1962, Parlophone R 4949: #17.
U.S.: "Love Me Do"/"P.S. I Love You"; April 27, 1964, Tollie 9008: #1.

LEGACY AND INFLUENCE

In 2010, *Rolling Stone* ranked "Love Me Do" as #87 on the magazine's list of *The Beatles' 100 Greatest Songs*.

ALBUM APPEARANCES: *Please Please Me*; *The Early Beatles*; *The Beatles, 1962–1966*; *Rarities* (U.S.); *20 Greatest Hits*; *Past Masters, Volume 1*; *Anthology 1*; *1*.

See also: Best, Pete; *Live at the BBC* (LP); *Please Please Me* (LP).

Love Songs (LP)

November 19, 1977, Parlophone PCSP 721
October 21, 1977, Capitol SKBL 11711

Love Songs is a compilation album, now deleted from the Beatles' catalogue, that was released on October 21, 1977, in the United States and November 19, 1977, in the United Kingdom.

BACKGROUND

Given its ornate packaging of a selection of Beatles classics, *Love Songs* finds the group in the act of rebranding themselves as a blue-chip commercial product. Capitol Records originally considered releasing a promotional single of "Girl" backed with "You're Going to Lose That Girl," but the release was withdrawn prior to the release of *Love Songs*.

Charting at #24 in the United States, *Love Songs* enjoyed the dubious distinction of being the first Beatles album since *The Early Beatles* not to achieve Top 10 status.

TRACK LISTING

Side 1: "Yesterday"; "I'll Follow the Sun"; "I Need You"; "Girl"; "In My Life"; "Words of Love"; "Here, There, and Everywhere."

Side 2: "Something"; "And I Love Her"; "If I Fell"; "I'll Be Back"; "Tell Me What You See"; "Yes It Is."

Side 3: "Michelle"; "It's Only Love"; "You're Going to Lose That Girl"; "Every Little Thing"; "For No One"; "She's Leaving Home."

Side 4: "The Long and Winding Road"; "This Boy"; "Norwegian Wood (This Bird Has Flown)"; "I Will"; "P.S. I Love You."

COVER ARTWORK

The album featured an elaborate packaging scheme, including a gold-foil reproduction of Richard Avedon's evocative 1967 *Look* magazine cover photograph of the band. The gatefold design involved a simulated-leather cover with the lyrics printed, calligraphy-style, on interior parchment paper.

CHART PERFORMANCE

U.K.: #7 (certified by the BPI as "Gold," with more than 100,000 copies sold).
U.S.: #24 (certified by the RIAA as "3x Multi Platinum," with more than 3 million copies sold).

See also: *The Early Beatles* (LP).

"Love You To" (Harrison)

"Love You To" is a song on the Beatles' *Revolver* album.

AUTHORSHIP AND BACKGROUND

Written by Harrison, "Love You To" marks one of the first pop songs to employ non-Western instrumentation and musical structures.

As Harrison later recalled, " 'Love You To' was one of the first tunes I wrote for sitar. 'Norwegian Wood' was an accident as far as the sitar part was concerned, but this was the first song where I consciously tried to use the sitar and tabla on the basic track. I overdubbed the guitars and vocals later" (Dowlding 1989, 137).

RECORDING SESSIONS

Produced by Martin, "Love You To" was recorded under the working title of "Granny Smith" at Abbey Road Studios on April 11, 1966, with an overdubbing session on April 13.

The song begins with an unhurried Hindustani overture—featuring the Asian Music Circle's Anil Baghwat on tabla and Ayana Deva Angadi on sitar—before launching into a full gallop in which Harrison examines the fleeting nature of existence. As Everett points out, "Love You To" wasn't Martin's first recording of Indian instrumentation. In addition to the previous year's "Norwegian Wood," Martin had worked with musicians playing the sitar and tabla for a 1959 track by Peter Sellers and the Goons in which they parodied *My Fair Lady*'s "Wouldn't It Be Loverly" (Everett 1999, 42).

As Baghwat later recalled,

A chap called Angadi called me and asked if I was free that evening to work with George. I didn't know who he meant—he didn't say it was Harrison. It was only when a Rolls Royce came to pick me up that I realised I'd be playing on a Beatles session. When I arrived at Abbey Road there were girls everywhere with Thermos flasks, cakes, sandwiches, waiting for the Beatles to come out. George told me what he wanted and I tuned the tabla with him. He suggested I play something in the Ravi Shankar style, 16-beats, though he agreed that I should improvise. Indian music is all improvisation. (Lewisohn 1988, 72)

PERSONNEL

McCartney: Backing Vocal
Harrison: Vocal, Sitar, Gibson J-160E, Epiphone Casino, Höfner 500/1
Starr: Tambourine

Bhagwat: Tabla
Studio Musicians: Sitar, Tamboura

ALBUM APPEARANCES: *Revolver* (U.K.); *Revolver* (U.S.); *Yellow Submarine Songtrack.*

See also: *Revolver* (U.K. LP); *Yellow Submarine* (Film).

"Lovely Rita" (Lennon–McCartney)

"Lovely Rita" is a song on the Beatles' *Sgt. Pepper's Lonely Hearts Club Band* album.

AUTHORSHIP AND BACKGROUND

Written by McCartney, "Lovely Rita" was inspired by traffic warden Meta Davis, who had recently issued a parking ticket to the unsuspecting Beatle.

As McCartney later recalled, "Yeah, that was mine. It was based on the American meter maid. And I got the idea to just—you know, so many of my things, like 'When I'm Sixty-Four' and those, they're tongue in cheek! But they get taken for real! And similarly with 'Lovely Rita'—the idea of a parking-meter attendant's being sexy was tongue in cheek at the time" (Miles 1997, 320). As Lennon remembered, "That's Paul writing a pop song. He makes 'em up like a novelist. You hear lots of McCartney-influenced songs on the radio now. These stories about boring people doing boring things—being postmen and secretaries and writing home. I'm not interested in writing third-party songs. I like to write about me, 'cuz I know me" (Lennon and Ono 2000, 197).

RECORDING SESSIONS

Produced by Martin, "Lovely Rita" was recorded at Abbey Road Studios on February 23, 1967, with additional overdubbing sessions on February 24, March 7, and March 21.

For the recording, Martin plays a nifty barrelhouse piano (courtesy of his trademark wound-up piano effect) and Harrison reaps all manner of musical color on his slide-driven Fender Strat. "Lovely Rita" also features Lennon, McCartney, and Harrison famously retiring to the Abbey Road Studios bathroom, where they toiled at forcing swathes of toilet paper through metal combs in order to achieve yet another unusual sound for the *Sgt. Pepper* album. Members of Pink Floyd later recalled witnessing the Beatles devoting their precious studio time to such a unique purpose. Pink Floyd was also in residence at Abbey Road studios, where the band members were working on their debut album *The Piper at the Gates of Dawn* (1967) under the supervision of Norman "Normal" Smith. The experience of witnessing the Beatles in the act of recording "Lovely Rita" allegedly inspired Pink Floyd to compose the instrumental "Pow R. Toc H.," a track from *The Piper at the Gates of Dawn.*

PERSONNEL

Lennon: Gibson J-160E, Comb and Toilet Paper
McCartney: Vocal, Rickenbacker 4001S, Piano, Comb and Toilet Paper
Harrison: Sonic Blue Fender Stratocaster, Gibson J-160E, Comb and Toilet Paper
Starr: Ludwig Oyster Black Pearl Drums
Martin: Piano

ALBUM APPEARANCE: *Sgt. Pepper's Lonely Hearts Club Band.*

See also: "Paul Is Dead" Hoax; *Sgt. Pepper's Lonely Hearts Club Band* (LP).

"Lucy in the Sky with Diamonds" (Lennon–McCartney)

"Lucy in the Sky with Diamonds" is a song on the Beatles' *Sgt. Pepper's Lonely Hearts Club Band* album.

AUTHORSHIP AND BACKGROUND

Written by Lennon with assistance from McCartney, the concept of imagined experience is the thematic focus of "Lucy in the Sky with Diamonds," the colorful, Lewis Carroll-inspired musical adventure that found its origins in three-year-old Julian Lennon's painting of a classmate named Lucy: "It's Lucy, in the sky, with diamonds," he told his father.

As Lennon remembered,

> My son Julian came in one day with a picture he painted about a school friend of his named Lucy. He had sketched in some stars in the sky and called it "Lucy in the Sky with Diamonds." Simple. The images were from "Alice in Wonderland." It was Alice in the boat. She is buying an egg and it turns into Humpty Dumpty. The woman serving in the shop turns into a sheep and the next minute they are rowing in a rowing boat somewhere and I was visualizing that. There was also the image of the female who would someday come save me—a "girl with kaleidoscope eyes" who would come out of the sky. It turned out to be Yoko, though I hadn't met Yoko yet. So maybe it should be "Yoko in the Sky with Diamonds." It was purely unconscious that it came out to be LSD. Until somebody pointed it out, I never even thought it, I mean, who would ever bother to look at initials of a title? It's *not* an acid song. (Harry 2011, 574)

As it turned out, by the time that he composed "Lucy in the Sky with Diamonds," Lennon had already met Ono on November 8, 1966, at the Indica Gallery. In Lennon's recollection, McCartney composed the song's organ introduction, as well as the line about "newspaper taxis."

RECORDING SESSIONS

Produced by Martin, "Lucy in the Sky with Diamonds" was recorded at Abbey Road Studios on March 1, 1967, with an additional overdubbing session on March 2.

In the composition's phantasmagoria, the Beatles achieve their most vivid instance of musical timbre by merging the nonsensicality and visual imagery of Lennon's lyrics with the ADT-treated sounds of McCartney's imaginative Lowrey organ introduction, Harrison's tamboura, and Lennon's dreamy lead vocal. The sense of mystery and adventure is heightened by shifts in both key and time signature. The verses float along merrily in 3/4 time, while common time establishes a more insistent mood for the chorus. According to Lennon, the song's principal images hail from *Through the Looking-Glass, and What Alice Found There* (1871), the sequel to Carroll's *Alice's Adventures in Wonderland* (1865). In this way, "Lucy in the Sky with Diamonds" invokes in particular the momentous scene in *Through the Looking-Glass* as Alice glides down the river in her boat—"Lingering onward dreamily"—setting her magical journey into motion.

As Julian Lennon later remarked, "I don't know why I called it that or why it stood out from all my other drawings, but I obviously had an affection for Lucy at that age. I used to show Dad everything I'd built or painted at school,

John Lennon poses with his four-year-old son, Julian, in front of Lennon's psychedelic Rolls-Royce in 1967. The Beatles' 1967 classic "Lucy in the Sky with Diamonds," a song filled with psychedelic imagery, was inspired by the young Julian, who came home one day with a painting of a classmate, telling his father, "It's Lucy, in the sky, with diamonds." (Keystone-France/Gamma-Keystone/Getty Images)

and this one sparked off the idea for a song about 'Lucy in the Sky with Diamonds.'" Julian sat next to Lucy O'Donnell, the subject of his painting, at Heath House School. The title's acrostic is often erroneously believed to be a not-so-subtle reference to the frequent acid trips that the Beatles had been taking during this period.

PERSONNEL

Lennon: Vocal, Epiphone Casino, Piano
McCartney: Rickenbacker 4001S, Lowrey Organ, Backing Vocal
Harrison: Sonic Blue Fender Stratocaster, Gibson J-160E, Tamboura, Backing Vocal
Starr: Ludwig Oyster Black Pearl Drums, Maracas

LEGACY AND INFLUENCE

In 2010, *Rolling Stone* ranked "Lucy in the Sky with Diamonds" as #19 on the magazine's list of *The Beatles' 100 Greatest Songs*.

CONTROVERSY

"Lucy in the Sky with Diamonds" was banned by the BBC for the LSD acronym. In the Beatles' defense, Pete Shotton, John's boyhood friend, later remarked that "I also happened to be there the day Julian came home from school with a pastel drawing of his classmate Lucy's face against a backdrop of exploding, multicolored stars. Unusually impressed with his son's handiwork, John asked what the drawing was called. 'It's *Lucy in the Sky with Diamonds*, Daddy,' Julian replied." Shotton added that "Though John was certainly ingesting inordinate amounts of acid around the time he wrote 'Lucy in the Sky with Diamonds,' the pun was indeed sheer coincidence" (Dowlding 1989, 166).

After years of denying that "Lucy in the Sky with Diamonds" had anything to do with LSD, McCartney seemed to reverse his position during a 2004 interview with the *Weekly Standard*'s Victorino Matus, stating that

A song like "Got to Get You into My Life"—that's directly about pot, although everyone missed it at the time. "Day Tripper"—that's one about acid. "Lucy in the Sky"—that's pretty obvious. There's others that make subtle hints about drugs, but, you know, it's easy to overestimate the influence of drugs on the Beatles' music. (*Washington Post* 2004)

ALBUM APPEARANCES: *Sgt. Pepper's Lonely Hearts Club Band*; *The Beatles, 1967–1970*; *Anthology 2*; *Love*.

See also: Ono, Yoko; *Sgt. Pepper's Lonely Hearts Club Band* (LP).

Lynne, Jeff (1947–)

Born in Birmingham, England, on December 30, 1947, Lynne was the leader and creative force behind the Electric Light Orchestra (ELO), a band that sold more than 50 million records and released such best-selling albums as *A New World Record* (1976) and *Out of the Blue* (1977). At the conclusion of ELO's heyday, he shifted his attention to record production. In addition to acclaimed albums by Roy Orbison and Tom Petty, he worked extensively with Harrison, with whom he coproduced the former Beatle's highly successful *Cloud Nine* album (1987), which spawned hit singles in "Got My Mind Set on You" and "When We Was Fab." He also performed a key role in the Traveling Wilburys, both as producer and musician. During the 1990s, he was invited to produce the surviving Beatles' recordings of the unreleased Lennon compositions "Free as a Bird" and "Real Love" as part of the band's blockbuster *Anthology* series. In the ensuing years, he produced McCartney's acclaimed *Flaming Pie* (1997) album, as well as Harrison's posthumously released studio album *Brainwashed* (2002). In 2002, he performed in the *Concert for George* at London's Royal Albert Hall, with contributing lead vocals on cover versions of Harrison's "The Inner Light," "I Want to Tell You," and "Give Me Love (Give Me Peace on Earth)." In 2012, he was nominated for induction into the Songwriters' Hall of Fame for such songs as "Mr. Blue Sky" and "Telephone Line."

See also: The Traveling Wilburys.

M

"Maggie Mae" (Harrison–Lennon–McCartney–Starr)

"Maggie Mae" is a song on the Beatles' *Let It Be* album.

AUTHORSHIP AND BACKGROUND

"Maggie Mae" is a traditional 19th-century Liverpool ditty about a thieving prostitute that the Beatles had performed throughout their early years. The group often used the song as a warm-up before live performances.

RECORDING SESSIONS

Produced by Martin with postproduction by Phil Spector, the Beatles recorded "Maggie Mae" at Apple Studio on January 24, 1969. A moment of pure spontaneity during the *Get Back* sessions, the Beatles concocted a hasty rendition of "Maggie Mae" between takes of "Two of Us." After a couple of false starts, they managed to play the song for some 40 seconds before it fell into total collapse.

PERSONNEL

> Lennon: Vocal, Gibson J-160E
> McCartney: Vocal, Martin D-28
> Harrison: Fender Rosewood Telecaster
> Starr: Ludwig Hollywood Maple Drums

ALBUM APPEARANCE: *Let It Be*.

See also: *Let It Be* (LP); *Let It Be . . . Naked* (LP).

"Magical Mystery Tour" (Lennon–McCartney)

"Magical Mystery Tour" is a song on the Beatles' *Magical Mystery Tour* album.

AUTHORSHIP AND BACKGROUND

Written by McCartney with assistance from Lennon, "Magical Mystery Tour" was explicitly conceived by the songwriter as the main title theme for the Beatles' next film project.

As McCartney later remarked,

> "Magical Mystery Tour" was co-written by John and I, very much in our fair-ground period. One of our great inspirations was always the barker: "Roll up! Roll up!" The promise of something—the newspaper ad that says "guaranteed not to crack," the "high class" butcher, "satisfaction guaranteed" from *Sgt. Pepper*. You'll find that pervades a lot of my songs. If you look at all the Lennon/McCartney things, it's a thing we do a lot. (Miles 1997, 352)

As Lennon remembered, "Magical Mystery Tour" was "Paul's song. Maybe I did part of it, but it was his concept" (Lennon and Ono 2000, 185).

RECORDING SESSIONS

Produced by Martin, "Magical Mystery Tour" was recorded at Abbey Road Studios on April 25, 1967. Additional overdubbing sessions were held on April 26 and 27, May 3, and November 7.

The Beatles convened at Abbey Road Studios in late April 1967, where they began working on "Magical Mystery Tour," the title track for their latest fantasia. During the first session, sound effects—including the *vroom* of a tour bus panning from the left to right sound channels—were drawn from the EMI tape library's *Volume 36: Traffic Noise Stereo.* After preparing the song's basic rhythm track with his trusty Rickenbacker, Lennon on his Jumbo, and Harrison on "Rocky," the nickname for his treasured Fender Strat, McCartney tasked Mal Evans with the job of canvassing bus stations in order to raid authentic mystery tour posters for lyric ideas, à la Lennon's found object for "Being for the Benefit of Mr. Kite!"

In addition to a glockenspiel, the Beatles added vocal tracks—including Lennon ad-libbing "Step right this way!"—before overdubbing a quartet of trumpets, led by the ubiquitous David Mason, who delivered a spirited barrage of high-velocity 16th notes. The music offers a panoply of styles and instrumentation—including a furtive "mock *misterioso*" section, in Tim Riley's words (1988, 237).

PERSONNEL

Lennon: Gibson J-160E, Percussion, Backing Vocal
McCartney: Vocal, Rickenbacker 4001S, Piano
Harrison: Sonic Blue Fender Stratocaster, Percussion, Backing Vocal
Starr: Ludwig Oyster Black Pearl Drums, Percussion
Neil Aspinall: Percussion
Evans: Percussion

Studio Musicians: Brass Accompaniment conducted by Martin
Roy Copestake, Elgar Howarth, David Mason, John Wilbraham: Trumpet

ALBUM APPEARANCES: *Magical Mystery Tour*; *The Beatles, 1967–1970*; *Reel Music*.

See also: Evans, Mal; *Magical Mystery Tour* (LP).

Magical Mystery Tour (LP)

November 27, 1967, Capitol MAL 2835 (mono)/SMAL 2835 (stereo)

As the soundtrack for the television movie of the same name, *Magical Mystery Tour* was released on the Capitol label on November 27, 1967, in the United States. In the United Kingdom, the Beatles released a truncated, two-disc EP version of the soundtrack on December 8, 1967. On November 19, 1976, Parlophone released the American LP version in the United Kingdom, thus standardizing the full-length version of *Magical Mystery Tour* among their album catalogue.

Magical Mystery Tour was released as a stereo compact disc (CD) on September 21, 1987. It was remastered and rereleased as a stereo CD on September 9, 2009. A remastered mono release was also made available at this time as part of a limited edition box set entitled *The Beatles in Mono*.

BACKGROUND AND RECORDING SESSIONS

Produced by Martin with Geoff Emerick, Keith Grant, and Ken Scott as his sound engineers, *Magical Mystery Tour* was recorded on four-track equipment during multiple, sporadic sessions from November 24, 1966, through November 7, 1967, at Abbey Road Studios, Chappell Sound Studio, and Olympic Sound Studios.

The idea for the Beatles' *Magical Mystery Tour* project found its roots in McCartney's April 11, 1967, return flight to London from the United States, where he had squired the touring Jane Asher around Los Angeles and Denver. With Evans in tow, McCartney hastily concocted lyrics for "Magical Mystery Tour," the title track for his proposed made-for-television movie about the popular British seaside tours that he remembered from his youth. As McCartney recalled,

> The *Mystery* show was conceived way back in Los Angeles. On the plane. You know they give you those big menus, and I had a pen and everything and started drawing on this menu and I had this idea. In England, they have these things called mystery tours. And you go on them and you pay so much and you don't know where you're going. So the idea was to have this little thing advertised in the shop windows somewhere called *Magical Mystery Tours*. (Gambaccini 1976, 47, 48)

Alive in McCartney's imagination before *Sgt. Pepper* even hit the stores, *Magical Mystery Tour* also offered an affectionate nod to Ken Kesey's Merry Pranksters, who conducted "Acid Tests" while trolling America's highways in a multicolored school bus.

For the *Magical Mystery Tour* project, the Beatles assembled a raft of new material in order to fill out the soundtrack for their impending made-for-television film. On September 1, 1967, the group had convened at McCartney's house on Cavendish Avenue, where he unveiled his *Magical Mystery Tour* schema. His outline for the movie consisted solely of a circle representing 60 minutes, with eight pie-shaped segments apportioned into sketches and musical numbers.

The release of the *Magical Mystery Tour* EP in early December 1967 met with similar runaway success throughout the holiday season, as did the LP release in the United States. *Magical Mystery Tour* later emerged as a central component of the 1969 "Paul Is Dead" hysteria. The album contains a number of so-called death clues, including the album's cover depicting the image of a black walrus, which is believed to represent death in some parts of Scandinavia. In addition to the image of McCartney wearing a black carnation during the "Your Mother Should Know" sequence, McCartney sits behind a desk in front of a sign bearing the prophetic words "I WaS." Such clues were later cited as evidence in support of an urban legend about McCartney's alleged demise and subsequent replacement by a look-alike after a 1966 automobile accident.

TRACK LISTING

Side 1: "Magical Mystery Tour"; "The Fool on the Hill"; "Flying"; "Blue Jay Way"; "Your Mother Should Know"; "I Am the Walrus."
Side 2: "Hello, Goodbye"; "Strawberry Fields Forever"; "Penny Lane"; "Baby, You're a Rich Man"; "All You Need Is Love."

COVER ARTWORK

Designed by pop artist John Van Hamersveld (1941–), the *Magical Mystery Tour* cover features Lennon costumed in black as a walrus, McCartney as a hippopotamus, Harrison as a rabbit, and Starr as a chicken. As with *Sgt. Pepper's Lonely Hearts Club Band*, the album's packaging included a gatefold sleeve design. Both the EP and LP releases of *Magical Mystery Tour* included a booklet consisting of song lyrics and still photographs from the movie.

CHART PERFORMANCE

U.K.: #31 (certified by the BPI as "Gold," with more than 100,000 copies sold).
U.S.: #1 (certified by the RIAA as "6x Multi Platinum," with more than 6 million copies sold).

LEGACY AND INFLUENCE

In 1969, *Magical Mystery Tour* was nominated for a Grammy Award for Album of the Year at the 11th Grammy Awards.

See also: Emerick, Geoff; *Magical Mystery Tour* (TV Film); *Magical Mystery Tour* (U.K. EP); Martin, George; "Paul Is Dead" Hoax.

Magical Mystery Tour (TV Film)

The idea for the Beatles' *Magical Mystery Tour* project found its genesis in McCartney's April 11, 1967, return flight to London from the United States, when he hastily composed lyrics for "Magical Mystery Tour." Later, on September 1, the group had assembled at McCartney's house on Cavendish Avenue, where he unveiled his *Magical Mystery Tour* schema. His outline for the movie consisted solely of a circle representing 60 minutes, with eight pie-shaped segments apportioned into sketches and musical numbers:

1. Commercial introduction. Get on the coach. Courier introduces.
2. Coach people meet each other / (Song, Fool on the Hill)
3. marathon—laboratory sequence.
4. smiling face. LUNCH. Mangoes, tropical (magician)
5. and 6. Dreams.
6. Stripper & band.
7. Song.

END. (Spitz 2005, 720, 721)

Postponing their plans to join the Maharishi in India for a lengthy retreat, the group decided to begin principal photography for their holiday-inspired lark during the week of September 11, 1967. Although he had begun working on the idea of filming a mystery tour since April, McCartney now had a far different motive in mind, given the leadership vacuum that had emerged within the band after Brian Epstein's death on August 27, 1967. "If the others clear off to India again now on another meditation trip," he confided in Tony Barrow, "I think there's a very real danger that we'll never come back together again as a working group. On the other hand, if I can persuade them today that we should go straight into shooting this film, it could save the Beatles" (Barrow 1999, [6]).

With the production of their film music firmly underway, the Beatles spent five days in mid-September 1967 on location in Surrey, Devonshire, Cornwall, and Somerset. Evans and Neil Aspinall rounded up 33 actors—including such British comic personalities as Jessie Robbins, Derek Royle, Ivor Cutler, and Victor Spinetti—along with four cameramen, a soundman, and a technical advisor. Amazingly, Ringo

John Lennon emerges from a tent during the filming of the made-for-television film *Magical Mystery Tour,* on September 16, 1967. The chaotic, nonsensical film, haphazardly directed by the band and largely improvised, was one of the group's rare critical and popular flops. (Chapman/Express/Hulton Archive/Getty Images)

Starr [as Richard Starkey] was credited as the director of photography, adding yet another layer of mythology to the drummer's ever-growing legend, while the Beatles were acknowledged collectively as the project's directors. Having rented a 62-seat bus as their mobile prop, the troupe patrolled the English countryside, hampered much of the time by a growing phalanx of media and fans who trailed their every move. Eventually, the production settled for another five days in the large empty hangars of Kent's West Malling Air Station, which doubled as their soundstage. At the end of October, McCartney traveled to Nice with a cameraman to film a daydream sequence, effectively bringing the movie's principal photography to a close.

As for the *Magical Mystery Tour* music, the songs in order of their appearance in the movie included

"Magical Mystery Tour"
"The Fool on the Hill"
"She Loves You" (played during the marathon on a fairground organ)
"Flying"
"All My Loving" (as orchestrated background music)
"I Am the Walrus"
"Jessie's Dream" (unreleased instrumental track)
"Blue Jay Way"
"Death Cab for Cutie" (performed by the Bonzo Dog Doo-Dah Band)

"Your Mother Should Know"
"Magical Mystery Tour"
"Hello, Goodbye" (end credits)

Having seen the finished product and sensing imminent disaster, Peter Brown recommended that the Beatles mothball the *Magical Mystery Tour* movie for the foreseeable future: "I tried to suggest writing off the £40,000 [in production expenses] and moving on. But Paul didn't know it was a mess and insisted on making the deal [with the BBC]" (Spitz 2005, 734).

As perhaps their single greatest artistic failure, the film version of *Magical Mystery Tour* showcases the band members in a beguiling series of burlesques that is memorable solely for its utter disarray. The film's chaotic narrative features musical iterations from Beatles films past, including a marching band's intentionally cloying version of "She Loves You" and a string arrangement of "All My Loving" during a romantic interlude involving Starr's wanton Aunt Jessie (Robbins) and staid courier Buster Bloodvessel (Cutler). In the movie's finest moments, it offers quasi-music videos for "The Fool on the Hill," "I Am the Walrus," and "Blue Jay Way." It reaches its ridiculous nadir in a variety of nonsensical skits—set in, of all places, an army recruiter's office and a strip club—that attempt to recall the zany vignettes inherent in *A Hard Day's Night* and *Help!* The poor reviews that *Magical Mystery Tour* received after its debut on Boxing Day (December 26, 1967) on the BBC—which premiered the film in black and white, thus mitigating its multicolored virtues—revealed the awful reality of its failure. ABC television, which owned the rights to broadcast *Magical Mystery Tour* in the United States, opted not to air the film at all.

The reviews themselves were swift and merciless. "The bigger they are, the harder they fall. And what a fall it was," James Thomas wrote in the *Daily Express*. "The whole boring saga confirmed a long held suspicion of mine that the Beatles are four pleasant young men who have made so much money that they can apparently afford to be contemptuous of the public" (Badman 2001, 332, 333). Meanwhile, the *Daily Sketch* couldn't help poking fun at the Beatles' recent forays into Eastern mysticism: "Whoever authorized the showing of the film on BBC1 should be condemned to a year squatting at the feet of the Maharishi Mahesh Yogi." For its part, the *Daily Mirror* condemned *Magical Mystery Tour* as "Rubbish . . . Piffle . . . Nonsense!" (Badman 2001, 332, 333). For the Beatles, it was a critical drubbing that proved difficult to stomach—especially after enjoying the artistic heights of *Sgt. Pepper's Lonely Hearts Club Band*.

As McCartney later recalled, "It was shown on BBC1 on Boxing Day, which is traditionally music hall and Bruce Forsyth and Jimmy Tarbuck time. Now we had this very stoned show on, just when everyone's getting over Christmas. I think a few people were surprised. The critics certainly had a field day and said, 'Oh, disaster, disaster!' " (Beatles 2000, 273).

See also: Aspinall, Neil; Evans, Mal; *Magical Mystery Tour* (LP).

Magical Mystery Tour (U.K. EP)

December 8, 1967, Parlophone MMT-1 (mono)/SMMT-1 (stereo)

Released on December 8, 1967, *Magical Mystery Tour* was the Beatles' 13th and final EP to be released in the United Kingdom.

BACKGROUND

Produced by Martin, the *Magical Mystery Tour* double EP consists of new Beatles composition associated with soundtrack for the television movie of the same name. As with *Sgt. Pepper's Lonely Hearts Club Band*, the album's packaging included a gatefold sleeve design. Both the EP and LP releases of *Magical Mystery Tour* included a booklet consisting of song lyrics and still photographs from the movie.

Of the Beatles' 13 EP releases in the United Kingdom, only two were composed of new material that had not been culled from one of their albums—*Magical Mystery Tour* and the 1964 U.K. release of the *Long Tall Sally* EP. On November 19, 1976, Parlophone released the American LP version in the United Kingdom, thus standardizing the full-length version of *Magical Mystery Tour* among their album catalogue.

TRACK LISTING

A: "Magical Mystery Tour"; "Your Mother Should Know."
B: "I Am the Walrus."
C: "The Fool on the Hill"; "Flying."
D: "Blue Jay Way."

CHART PERFORMANCE

U.K.: #2.

See also: *Magical Mystery Tour* (LP); *Magical Mystery Tour* (TV Film).

Maharishi Mahesh Yogi (1918–2008)

Born in Jabalpur, British Raj (now Madhya Pradesh, India), on January 12, 1918, Maharishi Mahesh Yogi was a central spiritual and philosophical influence upon the Beatles. Long before he came into the Fab Four's orbit, the Maharishi had been on a journey of spiritual regeneration for much of his life. In 1945, he began a personal program of solitary meditation in the Himalayas that lasted for more than a decade. When he literally came down from the mountain, he devoted himself to spreading traditional Indian teachings to the masses, a project that he started in 1957 with the founding of the Spiritual Regeneration Movement, the crusade that eventually brought him to London during the Summer of Love. On August 24, 1967, Harrison, Lennon, and McCartney attended a lecture given by the Maharishi at the Hyde Park Hilton. Of particular interest to the Beatles was the Maharishi's development of an increasingly popular technique known as Transcendental Meditation. He urged his followers to engage in a pair of 20-minute daily sessions in which they focus on their mantra, the simple phrase whose repetition promises to open new vistas of spirituality, inner calm, and human consciousness. Increasingly bemused by the prison-house of their celebrity, the Beatles gravitated rather naturally to the tiny, charismatic man in the lotus position, whose life and message were devoted to individual contentment and communal peace.

Swept up in their latest euphoria, the Beatles trundled off to Euston Station on August 25, 1967, where they boarded the train for University College in Bangor, Wales, the site of the Maharishi's upcoming Transcendental Meditation seminar. The Beatles' entourage included their significant others, save for Starr's wife Maureen, who had given birth to their son Jason six days earlier. The usual rock retinue was in tow, including Mick Jagger, Marianne Faithfull, and Donovan. Epstein

had been invited to attend the seminar by Lennon, but the manager refused, having already decided to go out on the town with Brown. As it turned out, the Beatles' spiritual excursion to Wales was short-lived, their exhilaration replaced by shock when they learned of Epstein's death, at the relatively tender age of 32, on August 27.

After the disastrous reception of the *Magical Mystery Tour* television film in December 1967, the Beatles resumed their studies with the Maharishi in February 1968, having rejoined the Maharishi in Rishikesh, India, the holy city that rests on the banks of the Ganges. The band's entourage included the Beatles' significant others, Pattie Harrison's sister Jenny Boyd,

Maharishi Mahesh Yogi, founder of the International Meditation Society and guru of the Beatles, poses in London on August 24, 1967. (AP Photo)

Donovan, the Beach Boys' Mike Love, jazz flautist Paul Horn, and the ever-present "Magic Alex" Mardas. Despite its remote location, the Maharishi's six-acre compound was replete with creature comforts, including a swimming pool, a laundry, a post office, and a lecture hall from which the holy man delivered his teachings to his assembled guests. At one point, the Maharishi arranged for a pair of helicopters to fly his distinguished visitors on a sightseeing tour up and down the Ganges. Each of the Beatles responded to their experience in the ashram in radically different ways. Complaining about the spicy cuisine, Starr left after only 10 days, having exhausted his secret supply of Heinz Baked Beans. For McCartney, life in Rishikesh offered a sublime opportunity to cleanse his mind and replenish his writerly muse. When he and girlfriend Asher left after six weeks in the compound, he graciously thanked their host: "Maharishi, you will never fathom what these days have meant to us. To have the unbroken peace and quiet and all your loving attention—only a Beatle could know the value of this" (De Herrera 2003, 237). For Harrison, it was one of life's great privileges to ponder the Maharishi's lectures and practice Transcendental Meditation in the ashram. But of all the Beatles' reactions to the experience, Lennon's ended up being the most peculiar. At one point, he announced, with uncharacteristic ebullience, that "we're going to build a transmitter powerful enough to broadcast Maharishi's wisdom to all parts of the globe—right here in Rishikesh" (De Herrera 2003, 238). He went so far as to fantasize about a new life for himself in the Maharishi's orbit, suggesting to the holy man that he and wife Cynthia retrieve young Julian from England and join the Maharishi in order to continue their spiritual training in Kashmir. Yet as Lennon gravitated ever closer to the Maharishi, Magic Alex grew increasingly suspicious of their host.

Within a few days, Lennon's mood abruptly shifted from exultance to gloom without explanation. To everyone's astonishment, Lennon gruffly declared that he and Harrison were leaving the compound immediately. When questioned by one of the Maharishi's followers about his sudden change of heart, Lennon angrily replied: "If you want to know why, ask your f—in' precious guru" (De Herrera 2003, 244). Lennon's motives later became clear in "Sexy Sadie," his *White Album*-era composition that explored the Beatles' experiences under the Maharishi's tutelage, with Lennon singing "We gave you everything we owned just to sit at your table." Lennon had written the song as a caustic critique of the Maharishi, the ostensibly celibate holy man who had, according to a rumor floating around the ashram courtesy of Magic Alex, made sexual advances upon a young woman staying at the compound. Having discovered what he believed to be an unforgivable hypocrisy, Lennon insisted that the Beatles' entourage depart the ashram immediately. When the incredulous Maharishi inquired about his guest's sudden impulse to leave, Lennon offered a bitter riposte: "Well, if you're so cosmic, you'll know why." Lennon had intended to entitle the song "Maharishi," although at Harrison's urging, he changed "Maharishi" to "Sexy Sadie" in advance of recording the Esher demos (Spizer 2003, 112).

As it turns out, the rumors about the Maharishi's behavior may have been fallacious—and perhaps even the vitriolic work of Magic Alex. According to Nancy Cooke de Herrera, the impetus for Lennon's sudden change of heart had relatively little to do with Magic Alex's act of character assassination, but rather with a competing movie deal in which the Maharishi had agreed to allow Four Star Productions to film his life story instead of Apple Corps (De Herrera 2003, 245). In 1993, Harrison asked the Maharishi for forgiveness for the events of 1968, claiming he had confirmed that the allegations were false. According to Deepak Chopra, the Maharishi told Harrison that "there's nothing to forgive—you're angels in disguise" (Waldman 2001).

Regardless of the background involving the unhappy conclusion to the Beatles' 1968 visit to the Maharishi's ashram, the group's experiences had far-reaching effects on their music, particularly in terms of the new and innovative musical innovations associated with *The Beatles* (*The White Album*), which commenced in May 1968. Years later, McCartney included the song "Cosmically Conscious," which he had composed in Rishikesh, as a hidden track on his *Off the Ground* album (1991). As for the Maharishi, he continued his work, particularly in terms of espousing the merits of Transcendental Meditation, until his death in the Netherlands on February 5, 2008, at age 90.

See also: *The Beatles* (*The White Album*) (LP); Epstein, Brian.

"Martha My Dear" (Lennon–McCartney)

"Martha My Dear" is a song on *The Beatles* (*The White Album*).

AUTHORSHIP AND BACKGROUND

Written by McCartney, "Martha My Dear" offers a musical valentine, presumably, to the songwriter's wooly Old English Sheepdog Martha. McCartney has also suggested that the song may concern itself with Asher, who broke off her engagement to the Beatle during the production of *The White Album*.

As McCartney later recalled, "I just start singing some words with a tune, you know what I mean. Mainly I'm just doing a tune and then some words come into my head, you know. And these happened to be 'Martha My Dear, though I spend my days in conversation.' So you can read anything you like into it, but really it's just a song. It's me singing to my dog" (Cadogan 2008, 206).

RECORDING SESSIONS

Produced and arranged by Martin, "Martha My Dear" was recorded at Trident Studios on October 4, 1968, with an additional overdubbing session on October 5.

PERSONNEL

McCartney: Vocal, Piano, Rickenbacker 4001S, Fender Esquire
Starr: Ludwig Oyster Black Pearl Drums
Studio Musicians: Brass and String Accompaniment conducted by Martin
Les Maddox, Dennis McConnell, Bernard Miller, Lou Soufier: Violin
Leo Birnbaum, Henry Myerscough: Viola
Frederick Alexander, Reginald Kilbey: Cello
Leon Calvert, Ronnie Hughes, Stanley Reynolds: Trumpet
Leon Calvert: Flügelhorn
Tony Tunstall: Horn
Ted Barker: Trombone
Alf Reece: Tuba

ALBUM APPEARANCE: *The Beatles* (*The White Album*).

See also: *The Beatles* (*The White Album*) (LP).

Martin, George (1926–2016)

The most widely acclaimed record producer of his generation, Martin enjoyed unparalleled success during a 50-year musical career in which he oversaw the production of some 30 #1 hits and more than 700 recordings. For many rock historians, he truly deserves the title of being the "fifth Beatle," despite "Murray the K." Kaufman's well-known comments to the contrary. Martin not only transformed the Beatles into popular music's most influential recording artists, but also handled key duties involving the musical arrangement and orchestration of their mid- to late-period recordings.

Born George Henry Martin on January 3, 1926, in Holloway, North London, Martin taught himself to play piano. By the age of 16, he was an active member of his school's dance band. During World War II, he served in the British Navy's aviation unit, where he achieved the rank of Lieutenant. McCartney credits Martin's military service with the leadership abilities that assisted the producer in shaping the Beatles as his musical protégées: "I think that's where George got his excellent bedside manner. He'd dealt with navigators and pilots. He could deal with us when we got out of line" (Houston 2000).

In 1947, Martin enrolled in London's Guildhall School of Music, where he pursued his studies in composition and classical music orchestration. After specializing in piano and oboe, he graduated in 1950 and found employment at the EMI Group's Parlophone Records, where his responsibilities included managing the label's catalogue of classical recordings. In the ensuing years, he served as producer for a variety of artists, ranging from Cleo Laine and Stan Getz to Humphrey Lyttelton and Judy Garland. He also made a name for himself producing comedy

The Beatles collaborate with their producer George Martin at a recording session for the Parlophone label, ca. 1963. (Keystone/Hulton Archive/Getty Images)

records by Peter Ustinov, Peter Cook, Dudley Moore, and the Goons. In 1955, he was appointed as head of Parlophone at the relatively youthful age of 29.

In the early 1960s, Martin planned to expand Parlophone's catalogue by venturing into the evolving world of pop music. He came into the Beatles' orbit via Brian Epstein. Having been rejected by EMI and Decca, as well as by two other major British record firms, Pye and Philips, Epstein was crestfallen as he left Decca House after learning about their most recent rejection of his charges following their failed New Year's audition with the prestigious label. With nothing to lose, he sought out Bob Boast, who managed London's HMV record store on Oxford Street. Although Boast was unimpressed with the Decca audition tapes, he suggested that Epstein cut an acetate of the best tracks in order to present his product more effectively to the city's A&R men. While Epstein waited, sound engineer Jim Foy cut the acetate in the studio below the HMV. Liking what he heard, Foy introduced Epstein to Sid Colman, who worked as the general manager of Ardmore and Beechwood, the influential London music publisher. As with the HMV, Ardmore and Beechwood were members of the EMI corporate family, and Colman felt that it was in the company's best interest to avoid losing the Beatles to their competitors. Recognizing that few, if any, of the EMI in-house producers were willing to take on the Beatles, Colman directed Epstein to Martin at Parlophone, the bottom of the proverbial barrel amongst EMI's numerous subsidiary labels. While Martin listened to Epstein's increasingly tiresome pitch that the Beatles were bigger than Elvis, he held firm on his resolve not to offer them a contract without auditioning them first.

A few months later, on May 9, 1962, Epstein made one last effort to win a contract from Parlophone. During a morning appointment with Martin at EMI Studios in St. John's Wood, London, Epstein toned down the overconfident approach that he had employed back in February. To Epstein's genuine surprise, Martin agreed to provide the Beatles with a recording contract without having met them, much less auditioned them. In truth, the contract saddled EMI with very little in the way of risk—the Beatles' contract would only become binding if Martin were satisfied with the audition; otherwise, it wasn't worth the paper upon which it was printed. But Epstein was ecstatic. After arranging for the Beatles' audition at EMI Studios on June 6, he telegrammed the Beatles in Germany: "Congratulations, boys. EMI request recording session. Rehearse new material." He posted a second message to the *Mersey Beat* that same day in which he announced that the Beatles had secured a recording contract from Parlophone. In both instances, he neglected to account for the extremely provisional nature of the agreement with Martin.

In the producer's mind, Martin had merely provided the band with a provisional recording contract contingent upon the outcome of an audition scheduled for June 6, 1962. Mark Lewisohn's meticulous research has unearthed an EMI "red form" indicating that the Beatles were already under contract—and, hence, not required to audition during a so-called artist test—at the June 6 session. When confronted with the evidence by Lewisohn, Martin refused to reconsider the circumstances of his first meeting with the Beatles: "Why on earth would I have signed a group before I even saw them? I would never have done that, it's preposterous" (Lewisohn 2004, 46). Yet additional testimony from Ken Townsend underscores Lewisohn's conclusion: "The difference between an artist test and a commercial test is that the former are not paid to undertake the test," Townsend recalled, "but the Beatles were paid official MU [Musicians Union] rates for that session" (Ryan and Kehew 2006, 346).

But as Elvis Costello notes, the Beatles, with their North Country roots, were fortunate to have a contract—*any* contract—at all: "The fact that four young musicians from Liverpool were assigned to the EMI comedy imprint, Parlophone, and the staff producer responsible for the comedy output, gives us a glimpse of a number of casual regional assumptions and the hierarchies of early '60s England" (Costello 2006, x). During the Beatles' historic first visit to Abbey Road Studios, Martin was impressed with their raw musical gifts, as well as with their good-natured sense of humor. At first glance, Martin's partnership with the Beatles seemed like an unlikely pairing; the classically trained, 36-year-old producer seemed to have little in common with four North Country lads from Liverpool. As

Beatles biographer Ray Coleman observes, though, their relationship "began as record producer and young pop stars and developed into that of a wise uncle, and eventually to friendship" ("A Day in the Life" 1999).

After producing the band's first #1 hit, "Please Please Me," and assisting them in crafting the sound that flowered into the global phenomenon known as Beatlemania, Martin challenged the Beatles as both songwriters and musicians by introducing them to classical influences and encouraging the experimentation that characterized their artistic heights in the late 1960s. In addition to providing them with nuggets of recording artistry such as the "wound-up piano" technique, he shared his own musical performances with the band—most notably, the piano solo on "In My Life"—while also composing such classical arrangements on their behalf as the groundbreaking "Yesterday" and "Eleanor Rigby" orchestrations, among a host of others. In terms of his own professional career, he eventually severed his relationship with the EMI Group after the conglomerate refused to increase his paltry salary despite his considerable role in the Beatles' international success. In 1965, he left EMI and established AIR (Associated Independent Recordings), an independent production company.

Peter Asher, the brother of McCartney's erstwhile fiancée Jane Asher and one of the stars of 1960s pop duo Peter and Gordon, and later a talented musical producer himself, lauds Martin for his significant role in shaping the Beatles' astounding musical development:

> The Beatles were brimming over with brilliant ideas and radical concepts, but it took extraordinary diplomacy, exceptional musical expertise, limitless patience, and visionary clarity to bring these ideas to fruition and greatness. Sometimes, George's genius was knowing when to jump in and offer musical advice; sometimes, it was knowing when to go down to the canteen and have a cup of tea, letting them get on with whatever they were up to. ("A Day in the Life" 1999)

During his post-Beatles career, Martin produced albums by a variety of different artists, including Jeff Beck, America, Elton John, Celine Dion, the Little River Band, and Cheap Trick. In addition to producing McCartney's celebrated *Tug of War* (1982) album, he supervised the Beatles' *Anthology* series during the mid-1990s, as well as the production of their remarkably successful compilation, *The Beatles 1*, in 2000. His career includes a number of noteworthy milestones. In 1963, for instance, recordings produced by Martin spent an unprecedented 37 weeks in the #1 position on British record charts. In 1995, he was honored with a knighthood. In 1996, he directed an acclaimed benefit concert starring McCartney, Eric Clapton, Elton John, and Sting on behalf of the volcano-ravaged island of Montserrat, the former home of one of AIR's recording studios. He produced his last #1 single, John's "Candle in the Wind '97," to commemorate the tragic death of Princess Diana. In 1998, he punctuated his musical career with the release of *In My Life*, an album of Beatles songs performed by several world-renowned musicians and actors, including Phil Collins, Celine Dion, and Sean Connery. Martin was the father of four children: Alexis and Gregory with first wife Sheena Chisholm, and Lucie and Giles with second wife Judy Lockhart-Smith. He authored four books about his experiences: *All You Need Is Ears* (1979), *Making Music* (1983), *With a Little Help from My Friends* (1994), and *Playback* (2002). He died in his sleep on March 8, 2016.

See also: Emerick, Geoff; Martin, Giles.

Martin, Giles (1969–)

Born on October 9, 1969, Giles is the son of Beatles producer George Martin and his second wife Judy Lockhart-Smith. As with his father, Giles pursued a career in music, serving as music director for high-profile productions such as the Party at the Palace concert held in honor of Queen Elizabeth II's Golden Jubilee. As a music producer, he has worked with such acts as Jeff Beck, Kate Bush, Costello, and INXS. He is perhaps most well-known for his collaborative work with his father on the Beatles' soundtrack for *Love*, the Cirque du Soleil theatrical production at the Mirage in Las Vegas. He later worked with director Martin Scorsese on his award-winning documentary *George Harrison: Living in the Material World*. He also lent his talents to the production of *The Beatles: Rock Band* video game. In 2008, he earned Grammy Awards for his work on *Love*, including Best Compilation Soundtrack Album and Best Surround-Sound Album at the 50th Grammy Awards.

See also: *The Beatles: Rock Band* (Video Game); *Love* (LP); Martin, George.

"Matchbox" (Perkins)

"Matchbox" is a song on the Beatles' *Long Tall Sally* EP, released in the United Kingdom on June 19, 1964.

AUTHORSHIP AND BACKGROUND

Written by Carl Perkins, "Matchbox" finds its origins in Blind Lemon Jefferson's 1927 recording "Match Box Blues." Released as a single on Sun Records in 1957, "Matchbox" became one of Perkins' best-known songs.

RECORDING SESSIONS

Produced by Martin, "Matchbox" was recorded at Abbey Road Studios on June 1, 1964. As Starr recalled in a 1964 interview, "I'm featured on it. Actually it was written by Carl Perkins about six years ago. Carl came to the session. I felt very embarrassed. I did it just two days before I went in the hospital (with tonsillitis) so please forgive my throat."

An earlier version of "Matchbox" was recorded by the newly minted Beatles in July 1960 in the McCartney family's bathroom using a Grundig tape recorder. Known as the Braun Tape, the recordings survived in the possession of Hans-Walther "Icke" Braun, one of the band's Hamburg friends, who was entrusted with the tape in the spring of 1961 (Winn 2003a, 4). Seventeen demos survive from the July 1960 recordings, including early versions of the Lennon–McCartney compositions "One After 909," "I'll Follow the Sun," and "Hello Little Girl." In addition to Lennon, McCartney, and Harrison, the July 1960 version of "Match-box" features Stuart Sutcliffe on bass.

In July 1963, the Beatles recorded yet another version of "Matchbox" with Starr on vocals for the BBC's *Pop Go the Beatles* radio show that was later included on the *Live at the BBC* album.

PERSONNEL

July 1960 Version:

> Lennon: Vocal, Guitar
> McCartney: Guitar, Backing Vocal
> Harrison: Guitar
> Sutcliffe: Bass

June 1964 Version:

> Lennon: Rickenbacker 325
> McCartney: Höfner 500/1
> Harrison: Gretsch Tennessean
> Starr: Vocal, Ludwig Oyster Black Pearl Drums
> Martin: Piano

CHART PERFORMANCE

> U.S.: "Matchbox"/"Slow Down"; August 24, 1964, Capitol 5255: #17.

LEGACY AND INFLUENCE

Perkins's recording of "Matchbox" is included among the Rock and Roll Hall of Fame's *500 Songs That Shaped Rock and Roll*.

ALBUM APPEARANCES: *Something New*; *Rock 'n' Roll Music*; *Live! at the Star-Club in Hamburg, Germany; 1962*; *Rarities* (U.K.); *Past Masters, Volume 1*; *Live at the BBC*; *Mono Masters*.

See also: *Live at the BBC* (LP).

"Maxwell's Silver Hammer" (Lennon–McCartney)

Written by McCartney, "Maxwell's Silver Hammer" is a song on the *Abbey Road* album. The song is notable for the Beatles' usage of a Moog synthesizer as part of their instrumentation.

AUTHORSHIP AND BACKGROUND

As the central theme of his composition, McCartney explores the "pataphysical" branch of metaphysics as explained in the work of Parisian playwright Alfred Jarry. Pataphysics is a form of antiphilosophy in which every occurrence throughout the universe, no matter how mundane or routine, is treated as an extraordinary and, hence, meaningful event. In "Maxwell's Silver Hammer," this phenomenon is made manifest in McCartney's song through Maxwell's unprovoked, largely motive-free, killing spree.

As McCartney later observed, " 'Maxwell's Silver Hammer' is my analogy for when something goes wrong out of the blue, as it so often does, as I was beginning to find out at that time in my life. I wanted something symbolic of that, so to me it was some fictitious character called Maxwell with a silver hammer. I don't know why it was silver." He added, "It just sounded better than Maxwell's hammer. It was needed for scanning. We still use that expression now when something unexpected happens" (Miles 1997, 554).

RECORDING SESSIONS

Produced by Martin, "Maxwell's Silver Hammer" finds its origins in the January 1969 *Get Back* sessions, during which McCartney began describing the song as "the corny one" (Dowlding 1989, 280). These sessions were also notable because Mal Evans played the telltale anvil part that Starr later replicated during the *Abbey Road* recording sessions. The final version of the song was recorded at Abbey Road Studios on July 9, 1969, with additional overdubbing sessions on July 10, 11, and August 6.

For Lennon, the recording sessions for "Maxwell's Silver Hammer" marked a decidedly low point in the Beatles' creative history: "I hate it. 'Cause all I remember is the track—he made us do it a hundred million times," Lennon later recalled. McCartney "did everything he could to make it a hit single and it never was and it never could've been" (Doggett 1998, 102).

PERSONNEL

Lennon: Epiphone Casino
McCartney: Vocal, Rickenbacker 4001S, Piano
Harrison: Gibson J-200, Moog Synthesizer

Starr: Ludwig Hollywood Maple Drums, Anvil
Martin: Hammond Organ

ALBUM APPEARANCES: *Abbey Road*; *Anthology 3*.

See also: *Abbey Road* (LP); *Get Back* Project.

McCartney, James (1902–1976)

Born in Everton, Liverpool, on July 2, 1902, James McCartney, Paul McCartney's father, was the third eldest of seven brothers and sisters. Jim left school at age 14, finding work for a Liverpool cotton broker. Over the years, he advanced from being a "sample boy" to becoming a full-fledged cotton salesman. In the 1920s, Jim led the Jim Mac Dance Band, who made a name for themselves on the local party and dancehall circuit. In his own way, his interest in period music later exerted a sizable influence on the Beatles' multifaceted musical directions.

In June 1940, Jim met Mary Patricia Mohin, a professional midwife. By April 1941, they were married. During World War II, the cotton exchange closed down, so Jim worked as an inspector at Napier's engineering works. James Paul McCartney was born on June 18, 1942, at Walton General Hospital, and Paul's younger brother Michael followed in 1944. The boys' youth was marked by the McCartneys' frequent moves from one government-subsidized council house to another—from Anfield to Speke, where they lived on Western Avenue before relocating to Ardwick Road. By 1955, the McCartneys had departed Speke for the relatively greener pastures of Allerton, where they lived in a council house at 20 Forthlin Road.

The young family's life was shattered by the breast cancer that quickly overcame Mary throughout the spring and summer of 1956. She died on October 31, leaving Jim to care for their young boys, with the assistance of his sisters Milly and Gin, on his meager income. As young Paul entered adolescence, Jim encouraged him to take piano lessons. For Paul's 14th birthday, his father presented him with a nickel-plated trumpet, which the boy struggled to play. While there was always music in the McCartney household—they were one of the few families in their social stratum who owned a piano—Paul's life was revolutionized by Radio Luxembourg's evening broadcasts of American music. He was particularly entranced by the soulful reverberations of African American R&B, rock 'n' roll's sedimentary bedrock that finds its roots in jazz, gospel, and the blues. Suddenly, Paul's world was ringing with the sounds of Ray Charles, Bo Diddley, Fats Domino, and—one of his all-time favorites—Little Richard. After seeing Lonnie Donegan live at Liverpool's Empire Theatre in 1956, Paul exchanged his trumpet for a Zenith, sunburst-model guitar. Before long, Paul realized that, despite the fact that he performed most tasks as a right-hander, he was a left-handed guitar player. After having the strings reversed on his guitar, the instrument, which had initially confronted him with great difficulty, came easily to him. "The minute he got the guitar that was the end," his brother Michael recalled. "He was lost. He didn't have time to eat or think about anything else" (Spitz 2005, 87).

After the advent of the Beatles' success, McCartney urged his father to retire, purchasing a home for him in Heswall, Cheshire. In 1964, Jim married Angela Stopworth Williams and adopted her daughter Ruth Ann (1959–). In November 1974, Wings (as "The Country Hams") recorded Jim's composition entitled "Walking in the Park with Eloise." On March 18, 1976, Jim died of bronchial pneumonia as Wings prepared for the European leg of the band's Wings Over the World tour. He was cremated at Landican Cemetery on March 22. His last words were reportedly "I'll be with Mary soon" (Miles 1997, 557).

See also: McCartney, Mary Patricia Mohin; McCartney, Paul; Wings.

McCartney, Linda Eastman (1941–1998)

Born on September 24, 1941, in New York City, Linda Louise Eastman had an older brother John and two younger sisters, Laura and Louise, Jr. Her father, Leopold Vail Epstein, later changed his name to Lee Eastman (1910–1991) and was a successful lawyer, later figuring prominently in the dissolution of the Beatles when McCartney attempted to engineer Eastman's selection as the band's manager. Eastman is often misidentified as a member of the George Eastman family associated with Eastman Kodak. At Lee Eastman's request, songwriter Jack Lawrence composed a song entitled "Linda" to commemorate Eastman's daughter's first birthday, which later became popular. Linda's mother, Louise Sara Lindner, was an heiress to her father's fortune from the Lindner Company in Cleveland, Ohio. In 1962, Louise died in an airplane crash in Queens, New York. Linda later studied fine art at the University of Arizona, where she met her first husband Joseph Melville See, Jr., with whom she had a daughter, Heather Louise, who was born on December 31, 1962. Heather was adopted by McCartney in 1969.

After the disintegration of her first marriage, Linda returned to New York City, where she found work as a receptionist for *Town and Country* magazine. She quickly made a name for herself as a photographer of rock musicians, photographing the Rolling Stones and eventually working as the house photographer for the Fillmore East, where she photographed such musicians as Bob Dylan, Aretha Franklin, Jimi Hendrix, the Doors, the Animals, and the Who, among others. Her photograph of Clapton adorned the May 11, 1968, cover of *Rolling Stone* magazine, marking the first cover photograph by a female photographer. Having later appeared on the January 31, 1974, cover of the magazine herself, she is the only photographer to have both taken a photograph and been the photographic subject for the cover of *Rolling Stone*. Her work as a photographer has been exhibited numerous times, while serving as the subject for the 1977 volume *Linda's Pictures* and 1993's *Linda McCartney's Sixties: Portrait of an Era*.

Linda Eastman in February 1969, a month before she wed Paul McCartney. The couple, who shared a dynamic post-Beatles music career, raised four children together (including her daughter from a previous marriage), and were together until her death in 1998. (AP Photo)

Linda first met McCartney at a Georgie Fame concert at London's Bag O'Nails club on May 15, 1967, seeing each other again four days later at the launch party for the Beatles' *Sgt. Pepper's Lonely Hearts Club Band* album. In May 1968, the couple met yet again for the Apple Corps launch party in New York City. In September, McCartney asked her to join him in London; the couple married on March 12, 1969, at the Marylebone Registry Office. The McCartneys welcomed a daughter, Mary, born August 28, 1969, and later adding two more children to their family, daughter Stella on September 13, 1971, and son James on September 12, 1977.

As a musician, Linda is known for her work with the enormously successful band Wings from 1971 through the early 1980s, as well as for her album with McCartney entitled *Ram* (1971) and her session work as a keyboard player on a host of McCartney solo albums, including *McCartney* (1970), *Tug of War* (1982), *Pipes of Peace* (1983), *Give My Regards to Broad Street* (1984), *Press to Play* (1986), *Flowers in the Dirt* (1989), *Off the Ground* (1991), and *Flaming Pie* (1997). At the time of her death, she was preparing a collection of solo material, which was released posthumously in 1998 as *Wide Prairie*. During her later years, she became known for her activism, especially vegetarianism, which resulted in two cookbooks—*Linda McCartney's Home Cooking* (1989) and *Linda's Kitchen: Simple and Inspiring Recipes for Meatless Meals* (1997)—as well as a line of frozen vegetarian meals called Linda McCartney Foods. She was also an outspoken advocate for the People for the Ethical Treatment of Animals (PETA).

After being diagnosed with breast cancer in 1995, Linda's condition continued to deteriorate, culminating in her death on April 17, 1998, at age 56. She died at the McCartneys' Tucson, Arizona, ranch. As she passed away, McCartney reportedly told her that "you're up on your beautiful Appaloosa stallion. It's a fine spring day. We're riding through the woods. The bluebells are all out, and the sky is clear-blue." Her ashes were scattered on the McCartneys' Sussex farm. In April 1999, McCartney performed at the "Concert for Linda" in London's Royal Albert Hall along with such rock luminaries as Costello, George Michael, and the Pretenders. In 2000, McCartney sponsored *A Garland for Linda*, a tribute album in Linda's honor and in support of the United Kingdom's Garland Appeal organization. PETA also honored Linda with the Linda McCartney Memorial Award. In 2002, a sculpture of Linda, designed by McCartney's cousin Jane Robbins, was installed in a memorial garden in Campbeltown, Scotland. Over the years, she has been portrayed in a number of television movies, including *John and Yoko: A Love Story* (1985), with Catherine Strauss playing Linda, and *The Linda McCartney Story* (2000), with Elizabeth Mitchell portraying Linda.

See also: Clapton, Eric; McCartney, Paul; Wings.

McCartney, Mary Patricia Mohin (1909–1956)

Born in Liverpool on September 29, 1909, Mary Patricia Mohin, Paul McCartney's mother, was of Irish descent. At age 14, she became a nurse trainee at Smithdown Road Hospital, followed by a three-year training course at Liverpool's Walton Road Hospital. Having become a state-registered nurse, she became a professional mid-wife. In June 1940, she met 40-year-old Jim McCartney, a cotton salesman. By April 1941, they were married. Their first son, James Paul McCartney, known as Paul, was born on June 18, 1942, at Walton General Hospital, and Paul's younger brother Michael followed in 1944. The boys' youth was marked by the McCartneys' frequent moves from one government-subsidized council house to another—from Anfield to Speke, where they lived on Western Avenue before relocating to Ardwick Road. By 1955, the McCartneys had departed Speke for the relatively greener pastures of Allerton, where they lived in a council house at 20 Forthlin Road.

The young family's life was shattered by the breast cancer that quickly overcame Mary throughout the spring and summer of 1956. At first, Mary associated the staggering pain in her chest with a severe bout of indigestion. Yet with her considerable background in nursing, Mary surely realized the perilous nature of her condition. One afternoon—while the McCartney children were away at Boy Scout camp—Mary shared her growing fears with her friend Olive Johnson: "I don't want to leave the boys *just* yet," she cried (Norman 1981, 29). As summer wore into autumn, her condition took a tragic turn. On October 30, she underwent an emergency mastectomy, but it was too late. By the next evening, Jim was taking the boys to visit their mother for the last time. Within a few short hours, she was stricken by an embolism and died. Devastated in his grief, young Paul could only contemplate the imminent practicalities of his mother Mary's death. "What are we going to do without her money?" he wondered aloud (Spitz 2005, 90). Mary was buried on November 3, 1956, at Yew Tree Cemetery in Liverpool.

McCartney composed his earliest song, "I Lost My Little Girl," about his mother's untimely demise and later immortalized Mary as "mother Mary" in "Let It Be." In August 1969, McCartney and wife Linda named their firstborn daughter Mary after his mother.

See also: McCartney, James; McCartney, Linda Eastman; McCartney, Paul.

McCartney, Paul (1942–)

Having joined the Quarry Men in 1957, McCartney was the Beatles' lead vocalist and bass guitarist, as well as a member of the exceedingly successful Lennon–McCartney songwriting team. He is, by a wide margin, the most successful solo artist among the former Beatles. During McCartney's post-Beatles years, he notched 11 #1 hits as a solo artist and with Wings, including "Uncle Albert/Admiral Halsey," "My Love," "Band on the Run," "Listen to What the Man Said," "Silly Love Songs," "Mull of Kintyre," "With a Little Luck," "Coming Up (Live at Glasgow)," "Ebony and Ivory" (with Stevie Wonder), "Say Say Say" (with Michael Jackson), and "Pipes of Peace." McCartney's final Top 40 hit—and the last Top 40 hit by any of the former Beatles—was "My Brave Face" in 1989. He continues to perform and compose music. In 1997, he was knighted as Sir Paul McCartney by Queen Elizabeth II.

EARLY YEARS

James Paul McCartney was born on June 18, 1942, at Liverpool's Walton General Hospital. His parents were Jim McCartney, a semiprofessional musician and cotton salesman, and Mary McCartney, a midwife. McCartney's younger brother Michael was born in 1944. The boys' youth was marked by the McCartneys' frequent moves from one government-subsidized council house to another—from Anfield to Speke, where they lived on Western Avenue before relocating to Ardwick Road. His formal education began at Stockton Road Primary School, where he received high marks for his work in English composition and art. His success on the Eleven Plus exams earned him entrance into the Liverpool Institute, the city's oldest grammar school, where he met Ivan Vaughan, who became one of his closest childhood friends. While he continued to excel in his studies—often after exerting surprisingly little effort in their stead—he drifted, rather naturally, toward the performing arts. In one very revealing instance, he auditioned for the role of Warwick in the Liverpool Institute's production of George Bernard Shaw's *Saint Joan* and became mortified when he was relegated to a minor role.

By 1955, the McCartneys had departed Speke for the relatively greener pastures of Allerton, where they lived in a council house at 20 Forthlin Road, scarcely a mile away—and just across the golf course—from Mimi Smith's home in Woolton. As he entered teenagehood, Jim encouraged him to take piano lessons. For his 14th birthday, his father presented him with a nickel-plated trumpet, which he struggled to play. While there was always music in the McCartney household—they were one of the few families in their social stratum who owned their own piano—his life was revolutionized by Radio Luxembourg's evening broadcasts of American music. He was particularly entranced by the soulful reverberations of African American R&B, rock 'n' roll's sedimentary bedrock that finds its roots in jazz, gospel, and the blues. Suddenly, his world was ringing with the sounds of Ray Charles, Bo Diddley, Fats Domino, and—one of his all-time favorites—Little Richard. After seeing Lonnie Donegan live at Liverpool's Empire Theatre in 1956, he exchanged his trumpet for a Zenith, sunburst-model guitar. Before long, he realized that, despite the fact that he performed most tasks as a right-

hander, he was a left-handed guitar player. After having the strings reversed on his guitar, the instrument, which had initially confronted him with great difficulty, came easily to him. "The minute he got the guitar that was the end," his brother Michael recalled. "He was lost. He didn't have time to eat or think about anything else" (Spitz 2005, 87).

Although the guitar changed Paul's world forever, the McCartney family's life was shattered by the breast cancer that quickly overcame Mary throughout the spring and summer of 1956. At first, Mary associated the staggering pain in her chest with a severe bout of indigestion. Yet with her considerable background in nursing, Mary surely realized the perilous nature of her condition. One afternoon—while the McCartney children were away at

Three members of the Liverpudlian skiffle beat band that would become the Beatles stand outside Paul McCartney's Liverpool home, ca. 1960. From left to right are George Harrison, John Lennon, and Paul McCartney. (Keystone/Getty Images)

Boy Scout camp—Mary shared her growing fears with her friend Olive Johnson: "I don't want to leave the boys *just* yet," she cried (Norman 1981, 29). As summer wore into autumn, Mary's condition took a tragic turn. On October 30, she underwent an emergency mastectomy, but it was too late. By the next evening, Jim was taking the boys to visit their mother for the last time. Within a few short hours, she was stricken by an embolism and died. Devastated in his grief, young Paul could only contemplate the imminent practicalities of his mother Mary's death. "What are we going to do without her money?" he wondered aloud (Spitz 2005, 90). Mary was buried on November 3, 1956, at Yew Tree Cemetery in Liverpool.

"My mother's death broke my Dad up," McCartney later recalled. "That was the worst thing for me, hearing my Dad cry. I'd never heard him cry before. It was a terrible blow to the family. You grow up real quick because you never expect to hear your parents crying. You expect to see women crying, or kids in the playground, or even yourself crying—and you can explain all that. But when it's your Dad, then you know something's *really* wrong, and it shakes your faith in everything" (Beatles 2000, 19).

As the McCartney family settled into their grief in the mid-1950s, they began, slowly but surely, to acquaint themselves with their new lives without Mary. Jim immersed himself in learning how to run the household, from cooking and cleaning to washing and ironing. Meanwhile, Paul absorbed himself in the power and whimsy of rock 'n' roll, mimicking the sounds of Elvis Presley, Buddy Holly, Carl Perkins, and Chuck Berry. By the summer of 1957, he was hooked. On July 6, he joined Vaughan at St. Peter's Church Hall, where he met Lennon after a performance by the Quarry Men.

"I remember coming into the fête," McCartney recalled. "There was the coconut shy over here and the hoopla over there, all the usual things—and there was a band playing on a platform with a small audience in front of them." His attention was drawn almost immediately to Lennon: "There was a guy up on the platform with curly, blondish hair, wearing a checked shirt—looking pretty good and quite fashionable—singing a song that I loved: the Del-Vikings' 'Come Go with Me.' He didn't know the words, but it didn't matter because none of us knew the words either. There's a little refrain, which goes, 'Come little darlin', come and go with me, I love you darling.' John was singing, 'Down, down, down to the penitentiary.' He was filling in with blues lines, I thought that was quite good, and he was singing well" (Beatles 2000, 20).

After the Quarry Men completed their afternoon performance, Vaughan and McCartney visited the band in a nearby Scout hut, where McCartney coolly performed renditions of "Twenty Flight Rock," "Be-Bop-a-Lula," and a trio of Little Richard tunes, including "Tutti-Fruitti," "Good Golly, Miss Molly," and "Long Tall Sally." "Right off, I could see John was checking this kid out," Pete Shotton recalled. "Paul came on as very attractive, very loose, very easy, very confident—*wildly* confident. He played the guitar well. I could see that John was very impressed" (Spitz 2005, 96). "I was very impressed by Paul playing 'Twenty Flight Rock,' " Lennon remembered. "He could obviously play the guitar. I half thought to myself, 'He's as good as me.' I'd been kingpin up until then. Now I thought, 'If I take him on, what will happen?' It went through my head that I'd have to keep him in line if I let him join. But he was good, so he was worth having. He also looked like Elvis. I dug him" (Davies 1968, 33).

Within a few weeks, the 15-year-old McCartney was a member of the band, with Harrison following several months later, and by the following year the Lennon–McCartney partnership was born. As with Lennon and Harrison, McCartney continued as a member of the Quarry Men through its various permutations as the Beatals, the Silver Beetles, and, finally, the

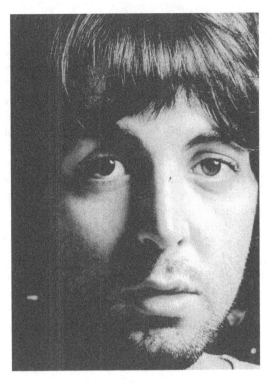

Paul McCartney in 1968. (Photofest)

Beatles in August 1960, when the group traveled to Hamburg for the extended musical apprenticeship that served as a prelude to the onset of their global fame in the early 1960s. In 1961, McCartney replaced Sutcliffe as the band's bass guitarist, a role that found him developing into a virtuoso musician. As Lennon later recalled, "I think Ringo's drumming is underrated the same way Paul's bass playing is underrated. Paul was one of the most innovative bass players ever. And half the stuff that is going on now is directly ripped off from his Beatles period" (Evans 2004, 385).

MARRIAGE AND FAMILY

During the 1960s, McCartney enjoyed a long-term relationship with Jane Asher. Having originally met the 17-year-old actress before the Beatles' April 18, 1963, performance at the Royal Albert Hall, he proposed to Asher in 1967, only to see their relationship come to an end in July 1968, partly due to Asher's discovery of McCartney's unfaithfulness to her. He met his first wife Linda Eastman at a Georgie Fame concert at London's Bag O'Nails club on May 15, 1967, seeing Linda again four days later at the launch party for the Beatles' *Sgt. Pepper's Lonely Hearts Club Band* album. In September 1968, he asked her to join him in London; the couple married on March 12, 1969, at the Marylebone Registry Office, after which McCartney adopted Linda's daughter Heather from a previous marriage. The McCartneys welcomed a daughter, Mary, on August 28, 1969, later adding two more children to their family, including Stella on September 13, 1971, and James on September 12, 1977. Stella later enjoyed international renown as a fashion designer, while James launched his own career as a recording artist. After being diagnosed with breast cancer in 1995, Linda's condition continued to deteriorate, culminating in her death at age 56 on April 17, 1998, at the McCartneys' Tucson, Arizona, ranch.

In April 1999, McCartney met activist and former model Heather Anne Mills at a Pride of Britain Awards event, where the former Beatle was presenting an award in honor of Linda Eastman McCartney. He proposed to Mills on July 23, 2001, and the couple were married on June 11, 2002, at Ireland's Castle Leslie. Their daughter, Beatrice Milly McCartney, was born on October 28, 2003. The couple separated in May 2006, with their eventual divorce being granted in May 2008 in which Mills was awarded a £24.3 million settlement. He married American Nancy Shevell on October 9, 2011, after dating the businesswoman for four years. He had originally met Shevell some 20 years earlier in the Hamptons, on New York's Long Island, where their respective families owned homes. The couple married at Old Marylebone Town Hall, where McCartney married Linda Eastman in March 1969.

SOLO YEARS

McCartney's initial foray as a solo artist commenced with his score for *The Family Way* (1967), directed by Roy Boulting. His solo career as a former Beatle commenced with *McCartney* (1970), a best-selling album that coincided with McCartney's public announcement of the Beatles' disbandment. *McCartney* featured "Maybe I'm Amazed," arguably the former Beatle's most recognizable solo composition. With wife Linda, he released the critically acclaimed *Ram* album the following year. The LP featured such standout tracks as the #1 single "Uncle Albert/ Admiral Halsey" and "The Back Seat of My Car."

In 1971, McCartney announced the formation of Wings, which included wife Linda on keyboards and backing vocals and mainstay Denny Laine. Over the years, the band featured a rotating cast of supporting players. The group's first album *Wild Life* (1971) offered an inauspicious, homespun beginning. After a string of impromptu university tours and successful early singles in "Hi, Hi, Hi" and "Live and Let Die," Wings began to enjoy international success with such albums as *Red Rose Speedway* (1973), which included the #1 single "My Love," and the block-buster *Band on the Run* (1973), which featured the best-selling title track and "Jet." In 1975, the album earned a Grammy Award for Best Pop Vocal Performance by a Duo, Group, or Chorus at the 17th Grammy Awards. That same year, Wings released *Venus and Mars*, which launched yet another chart-topping single in "Listen to What the Man Said." In the mid-1970s, the band engaged in the triumphant, multicontinent Wings Over the World tour in support of *Wings at the Speed of Sound* (1976), which included the hit singles "Silly Love Songs" and "Let 'Em In." The tour was commemorated with the release of the triple album *Wings Over America* (1976). In 1977, Wings galvanized U.K. listeners with "Mull of Kintyre," which displaced the Beatles' "She Loves You" as England's best-selling single. The band's *London Town* (1978) album featured yet another chart-topping single in "With a Little Luck." In addition to the disco hit "Goodnight Tonight," 1979 saw Wings release their final studio album in *Back to the Egg*. After completing their Winter UK Tour, the band intended to tour Japan, only to have their plans thwarted by McCartney's January 1980 arrest in Tokyo for possession of marijuana. After spending 10 days in a Japanese jail, he was deported back to the United Kingdom.

In 1980, McCartney released *McCartney II*, his first true solo album since 1970's *McCartney*. While the album included the former Beatle's studio version of "Coming Up," Wings' live version of the song became a #1 U.S. hit and served as a swan song for the group, which had all but disbanded after the failed Japanese tour. With Martin in tow, McCartney recorded a string of best-selling solo albums—most notably, *Tug of War* (1982), which featured "Ebony and Ivory" (with Stevie Wonder), "Take It Away," and the Lennon homage "Here Today," as well as *Pipes of Peace* (1983), which included McCartney's final chart-topping single in "Say Say Say," his duet with Michael Jackson. He interrupted his successful run with ill-conceived film *Give My Regards to Broad Street* (1984), which was notable for the Top 10 hit single "No More Lonely Nights." His solo career reached its nadir with the ineffectual *Press to Play* (1986), which finds the former Beatle attempted to effect a more contemporary sound.

McCartney enjoyed a remarkable return to form with *Flowers in the Dirt* (1989), which included "My Brave Face," his songwriting collaboration with Elvis Costello, as well as the final Top 40 hit by any of the former Beatles. He launched an international tour in support of the album. In 1993, he released the peace-oriented *Off the Ground*, for which he commenced yet another multicontinent tour. He rounded out the 1990s with a pair of highly successful solo releases, including *Flaming Pie* (1997) and *Run Devil Run* (1999), which found him exorcising his grief over Linda's recent death with a series of rock 'n' roll cover versions. His solo albums in the new century feature a quartet of critically acclaimed albums, including *Driving Rain* (2001), *Chaos and Creation in the Backyard* (2005), *Memory Almost Full* (2007), and *Kisses on the Bottom* (2012), a collection of jazz standards. Since 2002, he has launched a regular series of blockbuster concert tours with his supporting band, which includes Brian Ray and Rusty Anderson on guitars, Abe Laboriel, Jr., on drums, and Paul "Wix" Wickens on keyboards. In recent decades, he has supplemented his standard album releases with a series of classical music forays, including *Paul McCartney's Liverpool Oratorio* (1991), *Standing Stone* (1997), *Working Classical* (1999), *A Garland for Linda* (2000), *Ecce Cor Meum* (2006), and *Ocean's Kingdom* (2011). Since the 1990s, he has carried out an experimental collaboration in electronic music—known as the Fireman—with Youth (Martin Glover). Over the years, McCartney and Youth have produced three albums, including *Strawberries Oceans Ships Forest* (1993), *Rushes* (1998), and *Electric Arguments* (2008). Youth also participated in the production of McCartney's experimental album *Liverpool Sound Collage* (2000).

LEGACY

As with the other Beatles, McCartney was appointed as a member of the Order of the British Empire during the Queen's Birthday Honours on June 12, 1965, receiving his insignia from Queen Elizabeth II at Buckingham Palace on October 26. On July 11, 1983, his legacy was commemorated with the naming of a minor planet, 4148 McCartney, by Brian A. Skiff at the Lowell Observatory's Anderson Mesa Station outside of Flagstaff, Arizona. In 1988, the Beatles were inducted into the Rock and Roll Hall of Fame. He was knighted as Sir Paul by Queen Elizabeth II in March 1997; two years later, he was inducted into the Rock

Paul McCartney performs onstage at Olimpiyskiy Arena on December 14, 2011, in Moscow, Russia. The prolific and still-popular British musician was dubbed "the Most Successful Composer and Recording Artist of All Time" by *Guinness World Records*. (Aliaksandr Mazurkevich/Dreamstime.com)

and Roll Hall of Fame as a solo artist. In 2008, he was ranked #11 on *Rolling Stone* magazine's list of the 100 Greatest Singers of All Time. That same year, he received a BRIT Award for his Outstanding Contribution to Music. In 2010, U.S. President Barack Obama saluted McCartney with the Gershwin Prize; that same year, he was honored at the White House as a recipient of the Kennedy Center Honors. On February 10, 2012, he was honored with a star on Hollywood's Walk of Fame by the Hollywood Chamber of Commerce. As with the other Beatles, his star is located on North Vine Street in front of the Capitol Records Building. In September 2012, French President François Hollande awarded McCartney the Légion d'Honneur for his musical accomplishments. The *Guinness World Records* ranks him as "the Most Successful Composer and Recording Artist of All Time," with the former Beatle having amassed 60 gold discs, along with sales of more than 100 million albums, 100 million singles, and songwriting credit for 43 compositions that have sold more than 1 million copies each.

See also: Harrison, George; Lennon, John; Martin, George; McCartney, James; McCartney, Linda Eastman; McCartney, Mary Patricia Mohin; Mills, Heather Anne; Shevell, Nancy; Sutcliffe, Stuart; Wings.

"Mean Mr. Mustard" (Lennon–McCartney)

"Mean Mr. Mustard" is a song on the Beatles' *Abbey Road* album. It is the third song in the *Abbey Road* Medley.

AUTHORSHIP AND BACKGROUND

Lennon's "Mean Mr. Mustard" was written during the Beatles' 1968 visit to India. Lennon's inspiration for the song came from a newspaper article about a man who was so parsimonious that he hid £5 notes within his nether regions. As Lennon later recalled, "I'd read somewhere in the newspaper about this mean guy who hid his five-pound notes, not up his nose but *somewhere else*. No, it had nothing to do with cocaine" (Lennon and Ono 2000, 203).

The Beatles rehearsed the song during the *Get Back* sessions in January 1969. The song's original lyrics named Mean Mr. Mustard's sister as Shirley. She was later renamed as Pam during the recording sessions for "Mean Mr. Mustard." " 'Mean Mr. Mustard' was very John," McCartney later remarked. "I liked that. A nice quirky song" (Cadogan 2008, 220).

RECORDING SESSIONS

Produced by Martin, "Mean Mr. Mustard" was recorded as a single track along with "Sun King" at Abbey Road Studios on July 24, 1969. Additional overdubbing sessions occurred on July 25 and 29. An early version of "Mean Mr. Mustard" was recorded as a home demo by Lennon at his Kenwood estate. It was later included on *Anthology 3*.

PERSONNEL

Lennon: Vocal, Epiphone Casino, Piano, Lowrey Organ
McCartney: Fender Jazz Bass, Harmonium
Harrison: Gibson Les Paul Standard
Starr: Ludwig Hollywood Maple Drums, Tambourine

ALBUM APPEARANCES: *Abbey Road*; *Anthology 3*.

See also: *Abbey Road* (LP); *The Beatles: Rock Band* (Video Game).

Meet the Beatles! (LP)

January 20, 1964, Capitol T 2047 (mono)/ST 2047 (stereo)

Meet the Beatles! was the second Beatles album to be released in the United States. It was released on the Capitol label on January 20, 1964. Several of the songs on *Meet the Beatles!* were culled from *With the Beatles*, which had been released in the United Kingdom on November 22, 1963, as well as from the *Please Please Me* album, which had been released in the United Kingdom on March 22, 1963, and the "I Want to Hold Your Hand"/"This Boy" single, which had been released in the United Kingdom on November 29, 1963.

Meet the Beatles! was deleted from the Beatles' catalogue in 1987, when the group's U.K. albums were distributed as CD releases. A remastered mono and stereo release of *Meet the Beatles!* was released on November 15, 2004, as part of the box set entitled *The Capitol Albums, Volume 1*.

BACKGROUND

As Beatlemania brewed in Great Britain throughout the summer and fall of 1963, the EMI Group's American subsidiary, Capitol Records, remained eerily silent. On the advice of A&R executive Dave Dexter, Jr., Capitol president Alan Livingston passed, time and time again, on the opportunity to release Beatles records in the U.S. market. Things changed in a hurry, though, after the runaway success of *With the Beatles* in the United Kingdom. Within a week, Epstein traveled to New York in order to meet with American television personality Ed Sullivan. As luck would have it, the Beatles had come into Sullivan's orbit on the morning of October 31, having just landed at London's Heathrow Airport. Sullivan had flown in from the

United States to scout out talent for his popular CBS variety show, when he and his wife Sylvia encountered the thousands of ecstatic fans who had gathered at the airport to welcome their idols home.

On November 11, 1963, Epstein met with Sullivan in New York City, and the dueling impresarios quickly struck a deal: for $10,000, plus expenses, the Beatles would perform on three consecutive installments of Sullivan's program. Wasting little time, Epstein set his sights on Capitol Records, the EMI subsidiary that, for the balance of 1963, had refused to consider releasing the Beatles stateside. Afforded the right of first refusal by their parent company, Capitol had given the band a listen way back in January 1963 before scuttling them to their growing pile of rejected British imports. Having been rebuffed by Capitol, the group's wares had been considered, and passed on, by such American music luminaries as Columbia, RCA, Mercury, and United Artists before finding a home at Chicago's tiny Vee-Jay Records. But fate was clearly not on the Beatles' side. As EMI prepared the group's recordings for their conveyance to Vee-Jay, the company's president, Ewart Abner, Jr., had flown to Las Vegas to celebrate his 40th birthday. Within a week, he had accumulated massive losses at the tables that left Vee-Jay on the cusp of bankruptcy and without the necessary operating capital to promote the Beatles (Spitz 2005, 388, 389). Released without fanfare in February and March, respectively, Vee-Jay's single versions of "Please Please Me" and "From Me to You" languished in American obscurity, while their Parlophone counterparts topped the charts across the Atlantic.

By the time that Epstein arrived in New York City, Capitol Records had been ordered by EMI's managing director L. G. Wood to release the Beatles' next single without delay. Having racked up nearly 300,000 advance orders for *With the Beatles* alone, EMI could simply no longer wait for its American subsidiary to come around. With the band slated to perform on the *Ed Sullivan Show* on February 9, 1964, promoter Sid Bernstein signed them for a pair of shows at Carnegie Hall that same week. Having originally planned to press a mere 5,000 copies of "I Want to Hold Your Hand," Capitol earmarked the impressive sum of $40,000 to promote the single in the United States (Spitz 2005, 443, 444). As history had so resoundingly proved, it went down as one of the most astute investments in the annals of popular music.

As the long-playing vehicle for the group's American debut, the contents of *Meet the Beatles!* were carefully selected from the band's existing corpus. It pointedly includes original Lennon–McCartney material, while eschewing entirely the cover versions that the Beatles released on their first two U.K. albums. It also reflects a strikingly different marketing philosophy between U.S. and U.K. record executives. In the United States, singles releases drive album sales, while the U.K. marketplace during the early 1960s was generally more segmented among various levels of consumers; hence, the industry marketed itself to British fans with product gradations from relatively inexpensive 45-rpm singles through slightly more costly EP and, ultimately, higher-end LP releases. Explicitly designed with an

American audience in mind, *Meet the Beatles!* became a runaway success, rocketing to the top of the album charts, which the album reigned over for 11 blockbusting weeks until it was unseated by *The Beatles' Second Album.*

TRACK LISTING

Side 1: "I Want to Hold Your Hand"; "I Saw Her Standing There"; "This Boy"; "It Won't Be Long"; "All I've Got to Do"; "All My Loving."

Side 2: "Don't Bother Me"; "Little Child"; "Till There Was You"; "Hold Me Tight"; "I Wanna Be Your Man"; "Not a Second Time."

COVER ARTWORK

For the cover artwork of *Meet the Beatles!*, Capitol recycled Robert Freeman's August 1963 cover photograph from the *With the Beatles* album. The group's shadowy image appears under an erroneous banner describing *Meet the Beatles!* as "The First Album by England's Phenomenal Pop Combo." The album's liner notes serve as the Beatles' introduction to their new and eager American audience:

You've read about them in *Time, Newsweek, The New York Times.* Here's the big beat sound of that fantastic, phenomenal foursome: Meet the Beatles! A year ago the Beatles were known only to patrons of Liverpool pubs. Today there isn't a Britisher who doesn't know their names, and their fame has spread quickly around the world. Said one American visitor to England: "Only a hermit could be unaware of the Beatles, and he'd have to be beyond the range of television, newspapers, radio, records and rioting fans." Said another: "They're the biggest, hottest property in the history of English show business."

CHART PERFORMANCE

U.S.: #1 (certified by the RIAA as "5x Multi Platinum," with more than 5 million copies sold).

LEGACY AND INFLUENCE

In 2001, *Meet the Beatles!* was inducted into the National Academy of Recording Arts and Sciences Grammy Hall of Fame.

In 2003, *Rolling Stone* ranked *Meet the Beatles!* as #59 on the magazine's list of *The 500 Greatest Albums of All Time.*

In 2007, American band the Smithereens commemorated the Beatles' American album debut with a full-length cover version of *Meet the Beatles!* entitled *Meet the Smithereens!*

See also: With the Beatles (LP).

"Michelle" (Lennon–McCartney)

"Michelle" is a song on the Beatles' *Rubber Soul* album.

AUTHORSHIP AND BACKGROUND

Written by McCartney with assistance from Lennon, "Michelle" first emerged on a home demo that first surfaced way back in July 1963. As McCartney recalled, " 'Michelle' was like a joke French tune for when you go to a party or something. That's all it was. And then after a while you say, 'Well, that's quite a good tune. Let's put some real words to it' " (Dowlding 1989, 119).

McCartney was later assisted on the song's French phrases by Vaughan's wife Jan, the language teacher who helpfully translated McCartney's existing lyrics, "These are words that go together well," into *"Sont des mots qui vont très bien ensemble."* The composition finds its roots in Chet Atkins' instrumental "Trambone," while McCartney's vocal stylings emerge relatively unscathed, at Lennon's suggestion, from Nina Simone's "I Put a Spell on You."

As Lennon later remembered,

> He and I were staying somewhere and he walked in and hummed the first few bars, with the words, and he says, "Where do I go from here?" I had been listening to Nina Simone. I think it was "I Put a Spell on You." There was a line in it that went, "I love you, I love you." That's what made me think of the middle-eight for "Michelle." So, my contributions to Paul's songs was always to add a little bluesy edge to them. Otherwise, "Michelle" is a straight ballad, right? He provided a lightness, an optimism, while I would always go for the sadness, the discords, the bluesy notes. (Lennon and Ono 2000, 137)

RECORDING SESSIONS

Produced by Martin, "Michelle" was recorded at Abbey Road Studios on November 3, 1965. The song's musical foundation involves a trio of capoed acoustic guitars, with McCartney on his Epiphone Texan and Lennon and Harrison on their Jumbos. Harrison overdubbed the guitar solo on a heavily distorted Epiphone Casino.

PERSONNEL

Lennon: Gibson J-160E
McCartney: Vocal, Höfner 500/1, Epiphone Texan
Harrison: Gibson J-160E, Epiphone Casino
Starr: Ludwig Oyster Black Pearl Drums

LEGACY AND INFLUENCE

In 1967, "Michelle" earned a Grammy Award for Song of the Year at the 9th Grammy Awards.

In 1967, the Beatles received an Ivor Novello Award, awarded annually by the British Academy of Songwriters, Composers, and Authors, for "Michelle."

ALBUM APPEARANCES: *Rubber Soul* (U.K.); *Rubber Soul* (U.S.); *A Collection of Beatles Oldies*; *The Beatles, 1962–1966*; *Love Songs*.

See also: *Rubber Soul* (U.K. LP).

Mills, Heather Anne (1968–)

Born on January 12, 1968, in Aldershot, England, Mills is McCartney's former wife, as well as the mother of his daughter Beatrice Milly McCartney, who was born on October 28, 2003. She is an activist and former model. In later years, it was revealed that Mills had worked as an escort, while also performing in a soft-core pornographic video. She emerged as a public figure in 1993 after an accident involving a police motorcycle in London resulted in the amputation of her left leg below the knee. After selling her story to a London tabloid, she used the proceeds as seed money for the Heather Mills Health Trust, a charitable organization that recycles prosthetic limbs for amputees. She is also internationally renowned for her work on the banning and removal of land mines.

In April 1999, Mills met McCartney at a Pride of Britain Awards event, where the former Beatle was presenting an award in honor of his late wife Linda Eastman McCartney, who had died the previous year. Later that year, she and her sister recorded a song entitled "VO!CE" for the Heather Mills Health Trust with McCartney providing backing vocals. McCartney proposed to Mills on July 23, 2001; the couple were married on June 11, 2002, at Ireland's Castle Leslie in a lavish but private ceremony. Their marriage was relatively short-lived, however; after spending several months apart, the couple separated in May 2006, with Mills later citing tensions with McCartney's adult children as contributing to their problems. In February 2008, the McCartneys' divorce case was heard at London's Royal Courts of Justice. She requested a £125 million settlement, while McCartney countered with £15.8 million. After taking issue with McCartney's claims about his overall net worth, she was eventually awarded £24.3 million, and the divorce was granted in May 2008.

See also: McCartney, Paul.

"Misery" (McCartney–Lennon)

"Misery" is a song on the Beatles' *Please Please Me* album.

AUTHORSHIP AND BACKGROUND

Written by Lennon and McCartney, "Misery" was originally composed as a vehicle for 16-year-old Helen Shapiro. After Shapiro's producer turned down the song, Kenny Lynch recorded it, making his version of "Misery" the first cover version of a Beatles song.

As McCartney later recalled, "John and I were a songwriting team, and what songwriting teams did in those days was wrote for everyone. 'Misery' was for Helen Shapiro, and she turned it down. It may not have been that successful for her because it's rather a downbeat song. 'The world is treating me bad, misery.' It was quite pessimistic. And in the end Kenny Lynch did it. Kenny used to come out on tour with us, and he used to sing it. That was one of his minor hits" (Lewisohn 1988, 8).

RECORDING SESSIONS

Produced by George Martin, "Misery" was recorded at Abbey Road Studios on February 11, 1963. It offers an early example of Martin's knack for using studio trickery in order to achieve new-fangled soundscapes. In the case of "Misery," the producer superimposed a piano over the existing guitar introduction, played in 6/8 time, during an overdubbing session on February 20—while the Beatles were across town performing on a live BBC broadcast from the Playhouse Theatre. Years before, Martin had developed the technique of recording a piano at half-speed by itself or in unison with a guitar track that had been recorded an octave lower (Emerick and Massey 2006, 60). Played back at regular speed, the piano introduction assumes a quasi-harpsichord or music box effect, which Martin hailed as the "wound-up piano."

PERSONNEL

Lennon: Vocal, Rickenbacker 325
McCartney: Vocal, Höfner 500/1
Harrison: Gretsch Duo-Jet
Starr: Premier Mahogany Duroplastic Drums
Martin: Piano

ALBUM APPEARANCES: *Please Please Me*; *Rarities* (U.S.); *On Air: Live at the BBC, Volume 2*.

See also: Emerick, Geoff; Martin, George; *Please Please Me* (LP).

"Money (That's What I Want)" (Gordy–Bradford)

"Money (That's What I Want)" is a song on the *With the Beatles* album.

AUTHORSHIP AND BACKGROUND

Written by Janie Bradford and Berry Gordy, "Money (That's What I Want)" was recorded by Barrett Strong, who enjoyed a Top 40 hit with the song in 1960. It is one of the most widely covered compositions in the history of popular music.

RECORDING SESSIONS

Produced by George Martin, "Money (That's What I Want)" was recorded at Abbey Road Studios on July 18, 1963, with an overdubbing session on July 30.

PERSONNEL

Lennon: Vocal, Rickenbacker 325
McCartney: Höfner 500/1, Backing Vocal
Harrison: Gretsch Country Gentleman, Backing Vocal
Starr: Ludwig Oyster Black Pearl Drums
Martin: Piano

LEGACY AND INFLUENCE

Barrett Strong's recording of "Money (That's What I Want)" is included among the Rock and Roll Hall of Fame's *500 Songs That Shaped Rock and Roll*.

ALBUM APPEARANCES: *With the Beatles*; *The Beatles' Second Album*; *Rock 'n' Roll Music*; *Anthology 1*.

See also: *With the Beatles* (LP).

"Mother Nature's Son" (Lennon–McCartney)

"Mother Nature's Son" is a song on *The Beatles* (*The White Album*).

AUTHORSHIP AND BACKGROUND

Written by McCartney, "Mother Nature's Son" finds its origins during the Beatles' 1968 visit to India. As with Lennon's "Child of Nature" ["Jealous Guy"], "Mother Nature's Son" was written after McCartney and Lennon attended a lecture by the Maharishi regarding nature.

As McCartney remembered,

I've always loved the song called "Nature Boy." "Mother Nature's Son" was inspired by that song. I'd always loved nature, and when Linda and I got together we discovered we had this deep love of nature in common. There might have been a little help from John with some of the verses. (Cadogan 2008, 211)

An early version of "Mother Nature's Son" was recorded in May 1968 at Harrison's Kinfauns studio as part of the Esher Tapes.

RECORDING SESSIONS

Produced by Martin, "Mother Nature's Son" was recorded at Abbey Road Studios on August 9, 1968, with an overdubbing session on August 20. McCartney recorded the still unreleased "Et Cetera" during the latter session while awaiting the arrival of the session musicians.

McCartney can be heard tapping a copy of Henry Wadsworth Longfellow's *Songs of Hiawatha* during the latter half of "Mother Nature's Son," with Scott thoughtfully positioning a microphone over the book in order to capture its sound.

PERSONNEL

McCartney: Vocal, Martin D-28, Bass Drum, Tympani
Studio Musicians: Brass Accompaniment conducted by Martin

LEGACY AND INFLUENCE

In 2010, *Rolling Stone* ranked "Mother Nature's Son" as #80 on the magazine's list of *The Beatles' 100 Greatest Songs*.

ALBUM APPEARANCES: *The Beatles* (*The White Album*); *Anthology 3*.

See also: *The Beatles* (*The White Album*) (LP).

"Mr. Moonlight" (Johnson)

"Mr. Moonlight" is a song on the *Beatles for Sale* album.

AUTHORSHIP AND BACKGROUND

Written by Roy Lee Johnson, "Mr. Moonlight" was released as the B-side of the "Dr. Feelgood" single in January 1962 by Piano Red [William "Willie" Lee Perryman], who recorded the song under the name of Dr. Feelgood and the Interns. In addition to the Beatles, it was also covered by the Hollies and the Merseybeats.

RECORDING SESSIONS

Produced by Martin, "Mr. Moonlight" was recorded at Abbey Road Studios on August 14, 1964, and remade on October 18.

PERSONNEL

> Lennon: Vocal, Gibson J-160E
> McCartney: Höfner 500/1, Hammond Organ, Backing Vocal
> Harrison: Rickenbacker 360/12, African Drum
> Starr: Bongos

ALBUM APPEARANCES: *Beatles for Sale*; *Beatles '65*; *Live! at the Star-Club in Hamburg, Germany; 1962*; *Anthology 1*.

See also: *Beatles for Sale* (LP).

"My Bonnie" (Traditional)

"My Bonnie" was recorded by Tony Sheridan and the Beat Brothers [The Beatles] in Hamburg in June 1961. It was released as a single in the United Kingdom on January 5, 1962. More significantly, it was instrumental in bringing Epstein into the Beatles' orbit for the first time in November 1961.

AUTHORSHIP AND BACKGROUND

Often attributed to Bonnie Prince Charlie (Charles Edward Stuart), "My Bonnie Lies Over the Ocean" is a traditional Scottish folk song. Legend has it that after the Prince's 1746 defeat at the Battle of Culloden and his subsequent exile, his Jacobite supporters sang the song in his honor. In 1881, Charles E. Pratt published the song as "Bring Back My Bonnie to Me" under the pseudonyms of H. J. Fulmer and J. T. Wood.

Under its various titles, "My Bonnie Lies Over the Ocean" became a popular hit in both the British Isles and the United States during the latter years of the 19th century and into the first half of the new century as well. The song's role in popular music took a decidedly different turn on Saturday, October 28, 1961, when a patron named Raymond Jones reportedly entered NEMS (North End Music Stores)—the largest record outlet in Liverpool and throughout the North Country—and requested a copy of the Beatles' "My Bonnie" from the store's owner, 27-year-old Brian Epstein. The event served as the catalyst for Epstein's subsequent visit to the Cavern Club to see the Beatles perform during one of their regular lunchtime concerts. By January 1962, Epstein had signed a formal five-year contract with the Beatles.

In his autobiography *A Cellarful of Noise* (1964), Epstein claims to have been unfamiliar with the Beatles before Jones' visit on that fateful day:
"The name 'Beatle' meant nothing to me though I vaguely recalled seeing it on a poster advertising a university dance at New Brighton Tower, and I remembered thinking it was an odd and purposeless spelling" (Epstein 1998, 94, 95). Given his association with *Mersey Beat*—and its regular cover stories about the band—it is doubtful that the Beatles had so thoroughly eluded his notice. In addition to the *Mersey Beat*'s lavish attention upon the band, the Beatles were featured on numerous posters throughout Epstein's record stores. As Bill Harry pointed out, "He would have had to have been blind—or ignorant—not to have noticed their name" (Spitz 2005, 266). A number of music historians have gone so far as to suggest that Epstein manufactured Raymond Jones out of thin air (Lewisohn 1995, 34). Yet in Epstein's defense, Spencer Leigh located the elusive Raymond Jones, now retired and living in Spain. As Jones remarked, "No one will ever take away from me that it was me who spoke to Brian Epstein and then he went to the Cavern to see [the Beatles] for himself" (Leigh 2004, 21).

In a 2010 interview with the online *Beatles Bible*, Jones recalled that

My ex brother-in-law Kenny Johnson was the lead guitarist with a group called Mark Peters and the Cyclones. It was him that told me the Beatles had made a record in Germany. The following Saturday I went to NEMS to ask for the record, not realizing the person I spoke to was Brian Epstein. He started asking me questions: "Who were they?" "Where did they play?" "What type of music did they perform?" After I had answered his questions, I told him they were the best group I had ever seen. The next time I went to NEMS, I picked up the record. Shortly after that it was common knowledge that Epstein had become their manager. (*The Beatles Bible* 2008–2013)

RECORDING SESSIONS

Produced by German bandleader Bert Kämpfert with assistance from sound engineer Karl Hinze, "My Bonnie" was recorded at Hamburg's Friedrich-Ebert-Halle on June 22, 1961. Kämpfert had caught the Beatles' act with Sheridan at the Top Ten Club. He subsequently offered Sheridan a contract with Polydor Records and signed the Beatles as his backup band. For Sheridan's recordings, the Beatles temporarily refashioned themselves as the Beat Brothers. In German slang, *Pidels*, which sounds a lot like *Beatles*, is the plural form of penis. It was a connotation that Kämpfert was entirely unwilling to risk. The Beatles were paid 300 marks for the session.

"My Bonnie" was one of eight songs that the Beatles recording during their session with Sheridan at Friedrich-Ebert-Halle in June 1961. As Lennon remembered, "It's just Tony Sheridan singing, with us banging in the background. It's terrible. It could be anybody" (Beatles 2000, 59). McCartney later added that "they didn't like our name and said, 'Change to the Beat Brothers; this is more under-standable for the German audience.' We went along with it—it was a record" (Bea-tles 2000, 59).

PERSONNEL

Sheridan: Vocal
Lennon: Guitar, Backing Vocal
McCartney: Bass, Backing Vocal
Harrison: Guitar, Backing Vocal
Best: Drums

CHART PERFORMANCE

U.K.: "My Bonnie"/"The Saints"; January 5, 1962, Polydor NH 66–833 (as Tony Sheridan and the Beatles): #48.

U.S.: "My Bonnie"/"The Saints"; January 27, 1964, MGM K-13213 (as the Beatles with Tony Sheridan): #26.

ALBUM APPEARANCES: *Anthology 1*.

See also: Epstein, Brian; Sheridan, Tony.

N

Nerk Twins

In April 1960—after the Beatles briefly christened themselves as Johnny and the Moondogs—John Lennon and Paul McCartney dubbed themselves as the Nerk Twins for a pair of performances at the Fox and Hounds, a pub owned by McCartney's cousin Elizabeth Robbins, in Caversham, Berkshire. On April 23 and 24 of that year, Lennon and McCartney entertained bar patrons while sitting on stools, accompanied only by their guitars and without benefit of a sound system.

When they were children, McCartney and his brother Mike occasionally performed before their relatives as the Nerk Twins. Years later, Mike performed under the stage name Michael McGear, and he enjoyed a number of hit singles in the United Kingdom with the Scaffold, a trio that included McGear, Roger McGough, and John Gorman.

See also: Johnny and the Moondogs.

"The Night Before" (Lennon–McCartney)

"The Night Before" is a song on the Beatles' *Help!* album.

AUTHORSHIP AND BACKGROUND

Written by McCartney, "The Night Before" features a call-and-response vocal structure, as well as a guitar solo that McCartney overdubbed onto the final mix.

As McCartney later recalled, "I would say that's mainly mine. I don't think John had a lot to do with that" (Miles 1997, 195).

RECORDING SESSIONS

Produced by Martin, "The Night Before" was recorded at Abbey Road Studios on February 17, 1965.

PERSONNEL

Lennon: Electric Piano, Backing Vocal
McCartney: Vocal, Höfner 500/1, Epiphone Casino
Harrison: Gretsch Tennessean, Backing Vocal
Starr: Ludwig Oyster Black Pearl Drums

LEGACY AND INFLUENCE

In 2010, *Rolling Stone* ranked "The Night Before" as #49 on the magazine's list of *The Beatles' 100 Greatest Songs*.

ALBUM APPEARANCES: *Help!* (U.K.); *Help!* (U.S.); *Rock 'n' Roll Music*.

See also: *Help!* (U.K. LP).

"No Reply" (Lennon–McCartney)

"No Reply" is a song on *Beatles for Sale*.

AUTHORSHIP AND BACKGROUND

Written by Lennon, "No Reply" was influenced by the Rays' 1957 hit "Silhouettes."

As Lennon later recalled, "That's my song. That's the one where Dick James the publisher said, 'That's the first complete song you've written that resolves itself,' you know, with a complete story. It was sort of my version of 'Silhouettes.' I had that image of walking down the street and seeing her silhouetted in the window and not answering the phone, although I never called a girl on the phone in my life. Because phones weren't part of the English child's life" (Lennon and Ono 2000, 174).

RECORDING SESSIONS

Produced by Martin, "No Reply" was recorded on September 30, 1964, at Abbey Road Studios. Lennon double-tracked his vocal.

PERSONNEL

Lennon: Vocal, Gibson J-160E
McCartney: Höfner 500/1
Harrison: Gretsch Tennessean
Starr: Ludwig Oyster Black Pearl Drums
Martin: Piano

LEGACY AND INFLUENCE

In 2010, *Rolling Stone* ranked "No Reply" as #45 on the magazine's list of *The Beatles' 100 Greatest Songs.*

ALBUM APPEARANCES: *Beatles for Sale*; *Beatles '65*; *Anthology 1.*

See also: *Beatles for Sale* (LP).

Northern Songs/Sony ATV Publishing

Originally the brainchild of British entertainment impresario Dick James, Northern Songs was established in 1963 as a means for handling the Beatles' publishing concerns. Entitled Northern Songs in order to connote Lennon and McCartney's North Country roots, the company split the songwriters' royalties evenly after deducting James's 10-percent fee. The deal that they concocted required Northern Songs to purchase Lenmac Enterprises, a holding company that Epstein had established earlier in the year that already owned the rights to 59 original Lennon–McCartney compositions. The new agreement with Northern Songs required the songwriters to produce six new numbers per year over the next four years—a period in which they literally composed hundreds of songs. Initially, Northern Songs handled all of Lennon and McCartney's songs, as well as early composing efforts by Harrison and Starr, who later formed their own publishing companies—Harrisongs and Startling Music, respectively. The problems with Northern Songs began in 1965, when the company went public in order to save money on capital gains tax. Lennon and McCartney each maintained 15 percent ownership of Northern Songs, Epstein held 7.5 percent, Harrison and Starr owned some 1.6 percent, and James (along with his business partner Charles Silver) held a whopping 37.5 percent. The remaining shares subsequently traded on the London Stock Exchange.

In early 1969, the Beatles assigned Allen Klein and attorney Lee Eastman, McCartney's future father-in-law, with the task of cleaning up their business and legal affairs, respectively. Their first order of business was to win back control of NEMS Enterprises, which was now under the management of Clive Epstein, who was considering a bid for control from Triumph Investments, to whom he sold 70 percent of NEMS. The saga of Northern Songs came to a head in March 1969, when James threatened to sell his shares in Lennon and McCartney's publishing company to the United Kingdom's Associated Television (ATV), which had been founded in 1955 by Sir Lew Grade. Lennon was incensed: "I'm not going to be f—ed around by men in suits sitting on their fat arses in the City!" he remarked at the time (Koskimäki 2006, 58). To make matters worse, McCartney had been secretly buying shares of Northern Songs, which infuriated Lennon, although to his great credit, he forgave McCartney and resolved to work with his partner to effect a joint solution. In order to purchase Northern Songs outright, Lennon and

The Beatles sign documents for music publisher Dick James (left) in Studio Two at Abbey Road in London in July 1963. James' role in managing the Beatles' royalties through Northern Songs began a long saga of the band's battle, largely unsuccessful, over the ownership of the rights to their songs. (Terry O'Neill/Getty Images)

McCartney needed to come up with £9.5 million, but they simply didn't have access to that kind of cash, with Apple's dire financial straits no doubt contributing to their weak financial position (Koskimäki 2006, 41). By the time that Lennon and McCartney marshaled their forces in order to purchase a controlling interest in their publishing company, it was too late. London's money men in suits had prevailed. When ATV successfully negotiated their buyout later that year, Lennon and McCartney were powerless to do anything about it, other than voice their opposition. The songs that had earned for them international songwriterly acclaim were now the property of a faceless corporate entity.

But the Northern Songs calamity was far from over. After wresting control of the Lennon–McCartney songbook in September 1969, ATV maintained a majority interest in Northern Songs until 1985, when the company was put up for sale. McCartney was famously outbid for Northern Songs by Michael Jackson, with whom he had recently collaborated on a pair of hit singles ("The Girl Is Mine" on Jackson's *Thriller* [1982] and "Say Say Say" on McCartney's *Pipes of Peace* [1983]). The self-styled "King of Pop" paid $47.5 million for the publishing company. In 1995, Jackson agreed to merge ATV with Sony Music for some $95 million in order to ease his financial problems. In the ensuing years, Jackson's fiscal woes grew considerably, leaving his future ownership role with Sony ATV Music

Publishing in significant doubt—a situation that was further complicated by his untimely death in 2009. Following Jackson's passing, his estate retained 50 percent control of Sony ATV, with Sony retaining the other 50 percent. The company that McCartney might have purchased back in 1985 for some $50 million is now worth some $800 million, with Sony ATV having added to the Beatles' portfolio nearly 2 million other songs. While Sony ATV owns the copyrights for most of the Lennon–McCartney songwriting catalogue, the Beatles' sound recordings remain in the possession and control of the EMI Group.

See also: Epstein, Brian; Klein, Allen.

"Norwegian Wood (This Bird Has Flown)" (Lennon–McCartney)

"Norwegian Wood (This Bird Has Flown)" is a song on the Beatles' *Rubber Soul* album. It marks Harrison's first use of the sitar on a Beatles recording.

AUTHORSHIP AND BACKGROUND

Written by Lennon with assistance from McCartney, "Norwegian Wood (This Bird Has Flown)" was later described by McCartney—along with "Drive My Car"—as one of *Rubber Soul*'s two "comedy numbers."

For Lennon, the song's impetus involved an affair with a "prominent journalist," who has been widely speculated to be Maureen Cleave, a frequent contributor to the *London Evening News* and the *London Evening Standard* (Dowlding 1989, 115). As Lennon later remembered, " 'Norwegian Wood' is my song completely. It was about an affair I was having. I was very careful and paranoid because I didn't want my wife, Cyn, to know that there really was something going on outside of the household. I'd always had some kind of affairs going on, so I was trying to be sophisticated in writing about an affair, but in such a smoke-screen way that you couldn't tell. But I can't remember any specific woman it had to do with" (Lennon and Ono 2000, 178).

As McCartney recalled, "It was me who decided in 'Norwegian Wood' that the house should burn down—not that it's any big deal" (Dowlding 1989, 115).

RECORDING SESSIONS

Produced by Martin, "Norwegian Wood" went under the working title of "This Bird Has Flown." After recording a rough version of "Norwegian Wood" at Abbey Road Studios on October 12, 1965, the Beatles returned to the studio and produced an entirely new rendition of the song during a whirlwind session on October 21 with Lennon on guitar and vocals, McCartney on bass and harmony vocals, Harrison on sitar, and Starr on tambourine. Lennon later double-tracked his vocal.

"Norwegian Wood" features the exotic, microtonal flavor of Harrison's sitar lines accenting the flourishes of Lennon's haunting acoustic guitar, which he played in waltz-like 12/8 time on his capoed Jumbo. As sound engineer Norman Smith points out, recording the sitar at Abbey Road Studios proved to be difficult, given the instrument's unusual sonic properties: "It is very hard to record because it has a lot of nasty peaks and a very complex wave form. My meter would be going right over into the red, into distortion, without us getting audible value for money. I could have used a limiter but that would have meant losing the sonorous quality" (Lewisohn 1988, 65).

PERSONNEL

Lennon: Vocal, Gibson J-160E
McCartney: Höfner 500/1, Backing Vocal
Harrison: Sitar
Starr: Tambourine, Maracas, Finger Cymbals

LEGACY AND INFLUENCE

"Norwegian Wood (This Bird Has Flown)" is included among the Rock and Roll Hall of Fame's *500 Songs That Shaped Rock and Roll*.

In 2004, *Rolling Stone* ranked "Norwegian Wood (This Bird Has Flown)" as #83 on the magazine's list of *The 500 Greatest Songs of All Time*.

In 2010, *Rolling Stone* ranked "Norwegian Wood (This Bird Has Flown)" as #12 on the magazine's list of *The Beatles' 100 Greatest Songs*.

ALBUM APPEARANCES: *Rubber Soul* (U.K.); *Rubber Soul* (U.S.); *The Beatles, 1962–1966*; *Love Songs*; *Anthology 2*.

See also: Lennon, Cynthia Lillian; McCartney, Linda Eastman; Ringo Starr and His All-Starr Band; *Rubber Soul* (U.K. LP).

"Not a Second Time" (Lennon–McCartney)

"Not a Second Time" is a song on the *With the Beatles* album.

AUTHORSHIP AND BACKGROUND

Written by Lennon, "Not a Second Time" marked the first instance in which the Beatles received songwriting accolades beyond the low culture of the pop-music press. In a December 1963 article in the *Times*, William Mann famously saluted Lennon's composition for its deployment of an Aeolian cadence, a feature that Mann likened to the chord progression that concludes Gustav Mahler's *The Song of the Earth* (1907–1909).

Years later, Lennon remarked that "to this day I don't have *any* idea what [Aeolian cadences] are. They sound like exotic birds." Yet way back in 1963, Lennon could barely contain his excitement at Mann's sophisticated response to the band's work, going so far as to have the article framed: "That was the first time anyone had written anything like that about us" (Dowlding 1989, 57).

For Mann, the Beatles were already making an innovative and vital contribution to popular music. "They have brought a distinctive and exhilarating flavor into a genre of music that was in danger of ceasing to be music at all," he remarked. It makes "one wonder with interest what the Beatles, and particularly Lennon and McCartney, will do next" (Mann 1963).

RECORDING SESSIONS

Produced by Martin, "Not a Second Time" was recorded in nine takes at Abbey Road Studios on September 11, 1963. Lennon double-tracked his lead vocal.

PERSONNEL

Lennon: Vocal, Gibson J-160E
McCartney: Höfner 500/1
Harrison: Gibson J-160E
Starr: Ludwig Oyster Black Pearl Drums
Martin: Piano

ALBUM APPEARANCES: *With the Beatles*; *Meet the Beatles!*

See also: *With the Beatles* (LP).

"Not Guilty" (Harrison)

"Not Guilty" was recorded during the sessions for *The Beatles* (*The White Album*) and remained unreleased until the Beatles' *Anthology* project during the 1990s.

AUTHORSHIP AND BACKGROUND

Written by Harrison, "Not Guilty" was composed after the Beatles returned from their sojourn in India.

As Harrison recalled in an April 1979 *Rolling Stone* interview,

I wrote that in 1968. It was after we got back from Rishikesh in the Himalayas on the Maharishi trip, and it was for *The White Album*. We recorded it but we didn't get it down right or something. Then I forgot all about it until a year ago, when I found this old demo I'd made in the Sixties. The lyrics are a bit passé—all about upsetting "Apple carts" and stuff—but it's a bit about what was happening at the time. "Not guilty for getting in your way / While you're trying to steal the day"—which was me trying to get a space. "Not guilty / For looking like a freak / Making friends with every Sikh / For leading your astray / On the road to Mandalay"—which is the Maharishi and going to the Himalayas and all that was said about that. I like the tune a lot; it would make a great tune for Peggy Lee or someone. (*Rolling Stone* 1979)

RECORDING SESSIONS

Produced by Martin, "Not Guilty" was recorded in more than 100 takes at Abbey Road Studios on August 7, 1968, with additional overdubbing sessions on August 8, 9, and 12. Producer Chris Thomas contributed an uncredited harpsichord part.

For the recording, Harrison effected a distorted guitar part for "Not Guilty." As assistant engineer Brian Gibson later recalled, "George asked us to put his guitar amplifier at one end of the echo chambers, with a microphone at the other end to pick up the output. He sat playing the guitar in the studio control room with a line plugged through to the chamber" (Lewisohn 1988, 147).

An early version of "Not Guilty" was recorded in May 1968 at Harrison's Kinfauns studio as part of the Esher Tapes. In 1984, Geoff Emerick remixed "Not Guilty" in preparation for the unreleased Beatles *Sessions* project. In 1994, Martin remixed "Not Guilty" for release as part of the Beatles' *Anthology* project.

PERSONNEL

McCartney: Rickenbacker 4001S, Backing Vocal
Harrison: Vocal, Gibson Les Paul Standard
Starr: Ludwig Oyster Black Pearl Drums
Chris Thomas: Harpsichord

ALBUM APPEARANCE: *Anthology 3*.

See also: *The Beatles Anthology, Volume 3* (LP); *The Beatles* (*The White Album*) (LP); Thomas, Chris.

"Nowhere Man" (Lennon–McCartney)

"Nowhere Man" is a song on the Beatles' *Rubber Soul* album.

AUTHORSHIP AND BACKGROUND

Written by Lennon, "Nowhere Man" offers one of the songwriter's early explorations of interpersonal philosophy.

As Lennon recalled, "I'd spent five hours that morning trying to write a song that was meaningful and good, and I finally gave up and lay down. Then 'Nowhere Man' came, words and music—the whole damn thing—as I lay down. So letting it go is what the whole game is. You put your finger on it, it slips away, right? You know, you turn the lights on and the cockroaches run away. You can never grasp them" (Lennon and Ono 2000, 193).

RECORDING SESSIONS

Produced by Martin, "Nowhere Man" was recorded at Abbey Road Studios on October 21 and 22, 1965.

Musically, "Nowhere Man" offers a deep, trebly sound that the Beatles achieved through the studio trickery that became their standard modus operandi in 1966. As Walter Everett observes,

John and George ran their Strats through several sets of faders so the engineers could boost the treble to the utmost, multiple times, to enhance their silvery doubled part in "Nowhere Man," the solo of which culminates in the first natural harmonic featured in a Beatles recording. (Everett 2006, 80)

As McCartney later observed,

I remember we wanted very treble-y guitars—which they are—they're among the most treble-y guitars I've ever heard on record. The engineer said, "Alright, I'll put full treble on it," and we said, "That's not enough." He said, "But that's all I've got." And we replied, "Well, put that through another lot of faders and put full treble up on that. And if that's not enough we'll go through another lot of faders." They said, "We don't do that," and we would say, "Just try it—if it sounds crappy we'll lose it, but it might just sound good." You'd then find, "Oh it worked," and they were secretly glad because they had been the engineer who put three times the allowed value of treble on a song. I think they were quietly proud of those things. (Lange 2001, 133)

PERSONNEL

Lennon: Vocal, Gibson J-160E, Sonic Blue Fender Stratocaster
McCartney: Höfner 500/1, Backing Vocal
Harrison: Sonic Blue Fender Stratocaster, Backing Vocal
Starr: Ludwig Oyster Black Pearl Drums

CHART PERFORMANCE

U.S.: "Nowhere Man"/"What Goes On"; February 21, 1966, Capitol 5587: #3 (certified by the RIAA as "Gold," with more than 500,000 copies sold).

LEGACY AND INFLUENCE

In 2010, *Rolling Stone* ranked "Nowhere Man" as #66 on the magazine's list of *The Beatles' 100 Greatest Songs.*

ALBUM APPEARANCES: *Rubber Soul* (U.K.); *Yesterday . . . and Today; The Beatles, 1962–1966; Yellow Submarine Songtrack.*

See also: Rubber Soul (U.K. LP).

O

"Ob-La-Di, Ob-La-Da" (Lennon–McCartney)

"Ob-La-Di, Ob-La-Da" is a song on *The Beatles* (*The White Album*). It was released as a single backed with "Julia" on November 8, 1976, in the United States.

AUTHORSHIP AND BACKGROUND

Written by Paul McCartney, "Ob-La-Di, Ob-La-Da" finds its origins during the Beatles' 1968 visit to India. It found its inspiration in the words of Jimmy Scott, a Nigerian Conga player who was fond of repeating the Yoruban expression "*ob-la-di, ob-la-da*, life goes on."

As McCartney later recalled,

> A fella who used to hang around the clubs used to say, "Ob-la-di, ob-la-da, life goes on," and he got annoyed when I did a song of it, 'cuz he wanted a cut. I said, "Come on, Jimmy, it's just an expression. If you'd written the song, you could have had a cut." He also used to say, "Nothin's too much, just outta sight." He was just one of those guys who had great expressions, you know. (Dowlding 1989, 226)

An early version of "Ob-La-Di, Ob-La-Da" was recorded in May 1968 at George Harrison's Kinfauns studio as part of the Esher Tapes.

RECORDING SESSIONS

Produced by George Martin, the sessions for "Ob-La-Di, Ob-La-Da" began on July 3, 1968, at Abbey Road Studios, followed by overdubbing sessions on July 4 and 5. It underwent successive remakes on July 8 and 9, with additional overdubbing sessions on July 11 and 15. In an early rendition of the song later included on *Anthology 3*, the Beatles fashioned a south-of-the-border reading of "Ob-La-Di, Ob-La-Da," complete with John Lennon's enthusiastic preface: "Yes, sir! Take one, and the Magic Jumbo Band!"

Over the next several nights, the composition underwent numerous takes as the group attempted different versions of "Ob-La-Di, Ob-La-Da" and McCartney continuously tinkered with his vocal, testing his colleagues' patience in the process. Things finally came to head on July 9, 1968, when Lennon contrived the tune's jangly piano introduction. "I am f—ing stoned!" he announced upon entering the studio that evening. "And this is how the f—ing song should go," he said, before pounding out the famous piano opening (Emerick and Massey 2006, 247).

PERSONNEL

Lennon: Piano, Maracas, Backing Vocal
McCartney: Vocal, Fender Jazz Bass
Harrison: Gibson J-200, Backing Vocal
Starr: Ludwig Oyster Black Pearl Drums
Studio Musicians: Brass Accompaniment conducted by Martin

CHART PERFORMANCE

U.S.: "Ob-La-Di, Ob-La-Da"/"Julia"; November 8, 1976, Capitol 4347: #49.

CONTROVERSY

Jimmy Scott later attempted to claim authorship credit for "Ob-La-Di, Ob-La-Da," although McCartney countered by arguing that Scott's catchphrase was merely an expression. Scott agreed to drop his claim after McCartney paid Scott's unrelated legal expenses. McCartney borrowed yet another one of Scott's catchphrases as the inspiration for "Nothing Too Much Just Out of Sight"—a song on the Fireman's 2008 album, *Electric Arguments*.

LEGACY AND INFLUENCE

In 1969, the Beatles received an Ivor Novello Award, awarded annually by the British Academy of Songwriters, Composers, and Authors, for "Ob-La-Di, Ob-La-Da."

ALBUM APPEARANCES: *The Beatles* (*The White Album*); *The Beatles, 1967–1970*; *Anthology 3*.

See also: *The Beatles* (*The White Album*) (LP).

"Octopus's Garden" (Starr)

Written by Ringo Starr, "Octopus's Garden" is a song on the *Abbey Road* album.

AUTHORSHIP AND BACKGROUND

Composed by Starr on a family vacation in Sardinia during his August 1968 hiatus from the Beatles, "Octopus's Garden" had been inspired by a fisherman's tale about undersea life: "He told me all about octopuses, how they go 'round the sea bed and pick up stones and shiny objects and build gardens," Starr recalled. "I thought, 'How fabulous!' 'cause at the time I just wanted to be under the sea, too. I wanted to get out of it for a while" (Dowlding 1989, 283).

RECORDING SESSIONS

Produced by Martin, "Octopus's Garden" was recorded at Abbey Road Studios on April 26, 1969, with additional overdubbing sessions on April 29, July 17, and July 18.

The distinctive underwater ambience in "Octopus's Garden" was created by Harrison on the Moog Synthesizer, although Starr was especially keen on effecting the sound of blowing bubbles in order to enhance his lead vocal: "After some experimentation," Emerick later remembered, "I discovered that feeding the vocals into a compressor and triggering it from a pulsing tone (which I derived from George Harrison's Moog synthesizer) imparted a distinctive wobbly sound, almost like gargling. It was weird, almost like something out of a cheesy science-fiction movie, but Ringo loved the result" (Emerick and Massey 2006, 283).

PERSONNEL

> Lennon: Epiphone Casino, Backing Vocal
> McCartney: Rickenbacker 4001S, Piano, Backing Vocal
> Harrison: Fender Stratocaster, Moog Synthesizer, Backing Vocal
> Starr: Vocal, Ludwig Hollywood Maple Drums

ALBUM APPEARANCES: *Abbey Road*; *The Beatles, 1967–1970*; *Anthology 3*; *Love*.

See also: *Abbey Road* (LP).

"Oh! Darling" (Lennon–McCartney)

Written by McCartney, "Oh! Darling" is a song on the *Abbey Road* album.

AUTHORSHIP AND BACKGROUND

Produced under the working title of "I'll Never Do You No Harm," "Oh! Darling" was inspired by the rock 'n' roll ballads of the late 1950s—particularly such bombastic vocal showcases as Jackie Wilson's "Lonely Teardrops." One of McCartney's most searing vocal performances, "Oh! Darling" is performed by the group in a 12/8 time signature.

RECORDING SESSIONS

The Beatles debuted "Oh! Darling" at a January 27, 1969, rehearsal in Apple Records' basement studio. Produced by George Martin, "Oh! Darling" was recorded at Abbey Road Studios on April 20, with additional overdubbing sessions on April 26, July 23, and August 8 and 11.

"Oh! Darling" offers one of McCartney's most deftly crafted vocal performances: "When we were recording this track," he later remembered, "I came into the studios early every day for a week to sing it by myself because at first my voice was too clear. I wanted it to sound as though I'd been performing it on stage all week" (Dowlding 1989, 282).

PERSONNEL

Lennon: Backing Vocal
McCartney: Vocal, Rickenbacker 4001S, Piano
Harrison: Fender Rosewood Telecaster, Backing Vocal
Starr: Ludwig Hollywood Maple Drums

LEGACY AND INFLUENCE

In 2010, *Rolling Stone* ranked "Oh! Darling" as #67 on the magazine's list of *The Beatles' 100 Greatest Songs*.

ALBUM APPEARANCES: *Abbey Road*; *Anthology 3*.

See also: *Abbey Road* (LP).

"Old Brown Shoe" (Harrison)

"Old Brown Shoe" is the B-side of the Beatles' "The Ballad of John and Yoko" single, which was released in the United Kingdom on May 30, 1969, and in the United States on June 4, 1969.

AUTHORSHIP AND BACKGROUND

Written by Harrison, "Old Brown Shoe" was rehearsed by the Beatles during the January 1969 *Get Back* sessions. As Harrison later recalled, "I started the chord sequences on the piano, which I don't really play, and then began writing ideas for the words from various opposites. Again, it's the duality of things—yes no, up down, left right, right wrong, etc." (Dowlding 1989, 271).

RECORDING SESSIONS

Harrison recorded a demo for "Old Brown Shoe," along with "All Things Must Pass" and "Something," on February 25, 1969. Produced by Martin, "Old Brown Shoe" was recorded at Abbey Road Studios on April 16, with an additional over-dubbing on April 18.

"Old Brown Shoe" features an ecstatic guitar solo from Harrison, whose sizzling Rosewood Telecaster benefits from a heavy dose of ADT [automatic double-tracking]. A second guitar part by Lennon on his Epiphone Casino was later deleted from the final mix. There is some debate about whether or not McCartney played the song's galloping bass part. During an interview with *Creem* magazine, Harrison later reported that he was doubling his guitar part on the bass, remarking, "That was me going nuts. I'm doing exactly what I do on the guitar" (*Creem* 1987–1988).

PERSONNEL

Lennon: Epiphone Casino (deleted), Backing Vocal
McCartney: Piano, Backing Vocal
Harrison: Vocal, Fender Rosewood Telecaster, Fender Jazz Bass, Hammond Organ
Starr: Ludwig Hollywood Maple Drums, Backing Vocal

CHART PERFORMANCE

U.K.: "The Ballad of John and Yoko"/"Old Brown Shoe"; May 30, 1969, Apple [Parlophone] R 5786: #1. As the B-side of "The Ballad of John and Yoko," "Old Brown Shoe" did not chart.

U.S.: "The Ballad of John and Yoko"/"Old Brown Shoe"; June 4, 1969, Apple [Capitol] 2531: #8 (certified by the RIAA as "Gold," with more than 500,000 copies sold). As the B-side of "The Ballad of John and Yoko," "Old Brown Shoe" did not chart.

ALBUM APPEARANCES: *Hey Jude*; *The Beatles, 1967–1970*; *Past Masters, Volume 2*; *Anthology 3*.

See also: Clapton, Eric.

On Air: Live at the BBC, Volume 2 (LP)

November 11, 2013, Apple [Universal Music Group] B00F3VOL38

Released in 2013, *On Air: Live at the BBC, Volume 2* offers a selection of unreleased live performances by the band as a sequel to the Beatles' critically acclaimed 1994 album *Live at the BBC*.

BACKGROUND

On Air: Live at the BBC, Volume 2 features 40 songs, along with 23 dialogue tracks, recorded as BBC Light Programme radio shows between 1962 and 1965. As with *Live at the BBC*, the material on volume 2 was culled from some 275 performance of 88 different songs, the majority of which were cover versions. The band's first appearance on BBC Radio occurred in March 1962 with a recording for *Teenager's Turn: Here We Go*. Their run on BBC Radio ended with their appearance on the May 1965 special *The Beatles Invite You to Take a Ticket to Ride*.

On Air: Live at the BBC, Volume 2 was accompanied by the release of a remastered version of the original *Live at the BBC* album.

TRACK LISTING

Disc 1: "And Here We Are Again" (Speech); "Words of Love"; "How About It, Gorgeous?" (Speech); "Do You Want to Know a Secret"; "Lucille"; "Hey, Paul" (Speech); "Anna (Go to Him)"; "Hello!" (Speech); "Please Please Me"; "Misery"; "I'm Talking About You"; "A Real Treat" (Speech); "Boys"; "Absolutely Fab" (Speech); "Chains"; "Ask Me Why"; "Till There Was You"; "Lend Me Your Comb"; "Lower 5E" (Speech); "Hippy Hippy Shake"; "Roll Over Beethoven"; "There's a Place"; "Bumper Bundle" (Speech); "P.S. I Love You"; "Please Mister Postman"; "Beautiful Dreamer"; "Devil in Her Heart"; "The 49 Weeks" (Speech); "Sure to Fall (In Love with You)"; "Never Mind, Eh?" (Speech); "Twist and Shout"; "Bye, Bye" (Speech); "John: Pop Profile" (Speech); "George: Pop Profile" (Speech).

Disc 2: "I Saw Her Standing There"; "Glad All Over"; "Lift Lid Again" (Speech); "I'll Get You"; "She Loves You"; "Memphis, Tennessee"; "Happy Birthday Dear Saturday Club"; "Now Hush, Hush" (Speech); "From Me to You"; "Money (That's What I Want)"; "I Want to Hold Your Hand"; "Brian Bathtubes" (Speech); "This Boy"; "If I Wasn't in America" (Speech); "I Got a Woman"; "Long Tall Sally"; "If I Fell"; "A Hard Job Writing Them" (Speech);"And I Love Her"; "Oh, Can't We? Yes We Can" (Speech);"You Can't Do That"; "Honey Don't"; "I'll Follow the Sun"; "Green with Black Shutters" (Speech); Medley: "Kansas City/Hey-Hey-Hey-Hey!"; "That's What We're Here For" (Speech); "I Feel Fine" (Studio Outtake); "Paul: Pop Profile" (Speech); "Ringo: Pop Profile" (Speech).

COVER ARTWORK

On Air: Live at the BBC, Volume 2's front and back cover art depicts the Beatles in front of the BBC's Paris Studio in London's Waterloo Place. Shot in December 1963, the photograph was taken by Dezo Hoffmann (1918–1986). Originally photographed in black and white, Hoffmann's picture was reproduced in a color format.

CHART PERFORMANCE

U.K.: #12.
U.S.: #7.

See also: *Live at the BBC* (LP); Martin, George.

I (LP)

November 13, 2000, Apple [Parlophone] 7243 5 29325 2 8
November 13, 2000, Apple [Capitol] CDP 7243 5 29325 2 8

I is a compilation album that was released by EMI on November 13, 2000, and enjoyed tremendous worldwide success and acclaim, selling more than 31 million copies. In the United States, it was released on the Capitol Records label, while featuring the Apple/Parlophone imprint in the United Kingdom.

BACKGROUND

True to its name, the compilation reached the #1 chart position in 35 countries, becoming the best-selling album release of the 21st century. As a career retrospective, *I* features an amalgamation of the Beatles' #1 hits in both the United Kingdom and the United States.

I's contents are noteworthy for the exclusion of "Please Please Me," which failed to achieve #1 status in the key *Record Retailer* chart in the United Kingdom in 1963, and "Strawberry Fields Forever," which was blocked from the top spot in the United Kingdom in 1967 by Engelbert Humperdinck's international smash hit "Release Me." In each case, the choice of omission is somewhat controversial. For example, "Please Please Me" was counted as a #1 hit by two other U.K. charts at the time, while "Strawberry Fields Forever" fell victim to a U.K. policy during that era that only counted half of the double A-side's sales, with the other half going to "Penny Lane," which enjoyed slightly stronger returns.

The 27 tracks on *I* were remastered by Peter Mew of Abbey Road Studios using 24-bit resolution and processed via Sonic Solutions NoNoise technology. On November 6, 2015, the album was remixed by Giles Martin and reissued as *I+*. A deluxe edition included 50 promotional films and performances, along with commentary by McCartney and Starr.

TRACK LISTING

"Love Me Do"; "From Me to You"; "She Loves You"; "I Want to Hold Your Hand"; "Can't Buy Me Love"; "A Hard Day's Night"; "I Feel Fine"; "Eight Days a Week"; "Ticket to Ride"; "Help!"; "Yesterday"; "Day Tripper"; "We Can Work It Out";

"Paperback Writer"; "Yellow Submarine"; "Eleanor Rigby"; "Penny Lane"; "All You Need Is Love"; "Hello, Goodbye"; "Lady Madonna"; "Hey Jude"; "Get Back"; "The Ballad of John and Yoko"; "Something"; "Come Together"; "Let It Be"; "The Long and Winding Road."

COVER ARTWORK

Designed by Rick Ward, the cover art for *1* features a yellow, pop art numeral one in Helvetica typeface on a field of bright red. The album was packaged with a 32-page booklet featuring background information on each of the tracks, as well as more than 160 picture-sleeve photographs. Its back cover features photographs of the band from Richard Avedon's famous 1967 session with the Beatles.

CHART PERFORMANCE

- U.K.: #1 (certified by the BPI as "8x Platinum," with more than 2.4 million copies sold).
- U.S.: #1 (certified by the RIAA as "11x Multi Platinum," with more than 11 million copies sold; certified by the RIAA as "Diamond," with more than 10 million copies sold).

See also: Abbey Road Studios; Martin, Giles.

"One After 909" (Lennon–McCartney)

"One After 909" is a song on the Beatles' *Let It Be* album.

AUTHORSHIP AND BACKGROUND

Written by Lennon, "One After 909" was likely composed at the McCartney home on Liverpool's Forthlin Road in the late 1950s. As one of the earliest Lennon–McCartney compositions, "One After 909" was Lennon's obvious attempt to parrot skiffle's infatuation with life on the railroad in such tunes as Lonnie Donegan's "Rock Island Line," Johnny Duncan's "Last Train to San Fernando," and the Chas McDevitt Skiffle Group's "Freight Train." As John Mendelssohn observes, in "One After 909" the line " 'C'mon, baby, don't be cold as ice' may be at once the most ridiculous and magnificent line Lennon–McCartney ever wrote" (Doggett 1998, 127).

During one of his last interviews, Lennon remarked that "One After 909" was "something I wrote when I was about seventeen. I lived at 9 Newcastle Road. I was born on the ninth of October—the ninth month. It's just a number that follows me around, but numerologically, apparently I'm a number six or a three or something, but it's all part of nine" (Lennon and Ono 2000, 204).

Years later, McCartney remarked that

"One After 909" was one that we always liked doing, and we rediscovered it. There were a couple of tunes that we wondered why we never put out—either George Martin didn't like them enough to, or he favored others. It's not a great song but it's a great favorite of mine because it has great memories for me of John and I trying to write a bluesy freight-train song. There were a lot of those songs at the time, like "Midnight Special," "Freight Train," "Rock Island Line," so this was the "One After 909." She didn't get the 909, she got the one after it! (Miles 1997, 536)

RECORDING SESSIONS

Produced by Martin with postproduction by Phil Spector, "One After 909" was recorded during the Beatles' rooftop concert on January 30, 1969. The Beatles had conducted earlier rehearsals of the song at Apple Studio on January 28 and 29.

The Beatles' first recording of "One After 909" occurred during a July 1960 recording session in the McCartney family's bathroom using a Grundig tape recorder. Known as the Braun Tape, the recordings survived in the possession of Hans-Walther "Icke" Braun, one of the band's Hamburg friends, who was entrusted with the tape in the spring of 1961 (Winn 2003a, 4). Seventeen demos survive from the July 1960 recordings, including early versions of the Lennon–McCartney compositions "One After 909," "I'll Follow the Sun," and "Hello Little Girl." In addition to Lennon, McCartney, and Harrison, the July 1960 version of "One After 909" features Stuart Sutcliffe on bass.

The Beatles had recorded another early version of "One After 909" during the March 5, 1963, session in which they recorded their third single "From Me to You" and its B-side "Thank You Girl."

In 1984, Emerick remixed a 1963 version of "One After 909" in preparation for the unreleased Beatles *Sessions* project. In 1994, Martin remixed "One After 909" for release as part of the Beatles' *Anthology* project. For the song's *Let It Be . . . Naked* release (2003), "One After 909" was remixed from the rooftop concert version, albeit without Lennon's ad-lib.

PERSONNEL

July 1960 Version:

Lennon: Vocal, Guitar
McCartney: Guitar, Backing Vocal
Harrison: Guitar
Sutcliffe: Bass

January 1969 Version:

> Lennon: Vocal, Epiphone Casino
> McCartney: Höfner 500/1, Backing Vocal
> Harrison: Fender Rosewood Telecaster, Backing Vocal
> Starr: Ludwig Hollywood Maple Drums
> Billy Preston: Fender Rhodes Electric Piano

ALBUM APPEARANCES: *Let It Be*; *Anthology 1*; *Let It Be . . . Naked.*

See also: *Let It Be* (LP); *Let It Be . . . Naked* (LP).

"Only a Northern Song" (Harrison)

"Only a Northern Song" is a song on the Beatles' *Yellow Submarine* album.

AUTHORSHIP AND BACKGROUND

Written by Harrison, "Only a Northern Song" was originally intended for the *Sgt. Pepper's Lonely Hearts Club Band* album.

As Harrison later observed, " 'Northern Song' was a joke relating to Liverpool, the Holy City in the North of England. In addition, the song was copyrighted Northern Songs LTD, which I don't own" (Dowlding 1989, 212). In a 1999 *Billboard* interview with Timothy White, Harrison later added:

> It was at the point that I realized Dick James had conned me out of the copyrights for my own songs by offering to become my publisher. As an 18- or 19-year-old kid, I thought, "Great, somebody's gonna publish my songs!" But he never said, "And incidentally, when you sign this document here, you're assigning me the ownership of the songs," which is what it is. It was just a blatant theft. By the time I realized what had happened, when they were going public and making all this money out of this catalog, I wrote "Only a Northern Song" as what we call a "piss-take," just to have a joke about it. (*Billboard* 1999)

RECORDING SESSIONS

Produced by Martin, "Only a Northern Song" was recorded at Abbey Road Studios on February 13, 1967, with additional overdubbing sessions on February 14 and April 20. After the sessions, the group, particularly Lennon, rejected "Only a Northern Song" for inclusion on the *Sgt. Pepper's Lonely Hearts Club Band* album. In its stead, Harrison presented "Within You, Without You," which was accepted as his contribution to the project.

PERSONNEL

> Lennon: Piano, Glockenspiel, Tape Effects
> McCartney: Rickenbacker 4001S, Distorted Trumpet, Tape Effects
> Harrison: Vocal, Hammond Organ, Tape Effects
> Starr: Ludwig Oyster Black Pearl Drums

ALBUM APPEARANCES: *Yellow Submarine*; *Yellow Submarine Songtrack*; *Anthology 2*.

See also: *Sgt. Pepper's Lonely Hearts Club Band* (LP); *Yellow Submarine* (Film); *Yellow Submarine* (LP); *Yellow Submarine Songtrack* (LP).

Ono, Yoko (1933–)

Born on February 18, 1933, in Saitama, Japan, Yoko Ono is Lennon's second wife, as well as an internationally renowned peace activist and artist. She enjoyed a privileged upbringing as the oldest child of Isoko Yasuda, a wealthy heiress, and Eisuke Ono, a banker who, in his younger days, had pursued a career as a classically trained pianist. Yoko, whose name translates as "Ocean Child," attended Tokyo's elite Gakushuin academy. Her early years at the institution found her rebelling against her conventional education, as well as her disciplinarian-mother: "I was like a domesticated animal being fed information," she later remarked. "I hated it. And particularly music. I used to faint before my music lessons—literally. I suppose it was my way of escape" (Goldman 1988, 211). During the Second World War, her family—including her brother Keisuke and sister Setsuko—fled the city for the countryside, where their well-heeled existence clashed with the harsh poverty of the nation's peasantry.

After the war, Yoko's family immigrated to Scarsdale, New York, where she continued her education at Sarah Lawrence College. During this period, she fell in with a bohemian crowd of artists and writers, dropping out of college during her junior year. In 1956, she married Japanese experimental composer Toshi Ichiyanagi, whose inferior class status enraged her mother to no end. The couple became estranged in the early 1960s, and she engaged in a succession of sexual affairs, including a lengthy liaison with radical American composer La Monte Young, who introduced her to the New York art world, including composer John Cage and a host of other influential figures. In 1962, emissaries of her family escorted her back to Japan, where she became suicidal and was briefly institutionalized. During her stay in the mental hospital, she met American jazz musician and film producer Tony Cox, who had sailed to Asia after hearing tales from Young about a Japanese artist who had left New York City under mysterious circumstances. In November 1962, she married Cox—but without first having bothered to divorce Toshi. In order to untangle the ensuing legal mess, her lawyers advised her in March 1963 to annul her marriage with Cox. They remarried in June 1963, and their daughter Kyoko was born on August 8 of that year. Cox and Ono's marriage deteriorated rapidly in the wake of Kyoko's birth. At one point, their growing animus led to a knife fight that was broken up in the nick of time by Al Wunderlich, a visiting friend from the United States. Yet despite their tempestuous relationship, the couple remained together in order to nurture their respective careers.

In September 1964, Ono returned to New York, where she attempted to resurrect her artistic standing among the city's growing avant-garde community. Although it was slow going at first, she eventually found her place amongst the Dadaesque group of artists known as Fluxus (from the Latin word "to flow"), whose founder, George Maciunas, promoted her growing interest in performance art. Maciunas' whimsical approach to the genre was a driving force in her aesthetic, which explored, often playfully, the ironic interrelationships that exist between the natural and industrial worlds. Maciunas also influenced her creation of imaginary objects and works of interactive art. Under Cage's tutelage, she added a variety of natural and mechanized sounds to her creative repertoire. As a performance artist, she appreciated the power of shock value, often realized through nudity, as a means of conceptualizing her aesthetic. In her work entitled *Cut Piece*, for example, she reclined onstage, while audience members cut off her clothing with a pair of scissors until she was naked. Her desire to provoke her audience continued with her film *No. 4*, known colloquially as *Bottoms*, which exhibited a series of human buttocks as the subjects walked upon a treadmill accompanied by their own words in candid voiceover. In his review of Ono's film in the *Sunday Times* on February 12, 1967, Hunter Davies famously dismissed *Bottoms*, writing "Oh no, Ono" (Cross 2005, 196).

Yoko Ono poses at the 2012 MusiCares Person of the Year Awards honoring Paul McCartney, held at the Los Angeles Convention Center on February 10, 2012. (Sbukley/Dreamstime.com)

By the summer of 1966, Ono had left New York in order to attend the *Destruction in Art Symposium*, an international congress that Fluxus was hosting in London. Before long, she and Cox took to hanging out with the gaggle of other hipsters who frequented the Indica Gallery. At one point, she even met McCartney, whom she regaled with tales about her work with Cage. Without missing a beat, she invited him to contribute to *Notations* (1969), Cage's forthcoming anthology of musical scores by contemporary composers. But the Beatle balked at her offer, suggesting that she consider sharing her ideas with his songwriting partner instead. After all, with the recent triumph of "Tomorrow Never Knows" on the *Revolver* album, Lennon had been developing his own interest in the avant-garde of late.

After summoning up the necessary resolve to walk into the Indica Gallery on that fateful November evening, Lennon came face to face with Yoko Ono, the Ocean Child herself. As a way of introducing her exhibition, which would be opened to the public the next evening, Ono handed him a white card embossed with the word BREATHE. "You mean, like this?" Lennon responded, before breaking into a pant. Almost immediately, Lennon found himself enjoying the humor behind her art. Following the diminutive Japanese woman around the gallery, Lennon happened upon a ladder, above which hung Ono's *Ceiling Painting*. "It looked like a black canvas with a chain with a spyglass hanging on the end of it," Lennon remembered. At the top of the ladder, Lennon peered through the magnifying glass at the canvas, which sported a single word: YES.

One of the final works in the exhibition encouraged visitors to hammer a nail into a piece of white plasterboard. But Ono would have none of it. It was alright for Lennon to preview the exhibit, but the plasterboard should remain unspoiled for the opening. Dunbar pulled the artist aside: "I argued strongly in favor of Lennon's hammering in the first nail," the curator later remarked. "He had a lot of loot—chances are, he would buy the damn thing." An angry Ono finally relented, given the wealth and stature of her distinguished guest. "Okay, you can hammer a nail in for five shillings," she told him. "I'll give you an imaginary five shillings, if you let me hammer in an imaginary nail," Lennon retorted, a sly grin growing across his face. It was the defining moment of the artist's life. "My God," Ono thought to herself. "He's playing the same game I'm playing" (Spitz 2005, 652, 653).

Over the next several months, Ono embarked upon a spirited campaign to win Lennon's patronage for her aspiring art. In addition to showering him with notes and letters, she presented him with a copy of her book *Grapefruit* (1964), which was half-autobiography, half-artistic statement. As Cynthia Lennon later recalled, "I didn't know then that Yoko was beginning a determined pursuit of John. She wrote him many letters and cards over the next few months, but I knew nothing about them at the time, or that she had even come to our house looking for him several times" (Lennon 2005, 257). Lennon was impressed with Ono's Zen-like directives, particularly *Cloud Piece*, in which she entreated her readers to "Imagine the clouds dripping. Dig a hole in your garden to put them in."

Lennon and Ono's relationship finally advanced in the late spring of 1968. With wife Cynthia away on vacation in Greece, Lennon decided to invite Ono out to his

Weybridge estate in Surrey. Unbeknownst to Cynthia at the time, Ono had been bombarding Lennon on a daily basis with postcards, which he eagerly retrieved at the Maharishi's post office back in Rishikesh when he was staying there. Shortly before midnight on May 19, Ono took a taxi to Lennon's estate. They stayed up all night improvising recordings, with Lennon manipulating his pair of Brenell reel-to-reel tape recorders while Ono shrieked a series of wordless, discordant vocals into the growing cacophony.

A few days later, Cynthia returned from her Grecian holiday just in time to experience the great shock of her life. Kenwood was eerily silent, its front door strangely unlocked. As she prepared to open the sunroom door, Cynthia "felt a sudden frisson of fear": "John and Yoko were sitting on the floor, cross-legged and facing each other, beside a table covered with dirty dishes. They were wearing the toweling robes we kept in the poolhouse, so I imagined they had been for a swim. John was facing me. He looked at me, expressionless, and said, 'Oh, hi.' Yoko didn't turn around" (Lennon 2005, 284). Lennon's indifference spoke volumes, and Cynthia understandably fled the scene, finding temporary shelter in the house that Jenny Boyd, Pattie Boyd's sister, shared with Magic Alex. Ono and Lennon were married the following year, on March 29, 1969, near the Rock of Gibraltar.

Within slightly more than a year, the Beatles had disbanded, a turn of events that fans often attributed to Ono's influence. When asked about her own ostensible role in the band's demise, Ono suggests that they were responding to internal forces—perhaps even involving individual needs and desires related to growing up—rather than to external pressures: "I don't think you could have broken up four very strong people like them, even if you tried. So there must have been something that happened within them—not an outside force at all" (Lennon and Ono 2000, 144). McCartney couldn't have agreed more, as he remarked during an interview with CNN's Larry King, "I think it was time. I always remember the old song 'Wedding Bells (Are Breaking Up That Old Gang of Mine),' you know. The army buddies, the band, and you're going to grow up. You're going to get married. You're going to get girlfriends and have babies and things, and you don't do that in a band" (CNN 2001). Starr seconded McCartney's conclusions about the group's dissolution in an interview with *Rolling Stone* magazine's John Harris: "I think the reason the Beatles split up was because we were 30, and it was, 'Hey, I've got married, I've got kids, I've got a few more friends.' We didn't have the energy to put into it" (*The Washington Times* 2001).

In the post-Beatles years, Ono and Lennon collaborated on numerous albums, as well as with the conceptualization of the Plastic Ono Band, an experimental rock band with a shifting slate of performers. In addition to their first two avant-garde LPs recorded as the *Unfinished Music* series, Ono and Lennon released their *Wedding Album*, along with the activist-oriented *Some Time in New York City*. The couple took an 18-month hiatus from their marriage beginning in 1973 that Lennon later referred to as his "Lost Weekend." By 1975, Ono and Lennon had ended their separation. Their son Sean Taro Ono was born on Lennon's birthday on October 9, 1975. Over the next five years, Ono broadened her role in the Lennons' business affairs, making headlines in the late 1970s for her lucrative investments in Holstein cows, for example. In 1980, Ono and Lennon continued their collaboration with the *Double Fantasy* album, although their return to the music scene was to be short-lived. Lennon was murdered on December 8, 1980, in the entryway to the Dakota, the couple's New York City apartment building.

After the former Beatle's murder, Ono has continued to function as the custodian of his memory, overseeing the production of his posthumous compilations, while also looking out for the estate's interests. She continues to work as an artist, releasing the solo album *Season of Glass* not long after her husband's murder. She also enjoyed a hit single with "Walking on Thin Ice," the track that she and Lennon were working on the night that he was killed. In 2007, her early 1970s track "Open Your Box" enjoyed a resurgence on U.S. dance music charts.

On October 9, 1985, Ono dedicated the Strawberry Fields memorial in New York City's Central Park. Funded by her, the memorial was constructed across the street from the Dakota apartment building and features the famous "Imagine" mosaic. In 1995, she collaborated with McCartney on the track "Hiroshima Sky Is Always Blue" in honor of the 50th anniversary of the bombing of Hiroshima. On October 9, 2007, she dedicated the Imagine Peace Tower located on Viðey Island in Kollafjörður Bay near Reykjavík, Iceland. In 2009, she established the Rock and Roll Hall of Fame exhibit entitled "John Lennon: The New York City Years."

See also: Lennon, John.

Our World (TV Special)

The brainchild of BBC producer Aubrey Powell, the *Our World* television special marked the world's first live international satellite television production. The BBC's marketing department described the event as being "for the first time ever, linking five continents and bringing man face to face with mankind, in places as far apart as Canberra and Cape Kennedy, Moscow and Montreal, Samarkand and Söderfors, Takamatsu and Tunis" (Martin 1994, 159).

Most notable because of the world premiere and performance of the Beatles' "All You Need Is Love," the two-and-a-half-hour production featured performances from 19 different nations and required 10 months of planning and more than 10,000 technicians. Using four satellites, *Our World* was broadcast to 31 countries and an estimated audience of some 400 million people. It was altered at the last minute by the sudden cancellation of the Soviet Union and Eastern bloc nations in protest over Western responses to the Six Day War.

In addition to such luminaries as opera star Maria Callas and artist Pablo Picasso, the Beatles closed the program with their live performance of "All You Need Is

Love." As Starr later recalled, "We were big enough to command an audience of that size, and it was for love. It was for love and bloody peace. It was a fabulous time. I even get excited now when I realize that's what it was for: peace and love, people putting flowers in guns" (Lange 2001, 159). The Beatles' live performance occurred at 8:45 PM GMT, from Abbey Road Studios, with such rock luminaries as Eric Clapton, Mick Jagger, Marianne Faithfull, Keith Moon, and Graham Nash in attendance.

See also: Abbey Road Studios; Clapton, Eric.

P

"Paperback Writer" (Lennon–McCartney)

"Paperback Writer" was the band's 11th consecutive #1 single in the United Kingdom, where it was released on June 10, 1966.

AUTHORSHIP AND BACKGROUND

Written by McCartney with assistance from Lennon, "Paperback Writer" is a groundbreaking recording for the Beatles—both in terms of their use of studio technology as well as McCartney's innovative bass performance.

Legend has it that McCartney was inspired to write the song by an aunt, who dared him to compose a song that wasn't primarily concerned with love's trials and tribulations. As McCartney later recalled,

> I arrived at Weybridge and told John I had this idea of trying to write off to a publishers to become a paperback writer, and I said, "I think it should be written like a letter." I took a bit of paper out and I said it should be something like, "Dear Sir or Madam, as the case may be," and I proceeded to write it just like a letter in front of him, occasionally rhyming it. And then we went upstairs and put the melody to it. John and I sat down and finished it all up, but it was tilted towards me—the original idea was mine. I had no music, but it's just a little bluesy song, not a lot of melody. Then I had the idea to do the harmonies, and we arranged that in the studio. (Miles 1997, 279)

As Lennon remembered, " 'Paperback Writer' is son of 'Day Tripper'—meaning a rock 'n' roll song with a guitar lick on a fuzzy loud guitar" (Lennon and Ono 2000, 179).

RECORDING SESSIONS

Produced by Martin, "Paperback Writer" was recorded at Abbey Road Studios on April 13, 1966, with an additional overdubbing session on April 14. It required some 10 hours to complete in the studio.

With sound engineer Geoff Emerick at the helm in place of Norman Smith, the "Paperback Writer" recording benefits from the usage of STEED (single tape echo and echo delay) during vocal fermata or pauses in order to achieve a live-sounding

The Beatles perform "Paperback Writer" and "Rain" on the BBC show *Top of the Pops* on June 16, 1966. Ringo Starr is in front, and from left to right in back are John Lennon, Paul McCartney, and George Harrison. (Cummings Archives/ Redferns/Getty Images)

echo effect. The revolution track also finds McCartney playing a new bass—in this case, the melodic Rickenbacker 4001S. Inspired by recent recordings by Otis Redding and Wilson Pickett in which the bass had figured prominently—as well as by the groundbreaking bass work of McCartney's Motown idol James Jamerson—McCartney's roving, fluid bass is brought vividly to life by Emerick, who employed a loudspeaker as a microphone for the Beatle's Rickenbacker. The resulting effect renders the bass's already precise tonality even more dynamic and evokes an expansive and vibrant sound from the instrument. McCartney's bass playing and Emerick's engineering had come together in a recorded performance that hearkened a radical shift in terms of the bass guitar's role in popular music.

As Emerick later recalled, " 'Paperback Writer' was the first time the bass sound had been heard in all its excitement. To get the loud bass sound Paul played a different bass, a Rickenbacker. Then we boosted it further by using a loudspeaker as a microphone. We positioned it directly in front of the bass speaker and the moving diaphragm of the second speaker made the electric current" (Dowlding 1989, 128). Ironically, Emerick's colleague Ken Townsend was reprimanded by studio management—despite his innovative work at Abbey Road—for intentionally matching impedances incorrectly during the recording session.

Musically, "Paperback Writer" signals a breathtaking leap forward in terms of the band's ability to imagine new vistas of sound—and this is in comparison with their transformative work in the latter months of 1965, no less. Where *Rubber Soul* is buoyant, smart, and folk-minded, "Paperback Writer" is bright, colorful, and crisp. Lennon, McCartney, and Harrison's soaring three-part a cappella harmonies—fashioned after the Beach Boys' latest album *Pet Sounds* (1966)—give way to the fuzzy introductory guitar riff that Harrison strums on his Epiphone Casino, only to be followed by McCartney's peripatetic bass lines.

As with the "comedy numbers" on *Rubber Soul*, "Paperback Writer" serves to undercut its own musical virtuosity with impish humor. Witness, for example, Lennon and Harrison's comic backing vocals in which they sing "Frère Jacques" in broken falsetto.

The postrecording process associated with "Paperback Writer" also found the Beatles make innovative strides in the pop-music marketplace. The final recording was cut much louder than previous Beatles records through the deployment of EMI's new mastering process known as "Automatic Transient Overload Control."

PERSONNEL

Lennon: Gretsch Nashville, Backing Vocal
McCartney: Vocal, Rickenbacker 4001S
Harrison: Epiphone Casino, Backing Vocal
Starr: Ludwig Oyster Black Pearl Drums

CHART PERFORMANCE

U.K.: "Paperback Writer"/"Rain"; June 10, 1966; Parlophone R 5452: #1.
U.S.: "Paperback Writer"/"Rain"; May 30, 1966; Capitol 5651: #1 (certified by the RIAA as "Gold," with more than 500,000 copies sold).

LEGACY AND INFLUENCE

In 2010, *Rolling Stone* ranked "Paperback Writer" as #35 on the magazine's list of *The Beatles' 100 Greatest Songs*.

ALBUM APPEARANCES: *A Collection of Beatles Oldies*; *Hey Jude*; *The Beatles, 1962–1966*; *20 Greatest Hits*; *Past Masters, Volume 2*; *1*; *Tomorrow Never Knows*.

See also: Emerick, Geoff.

Past Masters, Volume I (LP)

March 7, 1988, Apple [Parlophone] CDP 7 90043 2
March 7, 1988, Apple [Capitol] CDP 7 90043 2

Past Masters, Volume 1 features the early, nonalbum tracks of the Beatles as released in the late 1980s when their catalogue was released on CD.

BACKGROUND

Compiled by Beatles historian Mark Lewisohn, the tracks on *Past Masters, Volume 1* include both rare recordings as well as hit singles not included on the Beatles' early albums ranging from *Please Please Me* through *Help!* Most notably, the compilation includes the contents of the U.K. *Long Tall Sally* EP in their entirety, as well as the Beatles' German-language recordings of "I Want to Hold Your Hand" and "She Loves You." It also includes "Bad Boy," which had previously only been released in the United States.

TRACK LISTING

"Love Me Do"; "From Me to You"; "Thank You Girl"; "She Loves You"; "I'll Get You"; "I Want to Hold Your Hand"; "This Boy"; "Komm, Gib Mir Deine Hand"; "Sie Liebt Dich"; "Long Tall Sally"; "I Call Your Name"; "Slow Down"; "Matchbox"; "I Feel Fine"; "She's a Woman"; "Bad Boy"; "Yes It Is"; "I'm Down."

CHART PERFORMANCE

U.K.: #49.
U.S.: #149 (certified by the RIAA as "Platinum," with 1 million copies sold).

See also: *Past Masters, Volume 2* (LP).

Past Masters, Volume 2 (LP)

March 7, 1988, Apple [Parlophone] CDP 7 90044 2
March 7, 1988, Apple [Capitol] CDP 7 90044 2

Past Masters, Volume 2 features the later, nonalbum tracks of the Beatles as released in the late 1980s when their catalogue was released on CD.

BACKGROUND

Compiled by Beatles historian Mark Lewisohn, the tracks on *Past Masters, Volume 2* include both rare recordings as well as hit singles not included on the

Beatles' later albums ranging from *Rubber Soul* through *Let It Be*. Most notably, the compilation includes the World Wildlife Fund version of "Across the Universe," along with such less-familiar B-sides as "Rain," "The Inner Light," and "You Know My Name (Look Up the Number)."

TRACK LISTING

"Day Tripper"; "We Can Work It Out"; "Paperback Writer"; "Rain"; "Lady Madonna"; "The Inner Light"; "Hey Jude"; "Revolution"; "Get Back"; "Don't Let Me Down"; "The Ballad of John and Yoko"; "Old Brown Shoe"; "Across the Universe" (World Wildlife Fund version); "Let It Be"; "You Know My Name (Look Up the Number)."

CHART PERFORMANCE

U.K.: #46.
U.S.: #121 (certified by the RIAA as "Platinum," with 1 million copies sold).

See also: *Past Masters, Volume 1* (LP).

"Paul Is Dead" Hoax

The "Paul Is Dead" hoax is an urban legend that emerged in the early fall months of 1969. The story line began to materialize after the publication of an article entitled "Is Beatles Paul McCartney Dead?" in the September 17, 1969, issue of Drake University's student newspaper. In October 1969, a DJ in Dearborn, Michigan, announced that McCartney had been dead since 1966. Later that month, the phenomenon grew by leaps and bounds after Roby Yonge, a DJ at New York City's WABC, broke the story for his station's massive audience. In the ensuing weeks, overzealous fans dissected a variety of "clues" regarding McCartney's death (and subsequent replacement by a look-alike) that the surviving Beatles had ostensibly secreted amongst the lyrics and artwork for *Sgt. Pepper's Lonely Hearts Club Band* (1967), *Magical Mystery Tour* (1967), *The Beatles* (*The White Album*) (1968), *Abbey Road* (1969), and *Let It Be* (1970).

The McCartney death clues include:

In the Beatles' May 1966 promotional film for "Rain," some viewers noted McCartney's chipped tooth and scarred lip—the results of a December 1965 Moped accident. Such details were interpreted by fans as evidence in support of McCartney's alleged demise and subsequent replacement by a look-alike.
During the coda for "Strawberry Fields Forever," Lennon famously mutters "cranberry sauce," a remark that was interpreted by some listeners as "I buried Paul."

Amid rumors of a conspiracy to cover up the death of Beatle Paul McCartney, Dr. Oscar Tosi, assistant professor of audiology at Michigan State University, compares the actual voice and a telephone voice recording of McCartney on a voice print machine in his lab on October 10, 1969. Tosi confirmed that the recordings were the same voice, defeating worldwide speculation that McCartney may have died as long ago as 1966. (Bettmann/Getty Images)

In *Sgt. Pepper's Lonely Hearts Club Band*'s "Lovely Rita," the song's comely traffic warden was cited as evidence for McCartney's alleged demise in a 1966 automobile accident, which had ostensibly been caused when McCartney was distracted by the meter maid's beauty.

In *Sgt. Pepper's Lonely Hearts Club Band*'s "A Day in the Life," Lennon sings, "He blew his mind out in a car," which interpreted by fans as evidence in support of McCartney's death in an automobile accident.

The *Magical Mystery Tour* album contains a number of so-called death clues, including the album's cover depicting the image of a black walrus, which is believed to represent death in some parts of Scandinavia. In addition to the image of McCartney wearing a black carnation during the "Your Mother Should Know" sequence, McCartney sits behind a desk in front of a sign bearing the prophetic words "I WaS."

On *The White Album*'s "Glass Onion," Lennon famously remarks that "Now here's another clue for you all / The walrus was Paul," referring to the walrus as a Scandinavian representation of death.

In *The White Album*'s "I'm So Tired," Lennon utters a series of nonsensical syllables before the beginning of "Blackbird." Some listeners interpret Lennon's words as sounding like "Paul is a dead man, miss him, miss him."

In *The White Album*'s "Don't Pass Me By," Ringo Starr sings, "You were in a car crash and you lost your hair," which some listeners interpreted as confirmation of McCartney's death in an automobile accident.

In *The White Album*'s "Revolution 9," some listeners maintain that playing the
"number nine" loop in reverse sounds like "turn me on, dead man."
Some fans interpret *Abbey Road*'s cover art as depicting a funeral procession,
with Lennon playing the role of priest.

In late October 1969, after Yonge broke the story on New York City's WABC,
the Apple press office was forced to make a statement. In addition to denying the
rumors about McCartney's death, the press office observed that "the story has been
circulating for about two years—we get letters from all sorts of nuts, but Paul is
still very much with us." A November 7 *Life* magazine cover story with the headline "Paul Is Still with Us" featured an interview in which the Beatle remarked
that "perhaps the rumor started because I haven't been much in the press lately. I
have done enough press for a lifetime, and I don't have anything to say these days.
I am happy to be with my family and I will work when I work. I was switched on
for ten years and I never switched off. Now I am switching off whenever I can. I
would rather be a little less famous these days" (Reeve 2004, 93). In spite of Apple
and McCartney's denials, the "Paul Is Dead" hoax continues to resound in pop culture, later spawning an array of books and television specials. The Beatles themselves have referred to the "Paul Is Dead" hoax on occasion. In Lennon's "How
Do You Sleep?" from his *Imagine* album, Lennon sings "Those freaks was right
when they said you was dead." Moreover, the title of McCartney's 1993 *Paul Is
Live* album offers its own pun on the urban legend, with McCartney posing on the
famous Abbey Road zebra crossing.

See also: *Abbey Road* (LP); *The Beatles* (*The White Album*) (LP); *Let It Be* (LP);
Magical Mystery Tour (LP); *Sgt. Pepper's Lonely Hearts Club Band* (LP).

"Penny Lane" (Lennon–McCartney)

"Penny Lane" was a hit double A-side single, backed with "Strawberry Fields Forever," which was released in the United Kingdom on February 17, 1967, and in
the United States on February 13, 1967. It was later included on the Beatles' *Magical Mystery Tour* album.

AUTHORSHIP AND BACKGROUND

Written by McCartney with assistance from Lennon, "Penny Lane" was inspired
by the songwriter's affinity for Dylan Thomas' nostalgic poem "Fern Hill."
As McCartney later recalled,

> John and I would always meet at Penny Lane. That was where someone would
> stand and sell you poppies each year on British Legion poppy day. When I came
> to write it, John came over and helped me with the third verse, as often was the

case. We were writing childhood memories—recently faded memories from eight or ten years before, so it was recent nostalgia, pleasant memories for both of us. All the places were still there, and because we remembered it so clearly we could have gone on. (Miles 1997, 308)

As Lennon remembered, "Penny Lane is not only a street but it's a district—a suburban district where, until age four, I lived with my mother and father. So I was the only Beatle that lived in Penny Lane" (Lennon and Ono 2000, 153).

RECORDING SESSIONS

Produced by Martin, "Penny Lane" was recorded at Abbey Road Studios on December 29, 1966, with additional overdubbing sessions on December 30 and seven additional sessions in January 1967.

At the end of December 1966, the Beatles began working on "Penny Lane," McCartney's latest composition, which, as with "Strawberry Fields Forever," explores the bandmates' Liverpudlian past. At this juncture, both songs were recorded as part of the group's planned follow-up album to *Revolver*, but by early the next year, they were allocated as the band's next single under pressure from both Epstein and the EMI Group, who were clamoring for new product. As Martin recalled,

Brian Epstein wanted a single and he was genuinely frightened that the Beatles were slipping. He wanted another single out that was going to be a blockbuster, and so I put together "Strawberry Fields Forever" and "Penny Lane" and said to him, "If this isn't going to be a blockbuster, then nothing is!"(Badman 2001, 263)

During a December 29, 1966, session, McCartney devoted several takes to playing the central piano figure that drives "Penny Lane," while adding a supplemental piano part that was played through a Vox guitar amplifier. The next evening, McCartney recorded his lead vocal, while Lennon provided a backing vocal, both of which were recorded at a slightly slower speed in order to sound faster—and, hence, brighter—during playback. The Beatles revisited "Penny Lane" during the new year, although work on the song was halted on January 5, 1967, while Lennon and McCartney attended to "Carnival of Light," an avant-garde recording that had been invited for presentation by the organizers of *The Million Volt Light and Sound Rave*, an art festival of electronic music and light shows that were debuted on January 28, 1967, at London's Roundhouse Theatre.

On January 6, 1967, the Beatles continued working on "Penny Lane," with Lennon, McCartney, and Harrison providing a guide vocal by scat singing during the bars where additional musical accompaniment—including four flutes, two piccolos, two trumpets, and a Flügelhorn—was overdubbed later. The next evening, a set of orchestral chimes was added to the mix, with a tubular bell being rung whenever the song referenced the fireman or his fire engine—his "clean machine." Studio musicians complemented the accompaniment from the January 6 session with two trumpets, two oboes, two cor anglais (English horns), and a double-bass. The Beatles finally completed "Penny Lane" during a whirlwind session on January 19. A few days earlier, McCartney had seen musician David Mason playing the trumpet on Bach's *Brandenburg Concerto #2 in F Major* for the BBC program *Masterworks*. A member of the New Philharmonia Orchestra, Mason was summarily recruited to play the piccolo trumpet solo on "Penny Lane."

PERSONNEL

Lennon: Gibson J-160E, Piano, Congas
McCartney: Vocal, Rickenbacker 4001S, Piano, Harmonium
Harrison: Sonic Blue Fender Stratocaster, Swarmandal, Maracas
Starr: Ludwig Oyster Black Pearl Drums, Bell
Martin: Piano
Studio Musicians: Orchestral Accompaniment conducted by Martin
Mason: Piccolo Trumpet Solo
P. Goody, Ray Swinfield, Manny Winters: Flute, Piccolo
Leon Calvert, Duncan Campbell, Freddy Clayton, Bert Courtley: Trumpet, Flügelhorn
Dick Morgan, Mike Winfield: Oboe, Cor Anglais
Frank Clarke: Double Bass

CHART PERFORMANCE

U.K.: "Penny Lane"/"Strawberry Fields Forever"; February 17, 1967, Parlophone R 5570: #2. As a double A-side with "Strawberry Fields Forever," "Penny Lane" charted at #2.

U.S.: "Penny Lane"/"Strawberry Fields Forever"; February 13, 1967, Capitol 5810: #8 (certified by the RIAA as "Gold," with more than 500,000 copies sold). As a double A-side with "Strawberry Fields Forever," "Penny Lane" charted at #1.

LEGACY AND INFLUENCE

In 2004, *Rolling Stone* ranked "Penny Lane" as #456 on the magazine's list of *The 500 Greatest Songs of All Time*.

In 2010, *Rolling Stone* ranked "Penny Lane" as #32 on the magazine's list of *The Beatles' 100 Greatest Songs*.

In 2011, "Penny Lane" was inducted into the National Academy of Recording Arts and Sciences Grammy Hall of Fame.

ALBUM APPEARANCES: *Magical Mystery Tour; The Beatles, 1967–1970; Rarities* (U.S.); *20 Greatest Hits; Anthology 2; 1.*

See also: *Magical Mystery Tour* (LP); Voormann, Klaus.

"Piggies" (Harrison)

"Piggies" is a song on *The Beatles* (*The White Album*).

AUTHORSHIP AND BACKGROUND

Harrison began composing "Piggies" in 1966, later completing it with assistance from his mother, who contributed the line "What they need's a damned good whacking!" Lennon later provided an additional line about piggies using utensils to eat bacon.

As Harrison later observed,

> "Piggies" is a social comment. I was stuck for one line in the middle until my mother came up with the lyric, "What they need is a damn good whacking" which is a nice simple way of saying they need a good hiding. It needed to rhyme with "backing," "lacking," and had absolutely nothing to do with American policemen or Californian shagnasties! (Harrison 1980, 126)

An early version of "Piggies" was recorded in May 1968 at Harrison's Kinfauns studio as part of the Esher Tapes.

RECORDING SESSIONS

Produced by Martin, "Piggies" was recorded at Abbey Road Studios on September 19, 1968, with additional overdubbing sessions on September 20 and October 10. Producer Chris Thomas contributed an uncredited harpsichord part.

The sounds of the pigs grunting in the barnyard were culled from the EMI tape library's *Volume 35: Animals and Bees*.

PERSONNEL

Lennon: Backing Vocal
McCartney: Rickenbacker 4001S, Backing Vocal
Harrison: Vocal, Gibson J-200
Starr: Tambourine
Thomas: Harpsichord
Studio Musicians: String Accompaniment conducted by Martin

ALBUM APPEARANCES: *The Beatles* (*The White Album*); *Anthology 3*.

See also: *The Beatles* (*The White Album*) (LP); Thomas, Chris.

Plastic Ono Band

The Plastic Ono Band is Lennon and Ono's revolving, concept-oriented super-group. Originally established in 1969, it included Lennon, Ono, Eric Clapton, Klaus Voormann, and Alan White. According to Ono, the band's name finds its roots in Ono's idea for a European art installation. In a recent interview, she recalled that "as I was asked to do a show in Berlin before John and I got together, I wanted to use four plastic stands with tape recorders in each one of them, as my band. I told that story to John, and he immediately coined the phrase Plastic Ono Band" (Britton 2013). Over the years, the supergroup was appropriated for solo releases by Lennon and Ono. The 1969 "Give Peace a Chance" recording marked the band's first singles release. The band's first album was the concert recording *Live Peace in Toronto 1969*, which was compiled from the one-day Sweet Toronto Peace Festival held on September 13, 1969, at the University of Toronto's Varsity Stadium. In subsequent years, Lennon and Ono released albums bearing the Plastic Ono Band's name, including *John Lennon/Plastic Ono Band* and *Yoko Ono/Plastic Ono Band*—both released in 1970—as well as *Some Time in New York City* (1972), which included members from Elephant's Memory. At times, Lennon variously presented the band as the "Plastic U.F. Ono Band" and the "Plastic Ono Nuclear Band."

While the notion of the Plastic Ono Band seemed to have concluded with Lennon's 1975 *Shaved Fish* compilation, Ono revivified the concept of the supergroup in 2009 with her *Between My Head and the Sky* album, which featured Ono, son Sean, Cornelius, and Yuka Honda. In 2010, the Plastic Ono Band staged a concert reunion with several past members, including Clapton, Voormann, and Jim Keltner.

See also: Clapton, Eric; Ono, Yoko; Voormann, Klaus.

"Please Mister Postman" (Dobbins–Garrett–Gorman–Holland–Bateman)

"Please Mister Postman" is a song on the *With the Beatles* album.

AUTHORSHIP AND BACKGROUND

Written by Georgia Dobbins, William Garrett, Freddie Gorman, Brian Holland, and Robert Bateman, "Please Mister Postman" was composed especially for the Marvelettes' April 1961 audition with Berry Gordy's Tamla/Motown record label.

As McCartney recalled, the Beatles' version of "Please Mister Postman" was "influenced by the Marvelettes, who did the original version. We got it from our fans, who would write 'Please Mister Postman' on the back of the envelopes.

'Posty, posty, don't be slow, be like the Beatles and go, man, go!' That sort of stuff" (Dowlding 1989, 53).

RECORDING SESSIONS

Produced by Martin, "Please Mister Postman" was recorded at Abbey Road Studios on July 30, 1963. Lennon doubled-tracked his lead vocal.

PERSONNEL

> Lennon: Vocal, Rickenbacker 325
> McCartney: Höfner 500/1, Backing Vocal
> Harrison: Gretsch Country Gentleman, Backing Vocal
> Starr: Ludwig Oyster Black Pearl Drums

ALBUM APPEARANCES: *With the Beatles*; *The Beatles' Second Album*; *On Air: Live at the BBC, Volume 2.*

See also: *With the Beatles* (LP).

Please Please Me (LP)

March 22, 1963, Parlophone PMC 1202 (mono)/PCS 3042 (stereo)

Please Please Me is the Beatles' first studio album. It was released on the Parlophone label on March 22, 1963, in the United Kingdom. In the United States, several of the songs on *Please Please Me* were released on Vee-Jay Records' *Introducing . . . the Beatles* in July 1963 (first issue) and January 1964 (second issue).

Please Please Me became standardized among U.S. album releases with the February 26, 1987, distribution of the band's first four albums as mono CD releases. *Please Please Me* was remastered and rereleased as a stereo CD on September 9, 2009. A remastered mono release was also made available at this time as part of a limited edition box set entitled *The Beatles in Mono*.

BACKGROUND AND RECORDING SESSIONS

Produced by Martin with Norman "Normal" Smith as his sound engineer, *Please Please Me* was recorded on February 11, 1963, with an overdubbing session on February 20, save for the extant recordings of "Ask Me Why," "Love Me Do," and "P.S. I Love You."

Initially, Martin had been determined to capture the exhilaration of a Beatles concert for the band's first long-playing record. "It was obvious, commercially, that once 'Please Please Me'—the single—had been a success, we should release an LP as soon as possible," the producer remembered (Lewisohn 1988, 24). For a while, he contemplated the notion of recording a live album at the Cavern before realizing that the venue's acoustics—given the building's unforgiving cement edifice—would make it all but impossible to achieve the necessary balance for the recording process. Instead, Martin came up with the idea of approaching their first studio album as though it were a Beatles concert in itself. Along with the four songs that comprised the band's first two singles, they assembled a selection of Lennon–McCartney compositions and an assortment of cover versions in order to reproduce the rhythm and musical range of a live show, albeit with the opportunity to refine their performances in the studio. The only problem was that, given the tight schedule that existed at Abbey Road Studios during that era, they only had a single day in which to bring the project to fruition.

On February 11, 1963, the Beatles arrived at Studio Two, where they had some 10 hours in which to record the album. To make matters worse, Lennon had been felled by a bad cold, which he had contracted during the band's recently completed tour with Helen Shapiro, the 16-year-old British pop sensation. When the tour began, Helen was the headlining act, while the Beatles were fourth on the bill. By the end of the tour, though, "Please Please Me" had worked its magic, and they were pop stars in their own right. As the *New Musical Express*'s Gordon Sampson later reported, the Beatles ended up dominating the last several concerts on the tour, so much so that "the audience repeatedly called for them while other artists were performing" (Spitz 2005, 370).

At the band's request, a jar of Zubes throat lozenges and two packs of Peter Stuyvesant cigarettes were placed atop the piano in Studio Two, thus beginning a Beatles tradition that continued for years. Martin was determined to complete the basic tracks for the entire album that day—the mixing process could be carried out later outside of the group's presence. In addition to the practical dilemma of booking studio time, Martin was also confronted with the fact that the Beatles were due to play for a youth-club dance at the Azena Ballroom the following evening in Sheffield, Yorkshire. The sessions began at 10 o'clock on the morning of February 11, 1963, and the Beatles, for the most part, were all business—deadly serious, in contrast with the jocularity that Martin had witnessed on previous occasions. Over a period of some 585 minutes, the band recorded 11 songs using Abbey Road Studios' two-track recording desk, 10 of which was included on their first album.

"We were performers," Lennon told *Rolling Stone*'s Jann Wenner. "What we generated was fantastic when we played straight rock, and there was nobody to touch us in Britain" (Lennon 1970, 20). For the Beatles, the recording studio was a revelation. "We gradually became the workmen who took over the factory," McCartney remarked in later years.

"In the end, we had the run of the whole building. It would be us, the recording people on our session, and a doorman. There would be nobody else there. It was amazing, just wandering around, having a smoke in the echo chamber. I think we knew the place better than the chairman of the company because we *lived* there. I even got a house just 'round the corner, I loved it so much. I didn't want ever to leave" (Beatles 2000, 93).

TRACK LISTING

Side 1: "I Saw Her Standing There"; "Misery"; "Anna (Go to Him)"; "Chains"; "Boys"; "Ask Me Why"; "Please Please Me."

Side 2: "Love Me Do"; "P.S. I Love You"; "Baby It's You"; "Do You Want to Know a Secret"; "A Taste of Honey"; "There's a Place"; "Twist and Shout."

COVER ARTWORK

Martin had originally suggested that the group entitle the album *Off the Beatle Track* and that the cover photo be taken in front of the Insect House at the London Zoo, an idea that was jettisoned when the zoo's director objected to the photo shoot. Martin was so fond of the title, though, that he eventually used it for the 1964 anthology of Beatles instrumental covers that was credited to "George Martin and His Orchestra." Instead, the Beatles opted to name the album after the recent chart-topping single. For the album's cover art, veteran theatrical photographer Angus McBean famously photographed the bandmates' fresh faces peering down the stairwell at London's EMI House on March 5, 1963. The album cover later adorned the cover of the compilation entitled *The Beatles, 1962–1966* (1973).

Beatles press officer Tony Barrow was tasked with compiling *Please Please Me*'s liner notes, writing that "between them the Beatles adopt a do-it-yourself approach from the very beginning. They write their own lyrics, design and eventually build their own instrumental backdrops, and work out their own vocal arrangements. Their music is wild, pungent, hard-hitting, uninhibited . . . and personal."

CHART PERFORMANCE

U.K.: #1 (In the United States, *Please Please Me* has been certified by the RIAA as "Platinum," with more than 1 million copies sold).

LEGACY AND INFLUENCE

In 2003, *Rolling Stone* ranked *Please Please Me* as #39 on the magazine's list of *The 500 Greatest Albums of All Time*.

See also: Martin, George.

"Please Please Me" (McCartney–Lennon)

"Please Please Me" is a song on the Beatles' *Please Please Me* album. It was the Beatles' first #1 single in the United Kingdom, where it was released on January 11, 1963. It was a hit single in the United States, where it was released on January 30, 1964.

AUTHORSHIP AND BACKGROUND

Written by Lennon, "Please Please Me" finds its origins in Bing Crosby's "Please," which Lennon's mother Julia sang to him during his youth. Lennon's imagination was piqued by the song's homonymic quality—"Please lend your ears to my pleas"—a conceit that he mimicked with the repetition of "please" in his new composition. Musically, Lennon had styled the song, a relatively slow number, after Roy Orbison's "Only the Lonely (Know the Way I Feel)."

The Beatles pose on the stairs of NEMS (North End Music Stores), Brian Epstein's Liverpool record shop, on January 24, 1963, where they performed with acoustic instruments and signed copies of their newly-released single "Please Please Me." (Mark and Colleen Hayward/Getty Images)

As Lennon remembered, " 'Please Please Me' is my song completely. It was my attempt at writing a Roy Orbison song, would you believe it? I wrote it in the bedroom in my house at Menlove Avenue, which was my auntie's place. I heard Roy Orbison doing 'Only the Lonely' or something. That's where that came from" (Dowlding 1989, 27).

The Beatles debuted "Please Please Me" for Martin during their September 11, 1962, session. But Martin felt that "Please Please Me" was "much too dreary" in its current state, and he encouraged the boys to prepare a more vigorous, upbeat version for their next session.

RECORDING SESSIONS

Produced by Martin, "Please Please Me" was reconsidered during a November 26, 1962, session at Abbey Road Studios. At this point, Martin was still considering the release of "How Do You Do It" as the Beatles' next single. But then he heard the band's revivified version of "Please Please Me," and everything changed. "We've revamped it," they informed him (Spitz 2005, 358).

For Martin, the recording of "Please Please Me" was simply transformative. Not only did he realize the band's considerable commercial potential, but he also recognized the awesome power of their original material. There was no more talk of "How Do You Do It" in the wake of "Please Please Me." "The whole session was a joy," Martin remembered. "At the end of it, I pressed the intercom button in the control room and said, 'Gentleman, you've just made your first number-one record' " (Everett 2001, 131).

PERSONNEL

> Lennon: Vocal, Harmonica, Rickenbacker 325
> McCartney: Vocal, Höfner 500/1
> Harrison: Gretsch Duo-Jet, Backing Vocal
> Starr: Premier Mahogany Duroplastic Drums

CHART PERFORMANCE

> U.K.: "Please Please Me"/"Ask Me Why"; January 11, 1963, Parlophone R 4983: #1.
> U.S.: "Please Please Me"/"Ask Me Why"; February 25, 1963, Vee-Jay VJ 498: did not chart.
> U.S.: "Please Please Me"/"From Me to You"; January 30, 1964, Vee-Jay VJ 581: #3.

LEGACY AND INFLUENCE

In 2004, *Rolling Stone* ranked "Please Please Me" as #186 on the magazine's list of *The 500 Greatest Songs of All Time*.

In 2010, *Rolling Stone* ranked "Please Please Me" as #20 on the magazine's list of *The Beatles' 100 Greatest Songs*.

CONTROVERSY

There is prevailing debate about whether or not "Please Please Me" captured the #1 spot on the British charts. While it charted at #2 on the *Record Retailer* charts, it became a #1 hit in both the *New Musical Express* and *Melody Maker* charts.

ALBUM APPEARANCES: *Please Please Me*; *The Early Beatles*; *The Beatles, 1962–1966*; *Anthology 1*; *1*; *On Air: Live at the BBC, Volume 2*.

See also: Epstein, Brian; Martin, George; *Please Please Me* (LP).

"Polythene Pam" (Lennon–McCartney)

"Polythene Pam" is a song on the Beatles' *Abbey Road* album. It is the fourth song in the *Abbey Road* Medley.

AUTHORSHIP AND BACKGROUND

Lennon's "Polythene Pam" was written during the Beatles' 1968 visit to India. Lennon drew his inspiration for the song from an eccentric Beatles fan named Pat Hodgett who was well known for eating polythene—the tough, light, translucent thermoplastic made by polymerizing ethylene (*OED*). Polythene Pam's deviant nature finds its roots in August 1963, when Lennon was introduced to Stephanie, the polythene-wearing girlfriend of British Beat poet Royston Ellis (Spizer 2003, 170).

"Perverted sex in a polythene bag," Lennon later recalled. "Just looking for something to write about" (Lennon and Ono 2000, 203). On the recording for "Polythene Pam," Lennon uses a thick Liverpudlian accent in order to connote his character's North Country origins and coarse demeanor.

RECORDING SESSIONS

Produced by Martin, "Polythene Pam" was recorded as a single track along with "She Came in Through the Bathroom Window" at Abbey Road Studios on July 25, 1969. Additional overdubbing sessions occurred on July 28 and 30. An early version of "Polythene Pam" was recorded as a home demo by Lennon at his Kenwood estate.

PERSONNEL

Lennon: Vocal, Framus 12-String Hootenanny
McCartney: Rickenbacker 4001S, Epiphone Casino, Piano

400 | Preston, Billy (1946–2006)

Harrison: Gibson Les Paul Standard
Starr: Ludwig Hollywood Maple Drums, Tambourine, Maracas, Cowbell

ALBUM APPEARANCES: *Abbey Road*; *Anthology 3*.

See also: *Abbey Road* (LP); *The Beatles Anthology, Volume 3* (LP).

Preston, Billy (1946–2006)

Born on September 2, 1946, in Houston, Texas, Preston is the only musician to receive co-billing with the Beatles—in Preston's case, for "Get Back" and "Don't Let Me Down," which are credited to the Beatles with Billy Preston. A gifted keyboard player, Preston toured with Ray Charles' band, which eventually brought him into the Beatles' orbit. In January 1969, the group invited him to play keyboards during their *Get Back* sessions. He famously performed with the band during their January 30 Rooftop Concert. In subsequent years, he enjoyed a lucrative solo career as an Apple Records artist, scoring international hits with "Outa-Space," "Will It Go Round in Circles," "Nothing from Nothing," and "Space Race." In addition to his work on Harrison's *The Concert for Bangladesh*, Preston had a starring role in the 1978 movie musical *Sgt. Pepper's Lonely Hearts Club Band*. In 1980, he enjoyed his last Top 5 hit, a duet with Syreeta Wright entitled "With You I'm Born Again."

After several years of bad fortune and drug abuse, Preston reached his personal nadir in 1991 when he was convicted of insurance fraud after setting fire to his Los Angeles home. He later served nine months in a drug rehabilitation center, followed by three months under house arrest. During the 1990s, he began to right himself while touring with the Band, Johnny Cash, Ray Charles, Eric Clapton, and Ringo Starr and His All-Starr Band. In 2002, he performed Harrison's "My Sweet Lord" and "Isn't It a Pity" during the *Concert for George* at London's Royal Albert Hall. In 2005, he promoted the rerelease of *The Concert for Bangladesh* film. It turned out to be his last public appearance, given that he fell into a coma in November 2005 after suffering respiratory failure as a complication from his long battle with kidney disease. Preston died on June 6, 2006, in Scottsdale, Arizona.

See also: Clapton, Eric; *Get Back* Project; *Let It Be* (Film); *Let It Be* (LP); *Let It Be . . . Naked* (LP); Ringo Starr and His All-Starr Band; The Rooftop Concert; *Sgt. Pepper's Lonely Hearts Club Band* (Film).

"P.S. I Love You" (Lennon–McCartney)

"P.S. I Love You" is a song on the Beatles' *Please Please Me* album. It was the B-side of the Beatles' first single in the United Kingdom, where it was released on October 5, 1962.

AUTHORSHIP AND BACKGROUND

Written by McCartney during the Beatles' 1961 venture to Hamburg, Germany, "P.S. I Love You" was influenced by the Shirelles' "Soldier Boy." As with "Love Me Do," the Beatles had been performing "P.S. I Love You" for the past few years as part of their set at the Cavern Club.

As McCartney remembered, "A theme song based on a letter. It was pretty much mine. I don't think John had much of a hand in it. There are certain themes that are easier than others to hang a song on, and a letter is one of them" (Miles 1997, 38).

RECORDING SESSIONS

Produced by Martin, the Beatles recorded the song in 10 takes on September 11, 1962. Given professional drummer Andrew "Andy" White's presence at the session, Starr was relegated to maraca duty.

PERSONNEL

Lennon: Vocal, Gibson J-160E
McCartney: Vocal, Höfner 500/1
Harrison: Gibson J-160E
Starr: Maracas
White: Drums

CHART PERFORMANCE

U.K.: "Love Me Do"/"P.S. I Love You"; October 5, 1962, Parlophone R 4949: #17.

U.S.: "Love Me Do"/"P.S. I Love You"; April 27, 1964, Tollie 9008: #1. As the B-side of the "Love Me Do," "P.S. I Love You" charted at #10.

ALBUM APPEARANCES: *Please Please Me*; *The Early Beatles*; *Love Songs*; *On Air: Live at the BBC, Volume 2*.

See also: *Please Please Me* (LP).

Q

The Quarry Men

As the skiffle craze reached its fever pitch in the United Kingdom, young John Lennon convinced his Aunt Mimi Smith to purchase a £5 guitar for him in March 1957. Having talked his friends Eric Griffiths, Ivan Vaughan, and Nigel Walley to start up a band with Pete Shotton and himself, Lennon formed the Black Jacks, which soon morphed into the Quarry Men. Not long afterward, Griffiths introduced them to drummer Colin Hanton. Griffiths remembered the boys' first experiences playing the guitar—and how Julia Lennon taught them to play chords: "John's mother had played the banjo, so she re-tuned our guitars to banjo tuning and taught us banjo chords, maybe three or four at the most. And that was it: instant guitar playing" (Babiuk 2001, 10).

The Quarry Men fashioned their name in reference to Quarry Bank High School, which they attended in the mid-1950s. In their early months, the band played at garden parties and entered into several talent contests. In addition to Lennon on guitar and vocals, the band included Shotton on washboard, Griffiths on guitar, with Vaughan and Walley sharing tea-chest bass duties. While Rod Davis played banjo, another high school friend, Bill Smith briefly played tea-chest bass, but was jettisoned from the band because of his unreliability. Len Garry eventually replaced Vaughan and Walley, who became the group's manager. Hanton later joined the band as their first drummer. In July 1957, the band's chemistry was irrevocably altered when Lennon met Paul McCartney after the Quarry Men's afternoon performance at a garden fête at St. Peter's Church Hall, Woolton, in Liverpool. McCartney performed "Twenty Flight Rock" for the assembled bandmates in a nearby Scout hut, and a few weeks later Lennon invited him to join the group. With McCartney shifting the band's sound toward rock 'n' roll, Davis left the group, feeling that the banjo was more appropriate for skiffle music. Shotton quit performing with the band soon thereafter, having tired of playing the washboard. By early 1958, McCartney succeeded in adding 14-year-old guitarist George Harrison to the Quarry Men. Not long afterward, Griffiths left the band. After suffering from an extended bout of tubercular meningitis, Garry left the group as well. During this period, John "Duff" Lowe occasionally performed with the group, sitting in on piano.

In July 1958, the Quarry Men recorded amateur versions of Buddy Holly's "That'll Be the Day" and the Harrison–McCartney composition "In Spite of All

Memorabilia of the early Quarry Men, including a view of the Grundig reel-to-reel tape recorder and tape, as well as the program for a performance by the Quarry Men skiffle group at Woolton Parish Church in Liverpool on July 6, 1957. At this performance, John Lennon first met Paul McCartney. (Mark and Colleen Hayward/Redferns/Getty Images)

the Danger" at Percy Phillips' recording studio in Liverpool. The session resulted in a shellac record that the bandmates shared. As McCartney later recalled, "I remember we all went down on the bus with our instruments—amps and guitars—and the drummer went separately. We waited in the little waiting room outside while somebody else made their demo and then it was our turn. We just went in the room, hardly saw the fella because he was next door in a little control booth. 'OK, what are you going to do?' We ran through it very quickly, quarter of an hour, and it was all over" (Lewisohn 1988, 7). In January 1959, Hanton quit the band after a drunken argument with McCartney, altering the band's chemistry yet again.

By May 1960, the Quarry Men had run their course. At Liverpool College of Art, Lennon met artist Stuart Sutcliffe and eventually convinced him to become the group's bass guitarist. With Sutcliffe in tow, the bandmates began to consider new names, including the Beatals, the Silver Beetles, and later, the Beatles, as they prepared to travel to Hamburg, West Germany, in August 1960. In 1997, the surviving original Quarry Men—Shotton, Davis, Gary, Griffiths, and Hanton—reunited for the 40th anniversary of the garden fête at St. Peter's Church where Lennon first met McCartney. Since 1998, the Quarry Men have performed across the globe. The group currently comprises Davis, Garry, and Hanton, with Lowe occasionally sitting in on piano, just as he did back in the late 1950s. The reunited Quarry Men recorded three albums, *Open for Engagements* (1994), *Get Back—Together* (1997), and *Songs We Remember* (2004).

See also: The Beatals; The Silver Beetles; Smith, Mimi Stanley; Sutcliffe, Stuart.

R

"Rain" (Lennon–McCartney)

"Rain" is the B-side of the Beatles' "Paperback Writer" single, released in the United Kingdom on June 10, 1966, and in the United States on May 30, 1966.

AUTHORSHIP AND BACKGROUND

Written by John Lennon, "Rain" was inspired by a remark by Beatles assistant Neil Aspinall when the Beatles endured a rainy arrival in Melbourne, Australia. Lennon later remarked that "I've never seen rain as hard as that, except in Tahiti," adding that "Rain" was "about people moaning about the weather all the time" (Beatles 2000, 212).

As Lennon remembered,

> That's me again—with the first backwards tape on record anywhere. I got home from the studio, and I was stoned out of my mind on marijuana, and, as I usually do, I listened to what I'd recorded that day. Somehow it got on backwards, and I sat there, transfixed, with the earphones on, with a big hash joint. I ran in the next day and said, "I know what to do with it, I know—listen to this!" So I made them all play it backwards. The fade is me actually singing backwards with the guitars going backwards. [sings] "Sharethsmnowthsmeanss!" That one was the gift of God—of Ja, actually—the god of marijuana, right? So Ja gave me that one. (Ryan and Kehew 2006, 303)

As Ringo Starr later recalled,

> My favorite piece of me is what I did on "Rain." I think I just played amazing. I was into the snare and hi-hat. I think it was the first time I used the trick of starting a break by hitting the hi-hat first instead of going directly to a drum off the hi-hat. I think it's the best out of all the records I've ever made. "Rain" blows me away. It's out in left field. I know me, and I know my playing—and then there's "Rain." (Dowlding 1989, 130)

RECORDING SESSIONS

Produced by George Martin, "Rain" was recorded at Abbey Road Studios on April 14, 1966, with an additional overdubbing session on April 16. The track is a landmark moment in the Beatles' usage of tape loops and backward recording.

Sound engineer Geoff Emerick's studio trickery rendered these effects possible by recording the rhythm track and Lennon's vocal at a faster speed, then slowing them down during the mixing process to create the song's purposefully idiosyncratic sound. Walter Everett likens Lennon's distinctive singing on the chorus to a Hindustani *gamak*, an ornamental vocal embellishment that is delivered in a forceful, oscillating style. His vocal, as with several tracks on *Revolver*, evinces an Eastern flavor that affords the Beatles' music with a more exotic sheen in contrast with their American rock 'n' roll heritage.

After the song's instrumental break, Lennon's voice—recorded backward—repeats the composition's opening phrase, "If the rain comes, they run and hide their heads." According to Emerick,

> With "Rain," the Beatles played the rhythm track really fast so that when the tape was played back at normal speed everything would be so much slower, changing the texture. If we'd recorded it at normal speed and then had to slow the tape down whenever we wanted to hear a playback it would have been much more work. It all seems very simple now—and, of course, tricks like this are easily accomplished in today's computers—but in 1966 it was a pretty revolutionary technique, one that we would repeatedly use to great effect on Beatles recordings. (Lewisohn 1988, 74)

Martin remembers bringing the backward effect to fruition:

> I was always playing around with tapes and I thought it might be fun to do something extra with John's voice. So I lifted a bit of his main vocal off the four-track, put it on another spool, turned it around and then slid it back and forth until it fitted. John was out at the time but when he came back he was amazed. (Lewisohn 1988, 74)

PERSONNEL

Lennon: Vocal, Gretsch Nashville
McCartney: Rickenbacker 4001S, Backing Vocal
Harrison: Gibson SG Standard, Backing Vocal
Starr: Ludwig Oyster Black Pearl Drums, Tambourine

CHART PERFORMANCE

U.K.: "Paperback Writer"/"Rain"; June 10, 1966; Parlophone R 5452: #1.
U.S.: "Paperback Writer"/"Rain"; May 30, 1966; Capitol 5651: #1 (certified by the RIAA as "Gold," with more than 500,000 copies sold). As the B-side of "Paperback Writer," "Rain" charted at #23.

LEGACY AND INFLUENCE

In 2004, *Rolling Stone* ranked "Rain" as #469 on the magazine's list of *The 500 Greatest Songs of All Time*.

In 2010, *Rolling Stone* ranked "Rain" as #88 on the magazine's list of *The Beatles' 100 Greatest Songs*.

ALBUM APPEARANCES: *Hey Jude*; *Rarities* (U.K.); *Past Masters, Volume 2*.

See also: Emerick, Geoff; Lindsay-Hogg, Michael; "Paul Is Dead" Hoax; *Revolver* (U.K. LP).

Rarities (U.K. LP)

October 12, 1979, Parlophone PCM 1001

Rarities is a compilation album, now deleted from the Beatles' catalogue, that was released on October 12, 1979, in the United Kingdom.

BACKGROUND

In contrast with the truly "rare" or unreleased tracks that were included on the American version of the LP, the contents of the British compilation consisted of B-sides, two German-language recordings, and, perhaps most notably, the World Wildlife Fund version of "Across the Universe," which had been exclusively released on a 1969 charity album.

Rarities was originally released on December 2, 1978, as part of *The Beatles Collection*, the British release of a deluxe box set of the Beatles' vinyl albums.

TRACK LISTING

Side 1: "Across the Universe" (World Wildlife Fund version), "Yes It Is"; "This Boy"; "The Inner Light"; "I'll Get You"; "Thank You Girl"; "Komm, Gib Mir Deine Hand"; "You Know My Name (Look up the Number)"; "Sie Liebt Dich."

Side 2: "Rain"; "She's a Woman"; "Matchbox"; "I Call Your Name"; "Bad Boy"; "Slow Down"; "I'm Down"; "Long Tall Sally."

COVER ARTWORK

The *Rarities* cover art mirrors the overall design of *The Beatles Collection*, which features gold lettering arrayed upon a field of blue.

CHART PERFORMANCE

U.K.: #71 (certified by the BPI as "Silver," with more than 60,000 copies sold).

See also: *Rarities* (U.S. LP).

Rarities (U.S. LP)

March 14, 1980, Capitol SHAL 12060

Rarities is a compilation album, now deleted from the Beatles' catalogue, that was released on March 14, 1980, in the United States.

BACKGROUND

In contrast with the British album of the same name, the American compilation consists of genuinely "rare" tracks, songs that existed in different versions on available releases or had never been released at all. As part of the album's package, the gatefold design included a full-sized photograph of the "butcher" cover that adorned the controversial release of the Beatles' *Yesterday . . . and Today* album.

The compilation's highlights include the mono single version of "Love Me Do" that featured Starr on drums, as opposed to session man Andy White. In addition to multiple, unreleased mono and stereo versions in the American marketplace, the album features alternate versions of "And I Love Her," which includes two additional bars in the conclusion, and "I Am the Walrus," which features a six-bar introductory piece. The version of "Penny Lane" is noteworthy for the piccolo trumpet solo that overlays its conclusion, while the album also includes a truncated version of "Helter Skelter" and an alternate take of "Don't Pass Me By," complete with variant violin stylings. The compilation is also noteworthy because of the inclusion of the World Wildlife Fund version of "Across the Universe," which had been exclusively released on a 1969 charity album. It concludes with the first American pressing of "Sgt. Pepper Inner Groove," a snippet of laughter, gibberish, and noise that concluded the British release of *Sgt. Pepper's Lonely Hearts Club Band*. The track was not included on the album in the American marketplace until 1987, when the band's albums were synchronized for worldwide CD release.

TRACK LISTING

Side 1: "Love Me Do" (single version); "Misery"; "There's a Place"; "Sie Liebt Dich"; "And I Love Her"; "Help!"; "I'm Only Sleeping"; "I Am the Walrus."
Side 2: "Penny Lane"; "Helter Skelter"; "Don't Pass Me By"; "The Inner Light"; "Across the Universe" (World Wildlife Fund version); "You Know My Name (Look up the Number)"; "Sgt. Pepper Inner Groove."

COVER ARTWORK

The *Rarities* cover art features a late-period Beatles photograph on a field of grey. The uncredited liner notes point out that "half of the fun of these recordings is comparing them to the 'standard' versions. As with any collection of songs, many 'rare' possibilities had to be left off for lack of space, but the ones included here were chosen because either collectors have searched for them for years or because musically these versions have something 'strange' about them to any listener who is familiar with the more common versions."

CHART PERFORMANCE

U.S.: #21 (certified by the RIAA as "Gold," with more than 500,000 copies sold).

See also: *Sgt. Pepper's Lonely Hearts Club Band* (LP); *Yesterday . . . and Today* (LP).

"Real Love" (Lennon)

Released some 26 years after their disbandment, "Real Love" was a 1996 hit single by the Beatles that the surviving band members recorded with a 1979–1980 demo by Lennon as the song's basic track.

AUTHORSHIP AND BACKGROUND

Written by Lennon, "Real Love" was composed by Lennon at his home with Yoko Ono in New York City's Dakota apartment building. In 1979 and 1980, Lennon recorded six takes for a demo version of the song, with vocal and piano or acoustic guitar accompaniment recorded on a single microphone, on a cassette player. In its early manifestations, "Real Love" went under the title of "Real Life," a song that Lennon was composing for a planned but unfinished stage play to be entitled as *The Ballad of John and Yoko*.

As the surviving Beatles—often referred to as "The Threetles"—compiled their *Anthology* documentary in the early 1990s, George Harrison and Aspinall approached Ono about the idea of enhancing Lennon's demos for release. After McCartney delivered his induction speech on Lennon's behalf at the Rock and Roll Hall of Fame's January 1994 induction ceremony, Ono provided him with Lennon's demo tapes for "Free as a Bird," "Real Love," "Now and Then," and "Grow Old with Me." Before leaving the Dakota, McCartney later recalled,

I checked it out with Sean, because I didn't want him to have a problem with it. He said, "Well, it'll be weird hearing a dead guy on lead vocal. But give it a try." I said to them both, "If it doesn't work out, you can veto it." When I told George and Ringo I'd agreed to that they were going, "What? What if we love it?" It didn't come to that, luckily. I said to Yoko, "Don't impose too many conditions on us, it's really difficult to do this, spiritually. We don't know—we may hate each other after two hours in the studio and just walk out. So don't put any conditions, it's tough enough." (Huntley 2004, 249)

RECORDING SESSIONS

While George Martin was originally considered for the production duties associated with "Real Love," the aging producer bowed out of the project because of problems with his hearing. As McCartney later remarked in a 1995 interview with *Bass Player* magazine, "George doesn't want to produce much any more 'cause his hearing's not as good as it used to be. He's a very sensible guy, and he says, 'Look, Paul I like to do a proper job,' and if he doesn't feel he's up to it he won't do it. It's very noble of him, actually—most people would take the money and run" (Badman 2001, 439). Jeff Lynne, who had produced Harrison's *Cloud Nine* album (1987), was subsequently tapped as the song's coproducer, along with Lennon, McCartney, Harrison, and Starr.

Given Lennon's glaring absence from the proceedings, Starr suggested a scenario in which his bandmates pretended that the fallen Beatle had gone out to lunch or for a cup of tea. Meanwhile, McCartney, Harrison, and Starr retired to McCartney's Hog Hill Mill studio in Sussex for a series of February 1995 recording sessions in which they recorded additional vocals and instrumentation around Lennon's basic track.

In the case of "Real Love," Lynne had to take special pains to counteract the inordinate amount of hiss on the source tape. As Lynne remarked in a December 1995 *Sound on Sound* interview,

> We tried out a new noise reduction system, and it really worked. The problem I had with "Real Love" was that not only was there a 60 cycles mains hum going on, there was also a terrible amount of hiss, because it had been recorded at a low level. I don't know how many generations down this copy was, but it sounded like at least a couple. So I had to get rid of the hiss and the main hum, and then there were clicks all the way through it. . . . We'd spend a day on it, then listen back and still find loads more things wrong. . . . It didn't have any effect on John's voice, because we were just dealing with the air surrounding him, in between phrases. That took about a week to clean up before it was even usable and transferable to a DAT [digital audio tape] master. Putting fresh music to it was the easy part!" (*Sound on Sound* 1995)

At the conclusion of the *Anthology* documentary project and the release of the "Free as a Bird" and "Real Love" singles, Starr observed that "recording the new songs didn't feel contrived at all, it felt very natural and it was a lot of fun, but emotional too at times. But it's the end of the line, really. There's nothing more we can do as the Beatles."

PERSONNEL

Lennon: Vocal, Piano

McCartney: Double Bass, Acoustic Guitar, Piano, Electric Baldwin Harpsichord, Backing Vocal

Harrison: Vocal, Model "T" Hamburguitar, Acoustic Guitar, Harmonium, Backing Vocal

Starr: Drums, Tambourine

CHART PERFORMANCE

U.K.: "Real Love"/"Baby's in Black (Live)"; March 4, 1996, Apple RP 6425: #4.

U.S.: "Real Love"/"Baby's in Black (Live)"; March 4, 1996, Apple NR 8 58544 7: #11 (certified by the RIAA as "Gold," with more than 500,000 copies sold).

CONTROVERSY

"Real Love" emerged as the center of a radio-programming controversy in March 1996 when BBC's Radio 1 purposefully excluded "Real Love" from the popular radio station's playlist, remarking that "it's not what our listeners want to hear. We are a contemporary music station." In a press release, Beatles spokesman Geoff Baker reported the band's response as "Indignation. Shock and surprise. We carried out research after the *Anthology* was launched, and this revealed that 41 percent of the buyers were teenagers." On March 9, 1996, McCartney published an 800-word retort in *The Daily Mirror*, writing, "The Beatles don't need our new single, 'Real Love,' to be a hit. It's not as if our careers depend on it. If Radio 1 feels that we should be banned now, it's not exactly going to ruin us overnight. You can't put an age limit on good music" (McCartney 1996).

ALBUM APPEARANCE: *Anthology 2.*

See also: *The Beatles Anthology, Volume 2* (LP); Lynne, Jeff; Ono, Yoko.

Reel Music (LP)

March 22, 1982, Parlophone TC PCS 7218
March 23, 1982, Capitol SV 12199

Reel Music is a compilation album, now deleted from the Beatles' catalogue, that was released on March 22, 1982, in the United States and March 23, 1982, in the United Kingdom.

BACKGROUND

Reel Music was released to coincide with the February 7, 1982, theatrical rerelease of the feature film *A Hard Day's Night* by Universal Pictures. It included the first true stereo mixes of "A Hard Day's Night" and "Ticket to Ride" to be released in the U.S. marketplace. A single entitled "The Beatles' Movie Medley" was released as part of the promotional blitz for the compilation, featuring excerpts from "Magical Mystery Tour," "All You Need Is Love," "You've Got to Hide Your Love Away," "I Should Have Known Better," "A Hard Day's Night," "Ticket to Ride," and "Get Back."

Compiled by Randall Davis and Steve Meyer, *Reel Music* was the first Beatles album released after Lennon's death.

TRACK LISTING

Side 1: "A Hard Day's Night"; "I Should Have Known Better"; "Can't Buy Me Love"; "And I Love Her"; "Help!"; "You've Got to Hide Your Love Away"; "Ticket to Ride"; "Magical Mystery Tour."

Side 2: "I Am the Walrus"; "Yellow Submarine"; "All You Need Is Love"; "Let It Be"; "Get Back"; "The Long and Winding Road."

COVER ARTWORK

Designed by Michael Diehl, *Reel Music* features a cover illustration by David McMacken depicted period incarnations of the Beatles from their film appearances in *A Hard Day's Night*, *Help!*, *Magical Mystery Tour*, *Yellow Submarine*, and *Let It Be*. The *Reel Music* LP package included a 12-page booklet entitled *The Beatles Souvenir Program*.

CHART PERFORMANCE

U.K.: Did not chart.

U.S.: #19 (certified by the RIAA as "Gold," with more than 500,000 copies sold).

See also: *A Hard Day's Night* (Film); *Help!* (Film); *Let It Be* (Film); *Magical Mystery Tour* (TV Film); *Yellow Submarine* (Film).

"Revolution" (Lennon–McCartney)

"Revolution" was a hit double A-side single, backed with "Hey Jude," which was released in the United Kingdom on August 30, 1968, and in the United States on August 26, 1968.

AUTHORSHIP AND BACKGROUND

Written by Lennon, "Revolution" finds its origins during the Beatles' 1968 visit to India. As with "Revolution 1," the song exists as Lennon's strident rejoinder to the bloody activities of the Communist Left and the Cultural Revolution in the People's Republic of China. After recording "Revolution 1," Lennon conceived of "Revolution" as a faster remake of the original track.

As Lennon later recalled,

> The statement in "Revolution" was mine. The lyrics stand today. It's still my feeling about politics. I want to see the plan. That is what I used to say to Abbie Hoffman and Jerry Rubin. Count me out if it is for violence. Don't expect me to be on the barricades unless it is with flowers. For years, on the Beatles' tours, Brian Epstein had stopped us from saying anything about Vietnam or the war. And he wouldn't allow questions about it. But on one of the last tours, I said, "I'm going to answer about the war. We can't ignore it." I absolutely wanted the Beatles to say something about the war. (Cadogan 2008, 203)

An early version of "Revolution" was recorded in May 1968 at Harrison's Kinfauns studio as part of the Esher Tapes.

RECORDING SESSIONS

Produced by George Martin, "Revolution" was rehearsed at Abbey Road Studios on July 9, 1968, and recorded the following day, with overdubbing sessions on July 11 and 12.

"Revolution" finds the Beatles complementing the slower, heavily distorted hopefulness of "Revolution 1" with the blistering, infectious sound of unvarnished rock 'n' roll. With ace session man Nicky Hopkins contributing a lightning-hot electric piano solo, the song sports a highly distorted sound that Emerick achieved by overloading the pre-amps and direct-injecting Lennon's Casino into the mixing desk.

PERSONNEL

Lennon: Vocal, Epiphone Casino
McCartney: Rickenbacker 4001S, Backing Vocal
Harrison: Gibson Les Paul Standard, Backing Vocal
Starr: Ludwig Oyster Black Pearl Drums
Hopkins: Electric Piano

CHART PERFORMANCE

U.K.: "Hey Jude"/"Revolution"; August 30, 1968, Apple [Parlophone] R 5722: #1. As a double A-side with "Hey Jude," "Revolution" did not chart.

U.S.: "Hey Jude"/"Revolution"; August 26, 1968, Apple [Capitol] 2276: #1 (certified by the RIAA as "4x Multi Platinum," with more than 4 million copies sold). As a double A-side with "Hey Jude," "Revolution" charted at #12.

LEGACY AND INFLUENCE

In 2010, *Rolling Stone* ranked "Revolution" as #13 on the magazine's list of *The Beatles' 100 Greatest Songs*.

CONTROVERSY

In 1987, "Revolution" became the first Beatles song to be licensed for commercial use. Nike paid $500,000 to the EMI Group for the right to air the song in their television advertisements, pitting McCartney, Harrison, and Starr against Ono, who had expressed approval for the Nike venture, believing that the commercials would bring Lennon's music into the orbit of a new generation of listeners. The surviving Beatles and EMI reached an out-of-court settlement in November 1989.

ALBUM APPEARANCES: *Hey Jude*; *The Beatles, 1967–1970*; *Rock 'n' Roll Music*; *Past Masters, Volume 2*; *Love*; *Tomorrow Never Knows*.

See also: *The Beatles* (*The White Album*) (LP).

"Revolution I" (Lennon–McCartney)

"Revolution 1" is a song on *The Beatles* (*The White Album*).

AUTHORSHIP AND BACKGROUND

Written by Lennon, "Revolution 1" finds its origins during the Beatles' 1968 visit to India. He composed the song as an explicit rejoinder to the bloody activities of the Communist Left, as his own gritty response to the Cultural Revolution in the People's Republic of China. Incensed by the Maoist exploitation of millions of youth militia forces in an express attempt to crush the Chairman's enemies, Lennon authored his fearsome screed in order to denounce the violence and destruction. For Lennon at least, the Beatles' initial effort at social protest had been long overdue.

An early version of "Revolution 1" (as "Revolution") was recorded in May 1968 at Harrison's Kinfauns studio as part of the Esher Tapes.

RECORDING SESSIONS

Produced by Martin, "Revolution 1" was recorded at Abbey Road Studios on May 30, 1968, with overdubbing sessions on May 31, June 4, and June 21.

The recording features heavily distorted electric guitars, with McCartney and Harrison supplying an intentionally jarring series of "bam shoo-be-doo-wop" backing vocals. As if to compound the incongruous nature of the composition's mêlée of competing styles and instrumentation, Martin scored an arrangement for two trumpets and a quartet of trombones. A sloppy edit at 0:02—intentionally retained in the mix at Lennon's request—witnesses Emerick muttering "take two" and adding an extra beat to the song's introduction. In an attempt to lend his voice a breathy quality, Lennon recorded his vocal lying flat on his back in the control room, with a microphone, courtesy of Emerick, hovering over his head.

The band's 20th take of "Revolution 1" clocked in at nearly 11 minutes and served as the impetus for the creation of "Revolution 9."

PERSONNEL

Lennon: Vocal, Epiphone Casino
McCartney: Fender Jazz Bass, Piano
Harrison: Gibson Les Paul Standard
Starr: Ludwig Oyster Black Pearl Drums
Studio Musicians: Brass Accompaniment conducted by Martin
Freddy Clayton, Derek Watkins: Trumpet
Don Lang, Rex Morris, J. Power, Bill Povey: Trombone

ALBUM APPEARANCE: *The Beatles* (*The White Album*).

See also: *The Beatles* (*The White Album*) (LP).

"Revolution 9" (Lennon–McCartney)

"Revolution 9" is a track on *The Beatles* (*The White Album*).

AUTHORSHIP AND BACKGROUND

Conceived by Lennon, "Revolution 9" is an experimental sound collage inspired by the musique concrète of Karlheinz Stockhausen. Literally defined as "concrete music," musique concrète refers to a form of electronic music in which artists combine fragments of natural and mechanized sounds through the editing process.

As Lennon later observed, "Revolution 9" was "just abstract, musique concrète, [tape] loops, people screaming." But the track is also striking for its author's self-described misreading of his own creation: "I thought I was painting in sound a picture of revolution—but I made a mistake, you know. The mistake was that it was anti-revolution" (Beatles 2000, 307).

RECORDING SESSIONS

Produced by Martin, "Revolution 9" finds its origins in the Beatles' May 30, 1968, sessions at Abbey Road Studios for "Revolution 1." The band's raucous 20th take of the song clocked in at nearly 11 minutes and served as the impetus for the creation of "Revolution 9." Additional overdubbing sessions occurred on June 6, 10, 11, 20, and 21.

Recorded on a series of Brenell tape recorders by Lennon and Ono, with assistance from Harrison, "Revolution 9" presents a sound collage of tape loops, backward recordings, and all manner of reconfigured noise. The track's eerily antiseptic spoken refrain, "number nine, number nine," was lifted from an examination recording for the Royal Academy of Music in the EMI tape library, while the tape loops include portions of Schumann's *Symphonic Etudes*, Vaughn-Williams's "O Clap Your Hands," Sibelius's *Symphony No. 7*, and even a violin trill from "A Day in the Life" (Everett 1999, 174–77).

Nonsequiturs abound in "Revolution 9," with a multitude of verbal fragments courtesy of Lennon, including the triumphant bequeathing of a sword, a weapon of honor in a dishonorable world: "Take this, brother, may it serve you well." In addition to the ambient noise of gunfire and crackling flame, the sound of a gurgling baby is oddly counterpoised by Ono's erotic nonchalance—"If you become naked"—while the entire sonic morass concludes with the welcome resolve and determination afforded by a football cheer.

PERSONNEL

Lennon: Voice
McCartney: Piano
Harrison: Voice
Starr: Voice
Ono: Voice
Martin: Voice

CONTROVERSY

Given the track's radically experimental nature, McCartney vehemently objected to the inclusion of "Revolution 9" on *The White Album*.

ALBUM APPEARANCE: *The Beatles* (*The White Album*).

See also: *The Beatles* (*The White Album*) (LP); Ono, Yoko; "Paul Is Dead" Hoax.

Revolver (U.K. LP)

August 5, 1966, Parlophone PMC 7009 (mono)/PCS 7009 (stereo)

Revolver is the Beatles' seventh studio album. It was released on the Parlophone label on August 5, 1966, in the United Kingdom. In the United States, several of the songs on *Revolver* were released on *Yesterday . . . and Today*, released on June 20, 1966.

Revolver became standardized among U.S. album releases with the April 30, 1987, distribution of *Help!*, *Rubber Soul*, and *Revolver* as stereo CD releases. *Revolver* was remastered and rereleased as a stereo CD on September 9, 2009. A remastered mono release was also made available at this time as part of a limited edition box set entitled *The Beatles in Mono*.

BACKGROUND AND RECORDING SESSIONS

Produced by Martin with Emerick as his sound engineer, *Revolver* was recorded on four-track equipment during multiple sessions from April 6 through June 21, 1966, at Abbey Road Studios. Its eclectic collection of songs engages in an "intra-album dialogue," to borrow a phrase from Russell Reising, that examines the ceaseless interplay between life and death, as well as the divergent forms of consciousness that we experience in our lives and afterlives (Reising 2002, 235). "*Revolver* is a

Album cover designed by art director Robert Fraser for the Beatles' 1967 album, *Sgt. Pepper's Lonely Hearts Club Band.* (Michael Ochs Archives/Getty Images)

very serious and a very heady album, both in terms of its sonic experiments as well as in its lyrical drift," Reising writes. "Even the love songs (and there are no 'silly love songs' on *Revolver*) relate deeply and seriously to its darker, more tragic elements" (Reising 2006, 127).

In March 1966, Lennon remarked in an interview that "Paul and I are very keen on this electronic music. You make it clinking a couple of glasses together or with bleeps from the radio, then you loop the tape to repeat the noises at intervals. Some people build up whole symphonies from it. . . . One thing's for sure," he added. "The next LP is going to be very different" (Ryan and Kehew 2006, 408). Anticipating the album's revolutionary soundscapes, McCartney commented in the June 24, 1966, issue of the *New Musical Express* that "I for one am sick of doing sounds that people can claim to have heard before" (Smith 1966, 3).

And while the album's astonishing textual worlds first found their being in the Beatles' fertile imaginations, it was 19-year-old Geoff Emerick who brought those very sounds and visions to life. Emerick's lucky break came in 1966, when Norman "Normal" Smith was promoted to become a full-fledged producer at Abbey Road Studios; in the process, he also became head of Parlophone, replacing the recently estranged Martin. Smith's first project was *The Piper at the Gates of Dawn*, the debut album by a fledgling band from the "London Underground" scene known as Pink Floyd. With Smith's absence, Martin wasted no time in inviting Emerick, whom the EMI staff affectionately nicknamed "Golden Ears," to be the Beatles' engineer for *Revolver*. But the project nearly didn't happen—at least not in the same fashion as history has foretold. In fact, the Beatles had originally considered recording the album in the United States after learning that Bob Dylan had made his latest LP *Blonde on Blonde* (1966) in Memphis. With Brian Epstein handling the negotiations, the band mulled over the possibility of working at either Detroit's Motown Studio, Memphis's Stax Studio, or New York City's Atlantic Studio. They even tinkered with the idea of having their next album produced by legendary soul guitarist Steve "The Colonel" Cropper, who was thrilled with the prospect of recording the Fab Four. Life had become complicated in the Beatles' camp, it seems, and a change of scenery—and possibly even in recording personnel—would "shake things up," in Harrison's reasoning (Spitz 2005, 599).

Things had indeed been shaking up since August 1965, when Martin had severed his official ties with EMI, shed his A&R duties with Parlophone, and became an independent producer who could record any act in any venue of his choice. Over the past few years, Martin had become fed up with the EMI Group, which paid him a paltry £3,000 for his work in 1963—a year in which the records he produced held the #1 position on the British charts for a phenomenal 37 weeks. Soon thereafter, Martin established AIR (Associated Independent Recording) Studios in London, and his liberation from EMI was complete. Meanwhile, Epstein's dealings with Cropper had disintegrated almost as quickly as they had begun. But it hardly mattered in the slightest to the Beatles: the group's plans to record in the United States, and perhaps even with a different producer at the helm, had already become moot. By the time that Epstein was ready to ink a deal with an American studio, the Beatles and Martin—in their typical breakneck fashion—had already finished recording much of the next album.

The creative team involving the Beatles, Martin, and Emerick was a veritable tour de force, and *Revolver* was their proving ground. Emerick ultimately succeeded in masterminding the sound of *Revolver* by violating Abbey Road Studios' highly proscriptive rules. As with the EMI Group itself, the studio was known for its austerity and tradition. Indeed, the production staff, from lowly assistant engineers on up, were required to wear white laboratory coats at all times. But Emerick was determined to test the limits of the recording studio, and the Beatles were the perfect vehicle for trying out his radical ideas. By placing microphones within inches of the group's amps and Starr's drums, for example, Emerick defied EMI's stipulated recording distances yet created a host of new sounds in the bargain. No matter how outlandish the group's requests, he made every effort to accommodate the Beatles' desires for formulating new sounds. When Lennon came up with an outrageous metaphor for how he wanted his vocal to sound—"Give me the feel of James Dean gunning his motorcycle down the highway"—Emerick never hesitated in dreaming up the necessary studio trickery with which to bring the songwriter's creative visions to life (Emerick and Massey 2006, 8).

In addition to Emerick's innovative engineering techniques, the band benefited from the invention of automatic double-tracking (ADT) by Abbey Road Studios' maintenance engineer Ken Townsend, who had devised the system at Lennon's behest. Fed up with the laborious task of double-tracking his voice on the Beatles' recordings, Lennon wanted a mechanism that could accomplish the job automatically. In contrast with double-tracking, which requires musicians to synchronize their voices or instruments with a preexisting track, ADT employs two studio tape decks that automatically feed the same signal through both decks, as well as through the mixing desk. In Townsend's design, ADT simultaneously duplicates the sounds of voices or instruments in order to create a layered effect. Townsend's system also enables its users to manipulate the second track by a few milliseconds in order to create a more expansive, trebly texture.

With Emerick's studio innovations and ADT in their stead, the Beatles' creative world had suddenly become all but limitless. Their lives on the road and in the studio were quite suddenly at artistic odds with each other, and *Revolver* had emerged as the great harbinger of things to come. As Tim Riley astutely argues, "*Revolver* single-handedly made Beatlemania irrelevant" (Riley 1988, 176).

TRACK LISTING

Side 1: "Taxman"; "Eleanor Rigby"; "I'm Only Sleeping"; "Love You To"; "Here, There, and Everywhere"; "Yellow Submarine"; "She Said She Said."
Side 2: "Good Day Sunshine"; "And Your Bird Can Sing"; "For No One"; "Doctor Robert"; "I Want to Tell You"; "Got to Get You into My Life"; "Tomorrow Never Knows."

COVER ARTWORK

When the Beatles embarked on June 23, 1966, for the first leg of their impending world tour—which began, as had their career as professional musicians not so many years ago, in West Germany—their new album remained untitled. Before settling on *Revolver*, they considered naming the album *Abracadabra*, or, at McCartney's suggestion, *Magic Circle*. Lennon jokingly proposed that they call it *The Beatles on Safari*. Eventually, McCartney floated the idea of calling it *Revolver*, the title stuck, and there was no turning back. *Revolver* it was. Pete Shotton remembered rifling through newspapers and magazines with Lennon and McCartney at the Lennons' Weybridge estate. After selecting various pictures of the Beatles, they cut out the faces and glued them together in a "surrealistic montage," which was then superimposed on a line drawing by the band's old friend from Hamburg, artist and bass player Klaus Voormann (Shotton and Schaffner 1983, 122). With its monochromatic imagery and intriguing assortment of photographs that seem to flower from Voormann's drawings of Lennon, McCartney, Harrison, and Starr, the result was the Beatles' most imaginative cover to date, a provocative sleeve design befitting a groundbreaking album such as *Revolver*. As McCartney later recalled,

> We knew [Voormann] drew and he'd been involved in graphic design; I must admit we didn't really know what he did, but he'd been to college. We knew he must be all right and so we said, "Why don't you come up with something for the album cover?" He did, and we were all very pleased with it. We liked the way there were little things coming out of people's ears, and how he'd collaged things on a small scale while the drawings were on a big scale. He also knew us well enough to capture us rather beautifully in the drawings. We were flattered. (Beatles 2000, 212)

Not surprisingly, in March 1967, the album cover earned "Best Album Cover/Graphic Arts" honors during the 9th Grammy Awards. As a kind of self-portraiture, Voormann depicts himself seated in Harrison's tousled hair on the *Revolver* album cover. As with *Rubber Soul*, *Revolver* does not include explanatory liner notes.

CHART PERFORMANCE

U.K.: #1 (In the United States, *Revolver* has been certified by the RIAA as "5x Multi Platinum," with more than 5 million copies sold).

LEGACY AND INFLUENCE

In 1998, the BBC ranked *Revolver* as #3 among its *Music of the Millennium* albums.

In 2000, *Q Magazine* ranked *Revolver* as #1 on the magazine's list of *The 100 Greatest British Albums Ever*.

In 2001, VH1 ranked *Revolver* as #1 among its *All Time Album Top 100*.

In 2003, *Rolling Stone* ranked *Revolver* as #3 on the magazine's list of *The 500 Greatest Albums of All Time*.

In 2004, *Q Magazine* ranked *Revolver* as #1 on the magazine's list of *The Music That Changed the World*.

In 2005, *Mojo* magazine ranked *Revolver* as #3 on the magazine's list of *The 100 Greatest Albums Ever Made*.

In 2006, *Mojo* magazine published a special issue that celebrated *Revolver*'s 40th anniversary, including a cover-mounted CD with contemporary cover versions of the album's entire contents entitled *Revolver Reloaded*.

In 2007, *Mojo* magazine ranked *Revolver* as #40 on the magazine's list of *Big Bangs: 100 Records That Changed the World*.

See also: Martin, George; Voormann, Klaus.

Revolver (U.S. LP)

August 8, 1966, Capitol T 2576 (mono)/ST 2576 (stereo)

Revolver was the 12th Beatles album to be released in the United States—the 10th on Capitol Records, along with Vee-Jay Records' *Introducing . . . the Beatles* and United Artists' soundtrack for the *A Hard Day's Night* feature film. It was released on the Capitol label on August 8, 1966. The American *Revolver* is a truncated edition of the U.K. version of *Revolver*, released on August 5, 1966, given that three of the original U.K. version's tracks had already appeared on the U.S. release of *Yesterday . . . and Today*, released on June 20, 1966.

The American version of *Revolver* was deleted from the Beatles' catalogue in 1987, when the group's U.K. albums were distributed as CD releases.

BACKGROUND

The American version of *Revolver* marked the last occasion in which Capitol Records released an altered version of a U.K. Beatles release.

TRACK LISTING

Side 1: "Taxman"; "Eleanor Rigby"; "Love You To"; "Here, There, and Everywhere"; "Yellow Submarine"; "She Said She Said."

Side 2: "Good Day Sunshine"; "For No One"; "I Want to Tell You"; "Got to Get You into My Life"; "Tomorrow Never Knows."

COVER ARTWORK

As with the U.K. release, the *Revolver* album cover features Voormann's line drawing, along with various pictures of the Beatles arrayed in what Shotton later described as a "surrealistic montage" (Shotton and Schaffner 1983, 122). In March 1967, the album cover earned "Best Album Cover/Graphic Arts" honors during the 9th Grammy Awards.

CHART PERFORMANCE

U.S.: #1 (certified by the RIAA as "5x Multi Platinum," with more than 5 million copies sold).

LEGACY AND INFLUENCE

In 1967, *Revolver* was nominated for a Grammy Award for Album of the Year at the 9th Grammy Awards.

In 1999, *Revolver* was inducted into the National Academy of Recording Arts and Sciences Grammy Hall of Fame.

See also: Martin, George; Voormann, Klaus.

"Rock and Roll Music" (Berry)

"Rock and Roll Music" is a song on *Beatles for Sale*.

AUTHORSHIP AND BACKGROUND

Written by Chuck Berry, "Rock and Roll Music" was a 1957 hit for the artist. One of the most widely covered compositions in the history of popular music, "Rock and Roll Music" is Berry's most recognized and influential song. Originally released by Chess Records, it charted at #6 on the U.S. Hot 100.

RECORDING SESSIONS

Produced by Martin, "Rock and Roll Music" was recorded in a single take on October 18, 1964, at Abbey Road Studios. Lennon's vocal is heavily treated with STEED (single tape echo and echo delay) in order to achieve a live-sounding echo effect. On November 25, the Beatles recorded another version of "Rock and Roll Music" for the BBC's *Saturday Club* radio show that was later included on the *Live at the BBC* album.

PERSONNEL

Lennon: Vocal, Rickenbacker 325
McCartney: Höfner 500/1

Harrison: Gibson J-160E
Starr: Ludwig Oyster Black Pearl Drums
Martin: Piano

LEGACY AND INFLUENCE

Berry's recording of "Rock and Roll Music" is included among the Rock and Roll Hall of Fame's *500 Songs That Shaped Rock and Roll*.

In 2004, *Rolling Stone* ranked "Rock and Roll Music" as #128 on the magazine's list of *The 500 Greatest Songs of All Time*.

ALBUM APPEARANCES: *Beatles for Sale*; *Beatles '65*; *Rock 'n' Roll Music*; *Live at the BBC*; *Anthology 2*.

See also: *Beatles for Sale* (LP).

Rock 'n' Roll Music (LP)

June 11, 1976, Parlophone PCSP 719
June 7, 1976, Capitol SKBO 11537

Rock 'n' Roll Music is a compilation album, now deleted from the Beatles' catalogue, that was released on June 7, 1976, in the United States and June 11, 1976, in the United Kingdom.

BACKGROUND

Presumably named after the eponymous Berry song, *Rock 'n' Roll Music* was released to capture the Beatles' rock 'n' roll roots, as well as their own contributions to the genre. In addition to such Beatles standards as "Drive My Car," "Revolution," and "Get Back," it contains several early cover versions. It is notable because it marks the first LP release of "I'm Down," which was previously only available as the B-side of the "Help!" single.

Rock 'n' Roll Music was promoted by the release of a pair of singles in the United States and the United Kingdom, respectively, including the American release of "Got to Get You into My Life" backed with "Helter Skelter" and the British release of "Back in the USSR" backed with "Twist and Shout." The A-side for the American release was originally slated to be "Helter Skelter," but the contemporaneous release of the *Helter Skelter* television movie about the 1969 Manson Family murders prompted Capitol Records to reverse the sides of the record.

In October 1980, Capitol Records released the albums as a pair of single LP releases, *Rock 'n' Roll Music, Volume 1* and *Rock 'n' Roll Music, Volume 2*, replacing the compilation's original controversial artwork with a Beatlemania-era photograph of the band.

TRACK LISTING

Side 1: "Twist and Shout"; "I Saw Her Standing There"; "You Can't Do That"; "I Wanna Be Your Man"; "I Call Your Name"; "Boys"; "Long Tall Sally."

Side 2: "Rock and Roll Music"; "Slow Down"; Medley: "Kansas City"/"Hey-Hey-Hey-Hey!"; "Money (That's What I Want)"; "Bad Boy"; "Matchbox"; "Roll Over Beethoven."

Side 3: "Dizzy, Miss Lizzy"; "Any Time at All"; "Drive My Car"; "Everybody's Trying to Be My Baby"; "The Night Before"; "I'm Down"; "Revolution."

Side 4: "Back in the USSR"; "Helter Skelter"; "Taxman"; "Got to Get You into My Life"; "Hey Bulldog"; "Birthday"; "Get Back" (*Let It Be* version).

COVER ARTWORK

Rock 'n' Roll Music is one of the more controversial releases among Beatles fans— even the Beatles themselves—because of its cover artwork, which features nostalgic, 1950s-oriented illustrations of Marilyn Monroe and a '57 Chevy. As Starr later remarked, "It made us look cheap, and we were never cheap. All that Coca-Cola and cars with big fins was the Fifties!" (Schaffner 1977, 188). Lennon wrote a pointed letter to Capitol Records, writing that the cover "looks like a Monkees reject" and suggesting alternative cover artwork adorned by period photographs of the early Beatles by Kirchherr, or, barring that, designing the cover himself.

CHART PERFORMANCE

U.K.: #11 (certified by the BPI as "Gold," with more than 100,000 copies sold).

U.S.: #2 (certified by the RIAA as "Platinum," with more than 1 million copies sold).

See also: Kirchherr, Astrid.

"Rocky Raccoon" (Lennon–McCartney)

"Rocky Raccoon" is a song on *The Beatles* (*The White Album*).

AUTHORSHIP AND BACKGROUND

Written by McCartney, "Rocky Raccoon" finds its origins during the Beatles' 1968 visit to India, when the songwriter improvised the song while playing acoustic guitars on the roof of one of the buildings in the Rishikesh compound with Lennon and Donovan. McCartney drew his inspiration for the song from Robert Service's poem entitled "The Shooting of Dan McGrew."

As McCartney later recalled,

> I like talking-blues so I started off like that, then I did my tongue-in-cheek parody of a western and threw in some amusing lines. The bit I liked about it was him [Rocky] finding *Gideon's Bible* and thinking, "Some guy called Gideon must have left it for the next guy." I like the idea of Gideon being a character. You get the meaning, and at the same time get in a poke at it. All in good fun. (Turner 1994, 162)

An early version of "Rocky Raccoon" was recorded in May 1968 at Harrison's Kinfauns studio as part of the Esher Tapes. It went under the working title of "Rocky Sassoon."

RECORDING SESSIONS

Produced by Martin, "Rocky Raccoon" was recorded at Abbey Road Studios on August 15, 1968.

Given the song's Old West feel, the sound effects abound, with Starr signaling the loud report of a gun with a rim-shot and Martin establishing a saloon-like ambience on the studio's Challen "jangle box" piano, which he played at half-speed, honky-tonk style, and created using his wound-up piano technique.

PERSONNEL

Lennon: Fender Bass VI, Harmonica, Harmonium, Backing Vocal
McCartney: Vocal, Martin D-28
Harrison: Gibson J-200, Backing Vocal
Starr: Ludwig Oyster Black Pearl Drums
Martin: Honky-Tonk Piano

ALBUM APPEARANCES: *The Beatles (The White Album); Anthology 3.*

See also: The Beatles (The White Album) (LP).

"Roll Over Beethoven" (Berry)

"Roll Over Beethoven" is a song on the *With the Beatles* album.

AUTHORSHIP AND BACKGROUND

"Roll Over Beethoven" was written by Chuck Berry, who was referencing his sister Lucy's fondness for playing classical music on the same family piano upon which he wanted to play contemporary songs. It became a hit single for Berry in 1956 after being released by Chess Records. It is one of the most widely covered compositions in the history of popular music.

RECORDING SESSIONS

Produced by George Martin, "Roll Over Beethoven" was recorded at Abbey Road Studios on July 30, 1963. On February 28, 1964, the Beatles recorded a second cover version of "Roll Over Beethoven" for the BBC's *From Us to You* radio show that was later included on the *Live at the BBC* album. Overall, they recorded seven versions of "Roll Over Beethoven" for BBC radio between June 1963 and February 1964. Yet another live recording of "Roll Over Beethoven" from the band's BBC sessions was later included on the Beatles' *On Air: Live at the BBC, Volume 2*.

PERSONNEL

Lennon: Rickenbacker 325
McCartney: Höfner 500/1
Harrison: Vocal, Gretsch Country Gentleman
Starr: Ludwig Oyster Black Pearl Drums

LEGACY AND INFLUENCE

In 2004, *Rolling Stone* ranked "Roll Over Beethoven" as #97 on the magazine's list of *The 500 Greatest Songs of All Time*.

ALBUM APPEARANCES: *With the Beatles*; *The Beatles' Second Album*; *Rock 'n' Roll Music*; *The Beatles at the Hollywood Bowl*; *Live! at the Star-Club in Hamburg, Germany; 1962*; *Live at the BBC*; *Anthology 1*; *On Air: Live at the BBC, Volume 2*.

See also: *With the Beatles* (LP).

The Rooftop Concert

The Rooftop Concert took place on Friday, January 30, 1969. Staged on the rooftop of 3 Savile Row, the London building that housed the corporate offices of Apple Corps and a newly outfitted basement recording studio, the concert was the Beatles' final public performance.

With long-time associates Mal Evans and Neil Aspinall acting as the band's roadies for the last time, the Beatles performed for some 42 minutes, half of which later appeared in the *Let It Be* feature film, as an impromptu lunchtime crowd gathered in the streetscape below. As a blustery wind whipped among the roof-tops and chimneys of the city's Mayfair district, Michael Lindsay-Hogg captured the action on film, while George Martin supervised the recording of the event six floors below in the band's basement studio using converted eight-track equipment that had been borrowed from Abbey Road Studios. Meanwhile, Martin's counter-part Glyn Johns observed the concert from the rooftop as Lindsay-Hogg dis-patched a team of 11 cameramen to record footage of both the performance itself and reaction shots from the audience that gathered below on Savile Row in the heart of the garment district.

But the concert itself nearly didn't happen at all. As Lindsay-Hogg's *Let It Be* footage reveals, Harrison heartily dismisses the idea on January 29, 1969, with Starr nodding nearby in stolid agreement. But Lennon and McCartney were not deterred. As Lindsay-Hogg later remembered, "We planned to do it about 12:30 to get the lunchtime crowds. They didn't agree to do it as a group until about twenty to one. Paul wanted to do it and George didn't. Ringo would go either way. Then John said, 'Oh f—, let's do it,' and they went up and did it" (Matteo 2004, 83). The band's instrumentation featured Lennon on his prized Epiphone Casino, a bearded McCartney playing his iconic Höfner bass—with the Beatles' set list for their final American tour still taped to its upper body—Harrison playing his Rose-wood Telecaster, Starr working a newly acquired set of maple-finished Ludwig Hollywood drums, and guest musician Billy Preston plying his Fender Rhodes electric piano. Throughout the concert, the bandmates struggled to fend off the bitter wintry wind, with Lennon borrowing Ono's fur coat and Starr donning his wife Maureen's vibrant orange raincoat for the occasion.

The concert itself, punctuated by a series of false starts, featured full perfor-mances of five songs, including "Get Back," "Don't Let Me Down," "I've Got a Feeling," "One After 909," and "Dig a Pony." In addition to taking multiple attempts at "Get Back," "Don't Let Me Down," and "Dig a Pony," the band made brief attempts at Frederick Weatherly's arrangement of the traditional "Danny Boy" and Irving Berlin's "A Pretty Girl Is Like a Melody," with slightly more extended, albeit truncated performances of "I Want You (She's So Heavy)" and the British royal anthem "God Save the Queen."

The concert concluded with a reprise performance of "Get Back" in which McCartney makes explicit reference to the London Bobbies who had arrived in response to complaints about the noise. The appearance of the London Bobbies was later depicted, both in the folklore of Beatles fandom and in the narrative of Lindsay-Hogg's film, as an express attempt to bring the group's concert to a sud-den close. Starr's own memories supported this claim, with Starr recalling that "I always felt let down about the police. I was playing away and I thought, 'Oh, great! I hope they drag me off!' I *wanted* the cops to drag me off—'Get off those drums!'— because we were being filmed and it would have looked really great, kicking the cymbals and everything" (Ryan and Kehew 2006, 506). But the truth was far less dramatic, even anticlimactic, as the police settled in to enjoy the proceedings, having realized the identity of the famous performers. "When they found out who it was," technical engineer Dave Harries later recalled, "they didn't want to stop it" (Matteo 2004, 86). The concert concludes in memorable fashion, as Lennon nostalgically remarks that "I'd like to say thank you on behalf of the group and ourselves, and I hope we passed the audition." Lennon's words offer a sly reference to the group's failed January 1962 Decca Records audition. His impromptu line brought the *Let It Be* film to a close, while also punctuating the soundtrack of the same name.

As EMI sound engineer Alan Parsons later recalled, the rooftop concert "was one of the greatest and most exciting days of my life. To see the Beatles playing together and getting an instant feedback from the people around them, five cameras on the roof, cameras across the road, in the road, it was just unbelievable" (Lewisohn 1988, 169).

Over the years, three recordings from the Rooftop Concert have been featured in various releases of the *Get Back* project and the eventual *Let It Be* soundtrack, including "I've Got a Feeling," "One After 909," and "Dig a Pony."

The concert has also emerged as an epochal cultural moment and has been parodied and restaged on a number of occasions, perhaps most famously in U2's

The Beatles perform their last live concert, an impromptu affair, on the rooftop of the Apple building, for director Michael Lindsey-Hogg's film documentary, *Let it Be*, in London on January 30, 1969. Lennon's wife Yoko Ono watches at right. (Express/Getty Images)

1987 music video, directed by Meiert Avis, for "Where the Streets Have No Name" in which the band performs on the rooftop of a Los Angeles liquor store.

SET LIST

"Get Back"
"Get Back" (Reprise)
"I Want You (She's So Heavy)"
"Get Back" (Reprise)
"Don't Let Me Down"
"I've Got a Feeling"
"One After 909"
"Dig a Pony"
"God Save the Queen"
"I've Got a Feeling"
"Don't Let Me Down"
"Get Back" (Reprise)

See also: Apple Corps, Ltd., Aspinall, Neil; Evans, Mal; *Let It Be* (Film); Lindsay-Hogg, Michael; Preston, Billy.

Royal Command Variety Performance

In the company of Aspinall and their recently acquired roadie Mal Evans, a former bouncer at the Cavern Club and a one-time postal engineer, the Beatles played a quartet of songs for their Royal Variety Command Performance on November 4, 1963, at the Prince of Wales Theatre. Before closing their set with "Twist and Shout," Lennon audaciously remarked to the venue's regal audience, "For our last number, I'd like to ask your help. The people in the cheaper seats, clap your hands, and the rest of you, if you'd just rattle your jewelry" (Spitz 2005, 434). During the band's rehearsals for the performance, Lennon claimed that he intended to ask the audience to "rattle your f—ing jewelry," a threat that left Epstein absolutely paralyzed with fear. "You could almost hear him exhale," the group's publicist Tony Barrow later recalled, after Lennon had delivered the line without using the expletive (Spitz 2005, 434).

In spite of their successful show that evening, the Beatles pointedly refused to appear at the Royal Variety Command Performance in subsequent years. As Lennon later remarked,

> We managed to refuse all sorts of things that people don't know about. We did the Royal Variety Show, and we were asked discreetly to do it every year after that, but we always said, "Stuff it." So every year there was a story in the

newspapers: "Why no Beatles for the Queen?" which was pretty funny, because they didn't know we'd refused. That show's a bad gig, anyway. Everybody's very nervous and uptight and nobody performs well. The time we did do it, I cracked a joke on stage. I was fantastically nervous, but I wanted to say something to rebel a bit, and that was the best I could do. (Beatles 2000, 105)

SET LIST

"From Me to You"
"She Loves You"
"Till There Was You"
"Twist and Shout"

See also: Aspinall, Neil; Epstein, Brian; Evans, Mal.

Rubber Soul (U.K. LP)

December 3, 1965, Parlophone PMC 1267 (mono)/PCS 3075 (stereo)

Rubber Soul is the Beatles' sixth studio album. It was released on the Parlophone label on December 3, 1965, in the United Kingdom. In the United States, several of the songs on *Rubber Soul* were released on *Yesterday . . . and Today*, released on June 20, 1966.

Rubber Soul became standardized among U.S. album releases with the April 30, 1987, distribution of *Help!*, *Rubber Soul*, and *Revolver* as stereo CD releases. *Rubber Soul* was remastered and rereleased as a stereo CD on September 9, 2009. A remastered mono release was also made available at this time as part of a limited edition box set entitled *The Beatles in Mono*.

BACKGROUND AND RECORDING SESSIONS

Produced by George Martin with Norman "Normal" Smith as his sound engineer, *Rubber Soul* was recorded on four-track equipment and draws upon the notion of "plastic soul" as its musical firmament. The Beatles recorded the album during multiple sessions in October and November 1965, having taken the month of September off after completing their latest American concert tour. On November 16, Martin concocted the running order for the album's tracks. Pointedly, it was one of the last times that he undertook such a role without the Beatles' express input. As McCartney had once predicted, the workmen were indeed taking over the factory. While it is genuinely difficult to establish a turning point in which they dismiss puppy love's vacuous simplicity in favor of more elaborate analyses of the human condition, their work on *Rubber Soul* demonstrates a considerable lyrical and musical leap from their previous efforts.

With songs like "Norwegian Wood (This Bird Has Flown)" and "In My Life," the Beatles' aesthetic clearly shifts from boy-band whimsy into narrative and impressionistic overdrive. The release of *Rubber Soul* was a groundbreaking musical and lyrical event in the larger scope of their career as songwriters. As John Covach points out, the album—particularly in songs such as "Nowhere Man" and "Michelle"—finds Lennon and McCartney discarding the standard patterns of their early "craftsperson" years, a fecund period in their development made possible by virtue of their creative approach, which "privileges repeatable structures." With *Rubber Soul*, Covach writes, Lennon and McCartney emerged as full-fledged "artists" who eschew repetition in favor of "adopting and adapting notions of inspiration, genius, and complexity" (Covach 2006, 38, 39).

Rubber Soul was truly a watershed moment—an unmistakable harbinger for innovative and even more provocative works of musical art. In 1965, the Beatles had clearly turned the corner into a new level of creative promise and possibility—and they had actually grown their fan base considerably in the bargain. As Gary Burns notes, Lennon and McCartney's nostalgic ventures in such songs as "Michelle" and "In My Life" during this era "softened and humanized" their recordings, thus "increasing their mass appeal" (Burns 2000, 186). Pointedly, *Rubber Soul* was released on December 3, the same day that the Beatles embarked upon a nine-day tour of the United Kingdom. On December 12, the curtain closed in front of the band at the Capitol Cinema in Cardiff, Wales. The show ended with a blistering performance of "I'm Down," which, amidst the tumult of screams, no one in the audience, much less the band, really heard. And what nobody knew, save for the increasingly weary lads from Liverpool, was that it was the last song of the last concert on the last tour that the Beatles ever played in their homeland.

TRACK LISTING

Side 1: "Drive My Car"; "Norwegian Wood (This Bird Has Flown)"; "You Won't See Me"; "Nowhere Man"; "Think for Yourself"; "The Word"; "Michelle."

Side 2: "What Goes On"; "Girl"; "I'm Looking Through You"; "In My Life"; "Wait"; "If I Needed Someone"; "Run for Your Life."

COVER ARTWORK

As with the band's four previous album covers, the *Rubber Soul* album cover photograph was shot by Robert Freeman. Its eye-catching cover was the last to feature Freeman's work. Shot in the garden of Kenwood, Lennon's Weybridge estate, the photograph was intentionally distorted at the group's request. In itself, the warped vision of the four Beatles on the cover was a hint of things to come—an arresting and skewed image of ambiguity for a new musical age. As with *Help!*, *Rubber Soul* does not include explanatory liner notes.

CHART PERFORMANCE

> U.K.: #1 (In the United States, *Rubber Soul* has been certified by the RIAA as "6x Multi Platinum," with more than 6 million copies sold).

LEGACY AND INFLUENCE

In 1998, the BBC ranked *Rubber Soul* as #39 among its *Music of the Millennium* albums.

In 2000, *Q Magazine* ranked *Rubber Soul* as #21 on the magazine's list of *The 100 Greatest British Albums Ever.*

In 2001, VH1 ranked *Rubber Soul* as #6 among its *All Time Album Top 100.*

In 2003, *Rolling Stone* ranked *Rubber Soul* as #5 on the magazine's list of *The 500 Greatest Albums of All Time.*

In 2005, *Mojo* magazine ranked *Rubber Soul* as #27 on the magazine's list of *The 100 Greatest Albums Ever Made.*

In 2005, *Rubber Soul* was commemorated with the release of *This Bird Has Flown: A 40th-Anniversary Tribute to the Beatles' Rubber Soul,* a compilation of various artists providing cover versions of the album's original tracks.

In 2006, *Rubber Soul* was commemorated with the release of *Rubber Folk,* a compilation of various artists providing cover versions of the album's original tracks.

See also: Evans, Mal; Martin, George; *Rubber Soul* (U.S. LP).

Rubber Soul (U.S. LP)

December 6, 1965, Capitol T 2442 (mono)/ST 2442 (stereo)

Rubber Soul was the 11th Beatles album to be released in the United States—the 9th on Capitol Records, along with Vee-Jay Records' *Introducing . . . the Beatles* and United Artists' soundtrack for the *A Hard Day's Night* feature film. It was released on the Capitol label on December 6, 1965. The American *Rubber Soul* is an amalgamation of the U.K. versions of *Help!*, released on August 6, 1965, and *Rubber Soul*, released on December 3, 1965.

The American version of *Rubber Soul* was deleted from the Beatles' catalogue in 1987, when the group's U.K. albums were distributed as CD releases. A remastered mono and stereo release of *Rubber Soul* was released on April 11, 2006, as part of the box set entitled *The Capitol Albums, Volume 2.*

BACKGROUND

Given the mergence of the acoustic-oriented tracks from the *Help!* and *Rubber Soul* album releases, the American version of *Rubber Soul* takes on a decidedly folkish orientation. In addition to the album's folk–rock veneer, it is noteworthy for its stereo version of "I'm Looking Through You," which includes a pair of false guitar introductions that are not included in the mix available on the U.K. *Rubber Soul*.

The American version of *Rubber Soul* sold an incredible 1.2 million copies within the first 9 days of the album's release.

TRACK LISTING

Side 1: "I've Just Seen a Face"; "Norwegian Wood (This Bird Has Flown)"; "You Won't See Me"; "Think for Yourself"; "The Word"; "Michelle."

Side 2: "It's Only Love"; "Girl"; "I'm Looking Through You"; "In My Life"; "Wait"; "Run for Your Life."

COVER ARTWORK

As with the U.K. release, the *Rubber Soul* album cover photograph was shot by Freeman. Shot in the garden of Kenwood, Lennon's Weybridge estate, the photograph was intentionally distorted at the group's request.

CHART PERFORMANCE

U.S.: #1 (certified by the RIAA as "6x Multi Platinum," with more than 6 million copies sold).

LEGACY AND INFLUENCE

In 2000, *Rubber Soul* was inducted into the National Academy of Recording Arts and Sciences Grammy Hall of Fame.

See also: *Rubber Soul* (U.K. LP).

"Run for Your Life" (Lennon–McCartney)

"Run for Your Life" is a song on the Beatles' *Rubber Soul* album.

AUTHORSHIP AND BACKGROUND

Written by Lennon, the acerbic "Run for Your Life" concludes *Rubber Soul*, although the song was ironically the first track to be recorded for the album. Lennon unabashedly based his composition on Presley's "Baby, Let's Play House," which had been written by Arthur Gunter, a Nashville preacher's son who fashioned the song around Eddy Arnold's 1951 country and Western hit entitled "I Want to Play House with You."

As Lennon recalled, "It has a line from an old Presley song. 'I'd rather see you dead little girl than to be with another man' is a line from an old blues song that Presley did once. Just sort of a throwaway song of mine that I never thought much of—but it was always a favorite of George's" (Dowlding 1989, 125).

RECORDING SESSIONS

Produced by George Martin, "Run for Your Life" was recorded at Abbey Road Studios on October 12, 1965.

PERSONNEL

Lennon: Vocal, Gibson J-160E
McCartney: Höfner 500/1, Backing Vocal
Harrison: Epiphone Casino, Backing Vocal
Starr: Ludwig Oyster Black Pearl Drums
Martin: Tambourine

CONTROVERSY

In 1992, Ottawa radio station CFRA banned "Run for Your Life" because of its misogynistic lyrics. The station also banned Presley's "Baby, Let's Play House."

ALBUM APPEARANCES: *Rubber Soul* (U.K.); *Rubber Soul* (U.S.).

See also: *Rubber Soul* (U.K. LP).

S

"Savoy Truffle" (Harrison)

"Savoy Truffle" is a song on *The Beatles* (*The White Album*).

AUTHORSHIP AND BACKGROUND

Written by George Harrison, "Savoy Truffle" had been inspired by Eric Clapton's notorious sweet tooth. The legendary guitarist simply couldn't get enough of Mackintosh's Good News Double Centre Chocolates, a candy assortment that featured such delectables as Creme Tangerine, Ginger Sling, and Coffee Dessert. Apple's Derek Taylor supplied the lyrics for the song's middle-eight: "You know that what you eat you are."

As Harrison remembered, " 'Savoy Truffle' is a funny one written whist hanging out with Eric Clapton in the '60s. At that time he had a lot of cavities in his teeth and needed dental work. He always had a toothache but he ate a lot of chocolates—he couldn't resist them, and once he saw a box he had to eat them all" (Dowlding 1989, 245).

RECORDING SESSIONS

Produced by Martin, "Savoy Truffle" was recorded at Trident Studios on October 3, 1968, with overdubbing sessions on October 5, 11, and 14.

Producer Chris Thomas contributed an uncredited electric piano part. Thomas also provided the song's saxophone arrangement. A quartet of studio musicians established the track's "beefy" sound with an ensemble of tenor and baritone saxophones.

PERSONNEL

McCartney: Rickenbacker 4001S
Harrison: Vocal, Fender Rosewood Telecaster, Hammond Organ
Starr: Ludwig Oyster Black Pearl Drums, Tambourine
Thomas: Fender Rhodes Electric Piano
Studio Musicians: Saxophone Accompaniment conducted by Martin
Derek Collins, Art Ellefson, Danny Moss: Tenor Saxophone
Bernard George, Harry Klein, Ronnie Ross: Baritone Saxophone

ALBUM APPEARANCES: *The Beatles* (*The White Album*); *Tomorrow Never Knows*.

See also: *The Beatles* (*The White Album*) (LP); Clapton, Eric; Thomas, Chris.

"Sexy Sadie" (Lennon–McCartney)

"Sexy Sadie" is a song on *The Beatles* (*The White Album*).

AUTHORSHIP AND BACKGROUND

Written by Lennon, "Sexy Sadie" finds its origins during the Beatles' 1968 visit to India.

Lennon had written the song as a caustic critique of the Maharishi, the ostensibly celibate holy man who had, according to a rumor floating around the ashram courtesy of Yanni Alexis "Magic Alex" Mardas, made sexual advances upon a young woman staying at the compound. Having discovered what he believed to be an unforgivable hypocrisy, Lennon insisted that the Beatles' entourage depart the ashram immediately. When the incredulous Maharishi inquired about his guest's sudden impulse to leave, Lennon offered a bitter riposte: "Well, if you're so cosmic, you'll know why." Lennon had intended to entitle the song "Maharishi," although at Harrison's urging, he changed "Maharishi" to "Sexy Sadie" in advance of recording the Esher demos (Spizer 2003, 112).

As Lennon remembered, "That was inspired by Maharishi. I wrote it when we had our bags packed and we're leaving. It was the last piece I wrote before I left India. I just called him, 'Sexy Sadie,' instead of [sings] 'Maharishi what have you done, you made a fool. . . .' I was just using the situation to write a song, rather calculatingly but also to express what I felt. I was leaving the Maharishi with a bad taste. You know, it seems that my partings are always not as nice as I'd like them to be" (Lennon and Ono 2000, 191).

An early version of "Sexy Sadie" was recorded in May 1968 at Harrison's Kinfauns studio as part of the Esher Tapes. In a post-"Sexy Sadie" home demo recorded by Lennon in March 1969, Lennon continues to address his February 1968 experiences with the Maharishi back in the ashram in India. Entitled "The Maharishi Song," the demo finds Lennon engaging in a protracted rant, with occasional interjections by Yoko Ono.

RECORDING SESSIONS

Produced by Martin, "Sexy Sadie" was recorded at Abbey Road Studios on July 19, 1968, and remade on July 24, with an overdubbing session on August 13.

PERSONNEL

Lennon: Vocal, Epiphone Casino, Gibson J-160E, Hammond Organ
McCartney: Fender Jazz Bass, Piano
Harrison: Gibson Les Paul Standard
Starr: Ludwig Oyster Black Pearl Drums, Tambourine

LEGACY AND INFLUENCE

In 2010, *Rolling Stone* ranked "Sexy Sadie" as #93 on the magazine's list of *The Beatles' 100 Greatest Songs*.

ALBUM APPEARANCES: *The Beatles (The White Album)*; *Anthology 3*.

See also: *The Beatles (The White Album)* (LP); Maharishi Mahesh Yogi.

"Sgt. Pepper Inner Groove" (Lennon–McCartney)

"Sgt. Pepper Inner Groove" is an unlisted track on the Beatles' *Sgt. Pepper's Lonely Hearts Club* album.

AUTHORSHIP AND BACKGROUND

Originally known as "Edit for LP End" on the EMI tape box, the unlisted "Sgt. Pepper Inner Groove" was concocted by the Beatles for insertion during the mastering process into the eventual *Sgt. Pepper's Lonely Hearts Club Band* record's concentric run-out groove. In so doing, they planned to detonate the silent afterglow of "A Day in the Life" with a sudden onslaught of sound effects, ambient noise, and gibberish that sound engineer Emerick had chopped up and reassembled in random and backward fashion. To conclude the experiment, Lennon suggested that they record a high-pitched 15-kilocycle whistle to rouse the family dog.

RECORDING SESSIONS

Produced by Martin, "Sgt. Pepper Inner Groove" was recorded on April 21, 1967, at Abbey Road Studios.

For the recording, the 15-kilocycle tone is followed by the gibberish and studio chatter that Emerick had assembled, spliced randomly, and played in reverse. With two seconds of Beatles sound effects, "Sgt. Pepper Inner Groove" was originally designed for playing endlessly on manual turntables until the listener lifts the tonearm on their record player. As a coda to the *Sgt. Pepper's Lonely Hearts Club Band* album, "Sgt. Pepper Inner Groove" was only included on the record's U.K.

release and was unavailable in the U.S. market until the 1980 release of the *Rarities* album. "Sgt. Pepper Inner Groove" was standardized in the Beatles' catalogue with the 1987 rerelease of the group's recordings on compact disc (CD). On the *Sgt. Pepper's Lonely Hearts Club Band* CD, "Sgt. Pepper Inner Groove" is looped 11 times before fading out.

For the album's original mastering process, Harry Moss conducted the process of cutting the record's run-out groove and inserting "Sgt. Pepper Inner Groove." As Moss recalled,

> I was told by chaps who'd been in the business a long time that cutting things into the run-out grooves was an old idea that they used to do on 78s. Cutting *Sgt. Pepper* was not too difficult except that because we couldn't play the masters I had to wait for white label pressings before I could hear whether or not I'd cut the concentric groove successfully. These were the things which, at the time, I used to swear about! It was George Martin who first asked me to do it. I replied, "It's gonna be bloody awkward, George, but I'll give it a go!" (Lewisohn 1988, 110)

PERSONNEL

Lennon, McCartney, Harrison, Starr: Sound Effects

ALBUM APPEARANCES: *Sgt. Pepper's Lonely Hearts Club Band*; *Rarities* (U.S.).

See also: Emerick, Geoff; Martin, George; *Rarities* (U.S. LP); *Sgt. Pepper's Lonely Hearts Club Band* (LP).

"Sgt. Pepper's Lonely Hearts Club Band" (Lennon–McCartney)

"Sgt. Pepper's Lonely Hearts Club Band" is a song on the Beatles' *Sgt. Pepper's Lonely Hearts Club Band* album.

AUTHORSHIP AND BACKGROUND

Written by McCartney with assistance from Mal Evans, "Sgt. Pepper's Lonely Hearts Club Band" finds the songwriter imaging alter egos for the Beatles. As McCartney remembered, "We were fed up with being Beatles. We really hated that f—ing four little mop-top boys approach. We were not boys, we were men. It was all gone, all that boy shit, all that screaming, we didn't want anymore, plus, we'd now got turned on to pot and thought of ourselves as artists rather than just performers—then suddenly on the plane I got this idea. I thought, 'Let's not be ourselves. Let's develop alter egos so we're not having to project an image which we know. It would be much more free'" (Frontani 2009, 127).

The fictitious band at the heart of "Sgt. Pepper's Lonely Hearts Club Band" allowed the Beatles to parody the mid- to late-1960s phenomenon of elongated names for pop groups. As Lennon remembered, " 'Sgt. Pepper' is Paul after a trip to America and the whole West Coast long-named group thing was coming in. You know, when people were no longer the Beatles or the Crickets—they were suddenly Fred and His Incredible Shrinking Grateful Airplanes, right? So I think he got influenced by that and came up with this idea for the Beatles" (Lennon and Ono 2000, 197). As McCartney later recalled, "It was an idea I had, I think, when I was flying from L.A. to somewhere. I thought it would be nice to lose our identities, to submerge ourselves in the persona of a fake group. We would make up all the culture around it and collect all our heroes in one place. So I thought, A typical stupid-sounding name for a Dr. Hook's Medicine Show and Traveling Circus kind of thing would be 'Sgt. Pepper's Lonely Hearts Club Band.' Just a word game, really" (Dowlding 1989, 159).

RECORDING SESSIONS

Produced by Martin, "Sgt. Pepper's Lonely Hearts Club Band" was recorded at Abbey Road Studios on February 1, 1967, with overdubbing sessions on February 2, March 3, and March 6.

Musically, "Sgt. Pepper's Lonely Hearts Club Band" was bolstered by direct injection, the technique devised by Ken Townsend in which electric guitars are plugged directly into the mixing desk, thus mitigating the need for amplifiers in the studio. "One of the most difficult instruments to record was the bass guitar," Townsend recalled. "The problem was that no matter which type of high-quality microphone we placed in front of the bass speaker it never sounded back in the control room as good as in the studio" (Ryan and Kehew 2006, 156). In the case of "Sgt. Pepper," McCartney had availed himself of direct injection during the song's initial recording session on February 1, 1967. It was the first usage of this technology on a Beatles track, and it afforded McCartney's bass with richer textures and tonal clarity. Meanwhile, the track was chockful of special effects, with the canned laughter and audience applause courtesy of the satirical British stage revue *Beyond the Fringe*, which had been borrowed from the EMI tape library's *Volume 6: Applause and Laughter* (Moore 1997, 27). The sound of the orchestra warming up was recorded on February 10 during the orchestral overdubs for "A Day in the Life," the album's climactic number.

PERSONNEL

Lennon: Epiphone Casino
McCartney: Vocal, Rickenbacker 4001S, Fender Esquire
Harrison: Gibson SG Standard
Starr: Ludwig Oyster Black Pearl Drums

Martin: Hammond Organ
Studio Musicians: Brass Accompaniment conducted by Martin
James W. Buck, John Burden, Tony Randell, Neill Sanders: Horn

CHART PERFORMANCE

U.K.: "Sgt. Pepper's Lonely Hearts Club Band/With a Little Help from My
Friends"/"A Day in the Life"; September 30, 1978, Parlophone R6022: #63.
U.S.: "Sgt. Pepper's Lonely Hearts Club Band/With a Little Help from My
Friends"/"A Day in the Life"; September 30, 1978, Capitol 4612: #71.

LEGACY AND INFLUENCE

In 1968, "Sgt. Pepper's Lonely Hearts Club Band" was nominated for a Grammy
Award for Group Vocal Performance at the 10th Grammy Awards. It was also nominated for a Grammy Award for Contemporary Vocal Group Performance.

In 2010, *Rolling Stone* ranked "Sgt. Pepper's Lonely Hearts Club Band" as #60
on the magazine's list of *The Beatles' 100 Greatest Songs*.

For all of the album's accolades and renown, McCartney was most gratified by
Jimi Hendrix's myth-making performance of the title track only scant days after
its release at the Saville Theatre. Hendrix's rendition of "Sgt. Pepper's Lonely
Hearts Club Band" was "the single biggest tribute" to *Sgt. Pepper*, McCartney
stated at the time (Badman 2001, 289). As Noel Redding, the bassist for the Jimi
Hendrix Experience, remembered:

Pepper came out on a Thursday, and we were playing on the Sunday, June 4th,
at the Saville Theatre, which was owned by Brian Epstein. We always used to
meet at [manager] Chas Chandler's flat before the gig and get a taxi around there,
or we'd meet in a pub near the theatre. Hendrix said, "Let's play 'Sgt. Pepper.'"
So there in the dressing room we learned the intro, which is A, C, and G. We
didn't do the middle part, because we didn't know it. . . . I found out later that
all the Beatles were in the audience and it freaked them out. (Babiuk 2001,
205–6)

In truth, only McCartney and Harrison were in attendance that evening. Although
the Experience hadn't bothered—nor had the time—to learn the middle-eight, it
hardly mattered to McCartney. As Hendrix began the set with his raw and thun-
derous rendition of "Sgt. Pepper's Lonely Hearts Club Band," it became abundantly
clear that the guitarist understood the song's mettle implicitly, having reduced
McCartney's splendid mergence of pop majesty and electric gusto into rock 'n'
roll gutturality. Condensed into its most primitive ingredients—guitar, bass, drums,
vocals—the song came alive with Hendrix's veritable tremble and roar. A live
recording of Jimi Hendrix and the Experience performing "Sgt. Pepper's Lonely

Hearts Club Band" on September 5, 1967, in Stockholm, Sweden, is included on the four-disc compilation entitled *The Jimi Hendrix Experience* (2000).

ALBUM APPEARANCES: *Sgt. Pepper's Lonely Hearts Club Band*; *The Beatles, 1967–1970*; *Yellow Submarine Songtrack*.

See also: Evans, Mal; *Sgt. Pepper's Lonely Hearts Club Band* (LP).

Sgt. Pepper's Lonely Hearts Club Band (LP)

June 1, 1967, Parlophone PMC 7027 (mono)/PCS 7027 (stereo)
June 2, 1967, Capitol MAS 2653 (mono)/SMAS 2653

Sgt. Pepper's Lonely Hearts Club Band is the Beatles' eighth studio album. It was released on the Parlophone label on June 1, 1967, in the United Kingdom. In the United States, it was released on June 2, 1967. It was the first Beatles album to receive a standardized release in both the United Kingdom and the United States.

Sgt. Pepper's Lonely Hearts Club Band was released as a stereo CD on June 1, 1987. It was remastered and rereleased as a stereo CD on September 9, 2009. A remastered mono release was also made available at this time as part of a limited edition box set entitled *The Beatles in Mono*.

BACKGROUND AND RECORDING SESSIONS

Produced by Martin with Emerick as his sound engineer, *Sgt. Pepper's Lonely Hearts Club Band* was recorded on four-track equipment during multiple sessions from December 6, 1966, through April 3, 1967, at Abbey Road Studios and Regent Sound Studio.

The album's elongated title takes its name from McCartney's conception of a fictitious, Edwardian military-style band. Flying back from the United States with Mal Evans, who had been working as his housekeeper on Cavendish Avenue for the past several months, McCartney came up with the idea of establishing alter egos for the band. After McCartney imagined the album's overarching concept, Evans coined the faux band's name—Sgt. Pepper's Lonely Hearts Club Band—in the tradition of the contemporary San Francisco area groups with long-winded handles such as Big Brother and the Holding Company or the Quicksilver Messenger Service. With a title track in hand, the Beatles' follow-up album to *Revolver* took shape in a hurry.

Yet for the Beatles and their production team, *Sgt. Pepper* was their most difficult and time-consuming project to capture on tape. As Emerick later recalled, "We were driving the equipment to its limit. . . . Technically *Pepper* still stands up as the best album, knowing what we were going through. I mean, although it was a bit laborious and it can't be done today, every time we either changed tape or we copied something everything was meticulously lined up and re-biased." He added that "On *Pepper* we were using the luxury of utilizing one track for bass overdub on some of the things. . . . We used to stay behind after the sessions and Paul would dub all the bass on. I used to use a valve C12 microphone on Paul's amp, sometimes on figure-eight, and sometimes positioned up to 8 feet away, believe it or not" (Dowlding 1989, 154).

With *Sgt. Pepper's Lonely Hearts Club Band*, the Beatles manufacture an artificial textual space in which to stage their art, having firmly ensconced themselves in their post-touring studio years. In so doing, they call their media-generated personae into question, revising and repackaging themselves in the process in order to create new spaces of possibility. "The 'Pepper' idea," Walter Everett points out, "allowed the Beatles to remove themselves from the public by an extra layer—they were now giving a performance of a performance" (1999, 99).

Perhaps even more intriguingly, *Sgt. Pepper's Lonely Hearts Club Band* was the first Beatles LP—indeed, the first pop recording—to be mastered without rills, eschewing any formal breaks between songs because Martin had explicitly instructed the engineers not to band the album into individual tracks. By doing away with the rills—the silent spaces of demarcation between songs on long-playing records—the Beatles succeeded in using every available creative space at their disposal, transitioning from one number into another without bothering to slow the pace of their art, while employing the ending of one song as the introduction to another. As Martin later observed, "*Sgt. Pepper* was the turning point, something that will stand the test of time as a valid art form, sculpture in music" (Dowlding 1989, 162).

Sgt. Pepper's Lonely Hearts Club Band was released to nearly universal praise on June 1, 1967—with the notable exception of *The New York Times'* Richard Goldstein—and the album's influence and acclaim has hardly ebbed in the interim. In the ensuing decades, British critic Kenneth Tynan lauded *Sgt. Pepper* as "a decisive moment in the history of Western civilization," while composer Leonard Bernstein once remarked that "three bars of 'A Day in the Life' still sustain me, rejuvenate me, inflame my senses and sensibilities" (Dowlding 1989, 161, 184). Having taken more than 700 hours and the unheard-of-sum of £75,000 to produce, the resulting album was a watershed moment in the history of popular music. *Sgt. Pepper* wasn't just an LP. It was an event—and one that still resounds, year in and year out, as the album continues to imprint itself upon world culture.

The Beatles had also considered making a television movie based on *Sgt. Pepper's Lonely Hearts Club Band*. The principal photography for the would-be production was scheduled for October and November 1967, with a screenplay by Ian Dallas under the direction of Keith Green. In addition to a mammoth "A Day in the Life" segment, the film was slated to feature 115 extras—including a troupe of motorcycle-riding "rockers" and a dozen "Model Rita Maids" (Lewisohn 1995, 245). In 1978, Stigwood produced a movie musical of *Sgt. Pepper's Lonely Hearts Club Band*, starring Frampton and the Bee Gees, that was met with widespread critical disdain.

TRACK LISTING

Side 1: "Sgt. Pepper's Lonely Hearts Club Band/With a Little Help from My Friends"; "Lucy in the Sky with Diamonds"; "Getting Better"; "Fixing a Hole"; "She's Leaving Home"; "Being for the Benefit of Mr. Kite!"

Side 2: "Within You, Without You"; "When I'm Sixty-Four"; "Lovely Rita"; "Good Morning, Good Morning"; "Sgt. Pepper's Lonely Hearts Club Band (Reprise)"; "A Day in the Life"; "Sgt. Pepper Inner Groove" [unlisted].

Originally included in the album's U.K. release, "Sgt. Pepper Inner Groove" was restored to the U.S. release with the 1987 CD release, as well as with the 2009 mono and stereo remasters.

COVER ARTWORK

Peter Blake's cover art for *Sgt. Pepper's Lonely Hearts Club Band* highlights the competing narratives of the paradigmatic Fab Four with the incarnation of the Summer of Love-era Beatles—decked out, as they are, in psychedelic military regalia as Sgt. Pepper's fabled troupe. The album cover depicts the group's former mythological selves standing stage right of their remythologized contemporary counterparts, themselves surrounded by similarly mythologized figures from the annals of history, religion, Hollywood, music, sports, and literature. In addition to the high literary presence of Lewis Carroll, Edgar Allan Poe, and Oscar Wilde, the cover montage ranges from Marlon Brando's steely visage in *On the Waterfront* (1954) and Bob Dylan in thoughtful repose to the stereotypically one-dimensional portrait of boxer Sonny Liston and the lost, penetrating gaze of Stuart Sutcliffe.

With its motley representation of cultural iconography, *Sgt. Pepper*'s cover reminds us that nuance and complexity have relatively little to do with the act of myth-making. With the album cover sporting obvious evidence of the band's forays into counterculture—*Sgt. Pepper* finds them replete with moustaches and sideburns while standing amidst a garden of flower power and faux cannabis—they were determined to undermine the fan-consoling notion of being four mild-mannered lads from Liverpool. It is little wonder that Epstein wanted to release the album in a plain-brown wrapper. For Epstein, the album cover proved to be a complicated legal tangle. The original artwork had been designed by the Fool, an avant-garde Dutch art collective, before their crude phantasmagoria was rejected in favor of the work of pop artist Peter Blake and photographer Michael Cooper, who assembled *Sgt. Pepper*'s renowned cover on a budget of some £2,800, at Cooper's Chelsea studio. With so many public personalities on display—many of whom were still among the living—NEMS (North End Music Stores) was forced to undergo the laborious task of securing permissions. At one point, actress Mae West famously remarked, "What would *I* be doing in a lonely hearts club?" In the end, only the Bowery Boys' Leo Gorcey demanded a fee, and he was subsequently deleted (Spitz 2005, 681). Released with a gatefold design, *Sgt. Pepper's Lonely*

Hearts Club Band included a series of cardboard cutouts—even a do-it-yourself moustache—and the printed lyrics on the back cover.

The LP's back cover also offered a seemingly innocuous acknowledgement for the production of the album's "cover by MC Productions and the Apple." The former refers to photographer Cooper's production company, while the latter was writ large on the band's future—after all, there was no Apple Corps in June 1967—and, by many accounts, figured prominently in the Beatles' demise.

CHART PERFORMANCE

U.K.: #1.

U.S.: #1 (certified by the RIAA as "11x Multi Platinum," with more than 11 million copies sold; certified by the RIAA as "Diamond," with more than 10 million copies sold).

LEGACY AND INFLUENCE

In 1968, *Sgt. Pepper's Lonely Hearts Club Band* earned Grammy Awards for Album of the Year and Best Contemporary Album at the 10th Grammy Awards.

In 1977, *Sgt. Pepper's Lonely Hearts Club Band* earned the British Phonographic Industry's Brit Award for the Best British Album.

In 1993, *Sgt. Pepper's Lonely Hearts Club Band* was inducted into the National Academy of Recording Arts and Sciences Grammy Hall of Fame.

In 1998, the BBC ranked *Sgt. Pepper's Lonely Hearts Club Band* as #1 among its *Music of the Millennium* albums.

In 2000, *Q Magazine* ranked *Sgt. Pepper's Lonely Hearts Club Band* as #13 on the magazine's list of *The 100 Greatest British Albums Ever*.

In 2001, VH1 ranked *Sgt. Pepper's Lonely Hearts Club Band* as #10 among its *All Time Album Top 100*.

In 2003, *Rolling Stone* ranked *Sgt. Pepper's Lonely Hearts Club Band* as #1 on the magazine's list of *The 500 Greatest Albums of All Time*.

In 2004, *Q Magazine* ranked *Sgt. Pepper's Lonely Hearts Club Band* as #3 on the magazine's list of *The Music That Changed the World*.

In 2005, *Q Magazine* ranked *Sgt. Pepper's Lonely Hearts Club Band* as #5 on the magazine's list of *The 40 Greatest Psychedelic Albums of All Time*.

In 2005, *Mojo* magazine ranked *Sgt. Pepper's Lonely Hearts Club Band* as #51 on the magazine's list of *The 100 Greatest Albums Ever Made*.

In 2007, *Mojo* magazine ranked *Sgt. Pepper's Lonely Hearts Club Band* as #16 on the magazine's list of *Big Bangs: 100 Records That Changed the World*.

In 2007, Cheap Trick celebrated *Sgt. Pepper's Lonely Hearts Club Band*'s 40th anniversary by performing the album in its entirety at the Hollywood Bowl. They were accompanied by the Hollywood Bowl Orchestra, conducted by Edwin Outwater, as well as guest vocalists Aimee Mann and Joan Osborne.

In 2007, *Mojo* magazine published a special issue that celebrated *Sgt. Pepper's Lonely Hearts Club Band*'s 40th anniversary, including a cover-mounted CD with contemporary cover versions of the album's entire contents entitled *Sgt. Pepper: With a Little Help from His Friends*.

See also: Emerick, Geoff; Evans, Mal; Martin, George.

"Sgt. Pepper's Lonely Hearts Club Band (Reprise)" (Lennon–McCartney)

"Sgt. Pepper's Lonely Hearts Club Band (Reprise)" is a song on the Beatles' *Sgt. Pepper's Lonely Hearts Club Band* album.

AUTHORSHIP AND BACKGROUND

Written by McCartney, "Sgt. Pepper's Lonely Hearts Club Band (Reprise)" was composed at the behest of Beatles associate Neil Aspinall, who came up with the idea of reprising "Sgt. Pepper's Lonely Hearts Club Band"—with the album having both a "welcome song" and a "goodbye song"—toward its conclusion and as an overture for "A Day in the Life."

RECORDING SESSIONS

Produced by George Martin, "Sgt. Pepper's Lonely Hearts Club Band (Reprise)" was recorded in nine takes at Abbey Road Studios on April 1, 1967, as McCartney prepared to leave for an extended break in the United States, where Jane Asher—Paul's girlfriend—had been traveling since mid-January with a touring company from the Old Vic.

"Sgt. Pepper's Lonely Hearts Club Band (Reprise)" brought the album's formal recording process to a close. The reprise was recorded in the relative largesse of EMI's Studio One, complete with ambient arena and audience sounds. The raw power of the Beatles' guitar work on the track likely found its inspiration in the high-wattage musicianship of Jimi Hendrix, whom McCartney had seen in concert on multiple occasions in recent months in various Soho nightclubs (Cross 2005, 433).

In the recording, "Sgt. Pepper's Lonely Hearts Club Band (Reprise)" emerges into being as a wayward lion's roar echoes in the distance at the conclusion of "Good Morning, Good Morning," while the sound of a clucking hen transforms into the cold-steel pluck of an Epiphone Casino courtesy of Martin's studio trickery. As the reprise begins, Sgt. Pepper's band begins to play once more, fueled by the thunder and growl of a hard-rocking combo, the stately brass quartet evidently having called it quits for the evening. Having reached its conclusion, the reprise of "Sgt. Pepper's Lonely Hearts Club Band" crashes into an oblivion of cheers and applause.

PERSONNEL

Lennon: Vocal, Epiphone Casino, Hammond Organ, Maracas
McCartney: Vocal, Rickenbacker 4001S
Harrison: Vocal, Epiphone Casino
Starr: Ludwig Oyster Black Pearl Drums

ALBUM APPEARANCES: *Sgt. Pepper's Lonely Hearts Club Band*; *Anthology 2*; *Love*.

See also: *Sgt. Pepper's Lonely Hearts Club Band* (LP).

"She Came in Through the Bathroom Window" (Lennon–McCartney)

"She Came in Through the Bathroom Window" is a song on the Beatles' *Abbey Road* album. It is the fifth song in the *Abbey Road* Medley.

AUTHORSHIP AND BACKGROUND

McCartney's "She Came in Through the Bathroom Window" may have been inspired by a March 1969 burglary at his Cavendish home, although the Beatles had actually rehearsed a version of the composition in January during the *Get Back* sessions. Harrison later described the track as "a very strange song with terrific lyrics, but it's hard to explain what they're all about!" (Dowlding 1989, 290).

RECORDING SESSIONS

Produced by George Martin, "She Came in Through the Bathroom Window" was recorded as a single track along with "Polythene Pam" at Abbey Road Studios on July 25, 1969. Additional overdubbing sessions occurred on July 28 and 30. The song was recorded under the working title of "Bathroom Window."

PERSONNEL

Lennon: Framus 12-String Hootenanny
McCartney: Vocal, Rickenbacker 4001S, Epiphone Casino, Piano
Harrison: Gibson Les Paul Standard
Starr: Ludwig Hollywood Maple Drums, Tambourine, Maracas, Cowbell

ALBUM APPEARANCES: *Abbey Road*; *Anthology 3*.

See also: *Abbey Road* (LP).

"She Loves You" (Lennon–McCartney)

"She Loves You" was the Beatles' third consecutive #1 single in the United Kingdom, where it was released on August 23, 1963. The single sold some 1.3 million copies by the end of 1963, and remained the biggest seller in the United Kingdom until McCartney and Wings' "Mull of Kintyre" surpassed it in 1978.

AUTHORSHIP AND BACKGROUND

Begun by Lennon and McCartney on June 26, 1963, in a Newcastle-upon-Tyne hotel room, "She Loves You" was completed the following night at Forthlin Road. It was inspired by the call-and-response structure of Bobby Rydell's recent hit "Forget Him," which counsels his young female fans to be wary of dubious male suitors.

In addition to offering the inaugural performance of the Beatles' famous "yeah yeah yeah" vocal stylings, "She Loves You" is significant for the different points of view that it affords their male and female listeners. In one sense, the speaker provides gentle and much-needed reassurance to a wayward boyfriend; yet at the same time, the speaker comforts the distraught girlfriend with his feelings of consolation and understanding, two facets that she is sorely lacking in her current romantic relationship.

As with "From Me to You," such lyrics—splayed against the optimistic, upbeat backdrop of Lennon and McCartney's vocals and the band's equally buoyant music, particularly informed by the guitar ornamentation of Harrison's recently acquired Gretsch Country Gentleman—find the Beatles speaking, quite literally, to their massive contingent of female listeners. Safe—but not *too* safe—the bandmates occupy a unique space in their fan's mindset: "The Beatles come across as being 'acceptable,'" Sheila Whiteley writes, "as ideal boyfriends who are sexy but tuned into a girl's perspective, thus allowing them both to enjoy and to explore their own sexuality through association with their respective idols" (2006, 61).

"She Loves You" pointedly marks the second appearance of "Lennon–McCartney," after their inaugural "Love Me Do" single, as the songwriters' authorship credit. Previously—from "Please Please Me" single and the *Please Please Me* album through the "From Me to You" single—their songs were pointedly credited to "McCartney–Lennon" on their record labels and album sleeves. McCartney alleged that Lennon plotted to reverse the order of their names during his spring 1963 Spanish vacation with Epstein, who later asserted that the reversal resulted from their collective effort to simplify the cadence of Lennon and

McCartney's authorial designation and create brand-name recognition—a tactic that clearly succeeded beyond their wildest dreams. According to McCartney, Lennon "had the stronger personality, and I think he fixed things with Brian" (Beatles 2000, 94). From "She Loves You" forward, the duo's songs were officially credited to "Lennon–McCartney."

RECORDING SESSIONS

Produced by Martin, "She Loves You" was recorded at Abbey Road Studios on July 1, 1963, using EMI's two-track machine.

As McCartney remembered, "Occasionally, we'd overrule George Martin, like on 'She Loves You,' we end on a sixth chord, a very jazzy sort of thing. And he said, 'Oh, you can't do that! A sixth chord? It's too jazzy.' We just said, 'No, it's a great hook, we've got to do it'" (Everett 2001, 175).

The Beatles recorded a German-language version, "Sie Liebt Dich," on January 29, 1964, at Pathé Marconi Studios in Paris.

PERSONNEL

Lennon: Vocal, Rickenbacker 325
McCartney: Vocal, Höfner 500/1
Harrison: Gretsch Country Gentleman
Starr: Ludwig Oyster Black Pearl Drums

CHART PERFORMANCE

U.K.: "She Loves You"/"I'll Get You"; August 23, 1963, Parlophone R 5055: #1.
U.S.: "She Loves You"/"I'll Get You"; September 16, 1963; rereleased January 25, 1964, Swan 4152: #1.

LEGACY AND INFLUENCE

A live recording of "She Loves You" from the band's BBC sessions was later included on the Beatles' *On Air: Live at the BBC, Volume 2.*

In 1964, the Beatles received an Ivor Novello Award, awarded annually by the British Academy of Songwriters, Composers, and Authors, for "She Loves You."

In 1964, "She Loves You" was honored as the *New Musical Express*'s "Single of the Year."

In 2004, *Rolling Stone* ranked "She Loves You" as #64 on the magazine's list of *The 500 Greatest Songs of All Time.*

In 2005, *Uncut* magazine listed "She Loves You" as the 3rd biggest song that changed the world behind Elvis Presley's "Heartbreak Hotel" and Dylan's "Like a Rolling Stone."

In 2010, *Rolling Stone* ranked "She Loves You" as #14 on the magazine's list of *The Beatles' 100 Greatest Songs*.

In October 2012, BBC Local Radio listeners ranked "She Loves You" as their 8th favorite Beatles song in a poll conducted in commemoration of the 50th anniversary of "Love Me Do," the band's first single.

ALBUM APPEARANCES: *The Beatles' Second Album*; *A Collection of Beatles Oldies*; *The Beatles, 1962–1966*; *The Beatles at the Hollywood Bowl*; *20 Greatest Hits*; *Past Masters, Volume 1*; *Anthology 1*; *1*; *On Air: Live at the BBC, Volume 2*.

See also: *The Ed Sullivan Show* (TV Series).

"She Said She Said" (Lennon–McCartney)

"She Said She Said" is a song on the Beatles' *Revolver* album.

AUTHORSHIP AND BACKGROUND

Written by Lennon, "She Said She Said" finds its roots in an August 1965 party that the Beatles attended in Benedict Canyon, Los Angeles. It was a wild affair in which the group's rented house was surrounded by thousands of fans held back by a cadre of L.A.'s finest. At one point, a pair of particularly motivated fans attempted, unsuccessfully, to land a helicopter in the house's garden. It was the kind of party that only the overwhelming tremors of Beatlemania could produce. Inside the house, Lennon, McCartney, Harrison, and Starr were joined by Roger McGuinn and David Crosby of the Byrds, as well as by actor Peter Fonda, with whom Lennon and Harrison shared a hit of acid. In the ensuing drug-addled malaise, Fonda famously claimed, "I know what it's like to be dead," to which Lennon angrily responded, "You're making me feel like I've never been born. Who put all that shit in your head?" before having Fonda expelled from the premises. Inspired by the actor's strange remark, Lennon decided to compose a song around the idea of being dead (Turner 1994, 11).

As Lennon remembered,

> That's mine. It's an interesting track. The guitars are great on it. That was written after an acid trip in L.A. during a break in the Beatles tour where we were having fun with the Byrds and lots of girls. Peter Fonda came in when we were on acid and he kept coming up to me and sitting next to me and whispering, "I know what it's like to be dead." He was describing an acid trip he'd been on. We didn't *want* to hear about that. We were on an acid trip and the sun was shining and the girls were dancing, and the whole thing was beautiful and Sixties, and this guy—who I really didn't know, he hadn't made *Easy Rider* or anything— kept coming over, wearing shades, saying, "I know what it's like to be dead,"

and we kept leaving him because he was so boring! And I used it for the song, but I changed it to "she" instead of "he." It was scary—I don't want to know what it's like to be dead! (Lennon and Ono 2000, 180)

As Peter Fonda later recalled, "I remember sitting on the deck with George, who was telling me that he thought he was dying. I told him that there was nothing to be afraid of and that all he needed to do was to relax. I said that I knew what it was like to be dead because when I was 10 years old, I'd accidentally shot myself in the stomach and my heart stopped beating three times because I lost so much blood. John was passing at the time and heard me say, 'I know what it's like to be dead'" (Cross 2005, 436).

RECORDING SESSIONS

Produced by Martin, "She Said She Said" was recorded at Abbey Road Studios on June 21, 1966. It took the Beatles some nine hours to rehearse and record "She Said She Said," which was the last track to be completed for the *Revolver* project.

As with "And Your Bird Can Sing" and "Doctor Robert," "She Said She Said" enjoys a bright, metallic sheen accomplished by Lennon and Harrison capoed Epiphone Casinos and a healthy dose of ADT.

PERSONNEL

Lennon: Vocal, Epiphone Casino
Harrison: Epiphone Casino, Höfner 500/1
Starr: Ludwig Oyster Black Pearl Drums

LEGACY AND INFLUENCE

In 2010, *Rolling Stone* ranked "She Said She Said" as #37 on the magazine's list of *The Beatles' 100 Greatest Songs*.

ALBUM APPEARANCES: *Revolver* (U.K.); *Revolver* (U.S.); *Tomorrow Never Knows*.

See also: *Revolver* (U.K. LP).

Shea Stadium (New York)

On August 15, 1965, the Beatles famously performed at New York City's Shea Stadium, where the band played for 55,600 fans. Promoted by Sid Bernstein, the Beatles' Shea Stadium appearance set a world record for attendance and for gross revenue, with the Beatles earning $160,000 from a box-office take of some $304,000.

In order to facilitate the performance, the Beatles were transported by helicopter to a nearby Port Authority heliport before taking a Wells Fargo armored truck into the stadium itself, where more than 2,000 security personnel monitored the enormous crowd. In spite of the additional security, several fans broke through the barricades. While the band had been outfitted with specially enhanced Vox 100-watt amplifiers for the show, their sound system was little match for Beatles' boisterous audience. Yet the band's legendary performance at Shea Stadium—not to mention the hype associated with the event—only succeeded in adding to the group's mystique, and the financial success of the Beatles' Shea Stadium performance ushered in a new era of big-time arena rock concerts.

In 2009, Shea Stadium, the home of the New York Mets professional baseball team, was demolished to make room for parking in the Mets' new stadium, Citi Field, next door.

SET LIST

"Twist and Shout"
"She's a Woman"
"I Feel Fine"
"Dizzy Miss Lizzy"

The Beatles perform at New York's Shea Stadium on August 15, 1965, as some 50,000 fans cheer them on. The concert set world records for attendance and gross revenue. From left to right are John Lennon, Paul McCartney, George Harrison, and Ringo Starr. (AP Photo)

"Ticket to Ride"
"Everybody's Trying to Be My Baby"
"Can't Buy Me Love"
"Baby's in Black"
"Act Naturally"
"A Hard Day's Night"
"Help!"
"I'm Down"

See also: Tours, 1960–1966.

Sheridan, Tony (1940–2013)

Born as Anthony Esmond Sheridan McGinnity on May 21, 1940, in Norwich, Norfolk, Tony Sheridan was the stage name for one of the Beatles' earliest collaborators. He made his name as an up-and-coming guitarist in the late 1950s, playing in a number of bands and in several national tours. By the early 1960s, though, his star had tarnished somewhat, and he found himself in Hamburg, West Germany, playing with a variety of pickup bands in the Reeperbahn clubs. Known as "The Teacher" among the other British expatriates, he caught a break in 1961, when Kämpfert caught his act with the Beatles as his latest pickup band at Hamburg's Top Ten Club. On June 22, 1961, Kämpfert, with assistance from Hinze, produced several recordings by the Beatles (as the Beat Brothers) and Sheridan at Hamburg's Friedrich-Ebert-Halle studio. In so doing, Kämpfert produced the Beatles' first commercial recordings, which were later marketed by Polydor and have been rereleased on numerous occasions since the rise of Beatlemania. More important, the sessions resulted in Sheridan's single with the Beat Brothers featuring "My Bonnie" backed with "The Saints," which later figured prominently in Brian Epstein's discovery of the Beatles. For Sheridan, the association proved to be a great boon, as "My Bonnie" scored a Top 5 hit in West Germany.

As the years wore on, Sheridan's rock 'n' roll sound transformed into a more jazz-oriented vein, although the guitarist continue to perform in Hamburg's clubs. In the late 1960s, he performed for the Allied troops during the Vietnam War, earning an honorary captaincy in the U.S. Army. In the 1970s, he made a living as DJ, while continue to pursue his musical interests in the Hamburg clubs. In 2002, he released a solo album, *Vagabond*, while also recording a concert video with Chantal in which Sheridan performed an original early 1960s composition coauthored with McCartney entitled "Tell Me If You Can." On February 16, 2013, Sheridan died in Hamburg after undergoing heart surgery.

See also: Epstein, Brian.

"She's a Woman" (Lennon–McCartney)

"She's a Woman" is the B-side of the Beatles' "I Feel Fine" single, released in the United Kingdom on November 27, 1964, and in the United States on November 23, 1964.

AUTHORSHIP AND BACKGROUND

"She's a Woman" was improvised and recorded by the Beatles on the same day. As McCartney recalled, "This was my attempt at a bluesy thing. Instead of doing a Little Richard song, whom I admire greatly, I would use the [vocal] style I would have used for that, but put it in one of my own songs" (Miles 1997, 173). "We were so excited to say 'turn me on,'" Lennon later observed, "you know, about marijuana and all that—using it as an expression" (Everett 2001, 266).

RECORDING SESSIONS

Produced by George Martin, "She's a Woman" was recorded at Abbey Road Studios on October 8, 1964. Starr can be heard playing a chocalho, a kind of Portuguese shaker. On November 17, 1964, the Beatles recorded a second version of "She's a Woman" for the BBC's *Top Gear* radio show that was later included on the *Live at the BBC* album.

PERSONNEL

Lennon: Rickenbacker 325
McCartney: Vocal, Höfner 500/1, Piano
Harrison: Gretsch Tennessean
Starr: Ludwig Oyster Black Pearl Drums, Chocalho

CHART PERFORMANCE

U.K.: "I Feel Fine"/"She's a Woman"; November 27, 1964, Parlophone R 5200: #1.

U.S.: "I Feel Fine"/"She's a Woman"; November 23, 1964, Capitol 5327: #1 (certified by the RIAA as "Gold," with more than 500,000 copies sold). As the B-side of "I Feel Fine," "She's a Woman" charted at #4.

ALBUM APPEARANCES: *Beatles '65*; *The Beatles at the Hollywood Bowl*; *Rarities* (U.K.); *Past Masters, Volume 1*; *Live at the BBC*; *Anthology 2*.

See also: *Live at the BBC* (LP).

"She's Leaving Home" (Lennon–McCartney)

"She's Leaving Home" is a song on the Beatles' *Sgt. Pepper's Lonely Hearts Club Band* album.

AUTHORSHIP AND BACKGROUND

Written by McCartney with a sizable contribution from Lennon, "She's Leaving Home" originally found its inspiration in the newspaper headlines—specifically, in the found object, the *objet trouvé*—of a *Daily Mail* article about the increasing phenomenon of teenage runaways. McCartney had been drawn to the case of 17-year-old Melanie Coe, who had run away from home to join a man whom she had met at a gambling casino. "My mother didn't like any of my friends," the troubled teen remarked after rejoining her distraught family. "I wasn't allowed to bring anyone home. She didn't like me going out. She didn't like the way I dressed." Her father was confused by his daughter's decision to leave the family home, particularly in light of the many material comforts that she enjoyed: "I can't imagine why she'd run away. She has everything here. She is very keen on clothes, but she left it all, even her fur coat" (Cross 2005, 438). The Beatles had actually met Coe in person in October 1963, when they made their inaugural performance on *Ready Steady Go!* Having won the show's lip-sync competition, Coe was presented with the top prize by the group themselves (Cross 2005, 438). "She's Leaving Home" is ultimately a song, in Bill Martin's words, "where growing up, 'liberation' if you will, and sorrow are inextricably intertwined" (Martin 2002, 17).

The lines about parental sacrifice in "She's Leaving Home"—"We gave her everything money could buy"—came directly from Lennon's experience growing up with his Aunt Mimi during the 1950s on Menlove Avenue. According to William J. Dowlding, "The line about the man from the motor trade might have been inspired by Terry Doran. He had been a car salesman and ran Brian Epstein's Bryder Auto car dealership in Hounslow, Middlesex, where the Beatles bought their many cars" (1989, 171).

RECORDING SESSIONS

Produced by George Martin, "She's Leaving Home" was recorded at Abbey Road Studios on March 17, 1967, with an overdubbing session on March 20.

When an enthusiastic McCartney arrived at EMI Studios in March 1967 to begin work on his latest composition, he learned that Martin was otherwise indisposed with a Cilla Black session. Caught up in the excitement of his new tune, McCartney simply didn't want to wait, enlisting the services of Mike Leander as the arranger for "She's Leaving Home": "I had one of those 'I've got to go, I've got to go!' feelings and when you get those, you don't want anything to stop you," McCartney recollected. "You feel like if you lose the impetus, you'll lose something valuable" (Cross 2005, 438). McCartney later recalled that "George Martin was offended that I used another arranger. He was busy and I was itching to get on with it; I was inspired. I think George had a lot of difficulty forgiving me for that. It hurt him; I didn't mean to" (Dowlding 1989, 171). Although he later conducted the studio musicians with his usual professionalism during the March 17, 1967, orchestral overdub, Martin was bothered by McCartney's impatience. "I minded like hell," the producer later recalled about McCartney's employment of a different arranger (O'Gorman 2004, 242).

As it turns out, Leander's arrangement coaxed a memorable harp performance from Sheila Bromberg, while also provided a moving palette for McCartney's quaint study of a young woman's need to discover a sense of identity and become a conscious participant in the world. During the overdubbing session on March 20, 1967, the vocals were doubled, affording Lennon and McCartney with the sound of a multivoiced chorale.

PERSONNEL

Lennon: Harmony Vocal
McCartney: Vocal
Studio Musicians: String Accompaniment conducted by Martin
Jose Luis García, Erich Gruenberg, Derek Jacobs, Trevor Williams: Violin
Stephen Shingles, John Underwood: Viola
Alan Dalziel, Dennis Vigay: Cello
Gordon Pearce: Double Bass
Sheila Bromberg: Harp

LEGACY AND INFLUENCE

In 1968, the Beatles received an Ivor Novello Award, awarded annually by the British Academy of Songwriters, Composers, and Authors, for "She's Leaving Home."

In 2010, *Rolling Stone* ranked "She's Leaving Home" as #82 on the magazine's list of *The Beatles' 100 Greatest Songs*.

ALBUM APPEARANCES: *Sgt. Pepper's Lonely Hearts Club Band*; *Love Songs*.

See also: Martin, George; *Sgt. Pepper's Lonely Hearts Club Band* (LP).

Shevell, Nancy (1959–)

After dating the former Beatle for nearly four years, Nancy Shevell became McCartney's third wife in 2011. Born in New York City on November 20, 1959, she enjoyed a successful career as vice president of her family-owned New England Motor Freight, as well as a member of the board of the New York Metropolitan Transportation Agency. She began dating McCartney in November 2007 following her separation from her first husband, Bruce Blakeman, with whom she had a son, Arlen. McCartney had originally met Shevell some 20 years earlier in the Hamptons, where their respective families owned homes. McCartney's children had nicknamed Shevell as "Jackie O.," given her striking sense of style.

McCartney and Shevell married on October 9, 2011—on what would have been Lennon's 71st birthday—at Old Marylebone Town Hall, where McCartney had married Linda Eastman in March 1969. On October 8, 2011, McCartney and Shevell attended Yom Kippur services in honor of Shevell's Jewish heritage. As with McCartney's previous wives, Shevell became Lady McCartney upon her marriage to her knighted husband. McCartney's "My Valentine," included on *Kisses on the Bottom* (2012), celebrates his love for Shevell.

See also: McCartney, Paul.

"Sie Liebt Dich" (Lennon–McCartney)

As the Beatles' German-language version of "She Loves You," "Sie Liebt Dich" was recorded specifically to stimulate the band's sales in the West German marketplace. It was released as a single by Swan Records in the United States on May 21, 1964.

AUTHORSHIP AND BACKGROUND

As with "Komm, Gib Mir Deine Hand," "Sie Liebt Dich" was translated into German by Luxembourg songwriter and musician Camillo Felgen, who used the pseudonym Jean Nicolas. Felgen acted at the request of EMI's Germany producer Otto Demler. Along with Martin and Norman Smith, Felgen traveled in January 1964 to Paris, where the Beatles were booked for an extended run at the Olympia Theatre, to join the group for a recording session to prepare German-language versions of "I Want to Hold Your Hand" and "She Loves You" for distribution by West Germany's Odeon label. EMI's West German division, Electrola Gesellschaft, had appealed to Epstein and Martin that the Beatles would make a greater impact upon the West German marketplace if their hits were translated into German-language versions. With a key EMI subsidiary pressuring their parent company for a Beatles release in their mother tongue, Epstein and Martin still had to persuade the Beatles, who were reluctant to comply because they believed foreign-language versions of their songs were unnecessary to break into non-English-speaking markets.

RECORDING SESSIONS

Produced by George Martin, the Beatles recorded "Sie Liebt Dich" in 13 takes on January 29, 1964, at Pathé Marconi Studios in Paris. In contrast with "Komm, Gib Mir Deine Hand," for which Martin still possessed the original instrumental track, "Sie Liebt Dich" had to be recorded from scratch, given that the July 1963 instrumental track for "She Loves You" had been destroyed by EMI. The mono mix of the song was dispatched to West Germany and the United States. On March 13— while the Beatles were filming *A Hard Day's Night*—Martin mixed a stereo version of "Sie Liebt Dich" for release.

During the January 29, 1964, session, Felgen assisted the Beatles in learning how to pronounce the songs' German-lyrics phonetically. For Martin, the experience of persuading the Beatles to join him at Pathé Marconi made for one of his less heartening memories of his life with the group. Relaxing in their suite at the George V Hotel, the band had decided, without informing their producer, not to attend the session. Martin was livid, to say the least: "I barged into their suite, to be met by this incredible sight, right out of the Mad Hatter's tea party. Jane Asher—Paul's girlfriend—with her long red hair, was pouring tea from a china pot, and the others were sitting around her like March Hares. They took one look at me and *exploded*, like in a school room when the headmaster enters. Some dived into the sofa and hid behind cushions, others dashed behind curtains. 'You are bastards!' I screamed, to which they responded with impish little grins and roguish apologies" (Lewisohn 1988, 38). Within minutes, to Martin's great relief, the Beatles were on their way to the studio.

Because Swan Records held the original rights to release "She Loves You" in the United States back in September 1963, the tiny distributor argued that it likewise held the rights to release the German-language version as well, which it released in May 1964 to relatively little fanfare.

PERSONNEL

Lennon: Vocal, Rickenbacker 325
McCartney: Vocal, Höfner 500/1
Harrison: Gretsch Country Gentleman
Starr: Ludwig Oyster Black Pearl Drums

CHART PERFORMANCE

U.S.: "Sie Liebt Dich" ["She Loves You"]/"I'll Get You"; May 21, 1964, Swan 4182: #97.

ALBUM APPEARANCES: *Rarities* (U.K.); *Rarities* (U.S.); *Past Masters, Volume 1.*

See also: *Past Masters, Volume 1.*

The Silver Beetles

In the spring of 1960, the Beatals scuttled their latest name at the encouragement of Brian Casser of Cass and the Casanovas. The bandmates had come into Casser's orbit through Allan Williams, the owner of the Jacaranda Club who became their first manager. The group had taken to hanging out at the club after their rehearsals at nearby Gambier Terrace. After staging the Merseyside and International Beat Show in May in collaboration with flamboyant promoter Larry Parnes, Williams had emerged as a central player on the local music scene. The Jacaranda Club had, quite suddenly, become a central hangout for a host of Liverpool bands, would-be managers, and music promoters.

During this time, Casser happened to witness McCartney singing "Tutti-Fruitti," and he couldn't believe his ears. He urged the band to obtain a drummer and to rid themselves of their "ridiculous" name in favor of a moniker that accented the band's leader. Hence, the Beatals refashioned themselves as Long John and the Silver Beetles, which they soon abridged as the Silver Beetles. Through Casser, the Silver Beetles—including Lennon, McCartney, Harrison, and Sutcliffe—met drummer

The Silver Beetles, on stage in 1960 in Liverpool, England. From left to right are Stuart Sutcliffe, John Lennon, Paul McCartney, substitute drummer Johnny Hutchinson, and George Harrison. (Michael Ochs Archive/Getty Images)

Tommy Moore. Soon thereafter, Williams arranged for the Silver Beetles to work as the opening act for a nine-date tour of Scotland in support of singer Johnny Gentle (born George Askew).

After the tour, Moore quit the group in disgust, having suffered several injuries during an automobile accident before the band's last performance as Johnny Gentle's supporting act. For a brief period, drummer Norman Chapman replaced Moore, although he was conscripted into the National Service after three gigs with the band. Not long afterward, the Silver Beetles altered the spelling of their name to the Silver Beetles, although their latest name was short-lived. In August 1960, Williams arranged for the group to accept an extended engagement in the port city of Hamburg, West Germany. After recruiting Best as their drummer, the band rechristened themselves as the Beatles and began the long journey to the Reeperbahn.

See also: Best, Pete; Sutcliffe, Stuart; Williams, Allan.

"Slow Down" (Williams)

"Slow Down" is a song on the Beatles' *Long Tall Sally* EP, released in the United Kingdom on June 19, 1964.

AUTHORSHIP AND BACKGROUND

Written by Larry Williams, "Slow Down" is a 24-bar blues song. It was released as a single by Williams in 1958, although it failed to become a hit. The original "Slow Down" single was backed with "Dizzy Miss Lizzy," another Williams composition covered by the Beatles.

RECORDING SESSIONS

Produced by George Martin, "Slow Down" was recorded at Abbey Road Studios on June 1, 1964, with an additional overdubbing session on June 4. Lennon double-tracked his lead vocal. On July 16, 1963, the Beatles recorded a version of "Slow Down" for the BBC's *Pop Go the Beatles* radio show that was later included on the *Live at the BBC* album.

PERSONNEL

Lennon: Vocal, Rickenbacker 325
McCartney: Höfner 500/1
Harrison: Gretsch Tennessean
Starr: Ludwig Oyster Black Pearl Drums
Martin: Piano

CHART PERFORMANCE

> U.S.: "Matchbox"/"Slow Down"; August 24, 1964, Capitol 5255: #17. As the B-side of "Matchbox," "Slow Down" charted at #25.

ALBUM APPEARANCES: *Something New*; *Rock 'n' Roll Music*; *Rarities* (U.K.); *Live at the BBC*; *Past Masters, Volume 1*.

See also: *Live at the BBC* (LP).

Smith, Mimi Stanley (1903–1991)

Born in Liverpool on April 24, 1903, Mimi Stanley was the oldest of five sisters, as well as Lennon's maternal aunt. In her early years, Mimi worked as a nurse trainee at the Woolton Convalescent Hospital and as a private secretary. On September 15, 1939, she married George Smith, who operated his family's dairy farm. After her sister Julia gave birth to Lennon on October 9, 1940, Mimi became increasingly disgusted with her sister's behavior, which included the still-married Julia setting up housekeeping with John Dykins, a Liverpool wine steward. After ensuring that her nephew was placed in the custody of herself and husband George, Mimi raised Lennon at her Menlove Avenue home in Liverpool. In 1955, George died of a liver hemorrhage at age 52. He was buried in the graveyard at nearby St. Peter's Church, where Lennon met McCartney in 1957.

In addition to serving a key parental role in his life, Mimi was also instrumental in securing her nephew's first guitar. As the skiffle craze reached its fever pitch in the United Kingdom, young Lennon convinced his Aunt Mimi Smith to purchase a £5 guitar for him in March 1957. Mimi continued to be a presence for the balance of Lennon's life, not only after the accidental death of her sister Julia in July 1958, but after the Beatles achieved worldwide fame. In 1965, Mimi was forced to leave Mendips, given the near-constant attention from the band's legions of fans. Lennon purchased a beachfront bungalow for his aunt for £25,000, known as Harbour's Edge, in Dorset, where Mimi lived for the remainder of her life. Lennon later presented Mimi with his MBE medal, although he asked for it back when he returned it to the British government in protest over the nation's involvement in the Nigeria–Biafra conflict. Lennon spoke with his aunt weekly for the rest of his life, including a final telephone call on December 5, 1980—three days before his murder—in which he announced that he would soon be returning to England for the first time since 1971, when he and Ono had moved to New York City.

Mimi died on December 6, 1991, at age 88. Lennon's first wife Cynthia, son Sean, and Ono, his widow, attended her funeral. Ono later purchased Mendips, donating it to the National Trust and renovating it to recapture its 1950s ambience. In 2010, Mimi was portrayed by actress Kristin Scott Thomas in *Nowhere Boy*.

See also: Lennon, Alfred; Lennon, Cynthia Lillian; Lennon, John; Lennon, Julia Stanley; McCartney, Paul; Ono, Yoko.

"Something" (Harrison)

"Something" is a song on the Beatles' *Abbey Road* album. It was also a hit double A-side single, backed with "Come Together," which was released in the United Kingdom on October 31, 1969, and in the United States on October 6, 1969. It was the only Harrison song released as the A-side of a single. It is second only to "Yesterday" in the number of cover versions of a Beatles composition.

AUTHORSHIP AND BACKGROUND

As Harrison later recalled, " 'Something' was written on the piano while we were making *The White Album*. I had a break while Paul was doing some overdubbing so I went into an empty studio and began to write. That's really all there is to it, except the middle took some time to sort out! It didn't go on *The White Album* because we'd already finished all the tracks" (Harrison 1980, 152). Harrison borrowed the song's opening lyric from Apple artist James Taylor's "Something in the Way She Moves."

During this period, Harrison had begun developing his signature slide-guitar sound, an aspect of his musicianship that was enhanced by the Leslie speaker that Clapton had given him several months earlier. With "Something," Harrison had finally come into his own. It "was the first time he ever got an A-side, because Paul and I always wrote both sides anyway," Lennon later observed. "Not because we were keeping him out, 'cause, simply, his material wasn't up to scratch" (Lennon and Ono 2000, 165).

RECORDING SESSIONS

Harrison recorded a demo for "Something," along with "All Things Must Pass" and "Old Brown Shoe," on February 25, 1969. Produced by George Martin, the band recorded multiple takes in April and May at Abbey Road Studios, along with numerous overdubs, including Martin's string arrangement and Harrison's guitar solo, in July and August. At one point, the Beatles created an eight-minute version of "Something" during the song's lengthy production, including a substantial countermelody and piano part played by Lennon (mostly deleted), as well as Billy Preston on Hammond organ.

The sessions for "Something" were generally convivial, although Emerick recalls Harrison asking McCartney to simplify his bass part. McCartney pointedly refused to oblige, ironically setting up one of the duo's finest moments on record. McCartney's jazzy, melodic bass provides a soulful palate for Harrison's sublime solo on his Gibson Les Paul Standard.

PERSONNEL

Lennon: Epiphone Casino
McCartney: Rickenbacker 4001S
Harrison: Vocal, Gibson Les Paul Standard
Starr: Ludwig Hollywood Maple Drums, Maracas
Preston: Hammond Organ
Studio Musicians: String Accompaniment conducted by Martin

CHART PERFORMANCE

U.K.: "Something"/"Come Together"; October 31, 1969, Apple [Parlophone] R 5814): #4.

U.S.: "Something"/"Come Together"; October 6, 1969, Apple [Capitol] 26543: #3 (certified by the RIAA as "2x Multi Platinum," with more than 2 million copies sold).

LEGACY AND INFLUENCE

Frank Sinatra famously described "Something" as "the greatest love song of the past 50 years," although the crooner often mistakenly ascribed it as a Lennon–McCartney composition.

In 1970, the Beatles received an Ivor Novello Award, awarded annually by the British Academy of Songwriters, Composers, and Authors, for "Something."

In 2000, *Mojo* magazine ranked "Something" as #14 on the magazine's list of *The 100 Greatest Songs of All Time*.

In 2005, McCartney and Clapton's version of "Something" for the *Concert for George* was nominated for a Grammy Award for Best Pop Collaboration with Vocals at the 47th Grammy Awards.

In 2010, *Rolling Stone* ranked "Something" as #6 on the magazine's list of *The Beatles' 100 Greatest Songs*.

ALBUM APPEARANCES: *Abbey Road*; *The Beatles, 1967–1970*; *Love Songs*; *Anthology 3*; *1*; *Love*.

See also: *Abbey Road* (LP).

Something New (LP)

July 20, 1964, Capitol T 2108 (mono)/ST 2108 (stereo)

Something New was the fifth Beatles album to be released in the United States—the third on Capitol Records, along with Vee-Jay Records' *Introducing . . . the Beatles* and United Artists' soundtrack for the *A Hard Day's Night* feature film. It was released on the Capitol label on July 20, 1964. Eight of the songs on *Something New* were culled from the *A Hard Day's Night* album, released in the United Kingdom on July 10, 1964. It also included tracks from the *Long Tall Sally* EP, released in the United Kingdom on June 19, 1964, and the German translation of "I Want to Hold Your Hand," which the Beatles had recorded at EMI's Pathé Marconi Studios in January 1964.

Something New was deleted from the Beatles' catalogue in 1987, when the group's U.K. albums were distributed as CD releases. A remastered mono and stereo release of *Something New* was released on November 15, 2004, as part of the box set entitled *The Capitol Albums, Volume 1*.

BACKGROUND

With United Artists having released the soundtrack for *A Hard Day's Night* some two weeks earlier, Capitol Records countered with *Something New*, a collection of eight songs from the original British release of *A Hard Day's Night*. As with other Beatles American releases, Capitol's Dave Dexter, Jr., added reverb and echo effects to the tracks. A number of other differences are in evidence, including alternate versions of "And I Love Her," "Any Time at All," "I'll Cry Instead," and "When I Get Home."

Something New was the first Beatles release on Capitol to feature true stereo as its audio format. In 1964, Parlophone released a special European edition of *Something New* for distribution among U.S. Armed Forces stationed abroad; Odeon released a similar edition in Germany. These versions of the album have become collector's items among Beatles fans.

TRACK LISTING

Side 1: "I'll Cry Instead"; "Things We Said Today"; "Any Time at All"; "When I Get Home"; "Slow Down"; "Matchbox."

Side 2: "Tell Me Why"; "And I Love Her"; "I'm Happy Just to Dance with You"; "If I Fell"; "Komm, Gib Mir Deine Hand" ["I Want to Hold Your Hand"].

COVER ARTWORK

Something New's front cover artwork consists of a color still photograph from their inaugural appearance on *The Ed Sullivan Show* on February 9, 1964. The album's liner notes describe *Something New* as the

> third great Beatles album for Capitol. And needless to say it's wonderful in the very special and exclusively marvelous Beatles way! Here are the latest, greatest new Beatles hits the boys have come up with since their first two phenomenal Capitol albums. All but two (including five hits from the picture) are written by John Lennon and Paul McCartney, the two busy Beatles who just keep on

turning out smash songs not only for their own foursome but for other singers as well. One of the most popular is "Komm, Gib Mir Deine Hand," the German-language version the boys made of their sensational Capitol hit, "I Want to Hold Your Hand."

CHART PERFORMANCE

U.S.: #2 (certified by the RIAA as "2x Multi Platinum," with more than 2 million copies sold).

LEGACY AND INFLUENCE

Unable to dethrone the United Artists soundtrack for *A Hard Day's Night*, *Something New* spent nine weeks in the #2 slot on the American album charts.

See also: *A Hard Day's Night* (Film); *A Hard Day's Night* (U.S. LP).

Spector, Phil (1940–)

Born as Harvey Phillip Spector on December 26, 1939, in the Bronx, New York, Spector is one of the most celebrated producers of all time and is often associated with his signature "wall of sound" recording technique. As his musical trademark, his wall of sound allowed him to imbue his orchestral arrangements with a more potent and expansive sound by feeding the signal from the studio into an echo chamber during the recording process. Between 1960 and 1965 alone, he produced and composed more than 25 Top 40 hits. He is a well-known progenitor of the 1960s-era girl-group sound. His 1965 song, "You've Lost That Lovin' Feelin,' " which he produced and coauthored with the Righteous Brothers, received more airplay than any other composition during the 20th century.

In 1970, Spector was invited by Beatles manager Allen Klein to produce Lennon's solo single "Instant Karma! (We All Shine On)." During the song's production, he was tasked by Lennon and Harrison with carrying out the postproduction work on the Beatles' *Get Back* project, which they had abandoned the previous year. Drawing upon his wall of sound production technique and adding orchestral arrangements to several tracks, he completed work on the album that was entitled *Let It Be* (1970). McCartney took particular issue with Spector's revisioning of his songs, later working to ensure that posthumous release of the Beatles' *Let It Be . . . Naked* (2003) album, which featured the band's songs as they had been originally produced by George Martin and Glyn Johns. In subsequent years, Spector worked extensively with Lennon (*John Lennon/Plastic Ono Band*, *Imagine*, and *Rock 'n' Roll*) and Harrison (*All Things Must Pass* and *The Concert for Bangladesh*). His relationship with Lennon became particularly overwrought during the production of the *Rock 'n' Roll* album in 1973. At times, he seemed to be suffering a nervous breakdown in the studio, brandishing a gun and, at one point, hijacking the album's master tapes and disappearing for several months.

In 1989, Spector was inducted into the Rock and Roll Hall of Fame for his work as record producer and composer. In 2009, he was convicted of second-degree murder in the 2003 death of actress Lana Clarkson for which he is currently serving a prison sentence of 19 years to life.

See also: *Get Back* Project; Johns, Glyn; Klein, Allen; *Let It Be* (LP); *Let It Be . . . Naked* (LP); Martin, George.

Starkey, Richard Henry Parkin, Sr. (1913–1981)

Born in 1913, Richard Henry Parkin Starkey, Sr., was a confectioner by trade. His family's surname had originally been Parkin until his mother was remarried, to a man named Starkey, and the entire family adopted her new last name. On October 24, 1936, Starkey married Elsie Gleave, whom he had met in the Liverpool dance halls. Known as "Big Ritchie" to prevent confusion with his infant son, Ritchie, born Richard Henry Parkin Starkey, Jr., on July 7,1940, Starkey was entirely unprepared for the responsibilities of fatherhood, preferring instead to continue making the rounds of the dance halls where he and Elsie had begun their courtship only a few years before. Within a year of their son's birth, the Starkeys had separated. By 1943, they had divorced, leaving Elsie to raise young Ritchie by herself until she married Harry Graves in 1953. Starr claimed that he saw his birth father no more than three more times throughout his life, observing that he had "no real memories" of Big Ritchie, who died in Cheshire in 1981.

See also: Graves, Harry; Graves, Elsie Gleave (Starkey); Starr, Ringo.

Starr, Ringo (1940–)

Born Richard Henry Parkin Starkey, Jr., Starr became the Beatles' drummer in August 1962 following the departure of Best. During his post-Beatles years, he scored two #1 hits in "Photograph" and "You're Sixteen."

EARLY YEARS

Starr was born to Elsie Gleave Starkey and Richard Starkey, a bakery worker, on July 7, 1940, in Liverpool's notoriously rough and impoverished Dingle neighborhood. After Starr's paternal grandmother remarried, the family altered its surname from Parkin to Starkey, her new husband's last name. Starr's parents were married in 1936, having met in the Liverpool dance halls. Known as "Big Ritchie" after his son's birth, Starr's father was unprepared for the responsibilities of father-hood, preferring instead to continue making the rounds of the dance halls where he and Elsie had begun their courtship only a few years before. Within a year of their son's birth, the Starkeys had separated. By 1943, they had divorced, leaving Elsie to raise Ritchie, as he was called, by herself. Eventually, Elsie found employ-ment as a barmaid, while devoting nearly all of her free time to her son, upon whom she doted. Most of the boy's childhood was overshadowed by illness. On July 3, 1947, he was felled by sharp pains in his abdomen, and he was hospital-ized for appendicitis. In the aftermath of his surgery, he developed peritonitis, a severe inflammation of the lining of the abdominal cavity, and slipped into a coma from which he awoke—lucky to have survived at all—on his seventh birthday. He spent the remainder of the year recuperating at the hospital. By the time that he returned to school, he had fallen woefully behind his classmates. For the next several years, he made little improvement at school, although he benefited greatly from the efforts of family friend Marie Maguire, who served as the boy's tutor at his home on Admiral Grove. Before long, he was even beginning to advance at reading. "He made incredible progress," Maguire recalled. "It seemed like we were *that* close to bringing him up to proper school standards when he got sick again" (Spitz 2005, 337).

In 1952, Starr was stricken with tuberculosis, which had reached epidemic pro-portions in Liverpool—particularly in the Dingle. Eventually, he ended up at Royal Liverpool Children's Hospital, where he convalesced in the sanitarium. During his lengthy stay at the hospital, he was encouraged to keep his mind alert by partici-pating in the makeshift hospital band, which consisted of young patients playing rudimentary percussion along with prerecorded music. He joined in by tapping a pair of cotton bobbins on the cabinet beside his bed (Spitz 2005, 338). In the autumn of 1953, he finally went home to the Dingle, where he found himself lagging even further behind in school, which he eventually stopped attending altogether. His sal-vation arrived in the form of Harry Graves, a bachelor who had left London after a failed marriage and found his true love in Starr's mother. Graves worked as a Liverpool Corporation housepainter, and his one abiding passion—in addition to Elsie—was music. He shared his wide-ranging tastes—from vocal stylists like Dinah Shore and Sarah Vaughan to pop stars in the vein of Frankie Lane and Johnnie Ray—with Starr, who became Graves' stepson in April 1954, when Elsie and Graves married.

Over the next few years, Starr went through an assortment of jobs. First, he tried his hand working for the British rail, although he was laid off in short order. Next, he took a position working as a waiter on daily boat trips from Liverpool to North Wales. Before long, Graves found Starr a job at Henry Hunt and Sons, a gymnas-tics equipment company, where he performed a range of chores. It was at Henry Hunt and Sons that Starr met Eddie Miles. A budding guitarist in his own right, Miles was the leader of the Eddie Miles Band, which evolved into Eddie Clayton and the Clayton Squares. Using an old washboard for percussion, Starr joined the group, which specialized—as with so many other bands across the United Kingdom—in the primitive musical sounds of skiffle. In December 1957, Graves presented his stepson with a used drum kit, which he had bought in London for £10. With Starr's drum set in tow, the Eddie Clayton skiffle group began booking a series of small-time local engagements. Soon, he had even started playing rock 'n' roll with Al Caldwell's Texans. In 1958, he left Miles behind as the band transformed into the Raging Texans, which became Jet Storm and the Raging Texans before settling in for the long haul as Rory Storm and

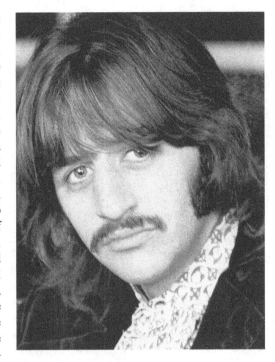

Ringo Starr in 1968. (Photofest)

the Hurricanes. Having borrowed £46 from his grandfather, Starr purchased a proper set of drums—a new Ajax drum kit, complete with pigskin heads.

As a member of Rory Storm and the Hurricanes, Starr came into his own. He quickly emerged as one of the group's most popular musicians, and his image was enhanced by the many rings that adorned his fingers. Before long, he became known as "Rings," which morphed into "Ringo." Likewise, Starkey was abbreviated into "Starr," and a stage name was born. Eventually, the band turned the spotlight on their drummer, who occasionally sang a song, and, during "Starr Time," he began playing extended drum solos. Like the Beatles, Rory Storm and the Hurricanes served an apprenticeship in Hamburg, where Starr got to know Lennon, McCartney, and Harrison in 1961. As with his earlier years, though, Starr had begun to develop a sense of wanderlust. At one point, he even pondered immigrating to Texas, where his blues idol, Lightnin' Hopkins, plied his trade. He went so far as to write a letter to the Houston Chamber of Commerce, but became dismayed by the mountain of registration forms that came in the return post. After playing drums behind Sheridan in Hamburg, Starr rejoined Rory Storm and the Hurricanes for their annual run at Butlin's Holiday Camp in England during the summer months of 1962. But what he really wanted was to be the drummer for the Beatles, and in August 1962, when the Beatles ousted Best, his dream came true.

Despite the apparent simplicity of his drum work, Starr possesses a unique, nonchalant playing style that acts, in its subtlety, as his musical signature:

I used to get put down in the press a lot for my silly fills, as we liked to call them, and that mainly came about because I'm a left-handed right-handed drummer; that means I'm left-handed but the kit's set up for a right-handed drummer, so if I come off the hi-hat and the snare . . . any ordinary drummer would come off with the right hand . . . so if I want to come off, I have to come off with the left hand, which means I have to miss a . . . miniscule of a beat . . . I can go around the kit from the floor tom to the top toms, which are on the bass drum easy, but I can't go the other way because the left hand has to keep coming in under the right one. (Everett 2001, 121)

As Lennon recalled,

Ringo was a star in his own right in Liverpool before we even met. He was a professional drummer who sang and performed and had Ringo Starr-time and he was in one of the top groups in Britain but especially in Liverpool before we even had a drummer. So Ringo's talent would have come out one way or the other as something or other. I don't know what he would have ended up as, but whatever that spark is in Ringo that we all know but can't put our finger on—whether it is acting, drumming, or singing I don't know—there is something in him that is projectable and he would have surfaced with or without the Beatles. Ringo is a damn good drummer. He is not technically good, but I think Ringo's drumming is underrated the same way Paul's bass playing is underrated. (Evans 2004, 385)

MARRIAGE AND FAMILY

Starr married Maureen Cox at London's Caxton Hall Registry Office on February 11, 1965. Together, Starr and Cox had three children, including sons Zak and Jason, as well as a daughter, Lee. Zak later became a professional drummer in his own right, becoming a regular member of the Who in 1996, while also working with Brit-Pop band Oasis. After Starr and Cox divorced in July 1975, Starr married Barbara Bach on April 27, 1981, having met the actress and *Playboy* model on the set of the film *Caveman* (1981).

SOLO YEARS

In his post-Beatles years, Starr has enjoyed a long, varied, and wholly uneven career. During the band's final years together, he began fashioning a career in film. Over the years, he has appeared in numerous films and made-for-television movies, including *Candy* (1968), *The Magic Christian* (1969), *200 Motels* (1971), *Blindman* (1971), *Born to Boogie* (1972), *That'll Be the Day* (1973), *Son of Dracula* (1974), *Lisztomania* (1975), *Sextette* (1978), *Ringo* (1978), *Caveman* (1981),

Ringo Starr gestures to the crowd during a ceremony to award him the 2,401st star on the Hollywood Walk of Fame in Los Angeles on February 8, 2010. (AP Photo/Chris Pizzello)

Princess Daisy (1983), *Give My Regards to Broad Street* (1984), and *Alice in Wonderland* (1985), among others. He also enjoyed key roles in the television series *Thomas the Tank Engine and Friends* and *Shining Time Station*. In 1991, he turned in a memorable cameo on *The Simpsons*.

As with his film career, Starr's solo musical career has been generally uneven, although it began auspiciously with several hit singles, including "Back Off Boogaloo" and "It Don't Come Easy," and culminating with the commercial blockbuster LP *Ringo* (1973), produced by Perry and featuring all four former Beatles on various tracks. Since the critical and commercial attainments associated with *Ringo*—which produced three hit singles in "Photograph," "You're Sixteen," and "Oh My My"—Starr has released a wide array of solo albums without, for the most part, achieving any sustained commercial success. With the exception of the *Ringo* album and its follow-up release *Goodnight Vienna* (1974), the highlight of his solo career is undoubtedly the establishment of his successful touring band, Ringo Starr and His All-Starr Band. Originally conceptualized by David Fishof, Ringo Starr and His All-Starr Band is a shifting collective of touring musicians who have worked with Starr since 1989. The revolving supergroup features hit songs by Starr from his solo and Beatles years, as well as material by each of the members from their own respective careers.

LEGACY

As with the other Beatles, Starr was appointed as a member of the Order of the British Empire during the Queen's Birthday Honours on June 12, 1965, receiving his insignia from Queen Elizabeth II at Buckingham Palace on October 26. On August 31, 1984, his legacy was commemorated with the naming of a minor planet, 4150 Starr, by Brian A. Skiff at the Lowell Observatory's Anderson Mesa Station. In 1988, the Beatles were inducted into the Rock and Roll Hall of Fame. He is the only former Beatle who has not been inducted for his solo career. In February 2010, he received a star on the Hollywood Walk of Fame from the Hollywood Chamber of Commerce. As with the other Beatles, his star is located on North Vine Street in front of the Capitol Records Building.

See also: Bach, Barbara; Best, Pete; Ringo Starr and His All-Starr Band; Starkey, Richard Henry Parkin, Sr.; Tigrett, Maureen Cox (Starkey).

"Strawberry Fields Forever" (Lennon–McCartney)

"Strawberry Fields Forever" was a hit double A-side single, backed with "Penny Lane," which was released in the United Kingdom on February 17, 1967, and in the United States on February 13, 1967. It was later included on the Beatles' *Magical Mystery Tour* album.

AUTHORSHIP AND BACKGROUND

Written by Lennon, "Strawberry Fields Forever" finds its origins during the production of Richard Lester's absurdist comedy *How I Won the War* in which Lennon had accepted a part in as Private Gripweed—a wisecracking fascist trapped in a war against the evils of fascism. Donning the National Health "granny" glasses for which he would forever be associated, the Beatle went on location in Almería, Spain. In no time, Lennon discovered that a movie set—especially for an actor in a supporting role—was a decidedly boring place to be. Relaxing in the beach house that he shared with Michael Crawford, the star of *How I Won the War*, Lennon gathered up his acoustic guitar and began picking out his first new composition in months. "Living is easy with eyes closed," the lyrics for the tune began.

As Lennon later recalled,

> Strawberry Field is a real place. After I stopped living at Penny Lane, I moved in with my auntie who lived in the suburbs—not the poor slummy kind of image that was projected in all the Beatles stories. Near that home was Strawberry Field, a house near a boys' reformatory where I used to go to garden parties as a kid with my friends Nigel and Pete. We always had fun at Strawberry Field. So that's where I got the name. (Lennon and Ono 2000, 158)

RECORDING SESSIONS

Produced by George Martin, "Strawberry Fields Forever" was recorded under the working title of "It's Not Too Bad" at Abbey Road Studios on November 24, 1966, with additional sessions on November 28 and 29. Work continued on the track on December 8, 9, 15, and 21.

On November 24, 1966, Lennon unveiled "Strawberry Fields Forever," the composition that he had begun back in Spain, for the Beatles. When he first heard the song in the studio that day, Martin couldn't believe his ears. "It was absolutely lovely," he recalled. "I was spellbound. I was in love" (Spitz 2005, 654). The composition was recorded over several sessions during a series of organic moments in which the song evolved from its folkish origins into the full-flower of psychedelia. The first session was marked by the introduction of the Mellotron Mark II into the studio. Played by McCartney on "Strawberry Fields Forever," the Mellotron is an electromechanical keyboard instrument that creates sound when its keys activate a bank of magnetic, 42-foot tape strips. The instrument's prerecorded tapes produce a wide variety of sounds, including string, woodwind, and brass instruments. Lennon had first seen a prototype of the Mellotron back in the summer of 1965. "I must have one of these!" he exclaimed (Babiuk 2001, 165). "It was a new

View of the distinctive red gates of Strawberry Field. A Salvation Army children's home in Liverpool, the grounds of the estate were a boyhood haunt of John Lennon's and the nostalgic inspiration for the title of his famous song "Strawberry Fields Forever." (Kenny1/Dreamstime.com)

instrument then," Geoff Emerick remembered. "John had one of the first ones, in a polished wooden cabinet. In the end, the Musicians' Union tried to stop manufacture because of the way it reproduced the sounds of other instruments" (Lewisohn 1988, 87). The first take of "Strawberry Fields Forever" featured Lennon's nasally lead vocal, McCartney playing the Mellotron with the instrument's flute setting toggled, and Harrison's twangy slide guitar. A few days later, the group added a rhythm track before treating Lennon's vocals with ADT and overdubbing McCartney's Rickenbacker bass part onto the composition.

On December 8, 1966, the Beatles continued shaping the track under the supervision of technical engineer Dave Harries, while Martin and Emerick attended the world premiere of Cliff Richards' film *Finders Keepers*. In their absence, the group recorded Starr's cymbals, which were replayed backward; McCartney and Harrison flailing away on the tympani; and Evans on the tambourine. Neil Aspinall provided additional percussion on the Güiro, a hollow gourd played by rubbing a wooden stick across the instrument's series of parallel notches. After numerous iterations that evening, the Beatles chose takes 15 and 24 for the next phase of the recording life of "Strawberry Fields Forever." That same evening, McCartney continued working on "When I'm Sixty-Four," a track that the band had started working on two nights earlier.

On December 9, 1966, Harrison added the sound of a swarmandal, or Indian harp, to "Strawberry Fields Forever," and four trumpets and three cellos were superimposed on tracks three and four of the burgeoning recording, whose two versions now included the original, breezier take of the song and the later, heavily orchestrated rendition. A few days before Christmas, Lennon came up with a solution for addressing the composition's competing versions, both of which met with his authorial approval. Why not splice the two takes together into a single, magnificent whole? "Well, there are only two things against it," Martin told him. "One is that they're in different keys. The other is that they're in different tempos." But for Lennon, there were no limits to the imagination, only temporary obstacles. "Yeah, but you can do something," Lennon told the producer. "You can fix it, George" (Everett 1999, 79). Martin and Emerick reasoned that if they sped up the remix of the original version, which was take 7, and then slowed down the remix of the latter version, which was take 26, they could align both recordings in terms of key and tempo. "We gradually decreased the pitch of the first version at the join to make them weld together," Emerick recalled (Lewisohn 1988, 91). After Martin and Emerick edited the two halves together—the join can be heard at 0:59—"Strawberry Fields Forever" was finally finished, complete with the "free-form coda," in Everett's words, that brings the track to its revolutionary conclusion (Everett 1999, 80).

PERSONNEL

Lennon: Vocal, Gibson J-160E, Mellotron Mark II, Bongos
McCartney: Rickenbacker 4001S, Mellotron Mark II, Tympani

Harrison: Sonic Blue Fender Stratocaster, Swarmandal, Maracas
Starr: Ludwig Oyster Black Pearl Drums, Tympani
Aspinall: Güiro
Terry Doran: Maracas
Mal Evans: Tambourine
Studio Musicians: Brass and String Accompaniment conducted by Martin
Greg Bowen, Tony Fisher, Stanley Roderick, Derek Watkins: Trumpet
John Hall, Norman Jones, Derek Simpson: Cello

CHART PERFORMANCE

U.K.: "Penny Lane"/"Strawberry Fields Forever"; February 17, 1967, Parlophone R 5570: #2.

U.S.: "Penny Lane"/"Strawberry Fields Forever"; February 13, 1967, Capitol 5810: #8 (certified by the RIAA as "Gold," with more than 500,000 copies sold).

LEGACY AND INFLUENCE

"Strawberry Fields Forever" is included among the Rock and Roll Hall of Fame's *500 Songs That Shaped Rock and Roll*.

In 1999, "Strawberry Fields Forever" was inducted into the National Academy of Recording Arts and Sciences Grammy Hall of Fame.

In 2004, *Rolling Stone* ranked "Strawberry Fields Forever" as #76 on the magazine's list of *The 500 Greatest Songs of All Time*.

In 2006, *Q Magazine* ranked "Strawberry Fields Forever" as #31 on the magazine's list of *The 100 Greatest Songs of All Time*.

In 2010, *Rolling Stone* ranked "Strawberry Fields Forever" as #3 on the magazine's list of *The Beatles' 100 Greatest Songs*.

In October 2012, BBC Local Radio listeners ranked "Strawberry Fields Forever" as their 10th favorite Beatles song in a poll conducted in commemoration of the 50th anniversary of "Love Me Do," the band's first single.

ALBUM APPEARANCES: *Magical Mystery Tour*; *The Beatles, 1967–1970*; *Anthology 2*; *Love*.

See also: *Magical Mystery Tour* (LP); "Paul Is Dead" Hoax.

"Sun King" (Lennon–McCartney)

"Sun King" is a song on the Beatles' *Abbey Road* album. It is the second song in the *Abbey Road* Medley.

AUTHORSHIP AND BACKGROUND

Influenced by Fleetwood Mac's wistful instrumental hit "Albatross," Lennon's "Sun King" originally came to him in a dream during the band's 1968 visit to India. The Beatles originally rehearsed the song under the working title "Los Paranoias" during the *Get Back* sessions in January 1969.

RECORDING SESSIONS

Produced by Martin, "Sun King" was recorded at Abbey Road Studios under the working title of "Here Comes the Sun King." The group recorded "Sun King" and "Mean Mr. Mustard" as a single track on July 24, 1969, with additional overdubbing sessions on July 25 and 29. During the recording, Lennon ad-libs a bizarre admixture of faux Romance languages.

As Lennon recalled,

> We just started joking, you know, singing "quando para mucho." So we just made it up. Paul knew a few Spanish words from school, you know. So we just strung any Spanish words that sounded vaguely like something. And of course we got "chicka ferdy" in. That's a Liverpool expression. Just like sort of—it doesn't mean anything to me but [childish taunting] "na-na, na-na-na!" "Cake and eat it" is another nice line too, because they have that in Spanish—"Que" or something can eat it. One we missed—we could have had "para noya," but we forgot all about it. We used to call ourselves Los Para Noias. (Beatles 2000, 337)

PERSONNEL

Lennon: Vocal, Maracas
McCartney: Rickenbacker 4001S, Harmonium
Harrison: Fender Rosewood Telecaster
Starr: Ludwig Hollywood Maple Drums, Bongos
Martin: Lowrey Organ

ALBUM APPEARANCES: *Abbey Road*; *Love*.

See also: *Abbey Road* (LP).

Sutcliffe, Stuart (1940–1962)

Born on June 23, 1940, in Edinburgh, Scotland, Stuart Fergusson Victor Sutcliffe was the Beatles' inaugural bassist, as well as a painter and influential early member of the band. He came into Lennon's orbit in January 1960, when the 19-year-old artist was a fellow student at the Liverpool College of Art. After entering the

Second Biennial John Moores Exhibition, one of his works, *The Summer Painting*, was selected to hang in Liverpool's Walker Art Gallery. Indeed, Moores was so impressed with Sutcliffe's art that he bought the painting himself for a rather lucrative £65. By this time, Lennon, McCartney, and Harrison had been regularly practicing in Sutcliffe's Gambier Terrace flat. They got on with the talented artist famously, and Lennon knew exactly what to do with his friend's sudden largesse: "Now [that] you've got all this money, Stu, you can buy a [bass] and join our group" (Spitz 2005, 173). Sutcliffe took Lennon up on his offer and purchased a sunburst Höfner 333, after making a £5 deposit, at Frank Hessy's music store. Fellow student Bill Harry recalled his dismay at Sutcliffe's decision to join the band. The painter calmed his friend by explaining that he felt their music was an art form in its own right. "And anyway," he added, "they're going to be the greatest. I want to be a part of it" (Spitz 2005, 174).

In addition to being the band's first bassist, Sutcliffe was instrumental in the Quarry Men rechristening themselves as the "Beatals." Legend has it that he suggested the notion of beetles as a reference to the biker gang in the 1953 Marlon Brando vehicle *The Wild One*, although Lennon and Sutcliffe later claimed to have chosen the name as an homage to Buddy Holly and the Crickets, changing the spelling from Beetles to Beatals in order to connote the idea of beat music. McCartney and Harrison took an immediate liking to the new name, and the days of the Quarry Men were over. While his bandmates appreciated his creative nature, Sutcliffe was roundly criticized for the quality of his musicianship. While Beatles folklore attributes his stage posture—playing either sideways or with his back to the audience—to shyness, McCartney alleges that, in truth, the bassist, and his bandmates, didn't want anyone to realize that he couldn't play his guitar properly. "We sometimes used to tell him to turn away when we were doing pictures because he sometimes wasn't in the same key we were in. We always used to look. I still do. . . . That was one of the things we loved about guys in the audience. The girls would look at us, the guys would look at the chords" (Babiuk 2001, 29).

After the band traveled to Hamburg in August 1960 for their first residency in the West German port city, Sutcliffe developed a fast friendship with fellow musician Klaus Voormann, who talked his former girlfriend, artist and photographer Astrid Kirchherr, into visiting the Kaiserkeller to see the Beatles in action. "I fell in love with Stuart that very first night," she remembered. "He was so tiny but perfect, every feature. So pale, but very very beautiful. He was like a character from a story by Edgar Allan Poe" (Norman 1981, 97). In the coming weeks, Kirchherr photographed the band in a variety of poses and in a range of locales, but most of her pictures capture Sutcliffe, with his ubiquitous sunglasses, shrouded in silence and mystery. Within two months, he and Kirchherr were engaged, much to his family's chagrin. The couple's affection for each other was palpable, but his newfound love was interrupted, as time went on, by intense seizures, as well as by paralyzing headaches that left him in a state of utter agony until the pain finally ceased.

In 1961, Sutcliffe made plans to attend Hamburg's prestigious State College of Art. For the time being, he remained as the Beatles' bassist, even boldly venturing into the spotlight to sing Presley's "Love Me Tender." Initially, he was the talk of the Reeperbahn for his innovative haircut. Kirchherr had apparently persuaded Sutcliffe to change his hairstyle to a "French cut" by shaping his locks to lie atop his forehead rather than towering above it, Teddy Boy style. Although they made fun of him relentlessly, Lennon, McCartney, and Harrison eventually followed suit, and the so-called Beatle haircut was born. As it turned out, the last straw in the band's relationship with Sutcliffe was McCartney, with whom a feud had been simmering for quite some time. McCartney had long been critical of Sutcliffe's bass playing, and, according to McCartney's girlfriend Dot Rhone, "he was jealous of Stu, especially of Stu's friendship with John" (Spitz 2005, 247). Things came to a head, of all places, on stage, when Sutcliffe threw down his bass in the middle of a song and leapt at McCartney. The die had been cast, and within a week Sutcliffe informed the others that he was leaving the band.

In April 1962, the Beatles' third residency in Hamburg was marred from the outset by an unexpected tragedy. Kirchherr met their plane on April 11 and reported that Sutcliffe had died of a brain hemorrhage the day before after complaining for months on end about a relentless series of headaches. While it is an accepted fact among many Beatles scholars that Sutcliffe's untimely death was related to head injuries that he sustained during a bloody scuffle in a parking lot after a 1960 performance with the Silver Beetles, Sutcliffe's autopsy declared the official cause of death as "cerebral paralysis due to bleeding into the right ventricle of the brain" (Harry 1992, 638).

For Sutcliffe's bandmates, his ethereal presence never really ceased. Lennon later referenced his memory of cherished friends such as Sutcliffe and boyhood pal Pete Shotton during "In My Life"—"some are dead and some are living"—while the group prominently featured Sutcliffe's image on the cover of *Sgt. Pepper's Lonely Hearts Club Band* (1967). Sutcliffe was also pictured on the cover of the Beatles' *Anthology 1* and *Anthology 3* album covers in the mid-1990. His role in the group's early years receives considerable attention in Ian Softley's *Backbeat* (1994). In 2011, his cover version of "Love Me Tender" was released as a posthumous Sutcliffe single nearly 50 years after the former Beatle's untimely death.

See also: The Beatals; Kirchherr, Astrid; The Quarry Men; *Sgt. Pepper's Lonely Hearts Club Band* (LP); Voormann, Klaus.

T

"A Taste of Honey" (Scott–Marlow)

"A Taste of Honey" is a song on the Beatles' *Please Please Me* album.

AUTHORSHIP AND BACKGROUND

Written by Bobby Scott and Ric Marlow, "A Taste of Honey" was originally written as an instrumental for the 1960 Broadway production of Shelagh Delaney's play *A Taste of Honey*. The Beatles fashioned their version of the song after Lenny Welch's 1962 vocal rendition.

RECORDING SESSIONS

Produced by George Martin, "A Taste of Honey" was recorded at Abbey Road Studios on February 11, 1963, with an overdubbing session on February 20. McCartney double-tracked his vocal by recording a second version along with the original, thus creating a layered effect and a fuller sound.

The Beatles also recorded "A Taste of Honey" on seven occasions for BBC Radio. The first instance, recorded on October 25, 1962, was broadcast on October 26 on the *Here We Go* program. They recorded "A Taste of Honey" on April 1, 1963, for May 13 broadcast on *Side By Side*, followed by a June 1, 1963 recording for a June 6 episode of *Pop Go the Beatles*. The Beatles recorded the song on June 19, 1963, for a June 23 episode of *Easy Beat*, followed by a July 3, 1963, recording for a July 4 broadcast on the *Beat Show*. The Beatles recorded "A Taste of Honey" a sixth time for the BBC on July 10, 1963, at London's Aeolian Hall for a July 23 broadcast of *Pop Go the Beatles*. This version was employed for the band's *Live at the BBC* album. The Beatles recorded "A Taste of Honey" for the BBC for the last time on September 3, 1963, for a September 10 episode of *Pop Go the Beatles*.

PERSONNEL

Lennon: Rickenbacker 325, Backing Vocal
McCartney: Vocal, Höfner 500/1
Harrison: Gretsch Duo-Jet, Backing Vocal
Starr: Premier Mahogany Duroplastic Drums

ALBUM APPEARANCES: *Please Please Me*; *The Early Beatles*; *Live! at the Star-Club in Hamburg, Germany; 1962*; *Live at the BBC*.

See also: *Live at the BBC* (LP); *Please Please Me* (LP).

"Taxman" (Harrison)

"Taxman" is a song on the Beatles' *Revolver* album.

AUTHORSHIP AND BACKGROUND

Written by George Harrison, "Taxman" depicts the guitarist's revelations about the realities of Great Britain's progressive income tax.

As Harrison later recalled, " 'Taxman' was when I first realized that even though we had started earning money, we were actually giving most of it away in taxes. It was and still is typical" (Cadogan 2008, 186).

As Lennon observed,

> I remember the day he [George] called to ask for help on "Taxman," one of his first songs. I threw in a few one-liners to help the song along because that's what he asked for. He came to me because he couldn't go to Paul. Paul wouldn't have helped him at that period. I didn't want to do it. I just sort of bit my tongue and said okay. It had been John and Paul for so long, he'd been left out because he hadn't been a songwriter up until then. (Evans 2004, 286)

RECORDING SESSIONS

Produced by Martin, "Taxman" was recorded at Abbey Road Studios on April 20, 1966, and remade on April 21, with additional overdubbing sessions on April 22 and May 16. Harrison double-tracked his lead vocal.

Interestingly, "Taxman" begins the *Revolver* album with a moment of faux spontaneity in which the Beatles simulate the sounds of a band in the act of warming up for a performance. But their simulation is intentionally skewed toward the unreal, with Harrison deliberately counting "one, two, three, four" out of rhythm and off-tempo. On the surface, the intro to "Taxman" seems like mindless studio noise—McCartney can be heard coughing in the background, and one can even make out the ambient sound of one of the Beatles idly sliding his fingers about the fretboard of an electric guitar. Yet the song's mock overture draws explicit attention to the fact of its studio creation, as opposed to any origins in live performance. In this way, "Taxman" "acts as a frame or doorway," in the words of Shaugn O'Donnell, "a boundary between reality and the mystical world of *Revolver*" (2002, 81).

"Taxman" is also noteworthy for McCartney's looping bass lines—reportedly inspired by legendary Motown bassist James Jamerson—as well as McCartney's intense, melodic guitar solo on his Epiphone Casino. As Harrison later remarked,

"I was pleased to have Paul play that bit on 'Taxman.' If you notice, he did like a little Indian bit on it for me" (Dowlding 1989, 133).

PERSONNEL

Lennon: Tambourine
McCartney: Rickenbacker 4001S, Epiphone Casino
Harrison: Vocal, Epiphone Casino
Starr: Ludwig Oyster Black Pearl Drums, Cowbell

LEGACY AND INFLUENCE

In 2010, *Rolling Stone* ranked "Taxman" as #55 on the magazine's list of *The Beatles' 100 Greatest Songs*.

ALBUM APPEARANCES: *Revolver* (U.K.); *Revolver* (U.S.); *Rock 'n' Roll Music*; *Anthology 2*; *Tomorrow Never Knows*.

See also: *Revolver* (U.K. LP).

"Tell Me What You See" (Lennon–McCartney)

"Tell Me What You See" is a song on the Beatles' *Help!* album.

AUTHORSHIP AND BACKGROUND

Written by McCartney with assistance from Lennon, "Tell Me What You See" presages the Beatles' folk aspirations with their next album, *Rubber Soul*. As McCartney later recalled, "I seem to remember it as mine. Not awfully memorable" (Miles 1997, 200).

RECORDING SESSIONS

Produced by Martin, "Tell Me What You See" was recorded at Abbey Road Studios on February 18, 1965. The Beatles used a wide assortment of percussion for the track, including the Güiro, a Latin American instrument involving a hollow gourd, open-ended with parallel notches on one side.

PERSONNEL

Lennon: Vocal, Rickenbacker 325, Tambourine
McCartney: Vocal, Höfner 500/1, Electric Piano
Harrison: Güiro
Starr: Ludwig Oyster Black Pearl Drums, Maracas, Claves

ALBUM APPEARANCES: *Help!* (U.K.); *Beatles VI*; *Love Songs*.

See also: *Help!* (U.K. LP).

"Tell Me Why" (Lennon–McCartney)

"Tell Me Why" is a song on the Beatles' *A Hard Day's Night* album.

AUTHORSHIP AND BACKGROUND

"Tell Me Why" was written by Lennon expressly for the film *A Hard Day's Night*. As Lennon remembered, "They needed another upbeat song and I just knocked it off. It was like a black, New York girl-group song" (Dowlding 1989, 71).

RECORDING SESSIONS

Produced by Martin, "Tell Me Why" was recorded in eight takes at Abbey Road Studios on February 27, 1964.

PERSONNEL

Lennon: Vocal, Rickenbacker 325
McCartney: Höfner 500/1, Backing Vocal
Harrison: Rickenbacker 360/12, Backing Vocal
Starr: Ludwig Oyster Black Pearl Drums

CHART PERFORMANCE

U.K.: "If I Fell"/"Tell Me Why"; December 4, 1964, Parlophone DP 562 (originally intended for export, this U.K. single was sold sporadically by British retailers; it did not chart).

ALBUM APPEARANCES: *A Hard Day's Night* (U.K.); *A Hard Day's Night* (U.S.); *Something New*.

See also: *A Hard Day's Night* (Film); *A Hard Day's Night* (U.K. LP).

"Thank You Girl" (McCartney–Lennon)

"Thank You Girl" was the B-side of the Beatles' "From Me to You" single.

AUTHORSHIP AND BACKGROUND

Written by Lennon and McCartney, "Thank You Girl" was the songwriters' explicit attempt to write a single. It went under the working title of "Thank You, Little Girl."

As with "From Me to You," "Thank You Girl" finds the Beatles attempting to make a strong interpersonal connection with their audience.

As McCartney later recalled in an interview with Mark Lewisohn, "We knew that if we wrote a song called 'Thank You Girl' that a lot of the girls who wrote us fan letters would take it as a genuine thank you. So a lot of our songs—'From Me to You' is another—were directly addressed to the fans. I remember one of my daughters, when she was very little, seeing Donny Osmond sing 'The Twelfth of Never,' and she said 'he loves me' because he sang it right at her off the telly. We were aware that that happened when you sang to an audience" (Lewisohn 1988, 9).

RECORDING SESSIONS

Produced by Martin, "Thank You Girl" was recorded in 13 takes at Abbey Road Studios on March 5, 1963. Lennon overdubbed the song's harmonica part on March 13. The Beatles recorded a second version of the song on June 19, 1963, at London's Playhouse Theatre and broadcast on the BBC radio program *Easy Beat* on June 23.

PERSONNEL

Lennon: Vocal, Gibson J-160E, Harmonica
McCartney: Vocal, Höfner 500/1
Harrison: Gretsch Duo-Jet
Starr: Premier Mahogany Duroplastic Drums

CHART PERFORMANCE

U.K.: "From Me to You"/"Thank You Girl"; April 11, 1963, Parlophone R 5015: #1. As the B-side of the single, "Thank You Girl" did not chart.

U.S.: "From Me to You"/"Thank You Girl"; May 27, 1963, Vee-Jay VJ 522: #116. As the B-side of the single, "Thank You Girl" did not chart.

U.S.: "Do You Want to Know a Secret"/"Thank You Girl"; March 23, 1964, Vee-Jay VJ 587: #2. As the B-side of "Do You Want to Know a Secret," "Thank You Girl" charted at #35.

ALBUM APPEARANCES: *The Beatles' Second Album*; *Rarities* (U.S.); *Past Masters, Volume 1*; *Live at the BBC*.

See also: *Live at the BBC* (LP).

"That Means a Lot" (Lennon–McCartney)

"That Means a Lot" was recorded during the sessions for *Help!* and remained unreleased until the Beatles' *Anthology* project during the 1990s.

AUTHORSHIP AND BACKGROUND

Written by Lennon and McCartney, "That Means a Lot" was composed expressly for the *Help!* feature film, although it ultimately wasn't selected for inclusion on the soundtrack.

As Lennon remembered, "This song is a ballad which Paul and I wrote for the film but we found we just couldn't sing it. In fact, we made a hash of it, so we thought we'd better give it to someone who could do it well" (Lewisohn 1988, 56). McCartney later added that "there were a few songs that we were just not as keen on, or we didn't think they were quite finished. This was one of them" (McCartney 1988, 12).

RECORDING SESSIONS

Produced by George Martin, "That Means a Lot" was recorded at Abbey Road Studios on February 20, 1965, with an additional overdubbing session on March 20.

In 1984, Geoff Emerick remixed "That Means a Lot" in preparation for the unreleased Beatles *Sessions* project. In 1994, Martin remixed "That Means a Lot" for release as part of the Beatles' *Anthology* project.

PERSONNEL

Lennon: Rickenbacker 325, Maracas, Backing Vocal
McCartney: Vocal, Höfner 500/1, Piano
Harrison: Gretsch Tennessean, Maracas, Backing Vocal
Starr: Ludwig Oyster Black Pearl Drums

ALBUM APPEARANCE: *Anthology 2.*

See also: *The Beatles Anthology, Volume 2* (LP); *Help!* (LP).

"That'll Be the Day" (Holly–Allison–Petty)

In July 1958, "That'll Be the Day" was the first song recorded by the Quarry Men. It was first released as part of the *Anthology* project in 1995.

AUTHORSHIP AND BACKGROUND

Written by Buddy Holly, Jerry Allison, and Norman Petty, "That'll Be the Day" was inspired by Holly, Allison, and Sonny Curtis's June 1956 viewing of *The Searchers* in which John Wayne employs the catchphrase "that'll be the day." Holly recorded a solo version of the song in February 1957 at Petty's Clovis, New Mexico, studio. Because of a complex of contractual obligations, Holly rerecorded the song with his band the Crickets for Coral Records, a Decca subsidiary. The Crickets' version of "That'll Be the Day" was released in May 1957, became a #1 hit, and was later included on the group's debut album *The "Chirping" Crickets*, which was released in November 1957.

RECORDING SESSIONS

The Quarry Men—Lennon, McCartney, Harrison, Colin Hanton, and John "Duff" Lowe—recorded "That'll Be the Day" on Saturday, July 12, 1958, three days before Julia Lennon's untimely death on Menlove Avenue. The Quarry Men had pooled their money in order to record a demo at P. F. Phillips Professional Tape and Disk Record Service, a fancy name for a back room in the 38 Kensington Street home of Percy F. Phillips, who had built a primitive recording studio with a Vortexion reel-to-reel tape recorder, an MSS portable disc-cutting machine, and a trio of microphones. With Phillips' assistance, the group cut a 78-rpm single. The Quarry Men had intended to record several takes in Phillips' studio, but their host was having none of it. For the bargain-basement price of 17 shillings, they were going "straight to vinyl," which meant that they were recording directly onto a shellac disc. It also meant that the band had to turn in flawless takes in order to get their money's worth.

As McCartney later recalled, "I remember we all went down on the bus with our instruments—amps and guitars—and the drummer went separately. We waited in the little waiting room outside while somebody else made their demo and then it was our turn. We just went in the room, hardly saw the fella because he was next door in a little control booth. 'OK, what are you going to do?' We ran through it very quickly, quarter of an hour, and it was all over" (McCartney 1988, 7).

For their first performance on record, the Quarry Men offered a cover version of Holly's "That'll Be the Day" with Lennon on lead vocals. The recording is distinguished by the driving force of Lennon's singing, as well as by a rollicking guitar solo from Harrison, who receives an audible shout of encouragement from one of his bandmates to "honky tonk!" As McCartney remembered, "John did 'That'll Be the Day,' which was one of our stage numbers, and George played the opening guitar notes and I harmonized with John singing lead" (McCartney 1988, 7).

The Quarry Men agreed to share the record amongst themselves, with each member taking temporary ownership of the prize for a week at a time. Lennon, McCartney, Harrison, and Hanton duly passed the disc amongst themselves, and when the record was in Hanton's custody, the drummer talked his friend Charles Roberts into playing it over the P. A. system in the lounge at Littlewood's gaming hall, where it received a surly response from the staff. The disc next alighted in the hands of Lowe, who stowed it away in a linen drawer where it languished for years. McCartney purchased the disc from Lowe in 1981 for an undisclosed amount.

PERSONNEL

Lennon: Vocal, Guitar
McCartney: Guitar, Backing Vocal
Harrison: Guitar, Backing Vocal
Lowe: Piano
Hanton: Drums

LEGACY AND INFLUENCE

Holly and the Crickets' recording of "That'll Be the Day" is included among the Rock and Roll Hall of Fame's *500 Songs That Shaped Rock and Roll*.

In 2004, *Rolling Stone* ranked "That'll Be the Day" as #39 on the magazine's list of *The 500 Greatest Songs of All Time*.

ALBUM APPEARANCE: *Anthology 1.*

See also: *The Beatles Anthology, Volume 1* (LP); The Quarry Men.

"There's a Place" (McCartney–Lennon)

"There's a Place" is a song on the Beatles' *Please Please Me* album.

AUTHORSHIP AND BACKGROUND

Written by Lennon, "There's a Place" was inspired by Motown rhythm and blues. Lennon borrowed the title from the lyrics of Leonard Bernstein and Stephen Sondheim's "Somewhere," the song from the musical *West Side Story* (1957) in which Tony and Maria sing dreamily that "there's a place for us" beyond the bitter turmoil of their feuding families. McCartney owned a copy of the soundtrack album at his family's Forthlin Road residence, where Lennon likely composed the song.

As Lennon later recalled, " 'There's a Place' was my attempt at a sort of Motown, black thing. It says the usual Lennon things: 'In my mind there's no sorrow . . .' It's all in your mind" (Lennon and Ono 2000, 193).

RECORDING SESSIONS

Produced by Martin, "There's a Place" was recorded at Abbey Road Studios in 10 takes on February 11, 1963, with an overdubbing session on February 20. It was the first number to be recorded during February 11's marathon session.

PERSONNEL

Lennon: Vocal, Harmonica, Rickenbacker 325
McCartney: Vocal, Höfner 500/1

Harrison: Gretsch Duo-Jet, Backing Vocal
Starr: Premier Mahogany Duroplastic Drums

CHART PERFORMANCE

U.S.: "Twist and Shout"/"There's a Place"; March 2, 1964, Tollie 9001: #2. As the B-side of "Twist and Shout," "There's a Place" charted at #74.

ALBUM APPEARANCES: *Please Please Me*; *Rarities* (U.S.); *On Air: Live at the BBC, Volume 2.*

See also: *Please Please Me* (LP).

"Things We Said Today" (Lennon–McCartney)

"Things We Said Today" is a song on the Beatles' *A Hard Day's Night* album.

AUTHORSHIP AND BACKGROUND

Written by McCartney, "Things We Said Today" finds its origins in McCartney's May 1964 Caribbean vacation with Jane Asher aboard the yacht *Happy Days*. McCartney was vacationing in the Bahamas with Asher, Starr, and Maureen Starkey. "Things We Said Today" is one of the three principal compositions that McCartney prepared, along with "Can't Buy Me Love" and "And I Love Her," for the film *A Hard Day's Night*.

As McCartney recalled, "I wrote 'Things We Said Today' on acoustic. It was a slightly nostalgic thing already, a future nostalgia: we'll remember the things we said today, sometime in the future, so the song projects itself into the future and then is nostalgic about the moment we're living now, which is quite a good trick" (Harry 2002, 837).

RECORDING SESSIONS

Produced by Martin, "Things We Said Today" was recorded at Abbey Road Studios in three takes on June 2, 1964. McCartney double-tracked his vocal. On July 14, 1964, the Beatles recorded a second version of "Things We Said Today" for the BBC's *Top Gear* radio show that was later included on the *Live at the BBC* album.

PERSONNEL

Lennon: Gibson J-160E, Piano, Tambourine
McCartney: Vocal, Höfner 500/1

Harrison: Rickenbacker 360/12
Starr: Ludwig Oyster Black Pearl Drums

CHART PERFORMANCE

U.K.: "A Hard Day's Night"/"Things We Said Today"; July 10, 1964, Parlophone R 5160: #1. As the B-side of "A Hard Day's Night," "Things We Said Today" did not chart.

LEGACY AND INFLUENCE

In 2010, *Rolling Stone* ranked "Things We Said Today" as #47 on the magazine's list of *The Beatles' 100 Greatest Songs*.

ALBUM APPEARANCES: *A Hard Day's Night* (U.K.); *Something New*; *The Beatles at the Hollywood Bowl*; *Live at the BBC*.

See also: *A Hard Day's Night* (U.K. LP); *Live at the BBC* (LP).

"Think for Yourself" (Harrison)

"Think for Yourself" is a song on the Beatles' *Rubber Soul* album.

AUTHORSHIP AND BACKGROUND

Written by Harrison, "Think for Yourself" went under the working title of "Won't Be There with You."

As Harrison later recalled, " 'Think for Yourself' must be written about somebody from the sound of it—but all this time later I don't quite recall who inspired that tune. Probably the government" (Dowlding 1989, 118).

RECORDING SESSIONS

Produced by George Martin, "Think for Yourself" was recorded at Abbey Road Studios on November 8, 1965. For the song's unusual texture, McCartney achieves a fuzz bass effect by playing his Epiphone Casino through a distortion box and doubling his bass part.

PERSONNEL

Lennon: Hammond Organ, Tambourine, Backing Vocal
McCartney: Höfner 500/1, Epiphone Casino, Backing Vocal
Harrison: Vocal, Sonic Blue Fender Stratocaster
Starr: Ludwig Oyster Black Pearl Drums, Maracas

LEGACY AND INFLUENCE

In 2010, *Rolling Stone* ranked "Think for Yourself" as #75 on the magazine's list of *The Beatles' 100 Greatest Songs*.

ALBUM APPEARANCES: *Rubber Soul* (U.K.); *Rubber Soul* (U.S.); *Yellow Submarine Songtrack*.

See also: *Rubber Soul* (U.K. LP).

"This Boy" (Lennon–McCartney)

"This Boy" was the B-side of the Beatles' "I Want to Hold Your Hand" single in the United Kingdom, where it was released on November 29, 1963.

AUTHORSHIP AND BACKGROUND

Written by Lennon, "This Boy" provides a gentle three-part harmony in 12/8 time.

As Lennon later remarked, "Just my attempt at writing one of those three-part harmony Smokey Robinson songs. Nothing in the lyrics—just a sound and a harmony. There was a period when I thought I didn't write melodies—that Paul wrote those and I just wrote straight, shouting rock 'n' roll. But of course, when I think of some of my own songs—'In My Life' or some of the early stuff—'This Boy,' I was writing melody with the best of them" (Everett 2001, 76).

RECORDING SESSIONS

Produced by Martin, "This Boy" was recorded in 15 takes at Abbey Road Studios on October 17, 1963.

PERSONNEL

Lennon: Vocal, Gibson J-160E
McCartney: Höfner 500/1, Harmony Vocal
Harrison: Gretsch Country Gentleman, Harmony Vocal
Starr: Ludwig Oyster Black Pearl Drums

CHART PERFORMANCE

U.K.: "I Want to Hold Your Hand"/"This Boy"; November 29, 1963, Parlophone R 5084: #1. As the B-side of "I Want to Hold Your Hand," "This Boy" did not chart.

ALBUM APPEARANCES: *Meet the Beatles!*; *Love Songs*; *Rarities* (U.K.); *Past Masters, Volume 1*; *Anthology 1*; *On Air: Live at the BBC, Volume 2*.

See also: *The Ed Sullivan Show* (TV Series).

Thomas, Chris (1947–)

Born in Perivale, Middlesex, on January 13, 1947, Chris Thomas is a celebrated record producer, particularly for his work on *The Beatles* (*The White Album*), as well as for his efforts on behalf of such artists as Elton John, Pink Floyd, Roxy Music, McCartney, the Sex Pistols, and INXS. Having studied violin and piano as a child, he began establishing himself in music production during the mid-1960s, working as an assistant to Beatles producer George Martin with Associated Independent Recording (AIR). His big break occurred in 1968, when Martin took a vacation, leaving *The White Album*'s production in his hands. In addition to his production duties, he played keyboards on "The Continuing Story of Bungalow Bill," "Long, Long, Long," "Not Guilty," and "Piggies." In his post-Beatles days, he produced albums by Procol Harum and Roxy Music, while also mixing Pink Floyd's legendary *The Dark Side of the Moon* (1973) LP. He later mixed Pink Floyd's *The Division Bell* (1994) and coproduced guitarist David Gilmour's *On an Island* solo album (2006). In addition to working with Apple Records' Badfinger, he produced "Anarchy in the U.K.," the debut singles release by the Sex Pistols, as well as influential albums by McCartney—including Wings' *Back to the Egg* (1979) and *Run Devil Run* (1999)— the Pretenders, the Who's Pete Townshend, and INXS.

See also: *The Beatles* (*The White Album*) (LP); Martin, George.

"Ticket to Ride" (Lennon–McCartney)

"Ticket to Ride" is a song on the Beatles' *Help!* album. It was the band's eighth consecutive #1 single in the United Kingdom, where it was released on April 9, 1965. It was the Beatles' third consecutive #1 hit single in the United States, where it was also released on April 9, 1965.

AUTHORSHIP AND BACKGROUND

Written by Lennon, "Ticket to Ride" was the last song prepared for the *Help!* feature film before the Beatles began principal photography for the movie.

Lennon and McCartney offer different origins for the song's title, with McCartney suggesting that it referred to "a British Railways ticket to the town of Ryde on the Isle of White" (Miles 1997, 193), while Lennon maintained that a "ticket to ride" connoted a clean bill of health for the German prostitutes that the Beatles encountered during their Hamburg days in the early 1960s.

RECORDING SESSIONS

Produced by Martin, "Ticket to Ride" was recorded at Abbey Road Studios on February 15, 1965. Lennon double-tracked his vocal.

As Lennon remembered, "That was one of the earliest heavy-metal records made. Paul's contribution was the way Ringo played the drums" (Lennon and Ono 2000, 196).

As McCartney later observed,

I think the interesting thing is the crazy ending—instead of ending like the previous verse, we changed the tempo. We picked up one of the lines, "My baby don't care," but completely altered the melody. We almost invented the idea of a new bit of a song on the fade-out with this song. It was quite radical at the time. (Miles 1997, 193)

In June 1965, the Beatles recorded another version of "Ticket to Ride" for the BBC's *Ticket to Ride* radio show.

PERSONNEL

Lennon: Vocal, Rickenbacker 325
McCartney: Höfner 500/1, Epiphone Casino, Backing Vocal
Harrison: Rickenbacker 360/12
Starr: Ludwig Oyster Black Pearl Drums, Tambourine

CHART PERFORMANCE

U.K.: "Ticket to Ride"/"Yes It Is"; April 9, 1965, Parlophone R 5265: #1.
U.S.: "Ticket to Ride"/"Yes It Is"; April 19, 1965, Capitol 5407: #1 (certified by the RIAA as "Gold," with more than 500,000 copies sold).

LEGACY AND INFLUENCE

In 2004, *Rolling Stone* ranked "Ticket to Ride" as #394 on the magazine's list of *The 500 Greatest Songs of All Time*.

In 2010, *Rolling Stone* ranked "Ticket to Ride" as #17 on the magazine's list of *The Beatles' 100 Greatest Songs*.

ALBUM APPEARANCES: *Help!* (U.K.); *Help!* (U.S.); *A Collection of Beatles Oldies*; *The Beatles, 1962–1966*; *The Beatles at the Hollywood Bowl*; *Reel Music*; *20 Greatest Hits*; *Anthology 2*; *1*.

See also: *Help!* (U.K. LP).

Tigrett, Maureen Cox (Starkey) (1946–1994)

Born on August 4, 1946, in Liverpool, Maureen Cox was Starr's first wife, as well as a regular at the Cavern Club during the Beatles' pre-fame days. Her birth name was Mary, although she changed it to Maureen when she began her brief career as a hairdresser's apprentice. Starr and Cox were married at London's Caxton Hall Registry Office on February 11, 1965. Together, they had three children, including sons Zak and Jason, as well as a daughter, Lee. In 1968, Frank Sinatra famously recorded a special version of "The Lady Is a Tramp" as a favor to Starr on Cox's 22nd birthday, singing "She married Ringo, and she could have had Paul, / That's why the lady is a tramp!" That same year, Cox sang backup vocals on the Beatles' "The Continuing Story of Bungalow Bill," later attending the Rooftop Concert on January 30, 1969. After concluding "Get Back," McCartney says "thanks, Mo" in response to her spirited applause. Her marriage to Starr began to disintegrate in the post-Beatles years. At one point, she engaged in an extramarital affair with Harrison, who was suffering his own marital woes at the time with Pattie Boyd. Starr and Cox divorced in July 1975. In 1976, she began living with Isaac Tigrett, one of the founders of the Hard Rock Café and the House of Blues, eventually marrying him in Monaco in May 1989. Together, Tigrett and Cox had one daughter—Augusta King Tigrett, born on January 4, 1987. Cox died in Seattle, Washington, on December 30, 1994, after suffering from complications from leukemia. At her bedside were Tigrett, Cox's four children, and Starr. McCartney later composed "Little Willow" from his *Flaming Pie* album in her memory.

See also: The Cavern Club; McCartney, Paul; The Rooftop Concert; Starr, Ringo.

"Till There Was You" (Willson)

"Till There Was You" is a song on the *With the Beatles* album.

AUTHORSHIP AND BACKGROUND

An American musical standard, "Till There Was You" was written by Meredith Willson for the hit Broadway show *The Music Man* (1957). It was originally performed by Robert Preston and Barbara Cook. The original Broadway cast album was released in 1958.

McCartney preferred Peggy Lee's interpretation of "Till There Was You," which became a minor hit in the United Kingdom in March 1961.

RECORDING SESSIONS

Produced by Martin, "Till There Was You" was recorded at Abbey Road Studios on July 18 and 30, 1963. In March 1964, the Beatles recorded a version of "Till

There Was You" for the BBC's *From Us to You* radio show. The live recording of "Till There Was You" from the band's BBC sessions was later included on the Beatles' *On Air: Live at the BBC, Volume 2.*

PERSONNEL

Lennon: Gibson J-160E
McCartney: Vocal, Höfner 500/1
Harrison: José Ramirez Studio Guitar
Starr: Bongos

ALBUM APPEARANCES: *With the Beatles*; *Meet the Beatles!*; *Live! at the Star-Club in Hamburg, Germany; 1962*; *Live at the BBC*; *Anthology 1*; *On Air: Live at the BBC, Volume 2.*

See also: *The Ed Sullivan Show* (TV Series); *Live at the BBC* (LP); Royal Command Variety Performance; *With the Beatles* (LP).

"Tomorrow Never Knows" (Lennon–McCartney)

"Tomorrow Never Knows" is a song on the Beatles' *Revolver* album.

AUTHORSHIP AND BACKGROUND

Written by Lennon, "Tomorrow Never Knows" is, in the songwriter's words, the Beatles' "first psychedelic song."

As Lennon remembered, "That's me in my *Tibetan Book of the Dead* period. I took one of Ringo's malapropisms as the title, to sort of take the edge off the heavy philosophical lyrics" (Beatles 2000, 209). As McCartney later added, "That was one of Ringo's malapropisms. John wrote the lyrics from Timothy Leary's version of the *Tibetan Book of the Dead*. It was a kind of Bible for all the psychedelic freaks. That was an LSD song. Probably the only one. People always thought 'Lucy in the Sky with Diamonds' was but it actually *wasn't* meant to say LSD" (Dowlding 1989, 146).

"Tomorrow Never Knows" came into being as the result of the confluence of two events in Lennon and McCartney's lives. Only scant days before the first recording session for "Tomorrow Never Knows," Lennon had purchased a copy of Timothy Leary's *The Psychedelic Experience: A Manual Based on the Tibetan Book of the Dead* (1964) at the trendy Indica Bookshop. In Leary's introduction to his reading of the *Tibetan Book of the Dead*, the American counterculture guru offers a morsel of advice that seized Lennon's attention: "Whenever in doubt, turn off your mind, relax, float downstream" (Leary, Metzner, and Alpert 1964, 14). Meanwhile, McCartney had immersed himself in London's diverse worlds of high and avant-garde culture. In the mid-1960s, he had embarked on a stringent personal program of reading the classics and theatergoing in order to broaden his literary and artistic intellect. "I vaguely mind anyone knowing anything I don't know," McCartney reported. "I'm trying to crowd everything in, all the things that I've missed" (Schaffner 1977, 65).

In terms of music, McCartney had become especially enamored with the electronic, experimental works associated with musique concrète—and with Karlheinz Stockhausen's *Gesang der Jünglinge* [*Song of the Youths*] in particular. McCartney was equally fond of the work of composer John Cage, the most famous pupil of the expressionist composer Arnold Schönberg. McCartney delighted in the concept behind Cage's experimental silent piano piece *4'33"*—a composition whose beginning and ending were indicated solely by the opening and closing of the piano lid. By the early 1960s, Cage took on a protégée of his own, a fledgling Japanese performance artist named Yoko Ono (Riley 2011).

RECORDING SESSIONS

Produced by Martin, "Tomorrow Never Knows" was recorded at Abbey Road Studios on April 6, 1966—the first session associated with the *Revolver* project. Additional overdubbing sessions were held on April 7 and 22.

"Tomorrow Never Knows" went under the working title of "Mark I" and "The Void." When Lennon debuted "Tomorrow Never Knows" for his mates in the studio, the composition's psychedelic underpinnings were already firmly in place. At this juncture, the only elements lacking in the production were the musical accompaniment and sound effects that would blast Lennon's ideas into the consciousness of a waiting world. During the first session, Lennon and Starr fashioned some rudimentary tape loops in a " 'weird sound' contest," according to Geoff Emerick. Meanwhile, the engineer improved the sound of Starr's percussion by moving the microphones closer to his drum kit and by stuffing an old woolen sweater inside his bass drum in order to deepen its resonance (Emerick and Massey 2006, 111).

Considerable studio time was also committed to recording Lennon's lead vocal. At Abbey Road Studios, Lennon had become famous for disliking the sound of his own voice, and he was constantly entreating Martin to alter his vocals during the recording process. For "Tomorrow Never Knows," he challenged the producer to make his "voice sound like the Dalai Lama chanting from a mountaintop, miles away" (Emerick and Massey 2006, 10). In an effort to satisfy Lennon's request, Emerick turned to the studio's Hammond organ, and, in particular, the instrument's Leslie speaker system, which was essentially a wooden cabinet containing two sets of speakers with rotating sound baffles. After Emerick and Ken Townsend rewired the system, they were able to project Lennon's voice through the Leslie cabinet, in front of which they had positioned a pair of microphones. After listening to the playback, Harrison suggested that he play the tamboura on "Tomorrow Never Knows": "It's perfect for this track, John," he explained. "It's just kind of a droning sound, and I think it will make the whole thing quite Eastern" (Emerick and

Massey 2006, 11). With the principal elements in place, the Beatles took their first pass at "Mark I"—a slower, pulsating version of the eventual "Tomorrow Never Knows"—and, after three takes on April 6, they called it a night.

The next evening, McCartney—having been inspired by Lennon and Starr's initial efforts—showed up with a plastic bag filled with tape loops that he had made at home on his Brenell reel-to-reel tape recorder. As McCartney recalled, "I would do them [tape loops] over a few days. I had a little bottle of EMI glue that I would stick them with and wait till they dried. It was a pretty decent join. I'd be trying to avoid the click as it went through, but I never actually avoided it. If you made them very well you could just about do it but I made 'em a bit ham-fisted and I ended up using the clicks as part of the rhythm" (Ryan and Kehew 2006, 304). After reviewing McCartney's collection of sound effects, the group selected five tape loops for "Tomorrow Never Knows," the most recognizable of which sounds like a seagull.

As it turned out, recording the tape loops was a chore in itself. Given that Studio Two had only one extra tape machine available that night, the complex's army of white-coated employees was forced to assemble the other machines at Abbey Road Studios and run the various tape loops through them, all the while steadying pencils in their hands in order to provide the necessary tension. In addition to the seagull sound, the tape loops afforded the track with industrial, machine-like noises. A few weeks later, Emerick grafted Harrison's tamboura drone onto the beginning of "Tomorrow Never Knows," and, at McCartney's suggestion, concluded the track by splicing in the recording of a spontaneous piano riff that the band had concocted on that very first evening.

As Nick Bromell writes, "The unearthly sounds that *Revolver* released into the world were at once the antithesis of the human and a provocative indication of the *mysterium tremendum*. They allowed the imagination to traverse the netscape of the future in which biology and technology would come full circle and touch" (Bromell 2000, 98).

PERSONNEL

> Lennon: Vocal, Tambourine, Tape Loops
> McCartney: Rickenbacker 4001S, Tape Loops
> Harrison: Sitar, Tamboura, Tape Loops
> Starr: Ludwig Oyster Black Pearl Drums
> Martin: Piano

LEGACY AND INFLUENCE

In 2006, *Pitchfork* ranked "Tomorrow Never Knows" as #19 on the Web magazine's list of *The 200 Greatest Songs of the 1960s*.

In 2006, *Q Magazine* ranked "Tomorrow Never Knows" as #75 on the magazine's list of *The 100 Greatest Songs of All Time*.

In 2010, *Rolling Stone* ranked "Tomorrow Never Knows" as #18 on the magazine's list of *The Beatles' 100 Greatest Songs*.

ALBUM APPEARANCES: *Revolver* (U.K.); *Revolver* (U.S.); *Anthology 2*; *Love*; *Tomorrow Never Knows*.

See also: *Revolver* (U.K. LP).

Tomorrow Never Knows (LP)

July 24, 2012, Apple
Tomorrow Never Knows is a compilation album released exclusively in digital format on iTunes on July 24, 2012. It also marks the Beatles' first compilation since the release of *The Capitol Albums, Volume 2* in 2006.

BACKGROUND

Borrowing its title from the intensely psychedelic closing number from the Beatles' *Revolver* album, *Tomorrow Never Knows* was billed on the band's website as "the Beatles' most influential rock songs in one powerful collection." A downloadable promotional video for "Hey Bulldog" was released in support of the album, with the compilation's liner notes including a prefatory note from the Foo Fighters' Dave Grohl. "If it weren't for the Beatles, I would not be a musician," Grohl writes. "It's as simple as that. From a very young age I became fascinated with their songs, and over the years have drowned myself in the depth of their catalogue. Their groove and their swagger. Their grace and their beauty. Their dark and their light. The Beatles seemed to be capable of anything. They knew no boundaries, and in that freedom they seemed to define what we now know today as 'Rock and Roll.'"

TRACK LISTING

"Revolution"; "Paperback Writer"; "And Your Bird Can Sing"; "Helter Skelter"; "Savoy Truffle"; "I'm Down"; "I've Got a Feeling" (*Let It Be . . . Naked* version); "Back in the USSR"; "You Can't Do That"; "It's All Too Much"; "She Said She Said"; "Hey Bulldog"; "Tomorrow Never Knows"; "The End" (*Anthology 3* version).

COVER ARTWORK

The cover art for *Tomorrow Never Knows* depicts the image of an orange vinyl record label inside a white LP sleeve, with the words "File Under: Rock" stamped on the sleeve.

CHART PERFORMANCE

U.K.: #44.
U.S.: #24.

See also: *The Capitol Albums, Volume 2* (Box Set).

Tours, 1960–1966

The Beatles began their touring career in 1960 in Scotland as "The Silver Bee-tles" (before Starr had joined), and as merely an opening act for other more popu-lar performers. Six years later when they had finished their final tour in the United States, they were performing as headliners and at enormous, sold-out venues around the world, but also suffering some criticism in the United States for Lennon's out-of-context remark about the Beatles' being more popular than Jesus.

JOHNNY GENTLE TOUR, SCOTLAND (1960)

At the behest of British promoter Larry Parnes, the Beatles' first manager Allan Williams was given the opportunity to promote a nine-date tour of Scotland in support of singer Johnny Gentle (born John Askew, 1936–). Needing an opening act, Williams offered the Silver Beetles the chance, after a hasty audition, to join the bill—which also included Ronnie Watt and the Chekkers Rock Dance Band—under the management and representation of Jacaranda Enterprises. For the first time in their career, the band had a manager, and, having borrowed the P.A. equip-ment from the Liverpool College of Art, they were about to embark upon their first concert tour.

For the tour, the Silver Beetles, save for Lennon and drummer Tommy Moore, adopted stage names. Sutcliffe dubbed himself Stuart de Staël, as an homage to Nicolas de Staël, the Russian abstract artist. McCartney took the name Paul Ramon, while Harrison called himself Carl Harrison in honor of his guitar hero, Carl Perkins.

The tour was an unqualified success for the unbilled Silver Beetles, who exhib-ited the electrifying stage presence of seasoned veterans. While Harrison and Moore lingered in the shadows with Sutcliffe—who was so uncomfortable onstage that he often played with his back to the audience—Lennon and McCartney single-handedly stole the show.

"Those two boys operated on a different frequency," Gentle recalled. "I used to watch them work the crowd as though they'd been doing it all their lives—and without any effort other than their amazing talent. I'd never seen anything like it. They were so tapped into what each other was doing and could sense their part-ner's next move, they just read each other like a book" (Spitz 2005, 190).

Dates

May 20—Town Hall, Alloa

May 21—Northern Meeting Ballroom, Inverness

May 23—Dalrymple Hall, Fraserburgh

May 25—St. Thomas' Hall, Keith

May 26—Town Hall, Forres

May 27—Regal Ballroom, Nairn

May 28—Rescue Hall, Peterhead

Standard Set List

"It Doesn't Matter Anymore"

"Raining in My Heart"

"I Need Your Love Tonight"

"Poor Little Fool"

"(I Don't Know Why) But I Do"

"Come on Everybody"

"He'll Have to Go"

WINTER TOUR, SCOTLAND (1963)

Booked by the Cana Variety Agency for £42 per night, the Beatles' second bona fide concert tour included five shows in January 1963, although the first event, scheduled for the Longmore Hall in Keith, was canceled because of inclement weather. As Lennon later recalled, "Touring was a relief. We were beginning to feel stale and cramped. We'd get tired of one stage and be deciding to pack up when another stage would come up. We'd outlived the Hamburg stage and hated going back to Hamburg those last two times" (Harry 1992, 656).

Details about the Beatles' standard set list for their January 1963 Scottish tour have been lost to the shadows of time. As Gerry Scanlon, one of the attendees at the Aberdeen concert remembered,

> They still had a lot of rough edges and the sound system wasn't perfect, so they got a bit of a mixed reaction, but you could tell they had loads of energy. Most of the songs they did were by other people, like Chuck Berry, and Lennon and McCartney had still to write their biggest songs. But I'm still glad I was there. (Drysdale 2013)

The band's Winter U.K. Tour ensued immediately after the conclusion of their Scottish dates.

Dates

January 3—Two Red Shoes Ballroom, Elgin

January 4—Town Hall, Dingwall

Beatles fans try to break through a police line at Buckingham Palace in London on October 26, 1965, where the stars were each due to receive the Member of the British Empire (MBE) decoration from the Queen. (AFP/Getty Images)

January 5—Museum Hall, Bridge of Allan
January 6—Beach Ballroom, Aberdeen

WINTER TOUR, U.K. (1963)

In contrast with their comparatively brief January 1963 Scottish tour, the Beatles' Winter U.K. Tour saw the band enjoying much larger crowds at succeeding concert venues, with several of the events selling out in advance. The Beatles were paid £50 per event, a slightly larger fee than their previous tour. As with the January 1963 Scottish tour, the Beatles' standard set list remains unclear, although their fans relished their memories of the concerts some 50 years later. As Ian M. Millington recalled about the Beatles' concert in Mold, Flintshire:

> My enduring memories are: having to go to the pub across the alley to get a crate of beer and a bottle of Scotch for the bands because the Beatles could not go out without being mobbed by the girls that were outside in the cold; seeing John Lennon eating a hot dog covered with tomato ketchup whilst still wearing his leather gloves; seeing John Lennon signing his autograph on a girl's thigh;

getting the autographs of John, Paul and Ringo in the band room; catching George Harrison at the top of the stairs as he left early to visit his auntie in Hawarden on the way home to Liverpool. (BBC 2009)

Dates

January 10—Grafton Rooms, Liverpool
January 11—Cavern Club, Liverpool
January 11—Plaza Ballroom, Old Hill
January 12—Invicta Ballroom, Chatham
January 14—Civic Hall, Wirral
January 17—Cavern Club, Liverpool
January 17—Majestic Ballroom, Birkenhead
January 18—Floral Hall, Morecambe
January 19—Town Hall, Whitchurch
January 20—Cavern Club, Liverpool
January 23—Cavern Club, Liverpool
January 24—Assembly Hall, Flintshire
January 25—Cooperative Hall, Darwen
January 26—El Rio Club, Macclesfield
January 26—King's Hall, Stoke-on-Trent
January 27—Three Coins Club, Manchester
January 28—Majestic Ballroom, Newcastle-upon-Tyne
January 30—Cavern Club, Liverpool
January 31—Majestic Ballroom, Birkenhead
February 1—Assembly Rooms, Tamworth
February 1—Maney Hall, Sutton Coldfield

HELEN SHAPIRO TOUR, U.K. (1963)

Manager Brian Epstein succeeded in staging the Beatles' third concert tour through promoter Arthur Howes, who was seeking supporting acts for 16-year-old British pop sensation Helen Shapiro. When the package tour began, Shapiro was the headlining act, while the Beatles were fourth on a bill that included Danny Williams, Kenny Lynch, the Honeys, the Kestrels, and the Red Price Band. By the end of the tour, though, "Please Please Me" had worked its magic, and the Beatles were pop stars in their own right. As the *New Musical Express*' Gordon Sampson later reported, the Beatles ended up dominating the last several concerts on the tour, so much so that "the audience repeatedly called for them while other artists were performing" (Spitz 2005, 370).

For Starr, the tour proved to be a means for establishing himself as a bona fide member of the band. As he later recalled, "I was still the odd one out, the new boy. But the togetherness of the tour helped a lot. It made me feel more part of a team. At first I worried about who I'd share with at our hotels, but mostly it was me in with Paul, and George with John sharing another room" (Harry 1992, 657). For Lennon, "It really was a relief to get out of Liverpool and try something new. Back home we'd worked night after night on the same cramped stage. Bradford wasn't very far away, but at least it was different as a field. We'd all started feeling tired, jaded, tied down with the club scenes. Tour, with a different venue each night, was a real lift" (Harry 1992, 657, 658).

Dates
February 2—Gaumont, Bradford

February 5—Gaumont, Doncaster

February 6—Granada, Bedford

February 7—Regal, Kirkgate

February 8—ABC, Carlisle

February 9—Empire, Sunderland

February 23—Granada, Mansfield

February 24—Coventry Theatre, Coventry

February 26—Gaumont, Taunton

February 27—Rialto, York

February 28—Granada, Shrewsbury

March 1—Odeon, Southport

March 2—City Hall, Sheffield

March 3—Gaumont, Hanley

Standard Set List
"Chains"

"Keep Your Hands Off My Baby"

"A Taste of Honey"

"Please Please Me"

TOMMY ROE/CHRIS MONTEZ TOUR, U.K. (1963)

Following the Beatles' impressive turn on the recent Helen Shapiro tour, Arthur Howes immediately booked the group as a supporting act for American pop stars Tommy Roe and Chris Montez. The Beatles joined the Viscounts, Debbie Lee, the Terry Young Combo, and Tony Marsh on the package tour's bill. As the tour progressed, the Beatles continued to grow in popularity. As Beatlemania came into full force with "Please Please Me," the tour's promoter Howes shifted the bill in order to take advantage of the Beatles' incipient fame, much to the chagrin of Roe and Montez (Beatles 2000, 94).

Dates
March 9—Granada, East Ham
March 10—Hippodrome, Birmingham
March 12—Granada, Bedford
March 13—Rialto, York
March 14—Gaumont, Wolverhampton
March 15—Colston Hall, Bristol
March 16—City Hall, Sheffield
March 17—Embassy, Peterborough
March 18—Regal, Gloucester
March 19—Regal, Cambridge
March 20—ABC, Romford
March 21—ABC, Croydon
March 22—Gaumont, Doncaster
March 23—City Hall, Newcastle-upon-Tyne
March 24—Empire, Liverpool
March 26—Granada, Mansfield
March 27—ABC, Northampton
March 28—ABC, Exeter
March 29—Odeon, Lewisham
March 30—Guildhall, Portsmouth
March 31—De Montfort Hall, Leicester

Standard Set List
"Love Me Do"
"Misery"
"A Taste of Honey"
"Do You Want to Know a Secret"
"Please Please Me"
"I Saw Her Standing There"

SPRING TOUR, U.K. (1963)

The Beatles' Spring 1963 U.K. Tour was marked by the birth of Lennon's first son Julian in early April, as well as the band's first meeting with the Rolling Stones.

The tour also found the band continuing to grow their U.K. audience, as evidenced by *The Middleton Guardian*'s review of the band's April 11, 1963, concert:

> The music was deafening and the record fans were keyed up to a fever pitch. Almost hysterical enthusiasm hit you in the face as you walked in, but promoter Barry Chaytow had taken great care in making sure that if his patrons got over-excited there were sufficient "bouncers" to take care of the trouble. He could have saved himself a great deal of expense in that direction, because they were not needed. The teenagers were there to see and hear the Beatles and everything else became secondary. The boys and girls certainly got their money's worth. This group which turned professional almost as soon as it was formed two years ago has carved itself two unforgettable niches in the charts with "Love Me Do" and "Please, Please Me." Though their earlier work was confined to backing other artists on the Continent, they have now earned a place in show business with their undeniable talent and unassuming manner.

On April 14, the Beatles saw the Rolling Stones perform for the first time, taking in their show at the Crawdaddy Club in Richmond. As Harrison later recalled,

> We'd been at Teddington taping *Thank Your Lucky Stars*, miming to "From Me to You," and we went to Richmond afterwards and met them. They were still on the club scene, stomping about, doing R&B tunes. The music they were playing was more like we'd been doing before we'd got out of our leather suits to try and get onto record labels and television. We'd calmed down by then. (Beatles 2000, 101)

As McCartney added, "Mick [Jagger] tells the tale of seeing us there with long suede coats that we'd picked up in Hamburg, coats that no one could get in England. He thought, 'Right—I want to be in the music business; I want one of those coats'" (Beatles 2000, 101).

Dates
April 2—Azena Ballroom, Sheffield
April 4—Roxburgh Hall, Buckingham
April 5—Swimming Baths, Leyton, London
April 6—Pavilion Gardens, Buxton
April 7—Savoy Ballroom, Portsmouth
April 9—Gaumont State Cinema, Kilburn, London
April 10—Majestic Ballroom, Birkenhead
April 11—Cooperative Hall, Middleton
April 12—Cavern Club, Liverpool
April 15—Riverside Dancing Club, Tenbury Wells
April 17—Majestic Ballroom, Luton

April 18—Swimming Sound '63, Royal Albert Hall, London
April 19—King's Hall, Stoke-on-Trent
April 20—Mersey View Pleasure Grounds, Warrington
April 21—NME Poll Winners Concert, Empire Pool, Wembley
April 21—Pigalle Club, Piccadilly, London
April 23—Floral Hall, Southport
April 24—Majestic Ballroom, Finsbury Park, London
April 25—Fairfield Hall, Croydon
April 26—Music Hall, Shrewsbury
April 27—Memorial Hall, Northwich
May 11—Imperial Ballroom, Nelson
May 14—Rink Ballroom, Sunderland
May 15—Royalty Theatre, Chester
May 17—Grosvenor Rooms, Norwich

Standard Set List
"I Saw Her Standing There"
"Sweet Little Sixteen"
"Chains"
"Beautiful Dreamer"
"Misery"
"Hey Good Lookin' "
"Love Me Do"
"Baby It's You"
"Three Cool Cats"
"Please Please Me"
"Some Other Guy"
"Ask Me Why"
"Roll Over Beethoven"
"A Taste of Honey"
"Boys"
"Keep Your Hands Off My Baby"
"Do You Want to Know a Secret"
"From Me to You"
"Long Tall Sally"

ROY ORBISON/BEATLES TOUR, U.K. (1963)

Following on the heels of their Spring UK Tour, the Beatles' 1963 tour with American rockabilly star Roy Orbison saw the emergence of British Beatlemania.

The Beatles pose with Roy Orbison and Gerry and the Pacemakers backstage in their dressing room during a tour of the United Kingdom in May 1963. From left to right are: Paul McCartney, Freddie Marsden (behind), George Harrison, Gerry Marsden, Ringo Starr (back), Les Maguire (back), John Lennon, John "Les" Chadwick and Roy Orbison. (Harry Hammond/V&A Images/Getty Images)

Arranged via Manchester's Kennedy Street Enterprises, the bill-toppers were originally slated to be such acts as Duane Eddy, Ben E. King, and the Four Seasons. By the time that Orbison had been slated as the headliner, the Beatles' star had begun to shine considerably in their homeland, and Orbison agreed to share the top of the bill with the Fab Four. The package tour was rounded out by Gerry and the Pacemakers, David Macbeth, Louise Cordet, Erkey Grant, Ian Crawford, the Terry Young Combo, and Tony Marsh. It was during the Orbison tour that the Beatles began being pelted by jelly babies after Harrison remarked in a recent television appearance that he enjoyed the candied sweets. With the emergence of Beatlemania in Great Britain, the group was also serenaded during their shows with a torrent of screams from their adoring female fans—so much so that they could scarcely be heard above the din.

Dates
May 18—Adelphi, Slough
May 19—Gaumont, Hanley

May 20—Gaumont, Southampton

May 22—Gaumont, Ipswich

May 23—Odeon, Nottingham

May 24—Granada, Walthamstow

May 25—City Hall, Sheffield

May 26—Empire, Liverpool

May 28—Gaumont, Worcester

May 29—Rialto, York

May 30—Odeon, Manchester

May 31—Odeon, Southend-on-Sea

June 1—Granada, Tooting

June 2—Hippodrome, Brighton

June 3—Granada, Woolwich

June 4—Town Hall, Birmingham

June 5—Odeon, Leeds

June 7—Odeon, Glasgow

June 8—City Hall, Newcastle-upon-Tyne

June 9—King George's Hall, Blackburn

Standard Set List

"Some Other Guy"

"Do You Want to Know a Secret"

"Love Me Do"

"From Me to You"

"Please Please Me"

"I Saw Her Standing There"

"Twist and Shout"

SUMMER TOUR, U.K. (1963)

With the Roy Orbison tour having just been completed, the Beatles immediately returned to the road for a summer swing through the United Kingdom. They were supported on the bill by the Colin Anthony Combo and Chet and the Triumphs. Tony Philbin, a bartender at the Palace Theatre Club, recalled the Beatles' performance during this period:

> They were superb and the highlight for me was John Lennon singing "Twist and Shout." He really belted it out and it made the hairs on the back of my neck stand on end. The place was electric and they were so raw—I'd never seen anything

like it before. We were used to seeing crooners so it was like a breath of fresh air when the Beatles arrived. It was very exciting because they weren't polished at all, and it was that sheer energy that made the night so special and memorable. The place was in chaos with hordes of teenagers, mainly girls, screaming—which was unusual for the Theatre Club as it was a members club and the audience was generally older. Other staff had difficulty getting in due to the huge crowds milling about outside. The screaming could be heard in the club and every word the Beatles sung could be heard outside for the unfortunate people without tickets. (*Manchester Evening News* 2005)

The tour concluded on September 15 at London's Royal Albert Hall, where the Beatles were headlining the afternoon show entitled "The Great Pop Prom." An annual fund-raising event held by the Printers' Pension Corporation, "The Great Pop Prom" also featured the Rolling Stones, with whom the Beatles shared a photo session that same day. "The Great Pop Prom" marked the only occasion in which the two legendary bands performed during the same concert. As McCartney later recalled, "Standing up on those steps behind the Albert Hall in our new gear, the smart trousers, the rolled collar. Up there with the Rolling Stones we were thinking, 'This is it—London! The Albert Hall! We felt like gods!'" (Miles 1997, 120).

Dates

June 10—Pavilion, Bath

June 12—Grafton Rooms, Liverpool

June 13—Palace Theatre Club, Cheshire

June 13—Southern Sporting Club, Manchester

June 14—Tower Ballroom, New Brighton

June 15—City Hall, Salisbury

June 16—Odeon Cinema, Romford

June 21—Odeon Cinema, Guildford

June 22—Town Hall, Monmouthshire

June 25—Astoria Ballroom, Middlesbrough

June 26—Majestic Ballroom, Newcastle-upon-Tyne

June 28—Queen's Hall, Leeds

June 30—ABC Cinema, Great Yarmouth

July 5—Plaza Ballroom, Old Hill

July 6—Memorial Hall, Northwich

July 7—ABC Theatre, Blackpool

July 8—Winter Gardens, Margate

July 9—Winter Gardens, Margate

July 10—Winter Gardens, Margate

July 11—Winter Gardens, Margate
July 12—Winter Gardens, Margate
July 13—Winter Gardens, Margate
July 14—ABC Theatre, Blackpool
July 19—Ritz Ballroom, Flintshire
July 20—Ritz Ballroom, Flintshire
July 21—Queen's Theatre, Blackpool
July 22—Odeon Theatre, Weston-super-Mare
July 23—Odeon Theatre, Weston-super-Mare
July 24—Odeon Theatre, Weston-super-Mare
July 25—Odeon Theatre, Weston-super-Mare
July 26—Odeon Theatre, Weston-super-Mare
July 27—Odeon Theatre, Weston-super-Mare
July 28—ABC Cinema, Great Yarmouth
July 31—Imperial Ballroom, Nelson
August 2—Grafton Rooms, Liverpool
August 3—Cavern Club, Liverpool
August 4—Queen's Theatre, Blackpool
August 5—Abbotsfield Park, Urmston
August 6—The Springfield Ballroom, Jersey, Channel Islands
August 7—The Springfield Ballroom, Jersey, Channel Islands
August 8—Candie Gardens, Guernssey, Channel Islands
August 9—The Springfield Ballroom, Jersey, Channel Islands
August 10—The Springfield Ballroom, Jersey, Channel Islands
August 11—ABC Theatre, Blackpool
August 12—Odeon Cinema, Caernarvonshire
August 13—Odeon Cinema, Caernarvonshire
August 14—Odeon Cinema, Caernarvonshire
August 15—Odeon Cinema, Caernarvonshire
August 16—Odeon Cinema, Caernarvonshire
August 17—Odeon Cinema, Caernarvonshire
August 18—Princess Theatre Torquay
August 19—Gaumont Cinema, Bournemouth
August 20—Gaumont Cinema, Bournemouth
August 21—Gaumont Cinema, Bournemouth
August 22—Gaumont Cinema, Bournemouth
August 23—Gaumont Cinema, Bournemouth
August 24—Gaumont Cinema, Bournemouth

August 25—ABC Cinema, Blackpool
August 26—Odeon Cinema, Southport
August 27—Odeon Cinema, Southport
August 28—Odeon Cinema, Southport
August 29—Odeon Cinema, Southport
August 30—Odeon Cinema, Southport
August 31—Odeon Cinema, Southport
September 4—Gaumont Cinema, Worcester
September 5—Gaumont Cinema, Taunton
September 6—Odeon Cinema, Luton
September 7—Fairfield Hall, Croydon
September 8—ABC Theatre, Blackpool
September 13—Public Hall, Preston
September 14—Memorial Hall, Northwich
September 15—Great Pop Prom, Royal Albert Hall, London

Standard Set List
"Roll Over Beethoven"
"Thank You Girl"
"Chains"
"A Taste of Honey"
"She Loves You"
"Baby It's You"
"From Me to You"
"Boys"
"I Saw Her Standing There"
"Twist and Shout"

MINI-TOUR OF SCOTLAND (1963)

Promoted by Albert Bonici, the Beatles' October 1963 Mini-Tour of Scotland included Mike Berry on the bill, along with Freddy Starr and the Midnighters as a supporting act. The band followed up their Scottish concerts with their 1963 Tour of Sweden.

Dates
October 5—Concert Hall, Glasgow
October 6—Carlton, Kirkealdy
October 7—Caird Hall, Dundee

Standard Set List

"Roll Over Beethoven"
"Thank You Girl"
"Chains"
"A Taste of Honey"
"She Loves You"
"Baby It's You"
"From Me to You"
"Boys"
"I Saw Her Standing There"
"Twist and Shout"

TOUR OF SWEDEN (1963)

The Beatles' Tour of Sweden in October 1963 marked the group's first official tour abroad. As with the band's recently completed Mini-Tour of Scotland, Berry joined them on the bill, along with Ken Levy and the Phantoms and Trio Me Bumba, a Swedish act.

Dates

October 25—Nya Aulan, Karlstad
October 26—Kungliga Hall, Stockholm
October 27—Cirkus, Goteborg
October 28—Borashallen, Boras
October 29—Sporthallen, Eskilstuna

Standard Set List

"Long Tall Sally"
"Please Please Me"
"I Saw Her Standing There"
"From Me to You"
"A Taste of Honey"
"Chains"
"Boys"
"She Loves You"
"Twist and Shout"

AUTUMN TOUR, U.K. (1963)

Having returned from their October 1963 Tour of Sweden, the Beatles began their fourth British tour of the year. The package tour also featured Peter Jay and the

Jaywalkers, the Brook Brothers with the Rhythm and Blues Quartet, the Vernons Girls, the Kestrels, and comedian Frank Berry. After the Cheltenham performance on November 1, the *Daily Mirror* sported the headline "Beatlemania!: It's Happening Everywhere—Even in Sedate Cheltenham."

Dates

November 1—Odeon, Cheltenham

November 2—City Hall, Sheffield

November 3—Odeon, Leeds

November 5—Adelphi, Slough

November 6—ABC, Northampton

November 7—Adelphi, Dublin

November 8—Ritz, Belfast

November 9—Granada, East Ham

November 10—Hippodrome, Birmingham

November 13—ABC, Plymouth

November 14—ABC, Exeter

November 15—Colston Hall, Bristol

November 16—Winter Gardens, Bournemouth

November 17—Coventry Theatre, Coventry

November 19—Gaumont, Wolverhampton

November 20—ABC, Ardwick

November 21—ABC, Carlisle

November 22—Globe, Stockton-on-Tees

November 23—City Hall, Newcastle-upon-Tyne

November 24—ABC, Hull

November 26—Regal, Cambridge

November 27—Rialto, York

November 28—ABC, Lincoln

November 29—ABC, Huddersfield

November 30—Empire, Sunderland

December 1—De Montfort Hall, Leicester

December 3—Guildhall, Portsmouth

December 7—Odeon, Liverpool

December 8—Odeon, Lewisham

December 9—Odeon, Southend-on-Sea

December 10—Gaumont, Doncaster

December 11—Futurist, Scarborough

December 12—Odeon, Nottingham
December 13—Gaumont, Southampton

Standard Set List
"From Me to You"
"I Saw Her Standing There"
"All My Loving"
"Roll Over Beethoven"
"Boys"
"Till There Was You"
"She Loves You"
"This Boy"
"I Want to Hold Your Hand"
"Money (That's What I Want)"
"Twist and Shout"

WORLD TOUR (1964)

The Beatles' only world tour began on June 4, 1964, and took the Fab Four to the Netherlands, Hong Kong, Australia, and New Zealand. On June 3, the day after the recording sessions for *A Hard Day's Night* concluded, Starr collapsed from exhaustion during a photo session, later being diagnosed with acute tonsillitis. Starr's illness forced him to miss the Beatles' concerts in Denmark, the Netherlands, Hong Kong, and part of their Australia leg. During his absence, Jimmie Nicol filled in as his replacement as the band's drummer. Nicol enjoyed his brief taste of celebrity, later recalling that Lennon "drank in excess. In Denmark, for example, his head was a balloon! He had drunk so much the night before, he was on stage sweating like a pig." During Starr's absence, McCartney sent the fallen drummer a telegram: "Didn't think we could miss you so much. Get well soon" (The Internet Beatles Album 1995).

In Auckland, New Zealand, the Beatles attended a civic reception held by Mayor Dove-Myer Robinson at the city's Town Hall, during which the Beatles famously waved to a crowd of more than 7,000 enthusiastic well-wishers.

Dates
June 4—Tivoli Gardens, Copenhagen, Denmark
June 6—Exhibition Hall, Blokker, Denmark
June 10—Princess Theatre, Hong Kong
June 12—Centennial Hall, Adelaide, Australia
June 13—Centennial Hall, Adelaide, Australia

June 15—Festival Hall, Melbourne, Australia
June 18—Sydney Stadium, Sydney, Australia
June 19—Sydney Stadium, Sydney, Australia
June 20—Sydney Stadium, Sydney, Australia
June 22—Town Hall, Wellington, New Zealand
June 23—Town Hall, Wellington, New Zealand
June 24—Town Hall, Auckland, New Zealand
June 25—Town Hall, Auckland, New Zealand
June 26—Town Hall, Dunedin, New Zealand
June 27—Majestic Theatre, Christchurch, New Zealand
June 29—Festival Hall, Brisbane, Australia
June 30—Festival Hall, Brisbane, Australia

Standard Set List
"Twist and Shout"
"I Want to Hold Your Hand"
"I Saw Her Standing There"
"You Can't Do That"
"All My Loving"
"I Wanna Be Your Man"
"She Loves You"
"Till There Was You"
"Roll Over Beethoven"
"Can't Buy Me Love"
"This Boy"
"Long Tall Sally"

AMERICAN TOUR (1964)

The Beatles' first American concert tour began in San Francisco on August 19, 1964, the same city in which they brought their touring life to a close just two years later at Candlestick Park in August 1966. The Fab Four broke a number of attendance and box-office records, with the concert bill featuring such supporting acts as Jackie DeShannon, the Righteous Brothers, the Bill Black Combo, and the Exciters.

Dates
August 19—Cow Palace, San Francisco
August 20—Convention Hall, Las Vegas

August 21—Coliseum, Seattle
August 22—Empire Stadium, Vancouver
August 23—Hollywood Bowl, Los Angeles
August 26—Red Rock Stadium, Denver
August 27—The Gardens, Cincinnati
August 28—Forest Hills Stadium, New York
August 30—Convention Hall, Atlantic City
September 2—Conventional Hall, Philadelphia
September 3—State Fair Coliseum, Indianapolis
September 4—Auditorium, Milwaukee
September 5—International Amphitheatre, Chicago
September 6—Olympia Stadium, Detroit
September 7—Maple Leaf Gardens, Toronto
September 8—Forum, Montreal
September 11—Gator Bowl, Jacksonville
September 12—Boston Gardens, Boston
September 13—Civic Center, Baltimore
September 14—Civic Arena, Pittsburgh
September 15—Public Auditorium, Cleveland
September 16—City Park Stadium, New Orleans
September 17—Municipal Stadium, Kansas City
September 18—Memorial Coliseum, Dallas
September 20—Paramount Theatre, New York

Standard Set List
"Twist and Shout"
"I Want to Hold Your Hand"
"I Saw Her Standing There"
"You Can't Do That"
"All My Loving"
"I Wanna Be Your Man"
"She Loves You"
"Till There Was You"
"Roll Over Beethoven"
"Can't Buy Me Love"
"This Boy"
"Long Tall Sally"

AUTUMN TOUR, U.K. (1964)

Promoted by Arthur Howes, the Beatles' Autumn 1964 Tour of Great Britain began on Lennon's 24th birthday and marked the only occasion that the group toured their homeland that year. Having recently completed their first American tour, the Beatles were supported by Mary Wells, the Rustiks, Michael Haslam, Sounds Incorporated, and Tommy Quickly and the Remo Four.

Dates

October 9—Gaumont, Bradford

October 10—De Montfort Hall, Leicester

October 11—Odeon, Birmingham

October 13—ABC, Wigan

October 14—ABC, Manchester

October 15—Globe, Stockton-on-Tees

October 16—ABC, Hull

October 19—ABC, Edinburgh

October 20—Caird Hall, Dundee

October 21—Odeon, Glasgow

October 22—Odeon, Leeds

October 23—Gaumont State, Kilburn

October 24—Granada, Walthamstow

October 25—Hippodrome, Brighton

October 28—ABC, Exeter

October 29—ABC, Plymouth

October 30—Gaumont, Bournemouth

October 31—Gaumont, Ipswich

November 1—Astoria, Finsbury Park

November 2—King's Hall, Belfast

November 4—Ritz, Luton

November 5—Odeon, Nottingham

November 6—Gaumont, Southampton

November 7—Capitol, Cardiff

November 8—Empire, Liverpool

November 9—City Hall, Sheffield

November 10—Colston Hall, Bristol

Standard Set List
"Twist and Shout"
"I'm a Loser"
"Baby's in Black"
"Everybody's Trying to Be My Baby"
"Can't Buy Me Love"
"Honey Don't"
"I Feel Fine"
"She's a Woman"
"A Hard Day's Night"
"Rock and Roll Music"
"Long Tall Sally"

EUROPEAN TOUR (1965)

The Beatles' final European tour occurred during the summer of 1965, with the band playing brief stints in France, Italy, and Spain. The Yardbirds joined the Beatles on the package tour's bill. For the Beatles, the stifling nature of touring under the shadow of their incredible celebrity was beginning to take its toll. Later that year, the band embarked on their second American tour.

Dates
June 20—Palais De Sports, Paris
June 22—Palais d'Hiver, Lyon
June 24—Velodromo, Milan
June 25—Palazzo dello Sport, Genoa
June 27—Teatro Adriano, Rome
June 28—Teatro Adriano, Rome
June 30—Palais des Fetes, Nice
July 2—Plaza de Toros de Madrid, Madrid
July 3—Plaza de Toros de Madrid, Madrid

Standard Set List
"Twist and Shout"
"She's a Woman"
"I'm a Loser"
"Can't Buy Me Love"
"Baby's in Black"
"I Wanna Be Your Man"

"A Hard Day's Night"
"Everybody's Trying to Be My Baby"
"Rock and Roll Music"
"I Feel Fine"
"Ticket to Ride"
"Long Tall Sally"

THE BEATLES' AMERICAN TOUR (1965)

After making yet another appearance on *The Ed Sullivan Show*, the Beatles' second American tour opened in spectacular fashion at New York City's Shea Stadium, where the band performed for 55,600 fans. Promoted by Sid Bernstein, the Beatles' Shea Stadium appearance set a world record for attendance and for gross revenue, with the Beatles earning $160,000 from a box-office take of some $304,000. The Beatles' supporting acts on the tour included Brenda Holloway and the King Curtis Band, Cannibal and the Headhunters, Sounds Incorporated, and the Young Rascals.

Dates
15 August—Shea Stadium, New York
17 August—Maple Leaf Gardens, Toronto
18 August—Atlanta Stadium, Georgia
19 August—Sam Houston Coliseum, Houston
20 August—White Sox Park, Chicago
21 August—Metropolitan Stadium, Minneapolis
22 August—Memorial Coliseum, Portland
28 August—Balboa Stadium, San Diego
29 August—Hollywood Bowl, Los Angeles
30 August—Hollywood Bowl, Los Angeles
31 August—Cow Palace, San Francisco

Standard Set List
"Twist and Shout"
"She's a Woman"
"I Feel Fine"
"Dizzy Miss Lizzy"
"Ticket to Ride"
"Everybody's Trying to Be My Baby"
"Can't Buy Me Love"

"Baby's in Black"
"I Wanna Be Your Man"
"A Hard Day's Night"
"Help!"
"I'm Down"

WINTER TOUR, U.K. (1965)

The Beatles' Winter 1965 British Tour was their last tour of their homeland, with their supporting acts including the Moody Blues, the Paramounts, the Koobas, Beryl Marsden and Steve Aldo, and the Marionettes. *Rubber Soul* was released on December 3, the same day that the Beatles embarked upon the nine-day tour. On December 12, the curtain closed in front of the band at the Capitol Cinema in Cardiff, Wales, ending the Beatles' final tour of the United Kingdom, as well as their last performance there, save for the May 1, 1966, *New Musical Express* Annual Poll-Winners Concert and the January 30, 1969, Rooftop Concert.

Dates
December 3—Odeon, Glasgow
December 4—City Hall, Newcastle-upon-Tyne
December 5—Empire, Liverpool
December 7—Apollo, Ardwick, Manchester
December 8—City Hall, Sheffield
December 9—Odeon, Birmingham
December 10—Odeon, Hammersmith
December 11—Astoria, Finsbury Park
December 12—Capitol, Cardiff

Standard Set List
"I Feel Fine"
"She's a Woman"
"If I Needed Someone"
"Act Naturally"
"Nowhere Man"
"Baby's in Black"
"Help!"
"We Can Work It Out"
"Yesterday"
"Day Tripper"
"I'm Down"

TOUR OF GERMANY AND JAPAN (1966)

The Beatles began the last year in their touring life with a brief tour of West Germany, Japan, and the Philippines in June and July 1966. It proved to be the first of two harrowing tours that saw them self-consciously choosing to perform their final live appearance before a paying audience at San Francisco's Candlestick Park on August 29, 1966. Their support acts for the tour were Cliff Bennett and the Rebel Rousers, along with Peter and Gordon.

For the band, the difficulties on the road that summer began almost immediately. On June 25, the Beatles played the Grugahalle in Essen. During the concert, the venue's bouncers began taking overzealous fans outside of the concert hall and beating them senseless. As the situation deteriorated, a pack of Luger-carrying police officers was dispatched to quell the very thugs who had been hired to provide security for the band in the first place. The tour continued in Japan, where the Beatles began a series of five concerts in Tokyo on June 30. A succession of death threats ensued after it was revealed that the band would be playing in the city's celebrated Budokan, the octagon-shaped arena that had been reserved for traditional Japanese martial arts. Many Japanese felt that it was a sacred venue that shouldn't be desecrated by Western rock 'n' roll music. Afraid that the world's most famous musicians might be injured—or, worse yet, perish—on their soil, the Japanese government overreacted in spectacular fashion, dispatching some 35,000 police officers to protect the Beatles during their brief visit. The bandmates were held as virtual prisoners in the Tokyo Hilton, and the concerts themselves were sterile affairs in which some 3,000 police had been distributed among the venue's 10,000 spectators in order to maintain control. With such an overwhelming police presence, the Japanese fans were reluctant to go berserk in the same fashion as their Western counterparts. Gone were the screams and tumult to which the band had become accustomed, and suddenly, without the comforting veil of teenage chaos and clamor, the Beatles could be heard, loudly and clearly, as an unhappy quartet of sloppy, out-of-tune musicians. As a surviving television broadcast of the first concert plainly demonstrates, their stage act by this juncture was simply awful (Lewisohn 1986, 192).

On July 3, the tour pressed on, with the Beatles bringing their show to the Philippines for the first time. After landing in Manila, the bandmates were inexplicably whisked away to a yacht that was owned by a local media mogul. After some two hours, Brian Epstein demanded that the group be removed from the vessel and provided with hotel accommodations in the city. When they finally checked into the Manila Hotel, the Beatles were blissfully unaware of an invitation from President Ferdinand Marcos and First Lady Imelda Marcos requesting their appearance at Malacañang Palace at 11 o'clock the following morning. But "since the British embassy fiasco," the group's assistant Peter Brown recalled, "the policy was never to go to those things" (Spitz 2005, 620). The next morning, the Beatles' entourage ignored further demands from Filipino officials that they go to the Palace, where the First Lady and some 200 children were now anxiously awaiting their appearance. After playing an afternoon concert for some 35,000 fans and an evening performance for another 50,000 spectators at José Rizal Memorial Stadium, the band started to realize that they were in dire straits when news reports began detailing their snubbing of the royal family.

Later that night, a genuinely contrite Epstein attempted to ameliorate the situation by expressing his regrets to the First Family on the Channel 5 News, but a burst of suspicious static rendered his apology all but unintelligible. The next day, the Beatles were suddenly ordered to pay income tax on concert receipts that they still hadn't received from Filipino promoter Ramon Ramos. Worse yet, their governmental security detail had been suspended, given their allegedly rude treatment of the First Lady, and the group and their entourage were left to their own devices as they rushed to the Manila International Airport in order to make their KLM flight to New Delhi. But their ordeal wasn't over yet. They were jostled by an angry mob as they made their way to immigration, and things became even more dicey on the tarmac, when Mal Evans and press officer Tony Barrow were removed from the plane shortly before takeoff. The Beatles had been declared "illegal immigrants" by the Filipino government, and Evans and Barrow spent some 40 minutes negotiating the band's way out of the country. Stultified by what they considered to be their near-death experience in the South Pacific, the group roundly blamed Epstein for the disastrous turn of events. When the Beatles finally arrived back in London on July 8, Harrison joked to a reporter that "we're going to have a couple of weeks to recuperate before we go and get beaten up by the Americans" (Lewisohn 1986, 195). At that early juncture, Harrison could not have begun to imagine how prophetic his words would prove to be.

Dates

June 24—Circus Krone, Munich, Germany

June 25—Grugahalle, Essen, Germany

June 26—Ernst Merck Halle, Hamburg, Germany

June 30—Budokan Hall, Tokyo, Japan

July 1—Budokan Hall, Tokyo, Japan

July 2—Budokan Hall, Tokyo, Japan

July 4—Rizal Memorial Football Stadium, Manila, Philippines

Standard Set List

"Rock and Roll Music"

"She's a Woman"

"If I Needed Someone"

"Baby's in Black"

"Day Tripper"

"I Feel Fine"

"Yesterday"

"I Wanna Be Your Man"

"Nowhere Man"

"Paperback Writer"

"I'm Down"

FINAL AMERICAN TOUR (1966)

For the Beatles, their final American Tour in August 1966 proved to be their most difficult moment in the history of their celebrity. For Lennon especially, the 1966 American Tour came to be known as the "Jesus Christ Tour," given the furor associated with his notorious remarks, originally published in the *London Evening Standard* and later republished in the United States in *Datebook*, that the Beatles were more popular than Jesus. During his infamous interview with Maureen Cleave,

Lennon remarked, "Christianity will go. It will vanish and shrink. . . . We're more popular than Jesus now; I don't know which will go first—rock and roll or Christianity. Jesus was all right, but his disciples were thick and ordinary. It's them twisting it that ruins it for me" (Lange 2001, 143). On August 29, the tour concluded in San Francisco, and it spelled the end of the Beatles' touring lives forever.

For the Beatles, the 1966 American Tour was fraught with a cultural backlash and what seemed, at times, like imminent danger. Things began ominously enough in New York's Shea Stadium, where, only one year earlier, they had played to a sold-out crowd. This time around, seats were visibly empty in the venue's upper echelons. On August 19, the band played a concert at

Paul McCartney, left, on bass guitar, and George Harrison, on six-string, perform at Chicago's International Amphitheatre on August 13, 1966, early in the band's troubled final U.S. tour. (AP Photo)

the Mid-South Coliseum in Memphis, Tennessee, where the Ku Klux Klan staged a protest, and a firecracker exploded on the stage. They momentarily thought that they were under attack, that one of them had been assassinated.

On Monday, August 29, the group performed at San Francisco's Candlestick Park before some 25,000 fans, with the Ronettes, the Remains, and the Cyrkle as their trio of opening acts. As with numerous other venues on the calamitous "Jesus Christ Tour," Candlestick Park hadn't sold out—in fact, there were some 10,000 conspicuously empty seats that day. Having privately decided that Candlestick Park would be the scene of their last concert, the Beatles good-naturedly photographed themselves in order to commemorate the occasion. Meanwhile, McCartney instructed Barrow to make a cassette recording of their final set. It was a blustery evening—complete with a full moon, no less—and the Beatles took the stage at 9:27 P.M., having been escorted onto the baseball diamond in an armored car with a security detail of some 200 police officers in tow. The stage itself was five-feet tall, with a six-foot high wire fence around the perimeter as an extra precautionary measure. The Beatles opened the concert with a searing rendition of "Rock and Roll Music," and, as Molyneux had done in St. Peter's Church Hall way back in July 1957, Barrow held his cassette player's tiny microphone aloft in front of the stage and recorded the show for posterity. Barrow's tape of the Beatles' 33-minute performance ran out of space less than a minute into "Long Tall Sally," the group's final number before a paying audience. After some 1,400 concerts, their lives as working rock 'n' rollers were suddenly over.

Dates

August 12—International Amphitheatre, Chicago

August 13—Olympia Stadium, Detroit

August 14—Municipal Stadium, Cleveland

August 15—Washington Stadium, Washington, D.C.

August 16—Philadelphia Stadium, Philadelphia

August 17—Maple Leaf Gardens, Toronto

August 18—Suffolk Downs Racecourse, Boston

August 19—Memphis Coliseum, Memphis

August 20—Crosley Field, Cincinnati

August 21—Busch Stadium, St. Louis

August 23—Shea Stadium, New York

August 24—Shea Stadium, New York

August 25—Seattle Coliseum, Seattle

August 28—Dodger Stadium, Los Angeles

August 29—Candlestick Park, San Francisco

Standard Set List

"Rock and Roll Music"

"She's a Woman"

"If I Needed Someone"

"Day Tripper"

"Baby's in Black"

"I Feel Fine"

"Yesterday"

"I Wanna Be Your Man"

"Nowhere Man"

"Paperback Writer"

"Long Tall Sally"

See also: "The Beatles Are Bigger than Jesus Christ"; *The Ed Sullivan Show* (TV Series); Epstein, Brian; Evans, Mal; The Rooftop Concert; *Rubber Soul* (U.K. LP); The Silver Beetles.

"12-Bar Original" (Harrison–Lennon–McCartney–Starr)

"12-Bar Original" was recorded during the sessions for *Rubber Soul* and remained unreleased until the Beatles' *Anthology* project during the 1990s. It is one of the very few songs credited to all four Beatles as composers.

AUTHORSHIP AND BACKGROUND

"12-Bar Original" was improvised by all four Beatles in the studio. Lennon later described the song during a radio interview as "some lousy 12-bar," while Starr remembered in an interview with Peter Palmiere that "we all wrote the track, and I have an acetate of one of the versions."

RECORDING SESSIONS

Produced by George Martin, "12-Bar Original" was recorded at Abbey Road Studios on November 4, 1965.

PERSONNEL

Lennon: Rickenbacker 325
McCartney: Höfner 500/1

Harrison: Gretsch Tennessean
Starr: Ludwig Oyster Black Pearl Drums
Martin: Harmonium

ALBUM APPEARANCE: *Anthology 2.*

See also: *The Beatles Anthology, Volume 2* (LP); *Rubber Soul* (U.K. LP).

20 Greatest Hits (LP)

October 11, 1982, Parlophone PCTC 260
October 18, 1982, Capitol SV 12245

20 Greatest Hits is a compilation album, now deleted from the Beatles' catalogue and superseded by the *1* compilation, that was released on October 11, 1982, in the United States and October 18, 1982, in the United Kingdom, where the album commemorated the 20th anniversary of the release of "Love Me Do."

BACKGROUND

20 Greatest Hits features variant U.S. and U.K. editions, given the different hit singles that topped the charts in each country—namely, the U.S.-only singles releases of "Eight Days a Week," "Yesterday," and "The Long and Winding Road." Due to length limitations, the U.S. edition includes an edited version of "Hey Jude," a five-minute track that was originally released in 1968 by Capitol Records as a "Pocket Disc" and sold in vending machines. As a bonus for audiophiles, *20 Greatest Hits* included the first true stereo mixes of "I Want to Hold Your Hand" and "I Feel Fine" to be released in the U.S. marketplace. An expanded version of the album, featuring 23 tracks, was released in Australia as *The Number Ones.*

TRACK LISTING (U.K.)

Side 1: "Love Me Do"; "From Me To You"; "She Loves You"; "I Want to Hold Your Hand"; "Can't Buy Me Love"; "A Hard Day's Night"; "I Feel Fine"; "Ticket to Ride"; "Help!"; "Day Tripper"; "We Can Work It Out."

Side 2: "Paperback Writer"; "Yellow Submarine"; "Eleanor Rigby"; "All You Need Is Love"; "Hello, Goodbye"; "Lady Madonna"; "Hey Jude"; "Get Back"; "The Ballad of John and Yoko."

TRACK LISTING (U.S.)

Side 1: "She Loves You"; "Love Me Do"; "I Want to Hold Your Hand"; "Can't Buy Me Love"; "A Hard Day's Night"; "I Feel Fine"; "Eight Days a Week";

"Ticket to Ride"; "Help!"; "Yesterday"; "We Can Work It Out"; "Paperback Writer."

Side 2: "Penny Lane"; "All You Need Is Love"; "Hello, Goodbye"; "Hey Jude" (Edited Version); "Get Back"; "Come Together"; "Let It Be"; "The Long and Winding Road."

COVER ARTWORK

The cover art for *20 Greatest Hits* features the band's name in stencil format with period photographs within the interior spaces of the letters.

CHART PERFORMANCE

U.K.: #10.

U.S.: #50 (certified by the RIAA as "2x Multi Platinum," with more than 2 million copies sold).

See also: *1* (LP).

"Twist and Shout" (Medley–Russell)

"Twist and Shout" is a song on the Beatles' *Please Please Me* album.

AUTHORSHIP AND BACKGROUND

Written by Phil Medley and Bert Russell, "Twist and Shout" was originally called "Shake It Up, Baby." The Isley Brothers scored a Top 20 hit with "Twist and Shout" in 1962.

RECORDING SESSIONS

Produced by George Martin, "Twist and Shout" was recorded at Abbey Road Studios in two takes on February 11, 1963, with an overdubbing session on February 20.

"Twist and Shout" was the last number to be recorded during the marathon session on February 11, 1963. As the studio personnel prepared to close the facility around 10 P.M., a shirtless Lennon settled in for one more number. With his voice cut to shreds—Martin described the performance as a "real larynx-tearer"—Lennon captured the vocal on the first take (Spitz 2005, 375). A second attempt at the song proved to be a nonstarter, and the band decided to call it an evening, having completed their work on *Please Please Me* in a little under 10 hours' worth of studio time.

In "Twist and Shout," a sense of sexual abandon is inherent in Lennon's scream-ing lead vocal. "Sure, I'm a cynic," Lennon remarked in April 1963. "What we play is rock and roll under a new name. Rock music is war, hostility, and conquest. We sing about love, but we mean sex, and the fans know it" (Badman 2001, 57).

As McCartney later recalled, "There's a power in John's voice there that cer-tainly hasn't been equaled since. And I know exactly why—it's because he worked his bollocks off that day. We left 'Twist and Shout' until the very last thing because we knew there was one take" (McCartney 1988, 11).

PERSONNEL

Lennon: Vocal, Rickenbacker 325
McCartney: Höfner 500/1, Backing Vocal
Harrison: Gretsch Duo-Jet, Backing Vocal
Starr: Premier Mahogany Duroplastic Drums

CHART PERFORMANCE

U.K.: "Back in the USSR"/"Twist and Shout"; June 25, 1976, Parlophone R 6016: #19. As the B-side of "Back in the USSR," "Twist and Shout" did not chart.

U.S.: "Twist and Shout"/"There's a Place"; March 2, 1964, Tollie 9001: #2.

ALBUM APPEARANCES: *Please Please Me*; *The Early Beatles*; *Rock 'n' Roll Music*; *The Beatles at the Hollywood Bowl*; *Live! at the Star-Club in Hamburg, Germany; 1962*; *On Air: Live at the BBC, Volume 2*.

See also: *Please Please Me* (LP); Royal Command Variety Performance.

"Two of Us" (Lennon–McCartney)

"Two of Us" is a song on the Beatles' *Let It Be* album.

AUTHORSHIP AND BACKGROUND

Written by McCartney, "Two of Us" memorializes Paul and Linda McCartney's lengthy driving trips around the English countryside during the late 1960s.

RECORDING SESSIONS

Produced by George Martin with postproduction by Phil Spector, the Beatles recorded "Two of Us" under the working title of "On Our Way Home" at Apple

Studio on January 31, 1969, after having conducted extensive rehearsals on January 24 and 25.

During the song's early stages, McCartney fashioned an electric guitar format for "Two of Us"—despite Johns' suggestion on the very first day of rehearsals that the composition might be more effectively rendered using acoustic guitars instead. In an early iteration of "Two of Us," McCartney adopted his "Elvis voice" in an up-tempo version that features Lennon on a lively rhythm guitar part. When the composer eventually acquiesced to Johns' acoustic arrangement, "Two of Us" fell into place rather quickly, with McCartney and Lennon sharing lead vocals.

For the song, McCartney crafted a superb middle-eight: "You and I have memories longer than the road that stretches out ahead." Intuitively recognizing that it was the song's most essential feature, McCartney had led the group in a 13-minute rehearsal of the middle-eight on January 25, 1969 (Sulpy and Schweighardt 1997, 260). Lennon later appended a whistling solo during the song's coda.

The *Let It Be . . . Naked* (2003) version of "Two of Us" consists of a remix of the January 31, 1969, Apple Studio recording. An alternate take of "Two of Us" is included on the "Fly on the Wall" disc as part of the album package associated with the *Let It Be . . . Naked* release.

PERSONNEL

Lennon: Gibson J-160E, Whistling
McCartney: Vocal, Martin D-28
Harrison: Fender Rosewood Telecaster
Starr: Ludwig Hollywood Maple Drums

LEGACY AND INFLUENCE

In 2010, *Rolling Stone* ranked "Two of Us" as #54 on the magazine's list of *The Beatles' 100 Greatest Songs*.

ALBUM APPEARANCES: *Let It Be*; *Anthology 3*; *Let It Be . . . Naked*.

See also: *Let It Be* (LP); *Let It Be . . . Naked* (LP); Lindsay-Hogg, Michael.

U

The U.S. Albums (Box Set)

January 21, 2014, Apple [Capitol] B00H8XF9I0

The U.S. Albums box set was released in January 2014 in celebration of the 50th anniversary of the Beatles' inaugural appearance on *The Ed Sullivan Show*, as well as the original release of *Meet the Beatles!*

BACKGROUND

The U.S. Albums includes Capitol Records' 13 American album releases. Eight of the albums had been included in *The Capitol Albums, Volume 1* and *The Capitol Albums, Volume 2*. The other five U.S. albums made their debut appearance on compact disc with this release, including *A Hard Day's Night*, *The Beatles' Story*, *Yesterday . . . and Today*, *Revolver*, and *Hey Jude*. As with *The Capitol Albums, Volume 1* and *The Capitol Albums, Volume 2*, the discs in *The U.S. Albums* feature mono and stereo versions of each recording, save for *The Beatles' Story* and *Hey Jude*, which are available only in stereo. The recordings in *The U.S. Albums* are partially culled from the original 1960s-era master recordings, as well as from the 2009 remasters as presented in *The Beatles Stereo Box Set* and *The Beatles in Mono*.

CONTENTS

Disc 1: *Meet the Beatles!*
Disc 2: The Beatles' Second Album
Disc 3: *A Hard Day's Night*
Disc 4: *Something New*
Disc 5: *The Beatles' Story*
Disc 6: *Beatles '65*
Disc 7: *The Early Beatles*
Disc 8: *Beatles VI*
Disc 9: *Help!*
Disc 10: *Rubber Soul*
Disc 11: *Yesterday . . . and Today*
Disc 12: *Revolver*
Disc 13: *Hey Jude*

CHART PERFORMANCE

U.S.: #48.

See also: *The Beatles' Second Album* (LP); *Beatles '65* (LP); *The Beatles Stereo Box Set*; *The Beatles' Story* (LP); *Beatles VI* (LP); *The Early Beatles* (LP); *A Hard Day's Night* (LP); *Help!* (U.S. LP); *Hey Jude* (LP); *Meet the Beatles!* (LP); *Revolver* (U.S. LP); *Rubber Soul* (U.S. LP); *Something New* (LP); *Yesterday . . . and Today* (LP).

V

Val Parnell's Sunday Night at the London Palladium (TV Series)

The explosive power of the Beatles was ignited before a national television audience of some 15 million viewers on the evening of October 13, 1963, when the band performed on the popular British variety show *Val Parnell's Sunday Night at the London Palladium*. The group played a four-song set that included three new tunes—"From Me to You," "I'll Get You," and "She Loves You"—and concluded with "Twist and Shout." The scene at the Palladium was pure pandemonium. By the end of the show, more than 2,000 frenzied fans had collected outside on Oxford Street. "Screaming girls launched themselves against the police—sending helmets flying and constables reeling," the *Daily Herald* reported. The next morning, the Beatles dominated the London headlines, with the *Daily Mirror* trumpeting "BEATLEMANIA!" on newsstands across the nation (Spitz 2005, 427, 428). On November 1, the *Daily Mirror* sported the headline yet again, announcing "Beatlemania!: It's Happening Everywhere—Even in Sedate Cheltenham." Canadian journalist Sandy Gardiner is often erroneously credited with coining the term "Beatlemania," which appeared in his *Ottawa Journal* article entitled "Heavy Disc Dose Spreads Disease in England" on November 9, 1963—nearly a month after the *Daily Mirror*'s headline made its way into print in London. In February 1964, American Beatlemania ensued with the Beatles' legendary performance on *The Ed Sullivan Show*.

See also: *The Ed Sullivan Show* (TV Series).

Voormann, Klaus (1938–)

Born on April 29, 1938, in Berlin, Klaus Voormann has enjoyed a long career as an artist, musician, and record producer. Along with his then-girlfriend Astrid Kirchherr and friend Jürgen Vollmer, he met the Beatles during their summer 1960 residency in Hamburg. After the advent of the Beatles' worldwide fame, he joined them in London, where he began working as a session musician and producer. From 1966 to 1969, he played as Manfred Mann's bassist, and in the 1970s produced three albums by the band Trio, who enjoyed an international hit with "Da Da Da" in 1979. In 1967, his cover artwork for the Beatles' *Revolver* album earned "Best

Album Cover/Graphic Arts" honors during the 9th Grammy Awards. In the 1970s and beyond, he performed on several albums by the former Beatles. He also served as a member of the Plastic Ono Band. During the mid-1990s, his cover artwork was commissioned for *The Beatles Anthology* project. In November 2002, he performed during the *Concert for George* at London's Royal Albert Hall. In 2009, he released his first solo album. Entitled *A Sideman's Journey*, the album features McCartney and Starr as guest musicians. In 2010, his life and work were explored in the television documentary *All You Need Is Klaus*, produced on Franco-German TV.

See also: Kirchherr, Astrid; *Revolver* (U.K. LP).

"Wait" (Lennon–McCartney)

"Wait" is a song on the Beatles' *Rubber Soul* album.

AUTHORSHIP AND BACKGROUND

Written by John Lennon and Paul McCartney, "Wait" was originally slated for release on the *Help!* album and then shelved—possibly being discarded in favor of "Dizzy Miss Lizzy"—only to be resurrected during the final stages of the *Rubber Soul* recording sessions.

Years later, McCartney laid claim to solely writing the composition, recalling that he had written "Wait" in the Bahamas during filming for the *Help!* feature film. McCartney remembered completing the song in the presence of actor Brandon de Wilde: "He was a nice guy who was fascinated by what we did. A sort of Brat Pack actor. We chatted endlessly, and I seem to remember writing 'Wait' in front of him, and him being interested to see it being written. I think it was my song. I don't remember John collaborating too much on it, although he could have" (Miles 1997, 278).

RECORDING SESSIONS

Produced by George Martin, "Wait" was originally recorded at Abbey Road Studios on June 17, 1965, during the final session for the *Help!* album. Needing one more song to complete the *Rubber Soul* project, the Beatles revisited "Wait" on November 11, 1964, overdubbing additional instrumentation onto the original track, which included vocals, guitars, bass, and drums. George Harrison remade his guitar part, which he accented with volume-pedal effects. Lennon and McCartney also double-tracked their vocals.

PERSONNEL

Lennon: Vocal, Rickenbacker 325
McCartney: Vocal, Höfner 500/1
Harrison: Gretsch Tennessean
Starr: Ludwig Oyster Black Pearl Drums, Maracas, Tambourine

ALBUM APPEARANCES: *Rubber Soul* (U.K.); *Rubber Soul* (U.S.).

See also: *Rubber Soul* (U.K. LP).

"We Can Work It Out" (Lennon–McCartney)

"We Can Work It Out" was the band's 10th consecutive #1 single in the United Kingdom, where it was released on December 3, 1965, as a double A-side with "Day Tripper," which also topped the charts. In the United States, where it was also released on December 3, 1965, "We Can Work It Out" was the Beatles' sixth consecutive #1 single. Along with "Day Tripper," it was released contemporaneously with *Rubber Soul*.

AUTHORSHIP AND BACKGROUND

Written by Lennon and McCartney, "We Can Work It Out" is an example of one of the songwriters' truly shared contributions. Jane Asher was the likely inspiration for McCartney's work on this composition.

As Lennon recalled, "Paul did the first half, I did the middle-eight. But you've got Paul writing, 'We can work it out / We can work it out' real optimistic, you know. And me, impatient, 'Life is very short and there's no time / for fussing and fighting, my friend' " (Lennon and Ono 2000, 177).

As McCartney remembered,

> I wrote it as more of an up-tempo thing, country and western. I had the basic idea, the title, had a couple of verses, then I took it to John to finish it off and we wrote the middle together, which is nice—"Life is very short / And there's no time for fussing and fighting, my friend." Then it was George Harrison's idea to put the middle into waltz time, like a German waltz. The lyrics might have been personal. It is often a good way to talk to someone or to work your thoughts out. It saves you going to a psychiatrist, you allow yourself to say what you might not say in person. (Miles 1997, 210)

RECORDING SESSIONS

Produced by George Martin, "We Can Work It Out" was recorded at Abbey Road Studios on October 20, 1965, with an additional overdubbing session on October 29. The Beatles spent some 11 hours recording the song, allotting a significant amount of time for a single track during these pre-*Sgt. Pepper* days.

PERSONNEL

Lennon: Vocal, Gibson J-160E, Harmonium
McCartney: Vocal, Höfner 500/1
Harrison: Gibson J-160E
Starr: Ludwig Oyster Black Pearl Drums, Tambourine

CHART PERFORMANCE

U.K.: "We Can Work It Out"/"Day Tripper"; December 3, 1965, Parlophone R 5389: #1.

U.S.: "We Can Work It Out"/"Day Tripper"; December 6, 1965, Capitol 5555: #1 (certified by the RIAA as "Gold," with more than 500,000 copies sold).

LEGACY AND INFLUENCE

In 1966, the Beatles received an Ivor Novello Award, awarded annually by the British Academy of Songwriters, Composers, and Authors, for "We Can Work It Out."

In 2010, *Rolling Stone* ranked "We Can Work It Out" as #30 on the magazine's list of *The Beatles' 100 Greatest Songs*.

ALBUM APPEARANCES: *Yesterday . . . and Today*; *A Collection of Beatles Oldies*; *The Beatles, 1962–1966*; *20 Greatest Hits*; *Past Masters, Volume 2*; *1*.

See also: *Rubber Soul* (U.K. LP).

"What Goes On" (Lennon–McCartney–Starr)

"What Goes On" is a song on the Beatles' *Rubber Soul* album.

AUTHORSHIP AND BACKGROUND

Written by Lennon during his Quarry Men days with later assistance from McCartney and Starr, "What Goes On" was the first of three songs for which Starr enjoyed composing credit, including such later compositions as "Don't Pass Me By" and "Octopus's Garden."

As Lennon recalled, "That was an early Lennon, written before the Beatles when we were the Quarry Men or something like that. And resurrected with a middle-eight thrown in, probably with Paul's help, to give Ringo a song, and also to use the bits, because I never liked to waste anything" (Lennon and Ono 2000, 178).

As Starr later remarked, "I contributed about five words to 'What Goes On.' And I haven't done a thing since!" (Everett 2001, 329).

RECORDING SESSIONS

Produced by George Martin, "What Goes On" was recorded at Abbey Road Studios on November 4, 1965. In an effort to assist Starr with learning his vocal, McCartney provided the drummer with a tape recording to study in advance of the recording session.

PERSONNEL

Lennon: Rickenbacker 325, Backing Vocal
McCartney: Höfner 500/1, Backing Vocal
Harrison: Gretsch Tennessean
Starr: Vocal, Ludwig Oyster Black Pearl Drums

CHART PERFORMANCE

U.S.: "Nowhere Man"/"What Goes On"; February 21, 1966, Capitol 5587: #3 (certified by the RIAA as "Gold," with more than 500,000 copies sold). As the B-side of "Nowhere Man," "What Goes On" charted at #81.

ALBUM APPEARANCES: *Rubber Soul* (U.K.); *Yesterday . . . and Today*.

See also: *Rubber Soul* (U.K. LP).

"What You're Doing" (Lennon–McCartney)

"What You're Doing" is a song on the *Beatles for Sale* album.

AUTHORSHIP AND BACKGROUND

Written by McCartney, "What You're Doing" concerns the songwriter's relationship with Asher, a subject that came under increasing scrutiny in the coming years through songs such as *Rubber Soul*'s "I'm Looking Through You" and *Revolver*'s "For No One."

As McCartney remembered,

"What You're Doing" was a bit of filler. I think it was a little more mine than John's. You sometimes start a song and hope the best will arrive by the time you get to the chorus, but sometimes that's all you get, and I suspect this was one of them. Maybe it's a better recording than it is a song—some of them are. Sometimes a good recording would enhance a song. (Miles 1997, 176)

RECORDING SESSIONS

Produced by Martin, "What You're Doing" was recorded at Abbey Road Studios on September 29 and 30, 1964, and remade on October 26.

PERSONNEL

Lennon: Gibson J-160E, Backing Vocal
McCartney: Höfner 500/1
Harrison: Rickenbacker 360/12
Starr: Ludwig Oyster Black Pearl Drums
Martin: Piano

ALBUM APPEARANCES: *Beatles for Sale*; *Beatles VI*; *Love*.

See also: *Beatles for Sale* (LP).

"What's the New Mary Jane" (Lennon–McCartney)

"What's the New Mary Jane" was recorded during the sessions for *The Beatles* (*The White Album*) and remained unreleased until the Beatles' *Anthology* project during the 1990s.

AUTHORSHIP AND BACKGROUND

Written by Lennon, "What's the New Mary Jane" finds its origins during the Beatles' 1968 visit to India.

RECORDING SESSIONS

Produced by George Martin, "What's the New Mary Jane" was recorded in four takes at Abbey Road Studios on August 14, 1968, with an additional overdubbing session on November 26, 1969.

During the August 14 session, Lennon and Harrison were the only Beatles present for the recording, along with Yoko Ono and Mal Evans joining in the merriment with sound effects. As the Beatles prepared *The White Album* for release in October and November 1968, "What's the New Mary Jane" was the last song to be deleted from the project, bringing the album's song total to 30.

An early version of "What's the New Mary Jane" was recorded in May 1968 at Harrison's Kinfauns studio as part of the Esher Tapes. In 1984, Geoff Emerick remixed "What's the New Mary Jane" in preparation for the unreleased Beatles *Sessions* project. In 1994, Martin remixed "What's the New Mary Jane" for release as part of the Beatles' *Anthology* project.

PERSONNEL

Lennon: Vocal, Piano, Sound Effects
Harrison: Vocal, Gibson J-200, Sound Effects
Ono: Vocal, Sound Effects
Evans: Handbell, Sound Effects

ALBUM APPEARANCE: *Anthology 3*.

See also: *The Beatles Anthology, Volume 3* (LP); *The Beatles* (*The White Album*) (LP); Evans, Mal; Ono, Yoko; Plastic Ono Band.

"When I Get Home" (Lennon–McCartney)

"When I Get Home" is a song on the Beatles' *A Hard Day's Night* album.

AUTHORSHIP AND BACKGROUND

Written by Lennon, "When I Get Home" was influence by the Shirelles. As Lennon remembered, "That's me again—another Wilson Pickett, Motown sound—a four-in-the-bar cowbell song" (Dowlding 1989, 76).

RECORDING SESSIONS

Produced by George Martin, "When I Get Home" was recorded at Abbey Road Studios in 11 takes on June 2, 1964.

PERSONNEL

Lennon: Vocal, Rickenbacker 325
McCartney: Höfner 500/1, Backing Vocal
Harrison: Rickenbacker 360/12, Backing Vocal
Starr: Ludwig Oyster Black Pearl Drums

ALBUM APPEARANCES: *A Hard Day's Night* (U.K.); *Something New*.

See also: *A Hard Day's Night* (U.K. LP).

"When I'm Sixty-Four" (Lennon–McCartney)

"When I'm Sixty-Four" is a song on the Beatles' *Sgt. Pepper's Lonely Hearts Club Band* album.

AUTHORSHIP AND BACKGROUND

Written by McCartney, "When I'm Sixty-Four" is nothing short of a vaudevillian throwback and one of the songwriter's earliest compositions from the Beatles' Cavern-era days. It was undoubtedly inspired by McCartney's father Jim, who turned 64 in July 1966. The musical roots of "When I'm Sixty-Four" actually run much deeper to 1958, when McCartney composed the rudiments of the song on the family piano at 20 Forthlin Road, and the Beatles included an earlier version of the number in their stage act during their Hamburg period.

As Lennon remembered, " 'When I'm Sixty Four' was something Paul wrote in the Cavern days. We just stuck in a few more words, like 'grandchildren on your knee,' and 'Vera Chuck and Dave.' It was just one of those ones that he'd had, that we've all got, really—half a song. And this was just one of those that was quite a hit with us. We used to do it when the amps broke down, just sing it on the piano" (Beatles 2000, 247).

McCartney later recalled, "I wrote the tune when I was about 15, I think, on the piano at home, before I moved from Liverpool. It was kind of a cabaret tune. Then, years later, I put words to it" (Dowlding 1989, 175). Years later, he added, "I thought it was a good little tune but it was too vaudevillian, so I had to get some cod lines to take the sting out of it, and put the tongue very firmly in cheek" (Miles 1997, 319).

During one of his last interviews, Lennon remarked that "When I'm Sixty-Four" was "Paul's, completely. I would never dream of writing a song like that. There's some things I never think about, and that's one of them" (Lennon and Ono 2000, 183).

RECORDING SESSIONS

Produced by George Martin, "When I'm Sixty-Four" was recorded at Abbey Road Studios on December 6, 1967, the first day of recording sessions for the *Sgt. Pepper's Lonely Hearts Club Band* album. Additional overdubbing sessions were held on December 8, 20, and 21. In order to provide the song with a period feel, Martin scored an arrangement for a clarinet trio to perform on "When I'm Sixty-Four."

"When I'm Sixty-Four" was initially considered to be the B-side for the Beatles' first post-*Revolver* single until the band settled on the double A-side release of "Penny Lane"/"Strawberry Fields Forever." With "When I'm Sixty-Four" having been completed, the band began formal recording sessions for their next album instead.

An earlier recording of "When I'm Sixty-Four" is one of the 17 demos on the Hodgson Tape that find their origins in the band's April and July 1960 recording sessions. All of the tracks were recorded on a Grundig reel-to-reel tape recorder that McCartney had borrowed from Charles Hodgson. In a November 1994 interview with Mark Lewisohn, McCartney recalled that "sometimes I'd borrow a tape recorder, a Grundig with a little green eye, and we'd sort of go 'round to my house and try and record things. . . . But those were very much home demos. Very bad quality" (Winn 2003a, 3). "When I'm Sixty-Four" is rumored to be one of the songs recorded during these sessions, although any recording of the song has not been publicly released.

PERSONNEL

Lennon: Epiphone Casino
McCartney: Vocal, Rickenbacker 4001S
Starr: Ludwig Oyster Black Pearl Drums, Chimes
Studio Musicians: Woodwind Accompaniment conducted by Martin
Robert Burns, Henry MacKenzie, Frank Reidy: Clarinet, Bass

ALBUM APPEARANCES: *Sgt. Pepper's Lonely Hearts Club Band*; *Yellow Submarine Songtrack.*

See also: *Sgt. Pepper's Lonely Hearts Club Band* (LP).

"While My Guitar Gently Weeps" (Harrison)

"While My Guitar Gently Weeps" is a song on *The Beatles* (*The White Album*).

AUTHORSHIP AND BACKGROUND

During his composition of the song, Harrison had been thinking about the Chinese *I Ching*—specifically "The Book of Changes." "I wrote 'While My Guitar Gently Weeps' at my mother's house in Warrington," Harrison later recalled. "The Eastern concept is that whatever happens is all meant to be, and that there's no such thing as coincidence—every little item that's going down has a purpose. 'While My Guitar Gently Weeps' was a simple study based on that theory. I decided to write a song based on the first thing I saw upon opening any book—as it would be a relative to that moment, at that time. I picked up a book at random, opened it, saw 'gently weeps,' then laid the book down again and started the song" (Beatles 2000, 306).

RECORDING SESSIONS

Produced by Martin, Harrison recorded an acoustic version of "While My Guitar Gently Weeps" on July 25, 1968, at Abbey Road Studios. The band remade the song on August 16, with an overdubbing session on September 3. On September 5, Harrison invited Eric Clapton to join the group for a third remake of the song, for which they conducted an overdubbing session on September 6. For Harrison, Clapton's appearance altered the band's dynamics dramatically, changing their behavior for the better. "Just bringing in a stranger among us made everybody cool out," Harrison later remarked (Beatles 2000, 306). Clapton played his magnificent, driving solo on a Gibson Les Paul Standard. At Clapton's request, the solo was heavily treated with ADT in order to achieve a more "Beatley" sound. "I was given the grand job of waggling the oscillator on the 'Gently Weeps' mixes," Chris Thomas recalled. "We did this flanging thing, really wobbling the oscillator in the mix. I did that for hours" (Babiuk 2001, 229).

In 1984, Emerick remixed take 1 of "While My Guitar Gently Weeps" and appended an artificially looped ending in preparation for the unreleased Beatles *Sessions* project. In 1994, Martin remixed "While My Guitar Gently Weeps" for release as part of the Beatles' *Anthology* project.

PERSONNEL

Lennon: Epiphone Casino, Backing Vocal
McCartney: Fender Jazz Bass, Piano, Hammond Organ, Backing Vocal
Harrison: Vocal, Gibson J-200
Starr: Ludwig Oyster Black Pearl Drums, Tambourine, Castanets
Clapton: Gibson Les Paul Standard

LEGACY AND INFLUENCE

In 2004, *Rolling Stone* ranked "While My Guitar Gently Weeps" as #136 on the magazine's list of *The 500 Greatest Songs of All Time*.

In 2008, *Rolling Stone* ranked "While My Guitar Gently Weeps" as #7 on the magazine's list of *The 100 Greatest Guitar Songs of All Time*.

In 2010, *Rolling Stone* ranked "While My Guitar Gently Weeps" as #10 on the magazine's list of *The Beatles' 100 Greatest Songs*.

A 2008 issue of *Guitar World* magazine cites Clapton's solo on "While My Guitar Gently Weeps" as #42 on the magazine's list of the *100 Greatest Guitar Solos*.

A 2008 issue of *New Musical Express* magazine cites Clapton's solo on "While My Guitar Gently Weeps" as #27 on the magazine's list of the *50 Greatest Guitar Solos*.

A 2012 issue of *Guitar World* magazine cites "While My Guitar Gently Weeps" as the best of Harrison's Beatles-era compositions.

ALBUM APPEARANCES: *The Beatles* (*The White Album*); *The Beatles, 1967–1970*; *Anthology 3*; *Love*.

See also: *The Beatles Anthology, Volume 3* (LP); *The Beatles* (*The White Album*) (LP); Clapton, Eric.

"Why Don't We Do It in the Road?" (Lennon–McCartney)

"Why Don't We Do It in the Road?" is a song on *The Beatles* (*The White Album*).

AUTHORSHIP AND BACKGROUND

Written by McCartney, "Why Don't We Do It in the Road?" finds its origins during the Beatles' 1968 visit to India. McCartney was inspired to write the 12-bar blues piece after witnessing the sight of monkeys copulating in the Maharishi's compound.

RECORDING SESSIONS

Produced by George Martin, "Why Don't We Do It in the Road?" was recorded at Abbey Road Studios on October 9, 1968. An overdubbing session was held the following day in which Starr contributed a drum part to replace the one that McCartney had recorded the previous evening.

As Lennon later recalled, "That's Paul. He even recorded it by himself in another room. That's how it was getting in those days. We came in and he'd made the whole record. Him drumming. Him playing the piano. Him singing. But he couldn't—he couldn't—maybe he couldn't make the break from the Beatles. I don't know what it was, you know. I enjoyed the track. Still, I can't speak for George, but I was always hurt when Paul would knock something off without involving us. But that's just the way it was then" (Harry 2002, 389).

PERSONNEL

McCartney: Vocal, Rickenbacker 4001S, Epiphone Casino, Martin D-28, Piano
Starr: Ludwig Oyster Black Pearl Drums

ALBUM APPEARANCES: *The Beatles* (*The White Album*); *Anthology 3*.

See also: *The Beatles* (*The White Album*) (LP).

"Wild Honey Pie" (Lennon–McCartney)

"Wild Honey Pie" is a song on *The Beatles* (*The White Album*).

AUTHORSHIP AND BACKGROUND

Written by McCartney, "Wild Honey Pie" finds its origins during the Beatles' 1968 visit to India. McCartney improvised the song during a sing-along in the Maharishi's compound.

540 | Williams, Allan (1930–)

As McCartney later observed, "We were in an experimental mode, and so I said, 'Can I just make something up?' I started off with the guitar and did a multitracking experiment in the control room. It was very home-made—it wasn't a big production at all. I just made up this short piece and I multitracked the harmony to that, and a harmony to that, and a harmony to that, and built it up sculpturally with a lot of vibrato on the [guitar] strings, really pulling the strings madly—hence, 'Wild Honey Pie'" (Miles 1997, 497).

RECORDING SESSIONS

Produced by Martin, the session for "Wild Honey Pie" occurred on August 20, 1968, at Abbey Road Studios. McCartney is the sole performer on the song.

PERSONNEL

McCartney: Vocal, Martin D-28, Harpsichord, Ludwig Oyster Black Pearl Drums

ALBUM APPEARANCE: *The Beatles* (*The White Album*).

See also: *The Beatles* (*The White Album*) (LP).

Williams, Allan (1930–)

Born March 17, 1930, in Liverpool, Allan Williams served as the Beatles' first manager. He was also instrumental in booking their first residencies in Hamburg, West Germany. He came into the Beatles' orbit through his coffeehouse, the Jacaranda, a former watch-repair shop that became a popular hangout for students at the Liverpool College of Art, including Lennon and Stuart Sutcliffe. In addition to arranging their Scottish tour with Johnny Gentle, he traveled with the Beatles, along with newly minted drummer Pete Best, to Hamburg in August 1960. The Beatles' managerial relationship with Williams disintegrated during the 1961 Hamburg residency over Williams's 10-percent fee, which the Beatles negated after negotiating their own contract at Hamburg's Top Ten Club without his knowledge. Later, when Brian Epstein prepared to stake his claim as the Beatles' manager, Williams warned him not to "touch them with a f—ing bargepole. They will let you down." In 1977, he published his autobiography entitled *The Man Who Gave the Beatles Away*. That same year, he was also instrumental in recovering the tapes from a 1962 Beatles performance at Hamburg's Star-Club. The recording was later released as *Live! at the Star-Club in Hamburg, Germany; 1962*.

See also: Best, Pete; Epstein, Brian; *Live! at the Star-Club in Hamburg, Germany; 1962* (LP); Sutcliffe, Stuart; Tours, 1960–1966.

Wings

Active from 1971 through their disbandment in 1981, Wings was enormously successful, with seven best-selling studio albums and the landmark Wings Over the World Tour in 1975–1976. The band notched six No. 1 U.S. singles releases, as well as one of England's best-selling recordings of all time in "Mull of Kintyre." Wings dissolved in the early 1980s after McCartney's drug arrest and brief incarceration resulted in the cancellation of the 1980 Japanese tour, as well as after Lennon's murder.

In 1971, with wife Linda and former Moody Blues member Denny Laine in tow, McCartney set about the business of naming his new band. As McCartney later recalled,

> We were thinking of all sorts of names. We had a new group and we had to think of a name. We had a letter from an old gentleman in Scotland, which said, "Dear Paul, I see you are looking for a name for your group. I'd like to suggest the Dazzlers." So we were nearly the Dazzlers, with the big sequined jackets. But we thought, no, we need something a little more earthy, so we thought of Turpentine. But I wrote to the guy in Scotland and told him that and he wrote back, "I don't think you'll be calling yourselves Turpentine because that's something used to clean paint off," so we thought of Wings. (Badman 2001, 71)

In the ensuing years, the group was often referred to as Paul McCartney and Wings, although the former Beatle preferred to refer to the band simply as Wings. As McCartney remarked, "It was never Paul McCartney and the Beatles, Paul McCartney and the Quarry Men, or Paul McCartney and the Moondogs. Wings is quicker and easier to say, and everybody knows I'm in the group anyway" (McGee 2003, 83). Over the course of the band's life, Wings' lineup shifted on a number of occasions, although the group's core trio of the McCartneys and Laine stayed intact for the balance of their career. The group went through a succession of lead guitarists, including Henry McCullough (1972–1973), Jimmy McCulloch (1974–1977), and Laurence Juber (1978–1981). The band's drummers included Denny Seiwell (1971–1973), Geoff Britton (1974–1975), Joe English (1975–1977), and Steve Holley (1978–1981). Over the years, the band performed nearly 150 concerts across five tours including the Wings University Tour (1972), the Wings Over Europe Tour (1972), the Wings 1973 UK Tour, the Wings Over the World Tour (1975–1976), and the Wings UK Tour 1979.

In one of his last interviews, Lennon praised his former collaborator for the manner in which he achieved post-Beatles success with Wings. As Lennon observed,

> I kind of admire the way Paul started back from scratch, forming a new band and playing in small dance halls, because that's what he wanted to do with the Beatles—he wanted us to go back to the dance halls and experience that again.

But I didn't. That was one of the problems, in a way, that he wanted to relive it all or something. I don't know what it was. But I kind of admire the way he got off his pedestal. Now he's back on it again, but I mean, he did what he wanted to do. (Jackson 2012, 136)

Wings disbanded in the early months of 1981 after abandoning work on the long-conceived *Cold Cuts* project. In April of that year, Laine announced that he was leaving the band, citing McCartney's reluctance to tour in the wake of Lennon's murder.

See also: McCartney, Linda Eastman; McCartney, Paul.

"With a Little Help from My Friends" (Lennon–McCartney)

"With a Little Help from My Friends" is a song on the Beatles' *Sgt. Pepper's Lonely Hearts Club Band* album.

AUTHORSHIP AND BACKGROUND

Written by McCartney with Lennon, "With a Little Help from My Friends" was written expressly for Starr to contribute a vocal on *Sgt. Pepper's Lonely Hearts Club Band*.

As McCartney recalled,

This was written out at John's house in Weybridge for Ringo. I think that was probably the best of our songs that we wrote for Ringo actually. I remember giggling with John as we wrote the lines, "What do you see when you turn out the light / I can't tell you but I know it's mine." It could have been him playing with his willie under the covers, or it could have been taken on a deeper level. This is what it meant but it was a nice way to say it—a very non-specific way to say it. I always liked that. (Miles 1997, 310)

As Lennon later recalled, "Paul had the line about 'a little help from my friends.' He had some kind of structure for it, and we wrote it pretty well fifty-fifty from his original idea" (Lennon 1970, 87).

RECORDING SESSIONS

Produced by George Martin, "With a Little Help from My Friends" went under the working title of "Bad Finger Boogie" and was recorded at Abbey Road Studios on March 29, 1967, with an additional overdubbing session on March 30. It reportedly earned its working title after Lennon injured his finger during the composition of "With a Little Help from My Friends."

In order to establish a segue between *Sgt. Pepper*'s title track and "With a Little Help from My Friends," Martin deftly masked the edit between the songs in a warm bath of screaming fans that he had recorded during one of the group's concerts at the Hollywood Bowl. Direct-injected on his Rickenbacker, McCartney's splendid, melodic bass lines imbue the composition with a heartfelt air, and the lyrics resonate with the charming sincerity of Starr's lead vocal, which affords the entire production with a sense of earnestness in sharp contrast with the ironic distance previously established by the title track.

PERSONNEL

Lennon: Epiphone Casino, Backing Vocal
McCartney: Rickenbacker 4001S, Piano, Backing Vocal
Harrison: Sonic Blue Fender Stratocaster
Starr: Vocal, Ludwig Oyster Black Pearl Drums, Tambourine

CHART PERFORMANCE

U.K.: "Sgt. Pepper's Lonely Hearts Club Band/With a Little Help from My Friends"/"A Day in the Life"; September 30, 1978, Parlophone R6022: #63.
U.S.: "Sgt. Pepper's Lonely Hearts Club Band/With a Little Help from My Friends"/"A Day in the Life"; September 30, 1978, Capitol 4612: #71.

LEGACY AND INFLUENCE

Joe Cocker's recording of "With a Little Help from My Friends" is included among the Rock and Roll Hall of Fame's *500 Songs That Shaped Rock and Roll*.

In 2004, *Rolling Stone* ranked "With a Little Help from My Friends" as #311 on the magazine's list of *The 500 Greatest Songs of All Time*.

In 2010, *Rolling Stone* ranked "With a Little Help from My Friends" as #61 on the magazine's list of *The Beatles' 100 Greatest Songs*.

CONTROVERSY

In his 1970 *Lennon Remembers* interview with Jann Wenner, Lennon argues that despite public misconceptions, "With a Little Help from My Friends" does not advocate drug abuse: "I just saw Mel Tormé on TV the other day saying that 'Lucy' was written to promote drugs and so was '[With] a Little Help from My Friends' and none of them were at all—'[With] a Little Help from My Friends' only says get high in it, it's really about a little help from my friends, it's a sincere message" (Lennon 1970, 86, 87).

ALBUM APPEARANCES: *Sgt. Pepper's Lonely Hearts Club Band*; *The Beatles, 1967–1970*; *Yellow Submarine Songtrack*.

See also: *Sgt. Pepper's Lonely Hearts Club Band* (LP).

With the Beatles (LP)

November 22, 1963, Parlophone PMC 1206 (mono)/PCS 3045 (stereo)

With the Beatles is the Beatles' second studio album. It was released on the Parlophone label on November 22, 1963, in the United Kingdom. In the United States, several of the songs on *With the Beatles* were released on Capitol Records' *Meet the Beatles!* on January 20, 1964, with any remaining tracks being held over in the United States for *The Beatles' Second Album*, released on April 10, 1964.

With the Beatles became standardized among U.S. album releases with the February 26, 1987, distribution of the band's first four albums as mono CD releases. It was remastered and rereleased as a stereo CD on September 9, 2009. A remastered mono release was also made available at this time as part of a limited edition box set entitled *The Beatles in Mono*.

BACKGROUND AND RECORDING SESSIONS

Produced by Martin with Norman "Normal" Smith as his sound engineer, *With the Beatles* was recorded, for the most part, over 11 sessions from July through October 1963. As with *Please Please Me*, Martin and the Beatles were limited by the capabilities of two-track recording, which necessitated the use of "bouncing down" as the group attempted to flex their creative muscles beyond the limits of EMI's two-track machine.

Bouncing down ultimately results in a generational loss with each successive bounce. As Kevin Ryan and Brian Kehew observe, "Several tracks on *With the Beatles* ('Little Child,' 'Devil in Her Heart,' 'Money [That's What I Want],' and 'I Wanna Be Your Man') saw three overdub bounces, meaning the final mix of each song was four generations removed from the initial take. In most cases, though, they generally tried to limit overdubs to a single bounce if possible" (Ryan and Kehew 2006, 359).

On November 22, 1963, Parlophone released *With the Beatles* to the hungry ears of the British record-buying public. In England, the sheer joy inherent in the record's release was palpable. Yet meanwhile, back in the United States, President John F. Kennedy was felled by a lone gunman in Dallas.

As with *Please Please Me*, *With the Beatles* was a runaway success in the United Kingdom. It was the second album, after the soundtrack to the 1958 film *South Pacific*, to sell more than a million copies. It knocked *Please Please Me* out of the #1 position, topping the album charts for an incredible 21 weeks. Between the two albums, the Beatles held the top spot in the album charts for 51 consecutive weeks.

TRACK LISTING

Side 1: "It Won't Be Long"; "All I've Got to Do"; "All My Loving"; "Don't Bother Me"; "Little Child"; "Till There Was You"; "Please Mister Postman."

Side 2: "Roll Over Beethoven"; "Hold Me Tight"; "You Really Got a Hold on Me"; "I Wanna Be Your Man"; "Devil in Her Heart"; "Not a Second Time"; "Money (That's What I Want)."

COVER ARTWORK

With its shadowy cover photograph by Robert Freeman, the album pointedly depicted the band as serious musicians, rather than mere pop sensations. He shot the iconic photograph on August 22, 1963, in the Palace Court Hotel in Bournemouth, England. He arranged the Beatles in a dark hotel corridor for their famous, moody portrait. As with *Please Please Me*, Beatles press officer Tony Barrow authored the liner notes for *With the Beatles*, writing that "Fourteen freshly recorded titles—including many sure-fire stage-show favourites—are featured on the two generously filled sides of this record. The Beatles have repeated the successful formula which made their first *Please Please Me* LP into the fastest-selling album of 1963. Again they have set eight of their own original compositions along side a batch of 'personal choice' pieces selected from the recorded repertoires of the American R&B artists they admire most."

CHART PERFORMANCE

U.K.: #1 (In the United States, *With the Beatles* has been certified by the RIAA as "Gold," with more than 500,000 copies sold).

LEGACY AND INFLUENCE

In 2003, *Rolling Stone* ranked *With the Beatles* as #420 on the magazine's list of *The 500 Greatest Albums of All Time*.

In 2005, *Mojo* magazine ranked *With the Beatles* as #63 on the magazine's list of *The 100 Greatest Albums Ever Made*.

See also: Martin, George.

"Within You, Without You" (Harrison)

"Within You, Without You" is a song on the Beatles' *Sgt. Pepper's Lonely Hearts Club Band* album.

AUTHORSHIP AND BACKGROUND

Written by Harrison, "Within You, Without You" was composed on the harmonium at Klaus Voormann's Hampstead home.

As Harrison later recalled, "I'm writing more songs now that we're not touring. The words are always a bit of a hang-up for me. I'm not very poetic. 'Within You, Without You' was written after dinner one night at Klaus Voormann's house. He had a harmonium, which I hadn't played before. I was doodling on it when the tune started to come. The first sentence came out of what we'd been doing that evening: 'We were talking.' That's as far as I got that night. I finished the rest of the words later at home" (Davies 1968, 321). As Lennon remembered, "Within You, Without You" is "one of George's best songs. One of my favorites of his, too. He's clear on that song. His mind and his music are clear. There is his innate talent. He brought that sound together" (Lennon and Ono 2000, 186).

RECORDING SESSIONS

Produced by George Martin, "Within You, Without You" was recorded at Abbey Road Studios on March 15, 1967, with additional overdubbing sessions on March 22 and April 3.

"Within You, Without You" was the final composition recorded for the album. It went under the working title of "Not Known," yet another clever nontitle from Harrison. The basic track was realized at the March 15, 1967, session, which featured Harrison on sitar with a gauzy ADT-treated vocal, Aspinall on tamboura, and session musicians from London's Asian Music Circle on dilruba, tamboura, tabla, and swarmandal. Martin later overdubbed eight violins and three cellos onto the composition, which features a tempo rubato—unique among the Beatles' corpus—which involves a flexible or fluctuating tempo that maximizes the song's capacity for expressiveness. "The best part of it for me," Harrison recalled in *I Me Mine*, "is the instrumental solo in the middle which is in 5/4 time—the first of the strange rhythm cycles that I caught on to—one-two; one-two-three; one-two-one-two-three" (Harrison 1980, 112). As Peter Blake later recalled, "I remember one evening George was recording ['Within You, Without You']. There was a carpet laid out, there was an Indian musician, and the whole atmosphere was different to other times" (Dowlding 1989, 174).

Interestingly, Harrison's planned contribution to the album, "Only a Northern Song," was recorded in February 1967 and rejected by his bandmates, especially Lennon, who felt that the composition's dour dismissiveness conflicted with the egalitarian spirit of *Sgt. Pepper*. By contrast, "Within You, Without You" represents, quite arguably, the album's ethical soul. Harrison based his composition on the Hindustani philosophy of *Māya*, which contends that the idea of humanity is the only genuine notion of reality, that mortals generally believe in false realities— "walls of illusion"—well beyond the scope of their corporeal selves. In "Within

You, Without You," Harrison sings "about the space between us all." Harrison's *Mayan* discourse establishes the firmament for the Beatles' utopian sentiments that ultimately propel the Summer of Love into being: "With our love we could save the world," Harrison sings. Chosen by the songwriter in an effort to sustain the album's convivial mood in spite of the song's weighty contents, the laughter over-dubbed at the conclusion of the song was selected from *Volume 6: Applause and Laughter* in the EMI tape library.

PERSONNEL

> Harrison: Vocal, Sitar, Tamboura
> Aspinall: Tamboura
> Studio Musicians: Indian Instrumental Accompaniment (Swarmandal, Dilruba, Tabla, Tamboura) and Orchestral Accompaniment conducted by Martin
> Ralph Elman, Julien Gaillard, Jack Greene, Erich Gruenberg, Alan Loveday, Jack Rothstein, Paul Scherman, David Wolfsthal: Violin
> Peter Beavan, Allen Ford, Reginald Kilbey: Cello

LEGACY AND INFLUENCE

In 2010, *Rolling Stone* ranked "Within You, Without You" as #96 on the magazine's list of *The Beatles' 100 Greatest Songs*.

ALBUM APPEARANCES: *Sgt. Pepper's Lonely Hearts Club Band*; *Anthology 2*; *Love*.

See also: Aspinall, Neil; *Sgt. Pepper's Lonely Hearts Club Band* (LP); Voormann, Klaus.

"The Word" (Lennon–McCartney)

"The Word" is a song on the Beatles' *Rubber Soul* album.

AUTHORSHIP AND BACKGROUND

Written by Lennon and McCartney, "The Word" finds its origins in the songwriters' efforts to write an intentionally simplistic track. As McCartney later remarked, "To write one song with just one note in it—like 'Long Tall Sally'—is really very hard. It's the kind of thing we've wanted to do for some time. We get near it in 'The Word' " (Dowlding 1989, 119).

As Lennon recalled, " 'The Word' was written together (with Paul), but it's mainly mine. You read the words, it's all about gettin' smart. It's the marijuana period. It's love. It's a love and peace thing. The word is 'love,' right?" (Dowlding 1989, 118).

RECORDING SESSIONS

Produced by Martin, "The Word" was recorded at Abbey Road Studios on November 10, 1965.

PERSONNEL

> Lennon: Vocal, Sonic Blue Fender Stratocaster
> McCartney: Vocal, Höfner 500/1, Piano
> Harrison: Vocal, Sonic Blue Fender Stratocaster
> Starr: Ludwig Oyster Black Pearl Drums, Maracas
> Martin: Harmonium

ALBUM APPEARANCES: *Rubber Soul* (U.K.); *Rubber Soul* (U.S.); *Love.*

See also: Ono, Yoko; *Rubber Soul* (U.K. LP).

"Words of Love" (Holly)

"Words of Love" is a song on the *Beatles for Sale* album.

AUTHORSHIP AND BACKGROUND

Written by Buddy Holly, "Words of Love" was recorded in April 1957, with Holly famously harmonizing with himself by "bouncing down" during the production process. He released "Words of Love" as a single in June 1957.

RECORDING SESSIONS

Produced by George Martin, "Words of Love" was recorded at Abbey Road Studios on October 18, 1964. Starr mimicked Holly's well-known percussion effects on "Everyday" by accenting the downbeats in "Words of Love" by banging on a packing case.

PERSONNEL

> Lennon: Vocal, Rickenbacker 325
> McCartney: Vocal, Höfner 500/1
> Harrison: Gretsch Tennessean
> Starr: Percussion

ALBUM APPEARANCES: *Beatles for Sale*; *Beatles VI*; *Love Songs*; *On Air: Live at the BBC, Volume 2.*

See also: *Beatles for Sale* (LP).

Y

Yellow Submarine (Film)

Directed by Canadian animator George Dunning, *Yellow Submarine* was produced by Al Brodax, one of the creative forces behind the Beatles cartoons. Cowritten by Brodax, Lee Minoff, and Erich Seagal—who later authored the screenplay for *Love Story* (1970)—*Yellow Submarine* featured little actual input from the band. Initially skeptical about the value of making another film, the Beatles only contributed four new songs ("All Together Now," "Hey Bulldog," "It's All Too Much," and "Only a Northern Song"), a few script alterations, and a brief appearance at the end of the movie. Yet, the finished product clearly exceeded their expectations. As Tony Barrow later remarked, the Beatles were "so pleased with the way the whole production had been put together that they were only too happy to associate themselves with it more closely from then on" (1993, 13).

For the movie, the voices of the Beatles were provided by Paul Angelis (Ringo/George), John Clive (John), and Geoffrey Hughes (Paul). *Yellow Submarine* premiered on July 17, 1968, at the London Pavilion with all four Beatles in attendance. For the 2011 holiday season, a downloadable *Yellow Submarine* commemorative booklet, complete with photos, music, and video, was made available as a free download from the iTunes bookstore.

As for the *Yellow Submarine* music, the songs in order of their appearance in the movie included

"Introduction Story" (George Martin and His Orchestra)
"Yellow Submarine"
"Eleanor Rigby"
"I Am the Walrus" (Excerpt)
"Love You To" (Excerpt)
"A Day in the Life" (Excerpt)
"All Together Now"
"When I'm Sixty-Four"
"Only a Northern Song"
"Nowhere Man"
"Lucy in the Sky with Diamonds"
"Sea of Green" (George Martin and His Orchestra)
"Think for Yourself" (Excerpt)
"Sgt. Pepper's Lonely Hearts Club Band"

"With a Little Help from My Friends" (Excerpt)
"All You Need Is Love"
"Baby, You're a Rich Man" (Excerpt)
"Hey Bulldog"
"It's All Too Much"
"All Together Now"

See also: *Yellow Submarine* (LP); *Yellow Submarine Songtrack* (LP).

"Yellow Submarine" (Lennon–McCartney)

"Yellow Submarine" is a song on the Beatles' *Revolver* album. It was the band's 12th consecutive #1 single in the United Kingdom, where it was released on August 5, 1966, as a double A-side with "Eleanor Rigby," which also topped the charts.

AUTHORSHIP AND BACKGROUND

Written by McCartney, "Yellow Submarine" succeeded, as did "In My Life," in opening up new demographics of listeners for the Beatles.

As McCartney later remarked,

> I was laying in bed in the Ashers' garret, and there's a nice twilight zone just as you're drifting into sleep and as you wake from it—I always find it quite a comfortable zone. I remember thinking that a children's song would be quite a good idea. I was thinking of it as a song for Ringo, which it eventually turned out to be, so I wrote it as not too rangy in the vocal. I just made up a little tune in my head, then started making a story—sort of an ancient mariner, telling the young kids where he'd lived. It was pretty much my song as I recall. I think John helped out. The lyrics got more and more obscure as it goes on, but the chorus, melody and verses are mine. (Evans 2004, 240)

As George Harrison remembered in a 1999 *Billboard* interview with Timothy White, "Paul came up with the concept of 'Yellow Submarine.' All I know is just that every time we'd all get around the piano with guitars and start listening to it and arranging it into a record, we'd all fool about. As I said, John's doing the voice that sounds like someone talking down a tube or ship's funnel as they do in the merchant marine. And on the final track there's actually that very small party happening! As I seem to remember, there's a few screams and what sounds like small crowd noises in the background" (*Billboard* 1999).

"Paul wrote the catchy chorus," Lennon recalled, "I helped with the blunderbuss bit" (Dowlding 1989, 138).

RECORDING SESSIONS

Produced by George Martin, "Yellow Submarine" was recorded on May 26, 1966, with an unusual overdubbing session—perhaps the most peculiar in Beatles' history—on June 1.

After recording a basic rhythm track on May 26, 1966, featuring Starr on drums, Lennon strumming his Jumbo, McCartney on bass, and Harrison on tambourine, Geoff Emerick overdubbed Starr's lead vocals and Lennon, McCartney, and Harrison's backing vocals at a slightly reduced speed in order to achieve a brighter quality during playback. A tape-to-tape reduction of take four left the Beatles with ample room for the later addition of the numerous sound effects that afford the song with its distinctively playful demeanor.

On June 1, 1966, the Beatles reconvened in Studio Two, where they were joined by a host of guests, including Rolling Stones' front men Brian Jones (who played the ocarina) and Mick Jagger, Jagger's girlfriend Marianne Faithfull, the Beatles' chauffeur Alf Bicknell, and Pattie Boyd. The group was rounded out by the band's ever-faithful roadies, Mal Evans and Neil Aspinall. The evening began with Lennon recording his famous superimposed voices in the studio's echo chamber: "Full speed ahead, Mr. Boatswain." Were Lennon's ad-lib voices a forgotten vestige of a Liverpudlian, seafaring past that he never really knew? As Emerick recalled,

> The whole marijuana-influenced scene that evening was completely zany, straight out of a Marx Brothers movie. The entire EMI collection of percussion instruments and sound effects boxes were strewn all over the studio, with people grabbing bells and whistles and gongs at random. To simulate the sound of a submarine submerging, John grabbed a straw and began blowing bubbles into a glass—fortunately, I was able to move a mike nearby in time to record it for posterity. Inspired, Lennon wanted to take things to the next level and have me record him actually *singing* underwater. First, he tried singing while gargling. When that failed (he nearly choked), he began lobbying for a tank to be brought in so that he could be submerged! (Emerick and Massey 2006, 120)

With Lennon's inspired voice work in the can, the glitterati in the studio assembled, conga-style, behind Evans, who led the bizarre proceedings with a bass drum strapped to his chest. As Mark Lewisohn observes, the resulting recording of "Yellow Submarine" is "either a weak Salvation Army band style sing-along or a clever and contagious piece of pop music guaranteed to please the kids, the grannies, and plenty others besides" (Lewisohn 1988, 80).

PERSONNEL

Lennon: Gibson J-160E, Backing Vocal, Blowing Bubbles through a Straw
McCartney: Epiphone Texan, Rickenbacker 4001S, Backing Vocal
Harrison: Tambourine, Swirling Water in a Bucket, Backing Vocal

Starr: Vocal, Ludwig Oyster Black Pearl Drums
Aspinall: Backing Vocal
Boyd: Backing Vocal
Bicknell: Sound Effects
Donovan: Backing Vocal
Evans: Backing Vocal, Bass Drum
Faithfull: Backing Vocal
Jagger: Backing Vocal
Jones: Backing Vocal, Sound Effects

CHART PERFORMANCE

U.K.: "Eleanor Rigby"/"Yellow Submarine"; August 5, 1966, Parlophone R 5493: #1. As a double A-side with "Eleanor Rigby," "Yellow Submarine" charted at #1.

U.S.: "Eleanor Rigby"/"Yellow Submarine"; August 8, 1966, Capitol 5715: #11 (certified by the RIAA as "Gold," with more than 500,000 copies sold). As a double A-side with "Eleanor Rigby," "Yellow Submarine" charted at #2.

LEGACY AND INFLUENCE

In 1967, the Beatles received an Ivor Novello Award, awarded annually by the British Academy of Songwriters, Composers, and Authors, for "Yellow Submarine."

In 2010, *Rolling Stone* ranked "Yellow Submarine" as #74 on the magazine's list of *The Beatles' 100 Greatest Songs*.

ALBUM APPEARANCES: *Revolver* (U.K.); *Revolver* (U.S.); *A Collection of Beatles Oldies*; *Yellow Submarine*; *The Beatles, 1962–1966*; *Reel Music*; *Yellow Submarine Songtrack*; *1*.

See also: Boyd, Pattie; Emerick, Geoff; Evans, Mal; Martin, George; *Revolver* (U.K. LP).

Yellow Submarine (LP)

January 13, 1969, Apple [Capitol] SW 153 (stereo)
January 17, 1969, Apple [Parlophone] PMC 7070 (mono)/PCS 7070 (stereo)

Yellow Submarine is the soundtrack for the Beatles' 1968 animated film of the same name. It was released on the Apple label on January 17, 1969, in the United Kingdom. In the United States, it was released on January 13, 1969.

Yellow Submarine was released as a stereo compact disc (CD), along with *The Beatles (The White Album)*, on August 24, 1987. On September 13, 1999, the

Beatles released *Yellow Submarine Songtrack*, which included remastered versions of the original sound-track recordings. *Yellow Submarine* was remastered and rereleased as a stereo CD on September 9, 2009.

BACKGROUND AND RECORDING SESSIONS

Produced by George Martin with Geoff Emerick as his sound engineer, *Yellow Submarine* was recorded on four-track equipment during multiple, sporadic sessions from February 13, 1967, through February 11, 1968, at Abbey Road Studios, De Lane Lea Recording Studios, and Olympic Sound Studios.

The Beatles devoted four new and unreleased tracks for the project—including "All Together Now," "It's All Too Much," "Only a Northern Song," and "Hey Bulldog"—along with the previously released "All You Need Is Love" and "Yellow Submarine," both of which featured prominently in the *Yellow Submarine* animated feature film that premiered at the London Pavilion on July 17, 1968. The Beatles originally considered the release of a five-song EP—as with the British *Magical Mystery Tour* EP—that would have included the four new Beatles songs along with "Across the Universe," although that plan was later dismissed in favor of a full-length album.

In addition to the four new Beatles recordings, the sound-track album itself was rounded out by *Yellow Submarine*'s incidental music, composed by Martin and performed courtesy of George Martin and His Orchestra. As Martin later recalled, "Everything had to be tailor-made for the picture. If a door opened or a funny face appeared at a window, and those moments needed to be pointed-up, it was the musical score that had to do the job." During the composition process, he added,

> You plan whatever tempo your rhythm is going to be, and then you lay down what is called a "click track." That is, a separate track which simply contains a click sound which appears every so many frames of film. You know that 35mm film runs at 24 frames per second, so knowing what tempo you want, you simply ask the film editor to put on a click at whatever interval you want. Then while conducting the orchestra, you wear headphones through which you can hear the clicks, and by keeping to that particular beat you "lock in" the orchestra to the film. In that way you can write your score knowing that, even if something happens a third of the way or halfway through a bar, you can safely put in whatever musical effect you want, with absolute certainty that it will match the picture—that is how I did it with "Yellow Submarine." I wrote very precisely even with *avant-garde* and weird sounds like "Sea Of Holes," keeping to their bar-lines, knowing that the click track would ensure it fitted. (Martin 1979, 227)

The sound-track album features six Martin instrumentals, including "Pepperland," the "Sea of Time"/"Sea of Holes" medley, "Sea of Monsters," "March of the Meanies," "Pepperland Laid Waste," and "Yellow Submarine in Pepperland."

For Martin, the soundtrack afforded the producer with the opportunity to push the boundaries of his work as composer. As Martin later wrote,

> "Yellow Submarine" saw some pretty strange experiments, too. In one sequence, in the "Sea Of Monsters," the yellow submarine is wandering around and all kinds of weird little things are crawling along the sea floor, some with three legs. One monster is enormous, without arms but with two long legs with wellington boots on, and in place of a nose there is a kind of long trumpet. This is a sucking-up monster—when it sees the other little monsters, it uses its trumpet to suck them up. Eventually it sucks up the yellow submarine, and finally gets hold of the corner of the [movie] screen and sucks that up too, until it all goes white. I felt, naturally, that scene required special "sucking-up" music—the question was how to do it with an orchestra! (Martin 1979, 228)

Eventually, Martin came up with a solution:

> Backwards music. Music played backwards sounds very odd anyway, and a trombone or cymbal played backwards sounds just like a sucking-in noise. So I scored about 45 seconds for the orchestra to play, in such a way that the music would fit the picture when we played it backwards. The engineer working at CTS at that time was a great character named Jack Clegg, and when I explained the idea to him he said, "Lovely! Great idea! I'll get the film turned 'round, and you record the music to the backward film. Then, when we turn the film 'round the right way, your music will be backwards." It sounded like something from a *Goon* script. (Martin 1979, 229)

George Martin and His Orchestra recorded the film's incidental music contemporaneous with the animated feature's production, leaving Martin with the task of merging his soundtrack with the film itself. As Martin later remembered, "Once all the music had been recorded, we dubbed it onto the film, and even then there was more messing about. In some places we cut out the music because sound-effects worked better—in others we eliminated sound-effects because what I had written sounded better. Yet, in spite of everything, that score proved enormously successful and earned me a load of fan mail" (Martin 1979, 229).

TRACK LISTING

Side 1: "Yellow Submarine"; "Only a Northern Song"; "All Together Now"; "Hey Bulldog"; "It's All Too Much"; "All You Need Is Love."

Side 2: "Pepperland" (Instrumental); "Sea of Time"/"Sea of Holes" (Instrumental); "Sea of Monsters" (Instrumental); "March of the Meanies" (Instrumental); "Pepperland Laid Waste" (Instrumental); "Yellow Submarine in Pepperland" (Instrumental).

COVER ARTWORK

The cover artwork for the *Yellow Submarine* album featured animated cells from the feature film. The artwork for the British release included the phrase "Nothing Is Real"—a lyric from "Strawberry Fields Forever"—underneath the film's title on the front cover. The back cover included a review of *The Beatles* (*The White Album*) from *The Observer*'s Tony Palmer, as well as liner notes from Apple press officer Derek Taylor. The American release omitted the Palmer review in favor of a fictitious biography of Sgt. Pepper's Lonely Hearts Club Band detailing their epic struggle in Pepperland against the evil Blue Meanies.

CHART PERFORMANCE

U.K.: #3.

U.S.: #2 (certified by the RIAA as "Platinum," with more than 1 million copies sold).

LEGACY AND INFLUENCE

In 1970, *Yellow Submarine* was nominated for a Grammy Award for Best Original Score Written for a Motion Picture or Television Show at the 12th Grammy Awards.

In 2012, *Mojo* magazine published a special issue in commemoration of *Yellow Submarine*, including a cover-mounted CD with contemporary cover versions of the album's entire contents entitled *Yellow Submarine Resurfaces*.

See also: Emerick, Geoff; Martin, George; *Yellow Submarine* (Film); *Yellow Submarine Songtrack* (LP).

Yellow Submarine Songtrack (LP)

September 14, 1999, Apple [Parlophone] 521 412
September 17, 1999, Apple [Capitol] CDP 7243 5 21481 2 7

Yellow Submarine Songtrack is the remastered soundtrack associated with the 1999 rerelease of the *Yellow Submarine* animated feature film.

BACKGROUND

Produced by Martin, *Yellow Submarine Songtrack* is fully remixed from the original multitrack tapes. In this way, it exists as a precursor for the fully remixed and remastered versions of the Beatles' official output that was released a decade later in September 2009.

In contrast with the original 1969 *Yellow Submarine* soundtrack, *Yellow Submarine Songtrack* omits Martin's incidental music as recorded by George Martin and His Orchestra. It includes a number of Beatles' tracks originally included in the animated feature in place of Martin's orchestral score. The additional tracks include "Baby, You're a Rich Man," "Eleanor Rigby," "Love You To," "Lucy in the Sky with Diamonds," "Nowhere Man," "Sgt. Pepper's Lonely Hearts Club Band," "Think for Yourself," "When I'm Sixty-Four," and "With a Little Help from My Friends." Although they feature in the original movie, "A Day in the Life" and "I Am the Walrus" were not included among the contents of the *Yellow Submarine Songtrack*.

TRACK LISTING

"Yellow Submarine"; "Hey Bulldog"; "Eleanor Rigby"; "Love You To"; "All Together Now"; "Lucy in the Sky with Diamonds"; "Think for Yourself"; "Sgt. Pepper's Lonely Hearts Club Band"; "With a Little Help from My Friends"; "Baby, You're a Rich Man"; "Only a Northern Song"; "All You Need Is a Love"; "When I'm Sixty-Four"; "Nowhere Man"; "It's All Too Much."

COVER ARTWORK

The cover art for *Yellow Submarine Songtrack* features a full-color film cell rendition of the yellow submarine, along with the logo for the animated feature film. The 1999 special LP release of the album included yellow vinyl, while the 2012 rerelease of *Yellow Submarine Songtrack* included an illustrated booklet.

CHART PERFORMANCE

U.K.: #8 (certified by the BPI as "Gold," with more than 100,000 copies sold).
U.S.: #15 (certified by the RIAA as "Gold," with more than 500,000 copies sold).

See also: Martin, George; *Yellow Submarine* (Film); *Yellow Submarine* (LP).

"Yer Blues" (Lennon–McCartney)

"Yer Blues" is a song on *The Beatles* (*The White Album*).

AUTHORSHIP AND BACKGROUND

Written by Lennon, "Yer Blues" finds its origins during the Beatles' 1968 visit to India. Written by Lennon in Rishikesh while he was "up there trying to reach God and feeling suicidal," the composition features a complex structure, as the song transitions among 12/8, 6/8, and 4/4 time signatures (Spizer 2003, 111).

"Yer Blues" was written as a tongue-in-cheek response to the British Blues Boom during the latter half of the 1960s. Lennon and McCartney disagreed about the song's title, with Lennon preferring the casual, lighthearted "Yer" and McCartney lobbying for "Your" instead.

An early version of "Yer Blues" was recorded in May 1968 at Harrison's Kinfauns studio as part of the Esher Tapes.

RECORDING SESSIONS

Produced by George Martin, "Yer Blues" was recorded at Abbey Road Studios on August 13, 1968, with overdubbing sessions on August 14 and 20. It was recorded in mid-August in Studio Two's closet-sized Annex, a relatively tiny room in which all four Beatles huddled with their instruments.

PERSONNEL

Lennon: Vocal, Epiphone Casino
McCartney: Fender Jazz Bass
Harrison: Gibson Les Paul Standard
Starr: Ludwig Oyster Black Pearl Drums

LEGACY AND INFLUENCE

In 2010, *Rolling Stone* ranked "Yer Blues" as #76 on the magazine's list of *The Beatles' 100 Greatest Songs*.

ALBUM APPEARANCE: *The Beatles* (*The White Album*).

See also: *The Beatles* (*The White Album*) (LP); Plastic Ono Band.

"Yes It Is" (Lennon–McCartney)

"Yes It Is" is the B-side of the Beatles' "Ticket to Ride" single, which was released in the United Kingdom on April 9, 1965, and in the United States on April 14, 1965.

AUTHORSHIP AND BACKGROUND

Written by Lennon with assistance from McCartney, "Yes It Is" offers another example of the Beatles' penchant for crafting harmony vocals.

As McCartney recalled, "I was there writing it with John, but it was his inspiration that I helped him finish off. 'Yes It Is' is a very fine song of John's" (Miles 1997, 176). As Lennon later observed, "That's me trying a rewrite of 'This Boy,' but it didn't work" (Lennon and Ono 2000, 196).

RECORDING SESSIONS

Produced by George Martin, "Yes It Is" was recorded in 15 takes at Abbey Road Studios on February 16, 1965. As with "I Need You," recorded the day before with overdubbing on February 16, "Yes It Is" finds Harrison employing volume pedal effects on his guitar part. Lennon, McCartney, and Harrison spent more than three hours working on their harmony vocals for the song.

PERSONNEL

Lennon: Vocal, Gibson J-160E
McCartney: Höfner 500/1, Backing Vocal
Harrison: Gretsch Tennessean, Backing Vocal
Starr: Ludwig Oyster Black Pearl Drums, Tambourine

CHART PERFORMANCE

U.K.: "Ticket to Ride"/"Yes It Is"; April 9, 1965, Parlophone R 5265: #1.
U.S.: "Ticket to Ride"/"Yes It Is"; April 19, 1965, Capitol 5407: #1 (certified by the RIAA as "Gold," with more than 500,000 copies sold). As the B-side of "Ticket to Ride," "Yes It Is" charted at #46.

LEGACY AND INFLUENCE

In 2010, *Rolling Stone* ranked "Yes It Is" as #99 on the magazine's list of *The Beatles' 100 Greatest Songs*.

ALBUM APPEARANCES: *Beatles VI*; *Love Songs*; *Rarities* (U.K.); *Past Masters, Volume 1*; *Anthology 2*.

See also: *The Beatles Anthology, Volume 2* (LP); *Past Masters, Volume 1* (LP).

"Yesterday" (Lennon–McCartney)

"Yesterday" was the Beatles' fifth consecutive #1 hit single in the United States, where it was released on August 6, 1965. It is the most widely covered composition in the history of popular music, with some 2,500 cover versions. It also widened the Beatles' audience, enlarging their fan base across multiple demographics.

AUTHORSHIP AND BACKGROUND

McCartney originally composed "Yesterday" during the band's January 1964 sojourn in Paris, and for more than 18 months, "Yesterday" had existed in the ether of his dreams—initially, as half-baked lyrics bespeaking an enduring love for

"Scrambled Eggs," the song's working title, and later as a tune that felt so fresh and original that the songwriter was certain that somebody else had composed it. For a while, the working lyrics included "Scrambled eggs / Oh, my baby how I love your legs."

There have been two principal theories about the inspiration for "Yesterday." British musicologist Spencer Leigh contends that McCartney was inspired by Nat King Cole's 1953 hit song "Answer Me, My Love," while Italian producer Lilli Greco suggests that "Yesterday" finds its roots in an 1895 Neapolitan composition entitled "Piccerè che vene a dicere."

As McCartney recalled,

> It fell out of bed. I had a piano by my bedside and I must have dreamed it, because I tumbled out of bed and put my hands on the piano keys and I had a tune in my head. It was just all there, a complete thing. I couldn't believe it. It came too easy. In fact, I didn't believe I'd written it. I thought maybe I'd heard it before, it was some other tune, and I went around for weeks playing the chords of the song for people, asking them, "Is this like something? I think I've written it." And people would say, "No, it's not like anything else, but it's good." (Dowlding 1989, 105)

McCartney later completed the lyrics for "Yesterday" while vacationing with Jane Asher in Portugal in May 1965. McCartney later claimed on *The Howard Stern Show* that he still possesses the original lyrics, which were written on the back of an envelope.

As Lennon recalled, "Paul wrote the lyrics to 'Yesterday.' Although the lyrics don't resolve into any sense, they're good lines. They certainly work, you know what I mean? They're good—but if you read the whole song, it doesn't say anything; you don't know what happened. She left and he wishes it were yesterday—that much you get—but it doesn't really resolve. So, mine didn't used to either. I have had so much accolade for 'Yesterday.' That's Paul's song, and Paul's baby. Well done. Beautiful—and I never wished I'd written it" (Lennon and Ono 2000, 177).

RECORDING SESSIONS

Produced by George Martin, "Yesterday" was recorded at Abbey Road Studios on June 14, 1965—the same day in which the Beatles recorded "I've Just Seen a Face" and the hard-rocking "I'm Down."

As McCartney prepared to record "Yesterday" with his trusty Epiphone Texan, Martin suggested that his solo performance might benefit from a string accompaniment. McCartney was initially skeptical, believing that a classical arrangement would be too precious for a Beatles' record. They were a rock 'n' roll band, after all, and a string quartet might detract from the image that they had been cultivating since teenagehood. But the producer was not to be deterred. Eventually, McCartney settled down at the piano with Martin, and they hammered out a suitably tasteful arrangement to the Beatle's liking. During Martin's years as the band's producer, the Beatles were unable to read or write musical notation due to their lack

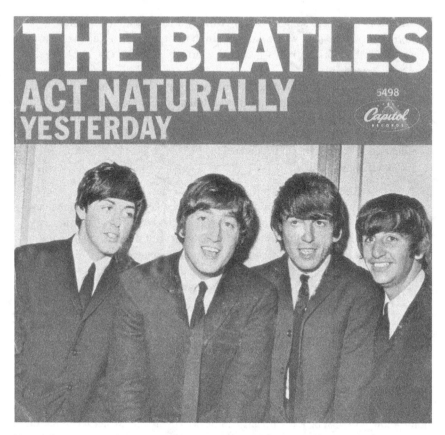

View of the cover of the 45-rpm single "Yesterday" by the Beatles, released in the U.S. by Capitol Records in 1965. From left to right are Paul McCartney, John Lennon, George Harrison, and Ringo Starr. (Blank Archives/Getty Images)

of formal training. (McCartney became somewhat adept at understanding musical notation during his later years as a solo artist.) Hence, Martin functioned as the Beatles' arranger and assist them in crafting the particular sounds that they wanted to achieve in their songs.

As Martin remembered,

Originally, I recorded Paul singing and playing at the same time, miking up both guitar and voice. Then later on I wrote and overdubbed the strings, and on my fourth track I got Paul to have another go at recording the voice, just in case we got a better performance. Well, we didn't—not in my opinion anyway—except in one particular part, which was at the end of the first section ("I said something wrong"). So I used that as an alternative voice, and during the past 20 years I've forgotten about it and have always thought that is where I decided to double-track the voice. But it's not double-tracked, because in fact its voice with leakage from a speaker, as we didn't use headphones. (Dowlding 1989, 106)

For the producer, it proved to be the most transformative moment in the group's career. As Martin recalled in *All You Need Is Ears* (1979),

> The turning point probably came with the song "Yesterday." . . . That was when, as I can see it in retrospect, I started to leave my hallmark on the music, when a style started to emerge which was partly of my making. It was on "Yesterday" that I started to score their music. It was on "Yesterday" that we first used instruments other than the Beatles and myself. On "Yesterday," the added ingredient was no more nor less than a string quartet; and that, in the pop world of those days, was quite a step to take. It was with "Yesterday" that we started breaking out of the phase of using just four instruments and went into something more experimental, though our initial experiments were severely limited by the fairly crude tools at our disposal, and had simply to be molded out of my recording experience. (Martin 1979, 166, 167)

As a musical achievement, the significance of "Yesterday" was not lost on the esteemed BBC critic Deryck Cooke, who—echoing William Mann's sentiments about "Not a Second Time" in December 1963—branded Lennon and McCartney as "serious" composers of a "new music" (Cooke 1982, 199).

PERSONNEL

McCartney: Vocal, Epiphone Texan
Studio Musicians: String Quartet Accompaniment conducted by Martin
Tony Gilbert, Sidney Sax: Violin
Kenneth Essex: Viola
Francisco Gabarro: Cello

CHART PERFORMANCE

U.S.: "Yesterday"/"Act Naturally"; September 13, 1965, Capitol 5498: #1 (certified by the RIAA as "Gold," with more than 500,000 copies sold).
U.K.: "Yesterday"/"I Should Have Known Better"; March 5, 1976, Parlophone R 6013: #8.

LEGACY AND INFLUENCE

"Yesterday" is included among the Rock and Roll Hall of Fame's *500 Songs That Shaped Rock and Roll.*

In 1966, the Beatles received an Ivor Novello Award, awarded annually by the British Academy of Songwriters, Composers, and Authors, for "Yesterday."

In 1997, "Yesterday" was inducted into the National Academy of Recording Arts and Sciences Grammy Hall of Fame.

In 1999, BBC Radio declared "Yesterday" as the #1 pop song of all time.

In 2000, *Mojo* magazine ranked "Yesterday" as #11 on the magazine's list of *The 100 Greatest Songs of All Time*.

In 2004, *Rolling Stone* ranked "Yesterday" as #13 on the magazine's list of *The 500 Greatest Songs of All Time*.

In 2006, *Q Magazine* ranked "Yesterday" as #52 on the magazine's list of *The 100 Greatest Songs of All Time*.

In 2010, *Rolling Stone* ranked "Yesterday" as #4 on the magazine's list of *The Beatles' 100 Greatest Songs*.

In October 2012, BBC Local Radio listeners ranked "Yesterday" as their 2nd favorite Beatles song in a poll conducted in commemoration of the 50th anniversary of "Love Me Do," the band's first single.

A January 2013 BBC documentary, *The Richest Songs in the World*, ranked "Yesterday" as the fourth highest-earning song in music history behind "Happy Birthday to You," "White Christmas," and "You've Lost That Lovin' Feelin'."

ALBUM APPEARANCES: *Help!* (U.K.); *Yesterday . . . and Today*; *A Collection of Beatles Oldies*; *The Beatles, 1962–1966*; *Love Songs*; *20 Greatest Hits*; *Anthology 2*; *1*; *Love*.

See also: *Help!* (U.K. LP); Martin, George.

Yesterday . . . and Today (LP)

June 20, 1966, Capitol T 2553 (mono)/ST 2553 (stereo)

Yesterday . . . and Today was the 11th Beatles album to be released in the United States—the 9th on Capitol Records, along with Vee-Jay Records' *Introducing . . . the Beatles* and United Artists' soundtrack for the *A Hard Day's Night* feature film. It was released on the Capitol label on June 20, 1966. Specifically released to take advantage of the phenomenal success of the "Yesterday" single on American shores, it is an amalgamation of the U.K. versions of *Help!*, released on August 6, 1965; *Rubber Soul*, released on December 3, 1965; and the upcoming *Revolver*, which was released on August 5, 1966. It also featured both sides of the hit double A-side single "Day Tripper"/"We Can Work It Out."

Yesterday . . . and Today was deleted from the Beatles' catalogue in 1987, when the group's U.K. albums were distributed as CD releases.

BACKGROUND

With the intense controversy that developed around its garish cover artwork, *Yesterday . . . and Today* is easily the most notorious of the Beatles' album releases on Capitol Records. As with other American Beatles releases during this era, it features variant mixes of Beatles tracks—in this case, different extant versions of "Day Tripper," "Doctor Robert," "I'm Only Sleeping," and "We Can Work It Out."

TRACK LISTING

Side 1: "Drive My Car"; "I'm Only Sleeping"; "Nowhere Man"; "Doctor Robert"; "Yesterday"; "Act Naturally."

Side 2: "And Your Bird Can Sing"; "If I Needed Someone"; "We Can Work It Out"; "What Goes On"; "Day Tripper."

COVER ARTWORK

The original cover artwork for *Yesterday . . . and Today* has come to be known as the "butcher" cover, given Robert Whitaker's gory photograph featured the Beatles dressed in white laboratory coats, clutching decapitated baby dolls, and surrounded by raw meat. Whitaker's photograph stems from an early 1966 photo session with the Beatles in which the photographer staged a conceptual art piece entitled *A Somnambulant Adventure*. In a 1980 interview, Lennon attributed the photograph to "our boredom and resentment at having to do *another* photo session and *another* Beatles thing. We were sick to death of it" (Cross 2005, 122). For McCartney, the photograph presented the Beatles' express critical statement about the bloody atrocities associated with the Vietnam War. Harrison was less supportive, describing the idea behind the photograph as "gross, and I also thought it was stupid. Sometimes we all did stupid things thinking it was cool and hip when it was naïve and dumb; and that was one of them" (Beatles 2000, 204). In addition to the *Yesterday . . . and Today* cover, the same photograph was used in promotional advertisements for the "Paperback Writer" single, which was released in the United Kingdom on June 10, 1966, and in the United States on May 30, 1966.

After advance copies of *Yesterday . . . and Today* were released in the United States to disc jockeys and record dealers, the backlash was swift. On June 15, 1966—a mere five days before the album's official release—the EMI Group's Chairman Sir Joseph Lockwood ordered the album's recall in a belated effort to replace its controversial cover photograph. In a hastily prepared statement, the president of Capitol Records, Alan W. Livingston, attempted to defend the album's cover as "'pop art' satire." Attempting to stem the negative publicity surrounding the album's inflammatory artwork, Capitol Records withdrew the cover photograph under Lockwood's orders and released the album five days later with a benign photograph, newly shot by Robert Whitaker, of the group playfully posing around a steamer trunk in a hotel room. The cover fiasco ensured that *Yesterday . . . and Today* became the only Beatles album to actually *lose* money, at least initially, for Capitol Records.

Ironically, the company ultimately failed in its effort to eradicate the offending cover. During the long weekend in which Capitol employees were busy removing *Yesterday . . . and Today*'s cover artwork—at a reported cost of more than

$200,000—many fatigued workers resorted to pasting the new photograph over the "butcher" cover. As a result, numerous fans discovered that they could carefully extricate the original photograph. The butcher cover has since emerged as a much-desired item of Beatles memorabilia among serious collectors.

In 1980, the U.S. release of *Rarities* included a full-cover photographic reproduction of the "butcher" cover. The *Rarities* liner notes state that "so few copies [of *Yesterday . . . and Today*] were distributed that many of today's fans had never even seen the famous and controversial picture which is why it is included in *Rarities*. When the shot was used on the original cover, it was cropped at knee level. Now for the first time, the entire butcher photo is reproduced."

CHART PERFORMANCE

U.S.: #1 (certified by the RIAA as "2x Multi Platinum," with more than 2 million copies sold).

See also: *Rarities* (U.S. LP).

"You Can't Do That" (Lennon–McCartney)

"You Can't Do That" is a song on the Beatles' *A Hard Day's Night* album.

AUTHORSHIP AND BACKGROUND

Written by Lennon, "You Can't Do That" was influenced by the 12-bar blues popularized by Wilson Pickett. As Lennon remembered, "I'd find it a drag to play rhythm all the time, so I always work myself out something interesting to play. The best example I can think of is like I did on 'You Can't Do That.' There really isn't a lead guitarist and a rhythm guitarist on that, because I feel the rhythm guitarist role sounds too thin for records. Anyway it drove me potty to play chunk-chunk rhythm all the time. I never play anything as lead guitarist that George couldn't do better. But I like playing lead sometimes, so I do it" (Dowlding 1989, 77).

RECORDING SESSIONS

Produced by Martin, "You Can't Do That" was recorded at Abbey Road Studios on February 25, 1964. On May 22, Martin overdubbed a piano part that was not used in the album's final mix.

PERSONNEL

Lennon: Vocal, Rickenbacker 325
McCartney: Höfner 500/1, Backing Vocal

Harrison: Rickenbacker 360/12, Backing Vocal
Starr: Ludwig Oyster Black Pearl Drums, Bongos, Cowbell

CHART PERFORMANCE

U.S.: "Can't Buy Me Love"/"You Can't Do That"; March 16, 1964, Capitol 5150: #1 (certified by the RIAA as "Gold," with more than 500,000 copies sold). As the B-side of "Can't Buy Me Love," "You Can't Do That" charted at #48.

LEGACY AND INFLUENCE

In 2010, *Rolling Stone* ranked "You Can't Do That" as #70 on the magazine's list of *The Beatles' 100 Greatest Songs*.

ALBUM APPEARANCES: *A Hard Day's Night* (U.K.); *The Beatles' Second Album*; *Rock 'n' Roll Music*; *Anthology 1*; *Tomorrow Never Knows*; *On Air: Live at the BBC, Volume 2*.

See also: *A Hard Day's Night* (Film); *A Hard Day's Night* (U.K. LP).

"You Know My Name (Look Up the Number)"
(Lennon–McCartney)

"You Know My Name (Look Up the Number)" was the B-side of the "Let It Be" single, which was released in the United Kingdom on March 6, 1970, and in the United States on March 11, 1970.

AUTHORSHIP AND BACKGROUND

Written and conceived largely by Lennon, "You Know My Name (Look Up the Number)" was an unfinished work-in-progress that the Beatles variously recorded between 1967 and 1969.

As one of the strangest songs in the Beatles' corpus, "You Know My Name (Look Up the Number)" originated from the 1967 London metropolitan telephone directory, which Lennon spotted during a visit to McCartney's Cavendish home. "You know their NAME?" the telephone directory's cover intoned, "Look up their NUMBER." With another quirky found object on his hands, Lennon began imagining a doo-wop number in the style of the Four Tops as he walked the short distance to EMI Studios with McCartney. By the time they set down to work on the track, it had been transformed, at McCartney's suggestion, into a zany, screwball comedy tune in the tradition of the Goons, or, more recently, the Bonzo Dog Doo-Dah Band. The Beatles' comedic efforts on "You Know My Name (Look Up the Number)" reveal the same zany brand of humor that they employed in the production of their annual fan-club Christmas records. Featuring a series of jokes, holiday music, and seasonal greetings, seven Beatles Christmas records saw release between 1963 and 1969, culminating in a special December 1970 compilation album. The Beatles' most recognizable holiday number, entitled "Christmas Time (Is Here Again)," was written by all four Beatles and released in December 1967.

As Lennon observed in 1969, "There was another song I wrote around *Pepper* time that's still in the can, called 'You Know My Name (Look Up the Number).' That's the only words to it. It just goes on all the way like that, and we did these mad backings. But I never finished it, and I must" (Winn 2003b, 282). During one of his final interviews, Lennon remarked that "You Know My Name (Look Up the Number)" "was a piece of unfinished music that I turned into a comedy record with Paul. I was waiting for him in his house, and I saw the phone book was on the piano with the words, 'You know the name, look up the number.' It was like a logo, and I just changed it. It was going to be a Four Tops kind of song—the chord changes are like that—but it never developed and we made a joke out of it" (Dowlding 1989, 295).

In a 1988 interview, McCartney noted that

People are only just discovering the B-sides of Beatles singles. They're only just discovering things like "You Know My Name"—probably my favorite Beatles track! Just because it's so insane. All the memories—I mean, what would you do if a guy like John Lennon turned up at the studio and said, "I've got a new song." I said, "What's the words?" and he replied, "You know my name look up the number." I asked, "What's the rest of it?" "No. No other words, those are the words. And I wanna do it like a mantra!" We did it over a period of maybe two or three years. We started off and we just did 20 minutes, and we tried it again and it didn't work. We tried it again, and we had these endless, crazy fun sessions. (Lewisohn 1988, 15)

McCartney later added that "we had a bit of a giggle doing those kind of tracks. Brian Jones [of the Rolling Stones] plays a funny sax solo. It's not amazingly well played but it happened to be exactly what we wanted. Brian was very good like that" (Miles 1997, 438).

RECORDING SESSIONS

Produced by Martin, "You Know My Name (Look Up the Number)" was recorded during four principal sessions on May 17, 1967, followed by June 7 and 8, 1967, and April 30, 1969. All of the sessions were conducted at Abbey Road Studios.

Nick Webb, an assistant sound engineer for the April 30, 1969, session, recalled, "John and Paul weren't always getting along that well at this time, but for this song they went out on the studio floor and sang together around one microphone. Even at this time I was thinking 'What are they doing with this old four-track tape, recording these funny bits onto this quaint song?' But it was a fun track to do" (Lewisohn 1988, 175).

"You Know My Name (Look Up the Number)" first came into being as an instrumental, complete with Rolling Stones guitarist Jones wailing away on an alto saxophone. The original track clocked in at more than six minutes and was composed of five discrete sections. With the assistance of the unwavering Evans, Lennon and McCartney finally overdubbed a series of uproariously funny vocals on April 30, 1969—nearly two years after the track's genesis. "You Know My Name (Look Up the Number)" begins with an intentionally overwrought, soulful introduction before cascading into "Slaggers," a smoke-filled cocktail lounge where McCartney adopts the smooth jazz stylings—as well as the breathy lower register—of nightclub singer Denis O'Bell, whose name was fashioned after Beatles assistant Denis O'Dell. As Slaggers fades out into obscurity, O'Bell surrenders the stage to none other than Lennon, who, adopting a pseudo-grandmotherly voice for the occasion, absurdly counts out loud, while singing the song's title, mantra-like, amidst a sea of penny whistles and percussion. The song's penultimate segment showcases McCartney's piano and Jones' alto sax before coalescing—with a trademark Beatles false ending—into Lennon's a cappella gibberish. Its inherent comedy owes little, if anything, to the repetition of its title, no matter how clever its origins. Instead, the track's humor develops out of the Beatles' effusive wit and obvious willingness to rush headlong into absurdity. Their sheer delight in producing the composition is made palpable at every turn.

"You Know My Name (Look Up the Number)" was finally mixed for commercial release in November 1969 as the A-side, rather amazingly, of a potential Plastic Ono Band single slated to feature "What's the New Mary Jane" as its flip side. Having been edited down to a more economical 4:19 in length, "You Know My Name (Look Up the Number)" eventually was released as the B-side of "Let It Be" in March 1970.

PERSONNEL

Lennon: Vocal, Maracas, Sound Effects
McCartney: Vocal, Piano, Double Bass, Sound Effects
Harrison: Xylophone, Backing Vocal
Starr: Vocal, Ludwig Oyster Black Pearl Drums, Bongos
Jones: Alto Saxophone
Evans: Sound Effects, Backing Vocal

CHART PERFORMANCE

U.K.: "Let It Be"/"You Know My Name (Look Up the Number)"; March 6, 1970, Apple [Parlophone] R 5833: #2. As the B-side of "Let It Be," "You Know My Name (Look Up the Number)" did not chart.

U.S.: "Let It Be"/"You Know My Name (Look Up the Number)"; March 11, 1970, Apple [Capitol] 2764: #1 (certified by the RIAA as "2x Multi Platinum," with more than 2 million copies sold). As the B-side of "Let It Be," "You Know My Name (Look Up the Number)" did not chart.

ALBUM APPEARANCES: *Rarities* (U.K.); *Rarities* (U.S.); *Past Masters, Volume 2*; *Anthology 2*.

See also: Evans, Mal.

"You Like Me Too Much" (Harrison)

"You Like Me Too Much" is a song on the Beatles' *Help!* album.

AUTHORSHIP AND BACKGROUND

Written by Harrison, "You Like Me Too Much" marks the guitarist's second contribution, after "I Need You," for the *Help!* album. It was the first time Harrison contributed original material since *With the Beatles*.

RECORDING SESSIONS

Produced by George Martin, "You Like Me Too Much" was recorded at Abbey Road Studios on February 17, 1965.

PERSONNEL

Lennon: Gibson J-160E, Electric Piano
McCartney: Piano, Höfner 500/1, Backing Vocal
Harrison: Vocal, Gretsch Tennessean, Tambourine
Starr: Ludwig Oyster Black Pearl Drums
Martin: Piano

ALBUM APPEARANCES: *Help!* (U.K.); *Beatles VI*.

See also: *Help!* (U.K. LP).

"You Never Give Me Your Money" (Lennon–McCartney)

"You Never Give Me Your Money" is a song on the Beatles' *Abbey Road* album. It is the first song in the *Abbey Road* Medley.

AUTHORSHIP AND BACKGROUND

McCartney's "You Never Give Me Your Money" was written in response to the Beatles' crippling managerial crisis. As McCartney later recalled, "This was me directly lambasting Allen Klein's attitude to us: no money, just funny paper, all promises and it never works out. It's basically a song about no faith in the person, that found its way into the medley on *Abbey Road*. John saw the humor in it" (Harry 2002, 930).

RECORDING SESSIONS

Produced by George Martin, "You Never Give Me Your Money" was recorded at Abbey Road Studios on May 6, 1969. In several July sessions, McCartney recorded his vocal and bass parts, along with chimes and other sound effects that would adorn the song's ending. In an August 5 session, the Beatles added the "One, two, three, four, five, six, seven / All good children go to heaven" refrain that concludes the track, displacing an organ part that was originally designed to segue into "Sun King," the medley's second song. As Wilfrid Mellers points out, the subsequent "electronic gibbering and beeping belies the nursery-rhyme paradise of the words," ultimately producing an emotional response that is "more scary than ecstatic" (1973, 119).

PERSONNEL

  Lennon: Epiphone Casino
  McCartney: Vocal, Rickenbacker 4001S, Piano, Epiphone Casino
  Harrison: Gibson SG Standard
  Starr: Ludwig Hollywood Maple Drums, Tambourine

ALBUM APPEARANCE: *Abbey Road.*

See also: *Abbey Road* (LP).

"You Really Got a Hold on Me" (Robinson)

"You Really Got a Hold on Me" is a song on the *With the Beatles* album.

AUTHORSHIP AND BACKGROUND

Originally written by Smokey Robinson, the song was recorded as "You've Really Got a Hold on Me" by Robinson and Miracles in 1962. It became a smash Top 10 hit for the Miracles. After "Shop Around," "You've Really Got a Hold on Me" was the group's second record to sell more than a million copies.

RECORDING SESSIONS

Produced by George Martin, "You Really Got a Hold on Me" was recorded in seven takes at Abbey Road Studios on July 18, 1963. The Beatles recorded "You Really Got a Hold on Me" on three occasions for BBC Radio, including a May 24, 1963, recording that was broadcast on *Pop Go the Beatles* on June 4. The Beatles also recording the song for BBC radio on July 30 and September 3. The July 30 recording was employed on the group's *Live at the BBC* album.

PERSONNEL

Lennon: Vocal, Rickenbacker 325
McCartney: Höfner 500/1, Backing Vocal
Harrison: Gretsch Country Gentleman, Harmony Vocal
Starr: Ludwig Oyster Black Pearl Drums
Martin: Piano

LEGACY AND INFLUENCE

The Miracles' recording of "You've Really Got a Hold on Me" is included among the Rock and Roll Hall of Fame's *500 Songs That Shaped Rock and Roll*.

ALBUM APPEARANCES: *With the Beatles*; *The Beatles' Second Album*; *Live at the BBC*; *Anthology 1*.

See also: *Live at the BBC* (LP); *With the Beatles* (LP).

"You Won't See Me" (Lennon–McCartney)

"You Won't See Me" is a song on the Beatles' *Rubber Soul* album.

AUTHORSHIP AND BACKGROUND

Written by McCartney, "You Won't See Me" was inspired by a crisis in the songwriter's relationship with Jane Asher. It bears a strong resemblance to the Four Tops' "It's the Same Old Song," from which McCartney borrowed the composition's three-chord sequence.

As McCartney later recalled, "Normally I write on guitar and have full chords, or on piano and have full chords, but this was written around two little notes, a very slim phrase—a two-note progression that I had very high on the first two strings of the guitar. Then I wrote the tune for 'You Won't See Me' against it. It was 100 percent me, but I am always happy to give John a credit because there's always a chance that on the session he might have said, 'That'd be better'" (Miles 1997, 271).

RECORDING SESSIONS

Produced by George Martin, "You Won't See Me" was recorded in two takes at Abbey Road Studios on November 11, 1965, the last session for *Rubber Soul*.

PERSONNEL

Lennon: Tambourine, Backing Vocal
McCartney: Vocal, Höfner 500/1, Piano
Harrison: Sonic Blue Fender Stratocaster, Backing Vocal
Starr: Ludwig Oyster Black Pearl Drums
Evans: Hammond Organ

LEGACY AND INFLUENCE

In 2010, *Rolling Stone* ranked "You Won't See Me" as #94 on the magazine's list of *The Beatles' 100 Greatest Songs*.

ALBUM APPEARANCES: *Rubber Soul* (U.K.); *Rubber Soul* (U.S.).

See also: Evans, Mal; *Rubber Soul* (U.K. LP).

"Your Mother Should Know" (Lennon–McCartney)

"Your Mother Should Know" is a song on the Beatles' *Magical Mystery Tour* album.

AUTHORSHIP AND BACKGROUND

Written by McCartney, "Your Mother Should Know" was composed explicitly for the soundtrack of the made-for-television *Magical Mystery Tour* film. It had already been chosen as the dancehall number to grace the conclusion of the *Magical Mystery Tour* made-for-television movie, with the Beatles swaying in unison down a staircase and across a glitzy soundstage brimming with costumed, sashaying extras.

RECORDING SESSIONS

Produced by George Martin, "Your Mother Should Know" was recorded at London's Chappell Sound Studio on August 22, 1967, with additional overdubbing sessions on August 23 and September 29. It was completely remade on September 16, although that version was not used in the track's final mix. The first two sessions for "Your Mother Should Know" were conducted at Chappell Sound Studio because Abbey Road Studios was unavailable.

During the second evening of production devoted to "Your Mother Should Know," the Beatles were visited at Chappell Sound Studio by Brian Epstein for what turned out to be his very last meeting with the group.

PERSONNEL

Lennon: Hammond Organ, Backing Vocal
McCartney: Vocal, Rickenbacker 4001S, Piano
Harrison: Tambourine, Backing Vocal
Starr: Ludwig Oyster Black Pearl Drums

ALBUM APPEARANCES: *Magical Mystery Tour*; *Anthology 2*.

See also: *The Beatles Anthology, Volume 2* (LP); Epstein, Brian; *Magical Mystery Tour* (LP); *Magical Mystery Tour* (TV Film); "Paul Is Dead" Hoax.

"You're Going to Lose That Girl" (Lennon–McCartney)

"You're Going to Lose That Girl" is a song on the Beatles' *Help!* album.

AUTHORSHIP AND BACKGROUND

Written by Lennon, "You're Going to Lose That Girl" was the last song prepared for the *Help!* feature film before the Beatles began principal photography for the movie.

RECORDING SESSIONS

Produced by George Martin, "You're Going to Lose That Girl" was recorded at Abbey Road Studios on February 19, 1965. As with "Help!" and "The Night Before," "You're Going to Lose That Girl" employs a call-and-response vocal structure.

PERSONNEL

Lennon: Vocal, Epiphone Casino
McCartney: Höfner 500/1, Piano, Backing Vocal
Harrison: Sonic Blue Fender Stratocaster, Backing Vocal
Starr: Ludwig Oyster Black Pearl Drums, Bongos

LEGACY AND INFLUENCE

In 2010, *Rolling Stone* ranked "You're Going to Lose That Girl" as #27 on the magazine's list of *The Beatles' 100 Greatest Songs*.

ALBUM APPEARANCES: *Help!* (U.K.); *Help!* (U.S.); *Love Songs*.

See also: *Help!* (Film); *Help!* (U.K. LP).

"You've Got to Hide Your Love Away" (Lennon–McCartney)

"You've Got to Hide Your Love Away" is a song on the Beatles' *Help!* album.

AUTHORSHIP AND BACKGROUND

Written by Lennon, "You've Got to Hide Your Love Away" offers another example of the songwriter's emerging forays into confessional and autobiographical lyrics.

As Lennon remembered,

> It's one of those that you sort of sing a bit sadly to yourself, "Here I stand / Head in hand." I started thinking about my own emotions. I don't know when exactly it started, like "I'm a Loser" or "Hide Your Love Away," or those kind of things. Instead of projecting myself into a situation I would just try to express what I felt about myself which I had done in me books. I think it was Dylan helped me realize that—I had a sort of professional songwriter's attitude to writing pop songs, but to express myself I would write *Spaniard in the Works* or *In His Own Write*—the personal stories which were expressive of my personal emotions. I'd have a separate "songwriting" John Lennon who wrote songs for the sort of meat market, and I didn't consider them, the lyrics or anything, to have any depth at all. Then I started being me about the songs—not writing them objectively, but subjectively. (Everett 2001, 255)

"You've Got to Hide Your Love Away" also benefits from an accidental moment of creative caprice. As Lennon's boyhood friend Pete Shotton remembered,

> The first Beatles song composed in my presence was "You've Got to Hide Your Love Away," to which I myself contributed the sustained *hey*'s that introduced the main chorus. This Dylan-inspired number originally included the line "I can't go on, feeling two foot tall"; when he first performed it for Paul McCartney, however, John accidentally sang "two foot *small*." He paused to correct himself, then burst into laughter. "Let's leave that in, actually," he exclaimed. "All those pseuds will really love it." (Dowlding 1989, 99)

RECORDING SESSIONS

Produced by George Martin, "You've Got to Hide Your Love Away" was recorded at Abbey Road Studios on February 18, 1965.

"You've Got to Hide Your Love Away" marks the Beatles' first usage of studio musicians—in this case, overdubbed flute parts by John Scott under Martin's arrangement and conduction. As the song comes to a close, Lennon and Harrison's acoustic guitars give way to a plush wall of flutes—recalling the first movement from Igor Stravinsky's *The Rite of Spring*—and the composition draws to a hasty finish, tying a neat bow around Lennon's tender fable about loneliness and it's all too real capacity for engendering self-effacement (Pollack 2000). In his deft arrangement for "You've Got to Hide Your Love Away," Martin's score calls for a concert flute to be played an octave above an alto flute, thus affording the track with its layered, velveteen effect.

PERSONNEL

Lennon: Vocal, Framus 12-string Hootenanny
McCartney: Höfner 500/1
Harrison: José Ramírez Studio Guitar
Starr: Tambourine, Maracas
Studio Musicians: Flute Accompaniment conducted by Martin
John Scott: Flute

LEGACY AND INFLUENCE

In 2010, *Rolling Stone* ranked "You've Got to Hide Your Love Away" as #31 on the magazine's list of *The Beatles' 100 Greatest Songs*.

ALBUM APPEARANCES: *Help!* (U.K.); *Help!* (U.S.); *The Beatles, 1962–1966*; *Reel Music*; *Anthology 2*.

See also: Epstein, Brian; *Help!* (U.K. LP).

Z

Zapple Records

A subsidiary of Apple Records, Zapple Records was a short-lived enterprise intended to be associated with the release of spoken-word and avant-garde recordings.

Led by Barry Miles, who later served as Paul McCartney's biographer, Zapple Records was in operation from October 1968 through June 1969, releasing two albums during this period: John Lennon and Yoko Ono's *Unfinished Music No. 2: Life with the Lions* (1969) and George Harrison's *Electronic Sound* (1969). A third album, a spoken-word production by writer Richard Brautigan, was never released, given that Allen Klein closed the Zapple label down when he dramatically reorganized the company in 1969. A fourth album, a spoken-word LP by writer Lawrence Ferlinghetti, was also in the works when Zapple closed for business.

See also: Apple Corps, Ltd.; Klein, Allen.

Discography

All songs and albums in this discography are listed in chronological order.

RECORDINGS RELEASED IN THE UNITED KINGDOM

U.K. Singles Releases

"My Bonnie"/"The Saints"; January 5, 1962, Polydor NH 66–833 (as Tony Sheridan and the Beatles)

"Love Me Do"/"P.S. I Love You"; October 5, 1962, Parlophone R 4949

"Please Please Me"/"Ask Me Why"; January 11, 1963, Parlophone R 4983

"From Me to You"/"Thank You Girl"; April 11, 1963, Parlophone R 5015

"She Loves You"/"I'll Get You"; August 23, 1963, Parlophone R 5055

"I Want to Hold Your Hand"/"This Boy"; November 29, 1963, Parlophone R 5084

"Can't Buy Me Love"/"You Can't Do That"; March 20, 1964, Parlophone R 5114

"A Hard Day's Night"/"Things We Said Today"; July 10, 1964, Parlophone R 5160

"I Feel Fine"/"She's a Woman"; November 27, 1964, Parlophone R 5200

"Ticket to Ride"/"Yes It Is"; April 9, 1965, Parlophone R 5265

"Help!"/"I'm Down"; July 23, 1965, Parlophone R 5305

"We Can Work It Out"/"Day Tripper"; December 3, 1965, Parlophone R 5389

"Paperback Writer"/"Rain"; June 10, 1966; Parlophone R 5452

"Eleanor Rigby"/"Yellow Submarine"; August 5, 1966, Parlophone R 5493

"Strawberry Fields Forever"/"Penny Lane"; February 17, 1967, Parlophone R 5570

"All You Need Is Love"/"Baby, You're a Rich Man"; July 7, 1967, Parlophone R 5620

"Hello Goodbye"/"I Am the Walrus"; November 24, 1967, Parlophone R 5655

"Lady Madonna"/"The Inner Light"; March 15, 1968, Parlophone R 5675

"Hey Jude"/"Revolution"; August 30, 1968, Apple [Parlophone] R 5722

"Get Back"/"Don't Let Me Down"; April 11, 1969, Apple [Parlophone] R 5777 (as the Beatles with Billy Preston)

"The Ballad of John and Yoko"/"Old Brown Shoe"; May 30, 1969, Apple [Parlophone] R 5786

"Something"/"Come Together"; October 31, 1969, Apple [Parlophone] R 5814

"Let It Be"/"You Know My Name (Look Up the Number)"; March 6, 1970, Apple [Parlophone] R 5833

"Yesterday"/"I Should Have Known Better"; March 5, 1976, Parlophone R 6013

"Back in the USSR"/"Twist and Shout"; June 25, 1976, Parlophone R 6016

"Sgt. Pepper's Lonely Hearts Club Band/With a Little Help from My Friends"/"A Day in the Life"; September 30, 1978, Parlophone R 6022

"The Beatles' Movie Medley"/"I'm Happy Just to Dance with You"; March 24, 1982, Parlophone R 6055

"Baby It's You"/"I'll Follow the Sun"/"Devil in Her Heart"/"Boys"; April 4, 1995, Apple [Parlophone] NR 7243 8 58348 1 3 [CD Maxi-Single]

"Free as a Bird"/"Christmas Time (Is Here Again)"; December 4, 1995, Apple R 6422

"Real Love"/"Baby's in Black (Live)"; March 4, 1996, Apple RP 6425

U.K. EP Releases

Twist and Shout, July 12, 1963, Parlophone GEP 8882 (mono)

A: "Twist and Shout"; "A Taste of Honey." B: "Do You Want to Know a Secret"; "There's a Place."

The Beatles' Hits, September 6, 1963, Parlophone GEP 8880 (mono)

A: "From Me to You"; "Thank You Girl." B: "Please Please Me"; "Love Me Do."

The Beatles (No. 1), November 1, 1963, Parlophone GEP 8883 (mono)

A: "I Saw Her Standing There"; "Misery." B: "Anna (Go to Him)"; "Chains."

All My Loving, February 7, 1964, Parlophone GEP 8891 (mono)

A: "All My Loving"; "Ask Me Why." B: "Money (That's What I Want)"; "P.S. I Love You."

Long Tall Sally, June 19, 1964, Parlophone GEP 8913 (mono)

A: "Long Tall Sally"; "I Call Your Name." B: "Slow Down"; "Matchbox."

Extracts from the Film A Hard Day's Night, November 6, 1964, Parlophone GEP 8920 (mono)

A: "I Should Have Known Better"; "If I Fell." B: "Tell Me Why"; "And I Love Her."

Extracts from the Album A Hard Day's Night, November 6, 1964, Parlophone GEP 8924 (mono)

A: "Any Time at All"; "I'll Cry Instead." B: "Things We Said Today"; "When I Get Home."

Beatles for Sale, April 6, 1965, Parlophone GEP 8931 (mono)

A: "No Reply"; "I'm a Loser." B: "Rock and Roll Music"; "Eight Days a Week."

Beatles for Sale (No. 2), June 4, 1965, Parlophone GEP 8938 (mono)

A: "I'll Follow the Sun"; "Baby's in Black." B: "Words of Love"; "I Don't Want to Spoil the Party."

The Beatles' Million Sellers, December 6, 1965, Parlophone GEP 8946 (mono)

A: "She Loves You"; "I Want to Hold Your Hand." B: "Can't Buy Me Love"; "I Feel Fine."

Yesterday, March 4, 1966, Parlophone GEP 8948 (mono)

A: "Yesterday"; "Act Naturally." B: "You Like Me Too Much"; "It's Only Love."

Nowhere Man, July 8, 1966, Parlophone GEP 8952 (mono)

A: "Nowhere Man"; "Drive My Car." B: "Michelle"; "You Won't See Me."

Magical Mystery Tour, December 8, 1967, Parlophone MMT-1 (mono)/SMMT-1 (stereo)

A: "Magical Mystery Tour"; "Your Mother Should Know." B: "I Am the Walrus." C: "The Fool on the Hill"; "Flying." D: "Blue Jay Way."

U.K. Album Releases

Please Please Me, March 22, 1963, Parlophone PMC 1202 (mono)/PCS 3042 (stereo)
Side 1: "I Saw Her Standing There"; "Misery"; "Anna (Go to Him)"; "Chains"; "Boys"; "Ask Me Why"; "Please Please Me." Side 2: "Love Me Do"; "P.S. I Love You"; "Baby It's You"; "Do You Want to Know a Secret"; "A Taste of Honey"; "There's a Place"; "Twist and Shout."

With the Beatles, November 22, 1963, Parlophone PMC 1206 (mono)/PCS 3045 (stereo)
Side 1: "It Won't Be Long"; "All I've Got to Do"; "All My Loving"; "Don't Bother Me"; "Little Child"; "Till There Was You"; "Please Mister Postman." Side 2: "Roll Over Beethoven"; "Hold Me Tight"; "You Really Got a Hold on Me"; "I Wanna Be Your Man"; "Devil in Her Heart"; "Not a Second Time"; "Money (That's What I Want)."

A Hard Day's Night, July 10, 1964, Parlophone PMC 1230 (mono)/PCS 3058 (stereo)
Side 1: "A Hard Day's Night"; "I Should Have Known Better"; "If I Fell"; "I'm Happy Just to Dance with You"; "And I Love Her"; "Tell Me Why"; "Can't Buy Me Love." Side 2: "Any Time at All"; "I'll Cry Instead"; "Things We Said Today"; "When I Get Home"; "You Can't Do That"; "I'll Be Back."

Beatles for Sale, December 4, 1964, Parlophone PMC 1240 (mono)/PCS 3062 (stereo)
Side 1: "No Reply"; "I'm a Loser"; "Baby's in Black"; "Rock and Roll Music"; "I'll Follow the Sun"; "Mr. Moonlight"; "Kansas City"/"Hey-Hey-Hey-Hey!" Side 2: "Eight Days a Week"; "Words of Love"; "Honey Don't"; "Every Little Thing"; "I Don't Want to Spoil the Party"; "What You're Doing"; "Everybody's Trying to Be My Baby."

Help!, August 6, 1965, Parlophone PMC 1255 (mono)/PCS 3071 (stereo)
Side 1: "Help!"; "The Night Before"; "You've Got to Hide Your Love Away"; "I Need You"; "Another Girl"; "You're Going to Lose That Girl"; "Ticket to Ride." Side 2: "Act Naturally"; "It's Only Love"; "You Like Me Too Much"; "Tell Me What You See"; "I've Just Seen a Face"; "Yesterday"; "Dizzy Miss Lizzy."

Rubber Soul, December 3, 1965, Parlophone PMC 1267 (mono)/PCS 3075 (stereo)
Side 1: "Drive My Car"; "Norwegian Wood (This Bird Has Flown)"; "You Won't See Me"; "Nowhere Man"; "Think for Yourself"; "The Word"; "Michelle." Side 2: "What Goes On"; "Girl"; "I'm Looking through You"; "In My Life"; "Wait"; "If I Needed Someone"; "Run for Your Life."

Revolver, August 5, 1966, Parlophone PMC 7009 (mono)/PCS 7009 (stereo)
Side 1: "Taxman"; "Eleanor Rigby"; "I'm Only Sleeping"; "Love You To"; "Here, There, and Everywhere"; "Yellow Submarine"; "She Said She Said." Side 2: "Good Day Sunshine"; "And Your Bird Can Sing"; "For No One"; "Doctor Robert"; "I Want to Tell You"; "Got to Get You into My Life"; "Tomorrow Never Knows."

A Collection of Beatles Oldies, December 9, 1966, Parlophone PMC 7016 (mono)/PCS 7016 (stereo)
Side 1: "She Loves You"; "From Me to You"; "We Can Work It Out"; "Help!"; "Michelle"; "Yesterday"; "I Feel Fine"; "Yellow Submarine." Side 2: "Can't Buy Me Love"; "Bad Boy"; "Day Tripper"; "A Hard Day's Night"; "Ticket to Ride"; "Paperback Writer"; "Eleanor Rigby"; "I Want to Hold Your Hand."

Sgt. Pepper's Lonely Hearts Club Band, June 1, 1967, Parlophone PMC 7027 (mono)/ PCS 7027 (stereo)

Side 1: "Sgt. Pepper's Lonely Hearts Club Band"/"With a Little Help from My Friends"; "Lucy in the Sky with Diamonds"; "Getting Better"; "Fixing a Hole"; "She's Leaving Home"; "Being for the Benefit of Mr. Kite!" Side 2: "Within You Without You"; "When I'm Sixty-Four"; "Lovely Rita"; "Good Morning, Good Morning"; "Sgt. Pepper's Lonely Hearts Club Band (Reprise)"; "A Day in the Life"; "Sgt. Pepper's Inner Groove" [unlisted].

The Beatles (*The White Album*), November 22, 1968, Apple [Parlophone] PMC 7067– 7068 (mono)/PCS 7067–7068 (stereo)

Side 1: "Back in the USSR"; "Dear Prudence"; "Glass Onion"; "Ob-La-Di, Ob-La-Da"; "Wild Honey Pie"; "The Continuing Story of Bungalow Bill"; "While My Guitar Gently Weeps"; "Happiness Is a Warm Gun." Side 2: "Martha My Dear"; "I'm So Tired"; "Blackbird"; "Piggies"; "Rocky Raccoon"; "Don't Pass Me By"; "Why Don't We Do It in the Road"; "I Will"; "Julia." Side 3: "Birthday"; "Yer Blues"; "Mother Nature's Son"; "Everybody's Got Something to Hide Except Me and My Monkey"; "Sexy Sadie"; "Helter Skelter"; "Long Long Long." Side 4: "Revolution 1"; "Honey Pie"; "Savoy Truffle"; "Cry Baby Cry"; "Can You Take Me Back" [unlisted]; "Revolution 9"; "Good Night."

Yellow Submarine, January 17, 1969, Apple [Parlophone] PMC 7070 (mono)/PCS 7070 (stereo)

Side 1: "Yellow Submarine"; "Only a Northern Song"; "All Together Now"; "Hey Bulldog"; "It's All Too Much"; "All You Need Is Love." Side 2: "Pepperland" (instrumental); "Sea of Time"/"Sea of Holes" (instrumental); "Sea of Monsters" (instrumental); "March of the Meanies" (instrumental); "Pepperland Laid Waste" (instrumental); "Yellow Submarine in Pepperland" (instrumental).

Abbey Road, September 26, 1969, Apple [Parlophone] PCS 7088 (stereo)

Side 1: "Come Together"; "Something"; "Maxwell's Silver Hammer"; "Oh! Darling"; "Octopus's Garden"; "I Want You (She's So Heavy)." Side 2: "Here Comes the Sun"; "Because"; "You Never Give Me Your Money"; "Sun King"; "Mean Mr. Mustard"; "Polythene Pam"; "She Came in through the Bathroom Window"; "Golden Slumbers"; "Carry That Weight"; "The End"; "Her Majesty" [unlisted].

Let It Be, May 8, 1970, Apple [Parlophone] PCS 7096 (stereo)

Side 1: "Two of Us"; "Dig a Pony"; "Across the Universe"; "I Me Mine"; "Dig It"; "Let It Be"; "Maggie Mae." Side 2: "I've Got a Feeling"; "One after 909"; "The Long and Winding Road"; "For You Blue"; "Get Back."

The Beatles, 1962–1966, April 19, 1973, Apple [Parlophone] PCSP 717

Side 1: "Love Me Do"; "Please Please Me"; "From Me to You"; "She Loves You"; "I Want to Hold Your Hand"; "All My Loving"; "Can't Buy Me Love." Side 2: "A Hard Day's Night"; "And I Love Her"; "Eight Days a Week"; "I Feel Fine"; "Ticket to Ride"; "Yesterday." Side 3: "Help!"; "You've Got to Hide Your Love Away"; "We Can Work It Out"; "Day Tripper"; "Drive My Car"; "Norwegian Wood (This Bird Has Flown)." Side 4: "Nowhere Man"; "Michelle"; "In My Life"; "Girl"; "Paperback Writer"; "Eleanor Rigby"; "Yellow Submarine."

The Beatles, 1967–1970, April 19, 1973, Apple [Parlophone] PCSP 718

Side 1: "Strawberry Fields Forever"; "Penny Lane"; "Sgt. Pepper's Lonely Hearts Club Band"; "With a Little Help from My Friends"; "Lucy in the Sky with Diamonds"; "A

Day in the Life"; "All You Need Is Love." Side 2: "I Am the Walrus"; "Hello, Good-bye"; "The Fool on the Hill"; "Magical Mystery Tour"; "Lady Madonna"; "Hey Jude"; "Revolution." Side 3: "Back in the USSR"; "While My Guitar Gently Weeps"; "Ob-La-Di, Ob-La-Da"; "Get Back"; "Don't Let Me Down"; "The Ballad of John and Yoko"; "Old Brown Shoe." Side 4: "Here Comes the Sun"; "Come Together"; "Something"; "Octopus's Garden"; "Let It Be"; "Across the Universe"; "The Long and Winding Road."

Rock 'n' Roll Music, June 11, 1976, Parlophone PCSP 719

Side 1: "Twist and Shout"; "I Saw Her Standing There"; "You Can't Do That"; "I Wanna Be Your Man"; "I Call Your Name"; "Boys"; "Long Tall Sally." Side 2: "Rock and Roll Music"; "Slow Down"; Medley: "Kansas City"/"Hey-Hey-Hey-Hey!"; "Money (That's What I Want)"; "Bad Boy"; "Matchbox"; "Roll Over Beethoven." Side 3: "Dizzy, Miss Lizzy"; "Any Time at All"; "Drive My Car"; "Everybody's Trying to Be My Baby"; "The Night Before"; "I'm Down"; "Revolution." Side 4: "Back in the USSR"; "Helter Skelter"; "Taxman"; "Got to Get You into My Life"; "Hey Bulldog"; "Birthday"; "Get Back" (*Let It Be* version).

Live! at the Star-Club in Hamburg, Germany; 1962, April 8, 1977, Lingasong LNL1

Side 1: "I Saw Her Standing There"; "Roll Over Beethoven"; "Hippy Hippy Shake"; "Sweet Little Sixteen"; "Lend Me Your Comb"; "Your Feet's Too Big." Side 2: "Twist and Shout"; "Mr. Moonlight"; "A Taste of Honey"; "Bésame Mucho"; "Reminisc-ing"; Medley: "Kansas City"/"Hey-Hey-Hey-Hey!" Side 3: "Nothin' Shakin' (But the Leaves on the Trees)"; "To Know Her Is to Love Her"; "Little Queenie"; "Falling in Love Again (Can't Help It)"; "Ask Me Why"; "Be-Bop-a-Lula"; "Hallelujah, I Love Her So." Side 4: "Red Sails in the Sunset"; "Everybody's Trying to Be My Baby"; "Matchbox"; "I'm Talking About You"; "Shimmy Like Kate"; "Long Tall Sally"; "I Remember You."

The Beatles at the Hollywood Bowl, May 6, 1977, Parlophone EMTV 4

Side 1: "Twist and Shout"; "She's a Woman"; "Dizzy Miss Lizzy"; "Ticket to Ride"; "Can't Buy Me Love"; "Things We Said Today"; "Roll Over Beethoven." Side 2: "Boys"; "A Hard Day's Night"; "Help!"; "All My Loving"; "She Loves You"; "Long Tall Sally."

Love Songs, November 19, 1977, Parlophone PCSP 721

Side 1: "Yesterday"; "I'll Follow the Sun"; "I Need You"; "Girl"; "In My Life"; "Words of Love"; "Here, There, and Everywhere." Side 2: "Something"; "And I Love Her"; "If I Fell"; "I'll Be Back"; "Tell Me What You See"; "Yes It Is." Side 3: "Michelle"; "It's Only Love"; "You're Going to Lose That Girl"; "Every Little Thing"; "For No One"; "She's Leaving Home." Side 4: "The Long and Winding Road"; "This Boy"; "Norwegian Wood (This Bird Has Flown)"; "I Will"; "P.S. I Love You."

Rarities, October 12, 1979, Parlophone PCM 1001

Side 1: "Across the Universe" (World Wildlife Fund version), "Yes It Is"; "This Boy"; "The Inner Light"; "I'll Get You"; "Thank You Girl"; "Komm, Gib Mir Deine Hand"; "You Know My Name (Look up the Number)"; "Sie Liebt Dich." Side 2: "Rain"; "She's a Woman"; "Matchbox"; "I Call Your Name"; "Bad Boy"; "Slow Down"; "I'm Down"; "Long Tall Sally."

Reel Music, March 22, 1982, Parlophone TC PCS 7218

Side 1: "A Hard Day's Night"; "I Should Have Known Better"; "Can't Buy Me Love"; "And I Love Her"; "Help!"; "You've Got to Hide Your Love Away"; "Ticket to Ride";

"Magical Mystery Tour." Side 2: "I Am the Walrus"; "Yellow Submarine"; "All You Need Is Love"; "Let It Be"; "Get Back"; "The Long and Winding Road."

20 Greatest Hits, October 11, 1982, Parlophone PCTC 260

Side 1: "Love Me Do"; "From Me To You"; "She Loves You"; "I Want to Hold Your Hand"; "Can't Buy Me Love"; "A Hard Day's Night"; "I Feel Fine"; "Ticket to Ride"; "Help!"; "Day Tripper"; "We Can Work It Out." Side 2: "Paperback Writer"; "Yellow Submarine"; "Eleanor Rigby"; "All You Need Is Love"; "Hello, Goodbye"; "Lady Madonna"; "Hey Jude"; "Get Back"; "The Ballad of John and Yoko."

Past Masters, Volume 1, March 7, 1988, Apple [Parlophone] CDP 7 90043 2

"Love Me Do"; "From Me to You"; "Thank You Girl"; "She Loves You"; "I'll Get You"; "I Want to Hold Your Hand"; "This Boy"; "Komm, Gib Mir Deine Hand"; "Sie Liebt Dich"; "Long Tall Sally"; "I Call Your Name"; "Slow Down"; "Matchbox"; "I Feel Fine"; "She's a Woman"; "Bad Boy"; "Yes It Is"; "I'm Down."

Past Masters, Volume 2, March 7, 1988, Apple [Parlophone] CDP 7 90044 2

"Day Tripper"; "We Can Work It Out"; "Paperback Writer"; "Rain"; "Lady Madonna"; "The Inner Light"; "Hey Jude"; "Revolution"; "Get Back"; "Don't Let Me Down"; "The Ballad of John and Yoko"; "Old Brown Shoe"; "Across the Universe" (World Wildlife Fund version); "Let It Be"; "You Know My Name (Look Up the Number)."

Live at the BBC, November 30, 1994, Apple [Parlophone] PCSP 726

Disc 1: "Beatle Greetings" (Speech); "From Us to You"; "Riding on a Bus" (Speech); "I Got a Woman"; "Too Much Monkey Business"; "Keep Your Hands Off My Baby"; "I'll Be on My Way"; "Young Blood"; "A Shot of Rhythm and Blues"; "Sure to Fall (In Love with You)"; "Some Other Guy"; "Thank You Girl"; "Sha La La La La!" (Speech); "Baby It's You"; "That's All Right (Mama)"; "Carol"; "Soldier of Love"; "A Little Rhyme" (Speech); "Clarabella"; "I'm Gonna Sit Right Down and Cry (Over You)"; "Crying, Waiting, Hoping"; "Dear Wack!" (Speech); "You Really Got a Hold on Me"; "To Know Her Is to Love Her"; "A Taste of Honey"; "Long Tall Sally"; "I Saw Her Standing There"; "The Honeymoon Song"; "Johnny B. Goode"; "Lucille"; "Can't Buy Me Love"; "From Fluff to You" (Speech); "Till There Was You." Disc 2: "Crinsk Dee Night" (Speech); "A Hard Day's Night"; "Have a Banana!" (Speech); "I Wanna Be Your Man"; "Just a Rumour" (Speech); "Roll Over Beethoven"; "All My Loving"; "Things We Said Today"; "She's a Woman"; "Sweet Little Sixteen"; "1822!" (Speech); "Lonesome Tears in My Eyes"; "Nothin' Shakin' (But the Leaves on the Trees)"; "Hippy Hippy Shake"; "Glad All Over"; "I Just Don't Understand"; "So How Come (No One Loves Me)"; "I Feel Fine"; "I'm a Loser"; "Everybody's Trying to Be My Baby"; "Rock and Roll Music"; "Ticket to Ride"; "Dizzy Miss Lizzy"; Medley: "Kansas City"/"Hey-Hey-Hey-Hey!"; "Set Fire to That Lot!" (Speech); "Matchbox"; "I Forgot to Remember to Forget"; "Love These Goon Shows!" (Speech); "I Got to Find My Baby"; "Ooh! My Soul"; "Ooh! My Arms" (Speech); "Don't Ever Change"; "Slow Down"; "Honey Don't"; "Love Me Do."

The Beatles Anthology, Volume 1, November 21, 1995, Apple [Parlophone] CDP 7243 8 34445 2

Disc 1: "Free As a Bird"; "We Were Four Guys . . . That's All" (Speech); "That'll Be the Day"; "In Spite of All the Danger"; "Sometimes I'd Borrow" (Speech); "Hallelujah, I Love Her So"; "You'll Be Mine"; "Cayenne"; "First of All" (Speech); "My Bonnie"; "Ain't She Sweet"; "Cry for a Shadow"; "Brian Was a Beautiful Guy" (Speech); "I Secured Them" (Speech); "Searchin' "; "Three Cool Cats"; "The Sheik of Araby";

"Like Dreamers Do"; "Hello Little Girl"; "Well, the Recording Test" (Speech); "Bés-ame Mucho"; "Love Me Do"; "How Do You Do It"; "Please Please Me"; "One After 909" (Sequence); "One After 909" (Complete); "Lend Me Your Comb"; "I'll Get You"; "We Were Performers" (Speech); "I Saw Her Standing There"; "From Me to You"; "Money (That's What I Want)"; "You Really Got a Hold on Me"; "Roll Over Beethoven." Disc 2: "She Loves You"; "Till There Was You"; "Twist and Shout"; "This Boy"; "I Want to Hold Your Hand"; "Boys, What Was I Thinking?" (Speech); "Moon-light Bay"; "Can't Buy Me Love" (Takes 1 and 2); "All My Loving" (*Ed Sullivan Show*); "You Can't Do That" (Take 6); "And I Love Her" (Take 2); "A Hard Day's Night" (Take 1); "I Wanna Be Your Man"; "Long Tall Sally"; "Boys"; "Shout"; "I'll Be Back" (Take 2); "I'll Be Back" (Take 3); "You Know What to Do" (Demo); "No Reply" (Demo); "Mr. Moonlight" (Takes 1 and 4); "Leave My Kitten Alone" (Take 5); "No Reply" (Take 2); "Eight Days a Week" (Sequence); "Eight Days a Week" (Complete); Medley: "Kansas City"/"Hey-Hey-Hey-Hey!" (Take 2).

The Beatles Anthology, Volume 2, March 18, 1996, Apple [Parlophone] CDP 7243 8 34448 2

Disc 1: "Real Love"; "Yes It Is" (Takes 2 and 14); "I'm Down" (Take 1); "You've Got to Hide Your Love Away" (Takes 1, 2, and 5); "If You've Got Trouble" (Take 1); "That Means a Lot" (Take 1); "Yesterday" (Take 1); "It's Only Love" (Takes 2 and 3); "I Feel Fine"; "Ticket to Ride"; "Yesterday"; "Help!"; "Everybody's Trying to Be My Baby"; "Norwegian Wood (This Bird Has Flown)" (Take 1); "I'm Looking Through You" (Take 1); "12-Bar Original" (Edited Take 2); "Tomorrow Never Knows" (Take 1); "Got to Get You into My Life" (Take 5); "And Your Bird Can Sing" (Take 2); "Tax-man" (Take 11); "Eleanor Rigby" (Take 14); "I'm Only Sleeping" (Rehearsal); "I'm Only Sleeping" (Take 1); "Rock and Roll Music"; "She's a Woman." Disc 2: "Straw-berry Fields Forever" (Demo Sequence); "Strawberry Fields Forever" (Take 1); "Strawberry Fields Forever" (Take 7 and Edit Piece); "Penny Lane" (Take 9); "A Day in the Life" (Takes 1, 2, 6, and Orchestra); "Good Morning, Good Morning" (Take 8); "Only a Northern Song" (Takes 3 and 12); "Being for the Benefit of Mr. Kite!" (Takes 1 and 2); "Being for the Benefit of Mr. Kite!" (Take 7 and Effects Tape); "Lucy in the Sky with Diamonds" (Takes 6, 7, and 8); "Within You, Without You" (Instru-mental); "Sgt. Pepper's Lonely Hearts Club Band (Reprise)" (Take 5); "You Know My Name (Look Up the Number)" (Composite); "I Am the Walrus" (Take 16); "The Fool on the Hill" (Demo); "Your Mother Should Know" (Take 27); "The Fool on the Hill" (Take 4); "Hello, Goodbye" (Take 16 and Overdubs); "Lady Madonna" (Takes 3 and 4); "Across the Universe" (Take 2).

The Beatles Anthology, Volume 3, October 25, 1996, Apple [Parlophone] CDP 7243 8 34451 2 7

Disc 1: "A Beginning"; "Happiness Is a Warm Gun" (Esher Demo); "Helter Skelter" (Edited Take 2); "Mean Mr. Mustard" (Esher Demo); "Polythene Pam" (Esher Demo); "Glass Onion" (Esher Demo); "Junk" (Esher Demo); "Piggies" (Esher Demo); "Honey Pie" (Esher Demo); "Don't Pass Me By" (Takes 3 and 5); "Ob-La-Di, Ob-La-Da" (Take 5); "Good Night" (Rehearsal and Take 34); "Cry Baby Cry" (Take 1); "Black-bird" (Take 4); "Sexy Sadie" (Take 6); "While My Guitar Gently Weeps" (Demo); "Hey Jude" (Take 2); "Not Guilty" (Take 102); "Mother Nature's Son" (Take 2); "Glass Onion" (Take 33); "Rocky Raccoon" (Take 8); "What's the New Mary Jane" (Take 4); "Step Inside Love"/"Los Paranoias"; "I'm So Tired" (Takes 3, 6, and 9); "I

Will" (Take 1); "Why Don't We Do It in the Road?" (Take 4); "Julia" (Take 2). Disc 2: "I've Got a Feeling"; "She Came in Through the Bathroom Window" (Rehearsal); "Dig a Pony"; "Two of Us"; "For You Blue"; "Teddy Boy"; Medley: "Rip It Up"/"Shake, Rattle, and Roll"/"Blue Suede Shoes"; "The Long and Winding Road"; "Oh! Darling" (Edited); "All Things Must Pass" (Demo); "Mailman, Bring Me No More Blues"; "Get Back" (Rooftop Concert); "Old Brown Shoe" (Demo); "Octopus's Garden" (Takes 2 and 8); "Maxwell's Silver Hammer" (Take 5); "Something" (Demo); "Come Together" (Take 1); "Come and Get It" (Demo); "Ain't She Sweet" (Jam); "Because" (a cappella version); "Let It Be"; "I Me Mine" (Take 16); "The End" (Remix).

Yellow Submarine Songtrack, September 14, 1999, Apple [Parlophone] 521 412

"Yellow Submarine"; "Hey Bulldog"; "Eleanor Rigby"; "Love You To"; "All Together Now"; "Lucy in the Sky with Diamonds"; "Think for Yourself"; "Sgt. Pepper's Lonely Hearts Club Band"; "With a Little Help from My Friends"; "Baby, You're a Rich Man"; "Only a Northern Song"; "All You Need Is a Love"; "When I'm Sixty-Four"; "Nowhere Man"; "It's All Too Much."

1, November 13, 2000, Apple [Parlophone] 7243 5 29325 2 8

"Love Me Do"; "From Me to You"; "She Loves You"; "I Want to Hold Your Hand"; "Can't Buy Me Love"; "A Hard Day's Night"; "I Feel Fine"; "Eight Days a Week"; "Ticket to Ride"; "Help!"; "Yesterday"; "Day Tripper"; "We Can Work It Out"; "Paperback Writer"; "Yellow Submarine"; "Eleanor Rigby"; "Penny Lane"; "All You Need Is Love"; "Hello, Goodbye"; "Lady Madonna"; "Hey Jude"; "Get Back"; "The Ballad of John and Yoko"; "Something"; "Come Together"; "Let It Be"; "The Long and Winding Road."

Let It Be . . . Naked, November 17, 2003, Apple CDP 7243 5 95713 2 4

"Get Back"; "Dig a Pony"; "For You Blue"; "The Long and Winding Road"; "Two of Us"; "I've Got a Feeling"; "One After 909"; "Don't Let Me Down"; "I Me Mine"; "Across the Universe"; "Let It Be."

Love, November 20, 2006, Apple [Parlophone] 0946 3 79808 2 8

"Because"; "Get Back"; "Glass Onion"; "Eleanor Rigby"/"Julia"; "I Am the Walrus"; "I Want to Hold Your Hand"; "Drive My Car"/"The Word"/"What You're Doing"; "Gnik Nus"; "Something"/"Blue Jay Way"; "Being for the Benefit of Mr. Kite!"/"I Want You (She's So Heavy)"/"Helter Skelter"; "Help!"; "Blackbird"/"Yesterday"; "Strawberry Fields Forever"; "Within You, Without You"/"Tomorrow Never Knows"; "Lucy in the Sky with Diamonds"; "Octopus's Garden"/"Sun King"; "Lady Madonna"; "Here Comes the Sun"/"The Inner Light"; "Come Together"/"Dear Prudence"/"Cry Baby Cry"; "Revolution"/"Back in the USSR"; "While My Guitar Gently Weeps"; "A Day in the Life"; "Hey Jude"; "Sgt. Pepper's Lonely Hearts Club Band (Reprise)"; "All You Need Is Love."

Mono Masters, September 9, 2009, Apple [Parlophone] 5099969945120

Disc 1:"Love Me Do"; "From Me to You"; "Thank You Girl"; "She Loves You"; "I'll Get You"; "I Want to Hold Your Hand"; "This Boy"; "Komm, Gib Mir Deine Hand"; "Sie Liebt Dich"; "Long Tall Sally"; "I Call Your Name"; "Slow Down"; "Matchbox"; "I Feel Fine"; "She's a Woman"; "Bad Boy"; "Yes It Is"; "I'm Down." Disc 2:"Day Tripper"; "We Can Work It Out"; "Paperback Writer"; "Rain"; "Lady Madonna"; "The Inner Light"; "Hey Jude"; "Revolution"; "Only a Northern Song"; "All Together Now"; "Hey Bulldog"; "It's All Too Much"; "Get Back"; "Don't Let

Me Down"; "Across the Universe" (World Wildlife Fund version); "You Know My Name (Look Up the Number)."

Past Masters, September 9, 2009, Apple 50999 2 43807 2 0

Disc 1: "Love Me Do"; "From Me to You"; "Thank You Girl"; "She Loves You"; "I'll Get You"; "I Want to Hold Your Hand"; "This Boy"; "Komm, Gib Mir Deine Hand"; "Sie Liebt Dich"; "Long Tall Sally"; "I Call Your Name"; "Slow Down"; "Matchbox"; "I Feel Fine"; "She's a Woman"; "Bad Boy"; "Yes It Is"; "I'm Down." Disc 2: "Day Tripper"; "We Can Work It Out"; "Paperback Writer"; "Rain"; "Lady Madonna"; "The Inner Light"; "Hey Jude"; "Revolution"; "Get Back"; "Don't Let Me Down"; "The Ballad of John and Yoko"; "Old Brown Shoe"; "Across the Universe" (World Wildlife Fund version); "Let It Be"; "You Know My Name (Look Up the Number)."

Tomorrow Never Knows, July 24, 2012, Apple [iTunes]

"Revolution"; "Paperback Writer"; "And Your Bird Can Sing"; "Helter Skelter"; "Savoy Truffle"; "I'm Down"; "I've Got a Feeling" (*Let It Be . . . Naked* version); "Back in the USSR"; "You Can't Do That"; "It's All Too Much"; "She Said She Said"; "Hey Bulldog"; "Tomorrow Never Knows"; "The End" (*Anthology 3* version).

On Air—Live at the BBC, Volume 2, November 11, 2013, Apple

Disc 1: "And Here We Are Again" (Speech); "Words of Love"; "How About It, Gorgeous?" (Speech); "Do You Want To Know a Secret"; "Lucille"; "Hey, Paul . . ." (Speech); "Anna (Go To Him)"; "Hello!" (Speech); "Please Please Me"; "Misery"; "I'm Talking About You"; "A Real Treat" (Speech); "Boys"; "Absolutely Fab" (Speech); "Chains"; "Ask Me Why"; "Till There Was You"; "Lend Me Your Comb"; "Lower 5E" (Speech); "The Hippy Hippy Shake"; "Roll Over Beethoven"; "There's a Place"; "Bumper Bundle" (Speech); "P.S. I Love You"; "Please Mister Postman"; "Beautiful Dreamer"; "Devil in Her Heart"; "The 49 Weeks" (Speech); "Sure To Fall (In Love With You)"; "Never Mind, Eh?" (Speech); "Twist and Shout"; "Bye, Bye" (speech); "John—Pop Profile" (Speech); "George—Pop Profile" (Speech); Disc 2: "I Saw Her Standing There"; "Glad All Over"; "Lift Lid Again" (Speech); "I'll Get You"; "She Loves You"; "Memphis, Tennessee"; "Happy Birthday Dear Saturday Club"; "Now Hush, Hush" (Speech); "From Me to You"; "Money (That's What I Want)"; "I Want to Hold Your Hand"; "Brian Bathtubes" (Speech); "This Boy"; "If I Wasn't in America" (Speech); "I Got a Woman"; "Long Tall Sally"; "If I Fell"; "A Hard Job Writing Them" (Speech); "And I Love Her"; "Oh, Can't We? Yes We Can" (Speech); "You Can't Do That"; "Honey Don't"; "I'll Follow the Sun"; "Green with Black Shutters" (Speech); "Kansas City/Hey-Hey-Hey-Hey!"; "That's What We're Here For"; "I Feel Fine" (Studio Outtake); "Paul—Pop Profile" (Speech); "Ringo—Pop Profile" (Speech).

The Beatles Bootleg Recordings 1963, December 17, 2013, Apple [iTunes]

"There's a Place" (Takes 5 and 6); "There's a Place" (Take 8); "There's a Place" (Take 9); "Do You Want to Know a Secret" (Take 7); "A Taste of Honey" (Take 6); "I Saw Her Standing There" (Take 2); "Misery" (Take 1); "Misery" (Take 7); "From Me to You" (Takes 1 and 2); "From Me to You" (Take 5); "Thank You Girl" (Take 1); "Thank You Girl" (Take 5); "One After 909" (Takes 1 and 2); "Hold Me Tight" (Take 21); "Money (That's What I Want)" (studio outtake); "Some Other Guy"; "Love Me Do"; "Too Much Monkey Business"; "I Saw Her Standing There"; "Do You Want to Know a Secret"; "From Me to You"; "I Got to Find My Baby"; "Roll Over Beethoven"; "A Taste of Honey"; "Love Me Do"; "Please Please Me"; "She Loves You"; "I Want to

Hold Your Hand"; "Till There Was You"; "Roll Over Beethoven"; "You Really Got a Hold on Me"; "The Hippy Hippy Shake"; "Till There Was You"; "A Shot of Rhythm and Blues"; "A Taste of Honey"; "Money (That's What I Want)"; "Anna (Go to Him)"; "Love Me Do"; "She Loves You"; "I'll Get You"; "A Taste of Honey"; "Boys"; "Chains"; "You Really Got a Hold on Me"; "I Saw Her Standing There"; "She Loves You"; "Twist and Shout"; "Do You Want to Know a Secret"; "Please Please Me"; "Long Tall Sally"; "Chains"; "Boys"; "A Taste of Honey"; "Roll Over Beethoven"; "All My Loving"; "She Loves You"; "Till There Was You"; "Bad to Me" (demo); "I'm in Love" (demo).

RECORDINGS RELEASED IN THE UNITED STATES

U.S. Singles Releases

"My Bonnie"/"The Saints"; April 23, 1962, Decca 31382 (as Tony Sheridan and the Beat Brothers)

"Please Please Me"/"Ask Me Why"; February 25, 1963, Vee-Jay VJ 498

"From Me to You"/"Thank You Girl"; May 27, 1963, Vee-Jay VJ 522

"She Loves You"/"I'll Get You"; September 16, 1963, Swan 4152

"I Want to Hold Your Hand"/"I Saw Her Standing There," December 26, 1963, Capitol 5112

"Please Please Me"/"From Me to You"; January 30, 1964, Vee-Jay VJ 581

"Twist and Shout"/"There's a Place"; March 2, 1964, Tollie 9001

"Can't Buy Me Love"/"You Can't Do That"; March 16, 1964, Capitol 5150

"Do You Want to Know a Secret"/"Thank You Girl"; March 23, 1964, Vee-Jay VJ 587

"Love Me Do"/"P.S. I Love You"; April 27, 1964, Tollie 9008

"Sie Liebt Dich" ["She Loves You"]/"I'll Get You"; May 21, 1964, Swan 4182

"A Hard Day's Night"/"I Should Have Known Better"; July 13, 1964, Capitol 5122

"I'll Cry Instead"/"I'm Happy Just to Dance with You"; July 20, 1964, Capitol 5234

"And I Love Her"/"If I Fell"; July 20, 1964, Capitol 5235

"Matchbox"/"Slow Down"; August 24, 1964, Capitol 5255

"I Feel Fine"/"She's a Woman"; November 23, 1964, Capitol 5327

"Eight Days a Week"/"I Don't Want to Spoil the Party"; February 15, 1965, Capitol 5371

"Ticket to Ride"/"Yes It Is"; April 19, 1965, Capitol 5407

"Help!"/"I'm Down"; July 19, 1965, Capitol 5476

"Yesterday"/"Act Naturally"; September 13, 1965, Capitol 5498

"We Can Work It Out"/"Day Tripper"; December 6, 1965, Capitol 5555

"Nowhere Man"/"What Goes On"; February 21, 1966, Capitol 5587

"Paperback Writer"/"Rain"; May 30, 1966; Capitol 5651

"Eleanor Rigby"/"Yellow Submarine"; August 8, 1966, Capitol 5715

"Strawberry Fields Forever"/"Penny Lane"; February 13, 1967, Capitol 5810

"All You Need Is Love"/"Baby, You're a Rich Man"; July 17, 1967, Capitol 5964

"Hello Goodbye"/"I Am the Walrus"; November 27, 1967, Capitol 2056

"Lady Madonna"/"The Inner Light"; March 18, 1968, Capitol 2138

"Hey Jude"/"Revolution"; August 26, 1968, Apple [Capitol] 2276

"Get Back"/"Don't Let Me Down"; May 5, 1969, Apple [Capitol] 2490 (as the Beatles with Billy Preston)

"The Ballad of John and Yoko"/"Old Brown Shoe"; June 4, 1969, Apple [Capitol] 2531

"Something"/"Come Together"; October 6, 1969, Apple [Capitol] 2654

"Let It Be"/"You Know My Name (Look Up the Number)"; March 11, 1970, Apple [Capitol] 2764

"The Long and Winding Road"/"For You Blue"; May 11, 1970, Apple [Capitol] 2832

"Got to Get You into My Life"/"Helter Skelter"; May 31, 1976, Capitol 4274

"Ob-La-Di, Ob-La-Da"/"Julia"; November 8, 1976, Capitol 4347

"Sgt. Pepper's Lonely Hearts Club Band/With a Little Help from My Friends"/"A Day in the Life"; September 30, 1978, Capitol 4612

"The Beatles' Movie Medley"/"I'm Happy Just to Dance with You"; March 24, 1982, Capitol B 5107

"Baby It's You"/"I'll Follow the Sun"/"Devil in Her Heart"/"Boys"; April 4, 1995, Apple [Capitol] NR 7243 8 58348 1 3 [CD Maxi-Single]

"Free as a Bird"/"Christmas Time (Is Here Again)"; December 12, 1995, Apple NR 7243 8 58497 7 0

"Real Love"/"Baby's in Black (Live)"; March 4, 1996, Apple NR 8 58544 7

U.S. EP Releases

Souvenir of Their Visit to America, March 23, 1964, Vee-Jay VJEP 1–903 (mono)
A: "Misery"; "A Taste of Honey." B: "Ask Me Why"; "Anna (Go To Him)."
Four by the Beatles, May 11, 1964, Capitol EAP 1–2121 (mono)
A: "Roll Over Beethoven"; "All My Loving." B: "This Boy"; "Please Mr. Postman."
4 by the Beatles, February 1, 1965, Capitol R 5365 (mono)
A: "Honey Don't"; "I'm a Loser." B: "Mr. Moonlight"; "Everybody's Trying to Be My Baby."

U.S. Album Releases

Introducing the Beatles [first issue], July 22, 1963, Vee-Jay VJLP 1062 (mono)/SR 1062 (stereo)
Side 1: "I Saw Her Standing There"; "Misery"; "Anna (Go to Him)"; "Chains"; "Boys"; "Love Me Do." Side 2: "P.S. I Love You"; "Baby It's You"; "Do You Want to Know a Secret"; "A Taste of Honey"; "There's a Place"; "Twist and Shout."
Meet the Beatles!, January 20, 1964, Capitol T 2047 (mono)/ST 2047 (stereo)
Side 1: "I Want to Hold Your Hand"; "I Saw Her Standing There"; "This Boy"; "It Won't Be Long"; "All I've Got to Do"; "All My Loving." Side 2: "Don't Bother Me"; "Little Child"; "Till There Was You"; "Hold Me Tight"; "I Wanna Be Your Man"; "Not a Second Time."
Introducing the Beatles [second issue], January 27, 1964, Vee-Jay VJLP 1062 (mono)
Side 1: "I Saw Her Standing There"; "Misery"; "Anna (Go to Him)"; "Chains"; "Boys"; "Ask Me Why." Side 2: "Please Please Me"; "Baby It's You"; "Do You Want to Know a Secret"; "A Taste of Honey"; "There's a Place"; "Twist and Shout."
The Beatles' Second Album, April 10, 1964, Capitol T 2080 (mono)/ST 2080 (stereo)
Side 1: "Roll Over Beethoven"; "Thank You Girl"; "You Really Got a Hold on Me"; "Devil in Her Heart"; "Money (That's What I Want)"; "You Can't Do That." Side 2:

"Long Tall Sally"; "I Call Your Name"; "Please Mister Postman"; "I'll Get You"; "She Loves You."

A Hard Day's Night, June 26, 1964, United Artists UA 6366 (mono)/UAS 6366 (stereo)

Side 1: "A Hard Day's Night"; "Tell Me Why"; "I'll Cry Instead"; "I Should Have Known Better" (instrumental); "I'm Happy Just to Dance with You"; "And I Love Her" (instrumental). Side 2: "I Should Have Known Better"; "If I Fell"; "And I Love Her"; "Ringo's Theme (This Boy)" (instrumental); "Can't Buy Me Love"; "A Hard Day's Night" (instrumental).

Something New, July 20, 1964, Capitol T 2108 (mono)/ST 2108 (stereo)

Side 1: "I'll Cry Instead"; "Things We Said Today"; "Any Time at All"; "When I Get Home"; "Slow Down"; "Matchbox." Side 2: "Tell Me Why"; "And I Love Her"; "I'm Happy Just to Dance with You"; "If I Fell"; "Komm, Gib Mir Deine Hand" ["I Want to Hold Your Hand"].

The Beatles' Story, November 23, 1964, Capitol TBO 2222 (mono)/STBO 2222 (stereo)

Side 1: Interviews plus extracts from "I Want to Hold Your Hand"; "Slow Down"; "This Boy." Side 2: Interviews plus extracts from "You Can't Do That"; "If I Fell"; "And I Love Her." Side 3: Interviews plus extracts from "A Hard Day's Night"; "And I Love Her." Side 4: Interviews plus extracts from "Twist and Shout" (live); "Things We Said Today"; "I'm Happy Just to Dance with You"; "Long Tall Sally"; "She Loves You"; "Boys."

Beatles '65, December 15, 1964, Capitol T 2228 (mono)/ST 2228 (stereo)

Side 1: "No Reply"; "I'm a Loser"; "Baby's in Black"; "Rock and Roll Music"; "I'll Follow the Sun"; "Mr. Moonlight." Side 2: "Honey Don't"; "I'll Be Back"; "She's a Woman"; "I Feel Fine"; "Everybody's Trying to Be My Baby."

The Early Beatles, March 22, 1965, Capitol T 2309 (mono)/ST 2309 (stereo)

Side 1: "Love Me Do"; "Twist and Shout"; "Anna (Go to Him)"; "Chains"; "Boys"; "Ask Me Why." Side 2: "Please Please Me"; "P.S. I Love You"; "Baby It's You"; "A Taste of Honey"; "Do You Want to Know a Secret."

Beatles VI, June 14, 1965, Capitol T 2358 (mono)/ST 2358 (stereo)

Side 1: "Kansas City"/"Hey-Hey-Hey-Hey!"; "Eight Days a Week"; "You Like Me Too Much"; "Bad Boy"; "I Don't Want to Spoil the Party"; "Words of Love." Side 2: "What You're Doing"; "Yes It Is"; "Dizzy Miss Lizzy"; "Tell Me What You See"; "Every Little Thing."

Help!, August 13, 1965, Capitol MAS 2386 (mono)/SMAS 2386 (stereo)

Side 1: "James Bond Theme" [unlisted]; "Help!"; "The Night Before"; "From Me to You Fantasy" (instrumental); "You've Got to Hide Your Love Away"; "I Need You"; "In the Tyrol" (instrumental). Side 2: "Another Girl"; "Another Hard Day's Night" (instrumental); "Ticket to Ride"; "The Bitter End"/"You Can't Do That" (instrumental); "You're Going to Lose That Girl"; "The Chase" (instrumental).

Rubber Soul, December 6, 1965, Capitol T 2442 (mono)/ST 2442 (stereo)

Side 1: "I've Just Seen a Face"; "Norwegian Wood (This Bird Has Flown)"; "You Won't See Me"; "Think for Yourself"; "The Word"; "Michelle." Side 2: "It's Only Love"; "Girl"; "I'm Looking through You"; "In My Life"; "Wait"; "Run for Your Life."

Yesterday . . . and Today, June 20, 1966, Capitol T 2553 (mono)/ST 2553 (stereo)

Side 1: "Drive My Car"; "I'm Only Sleeping"; "Nowhere Man"; "Doctor Robert"; "Yesterday"; "Act Naturally." Side 2: "And Your Bird Can Sing"; "If I Needed Someone"; "We Can Work It Out"; "What Goes On"; "Day Tripper."

Revolver, August 8, 1966, Capitol T 2576 (mono)/ST 2576 (stereo)
Side 1: "Taxman"; "Eleanor Rigby"; "Love You To"; "Here, There, and Everywhere";
"Yellow Submarine"; "She Said She Said." Side 2: "Good Day Sunshine"; "For No
One"; "I Want to Tell You"; "Got to Get You into My Life"; "Tomorrow Never Knows."
Sgt. Pepper's Lonely Hearts Club Band, June 2, 1967, Capitol MAS 2653 (mono)/SMAS
2653
Side 1: "Sgt. Pepper's Lonely Hearts Club Band"/"With a Little Help from My Friends";
"Lucy in the Sky with Diamonds"; "Getting Better"; "Fixing a Hole"; "She's Leav-
ing Home"; "Being for the Benefit of Mr. Kite!" Side 2: "Within You Without You";
"When I'm Sixty-Four"; "Lovely Rita"; "Good Morning, Good Morning"; "Sgt. Pep-
per's Lonely Hearts Club Band (Reprise)"; "A Day in the Life."
Magical Mystery Tour, November 27, 1967, Capitol MAL 2835 (mono)/SMAL 2835
(stereo)
Side 1: "Magical Mystery Tour"; "The Fool on the Hill"; "Flying"; "Blue Jay Way"; "Your
Mother Should Know"; "I Am the Walrus." Side 2: "Hello Goodbye"; "Strawberry
Fields Forever"; "Penny Lane"; "Baby, You're a Rich Man"; "All You Need Is Love."
The Beatles (The White Album), November 25, 1968, Apple [Capitol] SWBO 101
(stereo)
Side 1: "Back in the USSR"; "Dear Prudence"; "Glass Onion"; "Ob-La-Di, Ob-La-Da";
"Wild Honey Pie"; "The Continuing Story of Bungalow Bill"; "While My Guitar
Gently Weeps"; "Happiness Is a Warm Gun." Side 2: "Martha My Dear"; "I'm So
Tired"; "Blackbird"; "Piggies"; "Rocky Raccoon"; "Don't Pass Me By"; "Why Don't
We Do It in the Road"; "I Will"; "Julia." Side 3: "Birthday"; "Yer Blues"; "Mother
Nature's Son"; "Everybody's Got Something to Hide Except Me and My Monkey";
"Sexy Sadie"; "Helter Skelter"; "Long Long Long." Side 4: "Revolution 1"; "Honey
Pie"; "Savoy Truffle"; "Cry Baby Cry"; "Can You Take Me Back" [unlisted]; "Revo-
lution 9"; "Good Night."
Yellow Submarine, January 13, 1969, Apple [Capitol] SW 153 (stereo)
Side 1: "Yellow Submarine"; "Only a Northern Song"; "All Together Now"; "Hey Bull-
dog"; "It's All Too Much"; "All You Need Is Love." Side 2: "Pepperland" (instrumen-
tal); "Sea of Time"/"Sea of Holes" (instrumental); "Sea of Monsters" (instrumental);
"March of the Meanies" (instrumental); "Pepperland Laid Waste" (instrumental);
"Yellow Submarine in Pepperland" (instrumental).
Abbey Road, October 1, 1969, Apple [Capitol] SO 383 (stereo)
Side 1: "Come Together"; "Something"; "Maxwell's Silver Hammer"; "Oh! Darling";
"Octopus's Garden"; "I Want You (She's So Heavy)." Side 2: "Here Comes the Sun";
"Because"; "You Never Give Me Your Money"; "Sun King"; "Mean Mr. Mustard";
"Polythene Pam"; "She Came in through the Bathroom Window"; "Golden Slum-
bers"; "Carry That Weight"; "The End"; "Her Majesty" [unlisted].
Hey Jude, February 26, 1970, Apple [Capitol] SW 385 (stereo)
Side 1: "Can't Buy Me Love"; "I Should Have Known Better"; "Paperback Writer";
"Rain"; "Lady Madonna"; "Revolution." Side 2: "Hey Jude"; "Old Brown Shoe";
"Don't Let Me Down"; "The Ballad of John and Yoko."
Let It Be, May 18, 1970, Apple [Capitol] AR 34001 (stereo)
Side 1: "Two of Us"; "Dig a Pony"; "Across the Universe"; "I Me Mine"; "Dig It"; "Let
It Be"; "Maggie Mae." Side 2: "I've Got a Feeling"; "One after 909"; "The Long and
Winding Road"; "For You Blue"; "Get Back."

The Beatles, 1962–1966, April 2, 1973, Apple [Capitol] SKBO 3403
Side 1: "Love Me Do"; "Please Please Me"; "From Me to You"; "She Loves You"; "I Want to Hold Your Hand"; "All My Loving"; "Can't Buy Me Love." Side 2: "A Hard Day's Night"; "And I Love Her"; "Eight Days a Week"; "I Feel Fine"; "Ticket to Ride"; "Yesterday." Side 3: "Help!"; "You've Got to Hide Your Love Away"; "We Can Work It Out"; "Day Tripper"; "Drive My Car"; "Norwegian Wood (This Bird Has Flown)." Side 4: "Nowhere Man"; "Michelle"; "In My Life"; "Girl"; "Paperback Writer"; "Eleanor Rigby"; "Yellow Submarine."
The Beatles, 1967–1970, April 2, 1973, Apple [Capitol] SKBO 3404
Side 1: "Strawberry Fields Forever"; "Penny Lane"; "Sgt. Pepper's Lonely Hearts Club Band"; "With a Little Help from My Friends"; "Lucy in the Sky with Diamonds"; "A Day in the Life"; "All You Need Is Love." Side 2: "I Am the Walrus"; "Hello, Good-bye"; "The Fool on the Hill"; "Magical Mystery Tour"; "Lady Madonna"; "Hey Jude"; "Revolution." Side 3: "Back in the USSR"; "While My Guitar Gently Weeps"; "Ob-La-Di, Ob-La-Da"; "Get Back"; "Don't Let Me Down"; "The Ballad of John and Yoko"; "Old Brown Shoe." Side 4: "Here Comes the Sun"; "Come Together"; "Some-thing"; "Octopus's Garden"; "Let It Be"; "Across the Universe"; "The Long and Winding Road."
Rock 'n' Roll Music, June 7, 1976, Capitol SKBO 11537
Side 1: "Twist and Shout"; "I Saw Her Standing There"; "You Can't Do That"; "I Wanna Be Your Man"; "I Call Your Name"; "Boys"; Long Tall Sally." Side 2: "Rock and Roll Music"; "Slow Down"; Medley: "Kansas City"/"Hey-Hey-Hey-Hey!"; "Money (That's What I Want)"; "Bad Boy"; "Matchbox"; "Roll Over Beethoven." Side 3: "Dizzy, Miss Lizzy"; "Any Time at All"; "Drive My Car"; "Everybody's Trying to Be My Baby"; "The Night Before"; "I'm Down"; "Revolution." Side 4: "Back in the USSR"; "Helter Skelter"; "Taxman"; "Got to Get You into My Life"; "Hey Bulldog"; "Birthday"; "Get Back" (*Let It Be* version).
Live! at the Star-Club in Hamburg, Germany; 1962, June 13, 1977, Atlantic LS 2 7001
Side 1: "I'm Gonna Sit Right Down and Cry (Over You)"; "Roll Over Beethoven"; "Hippy Hippy Shake"; "Sweet Little Sixteen"; "Lend Me Your Comb"; "Your Feet's Too Big." Side 2: "Where Have You Been All My Life"; "Mr. Moonlight"; "A Taste of Honey"; "Bésame Mucho"; "Till There Was You"; Medley: "Kansas City"/"Hey-Hey-Hey-Hey!" Side 3: "Nothin' Shakin' (But the Leaves on the Trees)"; "To Know Her Is to Love Her"; "Little Queenie"; "Falling in Love Again (Can't Help It)"; "Sheila"; "Be-Bop-a-Lula"; "Hallelujah, I Love Her So." Side 4: "Red Sails in the Sunset"; "Everybody's Trying to Be My Baby"; "Matchbox"; "I'm Talking About You"; "Shimmy Like Kate"; "Long Tall Sally"; "I Remember You."
The Beatles at the Hollywood Bowl, May 4, 1977, Capitol SMAS 11638
Side 1: "Twist and Shout"; "She's a Woman"; "Dizzy Miss Lizzy"; "Ticket to Ride"; "Can't Buy Me Love"; "Things We Said Today"; "Roll Over Beethoven." Side 2: "Boys"; "A Hard Day's Night"; "Help!"; "All My Loving"; "She Loves You"; "Long Tall Sally."
Love Songs, October 21, 1977, Capitol SKBL 11711
Side 1: "Yesterday"; "I'll Follow the Sun"; "I Need You"; "Girl"; "In My Life"; "Words of Love"; "Here, There, and Everywhere." Side 2: "Something"; "And I Love Her"; "If I Fell"; "I'll Be Back"; "Tell Me What You See"; "Yes It Is." Side 3: "Michelle"; "It's Only Love"; "You're Going to Lose That Girl"; "Every Little Thing"; "For No

One"; "She's Leaving Home." Side 4: "The Long and Winding Road"; "This Boy"; "Norwegian Wood (This Bird Has Flown)"; "I Will"; "P.S. I Love You."

Rarities, March 14, 1980, Capitol SHAL 12060

Side 1: "Love Me Do" (single version); "Misery"; "There's a Place"; "Sie Liebt Dich"; "And I Love Her"; "Help!"; "I'm Only Sleeping"; "I Am the Walrus." Side 2: "Penny Lane"; "Helter Skelter"; "Don't Pass Me By"; "The Inner Light"; "Across the Universe" (World Wildlife Fund version); "You Know My Name (Look up the Number)"; "Sgt. Pepper Inner Groove."

Reel Music, March 23, 1982, Capitol SV 12199

Side 1: "A Hard Day's Night"; "I Should Have Known Better"; "Can't Buy Me Love"; "And I Love Her"; "Help!"; "You've Got to Hide Your Love Away"; "Ticket to Ride"; "Magical Mystery Tour." Side 2: "I Am the Walrus"; "Yellow Submarine"; "All You Need Is Love"; "Let It Be"; "Get Back"; "The Long and Winding Road."

20 Greatest Hits, October 18, 1982, Capitol SV 12245

Side 1: "She Loves You"; "Love Me Do"; "I Want to Hold Your Hand"; "Can't Buy Me Love"; "A Hard Day's Night"; "I Feel Fine"; "Eight Days a Week"; "Ticket to Ride"; "Help!"; "Yesterday"; "We Can Work It Out"; "Paperback Writer." Side 2: "Penny Lane"; "All You Need Is Love"; "Hello, Goodbye"; "Hey Jude" (edited version); "Get Back"; "Come Together"; "Let It Be"; "The Long and Winding Road."

Past Masters, Volume 1, March 7, 1988, Apple [Capitol] CDP 7 90043 2

"Love Me Do"; "From Me to You"; "Thank You Girl"; "She Loves You"; "I'll Get You"; "I Want to Hold Your Hand"; "This Boy"; "Komm, Gib Mir Deine Hand"; "Sie Liebt Dich"; "Long Tall Sally"; "I Call Your Name"; "Slow Down"; "Matchbox"; "I Feel Fine"; "She's a Woman"; "Bad Boy"; "Yes It Is"; "I'm Down."

Past Masters, Volume 2, March 7, 1988, Apple [Capitol] CDP 7 90044 2

"Day Tripper"; "We Can Work It Out"; "Paperback Writer"; "Rain"; "Lady Madonna"; "The Inner Light"; "Hey Jude"; "Revolution"; "Get Back"; "Don't Let Me Down"; "The Ballad of John and Yoko"; "Old Brown Shoe"; "Across the Universe" (World Wildlife Fund version); "Let It Be"; "You Know My Name (Look Up the Number)."

Live at the BBC, December 6, 1994, Apple [Capitol] CDP 7243–8-31796–2-6

Disc 1: "Beatle Greetings" (Speech); "From Us to You"; "Riding on a Bus" (Speech); "I Got a Woman"; "Too Much Monkey Business"; "Keep Your Hands Off My Baby"; "I'll Be on My Way"; "Young Blood"; "A Shot of Rhythm and Blues"; "Sure to Fall (In Love with You)"; "Some Other Guy"; "Thank You Girl"; "Sha La La La La!" (Speech); "Baby It's You"; "That's All Right (Mama)"; "Carol"; "Soldier of Love"; "A Little Rhyme" (Speech); "Clarabella"; "I'm Gonna Sit Right Down and Cry (Over You)"; "Crying, Waiting, Hoping"; "Dear Wack!" (Speech); "You Really Got a Hold on Me"; "To Know Her Is to Love Her"; "A Taste of Honey"; "Long Tall Sally"; "I Saw Her Standing There"; "The Honeymoon Song"; "Johnny B. Goode"; "Lucille"; "Can't Buy Me Love"; "From Fluff to You" (Speech); "Till There Was You." Disc 2: "Crinsk Dee Night" (Speech); "A Hard Day's Night"; "Have a Banana!" (Speech); "I Wanna Be Your Man"; "Just a Rumour" (Speech); "Roll Over Beethoven"; "All My Loving"; "Things We Said Today"; "She's a Woman"; "Sweet Little Sixteen"; "1822!" (Speech); "Lonesome Tears in My Eyes"; "Nothin' Shakin' (But the Leaves on the Trees)"; "Hippy Hippy Shake"; "Glad All Over"; "I Just Don't Understand"; "So How Come (No One Loves Me)"; "I Feel Fine"; "I'm a Loser"; "Everybody's Trying to Be My Baby"; "Rock and Roll Music"; "Ticket to Ride"; "Dizzy Miss Lizzy";

Medley: "Kansas City"/"Hey-Hey-Hey-Hey!"; "Set Fire to That Lot!" (Speech); "Matchbox"; "I Forgot to Remember to Forget"; "Love These Goon Shows!" (Speech); "I Got to Find My Baby"; "Ooh! My Soul"; "Ooh! My Arms" (Speech); "Don't Ever Change"; "Slow Down"; "Honey Don't"; "Love Me Do."

The Beatles Anthology, Volume 1, November 20, 1995, Apple [Capitol] CDP 7243 8 34445 2 6

Disc 1: "Free As a Bird"; "We Were Four Guys . . . That's All" (Speech); "That'll Be the Day"; "In Spite of All the Danger"; "Sometimes I'd Borrow" (Speech); "Hallelujah, I Love Her So"; "You'll Be Mine"; "Cayenne"; "First of All" (Speech); "My Bonnie"; "Ain't She Sweet"; "Cry for a Shadow"; "Brian Was a Beautiful Guy" (Speech); "I Secured Them" (Speech); "Searchin' "; "Three Cool Cats"; "The Sheik of Araby"; "Like Dreamers Do"; "Hello Little Girl"; "Well, the Recording Test" (Speech); "Bésame Mucho"; "Love Me Do"; "How Do You Do It"; "Please Please Me"; "One After 909" (Sequence); "One After 909" (Complete); "Lend Me Your Comb"; "I'll Get You"; "We Were Performers" (Speech); "I Saw Her Standing There"; "From Me to You"; "Money (That's What I Want)"; "You Really Got a Hold on Me"; "Roll Over Beethoven." Disc 2: "She Loves You"; "Till There Was You"; "Twist and Shout"; "This Boy"; "I Want to Hold Your Hand"; "Boys, What Was I Thinking?" (Speech); "Moonlight Bay"; "Can't Buy Me Love" (Takes 1 and 2); "All My Loving" (*Ed Sullivan Show*); "You Can't Do That" (Take 6); "And I Love Her" (Take 2); "A Hard Day's Night" (Take 1); "I Wanna Be Your Man"; "Long Tall Sally"; "Boys"; "Shout"; "I'll Be Back" (Take 2); "I'll Be Back" (Take 3); "You Know What to Do" (Demo); "No Reply" (Demo); "Mr. Moonlight" (Takes 1 and 4); "Leave My Kitten Alone" (Take 5); "No Reply" (Take 2); "Eight Days a Week" (Sequence); "Eight Days a Week" (Complete); Medley: "Kansas City"/"Hey-Hey-Hey-Hey!" (Take 2).

The Beatles Anthology, Volume 2, March 18, 1996, Apple [Capitol] CDP 7243 8 34448 4 7

Disc 1: "Real Love"; "Yes It Is" (Takes 2 and 14); "I'm Down" (Take 1); "You've Got to Hide Your Love Away" (Takes 1, 2, and 5); "If You've Got Trouble" (Take 1); "That Means a Lot" (Take 1); "Yesterday" (Take 1); "It's Only Love" (Takes 2 and 3); "I Feel Fine"; "Ticket to Ride"; "Yesterday"; "Help!"; "Everybody's Trying to Be My Baby"; "Norwegian Wood (This Bird Has Flown)" (Take 1); "I'm Looking Through You" (Take 1); "12-Bar Original" (Edited Take 2); "Tomorrow Never Knows" (Take 1); "Got to Get You into My Life" (Take 5); "And Your Bird Can Sing" (Take 2); "Taxman" (Take 11); "Eleanor Rigby" (Take 14); "I'm Only Sleeping" (Rehearsal); "I'm Only Sleeping" (Take 1); "Rock and Roll Music"; "She's a Woman." Disc 2: "Strawberry Fields Forever" (Demo Sequence); "Strawberry Fields Forever" (Take 1); "Strawberry Fields Forever" (Take 7 and Edit Piece); "Penny Lane" (Take 9); "A Day in the Life" (Takes 1, 2, 6, and Orchestra); "Good Morning, Good Morning" (Take 8); "Only a Northern Song" (Takes 3 and 12); "Being for the Benefit of Mr. Kite!" (Takes 1 and 2); "Being for the Benefit of Mr. Kite!" (Take 7 and Effects Tape); "Lucy in the Sky with Diamonds" (Takes 6, 7, and 8); "Within You, Without You" (Instrumental); "Sgt. Pepper's Lonely Hearts Club Band (Reprise)" (Take 5); "You Know My Name (Look Up the Number)" (Composite); "I Am the Walrus" (Take 16); "The Fool on the Hill" (Demo); "Your Mother Should Know" (Take 27); "The Fool on the Hill" (Take 4); "Hello, Goodbye" (Take 16 and Overdubs); "Lady Madonna" (Takes 3 and 4); "Across the Universe" (Take 2).

The Beatles Anthology, Volume 3, October 25, 1996, Apple [Capitol] CDP 7243 8 34451
2 7

Disc 1: "A Beginning"; "Happiness Is a Warm Gun" (Esher Demo); "Helter Skelter"
(Edited Take 2); "Mean Mr. Mustard" (Esher Demo); "Polythene Pam" (Esher Demo);
"Glass Onion" (Esher Demo); "Junk" (Esher Demo); "Piggies" (Esher Demo); "Honey
Pie" (Esher Demo); "Don't Pass Me By" (Takes 3 and 5); "Ob-La-Di, Ob-La-Da"
(Take 5); "Good Night" (Rehearsal and Take 34); "Cry Baby Cry" (Take 1); "Black-
bird" (Take 4); "Sexy Sadie" (Take 6); "While My Guitar Gently Weeps" (Demo);
"Hey Jude" (Take 2); "Not Guilty" (Take 102); "Mother Nature's Son" (Take 2);
"Glass Onion" (Take 33); "Rocky Raccoon" (Take 8); "What's the New Mary Jane"
(Take 4); "Step Inside Love"/"Los Paranoias"; "I'm So Tired" (Takes 3, 6, and 9); "I
Will" (Take 1); "Why Don't We Do It in the Road?" (Take 4); "Julia" (Take 2). Disc
2: "I've Got a Feeling"; "She Came in Through the Bathroom Window" (Rehearsal);
"Dig a Pony"; "Two of Us"; "For You Blue"; "Teddy Boy"; Medley: "Rip It
Up"/"Shake, Rattle, and Roll"/"Blue Suede Shoes"; "The Long and Winding Road";
"Oh! Darling" (Edited); "All Things Must Pass" (Demo); "Mailman, Bring Me No
More Blues"; "Get Back" (Rooftop Concert); "Old Brown Shoe" (Demo); "Octopus's
Garden" (Takes 2 and 8); "Maxwell's Silver Hammer" (Take 5); "Something" (Demo);
"Come Together" (Take 1); "Come and Get It" (Demo); "Ain't She Sweet" (Jam);
"Because" (a cappella version); "Let It Be"; "I Me Mine" (Take 16); "The End"
(Remix).

Yellow Submarine Songtrack, September 17, 1999, Apple [Capitol] CDP 7243 5 21481
2 7

"Yellow Submarine"; "Hey Bulldog"; "Eleanor Rigby"; "Love You To"; "All Together
Now"; "Lucy in the Sky with Diamonds"; "Think for Yourself"; "Sgt. Pepper's Lonely
Hearts Club Band"; "With a Little Help from My Friends"; "Baby, You're a Rich
Man"; "Only a Northern Song"; "All You Need Is a Love"; "When I'm Sixty-Four";
"Nowhere Man"; "It's All Too Much."

1, November 13, 2000, Apple [Capitol] CDP 7243 5 29325 2 8

"Love Me Do"; "From Me to You"; "She Loves You"; "I Want to Hold Your Hand";
"Can't Buy Me Love"; "A Hard Day's Night"; "I Feel Fine"; "Eight Days a Week";
"Ticket to Ride"; "Help!"; "Yesterday"; "Day Tripper"; "We Can Work It Out";
"Paperback Writer"; "Yellow Submarine"; "Eleanor Rigby"; "Penny Lane"; "All You
Need Is Love"; "Hello, Goodbye"; "Lady Madonna"; "Hey Jude"; "Get Back"; "The
Ballad of John and Yoko"; "Something"; "Come Together"; "Let It Be"; "The Long
and Winding Road."

Let It Be . . . Naked, November 17, 2003, Apple CDP 7243 5 95713 2 4

Disc 1: "Get Back"; "Dig a Pony"; "For You Blue"; "The Long and Winding Road";
"Two of Us"; "I've Got a Feeling"; "One After 909"; "Don't Let Me Down"; "I Me
Mine"; "Across the Universe"; "Let It Be."

Love, November 21, 2006, Apple [Capitol] CDP 0946 3 79810 2 3

"Because"; "Get Back"; "Glass Onion"; "Eleanor Rigby"/"Julia"; "I Am the Walrus";
"I Want to Hold Your Hand"; "Drive My Car"/"The Word"/"What You're Doing";
"Gnik Nus"; "Something"/"Blue Jay Way"; "Being for the Benefit of Mr. Kite!"/"I
Want You (She's So Heavy)"/"Helter Skelter"; "Help!"; "Blackbird"/"Yesterday";
"Strawberry Fields Forever"; "Within You, Without You"/"Tomorrow Never Knows";
"Lucy in the Sky with Diamonds"; "Octopus's Garden"/"Sun King"; "Lady Madonna";

"Here Comes the Sun"/"The Inner Light"; "Come Together"/"Dear Prudence"/"Cry Baby Cry"; "Revolution"/"Back in the USSR"; "While My Guitar Gently Weeps"; "A Day in the Life"; "Hey Jude"; "Sgt. Pepper's Lonely Hearts Club Band (Reprise)"; "All You Need Is Love."

Mono Masters, September 9, 2009, Apple [Capitol] 5099969945120

Disc 1:"Love Me Do"; "From Me to You"; "Thank You Girl"; "She Loves You"; "I'll Get You"; "I Want to Hold Your Hand"; "This Boy"; "Komm, Gib Mir Deine Hand"; "Sie Liebt Dich"; "Long Tall Sally"; "I Call Your Name"; "Slow Down"; "Matchbox"; "I Feel Fine"; "She's a Woman"; "Bad Boy"; "Yes It Is"; "I'm Down." Disc 2:"Day Tripper"; "We Can Work It Out"; "Paperback Writer"; "Rain"; "Lady Madonna"; "The Inner Light"; "Hey Jude"; "Revolution"; "Only a Northern Song"; "All Together Now"; "Hey Bulldog"; "It's All Too Much"; "Get Back"; "Don't Let Me Down"; "Across the Universe" (World Wildlife Fund version); "You Know My Name (Look Up the Number)."

Past Masters, September 9, 2009, Apple 50999 2 43807 2 0

Disc 1: "Love Me Do"; "From Me to You"; "Thank You Girl"; "She Loves You"; "I'll Get You"; "I Want to Hold Your Hand"; "This Boy"; "Komm, Gib Mir Deine Hand"; "Sie Liebt Dich"; "Long Tall Sally"; "I Call Your Name"; "Slow Down"; "Matchbox"; "I Feel Fine"; "She's a Woman"; "Bad Boy"; "Yes It Is"; "I'm Down." Disc 2: "Day Tripper"; "We Can Work It Out"; "Paperback Writer"; "Rain"; "Lady Madonna"; "The Inner Light"; "Hey Jude"; "Revolution"; "Get Back"; "Don't Let Me Down"; "The Ballad of John and Yoko"; "Old Brown Shoe"; "Across the Universe" (World Wildlife Fund version); "Let It Be"; "You Know My Name (Look Up the Number)."

Tomorrow Never Knows, July 24, 2012, Apple [iTunes]

"Revolution"; "Paperback Writer"; "And Your Bird Can Sing"; "Helter Skelter"; "Savoy Truffle"; "I'm Down"; "I've Got a Feeling" (*Let It Be . . . Naked* version); "Back in the USSR"; "You Can't Do That"; "It's All Too Much"; "She Said She Said"; "Hey Bulldog"; "Tomorrow Never Knows"; "The End" (*Anthology 3* version).

On Air—Live at the BBC, Volume 2, November 11, 2013, Apple

Disc 1: "And Here We Are Again" (Speech); "Words of Love"; "How About It, Gorgeous?" (Speech); "Do You Want To Know a Secret"; "Lucille"; "Hey, Paul . . ." (Speech); "Anna (Go To Him)"; "Hello!" (Speech); "Please Please Me"; "Misery"; "I'm Talking About You"; "A Real Treat" (Speech); "Boys"; "Absolutely Fab" (Speech); "Chains"; "Ask Me Why"; "Till There Was You"; "Lend Me Your Comb"; "Lower 5E" (Speech); "The Hippy Hippy Shake"; "Roll Over Beethoven"; "There's a Place"; "Bumper Bundle" (Speech); "P.S. I Love You"; "Please Mister Postman"; "Beautiful Dreamer"; "Devil in Her Heart"; "The 49 Weeks" (Speech); "Sure To Fall (In Love With You)"; "Never Mind, Eh?" (Speech); "Twist and Shout"; "Bye, Bye" (speech); "John—Pop Profile" (Speech); "George—Pop Profile" (Speech); Disc 2: "I Saw Her Standing There"; "Glad All Over"; "Lift Lid Again" (Speech); "I'll Get You"; "She Loves You"; "Memphis, Tennessee"; "Happy Birthday Dear Saturday Club"; "Now Hush, Hush" (Speech); "From Me to You"; "Money (That's What I Want)"; "I Want to Hold Your Hand"; "Brian Bathtubes" (Speech); "This Boy"; "If I Wasn't in America" (Speech); "I Got a Woman"; "Long Tall Sally"; "If I Fell"; "A Hard Job Writing Them" (Speech); "And I Love Her"; "Oh, Can't We? Yes We Can" (Speech); "You Can't Do That"; "Honey Don't"; "I'll Follow the Sun"; "Green with Black Shutters" (Speech); "Kansas City/Hey-Hey-Hey-Hey!"; "That's What We're Here For";

"I Feel Fine" (Studio Outtake); "Paul—Pop Profile" (Speech); "Ringo—Pop Profile" (Speech).

The Beatles Bootleg Recordings 1963, December 17, 2013, Apple [iTunes]

"There's a Place" (Takes 5 and 6); "There's a Place" (Take 8); "There's a Place" (Take 9); "Do You Want to Know a Secret" (Take 7); "A Taste of Honey" (Take 6); "I Saw Her Standing There" (Take 2); "Misery" (Take 1); "Misery" (Take 7); "From Me to You" (Takes 1 and 2); "From Me to You" (Take 5); "Thank You Girl" (Take 1); "Thank You Girl" (Take 5); "One After 909" (Takes 1 and 2); "Hold Me Tight" (Take 21); "Money (That's What I Want)" (studio outtake); "Some Other Guy"; "Love Me Do"; "Too Much Monkey Business"; "I Saw Her Standing There"; "Do You Want to Know a Secret"; "From Me to You"; "I Got to Find My Baby"; "Roll Over Beethoven"; "A Taste of Honey"; "Love Me Do"; "Please Please Me"; "She Loves You"; "I Want to Hold Your Hand"; "Till There Was You"; "Roll Over Beethoven"; "You Really Got a Hold on Me"; "The Hippy Hippy Shake"; "Till There Was You"; "A Shot of Rhythm and Blues"; "A Taste of Honey"; "Money (That's What I Want)"; "Anna (Go to Him)"; "Love Me Do"; "She Loves You"; "I'll Get You"; "A Taste of Honey"; "Boys"; "Chains"; "You Really Got a Hold on Me"; "I Saw Her Standing There"; "She Loves You"; "Twist and Shout"; "Do You Want to Know a Secret"; "Please Please Me"; "Long Tall Sally"; "Chains"; "Boys"; "A Taste of Honey"; "Roll Over Beethoven"; "All My Loving"; "She Loves You"; "Till There Was You"; "Bad to Me" (demo); "I'm in Love" (demo).

Recommended Resources

Starred titles (*) below are especially recommended.

Abbey Road Studios. Accessed September 20, 2013. http://www.abbeyroad.com.

Axelrod, Mitchell. 1999. *Beatletoons: The Real Story behind the Cartoon Beatles*. Pickens, SC: Wynn.

*Babiuk, Andy. 2001. *Beatles Gear: All the Fab Four's Instruments, from Stage to Studio*. San Francisco: Backbeat.

Badman, Keith. 1999. *The Beatles After the Breakup, 1970–2000: A Day-by-Day Diary*. London: Omnibus.

Badman, Keith. 2001. *The Beatles Off the Record: Outrageous Opinions and Unrehearsed Interviews*. London: Omnibus.

Barrow, Tony. 1993. "The Story behind A Hard Day's Night." *Beatles Monthly Book* 204 (September): 5–11.

Barrow, Tony. 1999. *The Making of the Beatles'* Magical Mystery Tour. London: Omnibus.

BBC. September 9, 2009. "When the Beatles Came to Town." Accessed September 7, 2013.

The Beatles. Accessed September 20, 2013. http://beatles.com.

*The Beatles. 2000. *The Beatles Anthology*. San Francisco: Chronicle.

*The Beatles Bible. 2008. Accessed September 20, 2013. http://www.beatlesbible.com

Billboard. 1999. "The Billboard Interview with George Harrison." Accessed September 7, 2013. http:// willybrauch.de/ In_Their_Own_Words/ harrison99. htm.

Britton, Luke Morgan. January 22, 2013. "Yoko Ono Celebrates 80th Birthday with One-Off Plastic Ono Band Gig." Accessed September 7, 2013. http:// thelineofbestfit.com/ news/ latest-news/ yoko-ono-celebrates-80th-birthday-with-one-off-plastic-ono-band-gig -116593.

Bromell, Nick. 2000. *Tomorrow Never Knows: Rock and Psychedelics in the 1960s*. Chicago: University of Chicago Press.

Cadogan, Patrick. 2008. *The Revolutionary Artist: John Lennon's Radical Years*. Raleigh, NC: Hulu.

Carlin, Peter Ames. 2009. *Paul McCartney: A Life*. New York: Touchstone.

Carr, Roy, and Tony Tyler. 1975. *The Beatles: An Illustrated Record*. New York: Harmony.

Clayson, Alan. 2003a. *George Harrison*. London: Sanctuary.

Clayson, Alan. 2003b. *Ringo Starr*. London: Sanctuary.

CNN. 2001. "CNN Larry King Live." Accessed September 7, 2013. http:// transcripts.cnn .com/ TRANSCRIPTS/ 0106/ 12/ lkl. 00. html.

Cooke, Deryck. 1982. "The Lennon-McCartney Songs." In *Vindications: Essays on Romantic Music*, edited by Deryck Cooke, 196–200. Cambridge: Cambridge University Press.

Costello, Elvis. 2006. "Foreword." In *Here, There, and Everywhere: My Life Recording the Music of the Beatles*. New York: Gotham: ix–xi.

Cott, Jonathan, and Christine Doudna, eds. 1982. *The Ballad of John and Yoko*. San Francisco: Rolling Stone.

Creem. 1987–1988. "The George Harrison Interview." Accessed September 7, 2013. http:// beatlesnumber9.com/creem.html.

Cross, Craig. 2005. *The Beatles: Day-by-Day, Song-by-Song, Record-by-Record*. New York: iUniverse.

Davies, Hunter. 1968. *The Beatles: The Authorized Biography*. New York: McGraw-Hill.

"A Day in the Life: A Biography of Sir George Martin." 1999. Accessed September 7, 2013. http:// members.pcug.org.au/ ˜ jhenry/ biography.html.

De Herrera, Nancy Cooke. 2003. *All You Need Is Love: An Eyewitness Account of When Spirituality Spread from the East to the West*. San Diego: Jodere.

Doggett, Peter. 1998. *Abbey Road/Let It Be: The Beatles*. New York: Schirmer.

Doggett, Peter. 2009. *You Never Give Me Your Money: The Beatles After the Breakup*. New York: Harper Collins.

*Dowlding, William J. 1989. *Beatlesongs*. New York: Simon and Schuster.

Drysdale, Neil. January 5, 2013. "So Were the Beatles Really Booed Off Stage in Aberdeen 50 Years Ago?" Accessed September 7, 2013. http:// news.stv.tv/ north/ 208517-s o-were-the-beatles-really-booed-off-stage-in-aberdeen-50-years-ago/.

Emerick, Geoff, and Howard Massey. 2006. *Here, There, and Everywhere: My Life Recording the Music of the Beatles*. New York: Gotham.

Epstein, Brian. 1998. *A Cellarful of Noise: The Autobiography of the Man Who Made the Beatles*. New York: Pocket.

Evans, Mike. 2004. *The Beatles Literary Anthology*. Medford, NJ: Plexus Publishing.

*Everett, Walter. 1999. *The Beatles as Musicians: Revolver through the Anthology*. Oxford: Oxford University Press.

*Everett, Walter. 2001. *The Beatles as Musicians: The Quarry Men through Rubber Soul*. Oxford: Oxford University Press.

Everett, Walter. 2006. "Painting Their Room in a Colorful Way: The Beatles' Exploration of Timbre." In *Reading the Beatles: Cultural Studies, Literary Criticism, and the Fab Four*, edited by Kenneth Womack and Todd F. Davis, 71–94. Albany: State University of New York Press.

Flippo, Chet. 1988. *Yesterday: The Unauthorized Biography of Paul McCartney*. New York: Doubleday.

Frontani, Michael. 2009. *The Beatles: Image and the Media*. Jackson: University Press of Mississippi.

Gambaccini, Paul. 1976. *Paul McCartney: In His Own Words*. New York: Flash.

Gibran, Kahlil. 1995. *Sand and Foam: A Book of Aphorisms*. New York: Knopf.

Goldman, Albert. 1988. *The Lives of John Lennon*. New York: Morrow.

Gorshin, Frank. June 27, 1999. "I Heard Nothing But the Screams." *The Daily Beast*. Accessed September 3, 2013. http:// www.thedailybeast.com/ newsweek/ 1999/ 06/ 27/ i-heard-nothing-but-the-screams.html.

Harrison, George. 1980. *I Me Mine*. San Francisco: Chronicle.

*Harry, Bill. 1992. *The Ultimate Beatles Encyclopedia*. New York: Hyperion.

Harry, Bill. 2002. *The Paul McCartney Encyclopedia*. London: Virgin.

Harry, Bill. October 30, 2011. "Two Who Knew Ex-Beatle Stu Sutcliffe Weigh in on Song Controversy." Accessed September 7, 2013. http:// www.examiner.com/ article/exclusive -two-who-knew-ex-beatle-stu-sutcliffe-weigh-on-song-controversy.

Hertsgaard, Mark. 1995. *A Day in the Life: The Music and Artistry of the Beatles*. New York: Delacorte.

Houston, Frank. July 25, 2000. "Sir George Martin." *Salon Magazine*. Accessed September 7, 2013. http:// www.salon.com/ 2000/ 07/ 25/ martin_6/.

Huntley, Elliot J. 2004. *Mystical One: George Harrison—After the Breakup of the Beatles*. Toronto: Guernica.

Inglis, Ian, ed. 2000. *The Beatles, Popular Music, and Society: A Thousand Voices*. New York: St. Martin's.

Inglis, Ian. 2009. "Revolution." In *The Cambridge Companion to the Beatles*, edited by Kenneth Womack, 112–24. Cambridge: Cambridge University Press.

The Internet Beatles Album. 1995. Accessed September 20, 2013. http://www.beatlesagain .com.

Jackson, Andrew Grant. 2012. *Still the Greatest: The Essential Songs of the Beatles' Solo Careers*. Lanham, MD: Scarecrow.

Koskimäki, Jouni. 2006. "Happiness Is . . . a Good Transcription: Reconsidering the Beatles' Sheet Music Publications." Dissertation. University of Jyväskylä.

Kozinn, Allan. 1995. *The Beatles*. London: Phaidon.

Lange, Larry. 2001. *The Beatles Way: Fab Wisdom for Everyday Life*. New York: Atria.

Leary, Timothy, Ralph Metzner, and Richard Alpert. 1964. *The Psychedelic Experience: A Manual Based on the Tibetan Book of the Dead*. New Hyde Park, NY: University Books.

Leigh, Spencer. 2004. "Nowhere Man?" In *The Beatles: Ten Years That Shook the World*, edited by Paul Trynka, 36, 37. London: Dorling Kindersley.

Lennon, Cynthia. 2005. *John*. London: Hodder and Stoughton.

Lennon, John. 1970. *Lennon Remembers*, interview by Jann Wenner. New York: Verso.

*Lennon, John, and Yoko Ono. 2000. *All We Are Saying: The Last Major Interview with John Lennon and Yoko Ono*, interview by David Sheff and edited by G. Barry Golson. New York: Griffin.

Lewisohn, Mark. 1986. *The Beatles Live!* London: Pavilion.

*Lewisohn, Mark. 1988. *The Complete Beatles Recording Sessions: The Official Abbey Road Studio Session Notes, 1962–1970*. New York: Harmony.

Lewisohn, Mark. 1995. *The Complete Beatles Chronicle*. London: Pyramid.

*Lewisohn, Mark. 2013. *Tune In: The Beatles—All These Years*. New York: Crown.

*MacDonald, Ian. 1994. *Revolution in the Head: The Beatles' Records and the Sixties*. New York: Holt.

MacFarlane, Thomas. 2004. "The Abbey Road Medley: Extended Forms in Popular Music." Dissertation. New York University.

Manchester Evening News. April 9, 2005. "Beatles Gig Feels Like It Was Yesterday." Accessed September 7, 2013. http:// www.manchestereveningnews.co.uk/ news/ local -news/ beatles-gig-feels-like-it-was-yesterday-1145090.

Mann, William. 1963. "What Songs the Beatles Sang." Accessed June 8, 2013. http:// jolomo .net/ music/ william_mann.html.

Martin, Bill. 2002. *Avant Rock: Experimental Music from the Beatles to Björk*. Chicago: Open Court.

Martin, George, with Jeremy Hornsby. 1979. *All You Need Is Ears*. New York: St. Martin's.

Martin, George, with William Pearson. 1994. *With a Little Help from My Friends: The Making of Sgt. Pepper*. Boston: Little, Brown.

Matteo, Steve. 2004. *Let It Be*. New York: Continuum.

McCabe, Peter, and Robert D. Schonfeld. 1972. *Apple to the Core: The Unmaking of the Beatles*. London: Martin Brian and O'Keeffe.

McCartney, Paul. Letter to the Editor. March 9, 1996. *The Daily Mirror*.

McGee, Garry. 2003. *Band on the Run: A History of Paul McCartney and Wings*. Austin, TX: Taylor.

McKinney, Devin. 2003. *Magic Circles: The Beatles in Dream and History*. Cambridge: Harvard University Press.

Mellers, Wilfred. 1973. *Twilight of the Gods: The Music of the Beatles*. New York: Schirmer.

*Miles, Barry. 1997. *Paul McCartney: Many Years from Now*. New York: Holt.

Moore, Allan F. 1997. *The Beatles: Sgt. Pepper's Lonely Hearts Club Band*. Cambridge: Cambridge University Press.

Neaverson, Bob. 1997. *The Beatles Movies*. London: Cassell.

Norman, Philip. 1981. *Shout!: The Beatles in Their Generation*. New York: Simon and Schuster.

O'Donnell, Jim. 1995. *The Day John Met Paul: An Hour-by-Hour of How the Beatles Began*. New York: Penguin.

O'Donnell, Shaugn. 2002. "Sailing to the Sun: Revolver's Influence on Pink Floyd." In *"Every Sound There Is": The Beatles' Revolver and the Transformation of Rock and Roll*, edited by Russell Reising, 169–86. Aldershot, U.K.: Ashgate.

O'Gorman, Martin. 2004. "Take 137!" In *The Beatles: Ten Years That Shook the World*, edited by Paul Trynka, 242, 243. London: Dorling Kindersley.

Peel, Ian. 2002. *The Unknown Paul McCartney: McCartney and the Avant-Garde*. London: Reynolds & Hearn.

Pollack, Alan W. 2000. "Alan W. Pollack's 'Notes On' Series." Accessed June 5, 2013. http://www.recmusicbeatles.com/public/files/awp/awp.html.

Reeve, Andru J. 2004. *Turn Me On, Dead Man: The Beatles and the "Paul Is Dead" Hoax*. Bloomington, IN: AuthorHouse.

Reising, Russell, ed. 2002. *"Every Sound There Is": The Beatles' Revolver and the Transformation of Rock and Roll*. Aldershot, U.K.: Ashgate.

Reising, Russell. 2006. "Vacio Luminoso: 'Tomorrow Never Knows' and the Coherence of the Impossible." In *Reading the Beatles: Cultural Studies, Literary Criticism, and the Fab Four*, edited by Kenneth Womack and Todd F. Davis, 111–28. Albany: State University of New York Press.

*Riley, Tim. 1988. *Tell Me Why: A Beatles Commentary*. New York: Knopf.

Riley, Tim. 2011. *Lennon: The Man, the Myth, the Music—The Definitive Life*. New York: Hyperion.

Roos, Michael E. 1984. "The Walrus and the Deacon: John Lennon's Debt to Lewis Carroll." *Journal of Popular Culture* 18: 19–29.

Russell, Jeff. 2006. *The Beatles Complete Discography*. New York: Universe.

*Ryan, Kevin, and Brian Kehew. 2006. *Recording the Beatles: The Studio Equipment and Techniques Used to Create Their Classic Albums*. Houston: Curvebender.

Schaffner, Nicholas. 1977. *The Beatles Forever*. Harrisburg, PA: Cameron House.

Scott, Ken. 2005. "Shooting to Thrill." Interview by Joe Chiccarelli. *EQ* (December): 38–53.

Shotton, Pete, and Nicholas Schaffner. 1983. *John Lennon: In My Life*. New York: Stein and Day.

Smith, Alan. 1966. "My Broken Tooth—By Paul McCartney." *New Musical Express* (June 24): 3.

Sound on Sound. December 1995. "The Story of the Beatles' Anthology Project." Accessed September 7, 2013. http:// www.soundonsound.com/ sos/ 1995_articles/ dec95/ the beatles.html.

Sounes, Howard. 2010. *Fab: An Intimate Life of Paul McCartney*. Cambridge, MA: Da Capo.

Southall, Brian. 2008. *Northern Songs: The True Story of the Beatles Song Publishing Empire*. London: Omnibus.

Spitz, Bob. 2005. *The Beatles: The Biography*. Boston: Little, Brown.

Spizer, Bruce. 1998. *Songs, Pictures, and Stories of the Fabulous Beatles Records on Vee-Jay*. New Orleans: 498 Productions.

*Spizer, Bruce. 2000a. *The Beatles on Capitol Records, Volume One: Beatlemania and the Singles*. New Orleans: 498 Productions.

*Spizer, Bruce. 2000b. *The Beatles on Capitol Records, Volume Two: The Albums*. New Orleans: 498 Productions.

*Spizer, Bruce. 2003. *The Beatles on Apple Records*. New Orleans: 498 Productions.

Spizer, Bruce. 2005. *The Beatles Solo on Apple Records*. New Orleans: 498 Productions.

Spizer, Bruce. 2007. *The Beatles Swan Song: "She Loves You" and Other Records*. New Orleans: 498 Productions.

Spizer, Bruce. 2011. *Beatles for Sale on Parlophone Records*. New Orleans: 498 Productions.

Sulpy, Doug, and Ray Schweighardt. 1997. *Get Back: The Unauthorized Chronicle of the Beatles' Let It Be Disaster*. New York: Griffin.

Taylor, Alistair. 2003. *With the Beatles*. London: John Blake.

Turner, Steve. 1994. *A Hard Day's Write: The Story behind Every Beatles Song*. New York: HarperCollins.

Unterberger, Richie. 2006. *The Unreleased Beatles: Music and Film*. San Francisco: Backbeat.

Waldman, Steve. 2001. "Deepak Chopra on His Friend George Harrison." Accessed September 7, 2013. http:// www.beliefnet.com/ Entertainment/ Music/ 2001/ 12/ Deepak -Chopra-On-His-Friend-George-Harrison.aspx? p = 1.

The Washington Post. November 17, 1992. "The Hours and Times." Accessed September 7, 2013. http:// www.washingtonpost.com/ wp-srv/ style/ longterm/ movies/ videos/ the hoursandtimesnrharrington_a0ab53. htm.

The Washington Post. June 3, 2004. "McCartney: Of Course Those Songs Were About Drugs." Accessed September 7, 2013. http://www.washingtonpost.com/wp-dyn/articles/ A11258 -2004Jun2.html.

The Washington Times. 2001. "Culture Briefs." Accessed September 7, 2013. http:// www .washingtontimes.com/ news/ 2003/ apr/ 16/ 20030416-090858-3040r/.

Whiteley, Sheila. 2006. " 'Love, Love, Love': Representations of Gender and Sexuality in Selected Songs by the Beatles." In *Reading the Beatles: Cultural Studies, Literary*

Criticism, and the Fab Four, edited by Kenneth Womack and Todd F. Davis, 55–69. Albany: State University of New York Press.

Wiener, Jon. 1991. *Come Together: John Lennon in His Time*. Champaign: University of Illinois Press.

Williams, Allan. 1975. *The Man Who Gave the Beatles Away*. London: Macmillan.

Winn, John C. 2003a. *Way Beyond Compare: The Beatles' Recorded Legacy, Volume One: 1957–1965*. Sharon, VT: Multiplus.

Winn, John C. 2003b. *That Magic Feeling: The Beatles' Recorded Legacy, Volume Two: 1966–1970*. Sharon, VT: Multiplus.

*Womack, Kenneth. 2007. *Long and Winding Roads: The Evolving Artistry of the Beatles*. New York: Continuum.

Womack, Kenneth, ed. 2009. *The Cambridge Companion to the Beatles*. Cambridge: Cambridge University Press.

Womack, Kenneth, and Katie Kapurch, eds. 2016. *New Critical Perspectives on the Beatles: Things We Said Today*. New York: Palgrave.

Womack, Kenneth, and Todd F. Davis, eds. 2006. *Reading the Beatles: Cultural Studies, Literary Criticism, and the Fab Four*. Albany: State University of New York Press.

Index

Note: Page numbers in **bold** indicate main entries.

About the Author

Kenneth Womack is Dean of the Wayne D. McMurray School of Humanities and Social Sciences at Monmouth University, where he also serves as Professor of English. He is the author or editor of numerous books, including *Long and Winding Roads: The Evolving Artistry of the Beatles* (2007), the *Cambridge Companion to the Beatles* (2009), and *The Beatles Encyclopedia: Everything Fab Four* (2014). Womack is also the author of three award-winning novels, including *John Doe No. 2 and the Dreamland Motel* (2010), *The Restaurant at the End of the World* (2012), and *Playing the Angel* (2013). He serves as Editor of *Interdisciplinary Literary Studies: A Journal of Criticism and Theory*, published by Penn State University Press, and as Co-Editor of the English Association's *Year's Work in English Studies*, published by Oxford University Press.

CPSIA information can be obtained
at www.ICGtesting.com
Printed in the USA
LVHW081342171120
671932LV00028B/365

9 781440 844263